D1505751

PRESIDENTIAL PROFILES
THE FDR YEARS

William D. Pederson

An imprint of Infobase Publishing

Presidential Profiles: The FDR Years

Facts On File, Inc.
An imprint of Infobase Publishing
132 West 31st Street
New York NY 10001

Library of Congress Cataloging-in-Publication Data

Pederson, William D., 1946–
    The FDR Years / William D. Pederson.
        p. cm. — (Presidential profiles)
    Includes bibliographical references and index.
    ISBN 0-8160-5368-5 (hardcover : alk. paper)
    1. Politicians—United States—Biography. 2. United States—Politics and government—1933–1945. 3. Roosevelt, Franklin D. (Franklin Delano), 1882–1945—Friends and associates. 4. United States—History—1933–1945—Biography. 5. United States—Biography. I. Title. II. Presidential profiles (Facts on File, Inc.)
    E747.P43 2006
    973.917—dc22   2005016260

Facts On File books are available at special discounts when purchased in bulk quantities for businesses, associations, institutions or sales promotions. Please call our Special Sales Department in New York at (212) 967-8800 or (800) 322-8755.

You can find Facts On File on the World Wide Web at http://www.factsonfile.com

Text design by Mary Susan Ryan-Flynn

Cover design by Nora Wertz

Printed in the United States of America

VB Hermitage 10 9 8 7 6 5 4 3 2 1

This book is printed on acid-free paper.

CONTENTS

PREFACE

The FDR Years is part of Facts On File's *Presidential Profiles* reference series. This volume contains biographical sketches of nearly 300 individuals during the longest presidential administration in American history, which shaped public policy during the Great Depression of the 1930s and World War II during the 1940s. Special emphasis is given to the executive branch officials, justices of the U.S. Supreme Court, members of Congress, and governors and cultural icons of the period, in addition to a few of the political leaders abroad with whom Franklin Delano Roosevelt (FDR) dealt.

Biographical entries begin with the name of the individual and his or her date of birth and death, followed by the name of the office held in the Franklin Roosevelt administration or the position or occupation for which the subject was most noted during that time. The entries are meant to capture the essence of each person's career in relation to FDR, the Great Depression, and World War II. Though most of these individuals interacted directly with the president, a few are selected because they reflect the larger social milieu on which the New Deal exerted influence.

Several appendices are contained in the volume, including a chronology of events during FDR's presidency. Because the FDR presidency was the nation's longest (1933–45), the chronology highlights Franklin Roosevelt's life, particularly the events in which FDR participated during his administration. This is followed by a list of Roosevelt's cabinet for each term, the members of the Supreme Court, and the leadership of the U.S. Congress. A number of FDR's most important speeches are also included. The volume concludes with a selected bibliography, with an emphasis on publications since 1995.

—William D. Pederson

INTRODUCTION

*F*ranklin Delano Roosevelt's presidency established a benchmark for democratic leadership. He proved worthy of Mount Rushmore status, not only for his unprecedented four presidential electoral victories, but also for meeting the two overlapping great challenges of the 20th century that spanned his presidency: the Great Depression and World War II. He prevailed against these two defining crises in American history and still managed to transform the presidency itself while altering the direction of American domestic and foreign policy. Moreover, FDR accomplished all this while remaining within the bounds of democratic constraints, unlike his major challengers at home and abroad. It is for these reasons that scholars rank FDR with George Washington and Abraham Lincoln, the triumvirate of greatest American presidents. Indeed, polls of scholars consider FDR second only to Abraham Lincoln.

FDR's democratic leadership becomes even more impressive when considered with respect to the world of that era. He was first elected in 1932 during an age when communist and fascist regimes, totalitarian systems in which dictators could conceive and implement executive decisions without constitutional checks, were romanticized as the wave of the future. Critics dismissed the ponderously slow and inefficient democratic model, whether in Germany's Weimar Republic or in the United States, as too outmoded to address the massive problems facing nations in the 20th century. However, Franklin Roosevelt, with his energetic and flexible character, working within the framework of the world's oldest written constitution, successfully transformed the executive branch by creating what is referred to as the modern presidency, thereby refuting critics and affirming the Founders' great experiment in democracy.

Born on January 30, 1882, into a secure and serene family of wealth and privilege among New York's Hudson River aristocracy, the boy who entered Groton School hardly seemed a future great leader who would transform America and the world. Like his role model and distant cousin Theodore Roosevelt, one of the four Mount Rushmore presidents, Franklin Delano Roosevelt graduated from Harvard University in 1903. He attended Columbia Law School without graduating but was admitted to the bar in 1907. FDR had found the law dull, and although he failed two law courses, the young aristocrat, as one might expect, soon joined a prestigious Wall Street law firm. Early on, he had given clues to the direction he wanted his career to take.

On St. Patrick's Day 1905, he married his fifth cousin, Anna Eleanor Roosevelt, favorite niece of President Theodore Roosevelt, who gave the bride away. Within five years FDR

Eleanor and Franklin D. Roosevelt at Hyde Park, N.Y., 1905 *(FDR Library)*

ran for political office for the first time. His role model "Uncle Ted" was Republican, but FDR ran as a Democrat and won a seat in the New York State senate. At the same time, former Princeton University president Woodrow Wilson also took electoral office for the first time as governor of New Jersey. FDR won reelection to the state senate in 1912, while Democrat Wilson was elected president of the United States, thanks to the Republican Party split that Teddy Roosevelt (TR) caused with his third-party Bull Moose campaign.

As TR's political star was fading, FDR's was in its ascendancy. FDR was on the same pathway that TR had followed to the White House. For example, he resigned his state senate seat in 1913 to become assistant secretary of state in

the Wilson administration; "Uncle Ted" had held the same position in the William McKinley administration. The Roosevelt name and World War I catapulted FDR to prominence as the Democratic vice presidential nominee in 1920. The Democratic ticket failed that year in voter backlash against the activism of the Wilson administration, but FDR's spirited campaign solidified his reputation as a rising star among national Democrats. Equally important, FDR had observed the blunders Wilson made in foreign policy because of his psychological rigidity as well as blunders that TR made because of his occasional excesses, and he learned from them. Franklin Roosevelt never achieved the scholarly heights of Woodrow Wilson or Teddy Roosevelt; he focused more on practical politics. Although not their academic equal, FDR nevertheless absorbed the intellectual lessons from pragmatism. He had been introduced to pragmatism, America's unique philosophical school, in classes at Harvard taught by the philosophy's founder, William James. This enabled FDR to avoid the costly political mistakes that TR and Wilson had made. His full grasp of pragmatism would soon reveal itself.

In 1921, FDR was stricken with polio. The devastating illness not only threatened his life and permanently paralyzed his legs but also threatened to halt his political momentum. In the same way that FDR had looked to TR as his political role model, TR's resiliency and triumph over major personal crises—overcoming a sickly childhood and enduring the deaths of his first wife and mother on the same day—served as inspiration for FDR as he battled polio and the paralysis that followed. Rather than yield to paralysis, Roosevelt spent several years in physical therapy with limited success while he focused on resuming his political career. Eleanor, one of the gifted inner circle that surrounded him, helped him to keep his name politically alive while he convalesced. She evolved into his full political partner and equal in the White House and remained a political power in her own right until her death.

New York governor Al Smith, the Democratic Party presidential candidate in 1928, persuaded FDR to run as his successor. Roosevelt narrowly won, becoming one of the few Democrats to survive Herbert Hoover's Republican landslide that year. Reelected governor in 1930, FDR experimented with programs to deal with the growing economic depression that had resulted from the 1929 Wall Street crash. As governor of the nation's most populous state and a successful campaign veteran, FDR was a leading contender for the 1932 Democratic presidential ticket.

Shown in this 1931 photograph is a breadline in Boston during the Great Depression, the most severe economic crisis in U.S. history. *(Library of Congress)*

After a deal was struck with the Texas delegation during the 1932 Democratic National Convention in Chicago to make John Nance Garner, speaker of the House of Representatives, his vice-presidential running mate, FDR won the presidential nomination on the fourth ballot. For only the second time in the history of national conventions, the presidential nominee showed up at the convention that year. Teddy Roosevelt had been the first in 1912; 20 years later, Franklin Roosevelt followed in his political footsteps. FDR promised "a New Deal for the American people" while also promising reduced governmental spending and a balanced budget. Despite the contradictions his promises suggested, the worsening Great Depression worked in the Democrats' favor. Herbert Hoover and Charles Curtis had been renominated as the Republican ticket at the Republican National Convention in Chicago. Voters, however, blamed the party in power for the nation's economic crisis and embraced the optimistic man with the enthusiastic smile to help the crippled nation get back on its feet, just as he had apparently overcome polio.

On November 8, 1932, Roosevelt garnered 22,821,857 votes (57.4%) to Hoover's 15,761,841 (39.6%). Moreover, by carrying 42 states, the Democrats achieved overwhelming majorities in the U.S. House of Representatives and the Senate.

FDR's first term as president began in March 1933, and during the first 100 days of his administration, he revealed his energetic and flexible character through an unprecedented ad hoc experimental program involving reform and regulation of the economy and public reassurances to the nation. Congress quickly enacted an ambitious legislative package that ranged from the Civilian Conservation Corps to the Tennessee Valley Authority Act. The legislation served to redefine the role of the national government in American society.

From the country's founding, "negative government"—championed by Thomas Jefferson, who asserted that "the best government is the least government"—had largely served as the basis for the federal government. The New Deal represented a switch to "positive government," which allowed the federal government to step in when conditions exceeded the power of individuals alone to deal with them. This new activist approach and FDR's confident pronouncements inspired the American public with hope. He was aided in implementing the New Deal by a large group of young lawyers who largely staffed many key positions in his administration. These lawyers were influenced by the new school of jurisprudence from the 1920s known as "legal realism." The legal realists thought the law should adapt to changing conditions. It was the most important school of jurisprudence during the 20th century and it helped to make the New Deal successful.

In 1935, Congress enacted two of the most significant pieces of legislation in its history. Based on a committee chaired by Secretary of Labor Frances Perkins, the first female cabinet member, and the energetic support of German-born senator Robert F. Wagner (D-N.Y.), often referred to as the chief legislative architect of the New Deal, Congress passed the Social Security Act. It was America's first social insurance system. In 1940, the Social Security Board began to issue monthly checks to eligible senior citizens. By 1997, one in seven Americans was receiving Social Security benefits. In 1935, Congress also enacted the landmark National Labor Relations Act (NLRA), often called the Wagner Act. Regarded by many as labor's Magna Carta, it recognized employees' right to organize for the first time and made collective bargaining a part of the economic recovery policy of the New Deal.

If the 1932 election primarily expressed public disgust with "Hoover's Depression," the sign of the changing times was that the Democrats gained congressional seats in the 1934 election, an atypical midterm elections outcome for the party in the White House. In 1936, the Republican National Convention met in Cleveland to chose Kansas governor Alfred E. Landon, a former Bull Mooser, as its presidential candidate on the first ballot. Frank Knox, publisher of the *Chicago Daily News,* was chosen as Landon's running mate.

Riding the crest of the New Deal, the FDR-Garner ticket was renominated by acclamation at the 1936 Democratic National Convention in Philadelphia. The New Deal, started as economic chicken soup for the nation, became the alphabet soup of federal agencies and laws. For example, the Agricultural Adjustment Administration (AAA) addressed the needs of farmers. The Works Progress Administration (WPA) employed the jobless. The Public Works Administration (PWA) helped state and local governments build highways and bridges. In keeping with national changes, FDR adapted a new persona for the 1936 election, that of a warrior fighting the "economic royalists." Funded by organized labor, his leadership attracted a coalition of ethnic voter groups. Pitted against demagogues on the left and right, FDR won in a landslide—27,751,597 (60.8%) to 16,679,583 (36.5%) popular votes. He carried every state except Maine and Vermont.

As typically happens during a second presidential term, FDR was considerably more controversial and less successful than he was in his first term. In early 1936, he appointed the President's Committee on Administrative Management, popularly known as the Brownlow Committee, and charged it with recommending changes that would enable the chief executive to manage efficiently the modern welfare state that had emerged with the New Deal. Justifiably considered the most important study on the executive branch since the *Federalist Papers,* the Brownlow Report was issued in early January 1937. Its conclusions recommended granting to the president managerial power commensurate with his role in overseeing the early stages of what would ultimately become the largest bureaucracy in the world. Uncharacteristically, FDR failed to lay the necessary political groundwork of consulting with Congress on the proposal, and his failure played into the hands of his opponents, who charged that he was merely trying to consolidate more power into his own hands. The stressful battle for the Brownlow bill caused its namesake, Louis Brownlow (1879–1963), to have a heart attack that removed him from the legislative struggle.

The battle between FDR and his congressional opponents intensified the next month with FDR's second, even larger political blunder, the Supreme Court packing plan, in which he repeated the misstep he had made with the Brownlow bill.

Between January 1935 and June 1936, the U.S. Supreme Court had issued a dozen judicial activist decisions declaring New Deal legislation unconstitutional. Believing that a constitutional amendment to change the court composition would take too long to pass, FDR had Attorney General Homer S. Cummings secretly draft a plan that would enable him to overcome Court opposition to the popularly supported New Deal legislation. On February 7, 1937, the president announced the Judicial Reform Bill of 1937, decried as the "Court packing plan." It allowed for the appointment of one new Supreme Court justice for each one of the justices who did not retire at age 70. At the time, six sitting justices were at least 70 years old. The proposal's real intent—to appoint enough justices who favored FDR's New Deal legislation to stop the decisions finding it unconstitutional—was only transparently cloaked by broadening it to allow for 44 new judges on the lower federal benches.

The number of justices on the high bench is fixed by statute rather than in the Constitution, and court enlargement schemes had precedents from the Civil War. The last attempt to assure a younger judiciary had come in 1913 when President Woodrow Wilson's attorney general, James C. McReynolds, devised a scheme that ultimately served as the basis for FDR's plan. Wilson had not pursued the plan, and in an ironic twist, McReynolds was now one of the four most conservative of the Supreme Court brethren, dubbed the Four Horsemen to invoke the biblical image of the Four Horsemen of the Apocalypse.

FDR went forward with his bold plan, drawing immediate and vocal opposition from Republicans, newspaper editors, and the organized bar. The proposal had considerable support among New Dealers, including future justices Fred Vinson (D-Ky.), then in the House of Representatives, and Hugo Black (D-Ala.), then in the U.S. Senate. Other heavyweights in FDR's corner were Solicitor General Stanley Reed and his immediate successor, Robert H. Jackson, who helped Roosevelt prepare the March 9, 1937, "fireside chat," a presidential radio broadcast justifying the proposal to the American people. FDR was also counting on the leadership of popular Joseph T. Robinson (D-Ark.), Senate majority leader, to ensure its passage. It was made clear to Robinson that he would be the president's first nominee to the expanded Court. However, the bill was doomed after Robinson suffered a fatal heart attack on July 14, eight days after Senate debate began on the bill. The president's position had weakened after the Court began handing down decisions that upheld New Deal measures, including the Wagner Act. Contemporaneously, Willis Van Devanter, one of the Four Horsemen, timed the announcement of his decision to retire from the Court for the same day that the House Judiciary Committee was scheduled to begin hearings on the bill.

The Court-packing scheme was a costly and avoidable political blunder for an activist president. FDR would have been better served by withdrawing the bill after the Court began changing its stance on New Deal legislation. FDR's Brownlow plan to reorganize and strengthen the Executive Branch was postponed for more than two years as a result and finally implemented in a much-weakened format in the Reorganization Act of 1939 and subsequent legislation. Roosevelt may have "lost the battle but won the war" in regard to the Supreme Court's reaction to the New Deal, but the victory was politically expensive: it contributed to the rise of the "conservative coalition" of southern Democrats and Republicans in Congress capable of blocking further New Deal legislation when they were united. Ironically, FDR, who had been unable to name a single justice to the High Court during his first term, would go on to name more justices than any other president since George Washington. In that way, he ultimately did "pack" the Court. Nonetheless, the ill-fated 1937 bills resulted in FDR being thwarted twice, something that had not happened since his initial inauguration in 1933.

The midterm congressional elections of 1938 amplified FDR's setbacks. He had tried to purge the most anti-New Deal conservative Democrats in the primary elections for Congress, but his campaign efforts failed. Republican gains in the U.S. House of Representatives increased from 88 to 170 and from 17 to 25 in the Senate. Whether FDR's political blunders resulted from hubris induced by the landslide reelection or because he was distracted from domestic issues by the mounting fascist threat in Europe and the Japanese threat in the Pacific remains an open question.

The 1940 election was set against the backdrop of the war in Europe. At the Republican National Convention in Philadelphia in June, political outsider Wendell Willkie was named presidential candidate on the sixth ballot, with Senator Charles L. McNary from Oregon as his running mate. Both were relative moderates.

The Democrats met in Chicago in July and on the first ballot nominated FDR for an unprecedented third term. He imposed Secretary of Agriculture Henry Wallace on the convention as his vice-presidential running mate. Wallace was a loyal and liberal New Dealer with prior family support for Theodore Roosevelt. Both Willkie and Roosevelt conducted active campaigns in an election race that returned FDR to the White House with 27,243,466 popular votes (54.7%) compared to Willkie's 22,304,744 votes (44.8%). Despite the win, the Democratic ticket carried only 38 states and gained only seven House seats in the 1940 election.

FDR's moniker "Dr. New Deal" rapidly morphed into "Dr. Win-the-War." He had already persuaded Congress to repeal the Neutrality Acts from the 1930s. In March 1941, Congress passed his Lend-Lease Act to help the British. Five months later, in August 1941, FDR officially met with British prime minster Winston Churchill for the first time aboard the American cruiser *Augusta* off Newfoundland. There they signed the Atlantic Charter, which called for an end to fascism as well as for the right to national self-determination. FDR recognized that the days of colonialism were doomed but Churchill stubbornly still clung to his traditional notion of preserving the British Empire. In November 1941, FDR extended lend-lease assistance to the Soviet Union as well. Then, on December 7, Japan conducted its sneak bombing attack on Pearl Harbor. The next day Congress declared war on Japan. Three days later, Germany and Italy declared war on the United States; Congress reciprocated the declarations of war. The largest war in history was under way.

FDR sought to make the war a bipartisan effort, appointing several Republicans to high office. He named Henry Stimson as secretary of war, Frank Knox as secretary of the navy, and Harlan Fiske Stone as chief justice of the Supreme Court. Once in the war, FDR quickly decided to focus on defeating the Nazis in Europe first before turning full military attention to Japan. In early 1942, he committed a moral blunder that stained America's democratic image with his decision to intern more than 100,000 Japanese Americans, two-thirds of whom were native-born American citizens.

FDR's level of physical activity as chief executive officer and commander in chief belied his physical paralysis. Well traveled during his youth and early adulthood, he vicariously followed international events daily as he worked on his beloved stamp collection. Moreover, he flew to Casablanca, Morocco, in January 1943 to meet with Churchill. In November that same year he flew to Tehran, Iran, for another meeting with Churchill and, for the first time, Joseph Stalin. Rather than exhausting him, the trips seemed to energize the president.

FDR continued his efforts toward planning a postwar world that began as early as August 1941 with the principles set forth in the Atlantic Charter. In July 1944, he convened an international conference at Bretton Woods, New Hampshire, that resulted in creation of the International Monetary Fund (IMF) and the International Bank for Reconstruction and Development. The Dumbarton Oaks conference was held in Washington, D.C., in August 1944 for representatives from the United States, Great Britain, the Soviet Union, and China to plan the groundwork for the United Nations.

During World War II, the conservative coalition (consisting of Republican and conservative Democrats) in Congress not only blocked the president from launching further social-reform legislation but also was able to dismantle many New Deal agencies. However, FDR helped to craft a third major piece of landmark legislation during his administration, the Servicemen's Readjustment Act of 1944—popularly known as the G.I. Bill of Rights. It was a worthy middle-class successor to Abraham Lincoln's Land Grant College Act of 1862, which

Winston Churchill, Franklin D. Roosevelt, and Joseph Stalin at Yalta *(Library of Congress)*

helped transform higher education in the United States. Almost half a million former American soldiers would go to college under provisions of the G.I. Bill of Rights legislation. (By 1956, almost 9 million veterans had taken advantage of the educational and vocational provisions of the programs that provided tuition, books, and living expenses. At the same time that the G.I. Bill of Rights was allowing veterans to improve their education, the Veteran Administration's low-interest loans for buying houses, farms, and small businesses were making home ownership a realistic goal for the returning veterans while at the same time stimulating a housing boom in growing suburbs.)

FDR's last hurrah came in 1944. Neither the war effort nor the midterm election had gone well in 1942, reflected in the Democrats' loss of 47 House seats. But in 1944, Americans went to the polls in the middle of a war for only the second time in U.S. history. The Republican National Convention had met in Chicago in late June and chosen New York governor Thomas E. Dewey on the first ballot; Ohio governor John Bricker was named as his running mate. The Democrats met in mid-July and picked FDR for an unprecedented fourth term. Political operatives forced Roosevelt to drop Henry Wallace from the ticket, and Harry Truman was nominated as the vice-presidential candidate on the second ballot. The stress of the war and ill health, however, were taking their toll on FDR, and it was beginning to show. Although he did not campaign until late in the election cycle, and the popular vote dropped by nearly 2 million votes, FDR still defeated Dewey, 25,602,504 (53.4%) to 22,006,285 (45.9%). The results were similar to 1940.

The Allied war effort was also clearly on the road to victory. Allied forces landed at Normandy on June 6, 1944, and by August had liberated Paris. In January 1945, FDR made his final trip abroad, flying to Yalta for a meeting with Churchill and Stalin. They agreed on the postwar occupation of Germany and the creation of what became the United Nations.

In April 1945, FDR left Washington for a vacation at his retreat in Warm Springs, Georgia. He died there on April 12 after suffering a massive stroke. Yet his legacy continued, in part because Eleanor Roosevelt worked to extend it through the United Nations during the postwar era. From a domestic perspective, FDR had helped to change the United States's philosophy of government from one that preferred the negative government advocated by Thomas Jefferson to one that approved of positive government, and he institutionalized the modern presidency. On the international front, he helped to create a new world order that ended American isolationism and European colonialism. Through his active leadership, FDR not only demonstrated to the world the potential of the United States's great experiment in self-government but achieved his early personal goal of surpassing Theodore Roosevelt's accomplishments. In the opinion of most historians and commentators, his was the finest political performance of the 20th century.

BIOGRAPHICAL DICTIONARY A–Z

Acheson, Dean Gooderham

(1893–1971) *assistant secretary of state for economic affairs*

Like many other ambitious pre–World War II lawyers, Dean Acheson proved his worth in the Roosevelt administration by performing yeoman political service. He was catapulted to a cabinet position by Harry Truman as secretary of state from 1949 to 1953 and was an informal adviser to Presidents Kennedy, Johnson, and Nixon.

Acheson was born into a prominent Connecticut family; his father was an Episcopal bishop of Connecticut and his mother had inherited family wealth. His performance at both Groton School and Yale University was lackluster. Acheson chose a legal career as his pathway to public service and attended Harvard Law School, where he studied with FELIX FRANKFURTER and was named to the law review. In 1917, he married Alice Caroline Stanley, and after earning his law degree in 1918, he served briefly in the Naval Auxiliary Reserve. His association with Frankfurter opened the door for Acheson to be hired by Supreme Court justice LOUIS BRANDEIS as his private secretary, a position Acheson held from 1918. In 1921 he joined the law firm of Covington, Burling and Rublee. He became a part-

ner in 1926 and was a senior partner when he retired from the firm in 1964.

In early 1933, Acheson became one of Frankfurter's many "Happy Hotdogs" when President Roosevelt appointed him as undersecretary of the Treasury. A liberal Democrat, he had campaigned for Roosevelt in 1932. Although he supported the New Deal, Acheson's rather rigid personal ethics led him to resign his position on November 15, 1933, in protest against the president's reduction of the dollar's gold content, an action he considered both unconstitutional and unwise. He resumed his private legal practice representing clients in the federal courts as well as before governmental agencies.

Despite leaving his appointment as undersecretary, Acheson's overall support for the New Deal and his relationship with Frankfurter (who often joined him for the morning walk to work) and Roosevelt resulted in his being named chair of a committee to study the operation of the federal government's administrative bureaus and advise the president on economic matters. His enthusiastic support of FDR's foreign policy prompted the president to bring him back into the administration as assistant secretary of state to CORDELL HULL. Working to aid the British, Acheson collaborated with fellow "Happy Hotdog" BENJAMIN

COHEN, a presidential aide, to draft the legal basis for a destroyer-bases swap in 1940. His legal-brief ingenuity impressed the president, who appointed him assistant secretary of state for economic affairs after reelection to a third presidential term.

During World War II, Acheson focused on the executive branch's relations with Congress and helped to coordinate the lend-lease program. He served as a delegate to the July 1944 Bretton Woods Conference, which led to the International Monetary Fund (IMF) and the Reconstruction and Development Bank (World Bank). In addition, he helped to persuade isolationist Republican senator ARTHUR VANDENBERG to support the United Nations in January 1945. This work led Acheson into contact with Harry Truman, another early-morning walker, who as president would name Acheson secretary of state. Each appreciated the other's loyalty, orderliness, and straightforward approach to politics in contrast to FDR's more indirect maneuvering. Had Acheson been more flexible and less moralistic, he might have risen much earlier to a key position in the Roosevelt administration. Acheson left the State Department in 1953, and then served as the Democratic Party's primary critic of Republican foreign policy during the remainder of the decade. He served as an informal adviser to John Kennedy and Lyndon Johnson during the 1960s. His final years were spent writing his memoirs until he died on October 12, 1971, in Silver Spring, Maryland.

Agee, James Rufus
(1909–1955) *writer*

Great personal and political crises occasionally conspire to produce not only great political leaders but also outstanding writers like James Agee. He was born on November 27, 1909, in Knoxville, Tennessee, and was 16 when his father—whom he later idealized—died. Agee's best-known and perhaps greatest work, *Let Us Now Praise Famous Men* (1941), captured the plight of impoverished Depression-era sharecroppers. The setting was reminiscent of his father's lower-class background; his mother had enjoyed a genteel upbringing.

Despite his border-state birthplace, Agee was educated at Phillips Exeter Academy and Harvard University. His first book of poems won the Yale Series of Younger Poets award. A staff writer for *Fortune* from 1932 to 1937, Agee wrote an article on the New Deal's Tennessee Valley Authority (TVA), and the magazine subsequently sent him and photographer WALKER EVANS to Alabama to gather material for a story on rural tenant farmers. They stayed for two months and focused on three sharecropper families. *Fortune* held their story for a year before finally rejecting it as too harrowing for publication. It was published in 1941 in book form as *Let Us Now Praise Famous Men* and earned Agee critical acclaim. Agee's empathy for his subject was transformed into one of the great works from the Depression era. His poetic prose captured both the suffering and the dignity of the three families. Like Abraham Lincoln and Walt Whitman, who both wanted the public "to think anew," Agee's experimental style captured the lives of those whom the New Deal attempted to assist. A decade later, he wrote a five-part television script about Lincoln's early years for the *Omnibus* program.

During the 1940s and 1950s, Agee wrote Hollywood screenplays and adaptations that included *The Blue Hotel, The African Queen, The Night of the Hunter,* and *Key Largo.* In 1951, he wrote his only other book published during his lifetime, the short novel *Morning Watch.* He completed his autobiographical novel, *A Death in the Family,* in 1955. It was published posthumously in 1957 and made into a play, *All the Way Home,* in 1960 and a film of the same name in 1963. He died on May 16, 1955, in New York City.

Marian Anderson is seen here shaking hands with a woman at the ceremony for the dedication of a mural commemorating Anderson's 1939 concert on the steps of the Lincoln Memorial. *(Library of Congress)*

Anderson, Marian
(1897–1993) *opera singer*

The pervasiveness of the New Deal throughout American culture is reflected in the operatic career of Marian Anderson, who became a symbol of both the talent of African Americans and their mistreatment in modern America.

Born on February 17, 1897, in Philadelphia, Pennsylvania, to parents able to offer few advantages, Anderson showed an early interest in music. She joined the children's choir of Union Baptist Church even before she taught herself to play the piano at age eight. Despite her ability, however, in high school she was refused admission to a local music school due to her race. After winning a vocal competition, she appeared with the New York Philharmonic in 1925 and then received a fellowship to continue her training. Her European debut was in Berlin in 1930. From 1935 through the remainder of her professional singing career, she was represented by the great impresario Sol Hurok, who turned her contralto voice into an international box office hit.

In 1938 Anderson performed 70 concerts in the United States, setting a concert tour record for an opera singer. The world of opera and politics collided shortly thereafter when Hurok tried to book her into the nation's capital at its then-premier auditorium, Constitution Hall, owned by the Daughters of the American Revolution (DAR). At that time, Washington, D.C., was still a southern outpost, and like the rest of the South, it was segregated. The DAR denied Anderson the opportunity to sing there.

The denial sparked a national furor. ELEANOR ROOSEVELT, a life member of the DAR, resigned in protest. Secretary of the Interior HAROLD ICKES and the First Lady arranged to have Anderson appear instead on the steps of the Lincoln Memorial on Easter Sunday, April 9, 1939; despite her support for the singer, the First Lady did not attend. Anderson began her concert before a crowd of 75,000 by singing "America" and established a precedent for the Lincoln Memorial as the capital site for public demonstrations. In 1943, the concert was depicted in a New Deal mural at the Interior Department, which was presented at a commemorative event by the DAR to benefit United China Relief.

Anderson became a symbol of integrated America by becoming the first black American to appear at the Metropolitan Opera House in New York City on January 7, 1955. She sang the national anthem at the 1957 inauguration of President Dwight Eisenhower and again in 1961 when President John F. Kennedy was inaugurated. After her retirement in 1964, she made guest appearances as the narrator of Aaron Copland's *A Lincoln Portrait*, often with her nephew James DePriest, who became the conductor of the Oregon Symphony and was Anderson's only living relative in her later years. In 1978, she was selected as one of the first five performing artists to receive the Kennedy Center Honors in the nation's capital. Her professional and symbolic careers had overlapped and come full circle. She died on April 8, 1993, in Portland, Oregon.

Armstrong, Louis
(Louis Daniel Armstrong)
(1901–1971) *jazz musician*

During the 1930s and 1940s, while Franklin Roosevelt was reshaping the American presidency, and AARON COPLAND was defining American classical music, Louis Armstrong was creating a world market for American jazz while establishing himself as the most famous trumpet player in the world. The giant shadows cast by all three extended around the globe. Each carved his place in American history using innate talents and modeling for the world the United States's embodiment of democratic values regardless of class or color. And while doing so, each seemed the epitome of an individual who derived personal and professional satisfaction from his public contributions. Through the medium in which each excelled, they were able to communicate their gifts easily to the public.

Louis Daniel Armstrong was born in New Orleans, Louisiana, on August 4, 1901, the illegitimate son of African-American parents in a segregated society. In 1911, while still a schoolboy, he bought his first cornet. He soon dropped out of school and ended up in the New Orleans Colored Waif's Home for Boys (1913–14), where he received his first formal music instruction. With incredible native talent and seemingly endless energy, Armstrong began to forge his career in music despite his minimal training. As a teenager he played in street parades as well as for christenings and funerals, and he held a variety of day jobs. By 1918, he was married to the first of his four wives.

He soon came under the influence of his mentor, Joe "King" Oliver and his Creole Jazz Band, with whom Armstrong made some of his early recordings. In 1922, he moved to Chicago to play second cornet in Oliver's band at the Lincoln Garden's Café. After his second marriage in 1924, he moved briefly to New York City, where he played with the Fletcher Henderson orchestra at the Roseland Ballroom. It was in New York that he developed the new swing jazz style on his trumpet. The next year, he was back in Illinois to make his first recordings as the leader of his own band. Over the next three years, Satchmo—the nickname eventually bestowed on him in England by the editor of a music magazine—helped to create the cornet and trumpet virtuoso jazz solo within an ensemble piece. He not only improvised in the best tradition of jazz, he also composed and sang, all the while expanding jazz's expressive dimensions.

By 1929, Armstrong had returned to New York with his own band, known as the Hot Five and Hot Seven ensembles. His improvisatory singing popularized the "scat" technique in which the voice is used as a musical instrument stringing together nonsensical syllables. He had picked up the basis for scat during his early years in New Orleans. Institutionalizing it on his recordings, Satchmo would influence other jazz singers, including Ella Fitzgerald. The naturally gravelly quality of his voice contributed to Armstrong's distinctive style. He toured Europe in 1932, and his music became a sensation there.

During the 1930s and 1940s, Satchmo reached a creative peak. By allowing Joe Glaser to serve as his business manager and agent from 1935 to 1969, Armstrong was free to focus on his musical genius. In doing so, he became a national celebrity. In 1937, he became the first African-American artist featured in a network radio series; by then he was appearing with a big band. He also appeared in more than 50 films, including *Rhapsody in Black and Blue* (1932), *She Done Him Wrong* (1933), *Pennies from Heaven* (1936), *Every Day's a Holiday* (1937), *Doctor Rhythm* (1938), *Cabin in the Sky* (1943), and *Jam Session* (1944). On a more personal level, he divorced his second wife in

1935 and married his third one in 1938. He wed for the fourth and final time in 1942 to Lucille Wilson. None of the marriages produced children.

Armstrong's popularity and fame continued throughout his life. On February 21, 1949, he appeared on the front cover of *Time* magazine. That same year, he returned to his birthplace and the roots of his music to serve as King of the Zulus for the annual Mardi Gras parade, an honor that brought him enormous personal satisfaction. Twenty years later, he appeared in the movie *Hello Dolly* (1969) with Barbra Streisand. He died on July 6, 1971, in Queens, New York.

Arnold, Henry Harley
(Hap Arnold)
(1886–1950) *assistant chief of the Army Air Corps, chief of the Army Air Force, member of the Joint Chiefs of Staff*

Born on June 25, 1886, in Gladwyne, Pennsylvania, to a physician father and housewife mother, Henry "Hap" Arnold attended local public schools before entering the U.S. Military Academy at West Point. On graduation in 1907, he ranked in the middle of his class. What he lacked in academic excellence he made up for with character and a genial personality. After serving as an infantry officer in the Philippines and New York, Arnold volunteered for flight training when aviation was in its infancy and found his true calling. Training with the Aviation Section of the Signal Corps in 1911, he briefly took flight instruction from the Wright brothers in Dayton, Ohio. Later that year, he became an army flight instructor in College Park, Maryland. In 1913, he returned to the Philippines with his bride, Eleanor Pool. They eventually had four children.

Arnold returned stateside in 1917, joining the Aviation Section at Rockwell Field in

San Diego, California, and later that year he became head of the 7th Aero Squadron in the Panama Canal Zone. During World War I, he served as the assistant director of the new Office of Military Aeronautics in Washington, D.C. During the interwar period, he served in a variety of military assignments on the West Coast.

At the beginning of the New Deal, Arnold was placed in charge of the army's attempt to deliver mail in the western United States via airplanes. The effort proved unsuccessful, but he was absolved of responsibility for the failure. By the end of summer 1934, Arnold had again demonstrated his aviation mettle by conducting a round-trip flight of 10 B-10 bombers from Washington, D.C., to Fairbanks, Alaska. The exercise confirmed the potential for strategic aerial bombing. He was made the assistant chief of the Army Air Corps in 1936, and in July 1941 he was promoted to chief of the Army Air Force.

Like his mentor, General William "Billy" Mitchell, Arnold understood the potential that air power held in modern warfare. Unlike Mitchell, however, Arnold—whose nickname *Hap* was short for "Happy"—was diplomatic, and he became the champion for army aviation at most of the conferences of the Allies. His experience, expertise, and personality earned him FDR's trust, allowing Arnold to create the world's largest air force during World War II. FDR's similar trust in GEORGE MARSHALL allowed the American service chiefs to come together informally in March 1942 as the Joint Chiefs of Staff, with Arnold representing the Army Air Corps. In May 1942, he developed the plan for daylight, precision bombing against Nazi Germany. By late 1944, he had earned his fifth star as an army general and directed B-29 bombings against Japan that would culminate in the atomic bombings of Hiroshima and Nagasaki in 1945. However, as early as 1943, Arnold had begun to experience heart problems that forced his retirement in

1946, a year before the United States Air Force was created as a separate military branch. In 1949, Congress formally recognized Arnold's role in American military aviation by making him the first General of the Air Force. When he died in California a few months later on January 15, 1950, Arnold's survivors included not only his widow and children, but the U.S. Air Force itself.

Arnold, Thurman Wesley
(1891–1969) *assistant attorney general*

Unlike most of the talented and ambitious "legal realist" lawyers who staffed the New Deal, Thurman Arnold was also a former military veteran, academician, and politician. He was born on June 2, 1891, in Laramie, Wyoming. After graduating Phi Beta Kappa from Princeton University in 1911, he entered Harvard Law School, graduating in 1914. He then practiced law in Chicago. In 1917, his Illinois National Guard unit was mobilized for service with General "Black Jack" Pershing's expedition against Pancho Villa in Mexico, and he also served in World War I. Following his return from Europe, Arnold joined his father's law practice in Laramie, Wyoming, and in 1921 he was elected to the Wyoming state legislature, the only Democrat. The next year, he was elected mayor of Laramie on a progressive platform. After his defeat as county prosecutor in 1924, he served as the judge advocate general of the Wyoming National Guard for the next three years.

A friendship with a Harvard classmate led to Arnold's appointment as dean of the West Virginia Law School from 1927 to 1930. His reform of West Virginia's court system led to his becoming a law professor at Yale University, where he taught for the next eight years; fellow faculty included WILLIAM O. DOUGLAS and political scientist Harold D. Lassell. Yale was a center of legal realism, which views the law in political terms. Arnold dismissed traditional casebook pedagogy and was responsible for beginning Yale's moot-court simulations. His two most influential legal realist books, *The Symbols of Government* (1935) and *The Folklore of Capitalism* (1937), were written during his Yale tenure.

At the same time that he taught and wrote, the politically engaged Arnold served as counsel to the Agriculture Department, as a legal adviser to the governor-general of the Philippines, and as a trial examiner for the Securities and Exchange Commission, which William O. Douglas had joined in 1936. In 1938, U.S. Attorney General ROBERT JACKSON recommended his good friend Arnold to head the Justice Department's antitrust division. Arnold served as the New Deal's trustbuster for five years, expanding his staff from fewer than 50 lawyers to more than 300. He filed 230 suits for monopoly practices or restraint of trade, involving most sectors of the national economy. Many

scholars consider his tenure (1938–43) as the most effective antitrust enforcement in American history. He was less interested in breaking up companies than in letting them know their activities were being monitored for monopolistic and unfair practices.

With the onset of World War II, the Roosevelt administration became less concerned with controlling big business, and Arnold became disillusioned. After he resigned from the Justice Department, Roosevelt appointed him to the Federal Court of Appeals for the District of Columbia, where he served two years of a lifetime appointment. He then established the law firm Arnold, Fortas, and Porter with former undersecretary of agriculture ABE FORTAS and attorney Paul Porter. During the 1950s McCarthy era, Arnold defended several individuals charged with communist espionage. The former army veteran became a hawk during the 1960s, viewing student protests of the Vietnam War as approaching treason. He died on November 7, 1969, in Alexandria, Virginia.

B

Bailey, Josiah William
(1873–1946) *U.S. senator*

Born on September 14, 1873, in Warrenton, North Carolina, Josiah Bailey became a Wilsonian Democrat. He was a southern progressive in education but also a states' rights fiscal conservative opposed to unions and integration. His lifelong moralistic streak derived from the influence of his father, who was a Baptist preacher and editor of North Carolina's second-largest periodical, a weekly Baptist newspaper. After graduation from Wake Forest College in 1893, Bailey assumed editorship of the newspaper. His restlessness, however, led to his resignation from the paper in 1908, and he became a lawyer. A mixture of progressive politics with a private law practice and his marriage in 1916 to Edith Walker Pou, from one of the state's leading families, led to Bailey's deeper involvement in state and national politics. He lost his 1922 bid for the Democratic gubernatorial nomination, but after the state's Democratic machine deserted AL SMITH's presidential bid in 1928, Bailey's loyalty to the party was rewarded, and he was elected senator in 1930.

The New Deal was too radical for Bailey's provincial regionalism, though he initially stuck by it in 1932 and 1936 out of party loyalty. After his 1936 reelection to the Senate, however, Bai-ley broke with FDR over his Court-packing plan and efforts to modernize the presidency. He joined Republican senator ARTHUR VAN-DENBERG in drafting a bipartisan "conservative manifesto" in opposition to further New Deal proposals. In the 1938 congressional elections, Bailey openly backed candidates Roosevelt had tried to purge. When he became chair of the powerful Senate Commerce Committee, he dropped his earlier isolationist views and helped the administration repeal the Neutrality Act of 1939, as did Vandenberg. Bailey supported taxes to finance U.S. participation in World War II, and his support in November 1943 for the Connally Resolution advocating an international organization was followed in February 1944 with his backing of the proposed United Nations. He died on December 15, 1946, in Raleigh, North Carolina.

Baker, Newton Diehl
(1871–1937) *Democratic presidential dark-horse candidate*

The son of a physician and former Confederate soldier, Newton Baker was born on December 3, 1871, in Martinsburg, West Virginia. He graduated in 1892 from Johns Hopkins University, where he took a class taught by future president Woodrow Wilson; when in Baltimore, Wilson would stay at the boarding house where Baker lived. Baker received his law degree from Washington and Lee University in 1894. He served as secretary to William L. Wilson, Grover Cleveland's second-term postmaster general, before moving to Cleveland, Ohio, to practice law. From 1911 to 1915, he was the progressive "Boy Mayor" of Cleveland. In 1916 President Wilson named Baker as secretary of war, a cabinet post he retained until the end of the administration. Never a crusader or an extremist, Baker remained loyal to the first president born in the South after the Civil War.

In 1921, Baker left public office and returned to a successful legal practice. At the 1924 Democratic convention, he argued the case for the League of Nations. Initially Baker was supportive of the New Deal, but at heart he remained a Cleveland conservative. In 1932, he was nominated for the presidency by anti-Roosevelt Democrats as a dark-horse candidate, but he was unable to block Roosevelt's nomination. During the 1930s, he served the army on various boards, including chairing the "Baker Board," which called for the reorganization of the Army Air Corps. He died on December 25, 1937, in Shaker Heights, Ohio.

Baldwin, Calvin Benham
(1902–1975) *Farm Security Administration official*

An assistant to Secretary of Agriculture HENRY WALLACE, Calvin Baldwin remained his close associate after Wallace's cabinet service in the Roosevelt administration. Baldwin was born on August 19, 1902, in Radford, Virginia. After attending Virginia Polytechnic Institute in the early 1920s, he began work with a railroad, rising quickly through the ranks from inspector to the general foreman's assistant. By 1928, he was proprietor of Electric Sales and Service

Company of East Radford, Virginia. From there he was recruited to the Roosevelt administration. He first served as assistant to Wallace from 1933 to 1935; then as assistant to REXFORD TUGWELL, the administrator of the Resettlement Administration from 1935 to 1936; and finally as assistant to Will W. Alexander, the first administrator of the Farm Security Administration (FSA), from 1937 to 1939. The FSA was designed to supervise the programs of the Resettlement Administration and the new farm ownership program.

Baldwin replaced Alexander as head of the Farm Security Administration in 1940. Although he did his best to defend the FSA from growing criticism leveled against it in Congress by the conservative coalition, he was unable to save it. Appropriations declined from 1941 to 1946, when it was replaced by the Farmers Home Administration. For his service to the New Deal, Roosevelt named Baldwin to his final federal government post with a State Department position in Italy, where he served from 1942 to 1943. He eventually became campaign manager for Henry Wallace's unsuccessful presidential campaign in 1948. Baldwin remained the national secretary of the Progressive Party until its dissolution in 1955. Baldwin died on May 12, 1975, in Bethesda, Maryland.

Baldwin, Stanley
(1867–1947) *British prime minister*

A conservative isolationist, Stanley Baldwin illustrates the lack of prescience in foreign affairs among British political leaders between World War I and World War II. He was born on August 3, 1867, in Worcestershire, England. His father supervised an inherited family steel business, and his mother's brother was Rudyard Kipling. He was educated at Harrow and Trinity College, Cambridge University, but he lacked intellectual ambition. In 1892, he married Lucy Ridsdale, with whom he enjoyed a happy and stable marriage. He entered the family business in 1898 and remained in it until 1908.

His father's death in 1908 was the impetus for Baldwin's transition into politics. The elder Baldwin had been a member of Parliament (MP). Although Stanley Baldwin had run unsuccessfully for parliament two years earlier, he replaced his father as a Conservative MP. "Like father, like son" was a recurring theme in Baldwin's life. His early career in the House of Commons reflected the lifelong tendency toward caution and mediocrity that had also characterized his educational record. However, World War I intervened, and Baldwin quickly rose through a series of political promotions. In 1917, he became parliamentary secretary to Andrew Bonar Law, and from 1917 to 1921, he was financial secretary to the Treasury. He next became a member of David Lloyd George's postwar coalition government. Bonar Law then became prime minister, and Baldwin was made chancellor of the exchequer, serving in that position briefly until Law died in 1923. Because of a split among Conservative leaders, Baldwin was chosen to succeed Bonar Law, the first of what would be three terms of service as prime minister.

Baldwin initially served as prime minister only a few months in 1923 due to his defeat later that year over the issue of a protective tariff to relieve unemployment. The first Labor government of Ramsay MacDonald took over until the Conservatives returned to power in 1924. Baldwin became prime minister for the second time, serving until May 1929, when the electorate replaced him with another Labor government. Baldwin remained the moderate leader of the Conservative Party and became prime minister for the third time on June 7, 1935, following MacDonald's retirement. During his third term, Italy invaded Ethiopia, Germany reoccupied the

Rhineland, and the Spanish civil war began. Because of Britain's perilous economic state, Baldwin concentrated on domestic economic affairs. Further, as an isolationist, he had little interest in foreign affairs. Many historians believe the roots of Neville Chamberlain's appeasement policy may be traced to the MacDonald and Baldwin governments. While Baldwin is credited with both skillfully handling the abdication of King Edward VIII and improving Britain's economic condition, it is felt by many that he underestimated Nazi Germany.

After the coronation of George VI, Baldwin retired as prime minister on May 28, 1937; he was replaced by Chamberlain. Politically inactive following his retirement, he died in Worcestershire on December 13, 1947.

Banister, Marion Glass
(1875–1951)   *assistant treasurer of the United States*

The daughter of a distinguished Virginia family, Marion Glass Banister was born in 1875 in Lynchburg. Her sister, Meta Glass, became president of Sweet Briar College, and her older brother, CARTER GLASS, served as a U.S. senator from Virginia. Marion Glass married the son of another old Virginia family, Blair Banister, who died in the mid-1920s.

Both Banister and her brother entered political life as Wilsonian Democrats. She wrote for the Committee on Public Information and then for the Democratic Party during the 1920s. In 1922 she became the first editor of the *Fortnightly Bulletin*, a pamphlet aimed at the Democratic Party's women's clubs in their effort to organize women voters. She remained as editor until 1924, the same year that she cofounded the Women's National Democratic Club (WNDC) in Washington, D.C. Banister supported her political work between 1924 and

1931 with employment in public relations for the Mayflower Hotel in Washington, D.C., until the Great Depression forced its temporary closure. Her active support of Roosevelt in the 1932 election led to her appointment in 1933 as assistant treasurer of the United States. Her position likely moderated her brother's differences with the New Deal. She died in Washington, D.C., in 1951.

Bankhead, John Hollis, Jr.
(1872–1946) *U.S. senator*

John H. Bankhead was born into a prominent southern family on July 8, 1872, in Moscow, Alabama. He first lived in the nation's capital as secretary for his father, a U.S. senator. He earned his undergraduate degree in 1891 from the University of Alabama and his law degree from Georgetown University in 1893. He practiced law with his brother, WILLIAM BROCKMAN BANKHEAD, for 12 years. After being elected to the Alabama legislature in 1902, he authored the Alabama Election Law that disenfranchised most black voters. He was legal counsel for the Alabama Power Company and for several railroads, and from 1911 to 1925 he was president of the Bankhead Coal Corporation, which had been founded by his father and operated one of the state's largest coal mines.

In 1926, Bankhead lost the Democratic primary for the U.S. Senate seat representing Alabama to HUGO LAFAYETTE BLACK, who had attacked him for his association with corporations. For the rest of his political career, Bankhead closely aligned himself with cotton farmers to compensate for Black's successful populist attack. However, the backing of Alabama's corporations was key to his 1930 senatorial victory.

Bankhead's senatorial career reflected general support for Franklin Roosevelt, especially in agriculture and defense. His concern about rural poverty, focusing on the fact that more than 65 percent of Alabama's farms were operated by tenants, and his support for agricultural commodity prices, especially for cotton, earned him the moniker "Parity John." He sponsored many measures to protect southern farm interests, including the Agricultural Adjustment Acts of 1933 and 1938, the Bankhead Cotton Control Act of 1934, the Soil Conservation and Domestic Allotment Act of 1936, and the Bankhead-Jones Farm Tenancy Act of 1937, which created the Farm Security Administration. Despite his support for some of Roosevelt measures, he voted against FDR's Court-packing plan in 1937. He participated in filibusters against anti-lynching legislation, abolition of the poll tax, and a permanent fair employment practices commission. Bankhead, who typified the amiable, bald, and portly old-style southern politician, died on June 12, 1946, in Bethesda, Maryland.

Bankhead, William Brockman
(1874–1940) *U.S. congressman, Speaker of the House*

The son of a former U.S. senator and the younger brother of Senator JOHN HOLLIS BANKHEAD, William Brockman Bankhead was born on April 12, 1874, in Moscow, Alabama. He grew up in a southern states' rights and segregationist environment, yet the Bankheads preferred compromise over rigidity in politics. An undergraduate degree in 1893 and a graduate degree in 1896 were followed in 1898 with a law degree from Georgetown University. Bankhead then moved to New York and briefly practiced law there while involved in Broadway theater productions before returning to Alabama in 1900 to practice law with his brother. His daughter was the actress Tallulah Bankhead.

Back in his home state, Bankhead followed family tradition and became active in politics, winning Alabama's seventh congressional district seat in 1916 and holding it until his death. The district included counties from the north Alabama hill country and the lowland Black Belt. His amiable personality and chairmanship of the powerful House Rules Committee (1934–39) enabled him to expedite New Deal legislation. His seniority allowed him to become the House majority leader in 1935–36 under Speaker of the House JOSEPH BYRNS. The next year he replaced Byrns as Speaker, and SAM RAYBURN assumed the post of majority leader.

Although Bankhead was in ill health, he unsuccessfully sought the Democratic vice-presidential nomination in 1940 without FDR's support. Bankhead had been sympathetic to FDR's 1937 Court-packing plan, but he felt the president had mismanaged the proposal by failing to inform him of the plan. Bankhead died on September 14, 1940, in Bethesda, Maryland.

Barkley, Alben William

(1877–1956) *Senate majority leader, vice president of the United States*

Alben Barkley rose from humble border-state origins to national prominence as the Senate majority leader during the New Deal and became vice president under HARRY S. TRUMAN. Born on November 24, 1877, in Wheel, Kentucky, he was the son of a former tobacco tenant farmer and railroad worker. Barkley failed to graduate from high school, but he received an undergraduate degree in 1897 from the tiny Methodist-run Marvin College. He struggled to obtain legal training in Georgia and Virginia and began practicing law in 1901 in Paducah, Kentucky, developing a reputation for public speaking. Within four years he had won local elections. He was elected to the U.S. House of Representatives in 1912 and developed a friendship with Woodrow Wilson, whose progressive "New Freedom" legislation offered him a policy program to champion.

After 14 years in the House, Barkley won a seat in the U.S. Senate in 1926. With the advent of the Great Depression, he became an advocate of the New Deal and served on the powerful finance and foreign affairs committees. He was also a keynote speaker at the 1932, 1936, and 1940 national Democratic conventions. With the exception of the Bonus Bill, to give early monetary stipends to veterans from World War I, he strongly backed the New Deal, including a federal antilynching bill. With the support of FDR, but by only a single vote, Barkley was chosen to replace the recently deceased JOSEPH ROBINSON as the Senate majority leader in 1937. He was known both for his talents as a stump speaker and his conciliatory personality. He was later accused of using Works Progress Administration (WPA) personnel and money during his 1939 reelection campaign, resulting in congressional cutbacks in WPA funding. The scandal also resulted in the Hatch Act of 1939, which forbids political activism and financial contributions by federal employees. In early 1944, he briefly resigned as majority leader in protest after FDR wrote a stinging message to veto a tax bill that Barkley had tried to make acceptable to the administration. The president quickly backed off, and the Senate unanimously reinstated the majority leader with FDR's support. Roosevelt, however, declined to support Barkley for the vice-presidential nomination in 1944, supposedly because of his age. Nevertheless, Truman chose him for his running mate in 1948. After his first wife's death in 1947, Barkley married Jane Rucker Hadley, who was 30 years younger. He died on April 30, 1956, in Lexington, Kentucky.

Baruch, Bernard Mannes
(1870–1965) *presidential adviser*

Bernard Baruch was born on August 19, 1870, in Camden, South Carolina. When he was 11, his physician father uprooted his southern Jewish family and transplanted it to New York City, where Simon Baruch became a leader in public health. After his graduation from City College of New York, Bernard Baruch became a Wall Street financier. In 1897, he married Annie Griffen, an Episcopalian. Just as he had bridged the personal religious divide between himself and his Christian wife and the cultural divide between North and South by owning a plantation in his native South Carolina, Baruch soon bridged the gap between Wall Street and politics. He became one of the most prominent American Jews during the first half of the 20th century.

Like FDR, Baruch entered national politics through his relationship with Woodrow Wilson, becoming one of Wilson's major financial supporters. His friendship with WILLIAM MCADOO, Wilson's Treasury secretary and another transplanted southerner, led to Wilson's appointment of Baruch as chairman of the War Industries Board (WIB) in 1917, leading the public to view him as the "czar" of industry. Baruch supported McAdoo's failed presidential bid as the Democratic nominee in 1924.

Baruch wanted to become FDR's secretary of state in 1932, but Roosevelt limited him to brief service as a participant during the London Economic Conference of 1933. He also added Baruch's associate HUGH JOHNSON to his so-called Brain Trust and later made Johnson—who had served on Baruch's WIB—head of the National Recovery Administration. FDR also appointed another Baruch friend and WIB member, GEORGE N. PEEK, to head the Agricultural Adjustment Administration. During World War II, Baruch worked to develop arti-

ficial rubber, and he assisted in a unit of the War Mobilization Office to develop postwar industrial reconversion.

FDR and Baruch were ambivalent about each other, and Baruch never became a New Dealer; however, he maintained a closer friendship with First Lady ELEANOR ROOSEVELT. He promoted her and helped to subsidize her Arthurdale project, a subsistence homestead community near Reedsville, West Virginia. He was known as the "Park Bench Statesman" for his unofficial Washington, D.C., office on a park bench in Lafayette Square across the street from the White House where he met informally with presidents and others. Decades later, the bench became a memorial to Baruch. He died on June 20, 1965, in New York City.

Bernard Mannes Baruch *(Library of Congress)*

Bennett, Harry Herbert
(1892–1979) *Ford Motor Company executive*

As personal assistant to HENRY FORD, founder and owner of the Ford Motor Company, Harry Bennett was the staff person directly in charge of negotiating with workers during their efforts throughout the 1930s and 1940s to unionize at the time in American history when the New Deal first recognized the rights of workers. In discharging his duties, Bennett was caught between the conflicting forces of his authoritarian employer's demands and the emergence of workers' rights supported by the New Deal. In Bennett, Ford had found a right-hand man who made up for his lack of formal training with abundant physical vigor, personal loyalty, and street smarts.

Bennett was born on January 17, 1892, in Ann Arbor, Michigan, to a blue-collar worker father and a school-teacher mother. When he was two years old, his father was killed in a fight. His mother soon remarried, but his step-father died just a few years later. Following his stepfather's death, he and his mother relocated in 1907 to Detroit, where Bennett received training as a commercial artist. Conflict at home drove him to escape by joining the U.S. Navy two years later. During the seven years he was enlisted, he performed a variety of assignments, including cartoonist for the navy magazine, ship gunner, and successful boxer.

Bennett's encounter with Henry Ford occurred after journalist Arthur Brisbane chanced to observe his performance in a New York street fight. Impressed, Brisbane brought Bennett to meet Henry Ford, who hired him in early 1916. Bennett first worked briefly in Ford's New York sales office before being transferred later that year to Detroit, where he worked for a short time in the Ford Motion Picture Department. Once in Ford's world, Bennett soon became the boss's personal assistant, although, like most of Ford's employees,

he served without an official job title. His emerging responsibilities included diverse duties such as supervising security at the new Ford River Rouge plant located in Dearborn near Detroit as well as serving as the company's liaison with local reporters.

Ford's authoritarian expectation was that his lieutenants' first devotion was to the Ford Motor Company, an attitude that helped to unravel the two of Bennett's three marriages that ended in divorce. (He had two children, one with his first wife and one with his third and final wife.) Ford's approach with top employees was to convert them into classic company men who had no time for personal lives. The energetic and ambitious Bennett was willing to comply, and by 1928, the year of his first divorce, he had become Ford's most trusted lieutenant.

Instead of the customary 10-round bout, Bennett's fight with Ford's workers was drawn out over 10 years. Throughout that decade, there were three deciding rounds fought from the opening bell in early 1932 until 1941, when Ford threw in the towel and accepted the New Deal's change in the rules between worker and employer relations. The opening round started on March 7, 1932, with a hunger march on the River Rouge, Michigan, plant by several thousand unemployed workers. Bennett's efforts to calm the angry marchers had the opposite effect: they threw rocks at him, triggering gunfire by either Bennett's own security force or by Dearborn police. In the violence, four marchers were killed and 20 more were wounded. Bennett was knocked unconscious during the melee.

The second round lasted for several years as the United Auto Workers (UAW) sparred with the Ford Motor Company in its attempt to organize at the River Rouge plant. Ford refused to negotiate and fired workers whom he suspected of union activity. By 1937, union officials, including WALTER REUTHER, had suffered severe beatings by Bennett's security force. This time, however, New Deal legislation was in place to make a difference. With the creation of the new National Labor Relations Board as part of the New Deal program and the Supreme Court's upholding of it in April 1937, the Ford Motor Company was found guilty of violating provisions of the National Labor Relations Act, which gave workers the right to join unions. Shortly afterward, in 1938, Henry Ford suffered a severe stroke.

By 1941, the final punches were being thrown. The union had forced a shutdown of the River Rouge plant, compelling Ford finally to negotiate with the UAW. He signed a contract with the union that involved wage and working condition concessions. In a de facto exchange, the Ford Motor Company received war contracts from the federal government. That same year, Ford suffered a second stroke. Two years later, Ford put the loyal Bennett on the company's board of directors and made him responsible for personnel, labor relations, and public relations. Within a few years, however, Henry Ford's senility led to assumption of the presidency by his grandson, Henry Ford II. Bennett's professional demise followed. He retired in September 1945 and lived on his ranches out West until his death on January 4, 1979.

Bennett, Hugh Hammond
(1881–1960) *chief, Soil Conservation Service, Department of Agriculture*

His gift for public relations and scientific showmanship earned Hugh Bennett recognition as the "father of soil conservation." Born on April 15, 1881, in Wadesboro, North Carolina, to a family of North Carolina farmers, he graduated from the University of North Carolina in 1903 and began work as a chemist in the Bureau of Soils in the Department of Agri-

culture in Washington, D.C. His life's work was influenced by the first-ever national governors' conference convened in May 1908 by THEODORE ROOSEVELT in Washington, D.C., to discuss conservation issues.

Bennett spent the next 25 years conducting soil surveys throughout the United States and Central America, while his reputation as a soils expert grew. He aroused national attention about the need to develop a national program to combat soil erosion, which in 1928 prompted Congress to establish erosion control stations and allowed Bennett to set up 10 of them across the nation. That work was expanded with the New Deal in 1933 when the National Industrial Recovery Act allocated soil conservation within the Department of the Interior. The department's secretary, HAROLD ICKES, chose Bennett as the director of the Soil Erosion Service. Bennett lobbied for an expanded program after the devastating effects of the Dust Bowl during the Great Depression. As a result, the Soil Conservation Act returned soil conservation to the Agriculture Department in 1935, with Bennett directing the Soil Conservation Service until his retirement in 1951. During his tenure, he used employees from the Civilian Conservation Corps and other federal work-relief agencies on conservation projects. He then decentralized soil conservation work, and in 1937, FDR persuaded states to create nearly 3,000 local conservation districts to oversee these projects while Bennett supported them with the necessary scientific and technology knowledge. He died on July 7, 1960, in Burlington, North Carolina.

Bennett, Richard Bedford
(1870–1947) *Canadian prime minister*

It was a caprice of fate that transformed Richard Bennett into the Canadian equivalent of U.S. president Herbert Hoover. Bennett served as the leader of Canada's Conservative Party from 1927 to 1938 and was prime minister from 1930 to 1935. Although Bennett was, unlike Hoover, a gifted orator, both were too wedded to tradition—imperialism and colonialism in Bennett's case—to address effectively the changing realities of their nations. Bennett would also become the Canadian scapegoat for the Great Depression just as Hoover would in the United States.

Born on July 3, 1870, in Hopewell, New Brunswick, Bennett attended local schools and then enrolled in Dalhousie University, Halifax, Nova Scotia. He began practicing law in his hometown in 1893, but in 1897 he moved to Calgary, Alberta, where he developed his law practice. He became one of Canada's wealthiest men through a combination of inherited wealth and prudent investments. His wealth and oratorical and legal skills quickly propelled him to prominence in the world of politics. He served in the North-West Assembly from 1898 to 1905 and in the Alberta legislature from 1909 to 1911. In 1911, he entered the Canadian House of Commons, where he served until 1917. As a bright light in the Conservative Party, Bennett was appointed director general of the National Service in 1917. By 1921, he was the minister of justice and attorney general in the cabinet of Arthur Meighen, succeeding him in 1927 as the leader of the Conservative Party.

It was the impact of the Great Depression that both allowed Bennett to rise to the prime ministership and led to his ultimate political failure. The 1930 election at the outset of the Depression resulted in the defeat of Prime Minister WILLIAM LYON MACKENZIE KING and the Liberal Party. Bennett, who defeated him, made huge promises to overcome the Depression on the basis of tariff protection. Although he is credited with establishment of the Bank of Canada and the Canadian Broadcasting Corporation, Bennett's economic policy—which went against the popular theories of British economist JOHN MAYNARD KEYNES—failed to bring relief to unemployed workers and drought-stricken farmers.

By the end of 1934, Bennett's fear of anarchy drove him to alter his course, and he tried to recast the Conservative Party in the successful model of Franklin Roosevelt's Democratic Party. However, his authoritarian manner failed to persuade either his own party or the general public, which had come to regard him as opportunistic, that a Canadian New Deal was needed. Much of his program was ruled unconstitutional by the Canadian Supreme Court. In the election of 1935, King's Liberals regained power with a resounding defeat of the Conservatives. Bennett remained the Conservative Party leader until 1938, when he retired from politics. Subsequently he moved to England and, in 1941, was made a member of the British House of Lords with the title of viscount. He died on June 26, 1947, in Mickleham, England.

Benton, Thomas Hart
(1889–1975) *New Deal muralist*

One of the most controversial artists of the New Deal, Thomas Hart Benton is associated with the American regionalist school of the 1930s. His innovative mural painting served as the basis of the Works Progress Administration of the 1930s, and he also received a commission from the federal Public Works of Art Project.

Benton's namesake was his great-uncle, U.S. Senator Thomas Hart Benton (1782–1858), who had championed westward expansion; his populist father served in Congress. Benton was born on April 15, 1889, in Neosho, Missouri. Although he lived in rural Missouri in the summers, he spent his winters in the nation's capital, where he viewed the murals in the Library of Congress. Benton's father discouraged his painting, but his mother supported it. After working briefly as a cartoonist for his first job, he spent a year at the Art Institute of Chicago training as a commercial artist and then spent time in France, where he was influenced by impressionism. He returned to Missouri for a year and then left for New York, where he was a struggling painter for a decade.

During World War I, Benton enlisted in the U.S. Navy, an experience that helped turn him from abstractionism to realist painting. His marriage in 1922 to Italian immigrant Rita Piacenza introduced stability into his life, and she acted as his manager and dealer. By 1934, his mural painting had captured national attention, and he was featured on the cover of *Time*.

In late 1936, Benton painted a bold, colorful mural for the Missouri State Capitol in Jefferson City that he considered his masterpiece. Yet it was so controversial that he failed to receive another mural commission for a decade. Conservatives thought his depiction of the United States was too negative. By then, however, his murals had achieved national recognition as capturing the New Deal spirit of the 1930s in the same way that WALKER EVANS used photography, JAMES AGEE used prose, and FRANK CAPRA used film to celebrate the dignity and triumph of the average person facing common economic adversity.

Benton's best-known student was Jackson Pollock, whose abstract expressionism of the 1940s seemed rooted in Benton's early, abbreviated stay in France. Benton's last best-known mural was done in 1961 for the Truman Library in Independence, Missouri. His relationship with the ex-president was his closest among former New Deal politicians. He died on January 9, 1975, in Kansas City, Missouri.

Berle, Adolf Augustus, Jr.
(1895–1971) *assistant secretary of state, ambassador to Brazil*

Born on January 29, 1895, in Brighton, Massachusetts, the son of a Congregational minis-

ter, Adolf Berle was raised and well schooled in the Social Gospel wing of progressive reform. He graduated from Harvard University at 18 and its law school at 21. His first job was with the law firm of LOUIS BRANDEIS in Boston. After doing army intelligence work—first during World War I, then in the Dominican Republic in 1918, and finally at the Paris Peace Conference the next year—he practiced corporate law in New York. In 1927, the same year that he married Beatrice Bend Bishop, daughter of a wealthy American aristocrat, he began teaching at Columbia University. Ever energetic, he also commuted to Massachusetts to teach at Harvard Business School and at the same time wrote for liberal magazines and law reviews.

Berle's first book, *Studies in the Law of Corporate Finance* (1928), reflected his "legal realism" approach to the law, which was echoed in the work of other young reform lawyers who staffed the New Deal—for example, THURMAN ARNOLD, JEROME FRANK, and WILLIAM O. DOUGLAS. His most influential book, *The Modern Corporation and Private Property* (1932), warned about the dangers of concentrated corporate wealth posing a threat to the health of the American democracy and suggested the need for greater government regulation.

Columbia University political science professor RAYMOND MOLEY invited Berle to join the FDR Brain Trust that also included another Columbia University professor, REXFORD TUGWELL. Berle's major contribution was drafting FDR's "Progressive Government" speech that was delivered at the Commonwealth Club of San Francisco on September 23, 1932, which foreshadowed the New Deal's approach to government planning. Berle accepted temporary assignments with the administration during the banking crisis and railroad emergency of 1933, and he participated in a State Department mission to Cuba to stabilize its government that same year. During this time, his home base was New York, where he was an adviser to Mayor FIORELLO LA GUARDIA, serving as chamberlain of the city (1934–37) and masterminding its financial recovery (1934–35), which depended on assistance from the New Deal's Reconstruction Finance Corporation and Public Works Administration. Berle built a political base in the city among labor liberals.

One of FDR's most influential advisers, Berle began his letters to the president with the jocular salutation "Dear Caesar." That greeting, however, may have been more revealing about Berle, who tended to have a Napoleonic complex. He was a short, chain-smoking ideologue obsessed with power. He met his match in his former Harvard law professor, FELIX FRANKFURTER, who was also short but even more insecure. Both were pontificators who preferred their own monologues to dialogues. Berle, one of the founding leaders of New York's Liberal Party, advocated control over the nation's largest corporations, while Frankfurter and Brandeis both merely favored enforcement of antitrust laws.

Following the recession of 1937–38, FDR brought Berle back to his administration as assistant secretary of state to advise on economic policy, indicating the president's desire to have someone advocating planning and control rather than more antitrust enforcement. Berle also focused on Latin American affairs and in the late 1930s organized Pan-American conferences to assist antifascist governments. During World War II, he ran the State Department's international intelligence network and became a critic of the Soviet Union. From 1944 to 1946, he served as ambassador to Brazil and then worked occasionally for the Central Intelligence Agency. During the 1960s, Berle became an anticommunist "cold war liberal." His Latin American expertise resulted in his appointment by President John F. Kennedy as chair of a task force that supported the Bay of Pigs invasion in Cuba. He also backed President Lyndon Johnson's intervention in the Dominican Republic in 1965 as well as his Vietnam policy. The world had changed, but Adolf Berle's ideological rigidity had not, for he remained a product of his early environment. He died on February 17, 1971, in New York City.

Bethune, Mary McLeod
(1875–1955) *director, Division of Negro Affairs, National Youth Administration; special assistant to the secretary of war*

When FDR appointed her director of the Division of Negro Affairs of the National Youth Administration, Mary Bethune became the first African-American woman to head a federal office. She remained the most influential African-American woman in the United States until well after her death.

Bethune overcame substantial obstacles to succeed. Born on July 19, 1875, in Mayesville, South Carolina, the 15th of 17 children of former slaves who became farmers in the South, she attended local schools. She went to Chicago to attend what became the Moody Bible Institute to train for a career as a missionary in Africa. After a year's training, she learned there were no openings there for black missionaries. Instead, she began her career as a missionary educator in the Deep South in 1896. Two years later, she married Albertus Bethune, a salesman, and they moved to Georgia, where their only son was born in 1899. Her husband lacked her interest in missionary work, and the couple separated.

In 1904, Bethune moved to Daytona, Florida, and founded a training school for African-American girls that evolved into the Bethune Cookman College in 1929. She gained national recognition as president of the college and helped to found other African-American organizations. She became vice president of the National Urban League in 1920, was president of the National Association of Colored Women from 1924 to 1928, and was founding president of the National Council of Negro Women.

Bethune's involvement with the national government commenced during the Calvin Coolidge and Herbert Hoover presidential administrations in the 1920s. It blossomed during the New Deal after she and ELEANOR ROOSEVELT established a close friendship. The First Lady arranged for her appointment to a voluntary position on the national advisory committee to the National Youth Administration (NYA) in 1935 that led the next year to a full-time NYA job overseeing activities involving African Americans. She became director of the Division of Negro Affairs in 1939. Eleanor Roosevelt and Bethune visited projects together, and both wrote newspaper and magazine columns.

Bethune remained the only African-American woman with open access to the White House. Until her health began to fail in the 1940s, she was as energetic and politically active as the First Lady. She organized a group of African Americans employed in the federal government, and they became known as the Black Cabinet. The couple of dozen members all were male except for Bethune, who headed the group and held its meetings in her home. When the NYA was terminated in 1943, she became a special assistant to the secretary of war and assistant director of the Women's Army Corps, establishing its first officer-candidate schools.

Bethune died on May 18, 1955, in Daytona Beach, Florida. The federal government dedicated the Mary McLeod Bethune Memorial Statue in Lincoln Park, across from the Lincoln statue located there, on July 10, 1974.

The park is located in southeastern Washington, D.C., near the Library of Congress.

Biddle, Francis Beverly
(1886–1968) *National Labor Relations Board chairman, U.S. solicitor general, U.S. attorney general*

Despite being from a wealthy, conservative patrician family, Francis Biddle developed into a progressive, supporting THEODORE ROOSEVELT's Bull Moose third-party effort in 1912 and then turning to the Democratic Party after Herbert Hoover neglected labor issues in the White House. Biddle identified with the poor and unemployed, so he enthusiastically supported FDR and became a Democrat.

He was born on May 9, 1886, in Paris, France. His father, Algernon Sydney Biddle, a law professor at the University of Pennsylvania, sent his son to Haverford Academy, Groton Academy, and Harvard University. He graduated cum laude from Harvard in 1909 and entered its law school, receiving his law degree in 1911. During the 1911–12 Supreme Court term, he acted as personal secretary to Justice Oliver Wendell Holmes, who embodied for Biddle a sense of noblesse oblige. He then returned to Philadelphia and practiced law for a decade before serving a four-year term as special assistant to the U.S. attorney for the Eastern District of Pennsylvania.

Biddle supported FDR in the 1932 presidential campaign, and in 1934 Roosevelt appointed him chairman of the National Labor Relations Board. He returned to his legal practice after a year but in 1938 returned to Washington, D.C., as the chief counsel for a congressional investigation of the Tennessee Valley Authority (TVA). The investigation disproved allegations of corruption and unfair competition at the TVA, thus restoring its reputation. In 1938 and 1939, he also served as a director and deputy chairman of the Federal Reserve Bank.

In return for his governmental service, Biddle was appointed as a judge on the Third Circuit of the U.S. Court of Appeals in Philadelphia in 1939 but gave up the lifetime appointment after only a year when he found the work too boring. Instead, he returned to the nation's capital to become the U.S. solicitor general, and in this role he won all the New Deal cases he argued before the Supreme Court. In 1941, Biddle briefly headed the Immigration and Naturalization Service.

After FDR named ROBERT JACKSON to the Supreme Court in September 1941, he chose Biddle to replace Jackson as the U.S. attorney general. Despite his civil libertarian beliefs, Biddle reluctantly approved the internment of Japanese Americans in 1942 and the enforcement of the Alien Registration Act. He expressed regret for both actions in his memoirs. After resigning as attorney general in June 1945, he served on the international tribunal for war criminals at Nuremberg. He died on October 4, 1968, on Cape Cod, Massachusetts.

Bilbo, Theodore Gilmore
(1877–1947) *U.S. senator*

Economic populist and white supremacist Theodore Bilbo epitomized a substantial segment of the Old South that Franklin Roosevelt was forced to deal with during his presidency. Although Bilbo supported the New Deal, many considered him an embarrassment to it as well as to the Democratic Party; the longer he served in office, the greater the embarrassment. A Mississippi contemporary of HUEY LONG from neighboring Louisiana, Bilbo came from an even more impoverished background and lacked Long's political ambition. However, they shared the political tendency to base their appeals on economic rather than racial grounds.

Born in Juniper Grove, Mississippi, on October 13, 1877, the last year of Reconstruction, Bilbo was the son of poor farmers. He attended local public schools and later took courses at Peabody College, Vanderbilt University, and the University of Michigan but never earned a degree. He taught school in Mississippi for two years and then attended Vanderbilt Law School. Although he did not receive a degree, he was admitted to the Mississippi state bar in 1907. In 1898, he married his first wife, who died two years later and left him with an infant daughter. He remarried in 1903 to Linda Gaddy Bedgood, and the couple had one son. Their marriage was troubled, and in 1938 they finally divorced. Sex and political scandals were recurring themes that emerged early in Bilbo's career. He sought political office the same year he remarried but lost his race for county clerk.

Bilbo's 40-year political career was a rollercoaster of electoral defeats and victories. His first electoral success came in 1907 when he won a four-year state senate seat. In 1911, he ran for lieutenant governor, a race that saw the emergence of his propensity for rhetorical excess to compensate for his small stature and poor background. He was easily elected governor in 1915 after a campaign that was pitched to the poor white tenant farmers and sharecroppers in southern and northeastern Mississippi. He championed their interests against the rich Delta planters. During his governorship (1916–20), Bilbo earned a progressive record for creating a new state tax commission and obtaining more state appropriations for public education and state charitable institutions.

Unable to succeed himself as governor, Bilbo ran unsuccessfully for Congress in 1918. He failed to recapture the governorship in 1923 but won the 1927 governor's race. The state legislature blocked his reform plans, so his second term was not a success. Despite his dismal second term as governor, he was elected to the U.S. Senate in 1934. His first term (1935–41) coincided with the peak of the New Deal, and Bilbo proved himself a genuine devotee of FDR's programs. He supported relief spending, social security, redistributive taxation, public power regulation, tenant resettlement, reorganization of the executive branch, and the controversial Court-packing plan. Through service on the Committee on Agriculture and Forestry, he protected his rural supporters. The only significant legislation that he initiated established regional agricultural research laboratories that sought new uses for farm products.

Just as his second gubernatorial term had been less successful than his first, Bilbo's second term as senator was less successful than his first, despite his easy reelection in 1940 as a strong supporter of FDR. He was generally supportive of the president's war policies, but he began to move from economic populism to entrenchment of the country's racial status quo. Race became his central message as the national Democratic Party began to champion civil rights. He battled an antipoll tax and antilynching legislation and obstructed the Fair Employment Practices Commission. Nevertheless, his blatantly racist 1946 reelection campaign drew his largest electoral win but he was plagued with scandals from it concerning conflict-of-interest charges and voting fraud. Soon afterward, he was admitted in declining health to the Ochsner's Clinic in New Orleans and died there from cancer on August 21, 1947.

Black, Hugo Lafayette

(1886–1971) *U.S. senator, U.S. Supreme Court justice*

Hugo Black had a strong instinctive sense of justice, perhaps shaped by his storekeeper father's misuse of alcohol. Born on February 27, 1886, in Horton, Alabama, he came from

Justice Hugo Black *(United States Supreme Court)*

relatively humble origins. Black's path to the education he needed to pursue the American dream was blocked when he failed to graduate from high school after he had intervened to prevent a high school teacher from punishing his sister with a switch. However, his father left an inheritance that Black used to attend medical school in Birmingham for a year. He then decided to change to the two-year University of Alabama Law School at Tuscaloosa, which had only two faculty members and did not require an undergraduate degree. He received his law degree in 1906.

Black became one of Birmingham's most successful personal-injury attorneys, practicing law for 20 years. A perennial "joiner," he was active in many civic organizations and taught a popular adult class at a Baptist church despite his own religious skepticism. Renowned for his charm and magnanimity, Black was a natural for elected office. He served as a part-time police court judge before being elected in 1914 as prosecutor for Alabama's Jefferson County. As a son of the South, he resigned that position in 1917 to join the army during World War I. He rose to the rank of captain in the 81st Artillery and served as adjutant of the 19th Artillery Brigade, never leaving the United States. After the war, he returned to Birmingham to resume his legal practice. His marriage to Josephine Foster in 1921 cemented his connection to the Birmingham elite.

Black also joined the Ku Klux Klan in 1921 as a means of furthering his political ambition. The underdog in Alabama's 1926 race for the U.S. Senate, he relied on his social connections and tireless energy to win a narrow victory in a three-man race in the Democratic primary, which assured he would win the fall election. His mistrust of big business grew during the Herbert Hoover administration. In 1932, he won reelection after defeating a former Alabama governor in the Democratic Party primary.

Aside from his opposition to antilynching proposals, Black became one of FDR's staunchest supporters from the South, even backing the Supreme Court packing plan that would have expanded the court membership to gain constitutional approval of the New Deal legislation. He proved even more liberal than FDR by urging a 30-hour workweek instead of 40 hours. Most impressive about Black's Senate years is that he demonstrated his autodidactic nature by using Library of Congress resources to compensate for his lack of a liberal arts education. Through constant reading, he developed a deep appreciation of the U.S. Constitution that would manifest itself during the next and final stage of his career.

In August 1937 Black became FDR's first nominee to the U.S. Supreme Court. He was confirmed by a vote of 63 to 13, despite the reservations of liberals about putting a native of

the Deep South on the high bench. The anti-New Deal press, however, created a national scandal shortly after his confirmation by uncovering evidence of Black's Klan membership. On October 1, 1937, he was forced to address the issue on the relatively new medium of radio, attracting one of the largest listening audiences of that time. He acknowledged his past membership, promised to defend the rights of all Americans, and asserted that since his long-ago resignation, he had had no further association with the organization. The media crisis was dispelled.

FDR's selection turned out to be among his best, since scholars rank Black as one of the dozen greatest justices in American history. Apart from supporting New Deal legislation, he became one of the Court's greatest civil libertarians with his literal "absolutist" standard for the Bill of Rights. He was unable to persuade the Court brethren to adopt his view of the immediate total incorporation of the Bill of Rights on the basis of using the Fourteenth Amendment to the states, but they ended up doing so incrementally over his three decades on the high court. He agreed with the constitutional framers' distrust of executive power as well as with Alexis de Tocqueville's warning about "the tyranny of the majority" in a democracy. Black's bulwark against the abuses of power was the U.S. Constitution. It was his "constitutional faith," and he always carried a small paperback copy of it with him. He died on September 25, 1971, in Bethesda, Maryland.

Blum, Leon
(1872–1950) *French premier*

Leon Blum, the first Jewish premier of France, helped create the modern French Socialist Party. Born on April 9, 1872, near the German border, he was educated at the prestigious École Normale Supérieure in Paris and graduated with the highest honors at the Sorbonne, where he received his legal education.

Following the dramatic and notorious anti-Semitic Dreyfus affair in 1898 during the Third Republic, which led to the 1905 separation of church and state, Blum joined the Socialist Party and was first elected in 1919 to the Chamber of Deputies, the French legislature. A split between the Socialists and the Communists in 1920 led to his rebuilding the Socialists and editing its publication *Le Populaire*. Defeated in the 1928 election, he was returned to the Chamber of Deputies in the 1932 election at the same time that Franklin Roosevelt was elected to the White House. Both politicians faced similar problems in their nations after the worldwide Great Depression.

Challenged by a resurgent right wing in the early 1930s, Blum built the Popular Front, which was a coalition of socialists, radicals, and others opposed to fascism. His coalition won the 1936 election, and he was elected premier.

Massive sit-down strikes in France, which influenced similar strikes at General Motors in the United States, were the impetus for Blum to launch his equivalent of the New Deal. His government began a 40-hour workweek and recognized the right of workers to bargain collectively. Concerned with BENITO MUSSOLINI and ADOLF HITLER's foreign threat, the government also nationalized the nation's defense industries and the Bank of France. Unfortunately, these measures produced a backlash from business and the Right, and the legislature failed to grant him emergency powers to deal with the depression. The political center failed, and Blum resigned.

After the Nazis invaded France in 1940, Blum was put on trial by the Vichy government for "war guilt"; he was exonerated, only to be put in a Nazi concentration camp, which the American military liberated in 1945. He died on March 30, 1950, in Jouy-en-Josas, France.

Bohlen, Charles Eustic
(1904–1974) *adviser to the president on Soviet affairs; chief, Division of Eastern European Affairs, U.S. State Department*

Charles Bohlen was born on August 30, 1904, in Clayton, New York. His mother was from a prominent New Orleans family, and he spent his early years in the South before moving to the North, from where he made frequent visits to Europe. His family background and accommodating, pleasant personality combined to produce one of the nation's key diplomats whose career spanned the Roosevelt, Truman, Eisenhower, Kennedy, and Johnson administrations.

Bohlen graduated in 1927 from Harvard, where he had majored in European history, and in 1929 he joined the U.S. State Department. His initial service assignment was in Prague, followed by Russian language training and time in Estonia. Following the Roosevelt administration's recognition of the Soviet government in 1933, Bohlen was sent to the new American embassy in Moscow. This was followed by his assignment to the Washington, D.C., office of the undersecretary of state and the Division of Eastern European Affairs. In 1938, he returned to Moscow, and the next year he learned from a German colleague about an impending German-Soviet rapprochement. The information reached Secretary of State CORDELL HULL, who shared it with the British and French to no avail.

After Bohlen was selected as FDR's interpreter at the Tehran conference in November 1943, HARRY HOPKINS, special assistant to the president, made him chief of the Division of Eastern European Affairs in the State Department. He was uniquely situated by background and personality to act as liaison between FDR and Hull, and he served again as FDR's interpreter at the Yalta Conference in February 1945. After FDR's death, Bohlen played a similar role for HARRY S. TRUMAN at the Potsdam Conference (July–August 1945). President

Dwight Eisenhower appointed him ambassador to the Soviet Union in 1953. President John Kennedy recruited Bohlen as an adviser during the Cuban missile crisis, and he again rendered useful service. Bohlen retired from the State Department in early 1969 and died on January 1, 1974, in Long Beach, California.

Borah, William Edgar
(1865–1940) *U.S. senator*

It is generally considered that William Borah was a better actor than statesman or political thinker. Defying his father's desire that he become a minister, Borah instead became an itinerant Shakespearean actor before becoming a flamboyant attorney and finally a nationally known senator who was often as inconsistent in his policy choices as he had been in his career choices. The constant in his life was his love of being both literally and figuratively "on stage," and he courted the media in his myriad political battles.

Borah was born on June 29, 1865, in Jasper, Illinois. His failure to follow through on his rhetorical battles may have resulted from his episodic education. He failed to graduate from either high school or college; poor health and lack of financial resources forced him to leave the University of Kansas after one year. Rather than pursue a formal education, he read law and passed the bar exam in 1887. For the next three years, he practiced law with his brother-in-law. He then headed for the West Coast, but he ran out of money in Boise, Idaho, and stayed there.

At the same time that he became recognized as a criminal lawyer in a frontier state, Borah improvised his political career. By 1892, he was chairman of Idaho's Republican State Central Committee. After briefly serving as the governor's secretary, he married the governor's daughter, a move that advanced him socially and politically. His entrance into national politics began when he joined the colorful Silver Republicans, who had deserted the Republican Party to support another great actor and orator, Williams Jennings Bryan, in his 1896 populist presidential crusade. Borah's split with Republican Party regulars resulted in his failure to win a seat in the U.S. House of Representatives and his subsequent failure to win a Senate seat in 1902. After he returned to the Republican Party fold, however, in 1907 the state legislature elected him to the U.S. Senate, where he served until his death.

Borah's idiosyncratic behavior was reflected in his voting in the Senate. After battling corporate interests, he voted against THEODORE ROOSEVELT's efforts to regulate them. He defended civil liberties during World War I when the Woodrow Wilson administration massively violated them, but he showed less concern for civil rights. At the same time that he wanted to limit the federal government's power, he supported the Prohibition amendment regardless of the preferences of individual states. Despite these and other inconsistencies like having a child with Alice Roosevelt Longworth, his seemingly maverick party behavior and oratorical gifts made him one of the best-known progressives of the era.

Borah's behavior during the Franklin Roosevelt presidency was similarly mixed. He supported New Deal relief legislation for the unemployed and pensions for the elderly but fought the National Industrial Recovery Act. Presidential ambitions always colored his actions. In 1939 he declared his candidacy for the White House but failed to capture the Republican nomination.

Borah had regretted his support for the United States's entry into World War I and had joined opposition in the Senate to block the United States from joining the League of Nations. His influence had increased when he became chairman of the Senate Foreign Relations Committee in December 1924. He came to believe that political violence around the world reflected the aspirations of other nations to determine their own fate, as the United States had done. Therefore he supported FDR's recognition of the Soviet Union in 1933 as well as the president's "Good Neighbor" policy toward Latin America. Still, his aversion to foreign entanglements led Borah to back neutrality legislation to block Roosevelt's desire to sell arms on a "cash and carry" basis. After Nazi Germany's invasion of Poland in September 1939, Congress ignored Borah's advice. He died on January 19, 1940, in Washington, D.C.

Bourke-White, Margaret
(1904–1971) *photojournalist*

One of the pioneering female photojournalists of the 1930s, 1940s, and beyond, Margaret Bourke-White preserved the history of her era through her compelling visual legacy. Because of her career successes, she became one of the best-known women in mid-20th century America. During the same male-dominated journalistic era when LORENA HICKOK became the first woman reporter hired by the Associated Press, Margaret Bourke-White became the first photographer at *Fortune* magazine and then one of the original photographers at *Life*. Through the lens of her camera, she witnessed history unfolding and documented it with photographs of the political leaders who were shaping it. Her camera also captured the plight of Dust Bowl farmers and inmates in Nazi concentration camps in stark images.

Born on June 14, 1904, in New York City, Margaret Bourke-White was the daughter of amateur photographer Joseph White and teacher Minnie Bourke. Her father died when she was 17, but he already had instilled in her not only his interest in photography but also in industrial and architectural life. Her early mar-

riage to a graduate student dissolved within a short time. She attended several universities before she graduated in 1927 from Cornell University with a degree in biology.

HENRY LUCE was attracted to Bourke-White's work on steel mills in Cleveland, where her mother then lived, and he invited her to join his new publishing venture, *Fortune*. She was an associate editor and its first photographer from 1929 to 1933. Her freelance work appeared in *Vanity Fair* from 1932 to 1937. Meanwhile, Luce created a new publication, *Life*, and he hired Bourke-White as one of the magazine's four original photographers. The other three *Life* photographers were Alfred Eisenstaedt, Thomas McAvoy, and Peter Stackpole. When the magazine premiered in November 1936, the cover photograph of Fort Peck Dam in Montana was Bourke-White's. During the more than 25 years that she was associated with *Fortune* and *Life*, Bourke-White photographed world leaders who included Franklin Roosevelt, WINSTON CHURCHILL, and JOSEPH STALIN.

In 1934, Bourke-White worked with JAMES AGEE to record drought conditions in the United States. For readers of *Fortune*, she graphically depicted the ruin wrought by the Dust Bowl on farm families who had lost everything. She worked with novelist ERSKINE CALDWELL to convey the story of impoverished southern sharecroppers in the book *You Have Seen Their Faces* (1937). By 1939, she and Caldwell were married, but they divorced three years later. Despite their personal differences, the couple had a successful professional collaboration. Their 1939 book *North of the Danube* recalled Czechoslovakia before the Nazi takeover. Next they offered a panorama of America entitled *Say, Is This the U.S.A.?* (1941).

During World War II, Bourke-White again broke boundaries for women. The first female photographer attached to the U.S. Air Force, she covered the Nazi bombardment of

Moscow and the 1945 liberation of the inmates of Buchenwald by General GEORGE PATTON. Although she developed Parkinson's disease, she continued to work for *Life* until 1957 but did not resign until 1969. She died in Stamford, Connecticut, on August 27, 1971.

Bowers, Claude Gernade
(1878–1958) *journalist, speechwriter, U.S. ambassador to Spain and to Chile*

Born on November 20, 1878, in Westfield, Indiana, Claude Gernade Bowers was the son of a storekeeper father and dressmaker mother. Reared in rural central Indiana, he moved to Indianapolis at age 13 following his parents' divorce. The year he graduated from Indianapolis High School, he won a state oratorical competition. Lack of funds prevented him from attending college, and he began working for the publishing firm that later became Bobbs-Merrill.

He launched his career in journalism in 1900 as chief editorialist for the *Sentinel*, the Indianapolis daily that aligned with the Democratic Party. Three years later, Bowers, an energetic individual with a gift for expressing himself both in print and orally, became an editorialist for newspapers in Terre Haute, where he also served on the city's Board of Public Works. He ran unsuccessfully for elective office as a Democrat in 1904 and 1906. His move to Washington, D.C., came in 1911 when U.S. senator John W. Kern appointed him as his secretary. That same year, Bowers married Sybil McCaslin of Indianapolis; the couple had one child.

Bowers worked closely with the influential Kern, who was the first Democratic Party whip in the Senate. Kern's job was to guide Woodrow Wilson's New Freedom legislation through the Senate. Following Kern's defeat in 1917, Bowers returned to Indiana as an editorial writer for the Fort Wayne *Journal-Gazette*, a position he held for six years. He had already begun pursuing a career as a historian while working in journalism. His first work, *The Irish Orators* (1916), was followed two years later by a biography of his former boss, Senator Kern. He then turned to his hero Thomas Jefferson, ultimately publishing a trio of works about him. In 1922 he published *The Party Battles of the Jackson Period*, followed three years later by *Jefferson and Hamilton* and, in 1929, *The Tragic Era: The Revolution after Lincoln.*

In 1923, Bowers moved to New York City, where he joined the editorial staff of *New York World* and gained greater national attention. Throughout the decade, his books and columns established his reputation as a scholar of the Democratic Party. He viewed the political world as a struggle between Hamiltonian elitism for the few and Jeffersonian democracy for the many. He blamed radical Republicans for hurting the South during Reconstruction. As a result of his defense of the Democratic Party, he delivered the major address at the 1928 Jackson Day Dinner in Washington, D.C., which led to his invitation to be keynote speaker at the 1928 Democratic National Convention.

In 1931, Bowers began writing editorials for New York City's *Evening Journal*, which distributed his columns to other newspapers owned by WILLIAM RANDOLPH HEARST. He also served on occasion as speechwriter for AL SMITH, ROBERT F. WAGNER, and Franklin Roosevelt, for whom he campaigned in 1932. That same year, he wrote another biography, this time on Albert J. Beveridge, the Indiana Republican.

In 1933, FDR appointed Bowers as U.S. ambassador to Spain, and he made efforts to improve trade between the two countries. During the Spanish civil war (1936–39), Bowers sympathized with the Loyalists defending the Spanish Republic against the rebel forces of General FRANCISCO FRANCO. FDR failed to support pleas by ELEANOR ROOSEVELT and Bowers to allow the Spanish Republic to buy arms; instead, the United States remained neutral. After the fall of the Loyalist government, Bowers was made U.S. ambassador to Chile, where he helped to persuade the Chilean government to sever relations with the Axis powers in 1943. He continued to serve in Chile after World War II until DWIGHT EISENHOWER was elected in 1952. Bowers then resigned from the Foreign Service and returned to New York, continuing to work with Eleanor Roosevelt and write accounts of his diplomatic service abroad. He died in New York City on January 21, 1958.

Bowles, Chester Bliss

(1901–1986) *head, Office of Price Administration*

Born on April 5, 1901, into an affluent Springfield, Massachusetts, business family, Chester Bowles attended exclusive prep schools in Connecticut and then followed in the footsteps of his father and brother by enrolling in Yale University. Although he was more interested in social and athletic college pursuits than academics, he graduated in 1924. He first worked briefly at his family's newspaper, the Springfield *Republican*, founded by his grandfather in the mid-19th century. Restless and energetic, he soon moved to New York, where he worked in a top advertising agency until 1929, when he and a fellow Yale alumnus founded their own agency, Benson and Bowles. Despite the Great Depression, by the mid-1930s their advertising agency had become the sixth largest in the nation. Bowles helped to pioneer the use of consumer surveys in market research.

Married in 1925, Bowles and his first wife had two children before they divorced in 1933. The next year he married Dorothy Stebbins, with whom he had three children. His business success made him a multimillionaire, and he left his advertising firm in 1941. A strong supporter of the New Deal who had begun working with ELEANOR ROOSEVELT in the 1930s, Bowles accepted an offer in 1942 from the governor of Connecticut to become state director of the newly established Office of Price Administration (OPA). He soon came to the attention of Franklin Roosevelt, who appointed him director of the national OPA in November 1943. Bowles served in that capacity until 1946. During his tenure, he managed to contain inflation and built both public support and congressional backing for fiscal discipline during World War II.

In the postwar period, Bowles served briefly as director of the newly established Office of Economic Stabilization for President HARRY S. TRUMAN. He resigned, however, after Congress refused to extend the price controls that he wanted. He returned to Connecticut and served as U.S. ambassador to India from 1951 to 1953 and again from 1963 to 1969. He was elected governor of Connecticut in 1953 and served until 1956. For a short while in 1961, he was undersecretary of state.

In the mid-1960s, Bowles developed Parkinson's disease. He died on May 25, 1986, in Essex, Connecticut.

Brandeis, Louis Dembitz

(Louis David Brandeis)

(1856–1941) *U.S. Supreme Court justice*

Born on November 13, 1856, Louis Brandeis grew up in Louisville, Kentucky. His parents were nonpracticing Jews who had fled Europe after the failed Austrian uprising of 1848. As a teenager, Brandeis changed his middle name from David in honor of his abolitionist lawyer uncle. His parents moved from Louisville to Boston, Massachusetts, and after the Civil War, in 1875, he entered Harvard Law School; his superlative academic performance there set a record.

Brandeis graduated in 1877 and a year later began practicing law in St. Louis, but he missed the intellectual environment of Harvard so much that he returned to Boston in 1879. There he set up a law practice and helped to create both the Harvard Law School Alumni Association and the *Harvard Law Review*. His practice increasingly moved in the direction of public matters, and he became known as "the people's attorney." Opposing the concentration of power both in business and in government, he came to view unions as necessary to balance the power of corporations and the need for individuals to have leisure in their lives for reasons of both health and opportunity to exercise their civic responsibilities.

Brandeis's focus on sociological jurisprudence—law being based on the needs of society—is illustrated in what became known as the Brandeis brief, which meant going beyond case-law precedents and using data to support one's legal position. During his support of Woodrow Wilson's presidential candidacy in 1912, he became one of the architects of the president's New Freedom program designed to regulate the excesses of big businesses. In return, Wilson nominated him to the Supreme Court in 1916. Despite the most intense confirmation battle ever waged by conservatives to block a trust-busting people's attorney, including former president William Howard Taft, Brandeis was confirmed, becoming the first Jew to sit on America's high court.

During most of his 23-year tenure as a Supreme Court justice, Brandeis's views were in the minority. Although he was much more a Wilsonian than a New Dealer, he supported FDR's programs overall since he also practiced judicial restraint in deferring to the elected branches of government. In the political world, he relied on FELIX FRANKFURTER, one of his disciples, to promote his preferred economic and labor reforms. Brandeis was unsympathetic to both big business and big government. He convinced the Court to stop striking down economic regulation while offering protection to free speech and even a right to privacy. Often referring to FDR as "Isaiah," Brandeis was pleased that the president picked WILLIAM O. DOUGLAS as his successor on the Court. He died on October 5, 1941, in Washington, D.C.

Bricker, John William
(1893–1986) *Ohio governor, Republican vice-presidential candidate, U.S. senator*

Born to farmer parents in Madison County, Ohio, on September 6, 1893, John Bricker graduated from Ohio State University in 1916. He was ordained as a minister so that he could serve as a U.S. Army chaplain during World War I. Following his military service, he continued his studies and received a law degree from Ohio State in 1920, then began his law practice in Columbus. The tall, handsome young attorney married Harriet Day, with whom he had one child.

Bricker, a conservative, gravitated toward local Republican politics immediately after receiving his law degree. He was appointed as solicitor for Grandview Heights, Ohio, serving from 1920 to 1928. He concurrently served as assistant attorney general from 1923 to 1927. From 1929 to 1932, he held an appointment to the Ohio Public Utilities Commission. During those years he traveled widely throughout Ohio, building a base of voter support.

Bricker sought office for the first time in 1928 when he ran unsuccessfully for state attorney general. Four years later, however, he was elected as attorney general and reelected in 1934. He insisted on a literal view of the Constitution in law enforcement. In 1936, Bricker ran for the Ohio governorship and lost, but two years later, he was elected during the period of public backlash over Franklin Roosevelt's Supreme Court packing plan. His political platform was founded on strong opposition to the New Deal and its expanding federal bureaucracy. He instead advocated for state and local governments, believing that the states should have control over unemployment relief, minimum wages, and retirement provisions. He also opposed federal support for organized labor. Bricker won reelection 1940 and 1942. Bricker was an isolationist in world affairs, and while his success was due in part to his reputation for honesty, it also was due, ironically, to the economic prosperity that accompanied U.S. involvement in World War II.

As a conventional conservative from the Midwest who had a successful electoral record, Bricker sought the Republican presidential nomination in both 1940 and 1944. In 1944, after the national convention selected New York governor THOMAS DEWEY instead, Dewey picked Bricker to be his running mate. Bricker was one of the first national Republicans to attempt to tie FDR and the entire Democratic Party to labor and communists; however, he and Dewey lost the election. In 1944, he also lost his reelection bid for the Ohio governorship to Democrat Frank J. Lausche.

Although his election efforts in 1944 failed, two years later Bricker was elected to the U.S. Senate, where he quickly aligned himself with the conservative Republicans, including Wisconsin senator Joseph McCarthy. In the early 1950s, he became associated with an amendment carrying his name that would have required congressional approval of executive agreements. Only the combined opposition of President DWIGHT EISENHOWER and liberal Democrats defeated it. Bricker was defeated when he sought a third Senate term in 1958. He returned to private law practice in Columbus, Ohio, and died there on March 22, 1986.

Bridges, Harry Renton
(Alfred Renton Bridges)
(1901–1990) *union leader*

Harry Bridges was born Alfred Renton Bridges in Melbourne, Australia, on July 28, 1901. His father was a real estate agent, and his mother, who was of Irish descent, was a shopkeeper. As a teenager, he began to refer to himself as Harry, the name of an uncle who was a socialist trade unionist, and in time the name became permanent. Bridges dropped out of school after 10th grade to become a merchant seaman. By 1920 he had emigrated to the United States and was employed as a seaman and dock worker. He first joined the Sailors' Union of the Pacific (SUP) in San Francisco. The next year, he participated in the national seaman's strike and briefly became a "Wobblie"—a member of the Industrial Workers of the World (IWW). Bridges then became active in the local chapter of the International Longshoremen's Association (ILA), joining a radical wing called "Albion Hall," which took its name from a local street. During these years, he had a daughter with Agnes Brown, whom he finally married in 1934.

A decade later, the radicals organized a wildcat strike against the established "Blue Book" union that was controlled by the Waterfront Employers Association (WEA). In 1934, the ILA's local unions along the entire West Coast sought a contract. After waterfront employers refused, a strike spread from the longshoremen to the seafaring unions. Bridges was elected chairman of his local's strike committee and soon gained notoriety. He refused a bribe from employers and opposed the leadership of the ILA. By early May 1934, more than 12,000 dockworkers had closed down every West Coast port except Los Angeles. The shutdown continued, and on July 5, San Francisco police attacked the strikers and California's governor called out the National Guard. As the situation escalated, on July 16, the ILA persuaded other unions to shut down the city for four days. With most economic activity terminated, both sides agreed to arbitration, which resulted in a victory for the longshoremen, who on July 26 received most of their demands from the WEA.

Bridges rode the strike to the presidency of Local 38-79 and then to the presidency of the entire Pacific Coast District. Within three years, he led the Pacific Coast District of the ILA out of the American Federation of Labor union to form the more radical International Longshoremen's and Warehousemen's Union (ILWU), which then affiliated with the Congress of Industrial Organizations (CIO). He became the first ILWU president in 1937 and served until 1977. JOHN L. LEWIS, the CIO president, appointed Bridges as the CIO western regional director in 1937, the same year that Bridges appeared on the front cover of *Time* magazine. During his entire tenure as ILWU president, Bridges's salary never exceeded a longshoreman's wages.

As a national labor leader, Bridges was involved in a series of court cases, and the significant pressure on him affected his personal life and health. Stress caused by his activities resulted not only in his divorce but also in ulcers. In *Bridges v. California* (1941), the Supreme Court upheld his First Amendment right to criticize a court order involving members of the ILA in Los Angeles. His sympathy toward the Communist Party prompted opponents' calls for his deportation. By 1939, Secretary of Labor FRANCES PERKINS had been drawn into the controversy, and she asked the Immigration and Naturalization Service (INS), which was within the Labor Department, to determine if Bridges could be deported. After the INS stated that he could not, the U.S. House of Representatives passed legislation in June 1940 that ordered his deportation, but the Senate killed the bill.

After FDR transferred oversight of the INS from the Labor Department to the Justice Department, U.S. Attorney General ROBERT JACKSON asked the FBI to investigate Bridges. This time, in 1941, the INS found against Bridges. Bridges appealed, and in *Bridges v. Wixon* (1945) the U.S. Supreme Court reversed the INS ruling. Bridges completed his naturalization process later that year. The next year, he married Nancy Feinstein Berdecio; the couple had two children before they divorced in 1953.

Bridges continued his activism throughout the postwar period. The CIO expelled both Bridges and the ILWU in 1948 for support of HENRY WALLACE's presidential bid. The next year the federal government tried to prove that Bridges was a communist. Once again, the U.S. Supreme Court overturned the case in *Bridges v. U.S.* (1953).

Bridges married his third and final wife, Noriko Sawada, in 1958 and had one child. He died in San Francisco on March 30, 1990.

Broun, Heywood
(Matthew Heywood Campbell Broun)
(1888–1939) *journalist*

Born Matthew Heywood Campbell Broun on December 7, 1888, in Brooklyn, New York, Heywood Broun was raised in Manhattan in a comfortable lifestyle. His father was an immigrant Scots businessman, and his mother was from a prosperous German-American family. Broun graduated from the elitist Horace Mann School in 1906 and subsequently entered Harvard University, but he failed to graduate due to his passions for poker, baseball, and the theater. Physically imposing, he was 6'4" tall and weighed more than 275 pounds. He was known for his careless dress and his tendency to act emotionally during alternating periods of great energy and laziness.

Broun was a talented writer who loved to drink. He landed his first job as a reporter with the *New York Morning Telegraph* and worked there from 1910 to 1912. He next worked at the *New York Tribune*, where he was a reporter, sportswriter, and, finally, drama critic. After serving as a war correspondent during World War I, he returned to the *Tribune* and in 1919 became the paper's literary editor, pioneering the signed syndicated column. In 1921, he moved to the *New York World*, where his liberal column "It Seems to Me" elevated him to the ranks of the nation's most highly regarded journalists.

Broun became one of the most passionate defenders of Sacco and Vanzetti, the immigrant anarchists accused of murder in 1927. The *World* temporarily suspended his column, which prompted him to attack it in the more radical *Nation* magazine. The *World* fired him the next year, and Broun moved to the *New York Telegram*. His columns became increasingly political, and he ran for the U.S. House of Representatives as a Socialist in 1930. He not only lost, he also split the Democratic vote, resulting in a narrow victory for the Republican incumbent.

In 1933, Broun helped to found the American Newspaper Guild, the first national organization of editorialists. He was elected as its first president and held that nonpaid position until his death. He guided the guild's transformation from a professional association to a modern industrial union and then worked for its affiliation with the American Federation of Labor (AFL), which occurred in 1936, and for the broader inclusion of workers in the union. In 1937, he helped to engineer the guild's switch from the AFL to the more radical Congress of Industrial Organizations (CIO).

Broun had married feminist Ruth Hale in 1917, and the couple had a son, Heywood Hale Broun. Hale helped her spouse produce some of his best work, and even after she obtained a Mexican divorce from him in 1933, the couple remained good friends until her death the next year. After her death, Broun married a widow, Maria Incoronata Fruscella, and adopted her nine-year-old daughter.

In 1935, Broun started writing a column for the *New Republic*, a liberal magazine. In 1938, his radical political views led to his subpoena to appear before the House Un-American Activities Committee, falsely accused of associating with communists, if not actually being one. The next year the *World-Telegram*, which had been created by a 1931 merger between the *World* and the *Telegram*, did not renew his contract. Broun was forced to find another newspaper and moved to the *New York Post* at a substantial cut in pay. At the *Post*, he wrote only one column before his death from pneumonia on December 18, 1939.

Browder, Earl Russell
(1891–1973) *Communist Party presidential candidate*

The son of an elementary schoolteacher father and homemaker mother, Earl Browder was born on May 20, 1891, in Wichita, Kansas. His boyhood was shaped by extreme poverty and political activism. He was forced to drop out of elementary school and go to work to help support his parents and five siblings after his father suffered a nervous breakdown. By 1906, he was an accountant as well as a member of the Socialist Party. He married his childhood sweetheart in 1911, and the following year they moved to Kansas City, Kansas, and they had a child.

Browder found a political cause in 1917 with his nonviolent resistance to the United States's participation in World War I. By the end of the year, he had been jailed for defiance of the Selective Service System. He transferred in July 1919 to Leavenworth Penitentiary in

Kansas and remained incarcerated there until November 1920. It was his actual imprisonment during the Russian Revolution that transformed him into a Bolshevik communist. His transformation took place in much the same way as reading Anton Chekhov's short story "Ward No. 6" propelled Vladimir Lenin—the father of the Russian Revolution—into political action in 1917, following the execution of his older brother by the czar while his sister was being treated in a tuberculosis sanitarium.

When Browder was released from prison, he deserted his family to move to New York City and become a full-time member of the Communist Party of the USA (CPUSA). For half a dozen years, he was associated with William Z. Foster, head of Chicago's Trade Union Educational League (TUEL); Foster had joined the Communist Party at the same time as Browder. Browder edited TUEL's paper, the *Labor Herald*, until 1926, when he broke with Foster and became a devoted follower of JOSEPH STALIN. He made several visits to the Soviet Union between 1934 and 1943 and developed close ties to Georgi Dimitrov, the leader of the Comitern (Communist International), the organization of communist parties worldwide. During this time, he had an affair with Raissa Luganovskaya, a legal scholar who subsequently moved to the United States to live with Browder. The couple eventually had three children.

Browder served briefly in China in the late 1920s as head of the Pan-Pacific Trade Union Secretariat, but he returned to the United States to battle for control of the divided Communist Party, which he gained by 1932. Two years later, he was made the party's general secretary. The CPUSA began to organize the unemployed and staged hunger marches and demonstrations to demand congressional passage of workers unemployment insurance. Although Browder personally advocated overthrow of the U.S. government, he modified his views to fit the Comitern's directive that called for a popular front in Western democracies to prevent fascism.

After William Z. Foster suffered a heart attack during the 1932 presidential election campaign and fell from Moscow's favor, Browder became the CPUSA candidate in the 1936 and 1940 elections. He spoke on national radio in 1936 and in 1938 appeared on the front cover of *Time* magazine. However, he won fewer than 100,000 votes in each of those presidential elections. He was imprisoned in the Atlantic Penitentiary for 14 months in 1941–42 for passport fraud. After the United States entered World War II and joined the Soviet Union's effort to fight ADOLF HITLER, the federal government halted its persecution of the Communist Party. FDR pardoned Browder by commuting his sentence on May 16, 1942.

Browder's second imprisonment had a largely negative impact on his personality, especially after the U.S. government's about-face, welcoming him to the nation's capital to discuss foreign policy with SUMNER WELLES, the undersecretary of state, on several occasions in 1942–43. Like Stalin, Browder began to nurture an exaggerated "cult of the personality" among his followers, who thought that by 1944 he could lead them into a coalition with the New Deal. However, following Hitler's defeat, the Soviet-American alliance crumbled, and Browder was quickly deposed by his party. He was expelled from the CPUSA in February 1946 without ever gaining reinstatement. He died on June 27, 1973, in Princeton, New Jersey, where he had lived with his youngest son's family.

Brownlow, Louis
(1879–1963) *chair, President's Committee on Administrative Management*

Louis Brownlow was born on August 26, 1879, in Buffalo, Missouri. Due to childhood illnesses, he was taught at home by his Ozark parents, who were former teachers. His early interest in reading and writing led him initially to a career in journalism. For 15 years he worked for newspapers in Tennessee and was a foreign correspondent also for a syndicated newsletter. Through his years in Tennessee, he became a longtime friend of Democratic congressman JOSEPH BYRNS.

Brownlow's career changed course when President Woodrow Wilson appointed him as a commissioner of the District of Columbia (1915–20). This developed his interest and expertise in city government, which led to his becoming city manager of Petersburg, Virginia, in 1920; he later held a similar position in Knoxville, Tennessee. In 1931, Brownlow became founding director of the Public Administration Clearinghouse in Chicago, Illinois, an agency funded by John D. Rockefeller that provided governmental advice; he held the position until the end of World War II.

In response to a request from former progressive Republican CHARLES E. MERRIAM, a pioneering American political scientist and cofounder of the Public Administration Clearinghouse, Brownlow drafted a page-long memo on what might be needed to improve the president's managerial role during the New Deal. Subsequently, he met with FDR in early 1936 and agreed to chair the President's Committee on Administrative Management, popularly known as the Brownlow Committee. The other committee members were Merriam and LUTHER GULICK. The committee faced a pressing nine-month deadline to assemble staff, conduct its research, and prepare its findings. The president's action was meant partly to counter congressional initiatives already under way to reorganize executive agencies. Senator HARRY F. BYRD (D-Va.) had already convened such a committee in the Senate, and Congressman James P. Buchanan (D-Tex.), chairman of the House Appropriations Committee and a conservative who wanted to abolish aspects of the New Deal, took similar action in the House.

A seasoned journalist used to deadlines, Brownlow acted fast. He and Gulick presented their draft findings to FDR by mid-November 1936, in keeping with the December final report date. The Brownlow Committee report called for strengthening the executive branch in five ways: (1) enlarging the president's staff by adding individuals who had a "passion for anonymity"; (2) expanding the merit system; (3) improving fiscal management; (4) creating a permanent planning agency; and (5) adding two additional cabinet posts and including agencies and independent commissions within the executive branch. Overall, the report called for the president to have managerial power commensurate with his developing role as the chief executive of the largest bureaucracy in the world.

On January 8, 1937, FDR informed the cabinet and congressional leaders of the report's contents, and on January 11, he held a news conference about it. Congressional hearings began in mid-February. Unfortunately, as with his Supreme Court packing plan, FDR made tactical errors by not asking members of Congress for suggestions and for having maintained total secrecy while the Brownlow Committee prepared its findings. His judgment errors were compounded when he introduced the report almost simultaneously with the highly controversial Court-packing plan. FDR focused on the Supreme Court battle and turned over the Brownlow legislation to his son James.

Left to fend for himself in getting legislation passed to implement the report recommendations, Brownlow suffered a heart attack on May 31, 1937. Fortunately, his heart attack was not fatal, like the one his friend House Speaker Joseph Byrns had suffered the previous year or the one that had killed majority leader

JOSEPH ROBINSON later in the summer amid the stress of dealing with New Deal legislation. With Brownlow sidelined, however, conservative opponents labeled the Brownlow bill as a call for executive dictatorship. The reorganization bill was finally defeated by a narrow margin in 1938. Opponents leading the defeat were Senators Harry Byrd and JAMES F. BYRNES.

FDR may have lost the battle, as he did with the Court-packing plan, but he mostly won the executive war the next year. Facing World War II, Congress passed the Reorganization Act of 1939, which began to enact what Brownlow had recommended. It institutionalized the modern presidency and, in doing so, permitted the abuses of the Watergate and the Iran-contra affairs in the 1970s and 1980s as later administrations violated most of what Brownlow had intended. He died on September 28, 1963, in Arlington, Virginia.

Buck, Pearl Sydenstricker

(1892–1973) *American novelist, Office of War Information writer*

A prolific and popular writer in the United States and abroad, Pearl Buck received the 1938 Nobel Prize in Literature, in large part for her best-known novel, *The Good Earth* (1931), an international best seller that had won a Pulitzer Prize in 1932. Both the book and the film version of 1937 presented a sympathetic picture of struggling Chinese peasants that allowed Western readers to identify with their triumph over a harsh economic struggle. It made China real for a generation of Americans and heavily influenced their view of China, creating sympathy after the Japanese invasion there in the 1930s.

Buck was born Pearl Sydenstricker on June 26, 1892, to Presbyterian missionaries in China. After an early education in China, she graduated from Randolph-Macon Woman's College in Lynchburg, Virginia, in 1904. She married John Lossing Buck in 1917, and in the early 1920s she began teaching English at several Chinese colleges. While on a year's leave of absence, she earned an M.A. degree in English from Cornell University in 1926 and then went back to China, but in the early 1930s she returned permanently to the United States. She divorced her first husband in 1934 and subsequently married Richard Walsh, president of the John Day Company, publisher of *The Good Earth*. During World War II, she wrote radio plays for the Office of War Information that were broadcast to China. They were meant to mobilize support for the Chinese. Buck died on March 6, 1973, in Danby, Vermont.

Bullitt, William Christian

(1891–1967) *special assistant to the secretary of state, ambassador to the USSR and to France*

Born into a wealthy old-line Philadelphia family on January 25, 1891, William Bullitt attended DeLancey Preparatory School and then went to Yale University, where he edited

Roosevelt says good-bye to William C. Bullitt, ambassador to the Soviet Union. *(Library of Congress)*

the campus newspaper. After his graduation in 1913, at the insistence of his lawyer father, he enrolled in Harvard Law School. However, after his father's death in 1914, he immediately switched to a career in foreign affairs. By the end of that same year, he had become a foreign correspondent for the Philadelphia *Public Ledger*, and he covered HENRY FORD's idealistic 1915 peace crusade to end World War I.

During World War I, Bullitt was appointed to the State Department's Bureau of Central European Information and subsequently to the United States Peace Commission to Paris. He led a secret mission to the Soviet Union in 1919 and obtained favorable terms to end the Russian civil war, but Woodrow Wilson refused even to meet with him after the president's negotiations with the Allied leaders broke down over personal differences among them. ADOLF BERLE, historian Samuel Eliot Morison, and Bullitt resigned from the U.S. peace delegation. In autumn 1920, Bullitt's testimony before the Senate Foreign Relations Committee contributed to Congress's decision not to approve the Treaty of Versailles.

Bullitt initially held a favorable view of Franklin Roosevelt, having known him while FDR was assistant secretary of the navy in the Wilson administration, and was an early supporter of Roosevelt's bid for the presidency in 1932. After the fall election victory, FDR dispatched Bullitt on secret missions to Europe regarding World War I debts. He was subsequently appointed as special assistant to Secretary of State CORDELL HULL, serving as executive officer to the London Monetary and Economic Conference in 1933. That fall, Bullitt helped to negotiate formal recognition of the Soviet Union with the Roosevelt-Litvinov Agreements, and FDR rewarded him by making Bullitt the first U.S. ambassador to the Soviet Union. Bullitt became increasingly critical of Soviet intentions, but FDR ignored his advice. Nevertheless, they remained friends,

and in 1936, FDR appointed Bullitt ambassador to France. Bullitt, who correctly forecast ADOLF HITLER's aggressive intentions, remained in this post until the surrender of France in 1940.

During World War II, Bullitt supported FDR's foreign policy. However, he urged FDR to fire Undersecretary of State SUMNER WELLES, with whom he had been engaged in a long feud. When the conflict was leaked to the press, Roosevelt personally blamed Bullitt and never forgave him. Frustrated, Bullitt volunteered to become an infantry commandant with the French Free Forces in mid-1944.

Just as Bullitt's professional relationships with both Wilson and Roosevelt ended in acrimony, his two marriages also failed. He had married Philadelphia socialite Ernesta Brinker in 1916, but their childless marriage ended in divorce in 1923. Later that year, he married Louise Bryant, widow of journalist John Reed, the author of *Ten Days That Shook the World.* His second marriage produced one daughter before it ended in divorce in 1930. He was involved with MISSY LEHAND, FDR's private secretary, during the 1930s.

During the postwar period, Bullitt lectured and wrote about foreign affairs from an increasingly anticommunist perspective. Though he had written an autobiographical novel during the interwar years, his first nonfiction book was published in 1946. *The Great Globe Itself* attacked FDR's foreign policy as well as the Soviet Union. The lifelong Democrat then joined the Republican Party. After the death of Woodrow Wilson's second wife, the biography of Wilson that Bullitt had written with Sigmund Freud in 1931, *Thomas Woodrow Wilson: 28th President, A Psychological Study,* was published in 1967. The first psychobiography ever written, it portrays Wilson as obsessed with his minister father. Ironically, Bullitt manifested some of the same behavior for which he condemned Wilson: both could be bright and charming, but they could also be extremely arrogant toward those with whom they worked.

Bullitt died on February 15, 1967, in Neuilly, France.

Burdick, Usher Lloyd
(1879–1960) *U.S. congressman*

Born to farmer parents in Owatonna, Minnesota, on February 21, 1879, Usher Burdick was reared in Grisham's Island, in the Dakota Territory, where he attended local schools. He graduated in 1900 from State Normal School in Mayville, North Dakota, and then worked for two years as the deputy superintendent of schools in Benson County, North Dakota. Following this, he entered the law program at the University of Minnesota, where he played on the university football team; he graduated in 1904.

Burdick returned to Munich, North Dakota, was admitted to the bar, and practiced law. Within three years, he was active in state politics. He was elected as a state legislator in 1907 and served until 1911, when he was elected lieutenant governor, a post he held until 1913. From 1913 until 1932, he served in various legal capacities—as state attorney, special prosecutor, and U.S. district attorney. At the same time, he farmed and wrote about western history.

Burdick's independent streak in politics first manifested itself in 1932 when he ran unsuccessfully for election to the U.S. House of Representatives as a Republican. Contrary to local popular opinion in his district, he supported Franklin Roosevelt over Herbert Hoover, and he favored the repeal of Prohibition in that election. Two years later, he won his congressional race, and he was reelected to five additional terms, which placed him in Congress throughout the entire New Deal as

well as World War II. During this period, he developed a reputation as a maverick who sometimes supported the New Deal, including work relief, the Wagner Housing Act, and even the Court-packing plan. Before the December 1941 bombing of Pearl Harbor, he was a midwestern isolationist in foreign affairs, but during World War II he supported FDR's wartime policies.

Burdick chose not to seek reelection in 1944, instead running unsuccessfully for a seat in the U.S. Senate. In 1948, he returned to the House and was reelected until 1958 when he stepped down and backed his son, Quentin Burdick, who was elected to replace him. Usher Burdick died on August 19, 1960, in Washington, D.C.

Burns, Eveline Richardson
(1900–1985) *research director, Committee on Long-Range Work and Relief Policies of the National Resources Planning Board*

Born on March 16, 1900, in London, England, where she was also educated, Eveline Richardson worked at the British Ministry of Labor and was a night student at the London School of Economics, from which she graduated with honors in 1920. She married Arthur R. Burns in 1920, the same year she entered graduate school. In 1926, she was awarded her doctorate from the London School of Economics.

Eveline Burns's academic career began in 1928 when she became a member of the Economics Department at Columbia University. There she conducted comparative research on the German and British unemployment insurance systems. At the same time, she became the president of the New York Consumer's League and served as the vice president of the American Association for Social Security from 1935 to 1943. From this academic and policy background, she became a staff member for

FDR's Committee on Economic Security in 1934. Her lobbying efforts helped to pass the Social Security Act of 1935. She wrote *Toward Social Security* (1936) to explain the new program and conducted training sessions for its administrators the same year.

While still teaching at Columbia, Burns was asked to review New Deal relief and public-works programs in 1939, as the research director to the Committee in Long-Range Work and Relief Policies of the National Resources Planning Board. Her report, "Social Insurance and Allied Services," was submitted by FDR to Congress in March 1943. It recommended a national system of unemployment insurance and federal relief programs when states failed to establish their own. Conservative congressional critics condemned the report and Burns for advocating socialism. She remained with the National Planning Agency until 1945 when it was abolished. During the postwar period she acted as a government consultant and wrote books on social security. She died on September 2, 1985, in Newton, Pennsylvania.

Bush, Vannevar
(1890–1974)   *head, National Defense Research Committee; director, Office of Scientific Research and Development*

The son of a minister and his wife, Vannevar Bush was born on March 11, 1890, in Everett, Massachusetts, and reared in Chelsea, Massachusetts. He earned his undergraduate and master's degrees from Tufts University before entering the doctoral program in engineering jointly offered by MIT and Harvard. He received his doctorate in 1916, the same year he married Phoebe Davis, with whom he had two sons.

Having begun teaching mathematics and electrical engineering at Tufts in 1914, he left

Vannevar Bush *(Library of Congress)*

that position five years later to join the MIT faculty as a professor of electrical power, which allowed him to combine his interests in mathematics and tinkering. By 1931, he had risen to become the vice president and dean of engineering at MIT. He then left MIT in 1938 to become the president of the Carnegie Institution of Washington (CIW), which helped him extend his network of contacts to both the nation's capital and New York. That same year, he was appointed to chair the National Advisory Committee for Aeronautics (NACA) while simultaneously serving as chair of the Division of Engineering and Industrial Research in the National Research Council (NRC), the operational branch of the National Academy of Sciences (NAS). He would later entrench himself even further in this milieu by becoming a member of the Committee on Scientific Aids to Learning in the NRC, which was chaired by Harvard's James B. Conant.

Bush's conservative background had led him to support the isolationist Liberty League's backing of ALF LANDON's 1936 presidential bid. However, he had come to appreciate the intersection of sciences and politics, just as earlier he had grasped intuitively the intellectual linkages between mathematics and engineering. Drawing on this broader understanding, he had Frederick Delano, a nephew of Franklin Roosevelt and a CIW trustee who headed the National Resources Planning Board, introduce him to HARRY HOPKINS. It proved to be a mutually advantageous connection between Bush and the Roosevelt administration as FDR later appointed him to head the National Defense Research Committee (NDRC).

The Roosevelt-Bush relationship not only clicked but deepened. For FDR, Bush was another extra pair of capable hands that helped the modern presidency in the way that the recommendations of the LOUIS BROWNLOW committee on administrative management had intended. FDR's bureaucratic experience as assistant secretary of the navy during World War I melded with Bush's frustrations with the navy during the same time over his invention of an electromagnetic tool for locating submarines. Often to the chagrin of both military and civilian bureaucrats, FDR bestowed upon Bush the freedom to act with a separate budget and direct access to the president. By 1941, FDR had enlarged Bush's role to director of the new Office of Scientific Research and Development (OSRD), which included the NDRC with Conant, who replaced him as chair, and the new Committee on Medical Research (CMR). This arrangement provided Bush's group of scientists and engineers the venue to develop new weapons outside of traditional bureaucratic channels. Bush came to admire FDR's leadership style and, in fact, adapted it to his own scientific and engineering realm. He networked, co-opted potential adversaries, and kept his multiple committees filled with the technically competent while acting as director of general policy and resolving lower-level conflicts.

Bush tried to limit OSRD to research and development. Whenever possible, he used its contracts with universities and industrial organizations to acquire what was necessary to win the war while avoiding getting into the more political thicket of military arms and supplies procurement. He also eschewed involvement in social policies and postwar planning. After the program to develop a nuclear device became too large, he turned it over to the Army Corps of Engineers while retaining oversight. Bush wanted to have the OSRD abolished after the war because he viewed it as an ad hoc emergency entity only. He was a bureaucratic entrepreneur who appreciated democratic restraint.

From 1946 to 1949, Bush headed the Research and Development Board before returning to the CIW, where he remained until he retired in 1955. His 1949 book, *Modern Arms and Free Men: A Discussion of the Role of Science in Preserving Democracy*, became a best seller. It captured the contribution to the Roosevelt administration that he had made through marrying basic and applied science to meeting national security needs and through creating the role of a science adviser to the modern presidency.

Bush died on June 28, 1974, in Belmont, Massachusetts.

Butler, Pierce
(1866–1939) *U.S. Supreme Court justice*

Born on March 17, 1866, in Pine Bend, Minnesota, Pierce Butler was the son of Irish Catholic immigrant farmers who came to the United States in 1848 due to the potato famine. After narrowly missing admission to the U.S. Military Academy, he attended nearby Carleton College, where he developed a conservative political philosophy. He graduated in 1887, and the next year he was admitted to the Minnesota bar after clerking and reading law in a St. Paul law office. After a brief stint as a county attorney, he began a two-decade legal practice representing utilities and railroads. In 1908 he became president of the Minnesota Bar Association, the same year he began what would be a long tenure on the University of Minnesota Board of Regents. He had made the transition from immigrant background to established society. During World War I, perhaps to provide proof of his national loyalty because of his Irish ancestry, he became a leader in the dismissal of professors who did not support the American war effort.

Despite the fact that Butler remained a lifelong Democrat, in 1922 Chief Justice William Howard Taft recommended that Butler fill the newly vacated opening on the U.S. Supreme Court. The traditional "Catholic seat" had been unfilled since the retirement in 1921 of Justice Edward D. White. Butler was confirmed as an associate justice on December 21, 1922, on a vote of 61 to 8, with an amazing 27 abstentions.

Taft and President Warren Harding got what they had sought. Butler was an energetic conservative ideologue who never wavered in upholding laissez-faire decisions. He became part of the Court conservative coalition known as the "Four Horsemen" by New Deal supporters frustrated by the justices' opposition to FDR's programs. The others were JAMES MCREYNOLDS, GEORGE SUTHERLAND, and WILLIS VAN DEVANTER. They rejected both sociological jurisprudence and legal realism, the legal-reform schools of jurisprudence during the 1920s. Butler may have been the most conservative justice of the 1920s and 1930s. He held the conservative bloc together with his proverbial Irish wit and congenial personality. In addition to voting against nearly every aspect of the New Deal, he demanded total loyalty from citizens rather than permitting dissent just as he had at the University of Minnesota.

Increasingly in ill health in the late 1930s, he died suddenly on November 16, 1939, in Washington, D.C. Scholars of the Court have rated him as one of the eight failures in its entire history. His judicial activism in promoting laissez faire government earned his place as the most overruled justice in Supreme Court history.

Byrd, Harry Flood
(1887–1966) *Virginia governor, U.S. senator*

Harry Byrd inherited a family name traceable to colonial Virginia, but it carried no financial advantages. Born on June 10, 1887, in Martinsburg, West Virginia, he attended public schools in Westchester, Virginia, until he quit high school to work for the failing family newspaper. Through hard work and thrift, he turned the paper around and soon developed an apple orchard business into one of the nation's largest. In the tradition of his uncle Hal Flood, who had been the Democratic state party boss during the Woodrow Wilson era, he created his own political machine. Byrd served in the Virginia state senate between 1915 and 1925 and then held the governorship from 1926 to 1930. With characteristic energy and drive, he established a record of progressive state leadership in terms of economy and industrial growth. Relying on the fame of his brother, Admiral Richard Evelyn Byrd Jr. (1888–1957), the polar explorer who flew over the North and South Poles, he encouraged development of airports and roads. He also supported creation of the Shenandoah National Park. In contrast to his later civil-rights record, as governor he backed a tough antilynching bill enacted in 1928. In 1932, he was Virginia's "favorite son" candidate at the Democratic national convention.

For more than three decades, as he rose in stature to become Virginia's most prominent 20th-century politician, Byrd was among the most intense critics of the New Deal and its legacy. His dynamic governorship regressed into a national leadership that blocked economic and social progress by advocating negative government and states' rights. He joined the conservation coalition in Congress, though he was a Democrat and not an isolationist. After FDR appointed Virginia senator Claude Swanson as secretary of the navy in 1933, Byrd filled Swanson's seat as a protégé of Senator CARTER GLASS. In 1944 he was a token protest presidential candidate against FDR, who prevailed in the contest with Byrd to enact historically significant legislation. Byrd, however, won his patronage battles to maintain control in Virginia. He died on October 20, 1966, in Berryville, Virginia.

Byrnes, James Francis
(Jimmy Byrnes)
(1879–1972) *U.S. senator; U.S. Supreme Court justice; director, Office of Economic Stabilization; director, Office of War Mobilization*

A third-generation Irish-Catholic American, James Byrnes was not yet born on May 21, 1879, when his father died. He had to quit school when he was a teenager to help support his family. He was a messenger for a law office, then a court stenographer, and two judges acted as father surrogates in guiding him to read law. He passed the South Carolina bar in 1903. After three years of both practicing law and working as a court stenographer, he married Maude Busch in 1906 and converted to the Episcopal faith. He also purchased the local newspaper and edited it for the next four years.

In 1908, Byrnes became the local solicitor in Aiken, South Carolina, which prepared him for politics. The next year he was elected to the U.S. House of Representatives, serving from 1911 to 1924. His ability to compromise made him well liked by members of both parties. While sitting on the Appropriations Committee, he forged a fast friendship with Assistant Secretary of the Navy Franklin D. Roosevelt when FDR sought naval funding during the Wilson administration.

Byrnes's only electoral defeat occurred in 1924 when a racist and anti-Catholic opponent used the Ku Klux Klan against him. Byrnes was openly a segregationist, but he never belonged to the KKK as charged. After his defeat, he joined a prominent law firm in Spartanburg. A few years later, with the endorsement of his Episcopal minister and the friendship and financial backing of BERNARD BARUCH, Byrnes defeated the reelection bid of his former electoral opponent and took his seat in the U.S. Senate in 1930. His alliance with Baruch enabled Byrnes to allocate Baruch's money to other Senate campaigns, making him a power broker in the nation's capital.

In Washington, D.C., Byrnes developed his reputation for accomplishing things and helped to get most New Deal legislation through the Senate. Although a central figure in the conservative coalition resisting the federal antilynching bill, the use of sit-down strikes, and the attempted congressional purge in 1938, the outbreak of World War II pushed him back in FDR's direction, and he helped steer the Reorganization Act of 1939 to reorganize the presidency through Congress. At the 1940 Democratic convention, Byrnes served as FDR's floor manger to secure the president's nomination for an unprecedented third term. He also helped to gain repeal of the Neutrality Acts as well as passage of the Lend-Lease Act to assist the British. As a reward, FDR nominated Byrnes to the U.S. Supreme Court in June 1941, and he was confirmed unanimously.

After slightly more than a year, Byrnes resigned from the Court to head the wartime Office of Economic Stabilization. The next year the president named him as the director of war mobilization. FDR referred to Byrnes as his "assistant president," an accurate description of his role in domestic affairs during World War II. The president delegated unprecedented and broad executive power to

Byrnes, enabling him to plan and coordinate military and civilian production. He received widespread praise for administrative ability.

Expecting the vice-presidential nomination and a chance for the presidency in 1948, Byrnes felt cheated when the 1944 vice presidency went to HARRY S. TRUMAN. He was also disappointed in 1944 when FDR chose EDWARD STETTINUS instead of him to succeed CORDELL HULL as secretary of state. However, FDR did invite Byrnes to accompany him to the Yalta Conference in February 1945. Later President Truman named him as his first secretary of state, but Byrnes was unable to harness the same power he had enjoyed with FDR. Similarly, his later governorship of South Carolina proved disappointing. Nonetheless, Byrnes was one of the most powerful national politicians during the 1930s and 1940s and ranks as one of South Carolina's greatest. He died on April 9, 1972, in Columbia, South Carolina.

Byrns, Joseph Wellington, Sr.

(1869–1936) *U.S. congressman, Speaker of the House*

Born on July 20, 1869, in Cedar Hill to Tennessee farmers, Joseph Byrns received his law degree from Vanderbilt University in 1890 and began practicing law in Nashville. His political career started in 1894 with his election to the Tennessee house, where he became the speaker during his third term. In 1900, he was elected to the state senate, but he lost his 1902 race for county district attorney. The Democrat began his career in the U.S. Congress with an upset election that put him in the House of Representatives from 1908 until his death.

A workhorse congressman, Byrns soon won a seat on the powerful Appropriations Committee. He aspired to the U.S. Senate, but health problems began in 1930, and he had to withdraw from the election. The next year, his legislative power in the House increased when he became chairman of the Appropriations Committee. In 1932, he became House majority leader. Byrns was very loyal to the New Deal, especially as it related to agriculture. He personally sponsored the Civilian Conservation Corps, which was FDR's original idea. With the death of House Speaker Henry T. Rainey, Byrns became a candidate for the position in January 1935. FDR preferred either WILLIAM BANKHEAD or SAM RAYBURN as Speaker, but the Democratic caucus elected Byrns, and Bankhead became the majority leader. Byrns instituted the initial expansion of the whip system to guide New Deal legislation through the House. He died suddenly of a heart attack on June 4, 1936, while in the Capitol.

Caldwell, Erskine
(1903–1987) *novelist, playwright*

The only child of a liberal southern minister father and schoolteacher mother, Erskine Caldwell was born on December 17, 1903, in Oak, Georgia. He was exposed as a child to the behavior of both poor whites and blacks as his family traveled throughout the South. After attending Erskine College in South Carolina, the University of Pennsylvania, and the University of Virginia in the early 1920s, Caldwell became a newspaper reporter and a prolific writer.

Caldwell achieved his greatest success in the 1930s and 1940s. His work of that time sympathetically portrayed the comic and absurd lives of rural Georgia's poor whites, first in *Tobacco Road* (1932), with its grotesque sexual behavior, then in *God's Little Acre* (1933). *Tobacco Road* was made into a 1933 Broadway play that ran for nearly eight years, and an obscenity trial turned *God's Little Acre* into a best seller. These literary efforts helped to provide the cultural rationale for the New Deal's Resettlement Administration and the Farm Security Administration. Caldwell spent the next 20 years in Hollywood. He turned to documentary writing during the height of the Great Depression as his politi-

cal leanings moved to the left. Pioneering photojournalist MARGARET BOURKE-WHITE, the third of his four wives, collaborated with him on the photos and text for *You Have Seen Their Faces* (1937), which captures the despair

Erskine Caldwell *(Library of Congress)*

on the faces of black and white farmers in the South. He worked as a correspondent during World War II. After the war he became a Hollywood screenwriter and wrote more novels without ever regaining his prewar popularity. He died on April 11, 1987, in Paradise Valley, Arizona.

Capper, Arthur
(1865–1951) *U.S. Senator*

Arthur Capper was the first native-born Kansan to become both the state's governor and a U.S. senator. He was initially a progressive Republican who favored Theodore Roosevelt's Bull Moose 1912 presidential bid but later became known in the Senate as a Republican New Dealer. Such exceptions notwithstanding, he remained a loyal Republican.

Capper was born on July 14, 1865, in Garnett, Kansas; his father was an English immigrant. After his graduation from Garnett High School in 1884, Capper began working for the Topeka *Daily Capital*, worked briefly for the *New York Tribune*, and in 1891 was a correspondent in the nation's capital for the *Daily Capital*. In 1892, he married Florence Crawford, the daughter of a former Kansas governor. Married for 34 years, the couple had no children.

Capper launched his midwestern business career in 1893 when he began purchasing newspapers that were in financial trouble. His first acquisition was a small weekly, the North Topeka *Mail*. He later bought the *Daily Capital*, where he had been a cub reporter years earlier. Eventually he owned at least a dozen newspapers that employed more than a thousand persons and boasted combined circulations of nearly 5 million. By the late 1920s, he had moved into the new communications field opened by radio.

Capper was a Republican in a state dominated by the Populist Party. Yet like the Populists, he opposed the domination of railroads in Kansas politics and came to endorse Progressive Republican reforms. When THEODORE ROOSEVELT launched his 1912 Bull Moose presidential campaign, Capper threw his hat into the state political ring, becoming the Republican candidate for governor. He lost that race by a narrow margin but defeated the incumbent two years later and was subsequently reelected in 1916. He ran successfully for the U.S. Senate in 1918 and served five consecutive terms before he retired in 1949.

Capper compensated for his lack of rhetorical skills by being as industrious in his senatorial committee work as he had been in building his newspaper empire. In both pursuits, he remained open to colleagues and the public, promptly responding to questions whether asked to him directly or by mail. He voted for the League of Nations, although he had reservations about it, and later became a foreign-policy isolationist. He became a leader of the farm bloc and sponsored the Capper-Volstead Acts of 1922 and 1926 and the Capper-Ketchum Act of 1928, which backed 4-H clubs.

Critical of conservative Republican presidents during the 1920s, Capper became an early supporter of New Deal legislation. He favored work relief, agricultural reform, and provisions for social security. While serving on the congressional District of Columbia Committee, he became a proponent of civil-rights legislation. On the other hand, he was critical of FDR's Court-packing plan. During World War II, he suspended his previous isolationist stance. Though he became known as a Republican New Dealer, he remained a member of the Republican Party.

Capper died in Topeka on December 19, 1951, and left the bulk of his estate to the Capper Foundation for Crippled Children and to his employees.

Capra, Frank
(1897–1991) *film director*

Frank Capra was born on May 18, 1897, in Bisaquino, Sicily. He was six years old when his Sicilian family emigrated to Los Angeles, and he was the only one among 14 children to attend college. Attending on scholarship, he graduated in 1918 with a degree in chemical engineering from what would become the California Institute of Technology. During World War I, he served as an artillery school instructor. He first began making short films in San Francisco and in 1923 moved to Hollywood, where he developed his knack for directing social comedies.

Capra's romantic comedy *It Happened One Night* (1934) was the first film ever to win five Academy Awards. It turned Columbia Pictures into a major studio, launched the screwball-comedy genre, and made him Hollywood's most sought-after director. His subsequent Great Depression films preached the basic goodness of humankind. *Mr. Deeds Goes to Town* (1936) set the formula for his other films with an honest, idealistic, and slightly naive hero confronting corrupt men and institutions and ultimately prevailing through the assistance of a more realistic girlfriend. He won Academy Awards for best picture and best director with *You Can't Take It with You* (1938) and nominations for *Mr. Smith Goes to Washington* (1939). Some have argued that the lead character, Jefferson Smith, was modeled in part on Senator BURTON WHEELER (D-Mon.). In *Meet John Doe* (1941), Capra presents a small-town hero who outwits an industrialist's attempted fascist coup to take over the United States.

During World War II, Capra became head of the Army Pictorial Service, directing and producing *Why We Fight*, a series of propaganda documentaries. Intended originally only for American soldiers, the series was released to the public and garnered him yet another Academy Award for the best documentary of 1942.

Some journalists during the postwar era derided his optimistic outlook as "Capracorn," but Capra had tapped into a basic dimension of the American democratic spirit that resonated with the public. He portrayed individuals who confronted crises like the Great Depression without giving in to defeat or cynicism but relied on bedrock American resourcefulness, ingenuity, and humor to survive and overcome. He died on September 3, 1991, in LaQuinta, California.

Caraway, Hattie Ophelia Wyatt
(1878–1950) *U.S. senator*

The daughter of a Tennessee farmer and shopkeeper, Hattie Wyatt was born on February 1, 1878, in Bakerville, Tennessee. She graduated from Dickson Normal College in 1896 and taught school in Tennessee before her 1902 wedding to Thaddeus H. Caraway, whom she had met in college. The couple moved to Jonesboro, Arkansas, where he began a law practice while she reared their three children and oversaw the family's cotton farm. After he was elected to the U.S. House of Representatives in 1912, they established a second home in Riverdale, Maryland.

Caraway was elected to the U.S. Senate in 1921 and served until his death on November 6, 1931. Following the precedent of widow appointments, Hattie Caraway assumed the vacant seat on December 9, 1931, and won the special election held in January 1932 to complete the remaining months of the term, thus becoming the first woman elected to the Senate. She stunned the Arkansas political establishment when she chose to seek reelection in her own right. Without other significant backing, Caraway accepted the offer of help from popular populist HUEY LONG, the Louisiana senator whose sympathy for the poor she had supported. In typical fashion, the ambitious Long wanted to show up his rival senator JOSEPH ROBINSON in his home state. Long accomplished his goal with a flamboyant road campaign for Caraway that used the latest technology of the time (radio and sound trucks) during the week before the Democratic primary. Campaigning with Long, she garnered nearly twice as many votes as her nearest rival in a crowd of prominent candidates.

Carraway became one of the New Deal's most loyal supporters, showing concern for the plight of the poor during the Great Depression. However, as with other white southerners, this compassion did not extend to racial justice, and she joined in the filibuster of the FDR administration's antilynching bill in 1938. Nevertheless, FDR backed her over Representative John L. McClellan in the Democratic primary that year, and she won reelection by a narrow victory. Not only did she support FDR's domestic New Deal, as a mother with two sons in the army, she also supported the president's foreign policy. In 1943, she became the first woman legislator to cosponsor the Equal Rights Amendment.

After a poor showing in the 1944 Democratic primary, which resulted in Caraway's losing her seat to freshman congressman J. William Fulbright, she was appointed to the Employees' Compensation Commission. President HARRY S. TRUMAN later promoted her to its Appeal Board, where she remained until her death on December 21, 1950, in Falls Church, Virginia.

Cárdenas, Lázaro

(1895–1970) *Mexican president*

Of Indian descent, Lázaro Cárdenas was born on May 21, 1895, in Jiquilpan de Juarez, Michoacan, the son of a weaver and small store owner; his mother was a seamstress. With only a primary school education, the energetic youth went from working in menial jobs to serving as a local public official at age eighteen. He joined the Mexican Revolution in 1913 and rose rapidly to become a general in the army.

Cárdenas was elected governor of his native state on September 15, 1928. He became a main leader in the formation of what became the Institutional Revolutionary Party (PRI in Spanish) and briefly served in a variety of leadership offices. In his run for the presidency in 1934, he undertook the most vigorous campaign for the office ever waged up to that time, even though the PRI's dominance nearly guaranteed his victory. With his promises of land reform and industrial development, he was elected at age 39, becoming Mexico's youngest president in the 20th century.

Aggressive implementation of Cárdenas's reforms began in the late 1930s. On assuming office he gave his full support to strikers. He expropriated the nation's foreign-owned oil companies on March 18, 1938, and then created the huge Petroleos, or Pemex, which would serve as a model for similar public corporations in other developing nations. The railroads owned by Southern Pacific, Missouri Pacific, and the Missouri-Kansas-Texas corporations were also expropriated and turned into public corporations. He distributed twice as much land to peasants as all of his predecessors combined and expanded government banks so they could borrow money. This was the equivalent of the New Deal in Mexico. Cárdenas created new organizations such as the National Peasant Confederation and the Confederation of Mexican Workers, a national trade union federation, to solidify his power base.

In foreign policy, Cárdenas opposed attacks on independent nations, such as the Italian fascist invasion of Ethiopia, the Soviet and Nazi German intervention in the Spanish civil war, Nazi Germany's annexation of Austria and invasion of Czechoslovakia, the Soviet invasion of Finland, and Japan's invasion of China. He extended political refuge to Leon Trotsky after JOSEPH STALIN forced him into exile.

In 1940, in the PRI tradition, Cárdenas picked his own successor, General Manuel Avila Camacho. Cárdenas was back in government when he served as minister of national defense (1943–45), and he served as a governmental adviser for most of his life. He died on October 19, 1970. His son Cuauhtemoc became mayor of Mexico City and nearly won the presidency in 1988 on an anti-PRI ticket.

Cardozo, Benjamin Nathan
(1870–1938) *U.S. Supreme Court justice*

Born on May 24, 1870, in New York City, Benjamin Cardozo was the only son of Sephardic Jewish parents whose forebears predated the American Revolution. His father was a successful lawyer elected to the New York State Supreme Court who resigned under clouded circumstances. Cardozo's mother died when he was nine, and his father died six years later; his sister, who was 10 years older, largely reared him. He was tutored at home with help from Horatio Alger, Jr., the rags-to-riches novelist, who prepared him for Columbia College. Cardozo graduated in 1889 and the next year received his master's degree in political science. He entered Columbia's School of Law as a member of its second class, but he withdrew after two years and passed the bar. During the ensuing two decades, he became a prominent New York City attorney, a lawyer's lawyer who specialized in preparing appeal briefs.

In 1913–41 years after his father's resignation—Cardozo won election to the New York Supreme Court. His tenure was brief because he was asked to serve temporarily on the New York Court of Appeals, but that turned into a 14-year elected term. He won the post of chief judge when he was unopposed in the 1926 election. During his tenure on the Court of Appeals, it became known as the most distinguished court in the nation, second only to the U.S. Supreme Court.

In addition to his many decisions on the bench, Cardozo wrote five books. His first, *The Nature of the Judicial Process* (1921), was his most important and it became a classic. He argued that judges did not "find" a preexisting law but rather "made" it. Though controversial at the time, he was essentially a pragmatist who viewed the U.S. Constitution as a living tradition that had to grow and adapt to changing conditions to fit human needs.

In 1932, President HERBERT HOOVER nominated Cardozo to replace Oliver Wendell Holmes, Jr., on the U.S. Supreme Court. With the backing of powerful senators such as WILLIAM BORAH, Cardozo's nomination trumped geographic and ethnic objections to win a rapid and unanimous confirmation. His belief in judicial restraint led him to emerge as the most persuasive member of the liberal faction approving most New Deal legislation, especially measures to regulate the economy. However, in the area of individual rights, he was less progressive. For example, his last and most influential decision, rendered in *Palko v. Connecticut* (1937), reflected his belief in selective incorporation of the Bill of Rights by the states, unlike HUGO BLACK, who favored total incorporation. Nonetheless, Cardozo is ranked as one of the nation's dozen greatest justices. He died on July 9, 1938, in Port Chester, New York.

Carmody, John Michael
(1881–1963) *federal bureaucrat*

Born in 1881 in Towanda, Pennsylvania, John Carmody attended the Free Academy at Elmira,

New York, and the Elmira Business College. He then moved to the Midwest and attended the Lewis Institute in Chicago and the Emerson School in Gary, Indiana. For a short time in 1926 he attended Columbia University. After initially working as a bookkeeper, he served from 1900 to 1914 as an inspector for steel firms in Pennsylvania, Illinois, and Indiana as well as in Ontario, Canada, and Havana, Cuba. During the next 10 years he worked for garment manufacturers including H. Black Company of Cleveland, Ohio, and Printz-Biederman.

Carmody's first federal job was with the Bituminous Coal Commission during President Warren Harding's administration. His work with that commission led to his appointment as vice president of industrial relations for the Davis Coal and Coke Company. From 1927 to 1933, he served as the editor of *Coal Age* and *Industrial and Factory Management*, published by McGraw-Hill. A trip to the Soviet Union in 1931 sponsored by McGraw Hill to survey industrial developments there later led extreme conservatives to question his loyalty to the United States.

Carmody's active involvement in the New Deal began after he was selected to head the Bituminous Coal Labor Board. Late in 1933, he was named chief engineer of the Civil Works Administration, and later he assumed the same position for the Federal Emergency Relief Administration. In 1934, he served with the National Mediation Board, and the next year, Franklin Roosevelt put him on the National Labor Relations Board and named him as a mediator in coal disputes and cases involving the National Recovery Administration. In 1936, MORRIS COOKE made him the deputy administrator of the Rural Electrification Administration (REA), and FDR selected Carmody to succeed Cooke as REA head the following year.

In all of these positions, Carmody acted as the quintessential "passionate anonym," as the

media had dubbed the additional bureaucrats that the LOUIS BROWNLOW Committee had recommended in its 1937 report on administrative management. Carmody avoided publicity and worked effectively with others behind the scenes. After the Executive Reorganization Act of 1939 was enacted until 1941, Carmody served as head of the new Federal Works Agency, supervising the Works Progress Administration, Public Works Administration, Public Roads Administration, and the United States Public Buildings Administration. His final post during the FDR years was as a member of the Maritime Commission from 1941 to 1946.

During the postwar era, Carmody served in a variety of government posts in HARRY S. TRUMAN's administration. He died on November 11, 1963.

Chamberlain, Neville
(1869–1940) *British prime minister*

The son of a distinguished Unitarian business family in Birmingham, England, Neville Chamberlain was born on March 18, 1869, in Edgboston, a suburb of Birmingham. He studied business at the local trade school and at age 21 was sent to the Bahamas to manage his father's new estate, growing sisal fiber for rope. The venture failed due to the soil, and he returned to Birmingham in 1897. After his family purchased a metal ship-berth-making company, he spent a number of years in that business until World War I began.

Chamberlain was increasingly drawn to civic duties and in 1911 won his first political office on the Birmingham city council; he then became lord mayor in 1915 and 1916. He briefly served in a minor position in David Lloyd George's coalition cabinet during World War I but resigned after half a year due to a disagreement with the prime minister. In 1918, he won a seat in Parliament representing Birmingham, a seat that he kept until his death.

Chamberlain was a progressive member of the Conservative Party. He served in a series of governmental posts, including postmaster general, health minister, and for five years during the Great Depression he was chancellor of the exchequer (finance minister). On May 28, 1937, at age 68, Chamberlain replaced STANLEY BALDWIN as prime minister. He immediately launched a three-year defense program, with an emphasis on building the British air force. He accepted Fascist Italy's takeover of Ethiopia and maintained British neutrality in the Spanish civil war. Due to the relative weakness of the British military, Chamberlain then began a series of meetings with ADOLF HITLER. These failed efforts at negotiations led to Chamberlain's name becoming synonymous with appeasement and defeatism in foreign policy. Though he took no action when Hitler annexed Austria and occupied Czechoslovakia, Central Europe's only democracy, Chamberlain finally declared war on Germany after Nazi armies invaded Poland on September 1, 1939.

Chamberlain quickly assembled a war cabinet that included WINSTON CHURCHILL, the only member who had disagreed with Chamberlain's prior appeasement policy. After Hitler's invasion of Norway in May 1940, Chamberlain's parliamentary consensus crumbled, and he resigned in favor of Churchill. Ill health forced his resignation from Churchill's cabinet on September 29. He died on November 9, 1940, in Birmingham.

Chiang Kai-shek
(Jiang Jieshi)
(1887–1975) *president of China and the Republic of China (Taiwan)*

Chiang Kai-shek was born in 1887 in the east coast province of Chekiang (Zhejiang), China, into a middle-class family. He was educated at military academies in China and Japan and served with the Japanese military (1909–11) before returning to China to fight for Sun Yat-sen (1866–1925) during the revolution of 1911. Sun was financially backed by Charlie Soong (Sung), who became wealthy as a Bible salesman in China and was the father of Chiang's second wife. Chiang joined the Kuomintang (Guomindang; the Nationalist Party) of Sun, who wanted to unify the nation under a central republican government based on democratic principles he had derived from Abraham Lincoln. After several years of fighting warlords unsuccessfully, Chiang traveled in 1923 to the Soviet Union to study Marxism. However, he remained an anticommunist. Chiang's wife, born Soong Mei-ling (Sung Meiling; 1897–2003), was the sister of Sun Yat-sen's wife, Soong Ch'ing-ling (Sung Qingling). The sisters all attended Wesleyan College in Macon, Georgia; Mei-ling transferred to and graduated from Wellesley College, in Massachusetts, however. The Sung family converted Chiang to Christianity in 1930 and was active in the rise of the Kuomintang, which in the 1930s was responsible for renaming a tiny island off the Vietnamese coast as Lincoln Island, the name it retains today.

Chinese Communists, eventually led by Mao Tse-tung (Mao Zedong; 1893–1976) and Chou En-lai (Zhou Enlai; 1896–1976), who had briefly worked for Chiang, were forced to flee to the mountains after Chiang's Nationalist army tried to crush them in the late 1920s. Chiang then tried to quell the warlords in northern China, capturing Peking (Beijing) in 1928. Chiang talked about reforms, but most of the country remained under the influence of warlords, provincial leaders, and the Communists. Compounding the Nationalists' problems, Japan took over Manchuria in 1931, which Chiang chose to ignore in launching another campaign against Mao that forced the Communists to retreat on the famous Long March.

Though Chiang wanted finally to crush the Communists, he was threatened with a coup if he did not unite with them to resist the Japanese. He was kidnapped by one of his military leaders in 1936 and held for 11 days until Madame Chiang intervened and quickly obtained his release in return for an agreement to fight the Japanese in conjunction with the Communists. Chiang and the Communists waged a desperate war against the better-equipped Japanese, controlling the large rural areas and keeping them confused in urban areas.

Beginning in 1945, the United States provided the Nationalists with massive economic aid. After meeting Madame Chiang earlier in the year, FDR invited the Chiangs to the Cairo Conference. Because her husband spoke little English, Madame Chiang undertook to speak on his behalf. She became the first Chinese citizen to address Congress, and she completely impressed and disarmed both the politicians and the American public. (It was before ELEANOR ROOSEVELT realized Madame Chiang's elitism and racism.) The Allies subsequently gave Nationalist China a seat on the new United Nations Security Council.

After World War II ended, the Chinese civil war resumed, and the Nationalists were finally forced to flee to Taiwan in 1949. The Chiangs ruled the island as dictators until his death in Taipei in 1975.

Churchill, Winston Leonard Spencer
(1874–1965) *British prime minister*

Winston Churchill was born on November 24, 1874, in Blenheim Palace in Oxfordshire, England. Despite his aristocrat lineage—he was the son of Lord Randolph Churchill and American-born Jennie Jerome, whose father was a New York financier—Churchill was only an average student at prestigious Harrow School. His father therefore decided to send him to Sandhurst Military Academy, the traditional training ground for British army officers. It took three attempts at the entrance examination before Churchill was admitted to Sandhurst. His parents focused most of their attention on his younger brother, and without the attention of a concerned nanny to compensate for parental disfavor, Churchill might have suffered more serious flaws than his lifelong tendency to depression (bipolarity). He dealt with parental rejection by idealizing his parents.

Churchill developed a unique career that intertwined the military and journalism. While on leave, he reported on the war of Cuban independence (1898) and also served in the British army in India and Africa in the 1890s. His military correspondent reports from India and Egypt brought him prominence. In 1899, he resigned his army commission to run unsuccessfully for a seat in the House of Commons. After losing, he traveled to South Africa to cover the Boer War. His dramatic adventures there led to his election to a seat in Parliament in 1900. He moved quickly up the political ladder, especially after changing his party affiliation from the Conservatives to the Liberals between 1904 and 1924. He would eventually hold numerous major positions with each party, including every principal cabinet post except foreign secretary.

In 1924, Churchill reversed course and returned permanently to the Conservative Party. During the 1920s and 1930s, he was in and out of office while at the same time becoming a prolific essayist. From 1929 to 1939, he remained a pariah among the consensus Tories for his vocal criticism of Prime Ministers STANLEY BALDWIN and NEVILLE CHAMBERLAIN. He considered Chamberlain's appeasement policy giving ADOLF HITLER what he wanted on the Continent to avoid another world war to be highly dangerous.

After Hitler invaded Poland in September 1939, Chamberlain resigned in April 1940, and

Churchill became prime minister. With Britain facing defeat, he provided inspirational leadership. Despite his age, he worked long, if unusual, hours and made numerous trips overseas. He was adamant that the British would never surrender to the Nazis after the fall of France in 1940 and the disaster of Dunkirk, which necessitated a mass evacuation of British soldiers across the English Channel.

Churchill recognized that British success depended on the United States's entrance into the war, thus triggering his friendship with Franklin Roosevelt, whom he had met once during World War I. FDR had not been favorably impressed by that first meeting or by the fact that Churchill had forgotten it. Nonetheless, the two world leaders were drawn to each other by Churchill's need for American support and Roosevelt's appreciation of world affairs.

Within a year, FDR's maneuverings around the isolationists in Congress allowed him to provide support to the British in the form of military surplus matériel and old destroyers. This escalated to massive military aid through the 1941 Lend-Lease Act, passed at a crucial time when British material resources were virtually exhausted. This was followed by a series of conferences between FDR and Churchill, the first in August 1941 aboard a ship off the eastern coast of Canada, where they issued the Atlantic Charter with principles that formed the basis for the United Nations Charter. In January 1943 came the Casablanca Conference in Morocco when General DWIGHT EISENHOWER was designated the commander of Allied forces in North Africa and Churchill reluctantly agreed to FDR's terms for the unconditional surrender of the Axis powers. The November and December Cairo Conferences in 1943 led to Eisenhower's designation as the commander of the Western Europe invasion. The Tehran Conference in Iran was held between the two Cairo meetings, and JOSEPH STALIN attended for the first time. The most

Prime Minister Winston Churchill addressing the U.S. Congress, December 1941 *(University of Kentucky Libraries)*

controversial Allied conference was held February 4–11, 1945, at Yalta in the Crimea and resulted in Stalin's being territorially rewarded for the Soviet Union's role during the war.

Churchill possessed an active, humorous, and magnanimous personality, and his record on domestic legislation and modern technology was progressive, yet at his core he was the true descendant of the First Lord of Marlborough, hero of the Battle of Blenheim. His leadership style was that of a traditional democrat who wanted to preserve the British Empire. He admired Napoleon I, in contrast to FDR, who admired Theodore Roosevelt (whose own political hero was Lincoln). The Roosevelts, like Lincoln, were rational democrats; FDR wanted to end colonialism.

Churchill was forced from office abruptly when the Conservative Party suffered a stunning defeat in the July 1945 election. He had admirably and heroically provided for the safety and security needs of the British when externally threatened by the Nazis. As soon as the threat ended, though, the British turned to the obscure leadership of Clement Attlee, whose Labor Party had a blueprint to address the

British people's emerging social needs. Churchill, unfortunately, was as blind to the need for change at home as he was to the emerging needs of British colonists. Nonetheless, he was briefly reelected prime minister in the mid-1950s. He died on January 24, 1965, in London.

Clapper, Raymond Lewis
(1892–1944) *journalist, radio commentator*

Born near LaCygne, Kansas, on May 29, 1892, Raymond Clapper was the son of farmers who moved to Kansas City, Kansas, shortly after his birth. Clapper developed an early interest in reading and began to read newspapers while in grade school. His interest in the printed word increased during the three years he worked for a local print shop, and he ultimately became a journeyman printer. While he was a teenager, his hero was fellow Kansan William Allen White, the well-known and influential editor of the *Emporia Gazette.* Clapper did not enter high school until age 17, and before he graduated, he married Olive Vincent Ewing in 1913; the couple eventually had two children. Both Clapper and his wife attended the University of Kansas after their marriage, and he became the campus correspondent for the *Kansas City Star.* They left college without graduating in 1916 and moved to Kansas City, Missouri, where he joined the *Star*'s staff. His work quickly caught the attention of United Press (UP). The news service recruited him and sent him to Chicago later in 1916. He was also assigned briefly to Milwaukee, St. Paul, and New York, before UP moved him to the nation's capital in 1923 to manage its Washington bureau. He held that post until 1933, when he published the book *Racketeering in Washington.*

In 1933, Clapper moved to the *Washington Post* as its bureau chief. The next year, he began his daily column, "Between You and Me." When his contract expired, he was hired by the Scripps-Howard papers, owner of the UP news service, which began to syndicate his column to its 176 papers, with a combined readership of 10 million. Clapper also wrote for magazines and served as a radio news anchor and commentator for the Mutual radio network.

Endeavoring to be an impartial reporter and commentator, Clapper never registered to vote. He characterized himself mostly as a New Dealer but criticized Franklin Roosevelt's third-term bid. Highly regarded by his colleagues, he was elected president of the Gridiron Club in 1939. In November 1943, the *Saturday Evening Post* described him as "The Average Man's Columnist." Although Clapper was seldom profound, he tried to convey his political analysis in clear, plain language that average readers could understand.

During World War II, Clapper moved away from political stories to the human dimensions of war. In 1943, he went to the Mediterranean theater to cover the Allied invasion of Italy, and early the next year he flew to the Pacific to report on the war there. While he was covering the invasion of the Marshall Islands, he was killed in an airplane accident on February 1, 1944.

Cohen, Benjamin Victor
(1894–1983) *legal counsel to the Roosevelt administration*

Ben Cohen was born on September 23, 1894, in Muncie, Indiana. The son of affluent Polish-Jewish immigrants, he received his undergraduate degree from the University of Chicago in 1914, a law degree from the University of Chicago the next year, and a second law degree from Harvard Law School in 1916. His legal talent attracted the attention of FELIX FRANKFURTER and LOUIS BRANDEIS, who arranged federal employment for him during Woodrow Wilson's administration. From 1922 to 1933, Cohen practiced law on Wall Street.

After the New Deal was launched in 1933, Brandeis and Frankfurter brought Cohen to the nation's capital. He worked with two other of Felix Frankfurter's legendary "Happy Hotdogs," JAMES LANDIS and THOMAS CORCORAN, to refine the Securities Act of 1933 and the Securities Exchange Act of 1934, which established the Securities Exchange Commission (SEC). The Cohen-Corcoran team drafted much New Deal legislation, including the acts establishing the Federal Housing Administration and the Tennessee Valley Authority; the extension of the Reconstruction Finance Corporation; the Public Utility Holding Company Act of 1935, designed to regulate giant utility corporations; the Rural Electrification Act of 1935; and the Fair Labor Standards Act of 1938. Indefatigable workers, Cohen and Corcoran drafted the legislation, helped to shepherd it through Congress, and defended it in court when needed.

Cohen's legal abilities continued to help FDR during World War II. He gave the president legal advice on the 1940 destroyers-for-bases deal with the British, and he was responsible for drafting the Lend-Lease Act. Serving as the general counsel to the Office of War Mobilization, he drafted the agreement for the Dumbarton Oaks conference in Washington, D.C., which led to the United Nations Charter. Cohen was the epitome of a presidential assistant with a "passion for anonymity," as White House adviser LOUIS BROWNLOW called for in the modern presidency. Never seeking the limelight, he was simply another pair of competent hands for the president when help was needed. He died on August 15, 1983, in Washington, D.C.

Collier, John
(1884–1968) *commissioner of Indian affairs*

Born on May 4, 1884, John Collier was the son of a prominent banker who was mayor of Atlanta, Georgia. His mother died when he was 13, and his father died three years later. Convinced that his father had committed suicide, Collier vowed to dedicate his life to public service instead of worldly success. He attended Columbia University and the Collège de France during the first decade of the 20th century but did not earn a degree. During the next decade, he worked with immigrants, mostly in New York City, and concluded that preserving one's heritage was consistent with becoming an American.

It was in 1920 that Collier found his calling after observing traditional Pueblo Indian dances in Taos, New Mexico. He was inspired by their culture and community spirit and made a lifelong commitment to preserving tribal life as an alternative to assimilation into modern American society. He worked as a lobbyist in Washington, D.C., for the American Indian Defense Association, which he founded in 1923, and attracted national attention as an Indian reformer.

Collier's efforts were recognized in 1933 when FDR appointed him as commissioner of Indian affairs. He thus became FDR's agent to bring a "New Deal" to Native Americans. He worked to enact the Johnson-O'Malley Act of 1934, which allowed the federal government to contract with the states to provide educational, medical, and social welfare services to American Indians. The cornerstone legislation was the Indian Reorganization Act of 1934 and the formation of an Indian Arts and Crafts Board in 1935 to market Indian-made items. Collier arranged for federal agencies to bring New Deal relief programs to reservations and he organized a separate Indian Civilian Conservation Corps.

Collier was an idealist who tended to romanticize American Indian culture, and his initiatives suffered setbacks from Congress, the administration, and Indians themselves. The Navajo voted against the Indian Reorganization Act, the Senate Indian Affairs Committee criticized him for advocating segregation, and Secretary of War HENRY STIMSON rejected Collier's call for separate Indian military units. He resigned as commissioner in early 1945. He died on May 8, 1968, in Talpa, New Mexico.

Connally, Thomas Terry
(Tom Connally)
(1877–1963) *U.S. congressman, U.S. senator*

Born on August 19, 1877, in Hewitt, Texas, the son of well-to-do Texas farmers, Tom Connally graduated in 1896 from Baylor College and earned his law degree from the University of Texas in 1898. He enlisted in the Second Texas Infantry Volunteers during the Spanish-American War, but illness kept him stateside. He began practicing law and was elected to the Texas House of Representatives for two terms and then served from 1906 to 1910 as a county prosecutor. He resumed a successful law practice until he was elected in 1916 to the U.S. House of Representatives. Two years later, he volunteered for military service and was commissioned as an army officer, but again illness kept him stateside. He returned to Congress, where, with the help of JOHN NANCE GARNER (D-Tex.), he landed a seat on the House Foreign Affairs Committee and supported Woodrow Wilson's foreign policy.

In 1928, Connally unseated a one-term incumbent for the U.S. Senate. An admirer of William Jennings Bryan, after whom he modeled his colorful oratory and appearance, Connally became an early FDR backer, helping to persuade Garner to support Roosevelt at the 1932 Democratic convention. He also supported the early New Deal. However, the court-packing scheme so enraged Connally that he and FDR did not speak to each other for two years. He also opposed the Reorganization Act of 1939, which strengthened the executive

branch. As a southerner, he supported states' rights against federal power and was against legislation that favored African Americans and organized labor.

Connally was, however, an internationalist and liberal on foreign policy. He served as either the chairman or the ranking minority member on the Senate Foreign Relations Committee from 1941 until his retirement. He died on October 28, 1963, in Washington, D.C.

Cooke, Morris Llewellyn
(1872–1960) *director, Rural Electrification Administration*

Morris Cooke was born on May 11, 1872, one of eight children; his father was a physician. Cooke received a degree in mechanical engineering from Lehigh University in 1895. Ever energetic, while in college he worked for several newspapers and as a machinist. He served as an assistant engineer in the navy in the Spanish-American War and then entered the printing business. In 1900, he married heiress Eleanor Bushnell, who shared his progressive beliefs.

One of the great influences on Cooke's professional life was Frederick W. Taylor, a mechanical engineer he met in 1903. Taylor selected Cooke as one of the four engineers to learn his approach to scientific management, which Cooke utilized after establishing his own engineering consulting firm in 1905. Philadelphia's reform mayor, Rudolf Blackenburg, appointed him as director of the city's Department of Public Works (1911–15), where Cooke applied Taylor's scientific management methods for industry to local government and achieved considerable savings. He performed similarly during World War I, serving on the War Industries Board and then as executive assistant to the chairman of the U.S. Shipping Board. As a progressive Republican himself,

Pennsylvania governor Gifford Pinchot made Cooke an economic adviser and appointed him to head a survey (1923–25) for rural electrification and state reorganization of the electric industry.

Cooke's work in Pennsylvania caught the attention of New York governor Franklin Roosevelt, who appointed him to the Power Authority of the State of New York in 1929. It also led Cooke to join the Democratic Party and support FDR's presidential bid in 1932. The next year, the president made him chair, first of the Mississippi Valley Committee of the Public Works Committee, then of the National Power Policy Committee, as well as a member of planning committees.

Cooke considered rural electrification as his most important contribution. FDR made him the first director of the Rural Electrification Administration (1935–37), which was established to finance construction of power distribution systems in rural areas that lacked electricity. As an advocate for national economic planning and conservation, he was on the cusp of those developing issues during the Great Depression when economic growth took precedence. He designed a 25-year economic and ecological plan for the Midwest when he was appointed in 1937 to chair the Great Plains Drought Area Committee. During World War II, Cooke became a technical consultant to the Office of Production Management and headed a technical mission to Brazil. He died on March 5, 1960, in Philadelphia.

Copland, Aaron
(1900–1990) *composer*

Born on November 14, 1900, in Brooklyn, New York, Aaron Copland was the youngest of five children of Russian Jewish immigrant shopkeepers. His mother had attended high school in Dallas and considered herself a Texan. Copland learned basic composition and harmony through a correspondence course and later regretted that he had never attended college. However, he went to France in 1920 and met Nadia Boulanger, considered one of the best teachers of musical composition of her era. Copland became her first great student; under her tutelage, he developed a compositional voice epitomizing American themes.

By the 1930s, Copland had become a staunch FDR Democrat. As FDR established his New Deal for America and Good Neighbor policy toward Latin America in the 1930s and 1940s, Copland completed some of his most famous works, musical equivalents to FDR's political programs, during the same time. For example, *El Salon Mexico* (1936), *A Lincoln Portrait* (1942), *Fanfare for the Common Man* (1942), and *Appalachian Spring* (1944) were the distinctly American musical works that reflected the spirit of FDR's leadership. Copland's mother's southwestern background was reflected in *Billy the Kid* (1938) and *Rodeo* (1932). That egalitarian dimension of his music, especially associated with America's West, was also reflected in his personal openness and unpretentiousness.

During the next two decades, Copland created music for films and orchestras before his retirement in 1970. He died on December 2, 1990, in Terrytown, New York.

Corcoran, Thomas Gardiner
("The Cork")
(1900–1981) *Reconstruction Finance Corporation lawyer, FDR speechwriter*

Born on December 29, 1900, in Pawtucket, Rhode Island, to an upper-class Irish-American family, Thomas Corcoran excelled in school. He was valedictorian at Brown University and editor of the law review at Harvard Law School, where he became a favorite pupil of Professor FELIX FRANKFURTER. After graduating in 1925,

Corcoran remained an extra year to earn a doctorate of juristic science. On Frankfurter's recommendation, he then served a year as secretary to Supreme Court justice Oliver Wendell Holmes, Jr. He practiced law on Wall Street for five years before accepting his first federal job in 1932. He joined the legal staff of the Reconstruction Finance Corporation (RFC), which had been established by HERBERT HOOVER to revive the nation's businesses and financial institutions. He remained with the RFC until 1940.

Like other important players in the Roosevelt administration, Corcoran's minor formal position belied his real status and the role he played in the New Deal. While Felix Frankfurter taught at Harvard Law School, Corcoran served as Frankfurter's designated agent in the capital for the first three years while establishing his own independent power base. Corcoran placed hundreds of attorneys in government jobs. His closest association was with legal counsel BENJAMIN COHEN, with whom he teamed to draft legislation and persuade Congress to accept it. Cohen acted as the primary drafter, and Corcoran lobbied the legislation using his intellect, wit, and personal charm. He was known as the life—and the music—of any party, for he would bring along his accordion to dinner parties and entertain. FDR enjoyed his company and appreciated his writing skills. He was the principal writer of FDR's 1936 acceptance speech at the Democratic National Convention in Philadelphia, coining the famous "rendezvous with destiny" phrase. He became too well known to conservative Democrats in Congress to remain a behind-the-scenes "passionate anonym" (as the media called the additional federal bureaucrats recommended by the LOUIS BROWNLOW committee). He had lobbied for the disastrous Court-packing plan of 1937, orchestrated FDR's campaign to purge conservatives from the Senate in 1938, and was an active member

of the covert team spearheading FDR's unprecedented third-term bid in 1940.

Corcoran resigned from the RFC in 1940 to campaign openly for FDR's reelection. Because of Senate hostility and a break with Frankfurter, who had declined to support Corcoran's nomination as solicitor general, he was not brought back into the administration. Instead, he married his longtime secretary and began a family as well as one of the most successful lobbying firms in the capital. He died on December 6, 1981, in Washington, D.C.

Coughlin, Charles Edward
(1891–1979) *radio personality*

Charles Coughlin was born on October 25, 1891, in Hamilton, Ontario, Canada. The only child of devout parents of Irish Catholic descent, he was shaped by his religion and

Father Charles Coughlin addressing a convention, 1936 *(Library of Congress)*

education in local parish schools in Ontario to become a priest. He was ordained in 1916 and taught in Canada for seven years. He then moved to Michigan, where he served as a parish priest for three years before being assigned to the new parish in Detroit where he would serve until his death. Because his church was under attack by the Ku Klux Klan and in financial trouble, he began to broadcast his Sunday sermons on a local radio station in 1926. The sermons became a hit, and in 1930 CBS radio began broadcasting them as "The Golden Hour from the Little Flower." The program attracted huge national audiences, in part because of Coughlin's made-for-radio voice—rich, mellifluous, and dramatic.

After the Great Depression struck, Coughlin's sermons took on political overtones, and they became a populist critique of corporate America. He became the most listened-to man in America and required a staff of more than 100 to answer mail. Coughlin met FDR in 1932 and initially admired him, endorsing Roosevelt's candidacy for president and telling his listeners it was "Roosevelt or ruin." As the White House staff began to distance itself from him, Coughlin changed his view of the New Deal, and by late 1934 he had created the National Union for Social Justice and the magazine *Social Justice*. The American public was sending more mail to him than to anyone in the United States, including the president.

In 1935, after Roosevelt proposed U.S. membership in the World Court, Coughlin, an isolationist, mounted a campaign that bombarded Congress with so much negative mail that it failed to ratify the treaty. It was FDR's first major legislative defeat. That same year, Coughlin formed an alliance with other New Deal critics, especially Senators HUEY LONG and FRANCIS TOWNSEND, called the Union Party. They hoped to run Long for president in 1936, but his assassination in September 1935 forced them to back WILLIAM LEMKE instead.

The campaign flopped, but some scholars believe it helped to push FDR in a more radical direction. He also may have learned his own mastery of the radio from listening to the "radio priest's" sermons.

After Coughlin's attacks became too extreme and openly anti-Semitic, his influence diminished, especially after America's entry into World War II. His magazine was banned from the U.S. mails as seditious, and the American Catholic hierarchy stopped his broadcasts in May 1942. He died in Detroit on October 27, 1979.

Couzens, James Joseph, Jr.
(1872–1936) *U.S. Senator*

James Couzens was born in Chatham, Ontario, Canada, on August 26, 1872. Not only was he geographically an outsider, but also he was the son of immigrants from England, a lower-class family who lived on the wrong side of town. With only two years of bookkeeping education at Chatham's Canada Business College, in 1890 he set out for Detroit to make his mark in the United States.

Couzens first began working for the Michigan Central Railroad. In 1895, he became a bookkeeper for Alex Malcomson's fuel company, work that brought him into contact with another highly energetic individual, HENRY FORD. Malcomson and Couzens entered into an arrangement to finance Ford's mechanical talent to manufacture automobiles. Couzens, who became the Ford company business manager in 1903, made Ford produce a vehicle that could be sold immediately rather than indulge Ford's tendency to invest endless time perfecting his model.

By 1913, Couzens's boundless energy was focused on Detroit's incomplete public transportation system. He resigned from his managerial position with Ford Motor Company in 1915 over disputes triggered by Ford's quirky personality, and in 1916 he was appointed as Detroit's police commissioner. Three years later, Couzens sold out his investment in the Ford Company, and he became a multimillionaire. By this time, he was already a full-time politician, having been elected as mayor of Detroit in 1918 and reelected in 1921. His persistence resulted in bringing about municipal ownership of the city's transportation system in 1922.

Couzens's reputation for honesty and accomplishment led to his appointment in 1922 to fill the unexpired term of Michigan's incumbent U.S. senator, who had resigned amidst a corruption scandal. Although he was a Republican, Couzens began his 14-year Senate career as an independent maverick who seemingly enjoyed tweaking the establishment. He opposed the scheme of his former business partner Henry Ford to buy the publicly owned Muscle Shoals and instead supported Nebraska senator GEORGE NORRIS's proposal that the hydroelectric facilities be operated by the federal government. He also opposed the tax proposals of the secretary of the Treasury, fellow Republican ANDREW MELLON, and instead sponsored a surtax on the wealthy.

Couzens's support of the New Deal was strong enough to earn him the appellation "New Deal Republican," although he personally objected to that characterization. Franklin Roosevelt tried in 1933 to co-opt him by including him as a U.S. representative to the World Economic and Monetary Conference in London. When American banks began collapsing in 1933, Couzens received much blame as a member of the Senate banking and currency committee. He supported FERDINAND PECORA's investigations of the nation's banking and investment networks. He also supported the Civilian Conservation Corps, the National Recovery Administration, Social Security, the National Labor Relations Act, the Public Util-ity Holding Company Act, and the Works Project Administration.

Through it all, Couzens seemed to remember his roots and so liked to chastise the Republican Old Guard, conservative Democrats, the American Liberty League, and the Hearst press. He also spent a large amount of his own fortune on establishing the Children's Fund of Michigan in 1934, yet he adamantly refused to let his name be used in association with the project.

Lacking the typical rhetorical and diplomatic skills of a politician, Couzens rejected an offer to run as a Democrat in the 1936 Senate race. Instead, he endorsed FDR's reelection bid before the September Republican primary in Michigan, dooming his own chance for reelection. His son, Frank, however, served as Detroit's mayor from 1933 to 1938. Couzens developed uremic poisoning and died in Detroit on October 22, 1936, leaving his wife of 38 years and their five children.

Cowley, Malcolm
(1898–1989) *literary critic, magazine editor*

A leftist intellectual, Malcolm Cowley not only served as editor of the *New Republic* magazine from 1929 to 1944 but also was involved in significant literary and political events that transpired during the Great Depression, World War II, and the postwar period. As his political views came under attack in the 1940s, he shifted his focus more to literary matters, with considerably greater success, through the 1970s.

Cowley was born on August 24, 1898, in Belsano, Pennsylvania, to a physician father and homemaker mother. His boyhood was spent on the family farm. He attended public schools in Pittsburgh and entered Harvard in 1915 but left three years later to serve with the American Field Service in France during World War I. He then returned to Harvard but stayed only briefly before leaving again to receive military training in Kentucky with the U.S. Army. After he married Marguerite "Peggy" Baird in 1919, he returned to Harvard and graduated in 1920.

Cowley and his wife, a painter, lived in New York's Greenwich Village for two years and then moved to France, where he studied French literature at the University of Montpellier, which granted him a diploma in 1922. While abroad, he met many American expatriate writers, including ERNEST HEMINGWAY, Ezra Pound, Gertrude Stein, Hart Crane, and Allen Tate. In 1929, he succeeded Edmund Wilson as the editor of *New Republic*. He divorced his wife in 1931 and the following year married Muriel Maurer, with whom he had his only child.

Cowley never joined the Communist Party, but he helped to move the *New Republic* further to the left. In September 1932, he joined more than 50 other prominent intellectuals in signing a letter that endorsed Communist Party leader WILLIAM Z. FOSTER in his presidential bid. Three years later, Cowley helped to organize the liberal League of American Writers, but he resigned in 1940 after it became affiliated with communists.

During World War II, ARCHIBALD MACLEISH recruited Cowley for the Office of Facts and Figures in the nation's capital. Cowley was soon under surveillance by the Federal Bureau of Investigation and under public attack. In 1942 he was criticized in the media by journalists Whittaker Chambers and WESTBROOK PEGLER as well as by Congressman MARTIN DIES (D-Tex.) for communist associations. Cowley resigned his government position that same year.

Moving from the political to the literary world afforded Cowley greater success, which including bringing public attention to a number of writers. He is credited for the renewed interest in WILLIAM FAULKNER during the postwar period. Cowley died on March 28, 1989, in New Milford, Connecticut.

Cox, Edward Eugene
(1880–1952) *U.S. congressman*

Edward Cox was born on April 3, 1880, near Camilla, Georgia, where he attended local public schools. He graduated from Mercer University with a law degree in 1902 and was admitted to the bar that same year. After beginning his law practice, Cox was soon involved in local politics, winning his first race and becoming mayor of Camilla for two years (1904–06). In 1908, he served as a delegate to the Democratic National Convention. He was first appointed and subsequently elected as a judge of the superior court of the Albany circuit, serving from 1912 to 1916 when he resigned to run as a Democrat for the U.S. House of Representatives. He lost the election but ran again and was elected in 1924. He was reelected 13 consecutive times through 1952.

Cox supported the Public Utility Holding Act of 1935 but turned against the New Deal during Franklin Roosevelt's second term. A typical white southerner who championed states rights and private property, he became enraged over "sit-down" strikes. He equated Franklin Roosevelt's tolerance for the newly organized Congress of Industrial Organizations (CIO) as evidence that FDR harbored radical intentions. Cox opposed FDR's Court-packing plan, the executive reorganization plan, the Works Projects Administration, and the National Labor Relations Board. He became a leader among members of the Conservative Coalition of southern Democrats who often voted with northern Republicans after 1937.

Cox died on December 24, 1952, in Bethesda, Maryland.

Crowley, Leo Thomas

(1889–1972) *Federal Deposit Insurance Corporation chairman, alien property custodian; head of Office of Economic Workforce and Foreign Economic Administration*

Leo Crowley was born in 1889 into a conservative Catholic family in Junction, Wisconsin. His family subsequently moved to Madison, where he was raised. His father's early death from tuberculosis and his older brothers' injuries in railroad accidents forced Crowley to quit school and find a job to support his mother and siblings. Always a hard worker, he was able to buy an interest in a wholesale paper and supply company by 1910. Applying his innate talents, personality, and industriousness, he worked his way to the top in eight years, becoming company president with investments in banking and real estate. By the 1920s, he was president of the State Bank of Wisconsin and director of First Wisconsin Bankshares, making him the most influential banker in the state by the end of that decade. Unfortunately, the stock-market crash plunged him deeply into debt, and he was forced to quit his position as bank president. The State Bank failed in 1932.

It was Crowley's Democratic Party political connections that provided him the avenue to make his comeback. Wisconsin governor PHILIP LA FOLLETTE named Crowley as chair of the Wisconsin Banking Review Board in 1932. La Follette's successor, Democratic governor Albert G. Schmedeman, came to rely on Crowley behind the scenes. Crowley previously had helped to direct Schmedeman's successful gubernatorial campaign in 1932; at the same time, he supported Franklin Roosevelt's presidential bid. He adeptly drafted Wisconsin's banking holiday proclamation in March 1933 and quickly gained FDR's approval for it. Addressing bank liquidity and farm mortgages in the state, he worked with JESSE JONES,

chairman of the Reconstruction Finance Corporation (RFC), and with Federal Farm Bureau chairman HENRY MORGENTHAU, JR., who in October 1933 appointed Crowley coordinator of the Seventh Farm District for the Farm Credit Administration. Crowley's typical energy and pluck earned him praise from both businessmen and politicians.

In 1934, FDR named Crowley to head the new Federal Deposit Insurance Corporation (FDIC), headquartered in the nation's capital and charged with oversight of the process to bring troubled banks into the insurance program. The next year, Crowley helped to gain congressional passage of banking regulatory legislation. He also acted as a liaison between the New Deal and La Follette and his brother ROBERT LA FOLLETTE in the 1936 and 1940 presidential elections. In 1939, he also became chairman of Standard Gas and Electric, a major public utility company.

Crowley had not only FDR's favor but also that of FDR's "assistant president," JAMES BYRNES, who acted as his patron during World War II. Over Morgenthau's objections, Crowley was appointed in 1942 as the alien property custodian. The next year, because of conflict between Vice President HENRY WALLACE and Jesse Jones, Byrnes persuaded FDR to appoint Crowley to head first the new Office of Economic Warfare and then the Foreign Economic Administration, which oversaw economic operations overseas, including the lend-lease program to Britain. After winning the extension of the lend-lease program in 1944, Crowley began to be criticized in the media, and by March 1944 he had resigned his alien property appointment. After HARRY S. TRUMAN became president, Crowley left the administration, and in December 1945 he became the head of the Chicago, Milwaukee, St. Paul and Pacific Railroad, a position he held through the 1960s. He died on April 15, 1972.

Crump, Edward Hull
(1874–1954) *political boss, U.S. congressman*

Born in Holly Springs, Mississippi, on October 2, 1874, Edward Crump was the son of a planter father and housewife mother. His father, a Confederate veteran, died when he was only three years old, forcing his mother to abandon the family plantation and move to town. During his youth, Crump held a series of odd jobs before he moved to Memphis, Tennessee, when he was 17 years old. There he took a job at a harness shop, which he bought from the owners eight years later. He married Bessie Byrd McLean in 1902, and they had three children.

Always ambitious, Crump was soon active in Democratic Party politics in his adopted state. He attended the state party conventions in 1902 and 1904. The next year, he won a seat on the Memphis city council while simultaneously serving on the city's Board of Public Works. In 1907, he was elected fire and police commissioner on a reform platform to rid collusion between public utilities and local government. He next ran for mayor of Memphis and was elected in 1910. From 1917 to 1923, he was treasurer of Shelby County, Tennessee's largest county.

Crump built a strong urban political machine that supported candidates for the next four decades. His machine's strength perhaps peaked at the 1940 Democratic National Convention in Chicago when it aligned with those of EDWARD KELLY in Chicago, FRANK HAGUE in Jersey City, EDWARD FLYNN in New York, and THOMAS PENDERGAST in Kansas City to deliver Franklin Roosevelt the nomination for an unprecedented third presidential term.

Crump also served as a delegate to many Democratic national conventions between 1912 and 1948 and was a member of the Democratic National Committee from 1936 to 1945. He also served in the U.S. House of Representatives from 1931 to 1935. He often combined politics with business and culture. The "Father of the Blues," W. C. Handy, composed a marching song for Crump that later became famous as the "Memphis Blues."

Despite his Deep South roots, Crump strongly opposed the Ku Klux Klan, which helped gain him the support of African-American voters. He supported the presidential candidacies of AL SMITH and Franklin Roosevelt. During Crump's reign as a political boss, the crime rate in Memphis declined, and he brought about a system of municipally owned public utilities. He demanded efficiency and honesty in the expenditure of public funds.

During the postwar period, Crump became critical of HARRY TRUMAN, ELEANOR ROOSEVELT, and Senator Estes Kefauver (D-Tenn.) for moving the Democratic Party too far to the left. He often accused others of having communist sympathies. He died on October 16, 1954, in Memphis.

Cummings, Homer Stille
(1870–1956) *U.S. attorney general*

The son of a Chicago businessman, Homer Cummings was born on April 30, 1870, in Chicago. He was educated at Heathcote School in upstate New York before entering Yale University for his undergraduate degree in engineering. He graduated from Yale Law School in 1893 and then began practicing law in Stamford, Connecticut. His first love, however, was politics, and he was a William Jennings Bryan partisan. In 1900, Cummings was elected to the first of three terms as Stamford's mayor. He was the state's attorney in Fairfield County from 1914 to 1924 and the Democratic Party national chairman from 1914 to 1920.

Cummings supported Franklin Roosevelt in 1932, helping FDR's delegate search at the Chicago convention and delivering a seconding speech for him. FDR reciprocated by first offering him the governor-generalship of the Philippine Islands. After the sudden death of his attorney general–designate Thomas Walsh, however, FDR named Cummings to that post. In his new position, Cummings expanded federal criminal prosecutions and recruited better lawyers, such as ROBERT JACKSON, into the Justice Department. But he faced a series of defeats in 1935–36 as the Supreme Court overturned New Deal statutes. Unfortunately, his judgment was clouded by the 1936 landslide presidential victory, and he shared FDR's overconfidence in the mandate as well as his desire for revenge against the Court's judicial activists. Rejecting the option of a constitutional amendment as too slow, he secretly drafted the Judicial Reorganization bill of 1937—commonly called the Court-packing plan—after discovering that former attorney general JAMES MCREYNOLDS had drafted a similar plan before he was appointed to the Supreme Court. The backlash against the proposal in Congress led to the emergence of a bipartisan conservative coalition against the New Deal. Cummings resigned in 1939 after having served one of the longest tenures of any attorney general. He died on September 10, 1956, in Washington, D.C.

Currie, Lauchlin

(1902–1993) *assistant for economic affairs, director of aid to China*

Lauchlin Currie was born on October 8, 1902, in New Dublin, Nova Scotia, Canada. He was a well-educated economist who received his education from St. Francis Xavier University, the London School of Economics, and Harvard University, where he received his doctorate. He taught at Harvard from 1927 to 1934, and he also taught at the Fletcher School of Law and Diplomacy. After he became a naturalized citizen of the United States in 1934, he began his involvement with the New Deal. He started working at the Treasury Department in Washington, D.C., where he became a friend of MARRINER ECCLES, the special assistant on monetary and credit matters.

After Eccles became the head of the Federal Reserve Board in November 1934, Currie began to work there as assistant director of the Research and Statistics Division. In that position, he helped draft the Banking Act of 1935, centralizing control of the Federal Reserve System through the new board of governors in Washington, D.C. The previous year he had published an influential book, *The Supply and Control of Money in the United States* (1934), which advocated government spending to recover from the Great Depression. Currie influenced Eccles to persuade FDR to resume federal expenditures to counter the recession of 1937. He became one of the most influential advocates of the theories of economist JOHN MAYNARD KEYNES.

The enactment of the Reorganization Act of 1939 led to the creation of a formal White House staff consisting of six new administrative assistants ("passionate anonyms," as the press referred to them) and the Executive Office of the President. FDR appointed Currie, the first economist on the White House staff, as "passionate anonym" responsible to the president for economic affairs. When the White House office staff later expanded from six to 600—never intended by the LOUIS BROWNLOW Committee—that position led to the larger postwar Council of Economic Advisers. A limited staff grew into a bureaucracy.

During World War II, Currie's attention turned toward foreign affairs. Serving on the

Foreign Economic Administration in China, Currie worked on the lend-lease program. In the postwar era of McCarthyism, he was investigated by the House of Representatives' Un-American Activities Committee, which led him ultimately to renounce his American citizenship in 1958. He died on December 23, 1993, in Bogotá, Colombia.

D

Daladier, Édouard
(1884–1970) *French premier*

Born in Carpentras, France, on June 18, 1884, Édouard Daladier was the son of a baker. He was a history teacher prior to being elected to the Chamber of Deputies in 1919, and he served as a leading Radical Socialist Party deputy from 1919 to 1940. During his career, Daladier held several cabinet posts, beginning as minister of colonies in 1924. In the late 1920s and early 1930s, he was minister of public instruction and minister of public works. Later he was minister of national defense in Premier LEON BLUM's cabinet from 1936 to 1937 and in successive cabinets, including his own, until May 1940. The French were looking for strong men, and Daladier, who had survived the battle of Verdun, seemed to fit the bill. He served as premier from January to October 1933; in January and February 1934; and, for the third and longest time, from April 1938 to March 20, 1940. His knowledge of history and experience should have served him well; unfortunately just the opposite proved to be true.

In 1935, Daladier led his Radical Party into the leftist Popular Front coalition with Premier Léon Blum's Socialist Party and the Communist Party. When the Popular Front coalition collapsed, he became the premier for the third time in 1938 by allying his party with conservatives in the Chamber of Deputies. Yet at the Munich Conference in September 1938, he misread ADOLF HITLER and followed British prime minister NEVILLE CHAMBERLAIN's appeasement policy by ceding Czechoslovakia's Sudetenland to Nazi Germany in the Munich Pact.

After Hitler invaded Poland in September 1939, Daladier joined the British in declaring war on Nazi Germany. On March 20, 1940, he was replaced as premier by his rival, Paul Reynaud, another leader seen as a strong man. Daladier continued to serve in the cabinet, first as minister of war and then as minister of foreign affairs, until June 16, 1940. Five days later, the Vichy government arrested him with other parliamentary leaders who were planning to set up a government in exile. He was put on public trial in 1941 after France's defeat. Accused with other republican leaders of causing the defeat, Daladier denounced the Vichy dictatorship. He defended himself so well that the proceedings were suspended, and he was deported to Nazi Germany as a political prisoner in 1943. He remained there until the April 1945 liberation by American troops.

During the postwar period, Daladier was elected once more to the Chamber of Deputies, where he served from 1945 until the collapse of the Fourth Republic in 1958. He died in Paris on October 10, 1970.

Davis, James John
(1873–1947) *U.S. senator*

Born on October 27, 1873, in Tredegar, South Wales, Davis was eight years old when his family emigrated to the United States. The family first settled in Pittsburgh and later moved to Sharon, Pennsylvania. He attended public schools and business college in Sharon while working in local mills. He made a fourth move in 1893, relocating to Elwood, Indiana, where he continued to work in steel and tin plate mills. He held several positions in the Amalgamated Association of Iron, Steel and Tin Workers of America, and within five years of moving to Elwood, he had become city clerk. In 1903, he became recorder for Madison County, Indiana, a position he held for five years.

Davis uprooted the life he had established for himself in Elwood when he moved to Pittsburgh, Pennsylvania, in 1907 to work for the Loyal Order of Moose, a civic and social organization, as its director general. He was chairman of the Loyal Order of Moose War Relief Commission in 1918, and in that capacity he made trips to visit relief camps throughout the United States, Canada, and Europe. He then came to the attention of President Warren G. Harding, who appointed Davis as his secretary of labor in 1921. Davis retained that post in the presidential cabinets of Calvin Coolidge and HERBERT HOOVER. He resigned in 1930 to run successfully as a Republican for a U.S. Senate seat made available by the Senate's refusal to seat Pennsylvania's William S. Vare.

Davis remained in the Senate until 1945. He was caught in the political middle, given his party affiliation versus his own labor and union background as well as the union strength within the state. He tried to reconcile these conflicting tensions and was successful in three out of the four senatorial campaigns he ran. He supported New Deal measures that favored minimum wages, maximum hours, collective bargaining, and unemployment assistance, while at the same time, he criticized the growing federal bureaucracy and budget deficits. Toeing the Republican line, he condemned FDR's Court-packing plan along with the recommendations of the LOUIS BROWNLOW committee on reorganization of the executive branch.

Davis was defeated in his 1944 reelection bid and returned to work for the Loyal Order of Moose in support of its educational and other organizational activities. He died in Takoma Park, Maryland, on November 22, 1947.

Dawes, Charles Gates
(1865–1951) *Reconstruction Finance Corporation director*

Born in Marietta, Ohio, on August 27, 1865, Charles Dawes was the son of a Civil War general who later established himself in the lumber business and was elected to Congress for one term. Dawes earned his undergraduate degree at Marietta College in 1884, entered Cincinnati Law School, from which he obtained his law degree in 1886, and then returned to Marietta and earned his graduate degree in 1887. He moved that same year to Lincoln, Nebraska, and opened his law practice. Two years later, he married Caro Blymyer of Cincinnati. The couple had two children and adopted two more.

Dawes's law practice and real-estate investments made him not only wealthy but also increasingly conservative. In Lincoln, he became friends with both John J. Pershing and William Jennings Bryan. During the 1890s, he became wealthier through his purchases of gas plants, one of which was located in Evanston, Illinois, where he relocated with his family.

Dawes also moved into the political world, serving as William McKinley's western treasurer during the 1896 presidential campaign. After McKinley became president, he appointed Dawes comptroller of the currency, a position that Dawes held until 1901, when he resigned to make an unsuccessful bid for the Republican nomination for the U.S. Senate.

In 1902, Dawes became the president of a newly founded bank, the Central Trust Company of Illinois, leaving that post during World War I to become part of the American Expeditionary Force. His old friend Pershing made him the head of the General Purchasing Board, the Military Board of Allied Supply, and the U.S. Liquidation Commission. This experience led to his 1921 appointment by President Warren Harding as the first director of the Bureau of the Budget. The next year, he chaired the commission charged with adjusting Germany's reparations from World War I by obtaining American loans, an approach dubbed the Dawes Plan. For this work, which helped to save the European financial system, he shared the 1925 Nobel Peace Prize with Sir J. Austen Chamberlain. Riding the crest of acclaim, he became Calvin Coolidge's vice-presidential running mate in 1924. Dawes campaigned not only against the Democrats but also against Progressive candidate ROBERT M. LA FOLLETTE and against the Ku Klux Klan.

In 1928, Dawes declined the opportunity to run for the presidency. HERBERT HOOVER appointed him as ambassador to Great Britain, and he held that post from June 1929 to January 1932. Hoover then named him to head the new Reconstruction Finance Corporation (RFC), the president's major effort to combat the Great Depression. The RFC's purpose was to lend federal funds to prop up the nation's economy. After less than six months, Dawes resigned the position to return to his own bank in Chicago and seek a large RFC loan himself. Dawes was criticized for his action, but his bank survived the crisis and it may have helped to stabilize other Chicago banks. His abrupt resignation from the RFC to save his bank suggested the dire condition of the nation's financial system that FDR faced on assuming the presidency.

Franklin Roosevelt's election in 1932 ended Dawes's political career and influence. He opposed American involvement in World War II. He died on April 23, 1951, in Evanston, Illinois.

Dawson, Mary Williams
(Molly Dawson)
(1874–1962) *director, Women's Division, Democratic National Committee; member, Committee on Economic Security; member, Social Security Board*

Molly Dawson was born on February 18, 1874. After graduating from Wellesley College, she worked as an economic researcher for the Women's Educational and Industrial Union in Boston, then served a dozen years as the superintendent of parole at the Massachusetts State Industrial School for Girls. A suffragette, she operated a dairy farm with her lifetime partner, Mary (Polly) Porter. The two served as social workers with the American Red Cross in France during World I and then returned to New York City. Dawson worked with the National Consumers League (1919–31) and as the civic secretary of the Women's City Club, the prominent reform organization, whose vice president was ELEANOR ROOSEVELT.

Through her connection with Eleanor Roosevelt, Dawson became a Democratic Party operative by working on AL SMITH's 1928 presidential campaign, Franklin Roosevelt's reelection campaign for the New York governorship in 1930, and as head of the women's activities in FDR's 1932 presidential bid. She successfully promoted FRANCES

PERKINS for secretary of labor in his cabinet. In 1933, National Democratic Committee chairman JAMES FARLEY named Dawson the chief leader of the Democratic Party women, and she headed the Women's Division of the Democratic National Committee and then its advisory committee through 1957.

In 1934, FDR appointed Dawson as a member of the Committee on Economic Security, where she contributed to the report that became the basis for the Social Security Act of 1935. The Roosevelts rewarded her loyal service by naming her in 1937 to the new Social Security Board. Ill health forced her retirement from government service the next year, although she worked briefly in the 1940 presidential campaign. In many ways her work epitomized the "passion for anonymity" that LOUIS BROWNLOW had recommended for an expanded presidential staff. Dawson died in Castine, Maine on October 24, 1962.

Dennis, Lawrence
(1893–1977) *writer*

Dennis was born on Christmas Day 1893 in Atlanta, Georgia, to an African-American mother and a Caucasian father. In 1897, he was adopted by African-American parents, Green Dennis and Cornelia Walker. Soon he became known as the "mulatto child evangelist" throughout Atlanta's African-American churches. As a teenager he toured the United States and Europe as an evangelist prodigy. Despite his lack of formal schooling, he applied to Phillips Exeter Academy at age 20 and graduated within two years. He entered Harvard University in 1915, received military training, and served during World War I as an officer stationed in France. After the war, he returned to Harvard and graduated in 1920. He had identified with the white establishment and been educated in two of its notable institutions.

Dennis joined the U.S. State Department in 1921 as a Foreign Service officer. He served both in Europe (Romania and France) and Central America (Haiti, Honduras, and Nicaragua). He became critical of how American corporations used the State Department to further their economic interests, and in 1927 he resigned to become the representative in Peru of J. W. Seligman and Company, an investment bank. He resigned that position three years later to serve as a witness against Wall Street during the PECORA investigations of the stock-market crash.

Dennis launched his writing career as an outgrowth of his criticisms of U.S. intervention in Latin America. His first book, *Is Capitalism Doomed?* (1932), criticized business and asserted that government was needed to resolve unemployment. He criticized the New Deal as an ad hoc program rather than a genuine revolution. The next year, he became the associate editor of the *Awakener,* a semimonthly reactionary magazine critical of Franklin Roosevelt. In 1935, he joined a New York brokerage firm as an economist. The next year, he published his second book, *The Coming American Fascism* (1936), which cemented his reputation as a fascist theorist. He traveled to Europe and met ADOLF HITLER and BENITO MUSSOLINI.

Dennis resigned from the New York brokerage firm in 1938 to edit and publish his own subscription newsletter, *Weekly Foreign Letter.* He was not anti-Semitic but was an isolationist searching for political leaders to promote fascism at home. Entry of the United States into World War II shattered his dream. In 1940, he published *The Dynamics of War and Revolution*, advocating a socialist revolution that he expected would result when the Allies fought the Axis powers. By 1944 the Justice Department had charged Dennis and others with sedition, but the seven-month trial ended after the death of the presiding judge. The indictments were dismissed in 1947. Ostracized as a fascist, Dennis continued to write until his death. He died in obscurity on August 20, 1977, in Spring Valley, New York.

Dewey, Thomas Edmund
(1902–1971) *New York district attorney, New York governor*

Thomas Dewey was born on March 24, 1902, in Owasso, Michigan, where he was reared in a Republican family of newspaper editors and publishers. He graduated from the University of Michigan and in 1923 moved to New York to attend Columbia Law School after he decided against further musical training to develop his baritone voice. He completed law school in 1928 and worked at Wall Street firms while also becoming active in local Republican Party politics. He developed a friendship with fellow New York lawyer Herbert Brownell, a progressive Republican who would become his closest political adviser.

Dewey first made a national name for himself after HERBERT H. LEHMAN, New York's Democratic governor, appointed him in 1935 to investigate racketeering. He became known as a "racket-buster" when he successfully prosecuted a criminal syndicate in New York City, which was the springboard he used to launch his political career. In 1937, he became the first Republican district attorney in a quarter century. He narrowly lost the governorship to Lehman in 1938 but won it in 1942, serving three terms in the tradition of a Theodore Roosevelt progressive. He was a fiscal conservative, but he established a strong civil rights record.

With Brownell's help, Dewey won the Republican presidential nominations in both 1944 and 1948. By securing 46 percent of the 1944 popular vote, he polled better than any other Republican since the 1920s. He had portrayed FDR's administration as worn out, warned of the dangers of one-man rule, and even alleged that the administration had sold out to communists.

Dewey had a progressive domestic record, strong civil libertarian convictions, and an internationalist view of foreign policy, but he was not a natural politician. He appeared aloof and rigid on the campaign trail. He narrowly lost the presidential race in 1948 to HARRY S. TRUMAN but in 1952 helped DWIGHT EISENHOWER secure the presidency, with Richard Nixon as his vice president. In 1968, as president, Nixon offered Dewey the chief justiceship of the U.S. Supreme Court, but he declined. He died on March 16, 1971, in Bal Harbor, Florida.

Dies, Martin, Jr.
(1901–1972) *U.S. congressman*

Martin Dies, Jr., a second-generation Democratic U.S. congressman whose father had served in the House for 10 years, was born in Colorado, Texas, on November 6, 1901. He received his undergraduate education at the University of Texas and his law degree from National University in Washington, D.C., in 1920. He then practiced law in Orange, Texas, for a decade before being elected to the U.S. House of Representatives in 1931. A protégé of JOHN NANCE GARNER, Dies received a seat on the powerful House Rules Committee after the Roosevelt-Garner ticket won the 1932 presidency. Initially, Dies supported the New Deal, but like his fellow southern Democrats he remained antiunion and anti-immigrant. Reflecting the values of his East Texas rural constituency and his own background, he had no sympathy for sit-down strikers in Michigan's auto factories or for ELEANOR ROOSEVELT's support for antilynching legislation and other activism.

By FDR's second term, which yielded the Court-packing plan of 1937 and the 1938 campaign to purge anti-New Deal members of Congress, Dies had become a leader in the conservative coalition of southern Democrats and Republicans who banded together to stop the New Deal and, if possible, reverse it with congressional action. In 1938, he introduced the bill to establish the Special Committee to Investigate Un-American Activities, which became known as the Dies Committee. Dies saw FDR's effort to manipulate the Supreme Court and modernize the presidency (in reaction to fascist and Marxist governments) as a larger threat to the checks and balances of the American political system than that posed by totalitarian governments abroad.

The Dies Committee conducted a series of media events during the late 1930s charging the Roosevelt administration with incompetence in handling domestic communists. He released purported reports of communist infiltration of the New Deal programs and labor organizations. These allegations peaked during the years 1938–40 and were a constant distraction to the White House. The committee persuaded Congress to terminate the Federal Theater Project and to pass the Hatch Act of 1939, which banned federal employees from being involved in electoral activities. His committee composed a list of hundreds of organizations and newspapers it regarded as possible communist fronts, including the American Civil Liberties Union, the Boy Scouts, and the Girl Scouts. FDR initially tried to ignore the committee but later met with Dies and used J. EDGAR HOOVER to investigate him. Hoover viewed Dies and his committee as a potential rival to his agency and therefore as a greater threat personally, so Hoover did not cooperate fully with the committee in investigating the loyalty of New Deal personnel.

Dies was unsuccessful in his bid for election to the Senate in 1941 and lost his interest in un-American activities. He retired from Congress in 1945 but returned to the House in 1952 during the heyday of McCarthyism. He was unable, however, to secure a seat on the committee he had started, by then a standing committee infamously known as the House Un-American Activities Committee. After a second failed attempt for the Senate in 1946, Dies soon faded from the political landscape. He died in Lufkin, Texas, on November 14, 1972.

Dos Passos, John
(John Roderigo Madison)
(1896–1970) *writer*

John Dos Passos was born John Roderigo Madison on January 14, 1896, in Chicago, Illinois. His mother was the mistress of a married corporate lawyer who did not marry her until 1910, after his wife died. Until this happened, Dos Passos spent a rootless life traveling Europe with his mother. He changed his last name to his father's when he was a teenager.

Due to his father's wealth, Dos Passos led a privileged life. He attended Choate Rosemary Hall in Connecticut and graduated from Harvard University in 1916. His first poetry and novels were published the following year; at the same time, he volunteered to be an ambulance driver in Italy during World War I. During the 1920s, he became a champion of leftist causes, and his participation in a protest march during the trial of the anarchists Sacco and Vanzetti led to his arrest; he published a book in their defense in 1927. In 1928, he visited the Soviet Union, a trip that served to disillusion him about communism.

During the 1920s and 1930s, Dos Passos became a prolific writer of poems, travel books, and plays. His most original work was the *U.S.A.* trilogy (*The 42nd Parallel* [1930], *1919* [1932], and *The Big Money* [1936]), which were difficult works in modernism that juxtaposed several elements: prose poem portraits of Thomas Jefferson, HENRY FORD, and others whom the author considered to be major contributors to the American culture; collages of newspaper headlines; and subjective prose poems of the author's state of being. Marxists and European intellectuals were impressed by Dos Passos's approach to the work.

Dos Passos also spent time in Spain in 1936 during its civil war, an experience that produced several books in 1937 and 1938. The Spanish civil war also led to the breakup of his friendship with ERNEST HEMINGWAY. For the first time in his life Hemingway became attracted to left-wing politics during his relationship with Martha Gellhorn. Dos Passos's personal friend José Robles, a left-wing aristocrat and professor at Johns Hopkins University, was shot during the Spanish civil war, probably as a result of a Stalinist purge. Feeling betrayed, Dos Passos came to see Hemingway as a tool of Stalin. The relationship between the writers was further complicated because he had married Katharine Smith, a writer who had been one of Hemingway's childhood friends in Michigan. His childless marriage to Smith ended with her death in a 1947 automobile accident; he lost an eye in the same accident.

Dos Passos published a second trilogy of novels and a series of books on major American political figures, including Thomas Jefferson and Tom Paine, in the late 1930s and 1940s. These works failed to receive the praise of his *U.S.A.* trilogy, however. He continued to publish during the postwar years, a period in which he grew increasingly conservative and lived a respectable life in the Deep South. In 1949, he married Elizabeth Holdridge, with whom he had one child. He died on September 28, 1970.

Doughton, Robert Lee
(1863–1954) *U.S. congressman*

Franklin Roosevelt was dependent upon the one-party South and the seniority system to achieve his political goals. This was particularly true among the most important permanent committees in the U.S. House of Representatives, which exercised considerable political muscle. As the chairman of its Ways and Means Committee during FDR's entire presidency, Robert Doughton played a crucial role in FDR's legislative success.

Born in Laurel Springs, North Carolina, on November 7, 1863, Robert Lee Doughton was the son of farmers. His first and middle names were testament to his father's service as a captain in the Confederate army during the American Civil War. Young Doughton was educated in local schools in Laurel Springs and Sparta before receiving his law degree from Catawba College. He became a farmer, banker, and businessman, and after the death of his first wife, he married Lillie Sticker Hix in 1898; they had four children.

Doughton's interest soon turned to local and state politics. For a decade, Doughton served on the North Carolina State Board of Agriculture. In 1908, he won his first elective office during his race for the state senate as a Democrat. He was appointed in 1909 as director of the state prison system, and he served in that position until he defeated the Republican incumbent in the U.S. House of Representatives in 1911. He would serve in the House until he retired in 1953, setting one of the longest career records in Congress.

Under the seniority system, Doughton rose to chairmanship of the Ways and Means Committee, which oversees taxation. His service as the chairman covered two periods, 1933–47 and 1949–53. During his first chairmanship, he played an important role in Franklin Roosevelt's presidency. Although he was a southern conservative, he proved to be a Roosevelt loyalist who was able to bring together southern and northern Democrats. Moreover, through persistent, diligent work, he first supported New Deal legislation that addressed the desperate state of the nation. Later, however, he rationalized the legislation as a temporary, ad hoc solution rather than a fundamental change in American government.

Doughton often modified New Deal proposals, but his banking background made him a champion of the Federal Deposit Insurance Corporation in 1933. As a lifelong supporter of lower tariffs, he favored the Reciprocal Trade Act of 1934. As a southerner who recognized the impact of poverty, he favored the Social Security Act of 1935 as a permanent program. Doughton is also viewed as an architect and defender of the graduated income tax. He was tempted to step down from his congressional perch to run for the governorship of his home state in 1936, but FDR persuaded Doughton that he was needed more at the helm of the Ways and Means Committee.

Doughton retired from Congress in 1953 and died on October 2, 1954, at his Laurel Springs home.

Douglas, Lewis William
(1894–1974) *budget director*

If background determines destiny, the fate of Lewis Douglas was sealed the moment he agreed to become Franklin Roosevelt's first director of the budget. Like FDR, Douglas was charming; however, he was also a throwback Grover Cleveland Democrat who believed in free trade, sound money, and small government with balanced budgets, while FDR was a flexible pragmatist who would experiment to find solutions to public-policy problems.

Douglas was born in Bisbee, Arizona, on July 2, 1894. His father was a mine owner and banker, and his mother was a housewife. His parents sent him east for his education, and he attended the Hackley School in Tarrytown, New York; the Montclair Military Academy in New Jersey; and Amherst College in Mas-

sachusetts, from which he graduated in 1916. He spent an additional year at the Massachusetts Institute of Technology studying geology and metallurgy. During World War I, he was an artillery officer, and after the war he returned to the United States and taught at two of his alma maters, Amherst and the Hackley School. In 1921, he returned to Arizona and married Margaret Zinsser, with whom he had three children.

State politics quickly caught Douglas's interest. He ran for the state legislature and was elected as a Democrat for a term that began in 1923 and ended in 1925. His next successful race was for the U.S. House of Representatives, and he served in Congress from 1926 to 1932. During his term, he served on the Military Affairs, Appropriations, and Reclamation committees and developed a reputation as a fiscal conservative. Douglas reluctantly gave up his congressional career in February 1933 when Senator JAMES F. BYRNES persuaded FDR to appoint him as the first director of the Bureau of the Budget.

By March 1933, Douglas had helped gain passage of the Economy Act, which cut federal spending. He was an insider with the president until FDR soon reversed course and advocated the creation of the Agricultural Adjustment Administration, the Federal Relief Administration, and the Civilian Conservation Corps. After FDR took the nation off the gold standard, Douglas became disillusioned and grew increasingly so after FDR called for drought relief in June 1934. Grown tired of Douglas's dissents, FDR excluded him from meetings and, in effect, forced Douglas to resign at the end of August 1934.

Thereafter, Douglas became a vocal critic of New Deal economics, publishing his objections in his book *The Liberal Tradition* (1939). He became an adviser to Republican presidential candidate ALFRED LANDON in 1936 and helped to organize Democrats for WENDELL

WILLKIE in 1940. During World War II, however, Douglas supported FDR's war policies. He became the deputy lend-lease expediter in Britain and from February 1942 to March 1944 was the deputy administrator of the War Shipping Administration.

After working briefly with the American Cyanamid Company in New York from 1934 to 1937, Douglas served as the vice chancellor of McGill University in Montreal, Canada from 1938 to 1939. In 1940, he became president of the Mutual Life Insurance of New York, serving until 1947. He served in the postwar period as HARRY S. TRUMAN's ambassador to Great Britain (1947–50). Following his service as ambassador, he returned to Tucson, Arizona, where he died on March 7, 1974.

Douglas, William Orville
(1898–1980) *chairman, Securities and Exchange Commission; U.S. Supreme Court justice*

Born on October 16, 1898, in Main, Minnesota, to a Presbyterian minister who subsequently moved his family from the Midwest to the West Coast, William O. Douglas contracted polio before he lost his father at age six. Douglas inherited his parents' Protestant work ethic, and he applied that diligence not only to hiking, which transformed his sickly body, but also to improving his mind. At an early age, he learned to work harder than most people; he excelled in everything he tried. He went east for his professional training and career, but always found his greatest pleasure in the outdoors.

After graduating in 1920 from Whitman College on the Washington and Oregon state border, Douglas moved to New York and attended Columbia Law School (1922–25). He was employed by a Wall Street law firm for the following two years and taught part-time at Columbia Law School. In 1928, at a time when

Justice William O. Douglas *(United State Supreme Court)*

Columbia pioneered the development of legal realism, which viewed the law in largely political terms, he was made an assistant professor. Following appointment of a new dean who opposed this approach to jurisprudence, a number of faculty, including Douglas, left the law school. He then began teaching at Yale Law School, which developed an even greater reputation in legal realism. Douglas was named the Sterling Chair of Commercial and Corporate Law and wrote seven casebooks from the legal-realist perspective.

Douglas's involvement with the New Deal began in 1934 after federal administrator JAMES LANDIS asked him to study bankruptcy and business reorganization for the new Securities and Exchange Commission (SEC). He soon became a close family friend of JOSEPH P. KENNEDY, the SEC chairman who lobbied FDR in 1936 to put

Douglas on the commission and then in 1937 to name Douglas to succeed him as chairman. As the New Deal's showcase regulatory agency of Wall Street, the SEC was designed to enforce the Securities Acts of 1933 and 1934, as well as the "death sentence" provisions of the Public Utilities Holding Company Act of 1935. Douglas's boyhood work ethic made him one of the best New Deal administrators, and he soon became a poker buddy and unofficial economic adviser to FDR.

Douglas was slated to become the next dean of the Yale Law School, but FDR nominated him to replace LOUIS BRANDEIS on the U.S. Supreme Court in early 1939. He became the second-youngest justice in Supreme Court history. With the legal realist's appointment, FDR got just what he wanted on the high bench. Though Douglas developed a major civil-libertarian reputation in his postwar years, he had served a short time in World War I and was equally patriotic in World War II. The author of many books, including one on Abraham Lincoln, Douglas shared the view of the majority of his brethren that civil liberties ended where the president's war powers began. As a result, he approved the Japanese-American relocation program during World War II.

FDR considered making Douglas his domestic policy czar during World War II and his vice-presidential running mate in both 1940 and 1944, but Douglas remained on the Court to become the longest-serving justice in its history. During his tenure, he not only developed into a major civil libertarian but also became a champion of the underdog and a pioneer in environmental protection. Apart from his role as a jurist, he organized a hike in 1954 along the Chesapeake and Ohio Canal towpath to protest a proposed parkway. Today the area is preserved by the National Park Service and dedicated to him. After a stroke, Douglas retired from the Court in 1975. He died in Washington, D.C., on January 19, 1980.

Dubinsky, David
(David Dubnievski)
(1892–1982) *union leader*

Born David Dubnievski on February 22, 1892, in Brest Litovsk, Russian Poland (now Brest, Belarus), David Dubinsky was the son of bakers. The family later moved to Łódź, where he attended elementary school, but at age 11, he left school to apprentice for his father. Four years later, he was a master baker and a member of the socialist General Jewish Workers Union. Committed to the union, Dubinsky led a strike against his own father's bakery. His activism brought him under the scrutiny of czarist police who jailed him and ultimately exiled him to Siberia. Eventually able to escape, he emigrated with his brother to New York City in 1911.

In the United States, Dubinsky abandoned baking for the garment-making business. He joined Local 10 of the International Ladies' Garment Workers Union (ILGWU) as well as the Socialist Party. In 1914, he married Emma Goldberg, a Lithuanian immigrant who also belonged to the ILGWU, and the couple had a daughter. After organizing a successful general strike in 1916, Dubinsky quickly rose in the union hierarchy and became chairman of the local in 1920. He was elected president of the entire ILGWU in 1932 and held that position until 1966.

It was Section 7(a) of the National Industrial Recovery Act (1933), which guaranteed the right to union recognition, that ensured Dubinsky's career. He shepherded the union from limited membership and near-bankruptcy during the early years of the Great Depression into a thriving organization with a vast treasury. He also became one of Franklin Roosevelt's strongest backers throughout his entire presidency. In FDR's 1936 reelection campaign, Dubinsky and fellow union leader SIDNEY HILLMAN quit the Socialist Party to help found the American Labor Party (ALP), which supported FDR and the New Deal. Dubinsky also joined Hillman and JOHN L. LEWIS to form the Committee for Industrial Organization, which in 1938 became the Congress of Industrial Organizations (CIO). In part because Lewis was indifferent to communists in the CIO, Dubinsky led the ILGWU out of the CIO in 1930 and then back into the American Federation of Labor (AFL) in 1940. Later that year, he condemned Lewis for endorsing the Republican presidential bid of WENDELL WILLKIE. In 1943, Dubinsky led an anticommunist faction out of the ALP to the Liberal Party of New York, which he had helped to form with ADOLF BERLE and others. The Liberal Party endorsed state and local Democrats and helped to reelect FDR in 1944.

In 1947, Dubinsky helped to organize Americans for Democratic Action (ADA) and in 1955 he helped to merge the AFL and CIO. He died in Manhattan on September 17, 1982.

Early, Stephen Tyree
(1889–1951) *presidential press secretary*

Distantly related to Confederate general Jubal Early, Stephen Early was born on August 27, 1889, in Crozet, Virginia. He attended public schools in Virginia and Washington, D.C., but did not attend college, instead beginning work as a news reporter. Early first met Franklin Roosevelt at the 1912 Democratic National Convention in Baltimore and later covered FDR's work as assistant secretary of the navy during Woodrow Wilson's presidency. During World War I, Early joined the officer's training program and won the Silver Star for participating in the Somme offensive and the battle of Meuse-Argonne. He was then placed in charge of *Stars and Stripes*, the soldier's newspaper, until he was discharged in 1919. He retained his commission in the Army Reserves.

After FDR won the vice-presidential spot on the 1920 Democratic ticket, he persuaded Early to become his advance man. Even though the Democrats lost, Early's professional reputation as one of the nation's best reporters continued to build during the 1920s; he was hired as the Washington, D.C., editor for Paramount Newsreel Company in 1927. In 1932, President-elect Roosevelt named Early his assistant secretary in charge of press rela-

tions. Early is credited with being the first designated presidential press secretary.

Early and FDR—a newspaper editor himself during his undergraduate college years—were a media- and public relations–savvy team. Their joint efforts to cultivate relationships with individual reporters, along with FDR's use of radio, helped to undercut the hostility of newspaper editors of the era. Loyal to the president and quick-tempered, Early was open to the media. In addition to working directly with the press corps accompanying FDR, he was the publicity agent for the New Deal until the late 1930s. He also advised ELEANOR ROOSEVELT, cabinet members, and agency heads about handling the media.

During World War II, the White House flow of information was more controlled, but at Early's recommendation, FDR continued to hold his legendary press conferences. The stress of his demanding job is considered to have played a part in Early's death on August 11, 1951, in Washington, D.C.

Eccles, Marriner Stoddard
(1890–1977) *assistant secretary of the Treasury; chairman, Federal Reserve System Board of Governors*

Born on September 9, 1890, in Logan, Utah, Marriner Eccles was the oldest of nine siblings;

his parents were a prosperous Mormon couple. Eccles graduated from Brigham Young College in 1909 and then served on a church mission to Scotland. Both his inheritance and his own business instincts made him an extremely successful banker with operations in three western states. However, monetary success was balanced by his Mormon upbringing, which emphasized a sense of community responsibility, and by the influence of English economist JOHN MAYNARD KEYNES. During the 1930s, he favored deficit financing of public works, minimum-wage laws, and agricultural regulations.

Eccles first attracted national attention after skillfully avoiding having a depositor run on his banks at the outset of the Great Depression. None of his banks failed. Secretary of the Treasury HENRY MORGENTHAU, JR., recruited Eccles to his department following Eccles's work in developing the Emergency Banking Act of 1933, the Federal Deposit Savings Corporation, and the Federal Housing Act. He joined the Federal Reserve Board in late 1934 and supported the Banking Act of 1935 for the purpose of creating a unified banking system. He also utilized his friendship with presidential adviser HARRY HOPKINS in influencing FDR to increase deficit spending in opposition to Morgenthau's advice. At one point Eccles debated Senator HARRY BYRD (D-Va.) on national radio and accused him of favoring the wealthy.

While he supported some elements of the New Deal, Eccles was against other programs, such as the Agriculture Adjustment Act, the Tennessee Valley Authority, and the National Recovery Administration. He also opposed deregulated banking and branch banking. He was reappointed in 1944 to the Board of Governors of the Federal Reserve Board and became concerned over the vast increase in the national deficit during World War II. After his government service, Eccles wrote his memoirs and returned to his family's corporations, including First Security Bancorporation and Amalgamated Sugar, as well as involvement in

civic and educational concerns. He died in Salt Lake City on December 18, 1977.

Einstein, Albert
(1879–1955) *physicist*

Born on March 14, 1879, in Ulm, Germany, Albert Einstein was the son of German Jewish parents; his father managed an electrical business. He attended local primary and progressive secondary schools in Munich. From 1896 to 1900, he studied at the Swiss Federal Polytechnic in Zurich, noted as one of Europe's best institutions for studying science. He had renounced his German citizenship in 1896 to avoid the German draft, and he became a Swiss citizen in 1901. Because of his independent nature, he failed to obtain a position at the Polytechnic. Instead, he held a series of temporary teaching jobs until he received a position in 1902 at the federal patent office in Bern. In his off hours he worked on his doctorate, which he received in 1905 from the University of Zurich. His first job in higher education was in 1908 as an unsalaried instructor at the University of Bern.

Einstein's published works between 1900 and 1909 transformed physics with his theory of relativity. From 1909 to 1913, he taught in Zurich and Prague, and the next year he went to Berlin, remaining there until 1933. During that time, he regained his German citizenship. In 1921, he was awarded the Nobel Prize in physics, which made him the best-known scientist of the 20th century. Following the 1933 Nazi revolution, Einstein again renounced his German citizenship. He accepted a position at the new Institute for Advanced Study at Princeton University since it permitted him the maximum amount of time to pursue independent research. In 1940, he was naturalized as an American citizen.

Though he had become a pacifist during World War I, the Nazi threat persuaded him to change his stance. With his knowledge of the German physics program, the most advanced in the world at the time, and at the urging of other exiled physicists, Einstein wrote to FDR in 1939, urging him to fund research to build an atomic bomb before Nazi Germany did it. He met with FDR, but he was branded a security risk, preventing his direct participation in the Manhattan Project, although scientists working on it consulted with him. Later in World War II, he was permitted to serve as a consultant to the U.S. Navy. He died in Princeton, New Jersey, on April 18, 1955.

Eisenhower, Dwight David
(Ike)
(1890–1969) *general, Allied Expeditionary Force in Western Europe supreme commander*

Born on October 14, 1890, in Denison, Texas, Dwight Eisenhower grew up in Kansas in a family of modest means. He was ambitious and athletic, but after a sports injury, he redirected his goals toward a military career. He graduated from the U.S. Military Academy at West Point in 1915. Frustrated by not being sent overseas in World War I, Eisenhower spent the following

In this photo, taken in England a few hours before their jump into France, General Dwight D. Eisenhower urges men of the U.S. 101st Airborne Division to "Full victory—nothing else." *(Library of Congress)*

years in staff assignments with DOUGLAS MACARTHUR and GEORGE C. MARSHALL. Although Eisenhower had expected a forced retirement as a lieutenant colonel in 1940, Marshall recognized his abilities and kept him on, making him the head of the War Plans Division (later called the Operations Division) in the War Department five days after the Japanese attack on Pearl Harbor in December 1941. The next year, Marshall put Eisenhower in charge of the American Forces in Great Britain, and he was made supreme commander of the American and British invasion of North Africa. In November 1942, Eisenhower concluded a controversial deal with Admiral Jean Darlan, commander in chief of the French Vichy forces, which resulted in a cease-fire in return for making Darlan governor general of French North Africa.

In December 1943, Franklin Roosevelt made Eisenhower Supreme Commander of the Allied Expeditionary Force for Operation Overlord, the D-Day invasion of France in June 1944. Eisenhower's diplomatic skills were tested in dealing with not only American general GEORGE S. PATTON and British general Bernard L. Montgomery, as well as rivals and publicity seekers like DOUGLAS MACARTHUR, but also JOSEPH STALIN and the Soviet army.

Eisenhower's innate ability to work with others and lack of vanity made him one of the greatest leaders in the Allied defeat of Nazi Germany. Emerging from World War II as the world's most successful and famous general, he went on to be elected the 34th president of the United States in 1952 and again in 1956. He died on March 28, 1969, in Bethesda, Maryland.

Evans, Luther Harris

(1902–1981) *director, Historical Records Survey of the Works Progress Administration; director, Legislative Reference Services; chief assistant librarian, Library of Congress*

Luther Harris Evans, the son of a railroad foreman, was born on October 13, 1902, on his grandmother's farm in Bastrop County, Texas. As a youngster, he attended local public schools before entering the University of Texas. He worked his way through college by teaching and by working on a farm. In 1923, Harris received his undergraduate degree, and the next year he earned his M.A. in political science. After graduation, he spent a summer in Europe before marrying a former college classmate in 1925; the couple had one child. Harris then attended Stanford University, where he received his doctorate in political science in 1927. He subsequently began teaching fulltime at New York University (1927–28). He later taught at Dartmouth University from 1928 to 1930 and at Princeton University from 1930 to 1935.

Presidential speechwriter RAYMOND MOLEY learned about Evans and in June 1935 invited him to Washington, D.C., to talk to FDR adviser HARRY HOPKINS about a national records survey. Evans wrote a proposal for the project that led to his appointment as the supervisor of historic projects in the Works Progress Administration (WPA) in October 1935. The next month, he was named director of the Historical Records Survey of the WPA within the Federal Writers' Project headed by Henry Alsberg. In 1936, the Historical Records Survey was made an independent program within Federal Project No. 1 of the WPA. During the next three years, Evans demonstrated his diplomatic skills working with a variety of state, local, and national politicians, historians, and archivists.

By autumn 1939, Evans's work had captured the attention of newly appointed Librarian of Congress ARCHIBALD MACLEISH, who offered him the job of directing the Legislative Reference Service (LRS). Evans accepted, and less than a year later he also became MacLeish's chief assistant librarian. MacLeish, who served as a wartime adviser to Franklin Roosevelt, was often absent, and Evans ran the Library of Congress during those intervals. During the

A mother and daughter from a sharecropper family in Hale County, Alabama, are featured in this photo by Walker Evans, 1936.

postwar period, he became the 10th Librarian of Congress (1945–53) and later was director-general of UNESCO. He died on December 23, 1981, in San Antonio, Texas.

Evans, Walker
(1903–1975) *photographer*

Born on November 2, 1903, in St. Louis and reared in Chicago, Walker Evans moved to New York City in 1918 after his affluent parents separated. After a series of boarding schools and a brief stint at Williams College, he spent 1926 in France, where he came under the influence of documentary photographer Eugène Atget. When he returned to New York, he enlisted the help of a friend to learn

photography and quickly gained recognition for his photographs of American architecture. His career got a boost after he met Lincoln Kirstein, who had good connections in the New York art world.

During the early 1930s, Evans began traveling throughout the South, establishing his national reputation by using what he called his "documentary style" to chronicle what he saw. He spent time in Florida, South Carolina, Georgia, and Louisiana. His association with the New Deal began in 1935 through the Division of Information of the Resettlement Administration, which was renamed the Farm Security Administration in 1937. Its Historical Section, headed by ROY E. STRYKER, built a large photographic record to document how the New Deal helped to alleviate the problems facing rural Americans. Evans was the senior photographer among a group that included DOROTHEA LANGE and Ben Shahn. Granted a leave of absence in 1936, he and writer JAMES AGEE went to Alabama to do an article on tenant farming. His transcendent images of sharecropper families in the Great Depression eventually were published in *Let Us Now Praise Famous Men* (1941). Even before the delayed publication, the photos constituted the most important part of a retrospective of his work exhibited at the Museum of Modern Art in 1938.

After his government employment ended in 1937, Evans photographed subway portraits from 1938 to 1941. In 1943, he served as the film, book, and art critic for *Time*. For 20 years, he was a postwar staff photographer at *Fortune*, and he later taught at Yale University. He died on April 10, 1975, in New Haven, Connecticut.

Ezekiel, Mordecai J.
(1899–1974) *economic adviser*

Mordecai Ezekiel was born on May 10, 1899, in Richmond, Virginia, and raised in the nation's capital. In 1918, he received his undergraduate degree in agriculture from the University of Maryland. Afterward, he served briefly in the military during World War I and then returned to Washington, D.C., where he took a job with the U.S. Census Bureau in 1919. In 1922, he changed jobs and became an economist with the Division of Farm Management, Department of Agriculture. The next year he received his master's degree from the University of Minnesota, and in 1926 he was awarded his doctorate in economics. In 1930, he began working as the assistant chief economist with the Federal Farm Board and also published his first book, *Methods of Correlation Analysis*. Ezekiel spent a

year in Europe as a Guggenheim Fellow, and when he returned, he began to propose a domestic allotment plan to solve farm problems. He met with President-elect Franklin Roosevelt, FDR adviser HENRY MORGENTHAU, JR., economist REXFORD TUGWELL, and M. L. Wilson, the chairman of the department of agricultural economics at Montana State College, to promote his plan.

After FDR took office and established his cabinet, Ezekiel was made chief economic adviser to Secretary of Agriculture HENRY A. WALLACE, a post he held from 1933 to 1944. He helped to draft the Agricultural Adjustment Act of 1933 and subsequently wrote two books in which he tried to promote the idea of planned production: *$2,500 A Year: From Scarcity to Abundance* (1936) and *Jobs for All Through Industrial Expansion* (1939). His effort to popularize national economic planning succeeded so well that Father CHARLES COUGHLIN called him a communist. Ezekiel's economic views that large corporations had effectively eliminated market competition had been influenced by the sociologist and economist Thorstein Veblen.

As the New Deal shifted from industrial planning to antitrust efforts, Ezekiel had little influence on the Roosevelt administration. Moreover, he came to support the economic spending approach advocated by JOHN MAYNARD KEYNES to deal with the Great Depression. In 1944, he transferred from the secretary of agriculture's office to become economic adviser in the Bureau of Agriculture Economics. During the postwar years, Ezekiel moved to the United Nations Food and Agriculture Organization, serving there from 1947 to 1962. He left that post for the U.S. Agency for International Development, where he served for five years. He died in Washington, D.C., on October 31, 1974.

Fahy, Charles

(1892–1979) *federal attorney, solicitor general of the United States*

Charles Fahy was born on August 27, 1892, in Rome, Georgia, where his Catholic parents were small-business owners. He attended the University of Notre Dame in 1910–11 before earning a law degree at Georgetown University in 1914. He then practiced law in the nation's capital for 10 years before health problems prompted him to relocate to Santa Fe, New Mexico. He married Mary Agnes Lane in 1929; the couple had four children.

Fahy became city attorney of Santa Fe in 1932 but continued his law practice. The next year, he was appointed as the assistant solicitor of the Department of the Interior and moved with his family to Washington, D.C. Later that same year, Secretary of the Interior HAROLD ICKES appointed Fahy as a member of the Petroleum Administrative Board; he was chairman in 1934–35. However, on January 7, 1935, in *Panama Refining Company v. Ryan*, the U.S. Supreme Court held that the Petroleum Administrative Board was unconstitutional in an 8:1 vote that was the first major challenge to the New Deal. Fahy then became the general counsel of the National Labor Relations Board, serving there for five years. A practitioner rather than a political or legal theorist, Fahy oversaw the effort to have the National Labor Relations Act of 1935 implemented by the federal courts. He won 18 cases that demonstrated labor problems could "obstruct the stream of commerce," thereby giving Congress jurisdiction to regulate the flow of interstate commerce. He also led the battle against the American Liberty League, which had sought an "injunction assault" against the National Labor Relations Act.

A loyal Democrat and supporter of the New Deal, Fahy was appointed assistant U.S. solicitor general in 1940. The following year, in his role as a member of the president's Naval and Air Base Commission to London, Fahy assisted in negotiating a deal to trade 50 American destroyers for British military bases in the Western Hemisphere, a major boost for WINSTON CHURCHILL. In November 1941, Franklin Roosevelt rewarded Fahy by appointing him as the solicitor general of the United States. He held this position until 1945, representing the federal government before the U.S. Supreme Court.

Fahy's legal style combined his origins as a southern gentleman with a narrow view of the law. He was an enforcer, not a theorist. He was always well prepared and modest in demeanor, and his reserve and restrained manner earned him the nickname "New Deal Sphinx." His many successful cases before the High Court included the relocation and internment of West Coast Japanese Americans, even though two-thirds of them were native-born American citizens. His actions in those cases were redeemed by his later postwar actions.

After World War II, Fahy continued to serve in advisory positions to the State Department and the United Nations. In 1947, he returned to private law practice in Washington, D.C. Two years later, HARRY S. TRUMAN made him chairman of the Committee on Equality of Treatment and Opportunity in the Armed Forces. Within four years, the American military was desegregated. In 1949, Truman appointed him to the United States Court of Appeals for the District of Columbia Circuit; Fahy served there until 1967. He died on September 17, 1979, in Washington, D.C.

Farley, James Aloysius

(1888–1976) *chairman, New York Democratic Committee and National Democratic Committee; postmaster general*

Born on May 30, 1888, in Grassy Point, New York, James Farley was from Irish Catholic immigrant stock. He graduated from Packard Commercial School of New York in 1905 and he worked briefly as a bookkeeper before becoming first a salesman and then sales manager for Universal Gypsum Company. In 1926, he formed his own company, which merged into a building supply corporation that he ran until the Franklin Roosevelt administration began.

With characteristic high energy, Farley had entered politics in 1912 when he was elected as the Stony Point, New York, town clerk, a post he held for six years. He ascended the local Democratic Party ladder quickly, becoming a county chairman, a New York

assemblyman (1923–24), and chairman of the state Athletic Commission (1924–33). After he helped AL SMITH take control of the state party from WILLIAM RANDOLPH HEARST, Farley worked to support Franklin Roosevelt's election as New York governor in 1928. His support was rewarded when he was made chairman of the state Democratic Committee (1930–44). Farley made an impression on FDR aide LOUIS M. HOWE and FDR himself, who made Farley his 1932 presidential campaign manager and also chairman of the Democratic National Committee, after Bronx boss EDWARD J. FLYNN declined. Farley expected a first-ballot victory for FDR, but it took four ballots at the Democratic National Convention in Chicago before Roosevelt secured the nomination. For his support, Farley was awarded the traditional plum, the postmaster generalship, and he became the main dispenser of political patronage during FDR's first two administrations. He also served as FDR's 1936 campaign manager.

Farley had political ambitions of his own, however, and in 1940 he opposed FDR's bid for a third term because he wanted the nomination for himself. He had begun to seek support from conservative Southern Democrats such as CORDELL HULL, CARTER GLASS, and JOHN NANCE GARNER, and he refused to join FDR's failed 1938 attempt to purge New Deal opponents from Congress. Furthermore, Farley's feelings had been injured because he was excluded from FDR's social circle. After receiving only 72 votes at the 1940 Democratic Party Convention, Farley resigned the party chairmanship as well as his cabinet post in August 1940. Not one to give up easily, though, he fought FDR for control of the New York State Democratic Party in 1942, which Farley wanted to use for his future political ambition. Though his nominee for governor won against FDR's, he was defeated in the general election by Republican THOMAS DEWEY. Farley resigned as state chairman in 1944 but remained a loyal

Democrat, supporting the national ticket in both 1940 and 1944. He died in New York City on January 9, 1976.

Faulkner, William
(William Cuthbert Falkner)
(1897–1962) *novelist*

Franklin D. Roosevelt termed the South the nation's number-one economic problem, and in a sense the post–Civil War South of the early 20th century also represented a profound national psychological problem. Its essence was captured by novelist William Faulkner, who created a fictional world in his greatest novels, published during the Great Depression and World War II. Faulkner's fictional world was inhabited by a cast of southern characters—black, white, mentally retarded, and all memorable—that provided readers with insights into the lasting, devastating imprint that Civil War and Reconstruction had left on the psyche of inhabitants of the defeated region. His eventual success can be attributed to the fact that Faulkner himself can be considered that era's most psychologically marginal writer, an outsider, based on the novelist's physical, social, and intellectual status. He came up literally short using several measures: physical stature (he was 5'6"), attempts at marriage that fell short, and academic shortcomings that caused him to drop out of high school. These personal shortcomings were overlaid on bruised family pride, so integral to the southern sense of worth. His Confederate great-grandfather, William Clark Falkner, was known for both his writing and his military exploits, but the reputations and fortunes of his male heirs fell far short of his revered status. Faulkner ultimately was able to restore pride in the family name—albeit a name of a different spelling—by becoming the author of some of the most creative short stories and novels of the 20th century.

Faulkner was born on September 25, 1897, as William Falkner—he later added the "u" to the spelling to set himself apart from his immediate relatives. He was born to Murry and Maud Falkner in New Albany, Mississippi, where his father was working briefly on the family's railroad, but the family soon moved to Ripley, another small town, before moving for the third and final time to Oxford, Mississippi, in 1902. Faulkner would spend most of his life there. He grew up subject to the demands of a strong mother, who was an amateur painter, and surrounded by a large, prominent north Mississippi family. His father's success never equaled that of either his grandfather or his writer great-grandfather, who had served in the Mexican War and then been a Confederate officer during the Civil War. After the Civil War, the family wealth declined with each successive generation, an embarrassment to Faulkner, who had social and intellectual aspirations early on. Still, the success he desired would be a long time in coming.

By the third grade, Faulkner had decided to become a writer like his great-grandfather. He read a great deal and as a child listened to stories told by others. His small physical size harmed his self-esteem, and although he could have been a good athlete and excellent student, he was neither. More than anything, he was an outsider during his year in Oxford's public schools, someone who primarily observed and listened to others. He eventually lost interest in formal academics, and to the consternation of his family, he dropped out of high school in 1915.

Faulkner's father had been forced to take a job as a secretary and then as a business manager at the University of Mississippi. Faulkner began to hang out on the campus but never enrolled as a student. His first published work was a drawing in the university's 1917 yearbook. The next year, his childhood sweetheart, Estelle Oldham, jilted him in favor of a more promising rival. The rejection prompted Faulkner to volunteer for the U.S. military, but he was rejected because of his height. His frustration over being unacceptable for the military was highlighted by the fact that a younger brother was wounded and decorated while serving during World War I. The military rejection underscored Faulkner's perception of himself as a failure. He moved to Canada to volunteer with the Royal Air Force and was accepted, but World War I ended before he had finished his training. He returned to Oxford, drank, and wrote poetry. His first published poem, "L'Apres-Midi d'un Faune," was initially published in the *New Republic* on August 6, 1919. Because he was a veteran, he was able to enroll in the University of Mississippi as a special student, but he dropped out at the beginning of the second year. Nevertheless, he continued to write and publish poetry, prose pieces, critiques, and drawings for university publications.

Faulkner's first governmental job was his appointment as postmaster of the University of Mississippi post office, 1921–24. He continued to write and in late 1924 published his first book, a long poem entitled *The Marble Faun.* He spent brief periods in New Haven, Connecticut, and Greenwich Village, New York, and moved briefly to the French Quarter in New Orleans. It was there that he made his transition from poetry to fiction and for the first time was in an environment that appreciated his artistic struggles. The successful novelist Sherwood Anderson befriended him and helped him to publish his first novel, *Soldier's Pay* (1926). He made a few close friends, but Faulkner remained an outsider, even when surrounded by other writers and artists. In July 1925, for example, he boarded a ship in New Orleans for a brief walking tour of Europe. Traveling alone, he visited Italy, Switzerland, England, and France, but by the end of the year he had returned to Oxford. For the second

time, he unsuccessfully pursued a woman, someone he had met while in New Orleans.

By the late 1920s, Faulkner had decided to construct an imaginary county named Yoknapatawpha, in which the southern characters from his imagination who populated it would reflect the human struggles of those in the wider world. His manuscript was rejected in 1927 by the publisher of his first novel, and his friends came to his rescue. After some 10 more rejections, a friend finally found a young editor at Harcourt Brace, and the heavily cut manuscript, newly entitled *Sartoris,* was published in 1929. Faulkner's second novel set in Yoknapatawpha, *The Sound and the Fury,* was completed during the extended quest to publish the first. Both novels were published in the fall of the same year. *The Sound and the Fury,* considered his first

William Faulkner *(Library of Congress)*

masterpiece, required four different voices to tell the twisted story of an extended southern family.

Between the publication of the first two novels set in his fictional kingdom, Faulkner married Estelle Oldham Franklin, his former childhood sweetheart, who had recently divorced. The stock-market crash came on the heels of publication of *The Sound and the Fury*, and Faulkner's marriage began to crash as well. It had been troubled from the start, and both turned to alcohol. Despite their problems, however, the couple had two daughters who kept them together, and their marriage endured.

Marriage was, in fact, Faulkner's spur to write. Shortly after he married in 1929, the decade of his greatest literary productivity began, just as the nation started to confront some of the same economic and social problems that the South had faced following the Civil War. During this prolific period, Faulkner published *As I Lay Dying* in 1930; *Sanctuary* in 1931; *Light in August* in 1932; and, in 1936, *Absalom, Absalom!*, considered by some to be his greatest novel. In this novel, southern and Canadian roommates at Harvard explore the burden and meaning of history, placing the southern past within terms of world history. Faulkner's native South is thus transmogrified into a universal place.

Two years later, Faulkner published *The Unvanquished*, followed in 1939 by *The Wild Palms*, in 1940 by *The Hamlet*, and in 1942 by *Go Down, Moses*. His stories present the voices of all three social classes, the elite aristocracy as well as the mentally retarded, parental conflict, kinship rivalries, wounded offspring, and the deterioration and dissolution of families. In the broadest sense, these were existential novels set in the traditional South and filled with characters trying to deal with lives disrupted by the twin crises of the Civil War and Reconstruction, as well as with a nation that subsequently had written it off as a backwater.

The postwar period proved to be Faulkner's denouement. By then, all of his novels were out of print until MALCOLM COWLEY edited the *Portable Faulkner* in 1946, which served to revive popular interest in his writing. Subsequently, he was awarded the Nobel Prize in literature in 1948, and he delivered one of the most memorable acceptance addresses. Like FDR's handling of the Great Depression and World War II, Faulkner's literary achievements showed the nation and the world that a devastated region could endure and even triumph at a time when the United States worked to restore its former enemies through the Marshall Plan of HARRY S. TRUMAN's administration.

Faulkner died in Wright's Sanitorium in Byhalia, Mississippi, near Oxford, on July 6, 1962, the birthday of the great-grandfather he had set out to emulate.

Fish, Hamilton
(1888–1991) *U.S. congressman*

Hamilton Fish was born on December 7, 1888, and it was a great stroke of irony when the attack on Pearl Harbor, triggering the U.S. entry into World War II, fell on the birthday of someone so opposed to American intervention in the war. Fish was the product of tradition, wealth, and Republican politics. His father was a congressman, and his grandfather had been a governor of New York, a U.S. senator, and U.S. secretary of state. In keeping with his family's position, he received an elite education at Chateau de Lancy near Geneva, Switzerland, and St. Mark's School in Southborough, Massachusetts. The 6'4" Fish then attended Harvard University, where he played football until he graduated in 1910. He began Harvard Law School but attended only one year and did not complete his degree.

Given his heritage, it was not surprising that Fish soon landed in New York politics.

Running as a member of the Progressive Party, he was elected to the state legislature in 1914 and served until 1916. He supported presidential primaries, workers' compensation, and penal reform. During World War I, he commanded the Harlem Hellfighters, a black infantry regiment, and returned home in 1919 as a decorated military officer. Upon his return, he helped to found the American Legion. In 1920, he was elected to the U.S. House of Representatives and ultimately served as a congressman for a quarter of a century. Through his congressional tenure, he became the ranking Republican on the House Rules Committee and Foreign Affairs Committee. He continued his interest in prison reform, and, drawing on his military experience, he championed the veteran's bonus as well as anti-lynching legislation. He introduced legislation for the burial of the Unknown Soldier in Arlington National Cemetery.

The Great Depression and World War II were not Fish's finest moments, although given his background one might have expected otherwise from a one-time Bull Moose Republican. He and Franklin Roosevelt were personal friends, but Fish lacked FDR's flexibility. His aristocratic sense of noblesse oblige allowed Fish to support minimum-wage and social-security legislation. As an Old Guard Republican, he was bound to balanced budgets, and tight money combined with the huge new bureaucracy, massive deficits, and labor unrest forced him to break with FDR. He was convinced that the Court-packing plan and the recommendations of the LOUIS BROWNLOW committee were the first steps to certain dictatorship in the White House.

After World War II broke out in Europe, Fish led the fight in the House against the "cash-and-carry" Neutrality Act of 1939, the Selective Service Act of 1940, and the Lend-Lease Act of 1941. He was a frequent speaker for the America First Committee. After the attack on Pearl Harbor, Fish changed his anti-interventionist stance. He was defeated for reelection in 1944 after gerrymandering occurred in redrawing his district in Orange, Putnam, and Dutchess counties.

After he left politics, Fish reentered private business and wrote a number of books during the postwar period in which he blamed FDR both for helping to launch World War II and for the spread of communism during the cold war. He died on January 18, 1991, in Cold Spring, New York.

Fisher, Irving
(1867–1947) *economist*

The son of a Congregationalist minister father and homemaker mother, Irving Fisher was born on February 27, 1867, in Saugerties, New York. He was the oldest of the couple's four children who survived past childhood. During his boyhood, Fisher's family lived in Rhode Island for 12 years and then moved to Missouri. He was sent back east to attend Yale University in 1884, just a few months before his father died of tuberculosis. He completed his undergraduate degree in 1888 and remained at Yale to begin his graduate studies in math and political economics. Political scientist William Graham Sumner persuaded Fisher to combine the two fields for his dissertation. Published in 1892, his dissertation became one of the first American works in mathematical economics. It also gained him an international reputation that resulted in Yale hiring him to teach math. He joined Yale's social and political science faculty permanently in 1895 and remained there for the rest of his life.

Fisher's greatest accomplishment may have been his marriage to Margaret Hazard, whose wealthy father built them the mansion in New Haven where they raised their three children. Fisher became a full professor in 1898, and soon afterward he began to suffer from tuberculosis, the disease that had caused his father's death. He took a three-year leave of absence while he recovered his health, and during that hiatus from teaching he wrote his successful book *How to Live*. Fisher had inherited his father's tendency for tireless proselytizing, and he applied those tendencies to his crusade for Americans to live in homes with fresh air ventilation and to abstain from alcohol and tobacco use. He also made regular pilgrimages to Battle Creek, Michigan, to engage in John Harvey Kellogg's health practices. Fisher changed his own health practices almost as frequently as he changed his mind about economic panaceas. He wrote little in mathematical economics after 1892 but became a prolific author over the next three decades. He favored a consumption tax rather than an income tax. In 1927, he arranged a visit in Rome with BENITO MUSSOLINI, who declined to adopt Fisher's monetary advice.

By the late 1920s, Fisher had become extremely wealthy from a card-index system that he had invented and marketed before Sperry Rand Corporation purchased it. He used his wealth to support his crusades to abolish war, fight disease, promote eugenics, and advocate a stable monetary system. None of his great reform campaigns succeeded, and during the Great Depression, which he had failed to predict, he lost his personal fortune; his sister-in-law saved him from bankruptcy.

Fisher always had answers, even if they were wrong. He urged FDR to abandon the gold standard and stabilize the currency. The president' gold-buying plan in 1933 and 1934 grew out of Fisher's position. But Fisher argued against the New Deal's effort to raise farm prices by restricting production. He began to criticize New Deal programs and by 1944 turned against FDR. Fisher's economic panaceas illustrated the conflicting advice that the president received from academics.

He died on April 29, 1947, in New York City.

Flanagan, Hallie Mae Ferguson
(1890–1969) *director, Federal Theatre Project*

Born on August 27, 1890, in Redfield, South Dakota, Hallie Mae Ferguson, the product of midwestern parents, graduated form Grinnell College in 1911 and taught school. She married Murray Flanagan, but her husband and older son died in 1922. After their deaths, she began teaching theater at her alma mater and wrote plays. She learned more about theater after becoming George Pierce Baker's assistant at Harvard University, and she was able to complete her M.A. degree at Radcliff College in 1924. She took a teaching job at Vassar College and then spent a year in Europe viewing modern European theater before returning to Vassar to implement what she had learned there in the Vassar Experimental Theatre.

Flanagan's connection to the New Deal came in 1935 after presidential adviser HARRY HOPKINS, a friend from her undergraduate years at Grinnell, asked her to become head of the Federal Theatre Project (FTP) within the Works Project Administration. The FTP consisted of four sections: a popular-price theater, the Living Newspaper, the Negro theater, and the experimental theater. It provided employment for more than 12,000 persons in 158 theaters across 28 states. Productions were staged in parks, halls, and hospitals. Flanagan had hoped to develop a national theater that would outlive the New Deal.

The most controversial section of the FTP was the so-called Living Newspaper, which was used to employ many out-of-work actors in productions dealing with current political issues. As a result, plays were performed about American foreign relations, Supreme Court decisions on the New Deal, slum life, and congressional legislation. The direct link between these performances and the New Deal forced Flanagan to defend the FTP before the House Un-American Activities Committee in 1938.

The program was accused of being tainted with communism. Congress ended its funding for the FTP in mid-1939. Flanagan became dean at Smith College in 1942 and served there until 1946. She died on July 23, 1969, in Old Tappan, New Jersey.

Flynn, Edward Joseph
(Boss Flynn)
(1891–1953) *political boss, National Democratic Committee, chairman*

Born on September 22, 1891, in New York City to Irish-Catholic immigrant parents who were relatively well-to-do, Edward Flynn graduated in 1912 from Fordham University Law School. He began a legal practice that he continued throughout his life. Despite having a reserved personality for a politician, he was selected by the head of the Tammany Hall political machine to run for the state legislature. After serving two terms, he was selected sheriff of Bronx County and then appointed city chamberlain by Mayor Jimmy Walker in 1925.

Flynn's formal association with Franklin Roosevelt began in 1929 after he was appointed as New York's secretary of state. By that time he already had been Tammany Hall's chairman of the Bronx County Democratic Executive Committee. He held this political machine "boss" position for more than 30 years, maintaining tight control to produce good government by backing candidates like FDR, AL SMITH, HERBERT LEHMAN, and HARRY S. TRUMAN. Flynn was an early FDR supporter, and he became an influential adviser to FDR throughout his governorship and presidency. In return, FDR appointed him as the regional administrator of the National Recovery Administration public works program and as U.S. commissioner general to the 1939–40 World's Fair. He was part of the informal White House inner circle whose members argued for urban and labor interests, which FDR had long cultivated.

Most important, Flynn was FDR's liaison with the big-city political machines in New York, Chicago, and elsewhere. He replaced JAMES FARLEY as chairman of the Democratic National Committee in 1940 after FDR decided to seek an unprecedented third term and split with Farley. As someone who was content to operate in the background, Flynn remained a principal confidant and adviser to the president. Recognizing FDR's health problems, Flynn maneuvered to have Truman on the Democratic presidential ticket in 1944. He also attended the Yalta Conference with the president in 1945. Flynn died in Dublin, Ireland on August 18, 1953.

Ford, Henry
(1863–1947) *Ford Motor Company founder*

Born on July 30, 1863, to farmer parents in Springwells (now Greenfield) Township, Michigan, Henry Ford attended local public schools for eight years. He rejected the farm life that faced him, and at age 16 he walked to Detroit, where he planned to become a mechanic. Fascinated with machinery but armed only with ability in math, Ford worked in a number of shops. In August 1880, he began an apprenticeship at Detroit's largest shipbuilding company, working in its engine shop. He completed his apprenticeship in 1882 and returned to the family farm. Soon, however, he caught the attention of a representative from Westinghouse Engine Company of Schenectady, New York, who recruited him to set up a shop and service Westinghouse steam engines throughout southern Michigan.

In 1888, Ford married Clara Bryant. His father gave him 40 acres of farmland on the condition that he would make it into a productive farm, but Ford refused and, instead, sold the timber on it and moved back to Detroit in autumn 1891. Beginning as a night engineer for the Edison Illuminating Company, the ever-energetic Ford became the chief engineer in the fall of 1893, the same year that the couple's only child, Edsel, was born.

By summer 1896, Ford had also produced his first experimental car. By 1899, with backing from JAMES COUZENS, who later became Detroit's mayor, and a local merchant, Ford began the Detroit Automobile Company. He became the superintendent in charge of production, but after producing only about a dozen autos, the company went out of business at the end of 1900. He then began his preoccupation with building race cars in the Henry Ford Company in 1901, but his fixation on the race cars led his financial backers to fire him. That company became the Cadillac Motor Car Company, named in honor of the founder of Detroit. Nevertheless, with his innate mechanical ability, Ford had proven himself by 1902 to be the nation's best race car designer.

With new backers, Ford returned to automobile manufacturing in 1903 with the formation of the Ford Motor Company. He assembled the components to his autos, and other small businesses actually built them. By the end of the decade, he had introduced the Model T, the first mass-produced car. More than 15 million Model Ts were eventually sold. Ford, who became one of the wealthiest industrialists in the United States, opened his 62-acre Highland Park plant in January 1910. The plant bred a new kind of semiskilled industrial worker who performed small, repetitive functions on an assembly line.

Ford soon proved to be his father's son in terms of exercising benevolent paternalism, which over time increasingly evolved into his being an autocrat. In 1914, he introduced the unprecedented five-dollar, eight-hour workday, a wage that nearly doubled the going rate for industrial workers while it shortened the standard workday by two hours. He also introduced the profit-sharing plan and an education department to monitor employees' work and private lives to make sure theirs were consistent with his own middle-class American morality. Nonetheless, his pay scale alone made him a hero among his own workers and the American working class.

By the end of World War I, Ford had bought out his remaining stockholders and his company became totally family owned and operated. Ford obtained a draft deferment for his son, Edsel, and immediately appointed him as president of the company, a position Edsel retained until his death in 1943. Although his son was president, the real power resided in Henry Ford, who was as autocratic in his control of his business fiefdom as his own father had been over the family farm. During World War I, he had recruited HARRY BENNETT, his most trusted associate, to deal with the labor unrest in the company. By 1920, the Ford Motor Company owned its main Highland Park plant, a huge new industrial Rouge Plant complex south of Detroit, and branch plants at home and abroad, including rubber plantations, iron mines, lumber mills, coal mines, glass plants, a railroad, and a fleet of ships. There were 21 assembly plants abroad, all controlled by Ford from Dearborn, Michigan.

Republicans and Democrats alike made political overtures to Ford, trying to entice him to run for office. Woodrow Wilson persuaded Ford to run for the Senate in 1918, and he narrowly won the Democratic nomination but lost the election. During autumn 1924, Ford endorsed Calvin Coolidge in exchange for Coolidge's endorsement of Prohibition and, some say, for his support of Ford's bid to develop a government-owned plant at Muscle Shoals, Tennessee, which Congress opposed.

The success of his industrial empire masked the flaws in Ford's personality and his limited education. His eccentric personality would manifest itself through subjecting his employees to his peculiar outlook. He purchased a newspaper in Dearborn, and by the early 1920s, numerous anti-Semitic articles had been published under his name in the newspaper. Some of these articles were gathered into a book, *The International Jew*, which blamed Jews for controlling the world's banks, starting World War I, and undermining moral values. The book appeared at a time when anti-Semitism was on the rise in Germany; Ford was the only American ADOLF HITLER praised in *Mein Kampf*.

The Great Depression in many ways proved to be Ford's undoing. Lacking the flexibility of either FDR or his fellow auto competitors, sales of Ford's namesake automobile dropped from first to third place among passenger cars. The longer he fought unionization, the more he shattered his popularity. He held out against unionization several years longer than General Motors and Chrysler, but the United Auto Workers finally forced Ford to sign a contract in mid-1941. The workers had broken free of Henry Ford's paternalism just as he had once rebelled against his own father's control.

Ford's stubbornness proved most costly in the toll it took on his mental and physical health. At age 75, he suffered his first stroke, which left him with reduced mental abilities and impaired his memory. Ford's son, Edsel, had been president of the company since 1919, but in reality most of the company decisions had to be approved by Henry. The stress from the criticism he directed at Edsel caused his son to develop stomach trouble.

On Ford's birthday in 1938—the same year he had his first stroke—Hitler awarded Ford the Grand Cross of the Supreme Order of the German Eagle. Two years later, however, the German dictator took control of the Ford plants in Europe, seizing them as "enemy property" after he declared war against the United States on December 11, 1941. That year, Ford suffered a second stoke.

To add insult to injury, Ford watched in early 1940 as FDR recruited William S. Knudsen, a former Ford executive who had left Ford Motor Company for General Motors, where he had become president, to be chairman of the National Advisory Defense Committee, a position he held without salary. Edsel persuaded his reluctant father to let the company participate in building aircraft engines for the U.S. Air Force. By autumn 1942, the entire American automotive industry had converted to war production. Following Edsel's death in 1943, Henry Ford briefly reassumed the presidency. In 1945, his grandson, Henry Ford II, succeeded him after Ford's wife and daughter-in-law forced him to relinquish the presidency. A mere shell of his former self, Ford died on April 7, 1947, at Fair Lane, his 2,000-acre estate in Dearborn, only two miles from the farm where he had been born.

Fortas, Abe

(1910–1982) *New Deal legal counsel, Department of the Interior undersecretary, Supreme Court justice*

Born on June 19, 1910, in Memphis, Tennessee, Abe Fortas was a first-generation American born to Russian and Lithuanian parents who had immigrated to the United States from England in 1905. His mother reared the children as Orthodox Jews, while his father tried to assimilate into the border state's Protestant community. Fortas was an outsider with enormous energy and musical talent. He graduated in 1930 from local Southwestern College, now Rhodes. The fall after his college graduation, he decided to attend Yale Law School on scholarship, and his life changed dramatically. At Yale, he came under the influence of WILLIAM O. DOUGLAS and the new school of jurisprudence called legal realism, which essentially viewed the law largely in political terms. Fortas served as editor in chief of the law journal. After completing his law degree in 1933, he took a temporary job on the legal staff of the Agricultural Adjustment Administration, headed by JEROME FRANK. From 1934 to 1937, he shuttled between Yale Law School, where he was a teacher, and Washington, D.C., where he accepted part-time assignments with the Roosevelt administration. In 1935, Fortas married Carolyn Eugenia Agger, whom he persuaded to study law at Yale. Their marriage was childless.

In 1937, Douglas recruited Fortas as the assistant director of the public utilities division at the Securities and Exchange Commission (SEC), which Douglas then chaired. After Douglas was nominated to the U.S. Supreme Court in 1939, Fortas became general counsel to the Public Works Administration, which was headed by Secretary of the Interior HAROLD ICKES. While the large number of Jews and legal realists in the FDR administration is often cited, it would be more accurate to say that it had an even larger number of social outsiders—individuals who were Irish, southerners, blacks, and others.

Fortas was appointed undersecretary of the interior in 1942 but soon resigned to enlist in the navy, returning to his old position in the Interior Department within a month after his discharge due to ocular tuberculosis. He subsequently participated in the relocation of 110,000 Japanese Americans, two-thirds of them native-born Americans, from temporary assembly centers to permanent internment camps.

Through the postwar period, Fortas's career would follow a pattern of similar rise and fall. He helped to found one of the best law firms in the nation's capital in 1946, remaining there until 1965, when President Lyndon Johnson appointed him as an associate justice of the U.S. Supreme Court. In May 1969, he became the first justice to resign in disgrace from the high bench. His resignation occurred under a barrage of public criticism for accepting payments from a wealthy financier and philanthropist who was under federal investigation. Fortas died on April 5, 1982, in Washington, D.C.

Foster, William Z.
(1881–1961)   *Communist Party leader*

Born in Taunton, Massachusetts, on February 15, 1881, William Foster was the son of an Irish immigrant father and English immigrant mother who had 23 children, most of whom died in infancy. His father was a horse carriage washer, and the family was very poor. When Foster was six years old, his struggling family moved to the Irish-Catholic slums of Philadelphia. He dropped out of school when he was 10 and subsequently worked in a series of menial jobs, including a stint as a seaman that took him from the east to the west coast.

Coming of age during the worst excesses of industrial America, Foster rejected his ties with Catholicism for other beliefs after a policeman in the City of Brotherly Love clubbed him on the head during a 1895 Philadelphia street car strike. He first embraced William Jennings Bryan's populism and later joined the Socialist Party. Moderation was never a Foster trademark. After briefly forming a Wage Workers party, he joined the "Wobblies" (Industrial Workers of the World). By the time he joined the Socialist Party in 1909 he had returned to the West Coast to take part in the Wobblies' "free speech fight" in Spokane, Washington, where he was arrested and held briefly.

In 1910, Foster traveled abroad for the second time since his seaman's days, this time to Europe, where he joined the syndicalist trade union movement. After returning to the United States, he published *Syndicalism*, the book marked the emergence of his career as an activist. He founded the Syndicalist League of North America in 1912, and that same year, he married a member of his organization, Esther Abramowitz, a Russian immigrant with three children. They had no children together.

The couple began working for the Chicago Federation of Labor. During World War I, Foster organized the meat packers, the trade about which UPTON SINCLAIR had written his classic novel *The Jungle*. After World War I, on behalf of the American Federation of Labor, Foster led a large but unsuccessful strike among mostly immigrant workers in the steel industry who wanted union recognition. The Red Scare hysteria in the postwar era assured the effort's defeat. Nonetheless, the perennial organizer formed yet another new group, the Trade Union Education League (TUEL), which espoused industrial unionism, a new labor party, and the Bolshevik Revolution. In 1921, Foster made his first trip to Moscow with a group of other radicals, including his chief assistant, EARL BROWDER, to attend the first congress of the Red International Labor Unions. Foster returned as a convert to communism, which caused the leadership of the American Federation of Labor to denounce TUEL as merely a communist front organization. His ties to the more moderate American labor movement were severed, which had not been the Kremlin's intended strategy. But he had found—or thought he had—his rock of support in communism.

In early 1924, Foster ran for the presidency as the candidate of the Workers Party, then the name of the American Communist Party, but pulled only 33,000 votes. Four years later, he ran again with similarly dismal results. Following his poor showing, the Kremlin delivered Foster a major blow when it anointed his charismatic lieutenant with boyish appeal, Browder, as its top leader in the United States. Nonetheless, having converted to his new political religion, Foster continued to work as a true

believer within the party during the onset of the Great Depression. He viewed Franklin Roosevelt and the New Deal as the last-ditch efforts to salvage American capitalism. In 1932, he was the Communist Party presidential candidate, winning more than 100,000 votes but losing badly to FDR. During the campaign, he suffered a near-fatal heart attack. Afterward, Browder, the Communist Party's general secretary, retained the real power, and Foster was relegated to the honorific post of chairman.

Foster thought that Browder's support of the Popular Front during the early days before World War II undermined the party's ideological purity. After the Molotov-Ribbentrop pact between the Soviet Union and Nazi Germany was signed in 1939, Foster's influence was on the ascendancy again until ADOLF HITLER invaded the Soviet Union in 1941, which reinstated Browder's leadership primacy until the first days of the cold war emerged. Browder was then soon excommunicated from the reformatted American Communist Party, and Foster was restored to his original leadership role.

Foster's fortunes turned bleak again after federal prosecution in 1948, and party membership dwindled significantly. In ill health, he died on September 1, 1961, while in the Soviet Union. He was honored with a state funeral in Red Square before his cremated remains were returned to Chicago for interment in Waldheim Cemetery.

Franco, Francisco
("El Caudillo")
(1892–1975) *Spanish head of state*

The youngest of three brothers, Francisco Franco was born on December 4, 1892, to a lower middle-class family in extreme northwestern Spain. He enrolled at the Toledo Military Academy when he was 15 years old and quickly identified with the frustrations of the Spanish army, which had been humiliated during the Spanish-American War in 1898. After his graduation in 1910, he volunteered to serve in Morocco, the best means for an ambitious soldier to achieve promotion. By 1915, he had become the youngest captain in the Spanish army during Spain's colonial campaigns in North Africa. He joined the Spanish Foreign Legion in 1920 and three years later improved his social standing by marrying into a wealthy business family. He took command of the Foreign Legion five years later, and in 1926 he became the youngest general in Europe. He was appointed head of the Zaragoza Military Academy in 1928.

With the end of the Spanish monarchy and the establishment of the new Second Republic with its antimilitary policy, Franco was forced on the inactive list. But after the conservative right regained power in 1933, he returned to active duty, crushed a miners' strike the next year, and was appointed in May 1935 as the army's chief of staff. The 1936 elections, however, returned the left wing to power, plunging the nation into political crisis. On July 18, 1936, Franco, then on the Spanish-held Canary Islands, rebelled against the Second Republic. He raised an army in Morocco and Spain to overthrow the government in Madrid but encountered resistance there. He subsequently obtained military aid from ADOLF HITLER and BENITO MUSSOLINI during the three-year Spanish civil war that raged between Franco's Falange (Spanish Fascist party) and the Republican government, aided by JOSEPH STALIN as well as international antifascist volunteers, including those from the United States who called themselves the International Lincoln Brigade. By April 1939, Franco had won, but not until after nearly 1 million Spaniards from both sides of the civil war had died.

Though privately pro-Axis, Franco's Spain remained technically neutral during World War II. His power remained based on the army and the Catholic Church. In 1947, Franco restored the monarchy in Spain, with himself as regent. He died on November 20, 1975.

Frank, Jerome New

(1889–1957) *New Deal legal counsel; chairman, Securities and Exchange Commission; judge, U.S. Court of Appeals for the Second Circuit*

Born on September 10, 1889, Jerome Frank was the only son among the three children born of his Jewish parents, in New York City; his father was a lawyer and his mother was a musician. The family moved to Chicago, where Frank was educated. At the University of Chicago, CHARLES MERRIAM, a renowned political scientist, changed the course of his life. By the time he received his undergraduate degree in 1909, Frank had taken all of Merriam's courses. Bowing to pressure from his father, he went to the University of Chicago Law School, where he encountered Roscoe Pound, who became the father of sociological jurisprudence. However, his first mentor's continued influence led Frank to take a year's leave to serve as Merriam's secretary while he was a reform alderman on Chicago's city council. Frank thus gained both an academic and a practical view of the link between law and politics. He graduated from law school in 1912, simultaneously beginning the practice of corporate law and becoming involved in local political reforms. While in Chicago, he met John Gunther, Sherwood Anderson, SINCLAIR LEWIS, and other intellectuals and writers of the period.

In 1928, Frank moved to New York City to take a job with one of the nation's premier law firms. Yet he found little satisfaction from Wall Street. Two years later, the publication of his classic book *Law and the Modern Mind*, which applied Freudian analysis to the law, enabled Frank to move from private practice into public service. The book became the most important work of the legal realism movement, and Frank soon became a research associate at Yale Law School, the epicenter of legal realism. His association with Yale continued until his death. While there, he formed friendships with WILLIAM O. DOUGLAS, THURMAN ARNOLD, ABE FORTAS, Harold Lasswell, and other leading figures.

After becoming acquainted with FELIX FRANKFURTER, FDR's legal adviser, Frank wrote to him in 1932 seeking a job with the New Deal. He was soon appointed the first general counsel in the Agricultural Adjustment Administration (AAA), and his office became a hotbed for reform. He assembled a talented staff, including Arnold, Fortas, and Alger Hiss, Adlai Stevenson, and Telford Taylor. These urban liberal lawyers championed tenant farmers and sharecroppers, thus coming in conflict with AAA head Chester Davis.

Frank lost his job over this but remained in good graces with FDR, who had included him in his famous "brain trust," which had helped to draft the National Industrial Recovery Act of 1933, especially the provision to guarantee labor's right to bargain collectively. Among Frank's enduring contributions was helping to create the *Federal Register*, which publishes the regulations of all administrative agencies of the federal government.

In 1933, Frank created the Federal Surplus Relief Corporation to administer procurement and distribution of agricultural surpluses to the hungry, establishing a precedent for future federal food programs. After he was dismissed from the AAA, Frank served briefly as a special counsel for the Reconstruction Finance Corporation in addition to performing legal work for Secretary of the Interior HAROLD ICKES that allowed the Public Works Administration to make loans to county power-development projects. He won the government's case, *Alabama Power Company v. Ickes*, in 1938.

On the suggestion of WILLIAM O. DOUGLAS, Frank was appointed to the Securities and Exchange Commission (SEC), and after Douglas's appointment to the U.S. Supreme Court in 1939, Frank succeeded Douglas as chairman of the SEC. In this role, he was often in conflict with conservative Wall Street businessmen. In 1941, at Douglas's urging, FDR nominated Frank to an opening on the U.S. Court of Appeals for the Second Circuit. It was an ideal position for Frank since his chambers were in New York City, allowing him to oversee Wall Street and also teach part-time at Yale Law School. During his judicial career on the Second Circuit, he wrote a number of decisions that influenced the U.S. Supreme Court to expand civil liberties. Frank died on January 13, 1957, in New Haven, Connecticut.

Frankfurter, Felix
(1882–1965) *U.S. Supreme Court justice*

Born on November 15, 1882, in Vienna, Austria, Felix Frankfurter was the son of Austrian Jewish immigrant parents who moved to New York City in 1894. He graduated from the City College of New York in 1902 and entered Harvard Law School before it became heavily influenced by legal realism and sociological jurisprudence. However, while enrolled there he heard LOUIS BRANDEIS deliver a presentation that motivated him to become involved in liberal political causes.

After his graduation in 1906, Frankfurter obtained a position with a prominent Wall Street law firm, becoming its first Jewish lawyer. He then became a staff member to HENRY L. STIMSON, who had become U.S. attorney for the Southern District of New York, and later served as Stimson's campaign manager in his unsuccessful bid for the governorship in 1910. After President William Howard Taft brought Stimson into his administration

Justice Felix Frankfurter *(United States Supreme Court)*

as secretary of war the next year, Stimson brought Frankfurter to Washington to serve as his special assistant. He subsequently rewarded Frankfurter for his work by helping to raise funds that allowed Harvard to hire Frankfurter, its first Jewish law faculty member, in 1914.

Frankfurter also worked as a special assistant to Woodrow Wilson's secretary of war, NEWTON D. BAKER, during World War I. As chairman of the War Labor Policies Board, Frankfurter worked with Franklin D. Roosevelt, assistant secretary of the navy. He subsequently acted as Roosevelt's legal adviser when FDR became governor of New York in 1929 and then president of the United States in 1933. FDR initially asked Frankfurter to become the solicitor general, but Frankfurter had already accepted a visiting professorship at Oxford University, where he developed a friendship with British economist JOHN MAY-

NARD KEYNES. He would later arrange for FDR to meet Keynes.

Using his law-school student contacts, Frankfurter became a one-person New Deal employment service for his "Happy Hot Dogs," furnishing legal talent for the Roosevelt administration in Washington. His influence expanded during FDR's second term, enabling him to push the administration leftward. After the death of BENJAMIN CARDOZO in 1938, FDR nominated Frankfurter as Cardozo's replacement on the Supreme Court. Liberals were overjoyed with the nomination, but conservatives were dismayed by Frankfurter's efforts to help found the American Civil Liberties Union and the *New Republic* magazine. To the surprise of both groups, he revealed himself to be a political liberal but a judicial conservative. Except for supporting New Deal economic reforms, Frankfurter typically sided with restrictions in free-speech cases, showing easy deference to majority consensus in society.

With an almost mystical belief in the melting pot, Frankfurter had married a Congregational minister's daughter, just as he was wedded to the pre-legal-realism jurisprudential tenets of Harvard Law School. His wife suffered several mental breakdowns during their marriage, and his brethren on the high tribunal finally turned against him because of his arrogant insistence on lecturing them about most cases. Frankfurter is considered a great justice in terms of historical rankings of justices, but he retired from the Court in 1962 embittered and frustrated after the majority rejected his leadership. He died on February 22, 1965, in Washington, D.C.

Frazier, Lynn Joseph
(1874–1947) *U.S. senator*

Lynn Joseph Frazier was born on December 21, 1874, near Medford, Minnesota, to a farm couple. When he was seven years old, the family moved to Pembina County, North Dakota, to homestead a tract of land. He earned a teaching degree from Mayville Normal School in 1895 and six years later received his bachelor's degree from the University of North Dakota. He returned to farm for several years near Hoople, North Dakota, and in 1903 married Lottie Stafford, with whom he had five children.

The lingering economic plight of farmers after the Civil War prompted Frazier to become active in the politics of the new Nonpartisan League, a farmers' organization founded in the state. It advocated restraints on railroads, bankers, and millers seen by members as exploiting small family farmers. Because of his farming experience and his unusually advanced education for that time and locale, the Nonpartisan League backed Frazier for the North Dakota governorship in 1916. Surprisingly, he won the Republican primary and overwhelmingly defeated his Democratic opponent in the fall general election. He was reelected in 1918 and 1920.

Frazier became an active governor, opposing U.S. involvement in World War I because he viewed it as diverting attention from domestic problems. He helped to create the state-owned Bank of North Dakota and a state-owned flour mill and grain elevator. Charges of the Nonpartisan League's support for socialistic policies and a scandal in the newly created bank precipitated a recall election in 1921, and he was narrowly defeated. The next year, however, he won the Republican Party's bid for a U.S. Senate seat by defeating four-term incumbent Porter J. McCumber in the primary. Frazier defeated his Democratic opponent in the fall general election. As with his governorship, he was reelected to the Senate twice, despite the fact that he was condemned in 1924 for endorsing the presidential bid of ROBERT LA FOLLETTE, JR. on the Progressive ticket.

While in the Senate, Frazier worked with other progressive Republicans, including Wisconsin's La Follette and Oregon's CHARLES MCNARY, in their efforts to help the unemployed and the underprivileged while regulating major corporations. His best-known pieces of legislation were the two Frazier-Lemke Acts of 1934 and 1935, which imposed moratoriums on foreclosures when farmers were unable to pay their mortgages. The U.S. Supreme Court held the 1934 act unconstitutional in *Louisville Joint Stock Land Bank v. Radford* (1935), but it was rewritten in August of that year as the Farm Mortgage Moratorium Act of 1935.

Frazier preferred to work behind the scenes while his flamboyant North Dakota colleague GERALD NYE reveled in the limelight. Frazier consistently supported farm relief and remained an isolationist in international affairs. He was defeated for reelection in 1940 when demagogue William Langer, the former League colleague from whom he had split, won the Republican primary. Frazier returned to farming in Pembina County, and his subsequent efforts to regain public office failed. He died on January 11, 1947, in Riverdale, Maryland.

Gannett, Frank Ernest
(1876–1957) *newspaper publisher*

Frank Ernest Gannett was born on September 15, 1876, in Bristol, New York, to farmer parents. He worked as a newspaper reporter while in high school and in college, graduating from Cornell University in 1898. Cornell's president, Jacob Gould Schurman, who was then head of the first Philippine Commission and knew Gannett as a student, recruited him to serve for a year as the commission's secretary. At the end of that commitment, Gannett returned to New York and newspaper work for the next five years.

Gannett moved into his long career in newspaper ownership in 1906 with his purchase of a half interest in the *Elmira Gazette*. His early trademarks included editorial brevity, separating news reporting from editorial writing, and refusing to sell space for liquor advertisements. Within a year, he had bought the city's other paper and merged the two, a move that foreshadowed another of his career trademarks. In 1920, he married Caroline Werner. The couple had a daughter, Sarah, and adopted a son, Dixon.

Gannett continued to replicate his pattern of newspaper acquisitions and mergers in New York cities in the early 1920s and finally headed the Gannett Company, Inc. In 1922, he expanded into the new communication medium of radio by launching a radio station in Rochester. By the end of that decade, the Gannett Company had gained Associated Press membership. Gannett's media empire had expanded to 22 newspapers in 16 cities, five radio stations, and three television stations in New York, Connecticut, New Jersey, and Illinois.

Gannett's early sympathy for the Democratic Party gradually transformed as his empire grew until he espoused an Old Guard Republican outlook. By the time of the New Deal and Franklin Roosevelt, he was a major critic of both, but he continued his practice of allowing local papers to develop their own editorial policies. His interests turned to politics after FDR's reelection in 1936. Gannett founded the National Committee to Uphold Constitutional Government in 1937 to fight FDR's Court-packing scheme as well as the LOUIS BROWNLOW committee recommendations for reorganizing the executive branch, which he viewed as efforts to create a dictatorship. He unsuccessfully sought the 1938 Republican nomination for the New York governorship and the party's presidential nod in 1940, losing the latter to WENDELL WILLKIE.

Gannett's National Committee to Uphold Constitutional Government continued to fight many New Deal reform and relief proposals until its contributor base faded by early 1941, at which time it morphed into a corporation named the Committee for Constitutional Government. Gannett served as the assistant chairman of the Republican National Committee from 1940 to 1942. He died on December 3, 1957, in Rochester. After his death, his newspaper chain continued to grow and eventually became the nation's largest.

Garner, John Nance
(Cactus Jack)
(1868–1967) *Speaker of the House, vice president of the United States*

Born in a log cabin on November 22, 1868, in Blossom Prairie, Texas, John Nance Garner later played semiprofessional baseball for a short time. He entered Vanderbilt University in 1886, but his poor educational background had not prepared him for college, and he soon dropped out. Returning home, he read law and set up a legal practice in 1890. He contracted tuberculosis and moved to the drier climate of Uvalde, west of San Antonio. After his health improved, he became involved in local community affairs as a publisher and county judge. In addition to his law practice, he became a banker and large landowner.

The energetic Garner entered state politics with his election to the Texas House of Representatives (1898–1902), where he favored populist measures to regulate insurance companies and railroads. He then moved into national politics with his election to the U.S. House of Representatives in 1902. "Cactus Jack," as he was called, maintained a homespun political style. His ability to cooperate and compromise led him to become the Democratic Whip in 1911 and obtain a spot on the powerful Ways

and Means Committee in 1913, allowing him to fund local projects for his constituents.

As a southerner, Garner loyally supported Woodrow Wilson's entry into World War I, but he opposed the Ku Klux Klan. His safe seat led him to become the senior Democrat on the Ways and Means Committee in 1923, where he typically worked behind the scenes. His closest friend in the House was Speaker Nicholas Longworth (R-Ohio), who was married to THEODORE ROOSEVELT's daughter. With Longworth, Democratic leader Garner ran the so-called Board of Education in the Capitol to keep their colleagues in line. By the narrow margin of three votes, Garner finally became Speaker on December 7, 1931, after the Democrats had regained the House.

John Nance Garner *(Library of Congress)*

Garner tended to be conservative on economic matters during the Great Depression. With the support of WILLIAM RANDOLPH HEARST's newspaper empire, he won the California primary and was a contender for the presidency in 1932. Fearing a divided convention, as had happened in 1924, Garner released his delegates after the third ballot and accepted Franklin Roosevelt's vice-presidential slot. Although initially supporting many New Deal programs only out of a sense of party loyalty, he was consulted by FDR and remained on the ticket in 1936. His differences with FDR grew, however, especially after the 1937 Supreme Court–packing plan. Differences over the plan aside, Garner engineered the final, watered-down, face-saving version of the Court-packing bill to reform only lower courts.

Garner's final split with FDR came after the president's attempted purge of conservative Democrats from the party in 1938. He made a bid for the 1940 presidential nomination but was thwarted by JESSE JONES, another Texan, especially after the state convention failed to oppose a third term for FDR. His favorite-son status proved meaningless as FDR obtained a first-ballot victory in 1940 at the national convention. Garner retired from national politics early in 1941. He died on November 7, 1967, in Uvalde, Texas.

Gaulle, Charles de
(1890–1970) *French head of state*

Born on November 22, 1890, to Catholic parents in northern France, Charles de Gaulle enlisted in the French army in 1909 and was accepted in the Saint-Cyr military academy, the equivalent of America's West Point. During World War I, he was wounded several times and held as a prisoner of war. Afterward, he was a history lecturer at Saint-Cyr. De Gaulle disagreed with the prevailing defensive strategy embodied in the Maginot Line intended to protect France against another German invasion and argued unsuccessfully for a mobile strike force instead. His criticism of French military strategy was responsible for repeated denials of promotion.

After Nazi Germany attacked France in May 1940 with the same kind of motorized armored attacks that de Gaulle had advocated for French defense, 84-year-old Marshal Philippe Pétain, his former patron and a World War I national hero, was named premier. Pétain, a known supporter of a cease-fire, agreed with the armistice the government signed with the Nazis that limited his government to the southern zone of France with headquarters in the spa town of Vichy while allowing Nazi occupation of the northern three-fifths of France. The French Vichy government collaborated with ADOLF HITLER, assuming that the dictator would soon defeat the British, and sentenced de Gaulle to death in absentia as a traitor.

De Gaulle, who had recently been promoted to general, refused to accept defeat. In early June 1940, he and his family fled to London, where he made a radio appeal for the French to resist. Without an electoral mandate, he renamed his Free France resistance movement "Fighting France" in 1942, and by the time of the Allied liberation in 1944, he had emerged as the undisputed, charismatic leader of the resistance. His hope was to restore French honor, which had been lost with the Nazi occupation. Largely because of this, de Gaulle was prickly toward British prime minister WINSTON CHURCHILL, who had been his host in exile, and even more so toward Franklin Roosevelt, who had withheld formal recognition of the Free French until a last resort shortly before the August 1944 liberation. De Gaulle was also excluded from both the Yalta and the Potsdam conferences. (FDR had recognized the Vichy government in 1941 to prevent French naval vessels and strategic overseas territory from falling into the hands of the Axis powers.)

Temporarily blocked by the Americans and British, de Gaulle eventually gained political power during the postwar period and established a stable Fifth Republic in 1959 with a strong presidency that he occupied. He often governed by plebiscite to terminate French colonialism, to develop a close relationship with West Germany, and to be a frequent irritant to both the British and Americans. He became the most effective democratic leader in France's history. He died in Colombey-les-Deux-Églises, France, on November 9, 1970.

Gellhorn, Martha
(1908–1998) *reporter*

Martha Gellhorn was born on November 8, 1908, in St. Louis, Missouri, the only daughter of a prominent Prussian-Jewish physician father and his progressive wife. She entered Byrn Mawr College but dropped out to work for United Press International as a correspondent from France. ELEANOR ROOSEVELT and her mother had worked together on the League of Women Voters and the Women's Division of the Democratic Party. In 1934, Gellhorn began her contact with the New Deal by working as one of a team of 16 writers hired by presidential aide HARRY HOPKINS to tour the nation and report on the impact of the Great Depression. His chief investigator, LORENA HICKOK, who also had a reporter background, arranged a meeting with Eleanor Roosevelt, who in turn introduced Gellhorn to FDR. Her reporter's knowledge provided the Roosevelts with firsthand observations about social conditions and the need for public relief.

After she left her brief assignment with Hopkins, Gellhorn returned to Europe to cover the Spanish civil war for *Collier's Weekly* in 1936 and 1937. She was a strong backer of the Loyalist (republican) side, as was ERNEST HEMINGWAY; their eventual five-year marriage (1940–45) grew from this episode. The couple made a movie of the Spanish civil war that showed the dangers of FRANCISCO FRANCO and fascism. The First Lady showed the film at the White House for FDR, but it failed to change his neutrality policy toward Spain. Gellhorn remained a welcome White House guest. After the war she moved to London covering military conflicts around the world. Gellhorn published articles, short stories and novels. She died on February 16, 1998, in London, England.

Giannini, Amadeo Peter
(1870–1949) *banker*

Born in San Jose, California, on May 6, 1870, Amadeo Giannini was the son of Italian immigrant parents. His father was killed when he was seven years old, and his mother remarried. Giannini's stepfather, Lorenzo Scatena, was an ambitious wholesale produce owner who moved the family to San Francisco. Giannini began working for him when he was 12 years old and still a student at Washington Grammar School, which he attended through the eighth grade. After briefly attending Heald's Business College, Giannini went to work full-time for his stepfather and at 19 was made a partner in the wholesale business. Three years later, he married Clorinda Agnes Cuneo, whose father was a wealthy real-estate investor. The couple had six children, but only three survived to adulthood.

In 1901, the Scatena wholesale produce firm was among the largest such businesses in San Francisco, and Giannini retired with a small fortune. His father-in-law died the following year, and the family asked him to manage the half-million dollar estate, which included shares in the Columbus Savings and Loan Society located in San Francisco's Italian quarter. Giannini unsuccessfully urged the institution to cultivate small borrowers and resigned to help found the Bank of Italy in late 1904. The new bank targeted small borrowers, and he actively advertised to attract such customers at a time when established banks did not solicit business.

Giannini applied his industriousness, business acuity, and humanity to building the new bank, and it flourished. After the California legislature enacted a law in 1909 that permitted branch banking, Giannini rapidly expanded the Bank of Italy by acquiring small banks and turning them into branches. By 1918, in addition to its headquarters location in San Francisco, there were 24 branches of the Bank of Italy, the nation's first large-banking system. He organized the Bancitaly Corporation in 1919 to further expand his banking system, acquiring New York banks and branch banks in Italy as well as the Bank of America in Los Angeles. Five years later, he retired as president of the Bank of Italy but retained the presidency of Bancitaly and bought more banks with branches, calling the group the Bank of America of California. By 1933, all these banks were brought together as the Bank of America National Trust and Savings Association, later known as the Bank of America, part of the Transamerica Corporation. Remarkably, despite his success, Giannini adhered to his original philosophy of putting emphasis on small borrowers, and he never succumbed to the corruption of power.

Under his careful management, Giannini's banking empire survived the Great Depression, although he was forced to obtain a loan from the Reconstruction Finance Corporation in 1932. He became a supporter of Franklin Roosevelt, and unlike others, he praised the Emergency Banking Act of 1933, the Banking Act of 1933, and the Banking Act of 1935. By 1939, Giannini had doubled the resources of his banks.

At the time of his death from a heart attack on June 3, 1949, in San Mateo, California, the Bank of America was the world's largest commercial bank. It had more than 500 branches in California as well as international branches abroad. Transamerica Corporation, a holding company, had 127 more banking offices in western states, in addition to real estate and industrial companies. The empire played a significant role in California's postwar economic growth.

Girdler, Tom Mercer
(1877–1965) *steel executive*

Tom Girdler was born on May 19, 1877, in Clark County, Indiana, to parents who owned a small farm as well as a cement plant. He attended a one-room country school as a boy and then went to Manual Training High School in nearby Louisville, Kentucky. In 1901, he earned his degree in mechanical engineering from Lehigh University. He then worked as a sales engineer in the London office of the Buffalo Forge Company for a year. In 1902, he left for Pittsburgh, Pennsylvania, and employment with the Oliver Iron and Steel Company. The next year, he married Mary Elizabeth Hayes, who died in 1917. (Girdler remarried three times after her death; all four of his children were from his first marriage.)

Girdler excelled at his job with Oliver Iron and Steel but soon left to work for Colorado Fuel and Iron Company in Pueblo for two years. He then went to Atlantic Steel Company in Atlanta, Georgia, staying for six years before being hired by Jones and Laughlin Steel Corporation in Pittsburgh in 1914. There he rose quickly in management and became the general superintendent of the corporation's plant at Aliquippa, Pennsylvania, in 1920. Girdler's "model town" at Aliquippa was considered "Little Siberia" by his workers. Still, however ruthless he may have been, his economic success during these years propelled him up the corporate ladder, and he became the company's president in 1928.

The next year, Girdler made his last career move when he unexpectedly left Jones and Laughlin at the pinnacle of his career to take over the newly organized Republic Steel Corporation. The new position in Cleveland, Ohio, gave him the opportunity to build an entire company that would bear his imprint. It soon had plants and mines in 77 cities, although it operated at a loss until 1935. Girdler had the foresight to see that railroads would be supplanted as steel's future by automobiles, airplanes, and home products. As a result, Republic moved toward specialization in lightweight steel alloys suitable for those products.

Girdler was a lifelong Republican, but he became a major booster of the New Deal's National Industrial Recovery Act (NIRA) of 1933 because it allowed the steel industry as a whole to establish a code that was pro-business. At the same time, it helped to prevent the steel giants from overwhelming the emerging ones like Republic with unfair price competition. Republic became a leader in backing the steel code, and even after the Supreme Court declared the NIRA unconstitutional in 1935, he continued to advocate voluntary code compliance.

Girdler became one of the major opponents of the National Labor Relations Act (NLRA) of 1935, which allowed labor to organize and bargain collectively with management. A collision occurred soon after JOHN L. LEWIS and his Committee for Industrial Organizations won a contract with United States Steel in March 1937. Similar contracts with Jones and Laughlin and others followed that one. However, Republic, Bethlehem, Youngstown Sheet and Tube, and Inland Steel refused

to recognize unions. Girdler became the authoritarian voice of what was dubbed "Little Steel," which responded to the threat of a strike with lockouts. Nearly 1 million workers went on strike and there were hundreds of instances of violence. On May 30, 1937, after a six-week strike at Republic's South Chicago plant, police shot and killed 10 workers, and more than 100 were injured. That gave the union its rallying cry, "Remember the Memorial Day Massacre." Franklin Roosevelt blamed both Girdler and Lewis, and neither backed his 1940 presidential campaign. FDR, in turn, denounced both of them as he campaigned for his third term.

Girdler had broken the strike by November 1937, turning public opinion against the strikers by playing the communist menace trump card. But his victory was short-lived after FDR's unprecedented third-term reelection in 1940 and the subsequent entrance of the United States into World War II. By 1942, the new National Labor Board had ruled that government contracts would be limited to companies that recognized the right of workers to bargain collectively. "Little Steel" was forced to bow to reality to retain a market for its product.

During World War II, Girdler was head of both the Republic Steel headquarters in Cleveland as well as the Consolidated Vultee Aircraft Corporation headquarters in San Diego. He introduced the assembly line to the production of aircraft, setting records in making the B-24 Liberator bomber for the army and the PBY Flying Boat for the navy. During the postwar era, he returned to his duties at Republic, continuing plant and market expansion for new company products using steel alloys. At age 79, he retired in 1955 with Republic at its peak of 70,000 employees and its greatest profit. He died a decade later at his home near Easton, Maryland, on February 4, 1965.

Glass, Carter
(1858–1946) *U.S. senator*

Carter Glass was born on January 4, 1858, into the political environment that surrounded his influential newspaper family in Virginia. Family financial hardship caused him to drop out of school at age 14, and he soon was following in his father's footsteps, working with local newspapers. In 1887, he became an editor for the *Lynchburg News,* and the next year he became the newspaper's owner. Over the ensuing decade, Glass acquired several more newspapers. He became involved in local politics as a state senator (1899–1903), favoring literacy tests and poll taxes to limit suffrage for blacks and whites.

Glass's long career in national politics began with his election to the U.S. House of Representatives, where he served from 1902 to 1918. He soon developed expertise in banking issues and became the main architect of the Federal Reserve Act of 1913, earning him the title Father of the Federal Reserve System. He became Woodrow Wilson's secretary of the Treasury (1918–20) until he was appointed to fill the vacant U.S. Senate seat from Virginia left by the death of Thomas S. Martin. He remained in that seat until his death. During his career, Glass also served as a member of the Democratic National Committee (1916–28).

FDR tried to co-opt Glass by inviting him to become his secretary of the Treasury, but Glass declined in 1933. However, FDR was successful in recruiting his sister, MARION GLASS BANISTER, as the assistant treasurer of the United States that same year. Nonetheless, Glass remained a conservative "states' rights" Democrat who believed in the gold standard and a balanced budget. He voted against the New Deal more than any other congressional Democrat. However, with a southern heritage shaped by having lost the American Civil War, Glass compensated by remaining a Wilsonian

internationalist who supported FDR's foreign policy. In 1938, FDR dedicated a bronze bas-relief of Glass, the self-described "unreconstructed rebel," in the lobby of the Federal Reserve Building, where it hangs across from a similar likeness of Wilson, another native Virginian. The inscription plaque for Glass reads "Defender of the Federal Reserve System." He died on May 26, 1946, in Washington, D.C.

Green, William
(1870–1952) *president, American Federation of Labor*

Born on March 3, 1870, in Coshocton, Ohio, William Green was the son of a poor immigrant coal miner and his wife. As a boy, he was slightly built and unusually energetic, bright, and religious. After completing the eighth grade, he worked for the local railroad for a short time before going to work in the coal mines, which he did for 19 years. In 1892, he married Jennie Mobley, the daughter of another local miner; the couple had six children.

Green and his father joined the Progressive Miners' Union in 1886, five years before it merged with the Knights of Labor District 35 to form the United Mine Workers of America (UMWA). Green was elected secretary of his local and then become the local president. By 1906 he was president of the entire Ohio district. After losing two elections to the presidency of the national UMWA he turned to state politics. In 1910, he won a seat in the state senate as a Democrat, and in 1912, he was reelected and became the Democratic floor leader.

When he was appointed statistician for the UMWA in 1911, Green returned to full-time union work. He was elected as secretary-treasurer of the UMWA in 1913 and held that position until 1924, serving during the early years of the presidency of JOHN L. LEWIS. In

1913, the president of the American Federation of Labor (AFL), Samuel Gompers, arranged for Green's election as vice president and member of the AFL executive council. Following Gomper's death in 1924, Lewis arranged for Green's succession to the AFL presidency. Having finally achieved leadership of the group with which he identified, though, Green grew increasingly conservative and moralistic.

As the Great Depression deepened, the conservative executive council of the AFL was forced to reverse its traditional opposition to federal legislation to protect labor. With pressure coming from rank-and-file workers for him to become a lobbyist on their behalf, Green assumed a new role and contributed to formulation of New Deal reforms that he then backed. In 1933, he became an enthusiastic supporter of Senator HUGO BLACK's 30-hour work-week bill. That same year, Green also supported passage of the National Industrial Recovery Act. Having helped to create Ohio's workmen's compensation program, he supported the Social Security Act of 1935. He also supported the 1935 National Labor Relations Act, which guaranteed labor's right to bargain collectively. In 1938, he helped gain passage of the Fair Labor Standards Act.

It was Green's traditional opposition to strikes that contributed to division within the AFL between the conservative craft union leaders who dominated the AFL executive council and the more radical industrial union advocates led by Lewis. Green personally believed in industrial unionism but deferred to the majority of the council. He voted with the majority to suspend the Committee for Industrial Organization in 1936, and two years later he voted to expel the group of unions that then became the Congress of Industrial Organizations (CIO). Green spent the remainder of his life fighting Lewis and the sit-down strike. By 1939, the executive council had named George Meany its secretary-treasurer, and he assumed many of Green's previous duties, transforming Green into a figurehead in the process.

Nonetheless, Green remained an influential labor leader during the New Deal and World War II. He served on FDR's Committee on Economic Security, the National Recovery Administration, the Management-Labor Policy Committee of the War Production Board, the Economic Stabilization Board of the Office of Economic Stabilization, the Management Labor Council of the War Production Board, and the advisory council to the Office of War Mobilization and Reconversion. Green had been thoroughly co-opted into FDR's administration just as he previously had been co-opted into the more conservative wing of the AFL. In contrast to Lewis, who called a miners' strike during World War II, Green collaborated with both the government and business to prevent strikes and maintain full production.

During the postwar period, Green opposed the Taft-Hartley Act but overall maintained his conservative union stance. He died on November 21, 1952, in Coshocton, Ohio, where he was born.

Gulick, Luther Halsey, IV

(1892–1993) *member, President's Committee on Administrative Management*

Luther Halsey Gulick was born in Osaka, Japan, on January 17, 1892. He shared his names with his Congregational church missionary father; his physical-educator grandfather, who is in the Basketball Hall of Fame and helped found the Boy Scouts of America; and his great-grandfather, who also was a missionary. Gulick also inherited the missionary zeal of his forebears but chose to apply his energies in a new field in political science, public administration.

After spending his boyhood in Japan, Gulick received both his undergraduate and master's degrees from Oberlin College in Ohio. For two years, he was a student of the progressive economic historian Charles A. Beard at the Training School for Public Service of the New York Bureau of Municipal Research, Columbia University. He ultimately replaced his mentor. During World War I, he worked for the Council of National Defense and the War Department in Washington, D.C., where he was a captain in the statistical branch of the general staff. After the war, he returned to Columbia and was awarded his doctorate in 1920.

Gulick was the founding president of the Institute of Public Administration at Columbia (1920–64) and simultaneously served as the director of the New York Bureau of Municipal Research. With the fervor of a missionary, he conducted a variety of municipal studies and lectured at a number of colleges and universities in the 1920s and 1930s. At that time a Republican, he helped to organize Massachusetts's budget system during Calvin Coolidge's governorship. During his tenure as the Eaton professor of municipal science and administration at Columbia University (1931–42), his work attracted national recognition, and he was appointed by the Social Sciences Research Council to direct the Commission of Inquiry on Public Service Personnel (1933–35).

Gulick's work at Columbia caught the attention of FDR, who appointed him to the presidential Committee on Administrative Management (the Brownlow Committee) in 1936 to study the administrative needs of a modern executive. Gulick served with LOUIS BROWNLOW and CHARLES MERRIAM on the study, which resulted in FDR's proposal of the Executive Office of the President and the concept of the modern White House staff. The study called for a small presidential staff composed of individuals described as having a "passion for anonymity." Because the proposal was submitted at virtually the same time as FDR's Court-packing plan, its implementation was diluted and delayed until Congress, recognizing the necessity of strengthening the presidency during an era of totalitarianism abroad, passed the Reorganization Act of 1939. If subsequent presidents had observed the recommendations of the Brownlow Committee (e.g., especially a small White House staff with assistants who did not make policy), episodes such as the Watergate and Iran-Contra affairs might have been avoided. The study remains one of the most significant documents on the American presidency. From 1921 to 1962, Gulick served as the president of the Institute of Public Administration, and then served as its chairman until 1982. He died on January 10, 1993, in New York City.

Hague, Frank
(1876–1956) *Jersey City mayor*

Born on January 17, 1876, to Irish immigrant parents, Frank Hague grew up in the Irish-American tenements of Jersey City, New Jersey, called the Horseshoe District, which would be his power base for the rest of his political life. He left school at age 14 and soon found opportunity in ward politics, being elected constable of the Second Ward in 1899. With street smarts, he worked his way up the Democratic ladder over the next two decades, serving as city commissioner before being elected as mayor in 1917. He became the boss and virtual dictator of the urban political machine, based on a 3 percent annual salary kickback from city workers, 10 percent from suppliers and contractors, and a cut from the rackets it protected. He provided the bacon; his patrons supplied voter loyalty.

Hague's urban machine served FDR loyally during all four presidential campaigns. In return, New Deal recovery programs and patronage in New Jersey were channeled primarily through Hague's operation. He worked with presidential aide HARRY HOPKINS to obtain thousands of federal jobs between 1935 and 1941. In turn, Hague delivered the repeated support needed on New Deal legisla-tion. Along with Hopkins and Chicago mayor EDWARD KELLY, he successfully managed FDR's third-term bid at the 1940 Democratic national convention in Chicago.

Unfortunately, Hague's power grew increasingly corrupt and tyrannical. He despised the newly formed Committee on Industrial Organization (CIO), using his police force to drive them violently from Jersey City in 1937. That same year he also barred socialist NORMAN THOMAS from speaking at a public rally in Jersey City, which resulted in a lawsuit from the CIO and the American Civil Liberties Union; the case was appealed to the U.S. Supreme Court, which in 1939 upheld the First Amendment. Regular junkets to Florida and the Jersey Shore turned Hague into the absentee mayor of a city with the highest tax rate of any comparably sized municipality in the nation. His police were the best paid in the United States, but teachers were slighted. A ruthless persona combined with policies that drove business and the middle class out of the city led to the defeat of his machine by 1949. Jersey City was changing, but Hague's policies lacked innovation, and his personality showed little flexibility. FDR and the New Deal had been willing to overlook the corruption as long as it served the administration's political purposes. Hague died on January 1, 1956, in New York City.

Hansen, Alvin Harvey
(1887–1975) *economic adviser to the Roosevelt administration*

Born on August 23, 1887, in Viborg, South Dakota, Alvin Hansen was the son of midwestern Baptist farmers. He was educated at Yankton College, the oldest private college in South Dakota, graduating in 1910 with a degree in English. In 1913, he began his study of economics at the University of Wisconsin, where he learned to use economics to address social issues. Hansen completed his dissertation in 1918 while teaching at Brown University in Providence, Rhode Island, and then began a successful teaching career at the University of Minnesota. After Franklin Roosevelt was elected president in 1932, Hansen became an economic adviser to Secretary of State CORDELL HULL.

In 1937, Hansen moved to Harvard University to become the first holder of the Lucius N. Littaurer chair of political economy. Many of his students, such as Paul Samuelson and John Kenneth Galbraith, would later become influential economists. While at Harvard, he acquired the nickname "the American Keynes" since he concluded that JOHN MAYNARD KEYNES had the appropriate solution to the Great Depression. Hansen always saw economics as a means to solving social problems. His appointment as an economic adviser to MARRINER ECCLES at the Federal Reserve Board (1940–45) furnished him a venue to promote American Keynesianism as well as Keynes's *Fiscal Policy and Business Cycles* (1941). Incurably optimistic, he believed in a mixed economy. In the same way that FELIX FRANKFURTER provided lawyers to staff the New Deal, Hansen provided a generation of Keynesian policy advisers to staff the war mobilization and the postwar Council of Economic Advisers. He died on June 6, 1975, in Alexandria, Virginia.

Harriman, William Averell
(1891–1986) *federal administrator, ambassador to the Soviet Union*

Born on November 15, 1891, in New York City, the son of a wealthy railroad magnate, Averell Harriman attended Groton School in Connecticut, where his academic performance was poor despite his father's pressure for him to excel; historians consider this a possible factor in his lifelong stammer. FDR and ELEANOR ROOSEVELT first met Harriman at Groton when he was a classmate with Hall Roosevelt, Eleanor's brother. After he graduated from Yale, Harriman began work at his father's Union Pacific Railroad and went on to create one of the largest merchant fleets in the world after World War I, earning him the nickname "the Steamship King." He became chairman of the Union Pacific board in 1932 but derived less pleasure from business success than from recreational pursuits like polo. He had been a member of the 1928 American polo team and later also earned a place in the Croquet Hall of Fame.

The Roosevelt presidency turned Harriman's interest to politics. He and his sister, Mary Harriman Rumsey, left the Republican Party fold in 1928 and voted for FDR in 1932. A friend of Brigadier General HUGH JOHNSON, Harriman accepted a position in the National Recovery Administration until it was declared unconstitutional by the Supreme Court in 1935. He then served as the chairman of the Business Advisory Council in the Commerce Department (1937–39) and joined the Office of Production Management during World War II. Combining his enjoyment of travel and public service, Harriman was FDR's representative to Britain to coordinate the lend-lease program. With his access to direct communication with the president and HARRY HOPKINS, Harriman's friend and protégé, he became friends with Prime Minister WINSTON CHURCHILL. (He would later marry Churchill's former daughter-in-law.) After

Soviet foreign minister V. M. Molotov, W. Averell Harriman, and British prime minister Winston Churchill *(Library of Congress)*

the Soviet Union entered World War II, Harriman eventually was appointed the American ambassador to Moscow (1943–46), and he attended the Tehran and Yalta conferences with FDR. His experience in the Roosevelt administration served as the basis for his assistance to subsequent presidential administrations as well as his later single and unsuccessful term as New York governor (1954–58). He died on July 26, 1986, in Westchester County, New York.

Harrison, Byron Patton
(Pat Harrison)
(1881–1941) *U.S. senator*

A classic Deep South character, Pat Harrison, born on August 29, 1881, was reared in Crystal Springs, Mississippi, and attended what became Louisiana State University in Baton Rouge. After briefly working as a public school teacher and lawyer, he found his calling in politics. He first served as a Mississippi district attorney and entered the national arena with his election to the U.S. House of Representatives (1911–19), where he took his lead from Deep South–born president Woodrow Wilson. In part because incumbent Senator James K. Vardaman, a former governor and race-baiter known as "the Great White Chief," failed to support Wilson's entrance into World War I, Harrison challenged him for election in 1918 and won. Harrison held his Senate seat until his death shortly before the United States entered World War II.

Because of his lively, energetic personality, Harrison was popular in the Senate. After the Democrats took control of Congress in March 1933, he became chairman of the Senate Finance

Committee. Initially, Harrison supported New Deal legislation, including the National Industrial Recovery Act, the Social Security Act, and the Reciprocal Trade Agreement Acts, as well as a series of revenue acts. However, he split with FDR after the president's failure to support him in his bid to become Senate majority leader in 1937; ALBEN BARKLEY won the position by a single vote. Nonetheless, by 1940, the Second World War had triggered Harrison's habitual support for defense revenue and preparedness. His long tenure in the Senate resulted in his being named president pro tempore in January 1941. FDR had the lend-lease bill sent to the Finance Committee instead of Foreign Relations because he knew that Harrison's loyalty in foreign affairs was unquestioned. He died of cancer on June 22, 1941, in Washington, D.C.

Hastie, William Henry
(1904–1976) *Roosevelt administration aide, federal judge*

William Hastie was born on November 17, 1904, to a lower-middle-class African-American family from Knoxville, Tennessee. His mother was a teacher, and his father was a clerk in the U.S. Pension Office. He attended the highly regarded Paul Lawrence Dunbar High School in Washington, D.C., and earned his undergraduate degree in mathematics from Amherst College in 1925. He taught briefly before going to Harvard University Law School, where he served on the law review. After he graduated in 1930, he returned to Washington, D.C., to practice law, and he joined the law faculty at Howard University. One of his first students was future Supreme Court justice Thurgood Marshall, who had been denied entry into the University of Maryland Law School because of his race. Hastie returned to Harvard to earn a second law degree in 1933. His roommate was Robert C. Weaver, who would earn a doctorate from Harvard University in 1934, and serve in the Department of the Interior during the presidency of FDR.

Hastie's association with the New Deal began late that same year when Secretary of the Interior HAROLD ICKES, a civil-rights activist, recruited him as assistant solicitor, and he drafted the Organic Act of 1936, which reorganized government in the Virgin Islands. Hastie and Weaver became members of FDR's so-called black cabinet. He was next appointed as district judge in the Virgin Islands, the first African-American federal judge in U.S. history. Two years later, he resigned that position to become dean of the Howard University Law School.

Hastie's service to the Roosevelt administration continued during World War II. In 1940, he took leave from Howard to assume a position with Secretary of War HENRY STIMSON and handled racial matters in the military, becoming known as the "father of the black air force." Yet he resigned his position in early 1943 over his inability to end discrimination in the military. FDR had already picked Hastie as a member of the Caribbean Advisory Committee to the Anglo-American Caribbean Commission. During the postwar period, reflecting his pro–human rights stance, President HARRY TRUMAN appointed Hastie as governor of the Virgin Islands, the first African-American governor since P. B. S. Pinchback, who had served briefly as Louisiana's acting governor during Reconstruction. Truman elevated him in 1950 to a Federal Court of Appeals judgeship, making Hastie the first African-American federal judge with life tenure. He died on April 14, 1976, in Norristown, Pennsylvania.

Hearst, William Randolph
(1863–1951) *newspaper publisher*

Born on April 29, 1863, in San Francisco, William Randolph Hearst was the son of a wealthy mine developer who was also a U.S. senator; his mother was Victorian in outlook and an art connoisseur in interest. Hearst developed a nearly split personality—part conventional and part rebel—and never reconciled his origins. Early evidence of this was that he never graduated from St. Paul's School or Harvard College, where he worked for the *Harvard Lampoon*. He later worked at Joseph Pulitzer's *New York World*. He acquired the *San Francisco Examiner* and focused both his father's money and his own energy on making it a success. He subsequently acquired the *New York Morning Journal* as a challenge to newspaper magnate Pulitzer.

From that start, the emerging publishing mogul poured his fortune into creating a media empire of newspapers, magazines, news services, and a film company. Hearst's trademarks were brash headlines, lots of photographs, and sensational stories to appeal to the masses, a style known as yellow journalism. His mean-minded and sensational columnists included Ambrose Bierce, WESTBROOK PEGLER, and Walter Winchell. Hearst was 6'2" tall, but his reputation was even larger than life as he developed a bully's reputation because of his papers. Perhaps due to his mother's influence, he was polite—sometimes even shy—in person and neither smoked nor drank, and his extremely high-pitched voice was at odds with his appearance.

Hearst's strategy was to use his journalism empire as a base to become president and win acceptance from the Northeast establishment. His political orientation was bifurcated and had begun on the left side of the political spectrum, but by the mid-1930s, it had swung to the extreme right. He was a Populist before World War I, supporting William Jennings Bryan's presidential bids in 1896 and 1900 along with muckraking journalist and novelist UPTON SINCLAIR and labor lawyer Clarence Darrow. He served two terms in the U.S. House of Representatives (1903–07) and was nearly selected by the 1904 Democratic National Convention as its presidential candidate. He was a Tam-

many Hall representative from New York and set a record for his absenteeism. He ran close but unsuccessful campaigns for mayor and governor in New York and in 1910 failed to win the lieutenant governorship on a third-party ticket.

Hearst favored Cuban independence. He exploited fear in California of Asian immigration at the same time that he favored Irish nationalism and supported the Germans over the English in the first two years of World War I. He opposed U.S. entrance into the war as well as U.S. membership in the postwar League of Nations. He supported the Russian Revolution and was against Woodrow Wilson's interventionist efforts to reverse it.

Initially Hearst supported the presidential candidacy of Texas congressman JOHN NANCE GARNER at the 1932 Democratic National Convention, but when that failed, he backed FDR to prevent Wilson's internationalist former secretary of war, NEWTON BAKER, from getting the nomination. He supported FDR during the campaign and for the first years of the New Deal, but once more his tendency to bifurcate views dominated, and he changed his mind. In 1934, he worked to defeat Upton Sinclair's bid for the California governorship. That same year, he traveled to Europe and met ADOLF HITLER and BENITO MUSSOLINI. He opposed U.S. entrance into World War II and warned about the threat of communism. After 1935, Hearst claimed that the New Deal was a "Raw Deal," reflecting his new concern about unions and increased taxation. In FDR's subsequent reelection campaigns, Hearst backed Republican challengers.

Growing out of touch with most Americans, Hearst increasingly retreated to his San Simeon estate near the California coast, where he lived for nearly three decades with actress Marion Davies, although he never divorced his wife. Despite Hearst's attempts to block its release, in 1941 ORSON WELLES's fictionalized biography of him, the classic *Citizen Kane*, was released. He died on August 14, 1951, in Beverly Hills, California.

Hemingway, Ernest
(1899–1961) *novelist*

Ernest Hemingway was born on July 21, 1899, in Oak Park, Illinois, to a physician father and a musician/voice teacher mother. Hemingway, his brother, and four sisters grew up in a seemingly conventional, well-to-do family. During the school year, they lived in an elitist enclave eight miles from downtown Chicago, but summers were spent mostly in the outdoors of northern Michigan at his parents' lakeside house. THEODORE ROOSEVELT, America's legendary turn-of-the-century outdoorsman, became Hemingway's childhood hero, just as he was FDR's role model. Like Teddy Roosevelt, Hemingway began to lead a strenuous physical life at an early age, and he developed a lifelong admiration for boxers, baseball players, and, eventually, bullfighters, who dared fate instead of seeking a safe, comfortable existence. Throughout his life, Hemingway remained energetic, intense, and competitive.

Although Hemingway was surrounded by external trappings that suggested a family to be envied, there was internal family dissent due to tension between his parents. The tension was further magnified by his father's slide into depression during Hemingway's teenage years. Those circumstances likely triggered his later rebellion against his family and rejection of his traditional middle-class upbringing. For example, while his family was well educated and involved in the Congregational Church, Hemingway never attended college and married four times. He, too, would eventually slip into depression and commit suicide just as his father had done in 1928 and as his brother and and one of his sisters would do as well. Although Heming-

way blamed his mother for his father's suicide, he remained the dutiful son who stayed in regular contact with her and ultimately supported her financially. Ties to his past were limited to that gesture, as he lived life on his own terms.

After he graduated from high school in 1917, Hemingway found a job as a cub reporter for the Kansas City *Star*, covering crime news about the same time that his boyhood hero, Teddy Roosevelt, was fighting crime as New York City's police commissioner. Thirsting for greater adventure, he volunteered to drive Red Cross ambulances in Italy during World War I. Within two weeks, the 18-year-old Hemingway was wounded, and he returned home in early 1919. In 1920, he began writing for the *Toronto Star*. The following year, he married Hadley Richardson, the first of his four wives, and the marriage produced one son. They soon moved to Paris, where Hemingway worked as a foreign news correspondent covering Georges Clemenceau, David Lloyd George, BENITO MUSSOLINI, and other post–World War I leaders. During this period, Hemingway's Oak Park Republicanism confronted European socialism, slowly pushing him into the political world while also contributing to his own emerging intellectual existentialism. In that world, he was an outsider without a religious or political home. Hemingway and his wife returned home in 1923, and by January 1924 he had quit his job at the *Toronto Star*. It was the last time in his life that he held a conventional full-time job.

Almost immediately the couple returned to Paris and lived on his wife's small trust and the periodic sale of his writing. They lived near the poet Ezra Pound, who became a mentor, and the writer Gertrude Stein, who not only was godmother to their son but also became Hemingway's surrogate mother figure. During this time, he also became friends with Ford Madox Ford and met Pablo Picasso, ARCHIBALD MACLEISH, James Joyce, and many other influential figures of the era. In Paris,

Hemingway was a restless man on the move, but he was moving upward. By the mid- to late 1920s, Hemingway was one of the best-known novelists of his generation. His breakthrough novel, *The Sun Also Rises*, was published in 1926, and in 1929 came *A Farewell to Arms*, his first war novel. He had been fortunate enough to find at his publisher, Charles Scribner's Sons, an extremely supportive editor, Max Perkins, who would become his surrogate father figure.

In 1927, as Hemingway was finally experiencing success, his wife divorced him; he gave her lifetime rights to income from *The Sun Also Rises*. He subsequently began an affair with Pauline Pfeiffer and married her. Pfeiffer, with a degree from the University of Missouri School of Journalism, was a devout Catholic with a large trust fund who had worked as a fashion editor for *Vogue* and *Vanity Fair*. In 1928, the couple returned to the United States, where Pauline gave birth to Hemingway's second son in 1931. During the Great Depression, the Hemingways depended partially on Pauline's trust fund for income. In 1933, he published a novel about Spain and bullfighting, *Death in the Afternoon*, followed in 1935 by *The Green Hills of Africa*, which dealt with African safaris. In September 1937, he reverted to his journalistic past and began covering the Spanish civil war. He appeared on the front cover of *Time* the next month.

At a time when the nation remained neutral and isolationist, Hemingway became anti-Franco and politically engaged. He bought a house in Key West, Florida, and wrote *To Have and Have Not* (1937), which lightly foreshadowed a Cuban revolt that paralleled the civil war in Spain. It was a less-successful novel that followed an ideological formula, and the title alone suggested Hemingway's growing existentialism. The following year, he wrote his only play, *The Fifth Column*, and contributed to the film *The Spanish Earth*.

By 1939, Hemingway's second marriage had also fallen apart. He began writing *For Whom the Bell Tolls*, considered his best novel, in his room at the Hotel Ambos Mundos in downtown Havana, Cuba. He then bought a house outside of Havana and completed work on *For Whom the Bell Tolls* by mid-1940. That same year, Pauline divorced him and he married MARTHA GELLHORN. Soon afterward, he began drinking heavily and stopped writing for the longest stretch in his career. He remained unproductive throughout World War II.

Despite his hiatus from writing novels, Hemingway could not sit still. He served as a correspondent in London and flew several missions with the Royal Air Force during World War II. By summer 1944, he was attached briefly to General GEORGE PATTON's Third Army. At the end of that summer, he led a small group of French irregulars and others during the liberation of Paris. A U.S. court martial subsequently cleared him of charges that he had acted illegally as a field officer. In November 1944, he rejoined the Fourth Army, participating for a couple of weeks in intense combat. During this time, he was also conducting an affair with Mary Welsh Monks, who became his fourth wife in 1946. They married in Havana.

Hemingway was not particularly productive during the postwar period. As his fourth marriage disintegrated, he returned to places he had visited previously. Despite the upheaval in his life, he completed *The Old Man and the Sea* (1952), which won the Pulitzer Prize the next year. In 1954, he was awarded the Nobel Prize for literature, but poor health prevented him from traveling to Stockholm to accept the award. Sympathetic to the Cuban revolution, he nonetheless moved to Ketchum, Idaho, to live. There, after two previous failed suicide attempts, Hemingway fatally shot himself on July 2, 1961.

Henderson, Leon

(1895–1986) *economic adviser to the Roosevelt administration; administrator, Office of Price Administration*

Born on May 26, 1895, in Millville, New Jersey, Leon Henderson was the son of a factory worker turned farmer. Attending college was not an immediate option for him, so he joined the army during World War I. Afterward he attended Swarthmore College, graduating in 1920, and went on to graduate school majoring in economics at the Wharton School of the University of Pennsylvania. He then began teaching at the Carnegie Institute of Technology, a job he held only briefly.

Henderson's entrance into the political world came in 1923 when he joined the administration of Pennsylvania governor Gilford Pinchot, who had been one of President THEODORE ROOSEVELT's cabinet members. Henderson served in a variety of positions with Pinchot before joining the Russell Sage Foundation (1925–43), where he worked to protect consumers from loan sharks. His entrée to the New Deal came in December 1933 after he had led a consumer delegation into the office of General HUGH JOHNSON, the National Recovery Administration director, with whom Henderson engaged in a shouting match. Johnson, however, appreciated a fellow wisecracker, hired Henderson as a consumer adviser, and soon made him the agency's chief economist. Henderson became an important economic adviser for the New Deal and was sent on a number of assignments.

A dedicated New Dealer, Henderson advised the Democratic National Committee in 1936, which led to his becoming the economic consultant for HARRY HOPKINS in the Works Progress Administration. Hopkins, Henderson, and fellow economist LAUCHLIN CURRIE were among those who led FDR to shift direction in administration policy to per-

mit more deficit spending and antitrust activity in what became known as the Second New Deal. WILLIAM O. DOUGLAS and MARRINER ECCLES supported their efforts against the balanced budget approach preferred by Secretary of the Treasury HENRY MORGANTHAU, JR. FDR then created the Temporary National Economic Committee to investigate monopolies and put Henderson in charge of it (1938–41); the following year, he appointed Henderson to the Securities and Exchange Commission (1939–41).

During World War II, FDR made Henderson the administrator of the Office of Price Administration and the head of the Civilian Supply Division of the War Production Board. His efforts against price hikes and use of rationing, combined with his personality, made him unpopular, but they held the cost of living down compared to what it was during World War I. At the end of 1942, he left government service. During the postwar period he engaged in a variety of professional and civic pursuits. He became president of the International Hudson Corporation, the chief economist for the Research Institute of America, and the chairman of the Americans for Democratic Action (ADA). He died on October 19, 1986, in Oceanside, California.

Hickok, Lorena Alice

(1893–1968) *reporter; Federal Emergency Relief Administration investigator; executive director, National Democratic Party, Women's Division*

Born on March 7, 1893, in East Troy, Wisconsin, to an abusive father who frequently moved his family, Lorena Hickok had an unhappy childhood. She was 13 when her mother died, and the next year she left home and began work as a domestic. Eventually she completed high school, and after several attempts at college, where she was discriminated against because of her weight, Hickok entered the male-dominated world of journalism. Making a name for herself through tenacity and native ability, she became one of the first women reporters hired by the Associated Press (AP).

Hickok became involved with the New Deal through her association with ELEANOR ROOSEVELT, whom she covered during the 1932 presidential campaign and who became her lifelong friend. She subsequently left her AP job to become the chief investigator for the Federal Emergency Relief Administration. Traveling through 32 states between 1933 and 1936, she used her reporter background to write concrete reports on the conditions that people at the grassroots faced: bureaucratic inefficiency, greedy politicians using the New Deal for personal benefit, and the upset that New Deal programs were causing in class and racial relationships. The reports went to presidential aide HARRY HOPKINS and reached FDR and others, helping to promote more public relief as well as the creation of the Civil Works Administration and the Emergency Relief Appropriation Act of 1935.

In 1937 Hickok worked as a publicist for the New York World's Fair. In 1940 she returned to Washington to join the staff of the Democratic National Committee, serving first as its publicist and then, until 1945, as executive secretary of the Women's Division. Eleanor Roosevelt invited her to live as a guest at the White House during this period so that Hickok could afford to maintain her home on Long Island. She developed a close relationship with Judge Marion Harron of the United States Tax Court and a political friendship with Helen Gahagan Douglas.

At the end of the FDR administration her health began to fail. Nonetheless, to support herself she was still able to work as a researcher for Representative Mary Norton of New Jersey and the New York State Democratic Committee from 1947 to 1952. The following year she

moved to Hyde Park, New York, to be near Eleanor Roosevelt. Hickok by then was partially blind, so the former First Lady aided her financially by collaborating with her on the book *Ladies of Courage* (1954), dealing with women in politics. Hickok lived first at Roosevelt's Val-Kill home and then in rental units. She went on to write several biographies for juveniles and a biography of Eleanor Roosevelt, *Reluctant First Lady*, in 1962. Hickok died on May 1, 1968, in Rhinebeck, New York.

Hicks, Granville
(1901–1982) *literary critic, novelist*

Many liberal intellectuals were blinded by their idealism in the 1930s as the despair in the United States produced by the Great Depression squeezed hope from millions of Americans. The 1917 Bolshevik Revolution in Russia had led them to believe that a utopia would emerge in the aftermath. Granville Hicks was among those who dismissed democratic principles in favor of idealism.

Hicks was born on September 9, 1901, in Exeter, New Hampshire; his father was the superintendent of a small factory, and his mother was a housewife. While at Harvard studying English, he attended the Universalist Church. After he graduated in 1923, he attended Harvard Theological School for two years before leaving it to teach and write. In 1925, he married his high-school sweetheart, Dorothy Dyer; the couple had one child.

In 1925, Hicks also became an instructor in religion and English at Smith College, where he was influenced by Newton Arvin's antibusiness views and Van Wyck Brooks's notions that artists are necessarily alien to a mass industrial society like the United States. He received his M.A. degree in English from Harvard in 1929 and accepted a professorship at Rensselaer Polytechnic Institute. By the time

FDR was sworn in as president for the first time, Hicks was advocating communism as the solution to America's economic problems. In 1934 he became the literary editor of the communist journal, *New Masses*, and lost his professorship the next year.

Hicks increasingly came to view literary criticism as the proper venue to promote revolutionary change, so he dismissed writers who failed to adopt a similar approach, such as PEARL BUCK and WILLIAM FAULKNER. He also dismissed ERNEST HEMINGWAY until the publication of Hemingway's most political and least commercially successful novel, *To Have and Have Not*, in 1937. On the other hand, Hicks supported the social realism of writers such as JOHN DOS PASSOS and JOHN STEINBECK.

Hicks and other leftist intellectuals were united in their opposition to fascism in Germany, Italy, and Spain during the 1930s. Like many of his contemporaries, Hicks supported the Republican side in Spain against FRANCISCO FRANCO during the Spanish civil war. But some of the leftist intellectuals grew disillusioned with their own Marxist views after JOSEPH STALIN entered into a nonaggression pact with ADOLF HITLER in August 1939. That shocking event led Hicks not only to resign his position at the *New Masses* but also to write a letter that appeared in the October 4, 1939, issue of the *New Republic* in which he publicly resigned his membership in the Communist Party.

Nonetheless, idealists tend to retain their basic worldviews, and though Hicks came to criticize literary Marxism and communism, he wrote a utopian novel, *The First to Awaken*, in 1940. In 1942 he wrote a second such novel, *Only One Storm*, dealing with life in small-town America. During the postwar period, his literary criticism became increasingly erratic. Hicks became overly critical of the New Criticism and in the process demonstrated considerable lack of understanding about its goals. The New

Criticism had emerged from the South during the 1930s by a new group of Southern intellectuals who insisted that society and fiction be interpreted on what was presented in the work of art itself without introducing outside historical and cultural forces to explain it. This group of so-called New Critics included the poets and writers John Crowe Ransom, Allen Tate, Robert Penn Warren, and Cleanth Brooks. In contrast, Hicks favored ideology to explain literary works. The New Criticism became the predominant literary school during the postwar era. He died on June 18, 1982, in Franklin Park, New Jersey.

High, Stanley
(1895–1961) *presidential speechwriter, Good Neighbor League organizer*

Born on December 30, 1895, in Chicago, Stanley High was a product of middle-class midwestern parents. He was a 1917 graduate of Nebraska Wesleyan University and graduated from Boston University School of Theology in 1923. He began his career by serving with the Methodist Mission to China (1919–20) and then was the European correspondent for the *Christian Science Monitor* (1921–24). He continued to blend journalism and religion during the 1920s with his work for the Board of Foreign Missions of the Methodist Church as a lecturer on international affairs. He became editor of the *Christian Herald* in 1928 and was a staff member of the National Broadcasting Company, delivering radio lectures on current events.

Although High was a Republican, SAMUEL ROSENMAN recruited him in 1936 to join the White House speechwriting staff after High had become disillusioned with HERBERT HOOVER's conservatism. His work helped to enhance FDR's inspirational addresses. FDR also used High to implement his secretary

LOUIS HOWE's idea of a Good Neighbor League to attract members of the religious, newspaper, and academic worlds, along with social workers, into the 1936 Roosevelt reelection campaign. By election time, more than 20 state chapters had been established, consisting in large part of Republicans who might not otherwise have voted Democratic. High tried but failed to get this organization to support FDR's Court-packing scheme in 1937.

After his departure from the administration, High returned to writing. He became a correspondent for the *Saturday Evening Post*, a senior editor of the *Reader's Digest* in 1952, and the author of *Roosevelt-And Then* in 1937. He died on February 3, 1961.

Hillman, Sidney
(1887–1946) *national union leader*

Born on March 23, 1887, to Jewish shopkeepers in Zagare, Lithuania, Sidney Hillman was educated at the Slobodka Rabbinical Seminary. He became caught up in revolutionary activity and was imprisoned. Afterward he fled to Manchester, England, and then emigrated to the United States in 1907. He went to Chicago, where he eventually found work under terrible conditions at the clothing factory of Hart, Schaffner and Marx. He emerged as the business agent of the new Local 39 of the United Garment Workers of America (UGW) after a strike in 1910. Four years later, he moved to New York and served as chief clerk of the Cloakmaker's Union.

After the more radical immigrants in Chicago broke from the UGW in 1914 and began the Amalgamated Clothing Workers of America (ACWA), Hillman became its first president and built it into one of the nation's most powerful unions. Following the onset of the Great Depression, he became a strong New Deal supporter and helped draft the pub-

lic works section of the National Industrial Recovery Act and was a member of the National Recovery Administration (NRA) board. After the American Federation of Labor, which initially had viewed the ACWA as an illegitimate rival of the UGW, admitted the ACWA in 1933, Hillman joined the insurgency of JOHN L. LEWIS, who wanted both unskilled and skilled workers in each industrial union. They formed the Committee for Industrial Organizations, which became the Congress of Industrial Organizations (CIO) in 1938. Hillman served as the CIO vice president until 1940.

In 1936, Hillman and Lewis founded Labor's Non-Partisan League to help reelect Franklin Roosevelt for a second term. Hillman also helped found the American Labor Party in New York to encourage Socialists and independents to back FDR. That support led Hillman to win passage of the Fair Labor Standards Act of 1938. After Lewis broke with FDR in 1940, Hillman became the senior union leader in the Democratic Party. He soon became cochairman of the Office of Production Management (1940–42) and then returned to the ACWA presidency. In 1943, as the new chairman of the CIO's Political Action Committee, Hillman helped to turn out labor for FDR's fourth-term presidential bid in 1944 and eventually backed HARRY S. TRUMAN for the second spot after HENRY WALLACE's effort failed. Hillman died on July 10, 1946, in Point Lookout, New York.

Hirohito
(1901–1989) *Japanese emperor*

Born April 29, 1901, Hirohito experienced a surreal upbringing as a god, not a human. The eldest son in the royal family, he became crown prince in 1916 while still a teenager and married Princess Kuni, in 1924. After the death of his father, the Taisho emperor, in late 1928, Hirohito became the 124th Showa emperor of the world's oldest monarchy. According to Japanese tradition, the emperor was not only Japan's ruler but also a god in human guise; his people were not even allowed to look upon him. On the other hand, Hirohito grew up during a period when Western standards, especially those of the United States, were in vogue. Emerging democratic political parties and cooperation with the West were the trend. As a student, Hirohito had three busts in his room: Charles Darwin, Abraham Lincoln, and Napoleon. Both Hirohito himself and the Japanese people were torn between tradition and modernization. He became the first crown prince to travel abroad when he visited Europe in 1921.

The great unresolved question about Hirohito is whether he might have used his godlike authority to suppress the influence of the Japanese military leading up to World War II. The Great Depression and the emergence of the Chinese Nationalist Party played into the hands of the militarists. After the assassination of the Japanese prime minister in 1931 and a failed major coup d'etat by young officers in early 1936, the military dominated the government until the end of the war. The militarists tried to resolve the tension between modernization and tradition by idealizing a warrior past. The policies held by the Japanese military eventually led Japan into the Sino-Japanese War and World War II. During World War II Hirohito formed alliances with Nazi Germany and Fascist Italy, resulting in the Rome-Berlin-Tokyo Axis.

After the war many believed that Hirohito had masterminded the Japanese war effort, while others claimed he was simply a powerless figurehead.

Some critics find Hirohito complicit in the brutalities committed by the Japanese army, yet the equivalent situation, to at least a degree, was Pope Pius XII's accommodation to fascism during World War II in order to preserve the Roman Catholic Church. Both the pope and Hirohito faced moral dilemmas and appear to have opted for the preservation of their historical institutions. Hirohito's personal intervention was critical in the decision for Japan to surrender in August 1945. General DOUGLAS MACARTHUR and General Tojo Hideki absolved the emperor of personal responsibility for the war and its atrocities in return for Hirohito's public renouncement of his divinity and willingness to accept a reduced status as Japan's constitutional monarch. He died in Tokyo on January 7, 1989.

Hitler, Adolf
(1889–1945) *German chancellor*

Both of Adolf Hitler's parents were illegitimate, but his authoritarian father managed to advance in society to become a customs official. His peasant mother, a much-younger third wife, was over-indulgent with her only child, born on April 20, 1889, in Braunau Inn, Austria. In the five years between his father's death in 1903 and his mother's in 1908, the teenage Hitler dropped out of school and drifted into a vagrant's life in Vienna, choosing not to receive the state's orphan benefits to which he was entitled. Cut loose from parental and school ties, he twice failed to gain entrance to the Vienna Fine Arts Academy, where he might have received training in art or architecture.

Hitler's physical, social, and intellectual marginality, the mental condition of feeling like an outsider, resolved initially when he volunteered for the German army in 1914 at the outset of World War I. Driven by his desire to belong, the Austrian-born Hitler would become more German than even native Germans. He first proved this through his service as a dispatch runner in a Bavarian infantry regiment. Twice wounded, he was evacuated to a military hospital near Berlin. Despite his low rank, he was awarded the Iron Cross, Second Class in 1914. The war afforded him his first success, and the experience made a lasting impression. Even more remarkable, he was awarded the Iron Cross, First Class four years later, an exceptional honor for a mere corporal.

From 1916 to 1918, Hitler was in a military hospital recovering from temporary blindness caused by a mustard-gas attack. It was there that he learned of Germany's defeat in World War I. He vowed immediately that he would become a politician and rescue Germany from Jews and Bolsheviks, the groups he blamed for Germany's defeat.

In summer 1919, while still serving in the army, Hitler was sent to investigate and report on political groups in Munich. One of them, a minor right-wing nationalistic party called the Germany Workers' Party, invited him to join. He found his political voice and quickly demonstrated both his oratorical and his organizational skills. In 1920, the party was renamed the National Socialist German Workers Party (Nazis), and Hitler became chairman. He quickly began using the then-new electrical loudspeaker as well as radio broadcasts, which allowed him to transmit his voice nationally, to spread his call for racial nationalism, the need for more territory, and an anti-Semitic and antidemocratic government.

Overestimating his early appeal, Hitler led the failed November 1923 Beer Hall Putsch to take over Bavaria and then marched on toward the capital, following the example of BENITO MUSSOLINI in Italy. Sixteen Nazis were killed, and Hitler was arrested and sentenced to a five-year imprisonment, but he served only nine months. The ensuing five years were not favorable to the Nazis since the economy had recovered, but the mission-driven Hitler wrote his major work, *Mein Kampf* ("my struggle" or "my battle"). Published in two volumes in

1925 and 1926, the book was a political manifesto that espoused German self-sufficiency, the suppression of trade unions, and the suppression of Jews.

Although the Nazis held only 12 of the 491 seats in the Reichstag (the German parliament) by 1928, Hitler led a revolution in Germany after the worldwide depression hit industrialized Germany especially hard, putting nearly a third of the nation out of work. In 1932, Hitler acquired German citizenship and ran for president. The Nazi Party had become the largest in the Reichstag, and he was appointed chancellor of Germany on January 30, 1933. On March 5 that year, in the last of the quasi-free elections, the Nazis achieved a 44.5 percent plurality of the vote. Lower-middle-class and middle-class voters had turned to Hitler, while the working class supported the communists. Hitler had particular appeal to a generation that had grown up without traditional parental influence because of fathers absent due to World War I military service—many of whom never came home—and mothers who replaced them in the factory. Hitler became a successful surrogate father figure with whom this generation could identify, and he offered a national face-saving explanation for Germany's military defeat.

Germany had been among Europe's last nations to unify, and its only experience with parliamentary democracy was short-lived—the Weimar Republic (1919–33). Many in Germany and abroad, including a number of FDR's critics at home, saw in Hitler and Nazism the basis for a new model of government as Hitler's Third Reich achieved results faster than the New Deal. Unemployment disappeared, the economy expanded, wages increased, and consumer goods appeared. Deficit spending allowed industrial expansion; public-works projects and rearmament were products of a mixed economy. Most Germans felt their pride and self-esteem return under their dynamic new leader. His programs were manifested in the *Autobahnen* (highways), construction of new public buildings, and workers' housing projects. The Berlin Olympics of 1936 put these impressive achievements and Germany in the international spotlight.

Yet like many dictators, Hitler tended to overextend himself—in his case, by trying to prove to native Germans that he was even more German than they were. Hitler's desire for more power escalated while satisfaction with their improved lives subdued Germans into submission, and they overlooked the concentration camps at home and extermination camps abroad where millions were executed, many in gas chambers. After his February 1938 takeover of Austria was followed by grabbing Czechoslovakia, his hubris led him to begin World War II through an unprovoked attack against Poland on September 1, 1939, followed by an assault on the Soviet Union in June 1941 and the declaration of war against the United States on December 11 that same year.

Franklin Roosevelt loathed both fascism and Adolf Hitler as the wave of the future. He condemned Hitler's totalitarian behavior, militarism, racism, and the glorification of the Nazi regime. On the other hand, Hitler resented America's wealth, and its cultural, racial, ethnic, and religious diversity. He sneered at FDR's infirmity. Hitler's grandiose thousand-year Reich (or empire) ended after a dozen years with his suicide in Berlin on April 30, 1945.

Hoover, Herbert Clark
(1874–1964) *president of the United States*

Neither fate nor history nor politics was particularly kind to the Oval Office occupant who preceded Franklin Roosevelt. Born August 10, 1874, in West Branch, Iowa, Herbert Hoover was the son of farmers who died before he was nine years old. He lived with relatives in Iowa and Oregon, and thanks to a prosperous uncle in the latter state, he studied mining engineering at the new Stanford University in California and graduated in its first class in 1895. During the next two decades, he traveled abroad as a mining engineer and businessman, becoming a millionaire by age 40.

World War I made Hoover famous. As a son of the Midwest, he had always admired Abraham Lincoln, as did Woodrow Wilson, who idealized the 16th president. Hoover had grown up in a home where a sketch of Lincoln that originally belonged to his grandfather was displayed; the same sketch hung in the White House during his presidency, the period during which Lincoln became a prominent influence on his life. Like Lincoln and Wilson, Hoover believed in "positive government," the notion that government could intervene when people needed help. Yet he believed more in volunteerism than what he labeled "the dole"—government relief—because he feared that taking government aid would become a habit. Wilson made Hoover head of the Commission for the Relief in Belgium. From 1917 to 1919 Hoover served as the president's U.S. food administrator, supervising voluntary rationing, and then was director general of the American Relief Administration in Europe from 1919 to 1920. His former reputation as "the Great Engineer" from developing mines in China, Burma, Australia, and Russia was transformed by his administrative skill into an international reputation as the "Great Humanitarian." Even FDR was impressed.

Hoover finally joined the Republican Party after both parties made overtures to him to run for the presidency in 1920. However, rather than seek the presidency, he opted for another administration capacity, serving as secretary of commerce for the duration of both the Warren Harding and Calvin Coolidge administrations. His scientific training made him almost apolitical, like many of the political progressives of the 1920s who wanted to remove the political dimensions from government. They favored "good government," which meant steering away from the large, corrupt Democratic urban machines dominant at the time. In keeping with his philosophy, he made the Commerce Department important, in part, by advocating a scientific approach to business cycles, industrial standards, and government regulation of the emerging radio and aviation industries. With his scientific background, the empirical approach to government seemed reasonable to him.

After Calvin Coolidge decided against seeking a second term, Hoover ran for his first elective office as the Republican presidential candidate. He won a landslide electoral victory in 1928, carrying with him a huge Republican majority in Congress. Initially it appeared he would bring an active scientific approach to the presidency, as he had done in mining, business, and administration. He established the Research Committee on Social Trends, which brought together social scientists and the recently established voluntary organizations, the National Institute of Public Administration

Shown in this photo is a Hooverville outside Seattle, Washington. *(Private Collection)*

and the Social Science Research Council. Hoover wanted to abolish poverty while promoting peace and prosperity.

Fate intervened after the Wall Street crash of 1929 and the onset of the Great Depression. The crisis magnified Hoover's inflexible beliefs and lifelong inability to admit mistakes. Initially he thought the economic crisis was merely an American recession, so he tried to increase volunteerism, held educational conferences, and established commissions. After his cooperative approach proved ineffective in restoring the economy, he became convinced that the source of the crisis was abroad. He fought congressional efforts to provide direct relief for the increasing millions of unemployed Americans. After he used General DOUGLAS MACARTHUR in July 1932 to drive the so-called Bonus Expeditionary Force of unemployed ex-servicemen from the nation's capital, he became the popular scapegoat for the Great Depression, which became "Hoover's Depression." His resounding defeat by FDR in 1932 branded him with a loser's image across the nation.

After keeping his silence for two years, Hoover published *The Challenge of Liberty* (1934), a book that reiterated his previous policies. From the next year, he became a major critic of the New Deal. Although he hoped for the Republican nominations in 1936 and 1940, his party turned to others. Nevertheless, both Franklin and ELEANOR ROOSEVELT wanted Hoover to head relief efforts abroad during World War II because of his demonstrated abilities. Hoover not only turned down the offer, he refused even to visit the White House during the entire Roosevelt administration. Like the only other engineer to occupy the White House in the 20th century, Jimmy Carter, Hoover tended to think that leadership was limited to a mastery of facts applied to public policy. Their successors proved them mistaken.

Hoover died on October 20, 1964, in New York City.

Hoover, J. Edgar
(1895–1972) *FBI director*

Born on New Year's Day 1895, John Edgar Hoover was the son of a Washington, D.C., government printer and his wife. He was reared in a middle-class neighborhood behind the Library of Congress and attended local public schools. He worked his way through the National University of Law School as a clerk at the Library of Congress. He graduated in 1916 and the next year was hired by the Alien Enemy Bureau in the Department of Justice. His work came to the attention of Woodrow Wilson's attorney general, A. Mitchell Palmer. Following the bombing of his home by radicals in retaliation for his violations of civil liberties, Palmer named Hoover to head the Radical Division. Hoover was the person in charge of the infamous Palmer raids in November 1919 and January 1920 that cracked down on alien radicals.

In 1921, Hoover was named assistant director of the Bureau of Investigation. As a result of the Teapot Dome scandals during the Warren Harding presidency, the bureau was reorganized in 1924, and Attorney General HARLAN FISKE STONE appointed Hoover as director of the bureau. Over the ensuing decade, Hoover built the bureau's reputation for professionalism through use of scientific methodology in fingerprint identification, a modern crime laboratory, and a system to analyze national crime statistics. In 1935, it was renamed the Federal Bureau of Investigation (FBI).

Hoover was adept at adjusting to new presidents, and when Franklin Roosevelt was elected, he acceded to the request of FDR's attorney general, HOMER CUMMINGS, and transformed the image of G-men (government men) into good-guy national heroes fighting celebrity gangsters and bank robbers. During the early days of Nazi Germany, FDR covertly put Hoover back into the business of political surveillance, and consequently several leaders of the American Nazi movement were put on trial. After World War II broke out abroad, FDR put Hoover in charge of domestic counterintelligence.

During the war, Hoover proved his skill at public relations to promote further the FBI's image as well as its budget, and he cooperated with authors and Hollywood producers who worked on projects dealing with the FBI. To his credit, Hoover opposed the government's internment of Japanese Americans, and he used groups like the American Legion as a network under the FBI's supervision to watch for espionage, in part to prevent the hysteria that had manifested during World War I.

Hoover became increasingly partisan during the postwar period and aligned himself with anticommunist zealots. An example of a successful bureaucratic entrepreneur, he increasingly came to symbolize governmental abuse of authority. Still, he headed the FBI until his death on May 2, 1972, in Washington, D.C.

Hopkins, Harry Lloyd
(1890–1946) *federal administrator, secretary of commerce, special assistant to the president*

Harry Hopkins, the son of a Midwest salesman, was born on May 19, 1890, in Sioux City, Iowa, into a family of modest means that moved frequently. In 1912, he graduated from progressive Grinnell College, where he had been an average academic student but a natural leader and great basketball player. A believer in the Social Gospel, expressing one's faith by providing social services to the less fortunate, Hopkins became a social worker on New York City's Lower East Side, where he learned firsthand about abject poverty amid great wealth. During his two decades there, he earned a streetwise reputation for his swearing as well as for his effective and energetic problem-solving

President Roosevelt and Harry Hopkins in the backseat of an automobile, 1938 *(Library of Congress)*

abilities. He could also inspire others with his optimistic confidence.

Hopkins's association with Franklin Roosevelt (then New York's governor) began in 1931 when he was made director of the New York Temporary Emergency Relief Administration, the nation's first executive agency to deal with unemployment during the Great Depression. In May 1933, FDR brought him to Washington, D.C., to direct federal relief. Hopkins came to believe that employment should be a right of American citizenship. When he headed the Works Progress Administration (WPA) from 1935 to 1938, he came in conflict with Secretary of the Interior HAROLD ICKES, who favored large construction projects supervised from Washington; Hopkins favored smaller projects involving more workers with greater local initiative. After several months, FDR sided with Hopkins. Nonetheless, most of the WPA involved construction projects, although it also allowed for grassroots art and music programs. Both FDR's secretary, LOUIS HOWE, and First Lady ELEANOR ROOSEVELT supported all these projects, which provided relief labor. Hopkins eventually employed more workers and spent more funds than probably any other person in American history, becoming known as the U.S. "minister of relief." He managed this without financial scandal or even caring about the partisan affiliation of those employed.

Hopkins's administrative skill led FDR to consider him as his successor in the Oval Office following the landslide victory of 1936, but personal tragedies struck Hopkins in the form of his wife's death in 1937 and his own stomach cancer. Health doomed not only his presidential aspirations but also his December 1938 appointment as secretary of commerce, the cabinet position that HERBERT HOOVER had used as a springboard to the presidency. After managing FDR's unprecedented third-term nomination at the 1940 Democratic National Convention, Hopkins resigned from the administration in August that year.

It was a brief hiatus. FDR named Hopkins as special assistant to the president—he served from 1941 to 1945—and moved him into the White House to live. He served as the first de facto national security adviser and became FDR's closest confidant during World War II. Despite his serious health problems, Hopkins acted as FDR's personal emissary to Great Britain and the Soviet Union, negotiating with WINSTON CHURCHILL and JOSEPH STALIN. He also became allies with Army Chief of Staff GEORGE C. MARSHALL; EDWARD STETTINIUS, who headed the lend-lease program before becoming secretary of state; AVERELL HARRIMAN, the lend-lease representative in London who later became ambassador to the Soviet Union; and CHARLES BOHLEN, who served as a liaison between the White House and the State Department. Hopkins's service was another example of the "passionate anonyms" that LOUIS BROWNLOW had advocated to work for the chief executive.

Less than a year after FDR's death, Hopkins died in New York City on January 29, 1946.

Horner, Henry
(1879–1940) *Illinois governor*

Born November 30, 1879, in Chicago, Illinois, Henry Horner went on to lead his native state during the Great Depression. Elected in 1932, he became the first Democratic governor of Illinois since World War I and was the first Jewish governor in its history. Confronting the Great Depression, which caused nearly half of Chicago's workers to be unemployed, he brought together politicians and academics to deal with the situation. In addition to facing massive economic problems when he entered office, Horner lost his friend and political ally, Chicago mayor Anton J. Cermak, who was accidentally killed in an assassination attempt on President-elect Franklin Roosevelt. Cermak's replacement, EDWARD KELLY, tried to wrest control of state politics from Horner. Horner fought back in an urban-rural, Cook County-versus-the-rest-of-the-state struggle that took its toll on the bachelor governor's health. Ironically, he was fighting for New Deal government at the same time New Dealers supported his major opponent.

Horner did his best to confront responsibly the dual economic and political crises facing him. He convinced the Illinois General Assembly to approve an unpopular two-cent sales tax and also persuaded a reluctant legislature to approve a $30 million bond to supplement money from the Federal Emergency Relief Administration. Moreover, he kept the legislature in session to pass a "Little New Deal" for the state, including measures to prevent farm foreclosures, provide public school funds, and implement the New Deal's National Recovery Administration's industrial codes.

Though Horner was a champion of the New Deal, the Roosevelt administration worked against him. Secretary of the Interior HAROLD ICKES understood that the Chicago machine used nondemocratic methods, but presidential adviser HARRY HOPKINS and other New Dealers were more interested in the dependable machine's votes from Chicago and Cook County. FDR sided with Hopkins and pulled the rug from under the governor in downstate Springfield by channeling federal patronage through Kelly's political machine. In addition, FDR backed the machine's candidate against Horner in the 1936 gubernatorial primary. The feisty governor fought back to win the primary and in the election carried every county in Illinois, except Cook County. Unfortunately, his choice for a running mate lost the lieutenant governor bid in the primary. Nonetheless, Horner and John Stelle, his unwelcome partner, carried the state in the November general election, winning 53.1 percent of the vote.

Like Abraham Lincoln, whose memorabilia he collected, Horner's executive days were plagued with ongoing political strife, in addition to labor mine violence and serious flooding in lower Illinois. The stress on him was enormous, and two days before the 1940 primary election, he suffered a stroke. Despite his health issues, Horner battled his opposition to a stalemate until his death on October 6, 1940, a few months before his second term would have expired.

Howe, Louis McHenry
(1871–1936) *secretary to the president*

The only child of a struggling Indianapolis, Indiana, businessman and his wife, Louis Howe was born on January 14, 1871. His family moved to Saratoga Springs, New York, when he was five years old. Poor health and poor finances prevented him from attending college, and he instead became a newspaper reporter. His major scoop was breaking the story of THEODORE ROOSEVELT's hasty travel adventure from Lake of the Clouds, New York,

to Buffalo after William McKinley's assassination in 1901. Five years later, he began covering state politics for the New York *Herald*. Physically unattractive—short and wiry, with a homely face scarred since childhood—Howe became fascinated with power. As he covered FDR in the New York State Senate in 1911, the characteristically gruff and rumpled reporter quickly saw potential in the man with a famous name, handsome appearance, and charismatic personality. After FDR caught typhoid the next year during his reelection campaign, Howe filled in as his campaign manager. FDR won not only reelection but also a political partner until Howe's death.

Following FDR's appointment as assistant secretary of the navy in 1913 during the Woodrow Wilson administration, he made Howe his chief of staff. The former reporter drafted FDR's speeches and took care of administrative details in the Washington, D.C., office while also handling federal patronage in New York and acting as his boss's agent to the state party. In 1920, he served as campaign manager for FDR's unsuccessful Democratic vice-presidential campaign. When FDR contracted polio in 1921, Howe teamed with ELEANOR ROOSEVELT to keep FDR's political career alive. He wrote articles with FDR's byline, issued press releases, and brokered a truce between FDR and Tammany Hall so that FDR could dramatically appear at the 1924 Democratic convention to nominate AL SMITH for president. Roosevelt was back in the political arena. In 1928, Howe served as FDR's campaign manager in his successful run for the New York governorship. He then worked with New York Democratic Committee chairman JAMES FARLEY to help FDR win the 1932 Democratic nomination for president as well as the subsequent presidential election.

Howe was named secretary to the president in 1933, and he held that post until his death. In the White House, the Roosevelts put

Howe in the Lincoln bedroom, where he could be accessible to both of them without having to deal with the public. He helped Eleanor Roosevelt to develop an unprecedented approach as First Lady, taking her to visit a group of World War I "bonus army" veterans, who were seeking a pension. Her obvious concern for them dissipated their anger and they sang old war songs. While Howe privately told the veterans that there would be jobs through the new Civilian Conservation Corps, the oft-quoted denouement was "Hoover sent the Army, Roosevelt sent his wife," in reference to the fact that General DOUGLAS MACARTHUR, acting on then-president HERBERT HOOVER's orders, had forcibly evicted a much larger group of them from Washington, D.C., on July 28, 1932.

Howe's power waned after he was actually inside the White House, partly due to his ill health and also because President Roosevelt had assembled new advisers who were much more liberal. After Howe's death on April 18, 1936, the Roosevelts gave him a state funeral in the East Room of the White House. He had helped FDR achieve the presidency and provided a political education for Eleanor Roosevelt that enabled her to set a new standard for First Ladies.

Hughes, Charles Evans
(1862–1948) U.S. Supreme Court chief justice

Charles Evans Hughes was born April 11, 1862, in Glens Falls, New York, the only child of an itinerant preacher and his wife. Hughes was particularly influenced by his Baptist father, who had converted from Methodism to placate his wife's Welsh immigrant parents and moved his family several times before settling in New York City. Hughes's parents also had a strong influence on his education, home-schooling him until he was a teenager. Hughes

originally planned to follow his father's example, and he entered Madison College (now Colgate University) in Hamilton, New York, to study for the ministry, but after two years he transferred to the larger and more cosmopolitan Brown University in Providence, Rhode Island. There he compiled a good social and academic record and developed an interest in the law.

After graduating in 1881, Hughes taught for a year at a private school to earn money for law school while reading law in his spare time. He entered Columbia Law School the next fall and graduated with highest honors in 1884. He then joined a prestigious New York City law firm and through hard work became a partner in the reorganized firm in 1887. The following year, he married Antoinette Carter, the daughter of one of his partners. It was a storybook marriage that resulted in three daughters and one son, Charles Evans Hughes, Jr., who became the U.S. solicitor general in 1929–30.

Hughes had a strong professional work ethic that repeatedly drove him to near exhaustion. For that reason, he left private practice in 1891 to teach law at Cornell University. After two years, he had regained his health and rejoined his old law firm, where the pay was much better than law school. He first gained national recognition as special counsel for two New York legislative committees investigating price gouging by gas, electrical, and life-insurance companies. His work led to a variety of reforms.

Never a glad-hander politician, the stern-looking Hughes entered politics through the orchestration of President THEODORE ROOSEVELT, who saw him as a fellow progressive Republican. As candidate for the New York governorship in 1906, Hughes narrowly defeated his Democratic opponent, newspaper mogul WILLIAM RANDOLPH HEARST. As a progressive, he distrusted politicians, and like many of them he wanted to take politics out of public business. He wanted good, clean government where reason (logic, efficiency, and fairness) trumped deal-making. In 1908, William Howard Taft, who also hated "politics," asked Hughes to be his vice-presidential running mate. Hughes declined in favor of running successfully for reelection as governor. President Theodore Roosevelt was subjected to Hughes's independence after his friendly efforts to referee a fight to oust Hughes's superintendent of insurance was rebuffed by the governor. It caused a permanent rift between them.

In 1910, President Taft made Hughes a second offer: to become an associate justice on the U.S. Supreme Court. Hughes accepted and was easily confirmed in early May. After two months, Chief Justice Melville Fuller died, and many expected Taft would elevate Hughes to the position, not knowing that Taft wanted to name someone older and in bad health so he himself could have a shot at becoming chief justice in the future. Taft settled on Associate Justice Edward D. White from Louisiana to be chief justice, and his plan worked perfectly, for Taft became White's replacement a decade later. It may have been serendipitous for Hughes and the nation that Taft did not elevate him to chief justice and put White into the position instead, since the ever-courteous gentleman from the Deep South introduced a new custom—handshakes among the justices—at a time when divisiveness was so prevalent that Oliver Wendell Holmes, Jr., referred to his brethren as "nine scorpions in a bottle." White's calming effect on the Court was so effective that Hughes would later hang a portrait of him over his fireplace at home; it is likely that White was Hughes's model when he later became chief justice.

As an associate justice, Hughes wrote the majority decision in the so-called Shreveport Rate Case (1914), which was fraught with irony because Louisianans, who had opted for seces-

sion during the Civil War and would later fight federal civil-rights intervention, asked for federal intervention to regulate unequal railroad rates imposed by neighboring Texas. The Court's decision prevented the abuse by strengthening the power of the Interstate Commerce Commission (ICC).

Hughes's service on the bench had allowed him to sit out the split between Roosevelt and Taft in the 1912 election that permitted Democrat Woodrow Wilson to gain the presidency. In 1916, Hughes reluctantly accepted the Republican Party's nomination, although he had not sought it, as its moderately progressive presidential candidate to heal the division between the conservative and progressive wings of the party. The only sitting justice ever to be nominated for president, he lost by a mere 13-vote margin in the electoral college.

Out of a job, Hughes was appointed secretary of state in March 1921 and retained that position after Calvin Coolidge succeeded to the presidency in 1923. He proved to be a gifted international diplomat who adapted his political and judicial views to the world that he wanted governed by reason that could be incorporated over time into the customs and laws of nations. Once again experiencing exhaustion from his hard work, Hughes returned to private legal practice while still serving in a part-time position as head of the U.S. delegation to the Sixth Pan-American Conference in 1928 and as a judge on the Permanent Court of International Justice.

On February 3, 1930, President HERBERT HOOVER nominated Hughes to be chief justice of the U.S. Supreme Court. Unlike his confirmation 20 years before, though, and to his chagrin, Hughes faced opposition from many progressives who believed he was too tied to corporate interests. Nonetheless, he was confirmed 10 days later and at age 67 became the oldest man ever confirmed to the post. Despite his age, he brought to the position his trademark work ethic, diplomacy, and independence. Usually he occupied the golden mean between the liberal and conservative wings on the court while trying to limit hostilities between them.

Both Hughes and Justice OWEN ROBERTS, also at the center of the ideological wings on the bench, sided with the conservatives in declaring New Deal legislation unconstitutional until 1936. They began to modify their stance during the private conference meetings of the justices by the end of that year, unbeknownst to Franklin Roosevelt, who, after his landslide election in 1936, made his first major political blunder in trying to outmaneuver the Court. Without seeking advice from his regular staff or Congress, Roosevelt proposed increasing the number of justices on the Court by six if the sitting justices over age 70 did not retire. This obvious manipulative ploy encountered considerable public and congressional opposition. Still, it might have gained legislative approval if Chief Justice Hughes had not taken the unusual step of writing a letter to the Senate Judiciary Committee, which undermined FDR's obviously false assertion that the current justices were unable to handle their caseload. Hughes's letter handed a defeat to yet another Roosevelt in the Oval Office who had been trying to interject unwelcome politics into his world.

It is often said that FDR lost the Supreme Court–packing battle but won the war. It is more accurate to say that he had won it already in private judicial conference meetings but did not know that he had. It is also accurate to say that his scheme produced a new coalition of conservative Democrats from the South and Republicans that could defeat him. It was primarily World War II that helped him to overcome the domestic battle that Hughes had won. Moreover, in terms of the rankings of scholars, only Hughes has achieved the greatness rating in all three of the political positions

that he held: governor, secretary of state, and Supreme Court justice. He truly was a competitor equal to FDR, whom he not only bested in the very political game that he disdained but also outlived. Hughes died on August 27, 1948, on Cape Cod, Massachusetts.

Hull, Cordell
(1871–1955) *secretary of state*

Born in Overton County (now Pickett), Tennessee, on October 2, 1871, Cordell Hull was part of a middle-class Baptist family. He was educated in local schools until he moved to Ohio for college. In 1893, he was elected to the state legislature, but like many other southern politicians, his term was interrupted by his military service. Hull served as a captain in the brief Spanish-American War (1898). In 1891 he attended Cumberland Law School for a year and then practiced law until 1903, when he was appointed to the Fifth Tennessee Judicial Circuit, a position he held until 1907.

Like many others, Hull used law as his path to politics. By 1906, he was prepared for the national political arena. A towering border-state political presence, the six-foot Hull won a seat in the U.S. House of Representatives that year on the traditional southern platform of preaching against the traditional protective tariffs, which he argued were contrary to the interest of his farmer constituents. In place of the protective tariff, he favored an income tax, and in 1913 he authored the first income-tax statute. It would become a constitutional amendment in 1917 during the Woodrow Wilson administration. Hull became a supporter of the southern-born president's policies, particularly Wilson's internationalist goals. Although he was never a dynamic speaker, Hull's appearance and his political style as a compromiser made him a lifelong popular leader in Congress. Unfortunately, in the short term, his loyalty to Wilson cost him his congressional office during the backlash against the administration in the 1920 Warren Harding electoral landslide. Hull bided his time as chairman of the Democratic National Committee until he was reelected to his former congressional seat in 1922. In 1930, he was elected to the U.S. Senate.

Hull's Wilsonianism first brought him into contact with FDR, who had supported his failed 1928 vice-presidential bid. In return, Hull made an early announcement in 1932 in support of FDR's presidential bid. Recognizing that he needed support from the southern wing of the Democratic Party, FDR appointed Hull as secretary of state, even though Hull lacked foreign-affairs experience. His physical appearance—white hair, tall height, and three-piece suits—added the diplomatic patina he needed to look the part, although FDR himself expected to dominate the role. As a subordinate

Cordell Hull *(Library of Congress)*

caught in that position, it was frustrating for Hull, especially since he tended to be more conservative than the New Dealers. However, he needed FDR to accomplish his goals just as FDR needed Hull's influence in Congress. In private, the president would often imitate Hull's slight lisp.

In 1934, in large part because of Hull's persistence, Congress passed the Reciprocal Trade Agreements, a cornerstone of New Deal foreign policy. This began the tradition of the most-favored-nation trading policy under which presidents were allowed to negotiate tariff agreements. Hull became the architect of free trade and the post–World War II trading pacts, such as the General Agreement on Tariffs and Trade (GATT). He believed that economic cooperation promoted peaceful relations among nations.

Hull was also a key figure and principal spokesman of the New Deal's approach to Latin American affairs. He supported FDR's Good Neighbor policy, which discouraged the earlier William McKinley–THEODORE ROOSEVELT–Woodrow Wilson policy of unilateral U.S. intervention in Latin American nations. The Good Neighbor policy instead promoted inter-American cooperation, which is still viewed today by Latin Americans as the high mark in U.S.–Latin American relations. FDR and Hull agreed to withdraw troops from Central American nations and to disavow the Platt Amendment, which had made a mockery of Cuba's sovereignty.

As a result of these policies, Hull became one of the most popular Democrats in the United States, and he traveled across the country campaigning for FDR's reelection in 1936. The White House staff, however, and especially HARRY HOPKINS, saw Hull as a rival to FDR, so despite the urgings of some Democratic Party leaders, he was denied a vice-presidential bid. Nonetheless, he helped to ease U.S. isolationism, found ways to circumvent the congressional neutrality acts, and worked for U.S. military aid to Great Britain and other nations fighting the Axis powers. He cooperated with FDR in providing old destroyers to the British through the Lend-Lease Act and denounced Nazi and imperial Japanese aggression in Europe and Asia.

Although he worked to achieve FDR's goals, Hull had to fight bureaucratic battles, primarily over FDR's desire to control the State Department and foreign policy through his own lieutenants. FDR's foreign trade adviser, GEORGE PEEK, was forced to resign, just as RAYMOND MOLEY resigned as assistant secretary of state after FDR tried to run foreign policy by circumventing his secretary of state. Hull successfully blocked Undersecretary of State SUMNER WELLES, Vice President HENRY WALLACE, and Secretary of the Treasury HENRY MORGENTHAU, JR., from interfering in what Welles considered his own turf. Most of these controversies involved FDR's inclination to want to act as his own secretary of state, which reflected his style of not relying on anyone except himself.

As a Wilsonian liberal internationalist, Hull backed the creation of a United Nations organization. He supported the Dumbarton Oaks conference in Washington, D.C., on August 21, 1944, by delivering an opening address there. Even after he left the State Department in late 1944, he accepted the honorary title of senior delegate to the UN conference in San Francisco in mid-1945. Later that year, he won the Nobel Peace Prize for his work toward that end. Some credit him as the father of the United Nations, though FDR deserves to share that honor.

Working for someone who preferred to be his own secretary of state took its toll on Hull. He endured many of the interferences because he wanted to run for the presidency in 1940, until FDR decided to break the two-term tradition. When Hull was finally forced to resign because of his tuberculosis and other medical complications, FDR at first refused the resignation and asked him to be his running mate in 1944. Hull declined but waited until the November election before stepping down as secretary of state. He remained a loyal southerner until his death on July 23, 1955, in Washington, D.C.

I

Ickes, Harold Leclair
(1874–1952) *secretary of the interior, Public Works Administration, director*

Born on March 15, 1874, in Hollidaysburg, Pennsylvania, Harold Ickes was the son of a mother who died while he was a teenager and an alcoholic father who abandoned him. He was sent to live with relatives in Chicago, where he graduated from high school in 1892 as senior class president and valedictorian. Insecure and sensitive to criticism, he was a tireless worker and a champion of minorities. In 1896, he graduated from the University of Chicago and began working as a local newspaper reporter, which taught him about urban political corruption. But he was also exposed to the social-reform movement led by political scientist CHARLES E. MERRIAM, Jane Addams of Hull House, and others. He was among the later New Deal participants influenced by the Social Gospel movement of service to one's community.

Ickes's entry into the political world grew from his work and volunteerism in settlement houses. In 1903, he was hired to manage the campaign of an unsuccessful Republican mayoral candidate. The next year, he returned to the University of Chicago for his law degree, which was awarded in 1907. He was soon practicing law and handling civil liberties cases pro bono.

Armed with journalistic, political, and legal skills, the independent Republican Ickes supported Charles Merriam in his 1911 campaign for mayor on a platform of clean and good government. In 1912, though, he joined THEODORE ROOSEVELT's unsuccessful Bull Moose third-party candidacy to regain the White House. Ickes served as the party's Cook County campaign manager and delivered the vote for Roosevelt. He remained the leader of the Progressive Party in Illinois until 1916, when he backed Supreme Court justice CHARLES EVANS HUGHES for president. During World War I, Ickes served overseas with the YMCA. In the 1920s, he joined the law firm of DONALD RICHBERG, and he fought conservative Republicans who had achieved political power both in Chicago and Washington, D.C. He had openly endorsed the 1920 Democratic Party ticket of James Cox as president and Franklin Roosevelt as vice president. By the end of the decade, he had developed a reputation for conservation and good-government reform in the mold of Teddy Roosevelt.

Ickes's association with FDR began in early 1932 when he was asked to head a Western Republican Committee for Roosevelt. After he lobbied for it, the progressive Republican Ickes

Secretary of the Interior Harold Ickes handing the first constitution issued under the Indian Reorganization Act to delegates of the Confederated Tribes of the Flathead Indian Reservation *(Library of Congress)*

was named to head the Interior Department in FDR's first cabinet. During his 13-year reign in that position, he set an unequaled standard, partly by enlarging his turf and partly by working harder than anyone else. He advocated conservation and national planning to develop natural resources as well as controls on private power companies. He also desegregated public facilities in the department and hired Robert Weaver, an African American, as an adviser.

In June 1933 Ickes's work paid off after FDR gave him a second, simultaneous job as director of the Public Works Administration (PWA), which spent $5–6 billion during the six-

year program on 19,000 public works projects in one of the first major unemployment programs of the New Deal. He lived up to his reputation for integrity. Meticulous in dispensing funds for this agency, which had been created by the National Industrial Recovery Act of 1933, Ickes proved indefatigable and incorruptible. He also made sure that African Americans received a fair share of construction jobs.

Ickes's lifelong insecurities manifested themselves in conflicts with Vice President HENRY WALLACE, presidential confidant HARRY HOPKINS, and even First Lady ELEANOR ROOSEVELT. These often grew out of FDR's characteristic vagueness in administrative matters. Ickes needed constant reassurance from FDR, who gave it with a certain bemusement, recognizing his talent, loyalty, and insecurities. His pugnacious personality also encouraged FDR to undertake the unsuccessful so-called purge of 1938 against conservative Democrats in Congress.

In 1939, Ickes helped Eleanor Roosevelt arrange MARIAN ANDERSON's Easter Sunday concert at the Lincoln Memorial and personally introduced the singer to the audience. He was the first person in the administration to speak out in favor of FDR's third term and campaigned for him in each election, serving as a colorful stump speaker. Despite his loyalty to FDR, he denounced the internment of Japanese-American citizens during World War II.

Ickes resigned from the cabinet after a dispute with President HARRY S. TRUMAN. Thereafter he wrote a political column for the *New Republic* until he died on February 3, 1952, in Washington, D.C.

Jackson, Robert Houghwout

(1892–1954) *solicitor general, attorney general, U.S. Supreme Court justice*

Born on February 13, 1892, in Spring Creek, Pennsylvania, Robert Jackson was the son of a small businessman. The family moved to western New York near Jamestown, where Jackson was raised. After his high school graduation, he clerked in the law office of his cousin, who was a prominent Democratic activist in Jamestown. After attending Albany Law School for a year, Jackson began legal practice in Jamestown, styling himself as a "country lawyer" and becoming one of the leading trial lawyers in western New York during his 20-year practice. He practiced very briefly in Buffalo but found the city too large.

Jackson first attracted the attention of Roosevelt, then the New York governor, when he was serving on a state commission investigating New York's judicial system. He worked in FDR's 1932 presidential campaign and reluctantly left Jamestown for Washington, D.C., where he served in several legal positions with the new administration. He led the government's investigation into income-tax evasion against former secretary of the Treasury ANDREW MELLON.

After Stanley Reed was elevated to the U.S. Supreme Court in March 1938, Jackson became one of the three highest-ranked members of the Justice Department. He was appointed solicitor general of the United States, the so-called 10th justice of the Supreme Court because the person who holds that office appears more often than any other lawyer before the high bench to represent the administration in cases. Jackson was so good at his job that Justice LOUIS BRANDEIS remarked that he deserved to be solicitor general for life. Yet his administration service led to conflicts in his personal life. FDR urged him to enter politics, but New York State Democratic Party leaders ignored his aspirations after he sought their backing in a bid for the governorship.

Jackson's loyalty to FDR was tested when he dutifully testified before Congress in support of the president's 1937 Supreme Court–packing scheme. He was better at law than politics, but FDR failed to name him when the next three openings occurred on the High Court. Instead, in 1940 the president named Jackson to succeed FRANK MURPHY as attorney general when Murphy was elevated to the Supreme Court. As attorney general, Jackson worked on the lend-lease deal involving the exchange of destroyers for military bases in Bermuda, Labrador, and other British possessions.

Jackson had been led to believe that he would be named to replace Chief Justice

CHARLES EVANS HUGHES when he retired in spring 1941, but FDR instead elevated Justice HARLAN FISK STONE to that position and made Jackson the associate justice's replacement. The problems arising from the rapid ascent of someone who was less educated about modern approaches to jurisprudence than WILLIAM O. DOUGLAS or HUGO BLACK, who had developed their own unique approaches, manifested soon after Jackson joined the High Court. Complicating his relationship with Douglas and Black was the fact that both harbored lingering presidential ambitions. During the postwar period, they would block Jackson from obtaining what he wanted most and thought his service merited: the chief justiceship.

Jackson was a master stylist who sprinkled his decisions with memorable phrases, but his civil-liberties record was erratic. Offered the chance to play to the crowds, the frustrated Jackson took leave from the Court to become the chief counsel for the United States in the prosecution of senior Nazi officials at Nuremberg, West Germany, in 1945–46. The results of the Nuremberg Trials were mixed for Jackson and the Court. His role in them ultimately prevented him from ever becoming chief justice. After the death of Chief Justice Stone on April 22, 1946, newspaper articles appeared that suggested HUGO BLACK's opposition to Jackson's elevation to chief justice. In response Jackson issued a public statement questioning Black's judicial propriety. President HARRY TRUMAN avoided the controversy by nominating his secretary of the Treasury, FRED M. VINSON, to succeed Stone. He died on October 9, 1954, in McLean, Virginia.

Johnson, Hiram Warren
(1866–1945) *U.S. senator*

Hiram Johnson, born September 2, 1866, and raised in Sacramento, California, was the son of a lawyer-politician who defended the interests of the Southern Pacific Railroad, California's most powerful corporation. He and a brother followed their father's career path. Johnson spent three years at the University of California at Berkeley and then dropped out in 1887 to study law in his father's office. He was admitted to the state bar the next year. Both Johnson and his brother initially practiced with their father and helped to run his political campaigns, but in 1897 the brothers opened their own law office and broke with their father's conservative politics. They moved their practice to San Francisco, and Hiram Johnson became a political rebel; his brother died an alcoholic in 1907.

Johnson's move into the electoral world grew from his work in the district attorney's office prosecuting graft, which earned him both publicity and the attention of California's Lincoln-Roosevelt League, an organization of progressive Republicans. With their support, he won the Republican nomination for governor in the state's first direct primary, having run on the single issue of removing the Southern Pacific Railroad from influence peddling in the state. A gifted orator, Johnson conducted an energetic and spirited campaign that landed him the governorship. He had the legislature's support to enact his reform agenda, including regulation of railroads and utility corporations; instituting a civil-service system; implementing the use of the initiative, referendum, and recall for voters; women's suffrage; labor reforms; conservation measures; and a variety of other measures that targeted partisan corruption in the political process.

An early supporter of THEODORE ROOSEVELT for the 1912 Republican presidential nomination, Johnson left the party after it refused to heed Roosevelt's primary wins. Johnson joined Roosevelt in forming the new Bull Moose Progressive Party and was made his running mate on the losing ticket. Although they placed ahead of William Howard Taft, the Roosevelt/Taft split among Republicans gave the election to Democrat Woodrow Wilson. Johnson subsequently gained popular support in 1913 by backing anti-Asian legislation that prevented Asian immigrants from owning property. In 1916, he returned to the Republican Party to run for the U.S. Senate after Roosevelt declined to run again as a Bull Moose. As CHARLES EVANS HUGHES lost California by fewer than 4,000 votes in his near presidential upset over Woodrow Wilson, Johnson won by more than two to one in the first of his five successful Senate elections.

Johnson's first Senate vote was to support Wilson's declaration of war in 1917. He became increasingly critical of the president's foreign policy and its domestic equivalent, the Sedition Act of 1918, which was used to silence criticism of the president's foreign policy. The next year, Johnson almost obtained congressional approval to withdraw American troops from Russia that had been sent there to signify Wilson's opposition to the Russian Revolution. Always an opponent of the railroads, he favored not only their regulation but also government ownership.

During the postwar era, Johnson became the most tireless orator of the Senate "irreconcilables" opposed to Wilson's League of Nations. When the president set out on his cross-country speaking tour to drum up popular support for it, Johnson shadowed him, packing local halls from city to city and urging defeat of U.S. entrance into the League. He feared that it would have a European focus rather than address the danger of Japan's rise in Asia. Like Theodore Roosevelt, Johnson advocated a stronger navy and merchant marine service. Wilson had a stroke on the campaign whirl while Johnson secured a new reputation as an isolationist.

In 1920, Johnson was a leading contender for the Republican presidential nomination.

He won seven of 12 primaries, yet his campaign was too disorganized and too radical for the conservatives. He placed third in initial balloting only to see his support dissipate, and refused requests from the three leading contenders to accept the vice presidency. He sought the presidency again in 1924, but his campaign was so poorly organized that he won only one primary and even lost California, his only electoral defeat in his native state. Meanwhile, he accomplished only one significant legislative measure during his first dozen years in the Senate. In the early 1920s, he cosponsored the Boulder Canyon Reclamation Project, legislation to dam the Colorado River at Boulder Canyon to prevent flooding, generate inexpensive electricity, and extend irrigation. As a result, Boulder Dam—later renamed Hoover Dam—opened in 1928 and provided a model for later New Deal projects.

Johnson's introduction to Franklin Roosevelt came through HAROLD ICKES, a fellow former Bull Moose Republican. Ickes urged him to challenge HERBERT HOOVER's reelection in 1932. Johnson declined and, like Ickes, supported FDR, campaigning for him. A grateful FDR offered Johnson the cabinet post of secretary of the interior, but he turned it down and recommended Ickes instead. During FDR's first term, Johnson supported the domestic New Deal. As a key member of the Senate Foreign Relations Committee, he pushed for neutrality in foreign policy.

Johnson suffered a serious stroke in 1936. FDR's Court-packing plan the next year triggered him to swing into his traditional rebel mode, opposing all further New Deal initiatives. He joined WILLIAM BORAH (R-Idaho) in leading Senate opposition to FDR's request to repeal the arms embargo provision in the Neutrality Act of 1937, which the president did not achieve until the Congress enacted the Neutrality Act of 1939. Johnson supported military and naval funding but opposed conscription the next year. The ranking minority member on the Senate Foreign Relations Committee, he failed to block FDR's lend-lease proposal. However, he did vote for war after the Japanese attack on Pearl Harbor in December 1941. His rebel behavior slowed only because of declining health. During the summer of 1945, Johnson's was the lone vote against sending the United Nations Charter to the Senate floor. He died on August 6, 1945, in Bethesda, Maryland.

Johnson, Hugh Samuel
(Old Iron Pants)
(1882–1942) *National Recovery Administration, director, columnist*

Born in Fort Scott, Kansas, on August 5, 1882, Hugh Johnson was the son of a lawyer/rancher who moved the family within the state four more times for enhanced business opportunities before finally settling in the newly opened Cherokee Strip (Alva, Oklahoma) in 1893. Johnson grew up there, attended Northwest Normal School, and gained admission to the U.S. Military Academy at West Point in 1899. Commissioned in 1903, Johnson led an adventurous military life. His assignments included delivering disaster relief after the 1906 San Francisco earthquake, serving in the Philippines during THEODORE ROOSEVELT's administration, and working in the national parks. He turned his experiences into a lucrative part-time writing career, publishing two books for juveniles and many short stories about military life that appeared in popular magazines of the era.

Following in his father's path, Johnson was admitted to the University of California Law School, which he attended from 1914 to 1916. He then served briefly with John J. Pershing's expeditionary force to Mexico before being transferred to the legal staff of the Bureau of Insular Affairs. Johnson rose to the rank of brigadier general during World War I when he worked with the Selective Service System and served on the War Industries Board (WIB) as its army representative and head of its Purchase and Supply Branch. He coordinated military procurement with the WIB, the federal agency that regulated the American economy during the war and was headed by BERNARD BARUCH, who later became his business partner. After resigning from the army in 1919, Johnson became an executive with the Moline Plow Company and he soon worked with GEORGE PEEK for agricultural relief, which was blocked by Republican presidential vetoes.

Working with Baruch from 1927 to 1932 as his economic investigator and assistant, Johnson gained entrée to the Franklin Roosevelt administration, joining FDR's so-called Brain Trust as the "Baruch man." In 1933, he contributed to implementing the National Recovery Act, which attempted to resurrect the business and government cooperation coordinated by the WIB during World War I. That same year, FDR chose Johnson to direct the National Recovery Administration (NRA), where he worked to establish codes to prevent cutthroat competition. Johnson came up with the NRA's Blue Eagle symbol and its motto "We Do Our Part," to show business compliance with governmental policy. FDR was careful to separate the employment side of the recovery program, which HAROLD ICKES directed. It was a wise separation of duties, for though Johnson was energetic and colorful, he was more a headstrong general than a diplomatic politician. The cross-pressures from business and labor demands triggered Johnson's mood swings and drinking binges, and market restrictions delayed the country's recovery. FDR gently eased Johnson out on October 15, 1934, by replacing his position with an administrative board.

Johnson served briefly as head of the Works Progress Administration in New York

City before channeling his abundant energy into a new journalism career as a syndicated columnist for the Scripps-Howard newspaper chain with his "Hugh Johnson Says," and as a radio commentator. By mid-1937, after the failed Court-packing plan and simultaneous effort to reorganize the executive branch, Johnson broke with the New Deal and FDR. He supported WENDELL WILLKIE for president in 1940 and helped organize the isolationist America First Committee. In response, FDR made sure that his reserve commission was not renewed. Johnson died on April 15, 1942, in Washington, D.C.

Jones, Jesse Holman

(1874–1956) *Reconstruction Finance Corporation chairman, Federal Loan Agency director, secretary of commerce*

Jesse Jones, born April 5, 1874, in Robertson County, Tennessee, was the son of tobacco farmers and merchants. His mother died when he was six years old, and three years later, in 1883, the family moved briefly to Dallas, Texas, but then returned to north central Tennessee,

Jesse H. Jones (right) with Howard Hughes
(Library of Congress)

where his father purchased a large farm. Jones left school at 14 to make money. After his father died in 1894, he moved back to Dallas to manage his uncle's lumber business. Four years later, his uncle died, and Jones moved to Houston, Texas. He married in 1920 but had no children. Jones embraced Houston and his businesses as an adopted extended family. He became one of the largest real-estate developers in the nation, the chairman of the largest bank in Texas, and the owner of the *Houston Chronicle.*

During World War I, Jones responded to Woodrow Wilson to become the director general of military relief for the Red Cross from 1917 to 1919, and he developed a close relationship with the president, who shared his southern roots. In 1928, Jones used his connections to bring the Democratic National Convention to Houston, showcasing his city. The next year, at the suggestion of Democratic congressional leaders, President HERBERT HOOVER appointed Jones as the token Democrat among the seven directors of the new Reconstruction Finance Corporation (RFC) (which was renamed the Small Business Administration during the Eisenhower administration).

When Franklin Roosevelt became president in 1933, he promptly elevated Jones to the head of the RFC, a post he would hold until 1945. During his tenure, the RFC made $50 billion in loans, and the agency became known as "the fourth branch of government." As was typical of FDR, in 1939 he named Jones to serve simultaneously as director of the new Federal Loan Agency, a position he also held until 1945. However, he turned over management of the RFC to Emil Schram, considered by Jones as one of his "RFC family" members. In addition, under special congressional legislation that allowed him to serve concurrently as an agency head and a member of FDR's cabinet, Jones also served as secretary of commerce from 1940 to 1945. He had become the "czar" of New Deal credit.

In both his business and governmental service, Jones was a strongly controlling person who based his trust on kinship and familial loyalty. His congressional influence as a southerner and New Dealer came to rival the president's, especially during World War II. His long-standing feud with Vice President HENRY WALLACE led FDR to side with Jones in 1943 on the abolition of Wallace's Board of Economic Warfare, which had purchased strategic raw materials. But Jones was infuriated by FDR's subsequent request that he step aside as secretary of commerce so that Wallace could be appointed to the post as a consolation after HARRY TRUMAN replaced Wallace on the 1944 ballot. Despite FDR's efforts to placate him, Jones resigned all his government positions and returned to Houston permanently. He opposed Truman's reelection in 1948 and supported DWIGHT EISENHOWER in 1952. Jones died on June 1, 1956, in his beloved Houston.

Kelly, Edward Joseph
(1876–1950) *Chicago mayor*

The son of an Irish policeman, Edward Kelly was born in Chicago, Illinois, on May 1, 1876, and left school early to help support his parents and eight siblings. He later was able to study civil engineering at night school at the Chicago Athenaeum. At age 18 he began working his way up in the Metropolitan Sanitary District, becoming chief engineer by 1920 during Mayor Anton Cermak's administration. Behind the scenes, Kelly and Patrick A. Nash, a former superintendent of sewers, ran the Cermak political machine. Four years later, he was appointed president of Chicago's South Park Board and became active in local Democratic Party politics.

Fate intervened to propel Kelly into elected office in 1933. The now-wealthy Nash, who had extensive business with the Sanitary District, engineered Kelly's selection as mayor by the City Council following Cermak's accidental death during an attempted assassination of President-elect Franklin Roosevelt. The Great Depression had left Chicago with a 40 percent unemployment rate, and Kelly acted quickly through the Illinois legislature and the new Democratic administration in Washington, D.C., to secure federal funding. At the same time, he expanded the Chicago–Cook County machine, based on an ethnic immigrant coalition that included African Americans and Italians. He delivered ethnically balanced tickets and patronage, and in return grateful recipients responded with votes. He also made deals with organized crime to overlook gambling in exchange for annual financial contributions.

Kelly's landslide electoral win in 1935 with more than 75 percent of the vote made him FDR's earliest and closest urban political-machine ally. In addition to funds he obtained from the Federal Emergency Relief Administration and the Civil Works Administration, the Works Progress Administration furnished millions of dollars more. Presidential aide HARRY HOPKINS and National Democratic Committee chairman JAMES FARLEY increasingly funneled federal money and patronage into the Chicago machine even as it sought to wrest control from Illinois's New Deal loyalist governor HENRY HORNER in downstate Springfield. As a result, Kelly became one of FDR's major supporters.

Kelly and Hopkins secretly orchestrated FDR's unprecedented third-term nomination at the 1940 Democratic National Convention in Chicago. Hopkins became the strategist, and Kelly worked to produce the staged draft that FDR requested. Kelly selected Chicago Stadium, packed the galleries with machine workers, and had the current superintendent of sewers anonymously boom out from the loudspeakers a call for FDR's nomination, triggering a spontaneous hour-long demonstration. The other big-city bosses (including New York's EDWARD FLYNN, Jersey City's FRANK HAGUE, and Kansas City's THOMAS PENDERGAST) reinforced the public display of support. Machine politics at its strongest manipulated its undemocratic agenda, appearing to the world to be democracy in action.

After Nash's death in 1943, Kelly turned the Chicago City Council into his rubber stamp. Ironically, it was the autocratic Kelly's call for open housing and desegregated schools that eroded his white ethnic support. Troubled by increasing health problems, he did not seek reelection in 1947, and he died in Chicago on October 20, 1950.

Joseph Patrick Kennedy *(Library of Congress)*

Kennedy, Joseph Patrick
(1888–1969) *Securities and Exchange Commission chairman, U.S. Maritime Commission chairman, U.S. ambassador to Britain*

The son of prosperous Irish parents and grandson of Irish immigrants, Joseph P. Kennedy was born on September 6, 1888, in Boston, Massachusetts. He learned quickly what it meant to be an Irish Catholic outsider in Protestant Brahmin Boston. He attended Boston High School and Harvard University, graduating in 1912, and married Rose Fitzgerald, the daughter of Boston mayor John F. "Honey Fitz" Fitzgerald, in 1914; the couple eventually had nine children. Building on his father's financial success, Kennedy became an investor and was a millionaire by the 1920s. He briefly moved his family from Boston to New York in the late 1920s, in part an attempt to escape the discrimination against the Irish in his native city. He dabbled in the stock market

and flirted with the movie business, including extramarital affairs with Hollywood actresses. He retired from the stock market before its 1929 crash, sparing him from the financial crisis many others experienced.

Kennedy turned to politics for acceptance and became an early financial backer of New York governor Franklin Roosevelt in his bid for the presidency. Kennedy claimed credit for persuading newspaper and Hollywood mogul WILLIAM RANDOLPH HEARST to support FDR. In 1932, he drafted a speech delivered by FDR that outlined the future Securities and Exchange Commission (SEC). After the SEC was established in 1934 for the purpose of reforming corrupt Wall Street trading practices, FDR made the politically conservative Kennedy its first chairman. As always, the energetic Kennedy worked vigorously to accomplish his mission by establishing new rules that outlawed some of the very techniques that he had used to increase his own wealth. Mission accomplished, he resigned in 1935, creating an opening for his friend WILLIAM O. DOUGLAS. The next year, he published *I'm for Roosevelt*, arguing that FDR had saved capitalism. Since Kennedy was an investor in shipbuilding, FDR brought him back to government service in March 1937 as chairman of the U.S. Maritime Commission to revive the shipbuilding industry.

Ever ambitious and driven, Kennedy wanted still more—social acceptance and even the presidency itself. Ironically, he achieved the first when the Protestant and socially secure FDR appointed his Irish Catholic associate as ambassador to the Court of St. James. Kennedy's informal style as America's ambassador to Great Britain initially pleased the British. In early 1938, he sided with the appeasement policy of NEVILLE CHAMBERLAIN, and even after WINSTON CHURCHILL assumed power two years later, Kennedy continued to argue that Nazi Germany would likely win the war and that the United States should remain isolationist. His Irish bias against the British leaked through in snide remarks about the king and queen, favorable views of European fascism, and criticism of Churchill's drinking. He resigned as ambassador in November 1940 during the German bombings of Britain.

During the postwar period, Kennedy became family friends with fellow Irish Catholic Joseph McCarthy, the first-term Republican senator from Wisconsin, who would later achieve notoriety in the 1950s for his investigations into suspected communists. After McCarthy's death from alcoholism, Kennedy devoted his last energy and fortune to assure that John F. Kennedy, his oldest surviving son who had entered Congress at the same time as McCarthy, would become the first Roman Catholic president of the United States in 1960. The elder Kennedy died on November 18, 1969, in Hyannis Port, Massachusetts, the patriarch of the American equivalent of a political dynasty.

Kerr, Florence Stewart

(1890–1975) *assistant director, Works Progress Administration*

Florence Stewart was born in Harriman, Tennessee, on June 30, 1890, and grew up in Iowa, where her parents had moved to live with her maternal grandmother. Along with HALLIE FLANAGAN, she became a classmate and lifelong friend with HARRY HOPKINS at progressive Grinnell College, from which she graduated in 1912. She married Robert Y. Kerr three years later and taught English at her alma mater.

In 1930, Kerr became a member of the Iowa Governor's Commission on Unemployment Relief that was established to deal with the effects of the Great Depression. Hopkins recommended her in July 1935 to serve as one of five regional directors of the Division of Women's and Professional Projects in the newly created Works Progress Administration (WPA), which he headed. The job required her to move to Chicago, and from there she oversaw work relief in 13 Midwestern states. She traveled in the region, consulting with state directors and women projects directors. When she was in her Chicago office, ELEANOR ROOSEVELT often came to visit. Kerr visited the numerous sewing and library projects for unskilled women and the Federal Art, Writers, and Theatre Projects for professional women. She developed the reputation of being the best of the regional directors.

In late 1938, when Ellen Woodward resigned as Hopkins's assistant, Kerr replaced her. Shortly after she moved to Washington, D.C., in early 1939, the WPA was reorganized as the Works Projects Administration within the new Federal Works Agency as a result of the Reorganization Act of 1939, which was the delayed congressional response to the 1937 report of the LOUIS BROWNLOW Commission. In April 1939, Kerr's division was renamed the Division of Professional and Service Projects. Even while WPA projects were subjected to increasing budgetary cuts, she was able to maintain her division's institutional and community service projects with backing from the First Lady, who had Kerr speak at one of her press conferences.

With the advent of World War II, the New Deal's Great Depression goals shifted to national defense. Kerr took steps to transform women's work relief into civilian defense. WPA day-care centers assumed an important niche in the national defense effort until they were transferred to local communities under the Lanham Act of 1942. Kerr was able also to maintain clothing and food production programs, public-health projects, and training for housekeeping aides until the WPA closed down in 1943. The next year, Kerr was named director of war public services under the Federal Works Agency, a post she held until the end of World War II. During the postwar period she left the federal government to work for Northwest Airlines. She died on July 6, 1975, in Washington, D.C.

Keynes, John Maynard, first Baron Keynes of Tilton
(1883–1946) *British economist*

Neither an American nor a New Dealer, British economist John Maynard Keynes nonetheless had a profound influence on both, reflecting the growing interdependency of the world in the 20th century. Born June 5, 1883, in Cambridge, England, he was reared in an intellectual environment. His father was registrar of Cambridge University for many years,

and his mother served as mayor of Cambridge. Keynes attended Eton and then entered King's College, Cambridge. After graduation, he served in the India Office of the British civil service for two years. He then returned to Cambridge University to write and edit the *Economic Journal*, Britain's most prestigious economics journal.

In 1919, Keynes attended the Versailles Peace Conference as the deputy director for the chancellor of the exchequer on the Supreme Economic Council, but he resigned in protest because he believed that reparations would wreck the German economy and trigger yet another chapter of military authoritarianism. The prescience of his protest and subsequent book, *The Economic Consequences of the Peace* (1919), established his international reputation.

During the 1920s, the ever-energetic and talented Keynes amassed a fortune by speculating on the international securities market while teaching at Cambridge and continuing to publish books including the *Treatise on Money* published in 1930, which critiqued the fixation on gold and currency. FELIX FRANKFURTER, who was on an academic sabbatical as the Visiting Eastman Professor at Oxford University in 1933, arranged for Keynes to meet Franklin Roosevelt the next year when he visited Washington, D.C. While there, Keynes urged New Dealers to spend even more on relief and public projects to stimulate private investment and income.

In 1936, he achieved in economics the equivalent to ALBERT EINSTEIN's achievement in physics with his publication of *The General Theory of Employment, Interest, and Money*. The work undermined classical economic theory by arguing that deficit spending was necessary to overcome depression. He reiterated these views in subsequent letters to FDR. World War II government spending and deficit financing accomplished the so-called Keynesian revolution. If the United States's material support saved the British during World War II and was necessary for both defeat of the Axis powers and postwar economic recovery, Keynes provided the economic theory for both dealing with the Great Depression and the generous postwar economic aid to avoid repeating the mistakes of World War I.

After his first meeting with FDR, Keynes returned to the United States several times, the last trip occurring in 1945 for the Bretton Woods Conference. Keynes was made Commander of the Order of the Bath (C.B.) in 1917 and Baron Keynes of Tilton in 1942. He died on April 21, 1946.

Keyserling, Leon
(1908–1987) *speechwriter, assistant to Senator Robert Wagner, federal administrator*

Leon Keyserling, like fellow New Dealers BERNARD BARUCH and JAMES BYRNES, had South Carolina roots that would prove useful later in getting congressional approval of his program. He was born January 22, 1908, in Beaufort, South Carolina, where he graduated from high school at age 16. Higher education was Keyserling's one-way ticket out of a small-town future. He majored in economics at Columbia University, where he came under the influence of REXFORD TUGWELL. After graduating in 1928, he immediately moved to Harvard, obtaining his law degree three years later. He then returned to Columbia to do graduate work in economics.

After the Democrats came to power in 1933, Tugwell, then the assistant secretary of agriculture, invited Keyserling to Washington, D.C., and urged him to join the legal staff of the Agricultural Adjustment Administration (AAA). JEROME FRANK, the general counsel for the AAA, immediately hired him when he learned that Keyserling's father was a personal friend of Senator ELLISON "Cotton Ed" SMITH, who had

entered the Senate in 1909 and was chairman of its Agricultural Committee. However, Keyserling held the position with Frank for only two weeks before leaving. In late 1933, he became the legislative assistant to liberal Democratic senator ROBERT WAGNER of New York.

Wagner championed much of the New Deal's reform package in Congress. He was instrumental in two of the landmark pieces of congressional legislation: the National Labor Relations Act of 1935 and the Social Security Act of 1935. Keyserling had drafted Section 7A of the National Industrial Recovery Act (NIRA) of 1933, which encouraged labor unions. It later became part of the Wagner Act (National Labor Relations Act of 1935) after the NIRA was declared unconstitutional. As Wagner's chief assistant, Keyserling prepared studies, wrote speeches, and testified before Congress on behalf of the reform package. He also played a major role in the Home Owners' Refinancing Act of 1933, the National Housing Act of 1934, and the Wagner-Steagall Housing Act of 1937. Because Wagner was the chairman of the Platform Committee to the Democratic National Conventions in 1936, 1940, and 1944, Keyserling wrote the presidential campaign platforms in those years. He also drafted occasional campaign speeches for FDR, e.g., refuting the charge by Republican presidential candidate ALF LANDON that the new Social Security system was a fraud without the means to pay pensions. In addition, he wrote FDR's 1942 executive order that created the National Housing Agency.

From 1937 to 1946, Keyserling worked in a variety of federal housing agencies. He married reform activist Mary Dublin, a former economics professor at Sarah Lawrence College, in 1940. During the postwar period, Senator Joseph McCarthy (R-Wis.) accused them both of being communists, charges that they successfully refuted in 1951. Keyserling's last major governmental post was as chairman of the Council of Economic Advisers during the

HARRY TRUMAN administration. He died on August 9, 1987, in Washington, D.C.

King, William Lyon MacKenzie
(1874–1950) *Canadian prime minister*

The eldest son of a prominent judge, William Lyon MacKenzie King was named for his maternal grandfather, a reform leader of the failed 1837 rebellion in Upper Canada. King earned his undergraduate degree from the University of Toronto in 1895. He held a master's degree from the University of Chicago and a doctorate in sociology and labor relations from Harvard University. He began public service in 1900 as the deputy minister of the new Department of Labor, where he helped to shape the Industrial Disputes Investigation Act of 1907, which was designed to encourage voluntary reconciliation in labor disputes. He was one of Canada's first politicians to urge recognition of labor unions.

King entered politics in 1908 when he won a seat in the House of Commons and was appointed minister of labor in the Liberal Party government of Sir Wilfrid Laurier, his lifelong political hero. After the Liberal Party lost in 1911, King lost his House seat. He spent the next decade developing an international reputation as an industrial negotiator in several strikes in the United States. His philosophy is reflected in his book *Industry and Humanity* (1918). Upon Laurier's death in 1919, King became his successor as leader of the Liberal Party, which he rebuilt.

King was first elected as prime minister in 1921 and would hold that position longer than any other person in the history of the British Commonwealth, serving three terms: 1921–26, 1926–30, and 1935–40. A bachelor, he viewed himself as a rebel—like his grandfather—on a divine mission. He essentially favored caution, compromise, and consensus. His lack of physical stature, public speaking skills, and inter-

personal warmth was compensated for by his belief in spiritualism and a shrewd sense of what was possible in Canada.

In the late 1920s, King forced the British Parliament to recognize the dominions as equals within the British Commonwealth, which was formalized in the 1931 Statue of Westminster. King's approach to the Great Depression and the dangers of European fascism lacked innovation, although he did nationalize the Bank of Canada. He approved of British prime minister NEVILLE CHAMBERLAIN's appeasement policy. He disliked the New Deal but liked Franklin Roosevelt, whose summer home was on Campobello Island in New Brunswick. The two North American leaders met 18 times. King hoped to become the mediator between the United States and Britain. He trusted Franklin Roosevelt more than Winston Churchill. Treated as a junior partner by both, he failed in that mission but joined with FDR in signing the August 17, 1940, Ogdensburg, New York, agreement declaring that the United States would come to Canada's defense if threatened with aggression. They also signed the April 1941 Hyde Park Declaration allowing for Canadian and American economic collaboration in defense production.

King's first steps to introduce a Canadian social-welfare state were not taken until after World War II, when he also recognized Newfoundland as the 10th Canadian province in the Confederation. He strongly supported the United Nations. Exhausted by his long tenure in office, King resigned in November 1948 and died on July 22, 1950, in Ottawa.

Knox, Frank
(1874–1944) *publisher, Republican vice-presidential candidate, secretary of the navy*

Born in Boston, Massachusetts, on January 1, 1874, Frank Knox was the son of an oyster dealer. After graduating from high school in Grand Rapids, Michigan, he entered Alma College in Alma, Michigan, in the late 1890s. During the Spanish-American War, he joined the First Volunteer United States Calvary (the Rough Riders), led by THEODORE ROOSEVELT, who became his lifelong hero.

After the war, Knox entered journalism as a reporter. In 1902, he became publisher of a small newspaper in Michigan. A decade later, he became the founding publisher and owner of New Hampshire's leading newspaper. In editorials, he called for U.S. intervention in World War I. He subsequently enlisted as a private and became an artillery officer. In 1927, WILLIAM RANDOLPH HEARST recruited Knox to become the general manager of his newspaper chain, a position he held for three years. In 1931, he became the publisher of Chicago's financially troubled *Daily News*, one of the nation's largest newspapers, and made it profitable during the Great Depression. He crusaded against Prohibition-era criminals and the corrupt Democratic political machine in Chicago.

Knox remained a Theodore Roosevelt Republican who wanted clean and efficient government. In 1911, he had managed Roosevelt's failed Midwest effort to wrest control of the party from the conservative Republicans, and for a brief period the next year he was the leader of the short-lived Bull Moose Republican Party. At the 1920 Republican National Convention he had been floor manager for former Rough Rider Leonard Wood's unsuccessful presidential bid. Knox's string of political setbacks had continued when he failed to win the Republican nomination for governor of New Hampshire in 1924.

Knox did not support the New Deal because he believed it placed too many burdens on businesses and that its social reforms bordered on socialism. He sought, but did not win, the Republican presidential nomination

in 1936; however, he ran as the vice-presidential candidate with ALF LANDON of Kansas. The Republican ticket lost in a Democratic electoral landslide. It was therefore ironic that Knox's first political success came during Democratic president Franklin Roosevelt's later administration. His ties to Theodore Roosevelt and his strong internationalist credentials led FDR to select him as the secretary of the navy at the same time that he made Republican HENRY STIMSON, another interventionist and former artillery officer, the secretary of war. The Republican duo lent a bipartisan cast to FDR's unprecedented third-term campaign in 1940.

FDR's selection proved to be a wise one. Knox backed the effort to provide destroyers for Britain in 1940 and helped to pass the Lend-Lease Act. He also presided over the greatest expansion in U.S. naval history. An energetic, blunt, and profane administrator, Knox relieved Admiral Husband E. Kimmel as commander of the Pacific fleet after the December 7, 1941, Pearl Harbor disaster. He died on April 28, 1944, in Washington, D.C.

Krock, Arthur
(1886–1974) *journalist*

The son of an accountant, Arthur Krock was born on November 16, 1886, in Glasgow, Kentucky. He entered Princeton University, but financial problems forced him to drop out during his freshman year. He obtained an associate of arts degree at the Lewis Institute in Chicago in 1906, and the next year he began his lifelong career in newspaper journalism by working for the *Louisville Times*. In 1910, he was sent to Washington, D.C., as the paper's capital correspondent. He returned to Louisville in 1915 to become editor in chief, and four years later, he covered the Versailles Peace Conference. During the 1920 presidential campaign, Krock served briefly as an aide to George White, chairman of the Democratic National Committee; this was his only direct political experience.

A dispute with *Louisville Times* owner Robert W. Bingham, who supported Prohibition and women's suffrage, led Krock to resign in protest in 1923. Later that year, he moved to New York to work for the *New York World* for four years until Adolph S. Ochs of the *New York Times* picked him up in 1927 as a member of that paper's editorial board. Krock moved back to the nation's capital in 1932 as the *Times* Washington correspondent and bureau chief, remaining there until he retired in 1966.

Krock was notably different in the world of reporters for his longevity with the *Times*, and he was an anomaly on the staff of a liberal newspaper at the time of the New Deal. Although he considered himself a liberal Democrat in the

tradition of Thomas Jefferson and Woodrow Wilson, he was personally quite conservative and grew increasingly so during his career. As a result, he distrusted executive power and the growth of the federal government. Personal views notwithstanding, he developed a reputation for journalistic objectivity. Ending the traditional practice of having only unsigned editorials, in 1933 Krock began a signed column, "In the Nation," for the *New York Times* editorial page. It became an innovative model for other newspapers. He eventually received four Pulitzer Prizes, more than any other journalist in history. The first was for his coverage of the New Deal in 1935 and the second was in 1937 after FDR granted him an exclusive interview and, in part, explained the rationale for the proposed Supreme Court–packing plan. Krock died in Washington, D.C., on April 12, 1974.

La Follette, Philip Fox

(1897–1965) *Wisconsin governor*

Born in Madison, Wisconsin, on May 8, 1897, Philip La Follette was the second son born to the well-known former governor and senator Robert Marion La Follette and his lawyer-journalist wife. Truly a second son, Philip La Follette was overlooked by his father, who was busy grooming his first son and namesake to become his political successor. It was Philip, however, who ultimately shared his father's personality, ambition, and career training. After serving as an army officer during World War I, he received his undergraduate and law degrees from the University of Wisconsin. His progressive politics masked his enormous ambition and relative provincialism.

After joining his father's law firm in 1922, La Follette was elected in 1924 as district attorney of Dane County, a position he held until 1927. Also in 1924, he participated in his father's independent Progressive Party campaign for president, during which the senior La Follette received a larger proportion of the popular vote than any third-party candidate between Theodore Roosevelt in 1912 and Ross Perot in 1992. After his father's death the next year, Philip La Follette served as the manager for the successful campaign of his brother, ROBERT M.

LA FOLLETTE, JR., to fill their father's vacant U.S. Senate seat. Philip then returned to private legal practice and teaching at the University of Wisconsin Law School from 1926 to 1931. He soon returned to the political arena, however, and won the Wisconsin governorship in 1930 as a progressive Republican.

Taking office during the Great Depression, when unemployment was extremely high, and saddled with a state legislature that refused to enact much of his programs, La Follette became unpopular with voters. In 1932, he was defeated for reelection by the same former Republican governor whom he had upset two years before. Because the New Deal usurped much of the traditional progressive Republican philosophy, in 1934 he left the Republicans and began the Wisconsin Progressive Party. He then won back the governorship by endorsing much of the New Deal.

Like Democratic Illinois governor HENRY HORNER, La Follette began a "Little New Deal," but the Wisconsin state legislature defeated most of his major bills. Nonetheless, to the consternation of local Democrats, FDR turned over control of the state's federal Works Progress Administration to the governor, and Wisconsin received a disproportionately high share of federal relief funds compared to neighboring states. In return, La Follette backed

FDR's reelection in 1936. Both president and governor were easily reelected that year, but their successful campaigns allowed both to be blinded by hubris, and each stumbled politically. La Follette gained national attention as he pushed his "Little New Deal" through the state legislature, earning him a reputation as an autocrat as well as the moniker "Wild Man of Madison," especially after he dismissed the president of the University of Wisconsin. With national ambitions that discounted the possibility that FDR would seek a third term, and without consulting others, La Follette launched the so-called National Progressives of America Party in 1938. Its symbol was a cross in a circle, which struck critics as being uncomfortably similar to Nazi Germany's swastika. La Follette blamed FDR for the Great Depression and moved left of the New Deal. He lost his bid for a fourth term as governor during the 1938 national Republican resurgence, ending his political career.

Though FDR had hoped that La Follette would return to support him, La Follette instead moved to the political right in defeat. He joined the America First Committee in 1939, becoming a prominent isolationist until the Pearl Harbor attack. In 1942, he reentered the army, serving on the staff of General DOUGLAS MACARTHUR in the Pacific. In 1944, La Follette participated in the failed effort to gain the Republican presidential nomination for MacArthur, which he tried again in 1948, also without success. He supported DWIGHT EISENHOWER in 1952. La Follette died on August 18, 1965, in Madison.

La Follette, Robert Marion, Jr.
(Young Bob)
(1895–1953) *U.S. senator*

The older of two sons of Senator Robert M. La Follette (R-Wis.) and his lawyer-journalist wife, Robert M. La Follette, Jr., was born on February 6, 1895, in Madison, Wisconsin. He was reared in an overly political environment. His crusading father, "Fighting Bob," groomed him as his successor even though he was less ambitious and would have preferred a different career. Health problems combined with a mediocre undergraduate record resulted in his dropping out of the University of Wisconsin. He went to Washington, D.C., to serve as his father's primary senate assistant until the senior La Follette died in 1925. Running as a Republican, "Young Bob" La Follette won the special election to fill his father's seat, becoming the youngest senator since Henry Clay, just as his father had been the youngest House member when he first entered Congress in 1885. The young senator married Rachael Young in 1930, and they had two sons.

La Follette championed his father's causes and moved beyond him in advocating bold action to deal with the Great Depression as he became one of the Senate's most liberal members. Though he played a significant role in formulating and passing New Deal economic measures, he also became a major administration critic who found FDR too cautious. In 1934, he reluctantly followed his younger brother, PHILIP LA FOLLETTE, in bolting the Republican Party and founding the Wisconsin Progressive Party, and he won reelection on the third-party ticket that same year. For the rest of the 1930s, Robert La Follette served as the subcommittee chairman to the Senate Committee on Education and Labor, popularly known as the La Follette Civil Liberties Committee, which investigated management violations of labor rights. Though this work enhanced his reputation as a hero of organized labor, he disliked the New Deal's emphasis on catering to well-organized interest groups. Reminiscent of his father's opposition to American entry into World War I, La Follette opposed U.S. entry into World War II until the Pearl Harbor attack of December 1941.

The elder La Follette's flamboyant behavior had alienated his Senate colleagues, but the junior La Follette's work ethic and respect for the legislative process generated bipartisan admiration. Also unlike his father, "Young Bob" showed little interest in political leadership outside the halls of Congress and hated to campaign. In 1946, the Wisconsin Progressive Party disbanded, and he rejoined the GOP. Waging only a token reelection campaign that year, he narrowly lost the Republican primary to Joseph R. McCarthy. Although he had been trapped in a career pursued only out of loyalty to his father, he found private life even more frustrating without a meaningful second career. He died from a self-inflicted gunshot wound on February 24, 1953.

La Guardia, Fiorello Henry
(1882–1947) *New York City mayor*

Born on December 11, 1882, in New York City to immigrant parents from southern Italy and Trieste, Fiorello ("Little Flower") La Guardia experienced frequent moves during childhood because his father was a bandmaster in the U.S. Army. In 1898, his father fell ill, probably due to contaminated "embalmed beef" sold to the army by corrupt contractors. He left the army and moved his family back to Europe, where he died six years later. Subsequently, La Guardia's mother was denied a military widow's pension, which instilled a lifelong hatred of corruption and bureaucrats in her firstborn son.

Returning to the United States, La Guardia went to law school at New York University, following which he began practicing law and became involved in progressive Republican politics. He lost his first congressional bid in 1914, but he won the seat from lower Manhattan in the next election, becoming the first Italian ever elected to Congress. In 1917, he resigned to become one of five con-

gressmen to serve in World War I. After he returned from the war in Europe, he became the successor to AL SMITH as president of the Board of Aldermen of New York City. He served in 1920–21, with the hope of running for mayor. In 1921, though, he suffered an electoral loss in the Republican primary for mayor that was overshadowed by his personal losses—the deaths of his daughter and wife from tuberculosis.

With the help of newspaper magnate WILLIAM RANDOLPH HEARST, La Guardia was reelected to Congress, this time representing East Harlem. He served from 1922 to 1933, fighting for the rights of labor and cosponsoring with Senator GEORGE W. NORRIS (R-Nebr.) the 1932 Norris-La Guardia Act, which prevented antilabor injunctions. He ran unsuccessfully for New York City mayor again in 1929, losing to Tammany Hall candidate Jimmy Walker. La Guardia finally achieved his goal in his third attempt by winning the mayoral election in 1933 and being reelected in 1937 and 1941. He became the first New York City mayor to serve three consecutive terms. Never very loyal to a political party, he was elected on more than four party tickets during

President Roosevelt (seated) with Mayor Fiorello La Guardia *(Library of Congress)*

the course of his entire political career. He was always in the minority.

During the 1930s, La Guardia enjoyed a larger-than-life reputation, despite his 5'2" stature, as the nation's most dynamic, popular, and incorruptible mayor. From 1936 to 1945, he also served as president of the United States Conference of Mayors, in which role he pursued a national urban coalition and federal assistance for cities. He developed close links with FDR, Secretary of the Interior HAROLD ICKES, and FDR special assistant HARRY HOPKINS, obtaining an increased and disproportionate share of federal funds to finance his many initiatives to rebuild the city. These included replacing tenements with public housing projects; building bridges, tunnels, parkways, libraries, schools, the nation's first airport, and the first sewerage system; putting the subway under city ownership; and creating parks, playgrounds, and zoos.

A tireless and a colorful public figure, La Guardia broadcast a weekly Sunday radio talk show that was the equivalent of FDR's occasional "fireside chat." It is perhaps best remembered for his dramatic reading of comic strips during a newspaper delivery strike. His aggressiveness led to excesses in abusing bureaucrats and civil liberties as well as an exaggerated sense of self-importance. During spring 1941, FDR appointed La Guardia as director of the Office of Civilian Defense, with quasi-cabinet rank, while he retained his mayorship. Yet like Theodore Roosevelt, whom he resembled in many ways despite their disparate backgrounds, La Guardia desperately wanted an appointment to a military position during World War II. When FDR failed to act, LaGuardia considered it to be his life's greatest disappointment. Still, historians consider La Guardia to be the greatest mayor in American history. He died on September 20, 1947, in the Bronx.

Landis, James McCauley

(1899–1964) *federal lawyer, Securities and Exchange Commission chairman, Office of the Civilian Defense director*

Born on September 25, 1899, in Tokyo, Japan, to Presbyterian missionary teachers, James Landis attended Tokyo Foreign School before arriving in the United States for the first time in 1912 to complete his education. He entered Princeton University in 1916 and graduated in 1921. He then entered Harvard Law School, graduating in 1924. While there, he was a student of FELIX FRANKFURTER, who arranged for him to clerk with Supreme Court justice LOUIS BRANDEIS in 1925–26. Landis was influenced by Brandeis's wary views about concentrated economic power and belief in market competition. While conducting research for Brandeis's dissent in *Myers v. United States*, Landis discovered the legal field of federal regulation, which became his focus. He returned to Harvard the next year to join the law faculty and coauthored *The Business of the Supreme Court* (1927) with Frankfurter.

After FDR was elected president, both Frankfurter and Landis arrived in the nation's capital to work on the Roosevelt administration's securities legislation. Landis, fellow lawyers BENJAMIN COHEN and THOMAS CORCORAN, and Congressman SAM RAYBURN (D-Tex.) drafted the Securities Act of 1933. That same year, FDR appointed Landis to the Federal Trade Commission, which was designed to provide the first governmental regulation over the sale of corporate stocks. The three "Happy Hotdogs," as the press dubbed Frankfurter's former students, and Congressman Rayburn repeated their performance in drafting the Securities and Exchange Act of 1934. FDR then named Landis, FERDINAND PECORA, and JOSEPH P. KENNEDY to the New Securities and Exchange Commission. Landis succeeded Kennedy as chairman in 1935, and he aimed for a pragmatic middle ground between federal regulation of industry and finance and outright governmental ownership. In 1937, Landis returned to Harvard as dean of the law school, the youngest in its history. He supported FDR's Supreme Court–packing plan.

Landis's lifelong struggle to live up to the expectations of his parents and others began to take its toll on his personal life. His 10-year marriage began to fail, and he increasingly turned to alcohol over the next decade. In early 1942, he succeeded FIORELLO LA GUARDIA as the director of the Office of Civilian Defense. His public legacy was undermined during the postwar era when his alcoholism led to income-tax evasion, a brief imprisonment, and disbarment. Nonetheless, he served as a special assistant to President John F. Kennedy. He accidentally drowned on July 30, 1964, in the pool at his home in Harrison, New York.

Landon, Alf
(Alfred Mossman Landon)
(1887–1987) *Kansas governor, Republican presidential candidate*

Alf Landon was born on September 9, 1887, in West Middlesex, Pennsylvania, the son of an oil and natural gas businessman; his mother was the daughter of a minister. He grew up in Marietta, Ohio, until 1904, when his family moved to Independence, Kansas. Although he obtained his law degree from the University of Kansas, he never practiced law. He worked as a banker for three years and then began a career—interrupted by brief service as an army officer during World War I—as an independent oil driller. When he returned to oil production after World War I, he diversified his business interests. Landon demonstrated sound business acumen, but he never became wealthy, in large part because he was distracted from

business by his interest in politics, which had been promoted by his politically active father.

Father and son worked for THEODORE ROOSEVELT's unsuccessful 1912 presidential bid. Alf Landon became Roosevelt's Progressive Party chairman in 1914 but returned to the Republic Party in 1916. He became secretary to the Republican governor of Kansas in 1922, and two years later he became a key leader in the independent gubernatorial campaign of journalist William Allen White against the Ku Klux Klan. In 1928, he organized the successful campaign to elect a moderate Republican governor and was chosen to become chairman of the Republican state committee. In 1930, conservative Republicans ousted both the governor and Landon from their positions.

Despite this, Landon's moderation and willingness to work with a broad political spectrum allowed him to stage a comeback the next year, and in 1932 he became the Republican candidate for governor with the goal of uniting the divided party. In a three-candidate race, Landon won with a scant 34.8 percent plurality. He championed governmental economy and efficiency while demonstrating his ability to work with Democrats to maintain a balanced budget. His shrewd dealings with Secretary of the Interior HAROLD ICKES allowed the state to receive a disproportionate share of New Deal funds in the Midwest.

Landon became the only Republican governor to win reelection in 1934. Always occupying the golden-mean, middle-of-the-road position between Republican conservatives and liberals, he won the presidential bid at the June 1936 national convention, a selection that marked the ascendancy of younger westerners in the Republican Party. Chicago publisher FRANK KNOX, who had also sought the nomination, was chosen as the vice-presidential candidate. Although the Republican Party remained divided, Landon was able to obtain the backing of former Democratic presidential nominees John W. Davis and AL SMITH. Once again, he tried to practice moderation during the campaign with denunciations of racial prejudice and religious bigotry. Republicans spent $14 million on Landon's candidacy, the most ever spent in American history up to that time. Conservative Republicans pushed him further right during the campaign, though neither Landon nor Democratic torchbearer Franklin Roosevelt turned their heated campaigns into personal vendettas. Lacking FDR's oratory skills, patronage, organization, name recognition, and platform, Landon was buried in the Democratic landslide that gave FDR every state except two. The election also reduced Republicans to a mere 89 seats in the U.S. House of Representatives and 16 in the U.S. Senate. Landon and FDR remained cordial after the election.

Landon chose not to seek public office again, although he remained an active head of the Republican Party until 1940. He received credit for the Republican resurgence in the 1938 elections, including the defeat of an anti-Semitic Republican senatorial nomination. He also became the only major-party politician to defend the right of Socialist Party leader NORMAN THOMAS to speak after Mayor FRANK HAGUE's Jersey City machine blocked him from doing so there. That same year, FDR named Landon vice chairman of the U.S. delegation to the Inter-American Conference in Lima, Peru. Picking up on political scientist Harold Lasswell's warning about the danger of the United States becoming a garrison state, Landon became a loyal Republican critic during World War II.

A politician educated in the law, Alf Landon was born during the centennial of the U.S. Constitution and help to uphold its democratic values. He had the satisfaction of seeing his similarly moderate Republican daughter, Nancy Landon Kassebaum, elected to the U.S. Senate in 1978. He died in Topeka, Kansas,

during the bicentennial year of the U.S. Constitution. His longevity was the only extreme in his otherwise moderate life.

Lange, Dorothea
(Dorothea Margaretta Nutzhorn)
(1895–1965) *photographer*

Dorothea Lange, the premier photographer of the New Deal, portrayed the grim reality of the Great Depression in her work just as Franklin Roosevelt, the premier politician of the New Deal, instituted programs that would improve life and restore hope to Americans. Born Dorothea Margaretta Nutzhorn on May 25, 1895, in Hoboken, New Jersey, Lange was the daughter of a lawyer who abandoned the family when she was about 12 years old. Her mother worked first as a librarian to support the family and then became a social worker in New York City, where Dorothea spent her girlhood and was educated. A bout with polio left her with a lifelong limp and sensitivity to outsiders. Deciding to become a photographer at age 18, she served a series of apprenticeships and briefly attended the Clarence White School of Photography.

In 1918, Lange moved to California, where she married western artist Maynard Dixon; the marriage lasted 15 years. The Great Depression changed Lange's life. She believed that photographs were better than written or spoken words to capture the tragedy that resulted from the Great Depression. Her work was viewed by Paul Schuster Taylor, a professor of agricultural economics at the University of California at Berkeley and beginning in 1934 an employee of FDR's State Emergency Relief Administration (SERA). Their relationship ultimately resulted in marriage in 1935, the same year he hired her at SERA. Together they documented a pea harvest in Nipomo, California, and brought

This classic photograph, "Migrant Mother, Nipuma, California" (1936), was taken by Dorothea Lange for the Resettlement Administration. *(Library of Congress)*

national attention to the plight of immigrant families, which eventually led to the first federal camps with sanitary facilities for farm workers. From 1936 to 1938, Lange and Taylor documented how farm mechanization and bad weather drove farmers from the South and Midwest to California. As a result, Congress enlarged the Resettlement Administration in 1937 into the enlarged Farm Security Administration, which commissioned more photographers to use Lange's and Taylor's approach. In all of her New Deal photographs, Lange considered families as a metaphor for the larger community in crisis.

During World War II, Lange photographed the internment of Japanese Americans, but the War Relocation Authority purposely prevented release of the images for fear that her photographs would elicit a sympathetic backlash. The State Department recruited her to record the founding of the United Nations Charter in 1945. Lange was one of the founders of *Aperture*, a photography magazine, but ill health then forced her into an early retirement. Lange died from cancer on October 11, 1965, in Berkeley.

Leahy, William Daniel

(1875–1959) *naval officer; Puerto Rico governor; ambassador to Vichy, France; chairman, Joint Chiefs of Staff; presidential chief of staff*

Born in Hampton, Iowa, William Leahy was the son of a lawyer and politician who moved his family to Wisconsin in 1882. Leahy entered the U.S. Naval Academy in 1893. He graduated in the lower third of his class in 1897 and then served in the Spanish-American War, the Boxer Rebellion intervention in China, and several interventions in Latin America. His introduction to Franklin Roosevelt came during the Woodrow Wilson administration while he was an aide to Secretary of the Navy Josephus Daniel and FDR was assistant secretary. Leahy obtained his first battleship command in 1926, and in 1933 FDR appointed him chief of the Bureau of Navigation, which permitted him the opportunity to advance the careers of fellow battleship officers. Four years later, the president named him chief of naval operations, and he served in that position until he reached mandatory retirement age in 1939.

In 1940, Leahy was appointed governor of Puerto Rico, and later that year, FDR asked him to become ambassador to Vichy, France. Leahy held the ambassadorship until May 1942. His most important posts came through his next assignment as chairman of the newly created Joint Chiefs of Staff and FDR's personal chief of staff. In those positions, he helped to moderate tensions between the army and navy, and generally supported GEORGE C. MARSHALL, the army chief of staff. For example, he backed Marshall's plan for an early cross-channel invasion of France and then DOUGLAS MACARTHUR's plan to retake the Philippines. Leahy also served on the British-American Combined Chiefs of Staff. He participated in the 1943 Tehran and 1945 Yalta conferences. Both FDR and Marshall valued his independent advice. In 1944, he became the first naval officer to be awarded a fifth star with the rank of fleet admiral. Leahy's final retirement, in March 1949, was forced by poor health. Nonetheless, he was able to complete a memoir of his wartime service. He died on July 20, 1959, in Bethesda, Maryland.

LeHand, Missy
(Marguerite Alice LeHand)
(1898–1944) *private secretary of the president*

Officially, Missy LeHand was the private secretary to President Franklin Roosevelt, but she was also his unofficial hostess. She had served as the Roosevelt family's housekeeper, and the Roosevelt children had bestowed her nickname on her. Unmarried, she was a loyal family employee, and readily provided the social companionship that the only-child FDR craved throughout adulthood.

Born on September 13, 1898, in Potsdam, New York, LeHand suffered childhood rheumatic fever. After she graduated in 1917 from Somerville High School in Massachusetts, she went to secretarial school. She worked at the national Democratic Party headquarters and on FDR's unsuccessful 1920 vice-presidential campaign. After he contracted polio the next year, LeHand became his personal secretary and accompanied him to Warm Springs, Georgia, instead of ELEANOR ROOSEVELT, who disliked the racial segregation in the South. LeHand also accompanied FDR during cruises on his houseboat, *Larooco*, which Eleanor preferred to avoid.

After FDR's election to the governorship of New York in 1928, LeHand moved into the executive mansion at Albany. In addition to supervising the household, she paid the bills as a de facto bookkeeper, occasionally presided as official hostess at dinner parties, played poker with FDR, and helped him sort stamps in his philatelic collection. Her employment at the governor's mansion freed Eleanor Roosevelt to teach part-time at the Todd Hunter School in New York City.

After FDR's election to the presidency, LeHand moved into a room in the White House and prepared his daily appointments. A member of his inner circle, she joined FDR for cocktail hours, which the First Lady eschewed. LeHand often arranged dinner parties and other social gatherings for FDR, including the selection of guests, with the result that those who wanted presidential access cultivated her.

LeHand suffered a major stroke in the early summer of 1941 and received treatment at Warm Springs, but she remained an invalid. FDR saw to it that her medical bills were covered, and he provided in his will for her care. She died on July 31, 1944, at her sister's home.

Lehman, Herbert Henry
(1878–1963) *New York governor; head, Office of Foreign Relief and Rehabilitation Operations; director general, United Nations Relief and Rehabilitation Administration*

The son of prosperous German Jewish immigrants, Herbert Lehman was born on March 28, 1878, in New York City. He was well educated, earning his undergraduate degree from

Williams College in 1899. He soon joined the investment banking firm of Lehman Brothers, which his father had helped to found. As soon as his business success was secured, he turned to philanthropic and government service. During World War I, he served as a military officer with the General Staff Corps in Washington, D.C.

Governor AL SMITH brought Lehman directly into the political arena after they met in 1922. Lehman served in Smith's political campaigns for half a dozen years, and in 1928, Smith backed Lehman for lieutenant governor and Franklin Roosevelt for governor. When FDR ran for the presidency in 1932, Lehman ran for New York governor and was elected in a record landslide. Reelected in 1934, 1936, and 1938, he became New York's longest-serving governor.

Lehman was humorless, colorless, and a poor speaker, traits that seemed to work to his advantage as a nonpartisan leader concerned not with himself but with the welfare of the state and its less-well-off citizens. As governor, he lobbied the legislature successfully to enact the "Little New Deal" of relief and reform measures between 1933 and 1938 that resembled FDR's New Deal. He was respected for his character and leadership.

During World War II, Lehman accepted FDR's offer to head the Office of Foreign Relief and Rehabilitation Operations, created in late 1942 within the U.S. Department of State to assist liberated nations during the war until international efforts were available. In late 1943, 44 nations established the United Nations Relief and Rehabilitation Administration (UNRAA), and its council elected Lehman director general. (This was the role that the Roosevelts had hoped HERBERT HOOVER would assume, but he refused.) The UNRAA provided relief to 16 nations. Lehman resigned from the position in early 1946 and soon reentered electoral politics. In

1946 he lost a bid for the U.S. Senate, the only election loss of his career. In 1949, he was appointed to the senate seat vacated by ROBERT WAGNER, and then the next year he defeated John Foster Dulles for a full six-year term. He remained in the senate until 1957, when he retired from politics. Lehman died on December 5, 1963, in New York City.

Lemke, William Frederick
(1878–1950) *U.S. congressman, third-party presidential candidate*

William Lemke was born in Albany, Minnesota, on August 13, 1878, to prosperous pioneer farmers and raised in Towner County, North Dakota. He graduated from the University of North Dakota in 1902 and remained there to complete his first year of law school before transferring to Georgetown University and later to Yale University, where he completed his law degree. He entered law practice in Fargo, North Dakota.

An idealist and champion of farmers, Lemke purchased land in Mexico to establish a socialist utopia, but he was left with failed plans and financial catastrophe by the Mexican Revolution (1910). He became associated with North Dakota's major farm groups, until he became a leader of the small-farm Nonpartisan League, which a group of discontented farmers had started in 1915. The league gained control of the state's Republican Party the next year, and Lemke became party chairman. In 1920, he was elected the state attorney general, but as a result of a banking scandal, he was defeated along with the governor in a recall election the following year. He lost bids for the governorship in 1922 and the U.S. Senate in 1926.

After returning to his law practice, Lemke reentered the political arena in 1932 with his election to the U.S. House of Representatives.

He promoted bankruptcy and mortgage legislation to help desperate farmers and small-business owners. Initially he was a strong supporter of Franklin Roosevelt but turned against the president when the administration opposed the Frazier-Lemke Farm Bankruptcy Act of 1934, which was subsequently struck down by the Supreme Court. It was reenacted in revised form in 1935 to liberalize bankruptcy proceedings for debt-ridden farmers. After FDR rejected the Frazier-Lemke Farm Refinance Bill, Lemke turned to radical fringe leaders offering similar inflationary panaceas for the Great Depression, including Father CHARLES COUGHLIN, Dr. FRANCIS TOWNSEND, and GERALD SMITH. He reluctantly agreed to be the presidential candidate in 1936 for their new Union Party.

However, the short, bald, heavy set Lemke, whose face was covered with freckles and pockmarks from childhood smallpox and who had lost an eye in a childhood accident, was hardly an attractive, charismatic leader. His limitations as a public speaker made him an ineffective voice for the angry dispossessed. He diverted less than 2 percent of the vote from the FDR landslide. In 1940, he was again defeated in a second close race for the U.S. Senate, but he returned to the U.S. House of Representatives in 1942 and served there until his death on May 30, 1950, in Fargo.

Lewis, John Llewellyn
(1880–1969) *national union leader*

John L. Lewis was born in 1880 in Cleveland, Ohio, to immigrant Welsh parents who subsequently moved to Iowa. There Lewis dropped out of high school to follow his father into the coal mines. In 1901, he became a charter member of the local United Mine Workers of America (UMWA). His 1907 attempt at elective public office failed when he

lost the race for the mayorship of Lucas, Iowa. Shortly afterward, the entire Lewis family moved to the new coal-mining town of Panama in south-central Illinois. By 1910, Lewis had been elected as president of the union local, one of the largest in the area. The next year, he became a field representative for the American Federation of Labor (AFL), which allowed him to travel across the country. Six years later, he became vice president of the UMWA, and by 1920 he was its president. The UMWA was the largest union in the AFL, and he held the presidency until he retired 40 years later.

Lewis remained in power partly through ruthless suppression of his opponents, consolidating power in his own hands. He was a lifelong Republican who found the New Deal useful to his ambitious agenda. He successfully

John L. Lewis (left) *(Library of Congress)*

lobbied for the right to organize and bargain collectively that was recognized in the National Industrial Recovery Act of 1933. By 1935, his desire to organize mass-production workers into an overall industrial union, contrary to the AFL's preference for separate craft unions, had caused a split. His supporters included SIDNEY HILLMAN, president of the Amalgamated Clothing Workers (ACWA). The Committee for Industrial Organization (CIO) emerged from this effort and came to dominate American labor during the next five years.

Known for his trademark eyebrows and bellowing voice, Lewis established unions in the automobile, steel, rubber, and appliance industries. In 1936, he helped to create labor's Non-Partisan League, which contributed more than half a million dollars in UMWA-CIO funds to Roosevelt's reelection campaign. In late 1938, the CIO was renamed the Congress of Industrial Organizations, formally splitting from the AFL. While Hillman and others hoped to reconcile with the AFL and remained New Dealers, Lewis soon split with FDR also. Perhaps partly due to his Welsh background, Lewis feared being drawn into World War II because of the British, and as a result he supported Republican presidential candidate WENDELL WILLKIE in 1940. Two years later, Lewis pulled the UMWA out of the CIO. Though he endorsed the war effort after the December 1941 Pearl Harbor attack and organized labor's No Strike Pledge, Lewis nonetheless led a series of strikes in 1943. FDR ordered strikers back to work. Near universal condemnation of the strike led Congress to enact the Smith-Connally Act of 1943, which subjected unions to stricter regulation.

By the time Lewis retired as UMWA president on January 1, 1960, the union was corrupt, in large part because of his authoritarian personality. He died on June 11, 1969, in Washington, D.C.

Lewis, Sinclair
(1885–1951) *novelist*

The son of a physician father and a mother who was a former teacher, Sinclair Lewis was born on February 5, 1885, in Sauk Centre, Minnesota. He received his undergraduate degree from Yale University in 1908 and began working as a journalist. Between 1912 to 1920, he began his prolific fiction career, writing a children's book, novels, and short stories during that period.

Lewis peaked as a writer in the 1920s with five best-selling novels. The first, *Main Street* (1920), was an exposé of small-minded, small-town life in the Midwest; the second, *Babbitt* (1922), exposed the sham life of a businessman; the third, *Arrowsmith* (1925), was a critique of the medical profession; the fourth, *Elmer Gantry* (1927), attacked the hypocrisy of a traveling evangelist; and the fifth, *Dodsworth* (1929), brought his work full circle by dealing with another businessman who finds himself. The first two of these novels were runners-up for the Pulitzer Prize, and when his next novel, *Arrowsmith*, received the award, Lewis refused the prize. In 1930, he became the first American to win the Nobel Prize in literature.

Lewis's best-known novel of the Great Depression era, *It Can't Happen Here* (1935), was his commentary on the rise of a fascist leader in the United States. The inspirations for these books were ADOLF HITLER's takeover of Germany's first democratic government (the Weimar Republic) and the emergence of Louisiana's HUEY LONG with his Share Our Wealth movement. Franklin Roosevelt considered Long to be one of the two greatest threats to American democracy; General DOUGLAS MACARTHUR was the other. *It Can't Happen Here* depicts a newspaper editor's struggle against a charismatic fascist leader and his American fascist supporters. The novel was adapted into a play that in 1935 was staged

Poster for the theatrical staging of Sinclair Lewis's *It Can't Happen Here* (1935) *(Library of Congress)*

simultaneously in 18 cities across the United States by the Federal Theater Project of the Works Progress Administration. Lewis himself played the lead role of Doremus Jessup in the New York City production. Metro-Goldwyn-Mayer (MGM) bought film rights to the novel but later dropped the project. Conservatives cited this play among the productions that they considered evidence of leftist and communist control of the Federal Theatre Project.

Lewis continued to churn out novels, but he also began to drink heavily and finally fled to Europe. Always an outsider, he died in Rome, Italy, on January 10, 1951.

Lilienthal, David Eli
(1899–1981) *Tennessee Valley Authority executive*

Born in Morton, Illinois, on July 8, 1899, David Lilienthal was the son of a Czech immigrant merchants. He became a light-heavyweight boxer at De Pauw University in Greencastle, Indiana, where he received his undergraduate degree in 1920. That fall he entered Harvard Law School, where he encountered FELIX FRANKFURTER, who influenced his interest in natural resources conservation. Ultimately, he would become one of the Roosevelt administration's "Happy Hotdogs," as the press dubbed Frankfurter's former pupils whom he placed in government service. First, however, after graduation from Harvard in 1923, Lilienthal practiced law in Chicago with DONALD RICHBERG. His handling of a telephone rate case before the Supreme Court impressed liberals, including Wisconsin governor PHILIP LA FOLETTE, who appointed Lilienthal to the Wisconsin State Utility Commission in 1931.

In 1933, as a result of Frankfurter's recommendation, FDR appointed Lilienthal as a director of the new Tennessee Valley Authority (TVA), the Depression-era project to improve living standards in a neglected region through flood control and inexpensive electric power. Government workers cleared 175,000 acres of land and built more than 20 dams on the Tennessee River. FDR appointed three directors to the TVA, and its first chairman was ARTHUR MORGAN, an engineer in charge of dam construction. HARCOURT MORGAN was the director in charge of fertilizer production, and Lilienthal was in charge of electric power. The philosophies of Morgan and Lilienthal clashed. Morgan preferred national economic planning through business-government cooperation, so he wanted to maintain close ties with the existing utilities companies. Lilienthal was more influenced by Supreme Court justice LOUIS BRANDEIS's suspicion of concentrated economic power, especially in the utility empire, so he advocated power offered at a cheaper rate to area municipalities. The conflict escalated, and FDR fired Arthur Morgan and replaced him with Harcourt Morgan as TVA chairman in 1938. Part of the conflict was due to the underlying change in the New Deal from national planning to favoring more antitrust legislation and greater economic competition.

Lilienthal's second political round was with WENDELL WILLKIE, who at the time was president of the huge Commonwealth and Southern Corporation, the major public utility in the Tennessee Valley. Willkie claimed the TVA would force his utility out of business through unfair competition. Despite harsh Republican criticism in Congress, Lilienthal survived. The TVA simply bought the Commonwealth and Southern Corporation in 1939, and Lilienthal was named vice chairman of the TVA; he was named chairman on September 15, 1941. The TVA continued to expand during World War II by producing ammunition and other war-related material for the government. At the end of the war, it was the leading producer of electric power in the nation.

Lilienthal prospered during HARRY TRUMAN's presidency. He and Secretary of State DEAN ACHESON developed the plan for the Atomic Energy Commission (AEC) to provide civilian control of the army's large atomic-energy programs. Truman named Lilienthal the first chairman of the AEC, and in April 1947 the Senate finally confirmed him after three months of hearings, during which he was unjustly accused of being a communist sympathizer. He resigned from the AEC in 1950. Lilienthal died on January 14, 1981, in New York City.

Lindbergh, Charles Augustus
(1902–1974) *aviator*

Born on February 4, 1902, in Detroit, Michigan, Charles Lindbergh was the son of a progressive Republican lawyer-congressman father and science-teacher mother. From an early age he wanted to fly airplanes, but he was too young during World War I to become a pilot. He enrolled in engineering at the University of Wisconsin but dropped out his second year to become an airline pilot. He purchased his first plane in 1923, enlisted in the Army Air Service, and then became a captain in the Missouri National Guard. He persuaded a St. Louis businessman to finance an airplane so that he could compete for a $25,000 prize offered to the first person to fly nonstop from New York to Paris. He claimed the prize in late May 1927, after a 33 1/2-hour flight. Garnering international celebrity status, he was awarded the Congressional Medal of Honor.

Two years later, Lindbergh married Anne Spencer Morrow, daughter of the U.S. ambassador to Mexico, and they eventually had six children. They also found that the publicity showered on them prevented a normal existence. In 1932, their first child, Charles Jr., was kidnapped and murdered. The subsequent trial and execution of Bruno Richard Hauptmann kept the Lindberghs in the public spotlight. As a result, they retreated to Europe in 1935. While there, they toured the German air industry, and Lindbergh was decorated by the Nazi regime. While he advocated avoidance of war, he urged Britain, France, and the United States to increase military aviation preparation. The Lindberghs returned home in spring 1939. Acting on a request from General HENRY ARNOLD, the Army Air Corps chief, Lindbergh assisted in promoting American air preparations.

Along with isolationist senator GERALD NYE (R-N.Dak.) and General Robert Wood,

Lindbergh formed the America First Committee in April 1941, becoming its leading crusader for nonintervention in World War II. He also resigned his commission in the Air Corps Reserve. After the Pearl Harbor attack on December 7 later that year, the America First Committee dissolved and he volunteered for the Army Air Force but was prevented from regaining his military commission. Nonetheless, he assisted the war effort as a civilian by testing military aircraft. He never apologized or retracted his prewar views.

During the postwar period, President DWIGHT EISENHOWER restored Lindbergh's commission in the Air Force Reserve and promoted him to brigadier general. His autobiography *The Spirit of St. Louis* (1953) won a Pulitzer Prize. Lindbergh secretly sired a bigamous family in Germany. He died on August 26, 1974.

Lippmann, Walter
(1889–1974) *journalist*

Born on September 23, 1889, into a prosperous Jewish family, Walter Lippmann attended private schools, including Harvard. There he was influenced by the pragmatist philosophy of William James, the detachment of George Santayana, and the British socialist Graham Wallas. Since the New Deal was essentially an ad hoc experiment rather than a grand blueprint for an ideal society, some suggest that William James had also influenced Franklin Roosevelt, who was a student at Harvard seven years before Lippmann.

Lippmann left Harvard shortly before he would have received his master's degree in 1910. He started work as a reporter for a socialist newspaper in Boston, and seven years later, he became the assistant to Lincoln Steffens, one of the nation's first muckrakers. In 1912, Lippmann moved to Schenectady, New York, to work for the new socialist mayor there. That summer he wrote *A Preface to Politics*, the first of his nearly two dozen books, combining ideas from William James, Sigmund Freud, and Henri-Louis Bergson. His book caught the attention of THEODORE ROOSEVELT, Lippmann's political idol, as well as Roosevelt's friend, Herbert Croly, who was launching the weekly magazine *New Progressive* to promote TR's "New Nationalism." Croly made Lippmann its first editor of the publication that debuted in late 1914.

That same year, the persistently energetic Lippmann published his second book, *Drift and Mastery*, in which he terminated his links to socialists and instead advocated a scientifically managed society run by a public-minded elite. It was an elitist philosophy that he retained for the rest of his life. Like many intellectuals of the time, Lippmann favored America's intervention in World War I, and he forged close ties with Colonel Edward House and the Woodrow Wilson administration. But by the end of the war and the peace process, he had grown disillusioned.

During the 1920s, Lippman left the magazine world and became a syndicated newspaper columnist, a career that lasted 36 years. His "Today and Tomorrow" column appeared in more than 250 newspapers in the United States and 25 nations around the world. He became an international figure who tried to interpret the meaning of the news for his readers from his elitist perch. Although he was the nation's first serious political columnist and an elegant writer, he could be inconsistent and commit occasional blunders. His most famous was his 1932 comment about Franklin Roosevelt's presidential bid: "He is a pleasant man who, without any important qualifications for the office, would like very much to be President." It was a view shared by other intellectuals of the day, including HEYWOOD BROUN, Edmund Wilson, and BERNARD BARUCH.

Lippmann supported the New Deal for its first two years and was one of the first Americans to champion the economic approach of JOHN MAYNARD KEYNES. He never feared that FDR would become a dictator, but he disliked what he viewed as the president's "devious methods," which he feared would provoke a backlash harmful to progressive reform. He especially objected to how FDR handled his tax bill in 1933 and the Court-packing plan of 1937.

After his divorce and remarriage, Lippmann moved to Washington, D.C., in 1938. During World War II, he became a realist in international relations, always believing that it was best to negotiate from strength. His heroes in international affairs were CHARLES DE GAULLE and WINSTON CHURCHILL. He basically agreed with FDR's goals, but the New Deal's inconsistency bothered him. However, he was conveniently able to ignore not only his own inconsistent views but also that he and FDR both were essentially the kind of pragmatists who would have drawn approval from William James. Lippmann died in New York City on December 14, 1974.

Long, Huey Pierce
(The Kingfish)
(1893–1935) *Louisiana governor, U.S. senator*

Even before the oppressive Great Depression, white farmers and others in Louisiana had struggled against similar economic conditions that resulted from the stranglehold on state politics by a conservative white oligarchy in alliance with large corporations. Fueled by political ambition, the charismatic Huey Long emerged from the piney woods of rural central Louisiana riding populist sentiments that propelled him first to the governor's seat and then to the U.S. Senate. Louisiana's impoverished environment created the climate in which Long's demagoguery took root and flourished.

A political pied piper luring the vulnerable with promises of shared wealth, Long would later attempt to turn the plight of the millions of Great Depression victims into his stepping-stone to the U.S. presidency. Unlike other southern demagogues of the era, his appeal was more to class than to race.

Born on August 30, 1893, in Winn Parish (county), Louisiana, to a relatively prosperous farm couple, Huey Long was always a man with the gift of gab who was in a hurry. Drawing on high-school debate skills and a brief law-school training, he became a lawyer without a degree, starting his law practice in 1915. Long only wanted a law background to open the doors to politics for him. Within three years, he had won election to the Louisiana Railroad Commission, forerunner of the Public Service Commission, and he held that posi-

Huey Pierce Long *(Library of Congress)*

tion for eight years. In 1924, he was defeated in the governor's election, but he won it in 1928, with his greatest support coming from voters in poor rural parishes.

As governor, Long put thousands of citizens to work. "The Kingfish," as he was nicknamed, built roads, bridges, and schools, in addition to building up and taking personal interest in Louisiana State University in Baton Rouge (including a sports facility and medical school). He built an airport in New Orleans, a new capitol, an improved public-health system, and a school-bus system, and he began providing free textbooks for students in both public and private schools. There were huge increases in both state spending and state debt under Long. He financed his statewide political machine through the "deduct box," the name for the system of automatic cash deductions from the salaries of all state employees, who depended upon his patronage for their jobs.

Long's political ambition, like his energy, was boundless. In 1930, he defeated the longtime senator from upstate Louisiana, Joseph E. Ransdell, a Catholic with a relatively progressive record that included cofounding what would become the National Institutes of Health. Long refused to take his Senate seat until after the 1932 gubernatorial election had installed his handpicked puppet, O. K. Allen. He continued to run the state political machine from his Senate seat, as reflected in an annual report of one of the state's charity hospitals. The report contained a full-page portrait of Long with the caption "Senator Huey P. Long, *The Master Builder*," with "Governor O.K. Allen, *his able assistant*" on the next page.

Long was a showman in the Senate who loved to grandstand. He resigned from Senate committees and challenged Democratic majority leader JOSEPH ROBINSON from neighboring Arkansas. Ever flamboyant, he pioneered the use of the sound truck in his whirlwind cam-

paign to return Arkansas senator HATTIE WYATT CARAWAY to her seat. Long did most of the talking, not only to show his strength beyond his home-state boundaries but also to assist a progressive ally and to embarrass the Senate leadership. In the Senate, he criticized President HERBERT HOOVER and advocated a redistribution of the nation's wealth to end the Great Depression.

In 1932, Long energetically supported Franklin Roosevelt's presidential bid at the Democratic National Convention and during the fall campaign. But by the end of the next year, he was disillusioned with the New Deal, considering it too conservative. He obstructed the administration's bills in the Senate with colorful filibusters. The White House retaliated by rewarding federal patronage in Louisiana to his opponents and withholding public-works funds.

Upping the ante, Long focused on building a national movement for a presidential bid in 1936. On February 23, 1934, he announced the "Share Our Wealth Society," designed to tax the rich to aid the poor. Poverty, Long asserted, would be eliminated by guaranteeing a minimum family income of $5,000 and by providing old-age pensions, cancellation of personal debt, and free public education through college. The society advocated high taxes on inherited fortunes greater than $1 million as well as limiting any individual's annual income to a maximum of $1 million. By 1935, more than 7 million members had signed up in one of the 27,000 "Share Our Wealth Society" clubs across America. That same year, Long wrote and published *My First Days in the White House*, which outlined what he would do as the chief executive. He appealed to the discontented during the Great Depression via radio addresses, his own newspaper, and propaganda sent through the mail.

His adversary FDR once dubbed Long as one of the "two most dangerous men in America." (The other was DOUGLAS MACARTHUR.)

Long epitomized the charismatic political leader. He had the ability at least to get people to watch him, especially the dispossessed who had previously been politically passive. His appeal to the dispossessed is best captured in Robert Penn Warren's classic novel *All the King's Men* (1946). He was probably the most serious threat to FDR's reelection bid in 1936. He tended to become more autocratic and was increasingly consumed by a need for power, which was more important to him than the accumulation of material wealth or his own family, which he seldom saw. By the end of 1935, he had basically eliminated local government in Louisiana and created almost total dependence on the state government, with repercussions that persist into the 21st century. Another by-product of his quest to rule Louisiana was the compromising of Louisiana's judiciary branch. His power in the state was nearly unchecked.

On September 8, 1935, Dr. Carl Austin Weiss shot Long, who was in the hallway of the Baton Rouge state capitol outside his old governor's office. Long died two days later, but his political machine survived him, perpetuating the state's Long and anti-Long factions well after his death.

Longworth, Alice Lee Roosevelt
(1884–1980) *daughter of Theodore Roosevelt, celebrity*

The life of Alice Lee Roosevelt Longworth foreshadowed the media phenomenon of the later 20th century in which personalities without much substance became famous for being famous. At the same time, she was a constant reminder of the political legacy of her father. Born in New York City on February 12, 1884, she was the only child born to THEODORE ROOSEVELT and his first wife, Alice Hathaway Lee. When she was only two days old, both her mother and her paternal grandmother died. A politician who later liked to lecture on morality, Teddy Roosevelt became an absentee father, essentially deserting his daughter and letting his sister Anna Roosevelt raise her until she was three years old, when he remarried. After his second marriage, Roosevelt did not speak with his daughter about her deceased mother, and her stepmother assumed responsibility for her upbringing.

A member of the Oyster Bay rather than the Hyde Park Roosevelts, Alice Roosevelt was part of the Roosevelt clan physically, socially, and intellectually, but not emotionally. As a girl, she was shy and wore leg braces because of polio. ELEANOR ROOSEVELT is typically cited as the proverbially ugly ducking of the clan, but when they were youngsters, Alice envied her cousin's looks. The only child of her father's first marriage in a family of half-siblings, Alice was as much of an outsider as Eleanor, who was orphaned as a child and taken in by relatives. Although Alice was bright, she refused to attend school and instead became an autodidact (self-taught). Never quite fitting in, she rebelled to attract attention. Rebelling became her trademark.

During her father's presidency, the politically sophisticated "Princess Alice" was allowed to make goodwill tours abroad for her father. She could be diplomatic, but she also enjoyed shocking others to gain attention. She smoked in public, bet on horses, and drove her own car, conduct bordering on scandalous for a lady of her position and time.

In 1906, Alice Roosevelt married Republican U.S. representative Nicholas Longworth of Ohio. Her White House wedding to the prominent politician who was 14 years her senior cemented her international celebrity status as well as her role in politics. Longworth was unfaithful and she followed suit. In 1925, she gave birth to her only child, fathered by U.S. senator WILLIAM E. BORAH (R-Idaho).

Longworth died in 1931. Rejecting tradition by declining to run for her deceased husband's congressional seat, Alice Longworth instead wrote her autobiography, *Crowded Hours* (1933). She campaigned for HERBERT HOOVER in 1932 against her distant cousin FDR, who had married her cousin Eleanor. She criticized FDR's New Deal and she served as a delegate to the 1936 Republican National Convention. Still, the White House Roosevelts went out of their way to invite her to functions, and she continued to attend the national conventions of both political parties.

Like most other Republicans of the time, Alice Longworth was a strong isolationist in foreign policy. She supported the 1940 and 1944 presidential bids of ROBERT TAFT and served as an officer on the national committee of the America First organization as well as director of its Washington, D.C., chapter in the 1940s. For the next 40 years she resided in the nation's capital as a local celebrity with a caustic tongue. She died on February 21, 1980, in Washington, D.C.

Lorentz, Pare
(1905–1992) *filmmaker, U.S. Film Service director*

Born in Clarksburg, West Virginia, on December 11, 1905, Pare Lorentz was the son of a printer. He studied at West Virginia Wesleyan College and the University of West Virginia until he moved to New York City in 1924. From 1925 to 1934, he reviewed films for *Judge*, a humor magazine, and he also was a film critic for a variety of popular magazines.

Lorentz supported the New Deal from its start. In 1934, he published *The Roosevelt Year: 1933*, in which he tried to capture the spirit of the New Deal through a survey of people, situations, and issues. The next year, he was hired by the Resettlement Administration to film a documentary about the Dust Bowl. On a small budget and with support from film director King Vidor and photographer DOROTHEA LANGE, he wrote, directed, and edited *The Plow That Broke the Plains*, with musical score by Virgil Thomson. Filmed on location across the Great Plains and the Texas Panhandle, the film premiered in May 1936 to critical acclaim. However, Hollywood studios saw the government-sponsored project as a commercial threat and refused to let it be shown in their theaters across the nation.

The Farm Security Administration soon recruited Lorentz to document the effects of flooding along the Mississippi River and the need for flood control. During the filming, the Ohio River flooded in January 1937, allowing Lorentz to capture the impact on entire communities. He again hired Virgil Thomson to compose the musical score, blended with folk songs and hymns, to evoke the mood and accent the theme of the film. *The River* won many awards, including first prize at the 1938 Venice International Film Festival. After FDR saw it, he appointed Lorentz as director of the U.S. Film Service, which was established in 1938 to produce documentaries about pressing social problems.

In 1940, in response to FDR's suggestion that he make a documentary showing the relationship of childbirth mortality to unemployment and slums, Lorentz made *The Fight for Life*, filmed in the Chicago Maternity Center. Its controversial nature angered many lawmakers who subsequently terminated the U.S. Film Service by refusing to fund it. It was reorganized under the Federal Security Agency and the Office of Education.

During World War II, Lorentz became an officer in the Army Air Corps, and he made briefing films for American pilots. During the postwar era, he became chief of the film section of the War Department's Civil Affairs Division, resigning his post in 1947. He died on March 4, 1992, in Armonk, New York.

Luce, Henry Robinson
(1898–1967) *publisher*

Henry Luce was born on April 3, 1898, in Teng-chow, China, to a missionary-educator father and a mother who was a former social worker. Growing up with a strong work ethic but a weak sense of humor, Luce spoke with a stammer, which led him to focus on the written word instead of oral communication. His parents sent him back to the United States for his education at the Hotchkiss School in Connecticut (1913–16). He then entered Yale University, where he helped edit the campus newspaper. He enthusiastically supported entry of the United States into World War I, but by the time he received his ROTC commission in late 1918, it was too late for him to serve abroad. He returned to Yale and graduated in 1920, then went on to study at Oxford University before beginning work at newspapers in Chicago and Baltimore.

Luce launched the first mass-circulation newsmagazine, *Time*, in 1923. It featured short news reports for people with limited time who were eager to understand the political world. He paid his staff well and motivated them by his own intense work ethic. His lifelong hero was THEODORE ROOSEVELT, and the magazine favored progressive Republican themes. By 1929, Luce had become a millionaire. Despite the Great Depression, Luce launched *Fortune* the next year, selling it for $1 per issue; it made him a force on Wall Street. In 1931, he began the radio series *The March of Time*, which in 1935 became the newsreel series of the same name that was shown in theaters worldwide. The next year, he divorced his first wife to marry Clare Boothe Brokaw, an aspiring playwright who sought the personal publicity Luce shunned. She served two terms in the U.S. House of Representatives (1943–47), where she echoed his political views.

In 1936, Luce began the photo magazine *Life*, which, with its emphasis on images, was in many ways the precursor to modern television. Ultimately, he proved to be his father's son, becoming a lay missionary who used his magazines as his pulpit. An internationalist, he was quick to support China's resistance to the Japanese invasion. He mistrusted FDR but initially backed the president's foreign-policy aims, especially conscription and the lend-lease proposal to aid Great Britain. By 1940, however, Luce turned to Republican WENDELL WILLKIE, supporting his presidential bid in an effort to move the Republican Party from isolationism to internationalism. He also helped to turn Madame CHIANG KAI-SHEK into a national celebrity during her 1943 visit to the United States while ignoring warnings from his own staff about the corruption and incompetence of the Chiang regime.

During the postwar era, Luce championed DWIGHT EISENHOWER's 1952 presidential bid and launched *Sports Illustrated* for a public with new leisure time. He resigned as editor in chief of *Time* in 1964 and died on February 18, 1967, in Phoenix, Arizona.

Ludlow, Louis Leon
(1873–1950) *U.S. congressman*

Born in southeastern Indiana on June 24, 1873, Louis Ludlow began his journalism career at age 18 in Indianapolis. In 1901, he moved to Washington, D.C., to become the capital correspondent for the *Indianapolis Sentinel*. Popular with his colleagues, he was president of the national press club in 1927. Always energetic, Ludlow wrote three of his five books in the 1920s. His autobiography, *From Cornfield to Press Gallery* (1924), was first, followed by *In the Heart of Hoosierland* (1925) and *Senator Solomon Spiffledink* (1927).

After 37 years of writing about politicians, Ludlow became one when he was elected to the U.S. House of Representatives in 1928; he represented the Indianapolis area until 1949. He supported both antilynching and equal rights for women legislation, but he opposed the repeal of Prohibition. Ludlow became known for his opposition to a more powerful executive branch of government. His fourth book, *America Go Bust: An Expose of the Federal Bureaucracy and Its Wasteful and Evil Tendencies* (1933) reflected his disdain for big government. However, he received the most attention two years later by proposing a war-referendum amendment that would have required a national vote prior to a declaration of war, except following a direct attack on or invasion of the United States. The House Judiciary Committee held hearings on the Ludlow amendment bill in June 1935, but it died in committee. During the next two years, he drummed up support for the legislation by giving speeches and radio addresses, writing letters and articles in newspapers and magazines, and publishing his fifth book, *Hell or Heaven* (1937). His media campaign worked to the degree that he was able to achieve popular support for his amendment in opinion polls, and his House colleagues considered a discharge petition to force the bill from the House judiciary committee to the floor of the House for a vote by the entire body. Ultimately the House voted 209-188 against considering the bill on January 10, 1938.

As the threat of World War II in Europe escalated, popular interest in the Ludlow amendment waned. During the postwar era, he favored an international war referendum and the creation of a Department of Peace and Good Will. The increasingly one-issue congressman died in Washington, D.C., on November 28, 1950.

MacArthur, Douglas
(1880–1964) *army chief of staff, commander of Southwest Pacific Theater army forces*

Douglas MacArthur was born in Little Rock, Arkansas, on January 26, 1880. His father was a Civil War veteran who went on to become one of the highest-ranking officers in the U.S. Army. Consequently, MacArthur was a "military brat" reared on army posts in Texas and the Southwest. He graduated at the top of his West Point class and became an officer in the engineering corps, assigned to posts in the United States, the Philippines, and Panama, and he served during the brief U.S. occupation of Vera Cruz (1914) during the Mexican civil war. He also served in France during World War I and briefly was among occupying forces in the German Rhineland after the war. During the interwar period, he became the reforming superintendent of West Point (1919–21) and served two tours of duty in the Philippines, where he became a friend of future Philippine President Manuel Quezon.

In 1930, President HERBERT HOOVER appointed MacArthur as army chief of staff (1930–35). In July 1932, he committed his first dramatic act of ill-advised independent judgment by using force to remove the Bonus Marchers, unemployed World War I veterans who were protesting for early government pensions, from the Anacostia Flats section of Washington, D.C. The House of Representatives had responded favorably to the veterans' request, but the Senate had refused. Hoover assumed responsibility for the actions of his overly eager army chief of staff.

Although Franklin Roosevelt considered MacArthur to be one of the two most dangerous men in America (HUEY LONG was the other), the two men worked together in establishing FDR's pet New Deal program, the Civilian Conservation Corps. After he stepped down as army chief of staff, MacArthur became the military adviser to the Philippine Commonwealth headed by Quezon. For the next half-dozen years, he was assisted by Major DWIGHT EISENHOWER. He retired from the U.S. Army in December 1937, but he continued to work privately as a military adviser to Quezon.

In late July 1941, MacArthur was recalled to active duty. Many critics were surprised by the U.S. military's lack of defensive preparedness as, nine hours after the December 7, 1941, attack on Pearl Harbor, the Japanese destroyed most of the American air force around Manila in the Philippines. Equally shocking was that MacArthur initially supported Quezon's plan to negotiate a truce with Japan and his acceptance of a $500,000 payment from Quezon.

General of the Army Douglas MacArthur on Luzon, the Philippines, 1945 *(Library of Congress)*

Despite this, FDR made MacArthur commander of the Southwest Pacific Area Theater, one of two Pacific theaters of operation during World War II. The president even approved awarding MacArthur a Congressional Medal of Honor, mostly to counter calls for a "Pacific first" rather than a European strategy for World War II. After MacArthur departed Corregidor for Australia in early 1942, he spent the following 30 months fulfilling his vow "I shall return" to free the Philippines. His effort was launched in New Guinea by the summer of 1942 and continued with successful amphibious operations during the next two years.

During the following three presidential elections (1944, 1948, 1952), MacArthur encouraged Republicans to promote a presidential bid for him. He had always been adept at using good public relations within the army, with the notable exception of the Bonus March veterans, but his efforts to be president failed, in part because he had spent so many years living outside of the United States. His greatest service to the nation may have been as occupation commander in Japan, and his autocratic tendencies may have contributed to his success in that environment. Both HARRY TRUMAN and MacArthur agreed to preserve a modified emperor system. HIROHITO's survival and support for the occupation gained crucial support from the Japanese people. The Korean War emphasized both his talents and limitations as a general. President Truman, after obtaining the agreement of most of his senior military and political advisers, fired MacArthur on April 11, 1951, in order to uphold the American principle of civilian supremacy. After DWIGHT EISENHOWER assumed the presidency, MacArthur faded from public life. He made occasional speeches but focused on completing his memoirs. He died on April 5, 1964, in Washington, D.C.

MacDonald, Ramsey
(1866–1937) *British prime minister*

Ramsey MacDonald was born out of wedlock on October 12, 1866, in Lossiemouth, Moraysluve, Scotland, to a domestic servant. His mother and grandmother raised him under very modest circumstances, and he attended the parish school at Drainie. Later he moved to Bristol, where he worked as a student-teacher. He subsequently moved to London, where he obtained a clerkship to Thomas Lough, a politician. A bright and energetic man determined to improve himself, MacDonald pursued his education, taking evening classes until he finally graduated from the British equivalent of high school in 1885. He immediately joined the Social Democratic Federation, and the following year he joined the socialist Fabian Society. By 1894, MacDonald was a member of the new Independent Labour Party. The next year, he married Margaret Gladstone, a distant relative of British prime minister William Gladstone. The marriage brought not only financial independence but also entrée into the elite social strata and personal happiness.

Believing that a labor party needed trade union support, MacDonald in 1900 became the first secretary of the Labour Representation Committee (LRC). By 1906, he had united with 28 other LRC members to successfully wage campaigns for seats in the House of Commons. That same year, the LRC became the Labour Party, and in 1911 MacDonald was selected as chairman of the party's parliamentary coalition. He was reelected to Parliament from Leicester in 1910, but because of his opposition to British entry into World War I, he was forced to resign his chairmanship on August 5, 1914. He was narrowly defeated in the 1918 parliamentary election.

The ever-resilient MacDonald came to support the war effort and the wartime coalition of Prime Minister David Lloyd George. Public sentiment had turned against George's politics by 1922, and MacDonald easily won his comeback election that year as Labour became the second-largest party in the House of Commons. In 1924, he became the first-ever Labour Party prime minister. His government granted diplomatic recognition to the Soviet Union and helped U.S. banker CHARLES DAWES to deal with the German financial crisis that allowed Germany to repay its reparations from World War I with loans from the United States. However, MacDonald's party turned against him after he arranged a trade agreement with the Soviet Union, and the Conservatives returned to power in late 1924.

MacDonald became prime minister again in 1929 after the Labour Party won the general election, and he therefore presided during the onset of the Great Depression. That same year his government revised the Old Age Pension Act, broadened the Unemployment Insurance Act, and passed a Coal Mines Act. Nonetheless, the government was unable to reach consensus about policies to address the serious financial problems faced by Great Britain. In 1931, MacDonald offered his resignation but changed his mind and, with a few other members of his own party, broke away to form a coalition government that was dominated by the Conservatives. MacDonald continued as prime minister under the new arrangement, but many Labourites viewed him as a traitor. The public, however, vindicated him in the general election of October 1931.

MacDonald remained in office through 1935. He appointed NEVILLE CHAMBERLAIN as his finance minister and took Britain off the gold standard while cutting government expenditures and raising tariffs. Despite continued high unemployment, overall the economic reforms seemed to work during the Great Depression. The constant pressures of his office took a toll on his health, however, prompting MacDonald to agree to exchange cabinet posts with STANLEY BALDWIN, lord president of the council. MacDonald resigned from that position soon afterward. He died on November 9, 1937, while on a trip to South America.

MacLeish, Archibald
(1892–1982) *poet; Librarian of Congress; director, Office of Facts and Figures; assistant director, Office of War Information; assistant secretary of state for cultural and public affairs*

Sometimes referred to as the "Poet Laureate of the New Deal," Archibald MacLeish was born on May 7, 1892, in Glencoe, Illinois. His father was a prosperous but emotionally distant Scottish businessman. His mother was a former educator who tried to inculcate in him a sense of social responsibility. MacLeish was the third of their five children, caught in the middle of his siblings and between his parent's differing wishes of what they wanted him to do with his life. Throughout his life, he craved approval and success. He attended Hotchkiss in Connecticut from 1907 to 1911 and Yale University, where he majored in English, from 1911 to 1915. His studies at Harvard Law School from 1915 to 1919 were interrupted

by one year of military service during World War I. After a brief stint as editor of the *New Republic*, MacLeish began a successful three-year law practice in Boston, but he then quit so that he and his wife could move to Paris to pursue his ambition of becoming a poet. He found his niche in poetry, and the MacLeishes returned to the United States in 1928 and bought a Berkshire farm in Conway, Massachusetts, that was their home for the rest of their lives.

Because MacLeish always needed the reinforcement of external approval, he was pulled between the private and public realms. HENRY LUCE recognized his talent and recruited him for his new magazine, *Fortune*, to write about American and international affairs. During that period, MacLeish wrote his long poem *Conquistador* (1932), which brought him the first of three Pulitzer Prizes. It was during this period that he concluded a poet should be involved in society, perhaps an echo of his mother's influence, and that America lacked a cultural vision, but a poet could furnish one. He was condemned by many modernist poets for wanting to write "public poetry," and he was also attacked by both conservatives and liberals for his political views. He came to admire Franklin Roosevelt and the New Deal.

MacLeish joined the Roosevelt administration in 1939 as the Librarian of Congress, which led New Jersey Republican conservative congressman J. Parnell Thomas to coin the term *fellow traveler*, a condemnation of both FDR and MacLeish as communists. The term would later reemerge during the McCarthy era to condemn other liberals. During the next five years, MacLeish also wrote speeches for FDR and served as director of the Office of Facts and Figures, then as assistant director of the Office of War Information from 1942 to 1943. He resigned from the administration in 1944 to return to private life. However, FDR brought him back one final time as assistant secretary of state for cultural and public affairs, a position he held until 1945.

During the postwar period, MacLeish served as the Boylston Professor of Rhetoric and Oratory at Harvard from 1949 to 1962, and it was during this time that he won his second and third Pulitzer Prizes for his *Collected Poems 1917–1952* (1952) and the poetic *J.B.* (1958). If his creative work is not as highly regarded today as the work of the American writers who were expatriates with him in Paris, such as E. E. Cummings, F. Scott Fitzgerald, and his friend ERNEST HEMINGWAY, it may be because he never realized his literary vision for Americans because he was trying to achieve success in his "public poetry." The critical view of MacLeish is that although he was immensely talented, he was too conventional. He died on April 20, 1982, in Boston.

Mao Zedong
(Mao Tse-tung)
(1893–1976) *Chinese revolutionary and Communist Party leader*

Mao Zedong was born in Hunan province, China, on December 26, 1893. While his father, a prosperous self-made grain dealer, was a harsh disciplinarian, his mother was kinder and more sympathetic to him. Mao attended local schools until he was 10, refusing to continue after he encountered a teacher who also was a rigid disciplinarian. In 1918, he graduated from Hunan First Normal School, located in Changsha, Hunan province's urban capital near his village. He then moved to Peking (Beijing), the ancient imperial capital, to work as a librarian's assistant at Peking University, China's leading university. His lowly position and southern dialect made Mao an outsider at the status-conscious institution. By summer 1920, he had embraced Marxism. The next year, he became one of the founding delegates of the Chinese Communist Party, which worked with Sun Yat-sen's Kuomintang (Chinese Nationalist Party; Guomindang) to subdue warlords and expel imperialist influence from China. After the death of Sun Yat-sen, who had been influenced by the writings of Abraham Lincoln, a split developed between the Nationalists and the Communists.

In 1927, CHIANG KAI-SHEK (Jiang Jieshi), Sun Yat-sen's successor, decided to launch the first of his several attempts to crush the Communists located in urban areas, forcing them to flee initially to southeastern China. Ironically, the campaign worked to reinforce Mao's identification with peasants and brought out his populist leanings, positioning him to emerge as the eventual political leader of the Chinese Communist Party in the mid 1930s. Soviet leader JOSEPH STALIN's support for a different faction at this time made Mao the first and only leader of a Communist Party without Stalin's support.

The New Deal era in the United States coincided with China's Yenan era, named for the remote northwest area where Mao staged the Chinese equivalent of the British withdrawal from Dunkirk in the early part of World War II. It began after Chiang started his "annihilation campaign" of 1934, forcing the Communists to flee Jianxi (Kiangsi) and leading to the so-called Long March. The march not only precipitated Mao's emergence as the main leader of the Communists but also elevated the lengthy retreat to Yenan into an instant legend. Until the end of World War II, Mao maintained his popular support among the peasantry of north China by treating them well. By 1936, Nationalist generals finally forced Chiang to abandon his annihilation campaign against the Communists and to replace it with an alliance forged with them to repel the Japanese invasion of China. In 1937, Mao divided his forces into smaller groups simultaneously to combat the Japanese and continue to build support among peasants.

Both the Communists and the Nationalists were receptive to postwar mediation efforts by GEORGE C. MARSHALL in 1945–46, maneuvering their troops to the greatest advantage during the talks. Mao's strategy proved more successful. Nationalism, modernization, and the appeal of equality trumped Karl Marx, V. I. Lenin, and Adam Smith. Despite the numerically superior armies of Chiang's Nationalists that controlled urban areas, Mao controlled the countryside and had the support of the peasantry. Finally, in 1949, his peasant soldiers "liberated" the urban working class, which had retreated into political passivity after Chiang's brutal 1927 campaign. The People's Republic of China was declared on October 1, 1949. For the first time in a century, mainland China was unified, based on the notion of equality (for example, ending the feudal custom of primogeniture), and would rapidly transform itself from an agrarian into a modern industrial giant, extracting a tremendous human cost in the process.

Mao would outlive the trio of other political giants of his time: Franklin Roosevelt, Joseph Stalin, and Chiang Kai-shek. In final twists of irony, his mausoleum in Beijing was modeled after the Lincoln Memorial in Washington, D.C., and he died on September 9, 1976, as the United States celebrated the bicentennial year of its independence.

Marcantonio, Vito Anthony
(1902–1954) *U.S. congressman*

Often considered one of the most radical members of Congress during his terms of service, Vito Marcantonio was born on December 10, 1902, in East Harlem, New York City, to an American-born, carpenter father and an Italian-born mother. Among his teachers at the local schools he attended was a history teacher at DeWitt Clinton High School who was a teachers' union organizer and former Socialist

candidate for Congress. Immediately after his graduation in 1921, Marcantonio became acquainted with FIORELLA LA GUARDIA, then serving on the New York City Board of Aldermen, who became his surrogate father. Marcantonio enrolled in New York University Law School and graduated in 1925, the same year he married Mariam Sanders, whom he had met at the Harlem House, a settlement house for immigrants. Their marriage was childless.

La Guardia was elected to Congress in 1922. When the Republican Party denied him the party nomination in 1924, he chose to run independently and selected Marcantonio as his reelection campaign manager. Marcantonio, who was multilingual like La Guardia, selected the Haarlem House with its immigrant constituency as the base for a La Guardia Political Club. It grew to more than a thousand members and also served as an informal organization independent of Democrats and Republicans. La Guardia won his campaign, and Marcantonio ran his local office, which provided maximum constituent service. By 1930, when Marcantonio was appointed an assistant U.S. district attorney, the 20th Congressional District was the largest Italian-American community in the nation.

La Guardia was defeated in the 1932 election that swept Franklin Roosevelt into the White House. However, the next year he ran successfully for election as mayor of New York City, freeing Marcantonio to seek La Guardia's former congressional seat. With backing from the new mayor, Marcantonio became one of only 123 Republicans to win in the off-year congressional election. However, he lost his seat in 1936 because he was unwilling to denounce communist support. He ran for another congressional seat in 1938 on the American Party ticket, won it, and remained in Congress for six terms.

Marcantonio joined MAURY MAVERICK of Texas and Ernest Lundeen of Minnesota in pressing for a more radical approach to the Great Depression than was offered under the New Deal. In foreign affairs, he advocated U.S. support for the Loyalists during the Spanish civil war, yet he remained a pacifist during the early years of World War II, changing his stance after Nazi Germany invaded the Soviet Union in June 1941. After that event, he became a major supporter of FDR's war policy.

Marcantonio's association with American communist leaders led to his marginalization in Congress, where he was relegated to the least-important committees. During the postwar period, his continued support for the Soviet Union grew out of fashion, and he was defeated for reelection in 1950. He resumed his law practice until his death on August 9, 1954, in New York City.

Margold, Nathan Ross
(1899–1947) *federal solicitor, chairman of Petroleum Administrative Board and Petroleum Labor Policy Board, special assistant attorney general, federal judge*

Nathan Margold was born on July 21, 1899, in Iaşi, Romania. His parents immigrated to the United States in 1901, and he was raised in Brooklyn, New York. After his graduation in 1919 from the City College of New York, he entered Harvard Law School, where he was editor of its law review and where FELIX FRANKFURTER developed his interest in social reforms and the rights of workers. After he graduated in 1923, he returned to New York City to practice law. He was the assistant U.S. attorney for the Southern District of New York from 1925 to 1927. He married Gertrude Weiner in 1927, and the couple had one son.

The same year that Margold married, Frankfurter recruited him to teach criminal law at Harvard. Harvard president A. Laurence Lowell objected to another Jewish reformer on the faculty, but law school dean Roscoe Pound initially supported FRANKFURTER; however, after two years of pressure, he acquiesced to the president, and Margold returned to his New York law practice in 1928. Between his return to New York and the beginning of the New Deal, Margold also served as a special counsel for the New York Transit Commission in 1928–29, and in 1930 he was the legal adviser on Indian affairs with the Institute for Government Research.

Ever industrious, Margold also wrote articles for law journals and coedited *Cases on Criminal Law*. At Frankfurter's suggestion, the National Association for the Advancement of Colored People (NAACP) recruited Margold as a special counsel in 1930, and he served in that capacity until 1933. In 1931, he wrote a book-length report that outlined a legal strategy for the NAACP to use to desegregate public schools in the South. It became the blueprint that culminated in *Brown v. Board of Education* (1954).

At the beginning of the New Deal, Margold left the NAACP to become one of Frankfurter's many "Happy Hotdogs," the term used to describe former Frankfurter students brought into the new administration. Both Frankfurter and Justice LOUIS BRANDEIS recommended Margold to FDR's new secretary of the interior, HAROLD ICKES. Ickes hired him as the solicitor for the department in 1933, and he remained in that role until 1942. First naming him as chairman of the Petroleum Administrative Board after the National Recovery Administration (NRA) developed the code for the industry, Ickes then appointed Margold as chairman of the Petroleum Labor Policy Board, which administered the code, from 1933 to 1935. However, the Supreme Court declared Section 9(c) of the National Industrial Recovery Act, which had delegated petroleum code-making authority to the president, unconstitutional in *Panama Refining*

Company v. Ryan (1935). Margold also acted as a special assistant attorney general from 1933 to 1935.

In return for his loyalty and legal expertise, FDR named Margold as a judge of the Municipal Court for the District of Columbia, where he served from 1942 to 1945, when he was moved to the U.S. District Court in the District of Columbia. He served on that bench until his death on December 16, 1947.

Marshall, George Catlett, Jr.
(1880–1959) *army chief of staff*

George C. Marshall, Jr., was born on December 31, 1880, in Uniontown, Pennsylvania. His successful father, a coal merchant, was distantly related to John Marshall, the great Supreme Court justice who had fought with George Washington's army during the American Revolution. George Marshall attended the Virginia Military Institute from 1897 to 1901. During and after World War I, he was one of General John J. Pershing's top aides. Among his many assignments was service with the 15th Infantry Regiment in Tienstin, China, from 1924 to 1927. Afterward, he returned to Washington, D.C., to serve briefly as an instructor at the naval War College before heading the Infantry School at Fort Benning, Georgia, from 1927 to 1932. There he created what would become the U.S. High Command during World War II.

From 1932 to 1936, Marshall commanded army posts in Georgia and South Carolina and he worked to organize some camps for Franklin Roosevelt's pet project, the Civilian Conservation Corps. He was promoted to brigadier general and afterward took command of the 5th Infantry Brigade in Washington State from 1936 to 1938. He returned to Washington, D.C., in 1938 to head the War Plans Division of the army general staff. Despite Marshall's relative lack of seniority, FDR made him the army chief of staff in April 1939. Marshall had impressed both the President and HARRY HOPKINS, even though his manner was very formal in comparison to FDR's style.

During early 1942, Marshall reorganized the War Department and became the leader of the new U.S. Joint Chiefs of Staff and Anglo-American Combined Chiefs of Staff, gradually emerging as FDR's key military adviser. His North-South links and military-civilian diplomacy made him effective with Congress as well as one of FDR's most trusted advisers. Marshall had the opportunity to lead the Normandy D-Day invasion, but he emulated George Washington's precedent of self-denial and selected his protégé, DWIGHT EISENHOWER, for the assignment. In 1944, Congress made him a five-star general with the title of General of the Army.

General George Catlett Marshall, Jr. *(Library of Congress)*

In late 1945, HARRY S. TRUMAN named Marshall as a special presidential envoy to China in an effort to help avoid a civil war between the Chinese Nationalists and Communists. Although the mission failed a year later, Truman named Marshall his secretary of state in early 1947, and he became the first professional soldier to occupy that position. During his two-year tenure, he obtained both public and Republican support for the European Recovery Program, better known as the Marshall Plan, which economically revived the war-torn continent. It also contributed to an integrated Western Europe, including West Germany, a direct contrast to the treatment of Germany after World War I. Despite his brief tenure in the cabinet post, scholars rank Marshall among the top five secretaries of state in American history. He became the first career military person to earn the Nobel Peace Prize, which he received in 1953. Marshall died on October 16, 1959, in Washington, D.C.

Martin, Joseph William, Jr.
(1884–1968) *U.S. congressman, Republican minority leader*

The second of eight children of an Irish black-smith and his wife, Joseph Martin was born in North Attleboro, Massachusetts, on November 3, 1884. He attended local public schools, graduating from North Attleboro High School in 1902. After he completed high school, he began working as a local newspaper reporter and playing semiprofessional baseball. By 1908, he and several local businessmen had jointly purchased one of the city's newspapers, and he became its publisher and editor. A decade later, he purchased an insurance agency, and in 1924 he bought a weekly newspaper in Massachusetts.

Martin became acquainted with local politics through his newspaper work and soon became involved in politics. He won a Repub-

lican seat in the state legislature in 1911 and served three one-year terms in the Massachusetts house before moving to the state senate, where he had a similar length of service. While in the senate, he came into contact with Calvin Coolidge, then serving as Massachusetts Senate president. In 1924, Martin challenged an incumbent for a U.S. congressional seat and lost. Six months later, however, the incumbent died, and Martin won the special election to fill the vacancy. He went on to serve in the U.S. House of Representatives from 1925 to 1967. At the request of Coolidge, by then president of the United States, Martin supported the 1925 bid by Ohio's Nicholas Longworth to become Speaker of the House. A friendly, low-key, and shrewd team player, Martin was appointed to the powerful House Rules Committee ("the traffic cop committee") in 1929. Following Longworth's death and the loss of the Republican majority in the House in 1931, Martin became friends with JOHN NANCE GARNER, the new Democratic Speaker. Martin served as the assistant minority whip from 1931 to 1933 and was the minority whip from 1933 to 1939.

Martin personally liked Franklin Roosevelt, but his new leadership position made him a strong opponent of the New Deal. He was an economic conservative representing small-town businessmen and the Republicans' Old Guard. In 1939, he was elected House minority leader, and he held that position throughout the remaining New Deal years as well as during World War II. A congressional technician, Martin drew on his whip experience to forge the bipartisan conservative coalition that emerged after 1937 and allowed southern Democrats and Republicans to defeat liberal legislation in two-thirds of the votes.

Martin supported most of the New Deal relief measures, but he battled the Agricultural Adjustment Act, Reciprocal Trade Agreements Act, and the Tennessee Valley Authority in particular. On the other hand, he supported the Roosevelt World War II policies despite the fact that he had sided with the isolationists before Pearl Harbor. In the 1940 presidential campaign, FDR had lampooned Martin and fellow isolationists Bruce Barton and HAMILTON FISH as "Martin, Barton and Fish" to the cadence of "Winkin, Blinkin and Nod." In 1940, Martin served as WENDELL WILLKIE's presidential campaign manager.

During the postwar period, Martin was twice elected Speaker of the House (1947–49 and 1953–55). He was minority leader from 1955 until 1959, when Charles A. Halleck from Indiana defeated him for reelection to that position. He remained in the House for eight more years and in 1966 was defeated in the Republican primary. Martin died a bachelor on March 6, 1968, in Hollywood, Florida.

Maverick, Maury, Sr.
(Fontaine Maury Maverick)
(1895–1954) *U.S. congressman, San Antonio mayor, federal administrator*

Born on October 23, 1895, to a San Antonio, Texas, real-estate investor and his wife, Maury Maverick had deep Texas roots. His grandfather had not only been a mayor of San Antonio but had also signed the Texas Declaration of Independence in 1835. Maverick entered the Virginia Military Institute in 1912 but soon transferred to the University of Texas, where he spent the next three years. In 1916, he began practicing law. As a loyal son of the South, he enlisted in the army the next year, and during World War I he earned both a Purple Heart and Silver Star. His crippling wounds made it impossible for him to raise his hands.

After practicing law for two more years, the ever-restless Maverick changed to the construction business, became active in local politics as an opponent of the Ku Klux Klan, and

participated in local relief programs. His first elective office was in 1929, when he became the tax collector of Bexar County; he was reelected in 1931. In 1934, he won a seat in the U.S. House of Representatives with support from Mexican Americans. Reelected in 1936, he allied himself in the House with other liberal Democrats as well as progressive Republicans, participating in the Progressive Open Forum Discussion Group. The media named Maverick as the group's chief, mainly because of his colorful personality, while others called it "Maury's Mavericks."

Unlike most southerners, Maverick supported civil rights for minorities and voted against racist poll taxes while he championed antilynching legislation and backed striking workers. He was virtually alone in backing Franklin Roosevelt's Court-packing plan in 1937. He had become a pacifist after World War I but changed his position to support FDR's foreign policy. His consistent and outspoken support for FDR and the New Deal angered Vice President JOHN NANCE GARNER and other conservative Texas Democrats, and this led to Maverick's defeat in the 1938 primary. Shifting gears, Maverick was elected mayor of San Antonio the next year, but when he sought reelection in 1941, he was again blocked by conservatives.

Because of his loyal support of FDR, the president appointed Maverick to several federal positions during the remainder of World War II. In 1941, he became a member of the Office of Price Administration (OPA), and after the OPA was transformed in April 1942 into the War Production Board, Maverick was made vice chairman in charge of the division of government requirements. From January 1944 to 1946, he headed the Smaller War Plants Corporation, whose aim was to secure more war contracts for small businesses.

During the postwar years, Maverick returned to San Antonio to practice law and made several unsuccessful attempts to return to elected office. He died in San Antonio on June 7, 1954.

McAdoo, William Gibbs
(1863–1941) *U.S. senator*

William McAdoo was born in Marietta, Georgia, on October 31, 1863. His father had been active in Tennessee politics before the Civil War and was a Confederate officer in Georgia during the war. His mother wrote and published several romantic novels of the Old South. McAdoo shared his father's interest in politics, but at the national level. He became a lawyer in 1883 and was counsel for a Tennessee railroad that soon built one of the nation's first electrified city railways. In early 1892, he moved to New York City, where he was responsible for completion of the first tunnel under the Hudson River and won an urban reputation as a progressive manager of a public utility (the Hudson and Manhattan Railway Company).

McAdoo soon became active in the Democratic Party and was a booster of Woodrow Wilson's bid for the presidency in 1912. Wilson appointed McAdoo to the influential post of secretary of the Treasury, which he ran as efficiently as his railway. His first wife died in 1912, and in 1914 he married Eleanor Wilson, the president's daughter. During World War I, he backed creation of the U.S. Shipping Board to assure efficient transatlantic traffic. In 1918, Wilson appointed McAdoo as director general of the nation's railroad to coordinate freight shipments. Just as when he was a private railway executive, McAdoo established a progressive record regarding the welfare of employees under his jurisdiction.

After the November 1918 armistice, McAdoo returned to private life, moving to California to align himself with the progressive wing of the Democratic Party. He wanted the 1920 presidential nomination, but Wilson stubbornly failed to endorse McAdoo's bid because he harbored a fantasy that the party would turn to him again as its candidate. During the 1924 presidential race, McAdoo tried to position himself as the successor to William Jennings Bryan. His reputation was marred in early 1924 when he was implicated in the Teapot Dome Scandal because he had provided legal work for one of the parties involved and also because he refused to disavow his association with the Ku Klux Klan for fear of losing his southern support. He ultimately lost his opportunity to be the presidential candidate.

With characteristic energy and resilience, McAdoo ran for the U.S. Senate in 1932 and was swept into office with the Franklin Roosevelt landslide. He had played a key role at the Chicago Democratic convention, heading the California delegation and participating in the switch of support from JOHN NANCE GARNER's presidential bid to a Roosevelt-Garner ticket. McAdoo became a loyal New Deal supporter. He was defeated for reelection to his Senate seat in 1938 by Sheridan Downey, who ran on an old-age pension platform. McAdoo died on February 1, 1941, in Washington, D.C.

McCarran, Patrick Anthony
(1876–1954) *U.S. senator*

The only son of Nevada sheep ranchers who were Irish Catholic immigrants, Patrick McCarran was born on August 8, 1876, during the nation's centennial year. He attended the University of Nevada, where he excelled in debate. He quickly developed an interest in local politics and in 1902 won a house seat in the Nevada legislature. He sought a state senate seat in 1904 but was defeated. Studying on his own, McCarran passed the state bar exam in 1905 and in 1906 was elected as a county district attorney. He was always ambitious and aimed next for the U.S. House of Representatives, challenging an incumbent Democrat in the 1908 election. He lost, and thereafter he turned his energy to law, becoming one of the state's leading defense attorneys (1909–12, 1919–32), specializing in criminal defense and divorce cases. McCarran's popular acclaim, never matched by members of the bar or the Democratic Party, allowed him to win a spot on the Nevada Supreme Court, where he served from 1913 to 1918. He attempted to win national office again in 1916, running against the incumbent Democrat for a U.S. Senate seat, and was defeated soundly. As a result, he lost his own bid for reelection to the Nevada Supreme Court in 1918. He ran again for the U.S. Senate in 1926 and lost again.

McCarran was finally successful in his third attempt, riding Franklin Roosevelt's coattails to a narrow victory in 1932. He became the first Nevada-born candidate elected by the state to the U.S. Senate. Because of Nevada's small population, McCarran was able to maintain personal relationships with voters and built up the strongest political machine in the state's history. He demanded complete loyalty in return for the patronage he distributed from his growing seniority in the U.S. Senate. His political opponents learned that he could be very vindictive.

Only a nominal Democrat, McCarran soon became part of the emerging conservative coalition that opposed much of the New Deal legislation. He was a vocal critic of FDR's Court-packing plan, opposed FDR's seeking a third term, and also opposed the president's interventionist policies toward Germany and Japan. Although he was an administration adversary, McCarran's seniority gained him the chairmanship of the Judiciary Committee in 1943, and he was a high-ranking member of the powerful Appropriations Committee. He was a loner and he was not well liked by his col-

leagues, Franklin Roosevelt, or HARRY TRUMAN, who did not endorse him in his reelection campaigns in 1938, 1944, or 1950.

During the postwar period McCarran was a vehement anticommunist. He joined Senator Joseph McCarthy (R-Wis.), a fellow Irish Catholic, in his attacks on alleged communists, and he stalled, and finally opposed, the eventual congressional censure of McCarthy. In 1952, McCarran's close links to Nevada's gambling interests were exposed. He died in Hawthorne, Nevada, on September 28, 1954. Only one of his fellow Democratic senators attended his funeral.

McCormack, John Williams
(1891–1980) *U.S. congressman*

John McCormack, born on December 21, 1891, in South Boston, Massachusetts, was the son of an Irish Catholic bricklayer. He quit school at age 13 following his father's death to help support his mother and two younger brothers. Like many other ambitious young men of the time, he studied law in a private office. He was admitted to the bar in 1913 and began his own law practice. In 1917, McCormack turned to politics as his path for advancement and won a slot as a delegate to the state's constitutional convention. During World War I, he resigned his delegate position to enlist as an army private but was stationed stateside. After the war, he won three consecutive one-year terms to the Massachusetts legislature, beginning in 1919. In 1920, he married Harriet Joyce, a South Boston Irish Catholic, who abandoned her opera career for marriage. The couple had no children.

In the same year as his marriage, McCormack won election to the state senate, moving up through the ranks to become the Democratic majority leader in 1925–26. Later in 1926, he unsuccessfully challenged James A.

Gallivan, the veteran incumbent Democrat in the South Boston–Dorchester–Roxbury U.S. congressional district. He eventually gained the seat in a 1928 special election by defeating eight competitors after Gallivan's death. It was the last time he ever faced serious opposition during his long congressional career. McCormack continued to make friends in his district and within Congress. One of his most important early friendships was with Democratic leader JOHN NANCE GARNER of Texas. The pair shared party loyalty and a love for playing poker. McCormack's appointment to the powerful House Ways and Means Committee in 1931 signified that he not only was a man to watch but that his relationship with Garner was cemented.

In 1934, McCormack was made chairman of the Special Committee on Un-American Activities. Although Democrat Samuel Dickstein of New York, who sponsored the bill, had intended the committee to undertake investigations of Nazi and anti-Semitic organizations, McCormack turned its focus to the Communist Party. It was a shrewd way for him to showcase his own American patriotism during a period when Irish Americans were put in a difficult situation because Ireland hoped to stay neutral in any future world war. Most credit McCormack with conducting an efficient investigation that avoided massive abuse of civil liberties. The committee's 1938 report resulted in the requirement that all agents of foreign powers in the United States had to register themselves.

McCormack's conservative ties to Texas as well as to conservative southern candidates in the Democratic caucus led to his support in early 1937 for Texan SAM RAYBURN as House majority leader. Three years later, after Rayburn had become Speaker of the House and after the death of WILLIAM BANKHEAD, the Democrat from Alabama, Roosevelt supported McCormack's bid to become House majority

leader, which was successful. With his election as majority leader, McCormack became the first New Englander to hold a Democratic leadership position in the House in more than a century; he held the post from 1940 to 1947. He remained generally supportive of the New Deal, staying in the background during Rayburn's cumulative long reign as Speaker.

McCormack acted more as a party facilitator than someone with a legislative agenda of his own; no major bills carry his name. Late in the postwar period, in January 1962, he became the first Roman Catholic Speaker of the House and served for nine years, his tenure length second only to Rayburn's. He retired from Congress in 1970 to care for his ill wife, who died the next year. He died on November 22, 1980, in Boston.

McCormick, Robert Rutherford
(1880–1955) *newspaper publisher*

Born on July 30, 1880, in Chicago, Illinois, and raised in an atmosphere of privilege, Robert McCormick was the son of a diplomat. His mother was the daughter of Joseph Medill, editor and publisher of the *Chicago Tribune*, and his illustrious family members included his great-uncle Cyrus McCormick, the inventor of the mechanical reaper and founder of the McCormick Reaper Company, now International Harvester. Sent first to England to attend Ludgrove, a preparatory school, McCormick later attended Elstree. He graduated in 1899 from the Groton preparatory school in Massachusetts, where his schoolmates included Franklin Roosevelt.

McCormick continued his education at Yale University, graduating in 1903. He returned briefly to Illinois to attend Northwestern University Law School but then temporarily dropped the law for politics, winning a term as an alderman on the Chicago City

Council in 1904. The next year, he won the Republican bid for the Chicago Sanitary District presidency, and he served a five-year term. Although he did not earn a law degree, he was admitted to the bar in 1908 and simultaneously practiced law while he also engaged in politics.

In 1910, after the death of his uncle Robert W. Patterson, Jr., McCormick and his cousin took over the *Chicago Tribune*. Ever the conservative, McCormick became president of the *Chicago Tribune* Company the next year and headed the business department. His cousin, Joseph Medill Patterson, a socialist, coedited the paper. Within half a dozen years, the unusual team built the paper's circulation from third to first among the eight Chicago dailies. To save money, McCormick acquired paper mills in Quebec and Ontario, Canada. It was during this time that "The World's Greatest Newspaper" was added to the paper's masthead.

The year 1915 proved to be a fateful one in McCormick's life. He turned from his legal and political interests to devote full attention to the *Tribune*. His family connections allowed for the governor to make him a colonel in the Illinois National Guard, giving him a military title when he traveled to Europe to cover World War I as a news correspondent. That same year, he published the first of his half-dozen books, *With the Russian Army*, based on his firsthand experiences abroad. It was also in 1915 that he wed Amie Irwin Adams; their marriage was childless.

McCormick had opposed American involvement in the war, but in 1916 he changed his position after Mexican bandits violated America's southern border. He supported Woodrow Wilson's plan to invade Mexico with General John J. Pershing in command and volunteered for the First Illinois Cavalry, a National Guard unit that was called to the border. That year, he was also elected as Chicago's mayor. McCormick criticized HENRY FORD's

opposition to American military preparedness, and when he accused Ford of threatening his employees' jobs if they left to defend the nation's border, Ford responded with a libel suit. Although Ford won the suit, he was awarded six cents in damages instead of the $1 million he had sought. It was McCormick who emerged victorious from the legal battle, hailed as a champion of the First Amendment.

In 1917, McCormick supported President Wilson's entry into World War I. He volunteered again, and he again served with Pershing, rising to the rank of colonel and receiving a Distinguished Service Medal. In 1919, he launched the *New York Daily News*, which eventually became the domain of his socialist cousin, who also had served with him in France during World War I. The *Daily News* became the most successful newspaper in the nation at the same time that under McCormick's guidance the *Chicago Tribune* broke the 1 million–reader mark to become the best-selling standard-size newspaper. Using his newspaper's powerful voice, he championed Prohibition, small government, and isolationism during the 1920s. In 1924, he began Chicago radio station WGN, the call letters taken from the initials of the *Tribune*'s claim of "World's Greatest Newspaper."

McCormick's *Tribune* became a leading advocate for archconservatism and midwestern isolationism during the 1930s. He labeled Franklin Roosevelt a communist and pronounced HERBERT HOOVER as "the greatest state socialist in history." He wrote public letters to his former Groton schoolmate, addressing FDR as "Dear Frank." He opposed organized labor and considered the New Deal to be totalitarianism, expressing greatest opposition to the National Recovery Administration.

McCormick also condemned American efforts to become involved in Europe and Asia. He blamed FDR personally for maneuvering the United States into World War II. He was against every congressional effort, including the Lend-Lease Act of 1941, to aid the British and others in the battle against Nazi Germany and Japan. The *Tribune* released a secret government report on military preparedness just prior to the December 1941 Pearl Harbor attack, which many criticized as a treasonous act. McCormick's denouncements continued until after Pearl Harbor. During World War II, he stuck with the Republican Party's candidates who challenged FDR, supporting WENDELL WILLKIE in 1940 and THOMAS DEWEY in 1944.

In 1944, five years after the death of his first wife, he remarried. His second wife was an old family friend, Maryland Mathison Hooper, and theirs was also a childless marriage. The postwar years were not conducive to McCormick's political views either. His nadir may have been after HARRY TRUMAN won election in 1948, when the jubilant new president posed holding the *Chicago Tribune* with its "Dewey Defeats Truman" banner headline. The photograph became famous and seemed to capture McCormick's legacy of misplaced predictions over the previous 20 years. He died on April 1, 1955, in Wheaton, Illinois.

McIntyre, Marvin Hunter
(1878–1943) *assistant secretary and secretary to the president*

Born in LaGrange, Kentucky, on November 27, 1878, Marvin McIntyre briefly attended Vanderbilt University. Between 1901 and 1908, he handled public relations for several railroads. He then switched to the field of journalism, working as a reporter for several newspapers during the next decade. During Woodrow Wilson's administration, he became special assistant to the secretary of the navy, returning to public relations as a press liaison for the Navy Department while Franklin Roosevelt was assistant secretary of the navy. McIntyre liked FDR from the first time they met.

During FDR's vice-presidential campaign in 1920, McIntyre acted as his general assistant for publicity. He left government employment in 1922 and until 1932 was the East Coast representative for several motion picture newsreel companies. During the 1932 presidential campaign, he rejoined the Roosevelts, serving as FDR's business manager and publicity representative. After his election, FDR made McIntyre an assistant secretary to the president in charge of appointments. After LOUIS HOWE's death in 1936, McIntyre replaced him but never exerted the level of influence that Howe had. He died on December 13, 1943.

McNary, Charles Linza
(1874–1944) *Senate minority leader, Republican vice-presidential candidate*

Born to farmer parents on June 12, 1874, in Salem, Oregon, Charles McNary was orphaned at age nine. From his work as a farmhand and in a tree nursery, he developed a lifelong appreciation of trees and the outdoors. He eventually developed two new trees, the American filbert and the Imperial prune.

After completing local public schools, McNary attended Stanford University for one year and then read law in his older brother's law office until he gained admission to the bar in 1898. He practiced the law with his brother and operated his family's old farm but also developed an interest in local politics. After serving as dean of Willamette University Law School from 1908 to 1913, he was appointed by the Democratic governor as an associate justice to fill a vacancy on the Oregon Supreme Court. In 1914, he lost the Republican primary election for a full term on the court by a single vote. Two years later, he became the Republican state chairman and manager of CHARLES EVANS HUGHES's presidential campaign in Oregon.

McNary's lengthy career in the U.S. Senate began unexpectedly in May 1917 with an appointment to fill a vacancy caused by the death of incumbent Harry Lane. McNary won a full term in 1918 and was reelected four times with little campaign effort on his part. He was a moderate, pragmatic, flexible, progressive middle-of-the-roader. Throughout his political career he retained the support of organized labor as well as both wings of the Republican Party. In time he also had support from Franklin Roosevelt and his vice presidents, HARRY TRUMAN, ALBEN BARKLEY, and HENRY WALLACE. McNary's ability to forge personal relationships, maintain his word, and reach a compromise were characteristics central to his success.

McNary first gained national prominence in the mid 1920s as the leader of the Senate farm bloc. Despite opposition from HERBERT HOOVER, he was elected Senate majority leader, and after the 1932 Democratic landslide, he was unanimously elected minority leader. He supported most of the early New Deal initiatives, including the Tennessee Valley Authority. FDR rewarded him by authorizing the Bonneville Dam on the Columbia River in Oregon. He kept Senate Republicans unified after the controversial Court-packing plan, allowing conservative Democrats to attack it instead.

To balance the 1940 Republican presidential ticket headed by WENDELL WILLKIE, McNary reluctantly accepted the 1940 nomination for vice president. He campaigned nonchalantly for a job he did not really desire. After FDR's reelection, he turned down offers to become a cabinet member and later declined the offer of a Supreme Court seat. Instead he chose to remain in the Senate until he died from a brain tumor on February 25, 1944, in Fort Lauderdale, Florida.

McNutt, Paul Vories

(1891–1955) *Indiana governor, U.S. high commissioner to the Philippines, Federal Security Agency director, War Manpower Commission chairman*

Born in Franklin, Indiana, on July 19, 1891, to a father who was a lawyer and a homemaker mother, Paul McNutt was raised in Martinsville, Indiana. In 1913, he graduated from Indiana University and entered Harvard Law School, graduating in 1916. McNutt served stateside during World War I and achieved the rank of major. He married Kathleen Timolat in 1918, and the couple had one daughter.

Energetic and handsome, McNutt was also political. He had become a law professor at Indiana University's law school in 1917 and resumed teaching there after the war. By 1925, he was dean of the law school. An ambitious Democrat, he used the American Legion as his springboard into state politics. He was commander of the Legion's Indiana Department in 1927, and the next year he became the national commander. After the onset of the Great Depression, the number and strength of the Indiana veterans propelled him into statewide consideration for the governorship.

McNutt's game plan worked, and after declaring his candidacy for the governorship in early 1932, he coasted to an easy victory over his Republican opponent in the November general election. His ambition cost him in the long run, however, after his belated endorsement of Franklin Roosevelt at the National Democratic Convention. He led an uncommitted delegation from Indiana and managed to infuriate FDR's campaign advisers. It later proved to have been a strategic blunder for the otherwise "platinum-haired knight," whose higher political ambitions were obvious.

Nevertheless, McNutt was an important New Dealer in Indiana during his single four-year term as governor. He was credited with instituting a state income tax, welfare laws, and state pensions. His governmental reorganization plan reduced the number of ever-increasing departments to only eight, eliminating debt so that by the time he left office, there was a surplus in the state treasury. On the other hand, liberals criticized his use of state troopers to control labor disturbances, and conservatives blasted the requirement for state employees to donate 2 percent of their salaries to the Hoosier Democratic Club.

Barred by the Indiana constitution from seeking a second term, McNutt was appointed by FDR in 1937 to serve as the U.S. high commissioner to the Philippines. He held that post until 1939, when FDR named him as the first director of the Federal Security Agency (FSA), which had been established by the Reorganization Act of 1939, a diluted form of the recommendations from LOUIS BROWNLOW's committee. The FSA consolidated a dozen organizations, agencies, and boards, including the Social Security Board, the Public Health Service, U.S. Office of Education, the National Youth Administration, the Civil Conservation Corps, the Food and Drug Administration, the U.S. Employment Service, and others. McNutt remained at FSA, where he was effectively co-opted or politically neutralized, until 1942, when FDR named him to chair the War Manpower Commission.

McNutt continued to harbor presidential ambitions, and "McNutt for President" clubs began emerging in early 1940. However, FDR's decision to run for his unprecedented third term ended that possibility. Rivals in the Roosevelt administration instigated an investigation by the Treasury Department into McNutt's finances, which left a cloud over his candidacy for the presidency or even the vice-presidential spot. He was forced to withdraw his name from consideration at the 1940 National Democratic Convention and FDR choose HENRY WALLACE to be his running mate.

President HARRY S. TRUMAN returned McNutt to the Philippines as high commissioner in the postwar period, and in 1946 he was named as the first U.S. ambassador to the newly independent Philippines. The following year, he ended his government service and returned to his law practice until his death on March 24, 1955, in New York City.

McReynolds, James Clark
(1862–1946) *U.S. Supreme Court justice*

James McReynolds was born on February 3, 1862, in rural Elkton, Kentucky. His father was a physician of Scots-Irish descent who was able to send his son to private educational institutions. While at Vanderbilt University, McReynolds spent additional time studying natural history and geology. He graduated in 1882, and the next year he earned his law degree from the University of Virginia. He returned to Nashville in 1884 and for the next two decades not only practiced law but also emerged as a successful businessman. For a few years, he taught at Vanderbilt, and he served briefly as Senator Howell Jackson's secretary prior to Jackson's appointment to the U.S. Supreme Court. One of Nashville's leading figures, McReynolds unsuccessfully ran for Congress in 1896 as a "Gold Democrat," who wanted to retain the gold standard, unlike the Democratic Party's candidate, William Jennings Bryan, who favored a silver standard.

It was THEODORE ROOSEVELT who opened the door to Washington for McReynolds, recruiting him as U.S. attorney general. It was a low-paying position that McReynolds, a bachelor of means, could afford to accept. From 1903 to 1911, he actively pursued trust-busting, but he resigned from office over the settlement against the American Tobacco Trust because he considered it too lenient. Personally, McReynolds so despised the use of tobacco that he forbade any-one from smoking in his presence. Following his resignation, he reentered law practice in New York City for two years until he was recruited by Woodrow Wilson, who shared southern roots, to be his first attorney general. Returning to Washington, McReynolds resumed his trust-busting efforts, but only for 18 months. He proved to be such an irritant to Wilson's cabinet that the president nominated him to become an associate justice on the Supreme Court as soon as the first opening occurred. Despite vocal oppo-sition from Senator GEORGE NORRIS (R-Nebr.), McReynolds was confirmed by a 44-6 vote.

As expected from his Jeffersonian/Jack-sonian southern perspective, McReynolds believed in states' rights and remained suspi-cious of distant concentrations of power that might threaten individual liberty. He was at odds with legal realism and sociological jurisprudence, which sought to adapt the U.S. Constitution to changing conditions. Prior to 1937, he was part of the conservative majority that repeatedly struck down New Deal legislation. He became the most con-servative of the so-called Four Horsemen—who included WILLIS VAN DEVANTER, GEORGE SUTHERLAND, and PIERCE BUT-LER—the High Court bloc hostile to Franklin Roosevelt's legislation to deal with the Great Depression.

McReynolds was personally autocratic, especially in dealings with his household maid, butler, and numerous legal secretaries. He was arrogant, abrasive, and rude to those whom he disliked, which included African Americans, Jews, and women, especially female lawyers. There were no regrets expressed by his brethren when he retired from the bench in 1941. He died on August 24, 1946, in Wash-ington, D.C., and none of his former brethren attended his funeral—an early indicator that his personal shortcomings would overshadow his professional legacy.

Mellon, Andrew William
(1855–1937) *financier, industrialist, art collector*

The son of a lawyer-banker, Andrew Mellon was born in Pittsburgh, Pennsylvania, on March 24, 1855. He attended local public schools before entering Western University of Pennsylvania, now the University of Pittsburgh. He dropped out of college in 1872 shortly before graduation to begin work in the business world. In 1880, he traveled with industrialist Henry Clay Frick to Europe, where he developed what would become his lifelong interest in collecting art. His father made him president of the family bank in 1882, and he was so successful in expanding it that by the end of the decade, his father had made him the virtual owner of all the family properties. At the same time that Mellon continued to build the family fortune, he also built his art collection. In 1900, he married Nora May McMullen, an Englishwoman 23 years his junior. They had two children before his deeper commitment to business resulted in the couple's divorce in 1912.

By then Mellon had become a powerful financial force within the Republican Party. An archconservative, he contributed to the presi-dential campaign of CHARLES EVANS HUGHES, who nearly defeated Woodrow Wilson in his 1916 bid for reelection. Mellon also helped finance the effort to defeat American partici-pation in the League of Nations. With his financial pockets filled with politicians, espe-cially the Pennsylvania delegation, Mellon was appointed secretary of the Treasury by Warren G. Harding. He held that position through the subsequent administrations of Calvin Coolidge and HERBERT HOOVER, despite the fact that Hoover considered Mellon's economic views too extreme. Mellon wanted to lower corporate taxes to encourage growth. His economic poli-cies as the most powerful presidential adviser in the 1920s may have encouraged stock-market speculation. Even after the stock-market crash in 1929, Mellon rejected Hoover's voluntary approach to help resolve the bank crisis. During his last year in office, Hoover finally rid himself of his Treasury secretary by appointing him ambassador to Great Britain.

While Mellon was serving as ambassador, the Congress began an unsuccessful effort to hold hearings on him for allegedly violating conflict of interest. Mellon returned home with the end of the Hoover administration and resumed the presidency of his Pittsburgh bank. In 1934, the Roosevelt administration alleged that Mellon had failed to pay the proper amount of income tax in 1931. He was cleared of that charge after many appeals. In the meantime, he followed through with his intent from the late 1920s to donate his art collection to the federal government. He had already contributed to the beautification of the nation's capital while serving in Washington, D.C. He ultimately provided not only his art collection but also funds to build and maintain the National Gallery of Art on the National Mall. Near the end of his life, he participated in the architectural planning of the largest granite building in the nation, which would house his personal collection.

Mellon died on August 26, 1937, in Southampton, New York. The following year, his estate paid a token settlement on technical grounds to resolve his income-tax violation of 1931. Ironically, the man intensely disliked while in public office—second only to Herbert Hoover—redeemed his disastrous economic policies, his family's name, and his personal reputation through the donation of his art collection, which preserves his better side in the public memory.

Mencken, Henry Lewis
(1880–1956) *journalist, editor*

The eldest among four children of a German couple in Baltimore, Maryland, Henry Louis Mencken—better known by his initials H. L.—was born on September 12, 1880. His father was a cigar manufacturer, and his mother was a housewife. He attended a private German school during his younger years but went to high school at Baltimore Polytechnic. After his high-school graduation, Mencken longed to become a newspaper reporter but instead worked in his father's growing cigar factory for two years that he considered the worst of his early life. When he was 18, his father died, freeing him to pursue his dream of becoming a newspaper reporter.

Within three months after his father died, Mencken was a cub reporter for the Baltimore *Herald*. In six years, he worked his way up the ranks from reporter to city editor to managing editor to editor. In 1906, he moved to the Baltimore *Sun* to become its Sunday editor, and he garnered local attention as a columnist and editorial writer. He soon began his part-time career as a prolific book author as well as a full-time editor from 1908 to 1923 for *Smart Set*, a New York monthly, and columnist for the Baltimore *Evening Sun*. He became one of the most influential social critics of the 1920s.

In 1923, Mencken cofounded the *American Mercury*, which he would edit for the next decade. Favoring literary naturalism in which humans are primarily viewed as victims of an indifferent environment, he published the fiction of Theodore Dreiser, SINCLAIR LEWIS, F. Scott Fitzgerald, Sherwood Anderson, and others. He was an agnostic who disliked literary romanticism and sentimentality. Though he disdained the American South for backwardness that he called "the Sahara of the Bozart," in 1930 he married Sara Haardt, a writer from Montgomery, Alabama. It was a happy marriage, but she died five years later at age 37.

During World War I, Mencken had favored Germany. He called himself a monarchist who disliked mass democracy, Anglo-Saxons in general, and Great Britain in particular.

He held bureaucrats and labor leaders in contempt. Especially during the early 1930s, his approach fell out of favor. Mencken also had a particular dislike for Franklin Roosevelt, whom he viewed not only as a betrayer of his social class but also as a duplicitous politician. FDR, in return, often satirized Mencken. The enlarged edition of Mencken's *The American Language* in 1936 helped to restore his popularity, as did the trilogy of autobiographical works, *Happy Days* (1940), *Newspaper Days* (1941), and *Heathen Days* (1943). Returning to his anti-British views during World War II, kept his political writing silenced. He confessed that the Germany that he once admired no longer existed.

The postwar years were even more unkind to Mencken and his reputation. In the late 1940s he suffered a series of strokes. He died on January 29, 1956, in Baltimore.

Merriam, Charles Edward
(1874–1953) *National Resources Planning Board member, President's Committee on Administrative Management member*

The son of a merchant-postmaster father and schoolteacher mother, Charles Merriam was born on November 15, 1874, in Hopkinton, Iowa, where he grew up in a Republican household. He attended Lenox College in his hometown before entering the University of Iowa, where he graduated in 1895. By then his interests had changed from the law to the emerging field of political science, and he pursued a doctorate at Columbia University from 1897 to 1900. While there, he was active in local politics and spent a year studying in Germany.

In 1900, Merriam became the first political scientist faculty member at the University of Chicago, where he remained until his retirement in 1940. In 1903, he became a founding member of the main professional organization of political science academics, the American Political Science Association. From 1904 to 1919, he was a progressive Republican and active in city government, serving as an alderman and city councilman. He unsuccessfully ran for mayor twice; HAROLD ICKES served as his campaign manager for his first campaign in 1911. Because Merriam favored efficiency in local government, Senator ROBERT LA FOLLETTE (R-Wis.) would dub him "the Woodrow Wilson of the West."

Merriam's academic work led him to promote an empirical rather than a strictly normative approach in studying politics. He would eventually be considered the father of the behavioral movement in political science. After playing a major role in the creation of the Social Sciences Research Council (SSRC) in 1923, he served as its first president from 1924 to 1927. The SSRC aimed to link academic social science with governmental policy making. Merriam was able to forge a funding alliance with the Rockefeller Foundation and recruited faculty to build his new department, which became known as the "Chicago School" of political science. During the HERBERT HOOVER administration, he helped to create and was vice chairman of the President's Research Committee on Social Trends (1929–33), an initiative funded by the Rockefeller Foundation.

It was his old tie to Ickes that brought Merriam into the New Deal on July 7, 1933, as a member of the National Resources Planning Board (NRPB), created under Title II of the National Industrial Recovery Act. The NRPB endeavored to link academic research and public policy, and Merriam became the academic philosopher of New Deal planning. He believed that industrialization and urbanization resulted in new, organized pressure groups that replaced individuals as activists. He also believed political parties should mediate cooperation among these groups. Conservative

Democrats and Republicans increasingly attacked the NRPB after 1939, fearful of "socialist" planning agencies. It was terminated during spring 1943.

Merriam's more enduring legacy to the New Deal and the presidency itself resulted from his encouraging FDR to establish the President's Committee on Administrative Management in 1936. Merriam collaborated with LUTHER GULICK and LOUIS BROWNLOW to issue the so-called Brownlow Report. Recommendations were delayed as well as diluted by the dissent arising from the Supreme Court–packing plan, but the report eventually led to the Reorganization Act of 1939, which created the Executive Office of the President and the White House Office. The Bureau of the Budget was transferred from the Treasury Department to the Executive Office. He retired from the University of Chicago in 1940, and died on January 8, 1953, in Rockville, Maryland.

Mitchell, Wesley Clair
(1874–1948) economist, member of National Planning Board and National Resources Board

Wesley Mitchell was born on August 5, 1874, in Rushville, Illinois, to parents who had been abolitionists. His father had been a surgeon in the 4th U.S. Colored Infantry during the Civil War. Mitchell's family moved throughout Illinois numerous times during his childhood. Mitchell entered the University of Chicago and was part of its first graduating class in 1896. While studying there, he was heavily influenced by several of the university's renowned faculty, including philosopher John Dewey and economists Thorstein Veblen and J. Laurence Laughlin. He chose to study economics, and his 1903 dissertation—the first of his prolific publications in the field—sought to link the use of greenbacks to the success of the Union Army in the Civil War. This was one of the first economic studies based on statistical accounting.

After he completed his doctorate in 1899, Mitchell worked briefly for the U.S. Census Bureau before returning the next year to the University of Chicago to begin his teaching career. After three years, he transferred to the University of California at Berkeley, remaining there until 1912. That same year, he married Lucy Sprague, the university's dean of women. His bride had inherited a fortune from her Chicago mercantile family, which afforded the academic couple greater independence than most educators. They eventually had four children.

After they married, Mitchell and his wife moved to New York City to become part of the faculty at Columbia University in 1913. He left in 1919 but returned in 1922 and remained until 1944. Mitchell soon became associated with economic historian Edwin Gay, who persuaded him to move to Washington, D.C., where Gay was the director of the Central Bureau of Planning and Statistics of the War Industries Board during World War I. Mitchell eventually became the head of the Price Division of the War Industries Board. Economic data convinced him of the utility of national economic planning. After World War I, Mitchell and Gay established the National Bureau of Economic Research, with Mitchell serving as the research director from 1920 to 1945.

Mitchell also was a founder of the New School for Social Research (1919–22). In 1921, HERBERT HOOVER, then secretary of commerce, tried unsuccessfully to recruit Mitchell as the department's economic adviser. Hoover shared Mitchell's quantitative obsession with economic data, and after the onetime engineer became the 31st U.S. president, he appointed Mitchell to chair his President's Research Commission on Social Trends. Mitchell conducted a comprehensive survey of American society, which resulted in the publication of

Recent Social Trends in the United States in 1933. Although it failed to predict the Great Depression, that study, along with his earlier *Recent Economic Changes* (1929), established Mitchell's reputation as the leading expert on economic cycles in American society, but it was an expertise markedly lacking in policy recommendations. Nonetheless, its political neutrality allowed Mitchell to receive an appointment in Franklin Roosevelt's Public Works Administration, first as a member of its National Planning Board and then on its National Resources Board in 1934–35.

During the postwar period, Mitchell continued his prolific economic writings. He worked with Arthur Burns, the husband of Social Security advocate EVELINE BURNS, on *Measuring Business Cycles* in 1946. Mitchell died in New York City on October 29, 1948.

Moley, Raymond

(1886–1975) *speechwriter, assistant secretary of state, economic adviser, editor*

Raymond Moley was born on September 27, 1886, in Berea, Ohio. His father was a local businessman, and he grew up in a traditional Democratic family in Olmstead Falls. He graduated from Cleveland's Baldwin-Wallace College in 1906 and then immediately returned to Olmstead Falls to be a teacher and superintendent of schools until 1910. After suffering a bout of tuberculosis, Moley began teaching high school in Cleveland in 1912, and in 1913 he obtained his M.A. degree in political science at Oberlin College. He went on to earn his Ph.D. from Columbia University in 1918, while he was teaching at Western Reserve University (1916–19). His dissertation adviser was the renowned economic historian Charles A. Beard, another midwesterner who became his lifelong friend. The pair shared similar political views, agreeing that easterners exploited

farmers and opposing U.S. involvement in both world wars. Moley was influenced by the populist tradition and admired "the Great Commoner" William Jennings Bryan. He also was influenced by the work of Henry George (1839–97), especially *Progress and Poverty* (1879), which critiqued concentrated economic power. The career of fellow political scientist Woodrow Wilson also influenced Moley.

Between 1919 and 1923, Moley served as the director of the Cleveland Foundation, the nation's first community trust for civic-improvement projects, which reflected the reform spirit of mayor NEWTON DIEHL BAKER. It was also the vehicle that brought national recognition to Moley. In 1922, the foundation sponsored the Cleveland Crime Survey, which became a model for other cities and for which he recruited Roscoe Pound and FELIX FRANKFURTER of Harvard Law School. The next year, he moved to Columbia University, remaining there until he retired in 1954.

Moley's work on the judicial process brought him to the attention of LOUIS HOWE, who as executive secretary of the National Crime Commission appointed him as research director of the New York State Crime Commission in 1926. Howe persuaded him to work on Franklin Roosevelt's 1928 bid for the governorship. As a political scientist, Moley recognized that FDR would likely become the Democratic presidential candidate, so he volunteered his services to FDR's campaign in January 1932. His writing skills, academic credentials, and taciturnity prompted Judge SAMUEL ROSENMAN to have Moley draft FDR's April 7, 1932, "Forgotten Man" speech that blamed rural poverty and collapsed commodity prices as causes of the Great Depression. Rosenman also had Moley assemble FDR's "Brain Trust"—sometimes referred to as the "Brains Trust"—of academic advisers. Moley recruited colleagues REXFORD TUGWELL and ADOLF BERLE, along with Basil O'Connor, FDR's law partner. Moley served as the de facto leader for the group that met during 1932 for discussions and rejected the Woodrow Wilson–LOUIS BRANDEIS emphasis on antitrust activity in favor of governmental regulation of the economy. The Brain Trust disbanded after the election.

From 1932 to 1935, Moley drafted most of FDR's speeches and fireside chats. He served as assistant secretary of state from March 4 to early September 1933. He was also FDR's principal economic adviser at the June 1933 World Monetary and Economic Conference held in London. Secretary of State CORDELL HULL, a free trader, forced Moley's resignation after the conference because, contrary to Hull's wishes, Moley had announced publicly that the United States would support global currency stabilization.

After leaving the administration, Moley became the founding editor of *Today* magazine, which later merged with *Newsweek*. Initially supportive of the New Deal, Moley began to perceive FDR as a captive of Frankfurter's anticorporate views as well as too responsive to the labor movement. His formal break with the administration in 1937 resulted from the Supreme Court–packing plan, which he denounced. He became a Republican the next year, developed an enduring friendship with HERBERT HOOVER, endorsed WENDELL WILLKIE in 1940, and then grew to oppose the eastern internationalist wing of the GOP. In 1974, Moley published his final book, a biography of his hero, Irish patriot Daniel O'Connell. He died on February 18, 1975, in Phoenix, Arizona.

Morgan, Arthur Ernest
(1878–1975) *Tennessee Valley Authority board chairman*

Born on June 20, 1878, in Cincinnati, Ohio, to Baptist schoolteacher parents, Arthur Morgan was reared in St. Cloud, Minnesota. His father was also a surveyor and taught those skills to his son, which influenced Morgan to become an engineer. In 1905, he took over his father's small surveying business. Two years later, he moved to Washington, D.C., to work for the Office of Drainage Investigations in the Department of Agriculture (1907–10). Despite his lack of a university degree, he operated his own engineering firm in Memphis, Tennessee, from 1910 to 1913. He became a certified member of the American Society of Civil Engineers and was elected as its vice president in 1927.

In 1913, Morgan was appointed chief engineer of what became the Miami (Valley) Conservancy District, headquartered in Dayton, Ohio. It consisted of five dams, the largest flood-control project of its time. In 1921, he assumed the presidency of the bankrupt Antioch College, which had been founded in 1853 by educational reformer Horace Mann. By the time he left the presidency in 1936, he had turned the financial condition of the college around as well as introduced work-study programs.

Although Morgan had voted for fellow engineer HERBERT HOOVER in 1932 and did not know Franklin Roosevelt, in May 1933 FDR appointed him as chairman of the new Tennessee Valley Authority's (TVA) three-member board of directors. The president also approved Morgan's recommendations for the two other board members, DAVID LILIENTHAL and HARCOURT MORGAN. Unfortunately, it proved to be a combustible trio. Morgan's idealistic nature and engineering background made him favor regional planning and the elimination of poverty, not just the pursuit of cheap power. The older Harcourt Morgan was more conservative than Arthur Morgan, and the younger Lilienthal viewed the chairman as a tool of the utility companies. By 1936, Arthur Morgan had begun criticizing his colleagues in public, and FDR finally fired him in 1938. As with Hoover, Morgan's supposedly apolitical engineering values proved too inflexible in the political arena.

Nonetheless, his implementation of the original dams and recruitment of the project staffs led to the TVA's early success. Ironically, his original idealistic vision is viewed more sympathetically in retrospect since the TVA evolved into a huge bureaucracy in the decades after World War II. Morgan outlived many of his critics, dying on November 15, 1975, in Xenia, Ohio.

Morgan, Harcourt Alexander

(1867–1950) *Tennessee Valley Authority board director; director and chairman*

Harcourt Morgan was born on August 31, 1867, in Strathroy, Ontario, Canada. He graduated from the University of Toronto in 1889 and pursued graduate work in science at Cornell University from 1891 to 1898. While employed as an entomologist and horticulturist at Louisiana State University in Baton Rouge from 1889 to 1894, Morgan worked with parish extension agents and the U.S. Department of Agriculture's experimental stations. He later became affiliated with the University of Tennessee, first as director of its Agricultural Experiment Station from 1905 to 1913 and then as dean of the College of Agriculture from 1913 to 1919. In 1919, he became president of the University of Tennessee.

Morgan's 1933 appointment by FDR to the three-person board of the Tennessee Valley Authority, which was backed by commercial farmers, marked the beginning of his involvement with the New Deal. He supervised fertilization production and agricultural policy while chairman ARTHUR MORGAN oversaw dam construction, education, and rural life, and DAVID LILIENTHAL was public-policy engineer. The chairman, suspicious of wealthy landowners, favored large-scale planning, which brought Arthur Morgan into conflict with Harcourt Morgan, a longtime resident of the Tennessee Valley. The more conservative Harcourt Morgan was equally suspicious of bureaucratic planning, instead advocating "grassroots democracy" that would not disrupt the local consensus.

After Arthur Morgan tried to oppose Lilienthal's reappointment to the board in 1936, Harcourt Morgan joined with Lilienthal to oppose the chairman, who began to criticize his colleagues publicly. As a result, FDR fired Arthur Morgan in 1938. Harcourt Morgan, who served on the board until 1948, replaced Arthur Morgan as chairman in 1938 and held the chairmanship until 1941, when Lilienthal became chairman. He retired in 1948 at the age of eighty. Harcourt Morgan died on August 25, 1950.

Morgenthau, Henry, Jr.

(1891–1967) *Federal Farm Bureau chairman, Farm Credit Administration governor, secretary of the Treasury*

Henry Morgenthau, Jr., born on May 11, 1891, in New York City, was the only son of affluent Jewish parents. The vast success of his businessman father caused him to suffer insecurities about his own abilities. His father's success extended to national politics: the senior Morgenthau served as the financial head of the Democratic National Committee in 1912 and 1916 and was Woodrow Wilson's emissary to Turkey. The junior Morgenthau entered Phillips Exeter Academy in 1904 but left after two years and completed his college preparation at the Sachs Collegiate Institute in New York City. The pattern was repeated in his less-than-impressive college performance: he entered Cornell University but never graduated.

While in Texas recovering from typhoid fever in 1911, Morgenthau developed an interest in agriculture. Two years later, his father helped him to purchase a large cattle and apple farm in southern Dutchess County, New York, 15 minutes from Franklin Roosevelt's Hyde Park estate. Within two years, gentlemen farmers Morgenthau and Roosevelt had developed what would become a lifelong friendship, and in FDR the younger Morgenthau found a substitute father figure.

In 1916, Morgenthau married Elinor Fatman, whose maternal grandfather had been a founding partner in the banking house of Lehman Brothers, and whose uncle was HERBERT LEHMAN. Morgenthau's wife and ELEANOR ROOSEVELT also became close friends. The Roosevelts and the Morgenthaus became especially close after FDR contracted polio in 1921. They spent countless hours playing board games and discussing farm issues and local politics. After FDR was elected governor of New York in 1928, he appointed Morgenthau as chairman of the Agricultural Advisory Committee and then as commissioner of conservation in 1930. In that role, Morgenthau worked closely with HARRY HOPKINS to accomplish a major state reforestation project.

After FDR was elected president, he appointed Morgenthau chairman of the Federal Farm Bureau. He also became the governor of the new Farm Credit Administration, helping farmers refinance their mortgages. By 1934, he was the secretary of the Treasury and eventually served longer in that position than all his predecessors except ANDREW MELLON. He was more conservative than FDR, and he lacked media skills—Roosevelt sometimes would refer humorously to him as "Henry the Morgue"—but Morgenthau was also honest, compassionate, hardworking, and efficient, as well as totally loyal to FDR. His basic decency was also reflected in his opposition to the relocation of Japanese Americans in 1941 as well as his assistance in creating the War Refugee Board to assist refugees from Nazi Germany. Although he helped to keep the dollar sound while financing America's participation in World War II, Morgenthau is sometimes faulted in the recession of 1937–38. At the 44-nation Bretton Woods conference in July 1944, he helped to establish the International Monetary Fund and World Bank. On the other hand, he advocated the so-called Morgenthau Plan for postwar Germany, under which Germany would have become an agricultural society. FDR initially had favored the idea at the second Quebec conference in 1944 but had come to reject it by the time of the February 1945 Yalta conference. Morgenthau resigned after FDR's death.

The Morgenthaus became the Roosevelts' closest Jewish family friends, and Henry Morgenthau was the only Jew in FDR's cabinet. When Elinor Morgenthau died on September 21, 1949, Eleanor Roosevelt delivered the eulogy at her funeral. In 1951 he married Margaret Puthon Hirsch, and spent the remainder of his life primarily as a philanthropist. Morgenthau died on February 6, 1967, in Poughkeepsie, New York.

Murphy, Frank

(1890–1949) Detroit mayor, governor-general of the Philippines, U.S. high commissioner to the Philippines, Michigan governor, U.S. attorney general, U.S. Supreme Court justice

Frank Murphy was born on April 13, 1890, in what is now Harbor Beach, Michigan. His father was a Canadian-born Irish-Catholic lawyer who in his youth had been jailed for Fenian (Irish Republican) sympathies; his great-grandfather had been hanged by the British as an insurrectionist. Murphy attended local public schools, and although he hated exams he was an enthusiastic debater during

Justice Frank Murphy *(Library of Congress)*

both high school and college. He earned his undergraduate degree in 1912 and his law degree in 1914, both from the University of Michigan. While Ireland remained neutral in World War I, Murphy proved his patriotism by serving with the American Expeditionary Force in France, but he never experienced combat. He briefly studied law at Lincoln's Inn in London and Trinity College in Dublin during the postwar period. Upon his return to the United States, he served as a U.S. attorney in Michigan and participated in the government's prosecution of radicals. He supported U.S. attorney general A. Mitchell Palmer's failed presidential bid in 1920. After Murphy was badly defeated in a congressional race that same year, he resigned as a federal prosecutor in early 1922 to practice and teach law. The next year, he won a seat on Detroit's Recorder's Court and was reelected in 1929. To appeal to

the urban political base he needed, he abandoned his previous "law and order" record and became a progressive judge who won local acclaim for his stance on the rights of labor and blacks.

In 1930, the politically ambitious and articulate Murphy was elected mayor of Detroit, and he won reelection in 1931. He became the first president of the U.S. Conference of Mayors. He was an early supporter of Franklin Roosevelt and campaigned for him in Michigan in 1932. After FDR won the presidency, he rewarded Murphy in 1933 by naming him governor-general of the Philippines, a post he held until 1936. Murphy supported the Filipino independence campaign, and during the 10-year commonwealth phase to independence, he became the Philippines' first high commissioner in 1935. In response to FDR's wishes, he returned to Michigan in 1936 and campaigned successfully for the governorship, implementing a "Little New Deal" in the state while he played to the crowds as a champion of prolabor principles. He was criticized for ignoring court injunctions against strikers. Mobilizing the National Guard for the limited purpose of restoring order during the 1937 General Motors sit-down strike, Murphy did not allow them to remove strikers from the factories even though he felt the strikes were illegal. He also allowed the families of strikers to collect state relief. Although he presided during one of the first times that state government had remained neutral in a major strike and had supported New Deal reforms, Murphy lost his bid for reelection in 1938.

FDR appointed him as U.S. attorney general the next year. Murphy investigated the THOMAS PENDERGAST machine in Kansas City with his characteristic energy, and the investigation led to its demise. He also created the first civil-liberties unit in the Department of Justice. In November 1939, against Murphy's personal wishes, FDR forced him to accept the opening on the U.S. Supreme Court following the death of conservative justice PIERCE BUTLER, a Roman Catholic from Minnesota. The move meant it would be unlikely that Murphy could pursue his presidential ambitions.

FDR got what he wanted with his fifth appointment to the Supreme Court as Murphy joined the liberals on the court, HUGO BLACK and WILLIAM O. DOUGLAS (and later WILEY RUTLEDGE, JR.). Accused of "voting his heart," he may have been the most liberal justice ever to serve on the bench. Justice FELIX FRANKFURTER came to view Murphy as part of the judicial "Axis" that would not loyally follow his governmental conformity during World War II, and as a result it may have been Frankfurter who sarcastically characterized Murphy's tendency to moralize his jurisprudence as "tempering justice with Murphy."

During World War II, Murphy stunned his brethren by volunteering for military service and undergoing infantry training at Fort Knox in 1942. Perhaps influenced by the legacy of his father and great-grandfather, Murphy stood up against those in power for what he believed, and he seemed to have matured while on the Supreme Court. For example, he sided with protection of the rights of Jehovah's Witnesses even though they attacked the Catholic Church. As mayor of Detroit, as a criminal court judge, and during his brief army stint in southern states, Murphy had witnessed racism and hated it. He became the only liberal on the Court to dissent in *Korematsu v. U.S.* (1944), insisting the majority decision against Japanese Americans was a "legalization of racism." He developed one of the strongest civil-liberties records ever on the bench. He supported the right to picket and the rights of conscientious objectors, Native Americans, and suspects, in addition to implementing a constitutional standard for the Tokyo War Crimes Trials. As a member of an ethnic and religious minority that had been subjected to discrimination, Murphy wanted the Bill of Rights applied on a universal basis. His best work on the Supreme Court emphasized a call for universal justice, and his record of personal generosity, although he was a person of limited means, left him penniless when he died in Detroit on July 19, 1949.

Murray, Philip
(1886–1952) *national union leader*

The son of Irish-Catholic parents who had recently moved from Ireland, Philip Murray was born on May 25, 1886, in New Glasgow, Scotland. His father had relocated to Scotland to find work in coal mines there, and he became the head of a local coal-miners union. Murray went to work in the coal mines with his father when he was 10 years old. When he was 16, his family immigrated to the United States, where both Murray and his father found jobs in the coal mines near Pittsburgh, Pennsylvania. Although he had left school, Murray managed to complete his education through correspondence courses.

In 1904, Murray triggered an unsuccessful strike after he accused a company official of cheating him. He lost that battle but went on to win the local presidency of the United Mine Workers of America (UMWA). Murray's energy, charm, and egalitarian style assisted his climb up the union ranks. In 1910, he married Elizabeth Lavery, and they subsequently adopted a son.

Murray was elected to the international executive board of the UMWA in 1912. Four years later, he was president of District 5, which included Pittsburgh. During World War I, he served as a member of the War Labor Board and the National Coal Production Committee. In 1920, JOHN L. LEWIS appointed him vice president of the union after Lewis became its president. Murray demonstrated both loyalty to Lewis and an ability to resolve disputes using his persuasive skills. He also aided Lewis in purging radicals from the union.

During the 1930s, Murray used the National Industrial Recovery Act (NIRA) to build up union membership. After the U.S. Supreme Court invalidated the NIRA in May 1935 (*Schechter Poultry Corporation v. U.S.*), Murray became a board member of the National Recovery Administration and aided in the drafting of the Guffey-Snyder Bituminous Coal Stabilization Act of 1935. The bill narrowly passed the Congress, and Franklin Roosevelt signed it into law on August 30, 1935, only to have the Supreme Court declare it unconstitutional the next year. Following FDR's landslide reelection in 1936, Congress passed the Guffey-Vinson Bituminous Coal Act of 1937, which FDR signed on April 26, 1937, and which reenacted most of the provisions that had been in the Guffey-Snyder version.

In 1935, Murray, Lewis, and SIDNEY HILLMAN of the Amalgamated Clothing Workers formed the Committee for Industrial Organization, later renamed the Congress of Industrial Organizations (CIO), breaking from the American Federation of Labor, which remained committed to only organizing unions by craft. In May 1936, Murray was appointed the head of the Steel Workers Organizing Committee (SWOC) and led one of the most successful industrywide mass-production strikes in American history. By spring 1937, Murray had negotiated a contract with United States Steel, which recognized SWOC as the bargaining agent for the company's employees. U.S. Steel thereby avoided the sit-down strikes that had occurred at General Motors during the same time. Though Murray was less successful in his actions against the "Little Steel" corporations, and a series of strikes culminated in the "Memorial Day Massacre" in South Chicago, his persistence in seeking legal sanctions through the National Labor Relations Board finally achieved success in 1941.

After the more belligerent and inflexible Lewis resigned as president of the CIO in 1940 with FDR's third-term victory, Murray was elected to replace him. As Murray became a close adviser to FDR and supported the president's war policies, tensions increased between Lewis and Murray. In 1942, Lewis led the UMWA out of the CIO, and SWOC became the United Steel Workers of America. Murray demonstrated his patriotism by agreeing to a "no-strike pledge" for the duration of the war, although his native country remained neutral in World War II, as it had in World War I. Murray supported the CIO's participation in the National War Labor Board. In 1943, he organized the CIO's Committee on Political Education to mobilize voter registration drives among union members. During the postwar period, he sought to remove communist-led unions from the CIO. Murray died on November 9, 1952, in San Francisco.

Murrow, Edward R.
(Egbert Roscoe Murrow)
(1908–1965) *broadcast journalist*

Edward R. Murrow became America's most important radio broadcaster of the 20th century. He was born in the Deep South, raised in the Northwest, and worked in the Northeast. His trans-American experiences would be crucial for his pioneering broadcasts from Europe during World War II, which brought his trusted voice into homes across the nation. He was born Egbert Roscoe Murrow on April 25, 1908, in Polecat Creek, near Greensboro, North Carolina. His father was a farmer and railroad man, and his mother was a teacher. The family moved to Washington State near Blanchard, where he attended high school and then worked his way through Washington

State College. His natural leadership ability emerged in high school and in college, where he majored in speech but also studied political science and international relations. There he changed his first name from Egbert to Edward.

After he completed college, Murrow became the assistant director of the Institute of International Education. In 1934, he married Janet Huntington Brewster, also a broadcast journalist, and the couple had one son. It was in 1935 that he began his career with Columbia Broadcasting System (CBS), then one of the nation's two major radio networks. In 1937, Murrow was sent to London as the network's European director. The next year, he traveled to Poland when ADOLF HITLER invaded Austria, and in the first of what would be 5,000 career broadcasts, he covered the so-called *Anschluss,* or union of Germany and Austria. He went on to cover the Munich Conference, at which the appeasement-seeking British prime minister NEVILLE CHAMBERLAIN acceded to Hitler's demand to annex the Sudetenland of Czechoslovakia.

Murrow became a household name in the United States during his coverage of the Battle of Britain in 1940. His resonant voice, vivid style, and the dramatic backdrop of bomb explosions and sirens captured the immediacy of the situation for listeners back home. The broadcasts also persuaded many that Nazi Germany's actions justified American support for the British. Murrow helped to create international on-the-scene global broadcast reporting, which attracted talented print journalists to the field, including Charles Collingwood, Eric Sevareid, William Shirer, and Howard K. Smith.

Murrow made the successful transition from radio to television news during the postwar period. With his trademark cigarette in hand, he interviewed ELEANOR ROOSEVELT, film stars, and politicians as well as scholars and scientists. He pioneered in-depth features,

the newsmagazine, and investigative reports like his critique of Senator Joseph McCarthy (R-Wis.) in 1954. Frustrated by CBS's preference for profits from entertainment programs over serious news, Murrow accepted the position as the director of the United States Information Agency in 1961. Due to lung cancer, he resigned three years later. He died on April 27, 1965, in Pawling, New York.

Mussolini, Benito
(1883–1945) *Italian dictator*

Benito Mussolini was born on July 29, 1883, to a socialist father and schoolteacher mother. His birthplace was Predappio in the east-central Romagna region of Italy known for its poverty as well as its political radicalism. An unruly student, he was expelled from several boarding schools. He obtained a certificate as a schoolteacher in 1902 and spent the next decade as an itinerant teacher, journalist, and socialist activist in Switzerland, Austria, and Italy. He was imprisoned briefly several times for advocating violence against employers. In 1915, he married Rachele Guidi, and they eventually had five children. His oldest daughter, Edda, married Count Galeazzo Ciano, who would become his foreign minister in 1936.

Mussolini's entry into politics came about in 1912 through his editorship of the Socialist Party's paper, published in Milan. His views on World War I changed from his initial argument against nationalism and Italy's entry into the war to the opposite view, which resulted in his dismissal and expulsion from the party. In 1914, he became editor of his own pro-war newspaper, which eventually became the voice of the fascist movement. When Italy entered World War I, Mussolini served briefly in the army as a sharpshooter. In 1917, he was wounded, and upon his return from the front, he denounced socialism and founded the Fascist Party in Milan on March 23, 1919, with support from war veterans and others.

Middle-class fears of a socialist revolution led to the May 1921 election of Mussolini and other fascists to the parliament as a coalition against the socialists. Disillusioned with democracy, Mussolini wanted to become the dictator who would restore order and grandeur to Italy. The next year, the fascists planned a coup d'état after the pugnacious bluffer threatened to have his Blackshirt followers "march on Rome." Caving in to his threat, King Victor Emmanuel III asked Mussolini to form a new government. As a result, Mussolini became the youngest prime minister in Italian history on October 30, 1922. The next month, the Italian parliament granted him unlimited authority to restore order. In January 1925, he declared a dictatorship, calling himself *Il Duce.*

Mussolini played on the disappointment that many Italians felt toward Woodrow Wilson and the Allies for not meeting their territorial expectations after World War I. After quashing the strikes and riots that had plagued the country, he launched massive public-works projects to put many Italians back to work. He venerated the state and wanted a hierarchical society with himself at the top. Only 5'7" tall but a charismatic bully, Mussolini came to believe he was infallible. Initially he had many diplomatic successes. Italy was among the first to recognize the Soviet Union in 1924, and the next year the Locarno Treaty allowed for collective security in the Rhineland and eastern Europe. In 1929, the Lateran Pact resolved a long-standing dispute with the Vatican, and in July 1934, Mussolini forced ADOLF HITLER to back down when he attempted a coup in Austria. He was furious after Britain and France refused to help Austria.

In 1935, Mussolini launched a successful attack against Ethiopia, the last independent kingdom in Africa, in large part to compensate for the 1869 Ethiopian defeat of Italy. In 1936, following German remilitarization of the Rhineland and failure by Britain and France to stand up to Hitler, Mussolini moved closer to Hitler despite the German leader's dismissal of him in 1934 as a funny little man of no consequence. After the League of Nations condemnations against Mussolini failed to include an oil embargo, Italy pulled out of the League in 1937. By abandoning Italy's traditional role as a balancer of power between the West and the Soviet Union, he fundamentally doomed himself by siding with Hitler. After a series of military defeats during World War II, the fascist Grand Council voted no-confidence in him, and the king deposed him on July 26, 1943. The Nazis came to his aid and installed him as the puppet head of the Italian Social Republic at Salo on Lake Garda until the collapse of the Third Reich. Attempting to flee Switzerland with his mistress, Claretta Petacci, Mussolini was captured by Italian partisans who executed the couple on April 28, 1945. Their bodies were strung up by the heels in dishonor and exposed to public view in a Milan piazza.

Nelson, Donald Marr
(1888–1959) *federal administrator*

Born the son of a locomotive engineer on November 17, 1888, in Hannibal, Missouri, Donald Nelson chose to become an engineer of a different kind, obtaining his degree in chemical engineering at the University of Missouri in 1911. He began his 30-year career with Sears, Roebuck and Company in 1912, working his way up the corporate ladder to executive vice president by 1939.

In contrast to most businessmen who opposed Franklin Roosevelt and the New Deal, Nelson was a liberal who supported organized labor. As a result, FDR recruited him in 1940 to assist in mobilizing the nation's economy for wartime. He initially headed the National Defense Advisory Committee in June 1940, switching in January 1941 to head the Division of Purchases of the Office of Production Management. In July 1941, he became head of the Supply, Priorities, and Allocation Board. An able administrator, Nelson was appointed by FDR in January 1942 as head of the War Production Board, which dealt with all aspects of economic mobilization, the economic conversion to wartime production, and the allocation of materials.

In 1944, Nelson was forced out of office when he lost a major battle with the military, which opposed early gradual reconversion of the economy to civilian production in order to maintain full employment. FDR then assigned him to missions in the Soviet Union and China as compensation. He left government service after the war and died in Los Angeles, California, on September 29, 1959. Married five times, he had no children.

Niebuhr, Reinhold
(1892–1971) *theologian, religious leader*

Born on June 21, 1892, in Wright City, Missouri, Reinhold Niebuhr was the son of an immigrant German preacher, a minister of the German Evangelical School of North America. His mother worked as parish assistant and church organist. One of four children, Niebuhr grew up in Missouri and Illinois. From his time in Illinois, he was influenced by Abraham Lincoln, who became his political hero. Appropriately enough, the Niebuhr family moved when he was 10 years old to Lincoln, Illinois, a city with a large German-American population. He completed the ninth grade at Lincoln High School and then attended boarding school at the German-Evangelical Synod's preseminary,

Elmhurst College near Chicago, graduating in 1910. Intending to follow his father into the ministry, Niebuhr went to the Synod's Eden Theological Seminary near St. Louis. After he received his divinity degree in 1913, he was ordained as a minister. Neibuhr's failure to obtain a regular Bachelor of Arts degree from a liberal arts college made him question his academic and scholarly background. During that same spring, his father died unexpectedly, and he subsequently served briefly as interim pastor of his father's church.

Niebuhr moved to the East Coast in the fall of 1913 to attend Yale Divinity School. He received his second B.D. degree there in 1914 and the next year earned his master of arts degree. After he completed his education, he was ordained a minister of the Evangelical and Reformed Church (now part of the United Church of Christ). From 1915 to 1928, he served as the pastor of Bethel Evangelical Church in Detroit, which would be his only congregation.

As a theologian, Niebuhr downplayed dogma and ritual in favor of magnanimity in one's personal and social existence. However, during World War I, he was less forgiving when he purged the German-Evangelical Synod of pro-German views, crusading against "disloyalty" within the church and banning German-language services.

Niebuhr developed a reputation as a great orator. In 1922, he became a contributor and editorial writer for the *Christian Century*. He defined politics as "seeking justice in an unjust world," and wanted to build a labor party like RAMSEY MACDONALD's in Britain. He campaigned against the Ku Klux Klan in 1925 by supporting the successful Catholic candidate in Detroit's mayoral race. He also campaigned against HENRY FORD's industrial policy, which in his view undermined workers. Niebuhr wanted to combine religious belief with political action to achieve justice in the world.

In 1928, Niebuhr left the pulpit and Detroit to teach at the Union Theological Seminary in New York. He became the most influential Protestant theologian during the Great Depression. The following year, he joined the Socialist Party, whose leaders included NORMAN THOMAS, also a Protestant minister. In 1930, Niebuhr became the party's candidate for the New York state senate from the Upper West Side of Manhattan, but he lost badly. In 1931, he married Ursula Keppel-Compton, a theology student from England with whom he had two children.

Although he had lost the state senate race, Niebuhr ran for Congress from the same district in 1932 but fared no better in that race. After the 1932 election, one of his most important books was published. *Moral Man and Immoral Society* reflected his "Christian realism" philosophy. In his view, a pluralist society consisted of conflicting power blocs so that large groups had to champion just causes. It was that position that, by 1940, had led him to turn from the Socialist Party because of its belief in pacifism. The rise of European fascism caused Niebuhr to turn from his pacifist beliefs to denounce ADOLF HITLER and BENITO MUSSOLINI. In 1941, he founded a new magazine, *Christianity and Crisis*, as an alternative to the pacifism of the *Christian Century*. He also chaired the Union for Democratic Action (UDA), which was composed of former Socialists who had grown frustrated with that party's isolationism. The UDA stood for promoting labor rights but was both anticommunist and antifascist.

Niebuhr supported the lend-lease program and traveled to England on behalf of the Office of War Information to support the British public and Allied troops. He also chaired a new group, the American Friends of German Freedom, to promote German democrats. He lobbied the Roosevelt administration to allow Jewish emigration to the

United States. In 1944, he supported the founding of the Liberal Party of New York. He remained a liberal anticommunist during the postwar period, and in 1947 he helped found the Americans for Democratic Action, which grew out of the UDA.

Perhaps Niebuhr's most enduring legacy from the 1940s is his "Serenity Prayer," later adopted by Alcoholics Anonymous. By 1952, he had suffered a series of strokes that left him partially paralyzed. Still, he continued to teach at the Union Theological Seminary until 1960, when he retired. He died on June 1, 1971, in Stockbridge, Massachusetts.

Norris, George William
(1861–1944) *U.S. senator*

The 11th of 12 children in an Ohio farm family, George Norris experienced the effects of war throughout his life, which began with his birth on July 11, 1861, during the Civil War and ended during World War II. In 1864, his father died from pneumonia and an older brother was killed in the Civil War. Norris attended local schools before entering Ohio's Baldwin University in 1877. He left in 1878 and subsequently taught school for a year and then graduated in 1880 from Northern Indiana Normal School. He graduated from its law school in 1883. After teaching school for two years in Ohio and Washington, he moved in 1885 to Nebraska and began his law practice.

By the early 1890s, Norris was involved in local politics. In 1892, he won election as a county prosecutor. Three years later, he won a district judgeship. His congressional career began in 1902 when, as a Republican he was elected to the U.S. House of Representatives, where he remained for a decade. He was then elected to the U.S. Senate and served for 30 years. Although he was a conservative when he entered politics, he gradually sided with the

progressives. He first attracted national attention when he participated in the 1910 St. Patrick's Day coup against the Speaker of the House, Joseph Cannon, the powerful conservative Republican from Illinois whose power was greatly reduced as the result of an alliance between progressive Republicans and Democrats. The Speaker's previous overwhelming power was divided among the chairmen of the permanent committees.

During the 1920s, Norris's support for the Republican Party continued to erode because of his belief that the Warren Harding, Calvin Coolidge, and HERBERT HOOVER administrations were too much under the influence of corporate wealth. In 1925, after the death of Wisconsin senator Robert M. La Follette, Sr., Norris became the de facto leader of the congressional progressives. The conservatives struck back in 1930 after Norris's public endorsement of AL SMITH for president in 1928. They found another George Norris and ran him unsuccessfully against Norris in the Republican primary. The courts blocked the political ploy.

In the 1932 presidential election, Norris not only endorsed Franklin Roosevelt publicly, but also campaigned for the Democratic candidate. Consequently the two became political allies as well as personal friends. Norris was the principal author of the Tennessee Valley Authority Act in 1933. He sponsored the Rural Electrification Act of 1936, the Farm Forestry Act of 1937, and a "little TVA" program for Nebraska. In keeping with the philosophy of progressives to eliminate politics from the political process, Norris played a major role in converting the bicameral Nebraska legislature into a unicameral body. In 1936, with FDR's support, he ran successfully for a fifth Senate term as an Independent Progressive rather than as a Republican.

Norris became the only leading Senate isolationist to abandon his former foreign-policy position to support most of FDR's prewar proposals. He became the first member of Congress to denounce publicly J. EDGAR HOOVER, the director of the Federal Bureau of Investigation. At age 81, Norris sought reelection to a sixth term, running again as an Independent Progressive, but lost. Despite FDR's offers of various positions in the administration, Norris declined and opted for retirement due to declining health. He completed his autobiography shortly before his death on September 2, 1944, in McCook, Nebraska. Post–World War II polls of scholars rank Norris among the top five greatest U.S. senators in American history.

Nye, Gerald Prentice
(1892–1971) *U.S. senator*

Gerald Nye, the son of a progressive Republican newspaper publisher, was born on December 19, 1892, in Hortonville, Wisconsin. He grew up in Wittenberg, Wisconsin, and graduated from high school there in 1911. Instead of attending college, Nye began his career as a newspaper editor on small-town newspapers in Wisconsin and Iowa before moving to North Dakota in 1916. There, in 1925, he was appointed as a progressive Republican to fill the vacancy caused by the death of an incumbent U.S. senator. He won a full term in 1926 and was reelected in 1932 and 1938.

Nye considered the American farmer to be the backbone of the nation and was suspicious of what he considered favoritism toward urban business interests. In the 1930s, he initially supported most of the New Deal. In 1934, he became the chair of the seven-member Senate Special Committee Investigating the Munitions Industry, which had grown out of the disillusionment with U.S. involvement in World War I. From September 1934 through February 1936, the colorful and articulate chairman of the so-called Nye Committee hearings attracted sensational national media coverage. Testimony came from nearly 200 witnesses, including business and financial giants J. P. Morgan and the du Ponts. The committee recommended governmental regulation of the munitions industry to lessen the likelihood of American involvement in foreign wars. It also suggested a link between business and the executive branch (war, navy, and state departments) in promoting the armaments race and war.

Though the Nye Committee failed to enact the legislation it proposed, it contributed to the enactment of neutrality legislation from 1935 to 1937. FDR initially supported the Nye Committee until war became likely. Nye first broke with FDR during the controversy over the Court-packing plan in 1937. Two years later, he became one of the leading opponents of FDR's attempt to repeal the neutrality acts. From 1940 until the December 1941 Japanese attack on Pearl Harbor, Nye was one of the leading orators for the America First Committee, which opposed American entry into World War II, charging that FDR was going to use intervention in the European war to cover the failure of the New Deal to end the Great Depression. Nye was defeated for reelection in 1944 and quickly faded from national attention. He died on July 17, 1971, in suburban Maryland.

Olds, Leland

(1890–1960) *member of federal commissions, chairman of Federal Power Commission*

Born on December 31, 1890, in Rochester, New York, Leland Olds was the son of an Amherst College mathematics professor. In 1912, he graduated from Amherst College, Massachusetts, where his father, who had become the chair of the mathematics department in 1891, would become president in 1924. Olds pursued graduate work in economics and sociology at Harvard University and then at Columbia University. He engaged in social work in Boston's South End, which led him to study for two years at Union Theological Seminary. Afterward, he served briefly as a minister in a poor section of Brooklyn.

During World War I, Olds worked for the Council of National Defense, the Shipbuilding Labor Adjustment Board, and the National War Labor Board. From 1920 to 1922, he served as head of the American Federation of Labor's research bureau. He next worked as industrial editor for the Federated Press, a labor news agency. In 1924, he married Maud Agnes Spear. The couple, who had four children, lived in Northbrook, Illinois, until 1929 and then moved to New York.

From 1931 to 1939, Olds was the executive secretary for the newly established New York Power Commission. It was during this period that he developed a strong belief in national economic planning. In 1937, Franklin Roosevelt appointed him to the Commission to Study Cooperative Enterprise Abroad. Olds wrote the commission's report, "Inquiry on Cooperative Enterprise in Europe." On June 22, 1939, FDR rewarded Olds's work with an appointment to a five-year term on the Federal Power Commission (FPC). He was made chair the next year and reappointed in 1944. HARRY TRUMAN reappointed him again in 1949, but senators from gas-producing states used the opportunity to red-bait him, and the Senate rejected his confirmation by a vote of 53 to 15. In reality, the opposition grew from senators representing gas-producing state who did not want the FPC to regulate wellhead prices for natural gas. Lyndon Johnson, the Texas Democrat, played a major role in Olds's defeat. Olds died from a heart attack in Bethesda, Maryland, on August 3, 1960.

Olson, Culbert

(1876–1962) *California governor*

Born to Scandinavian immigrant parents on November 7, 1876, Culbert Olson was a native of Millard County, Utah. He attended Brigham Young University and then became a newspaper reporter and city editor in Ogden, Utah. A Democrat, he admired William Jennings Bryan. After his cousin, William H. King, a Utah Democrat, was elected to the U.S. House of Representatives in 1897, Olson moved to Washington, D.C., to serve as his secretary. While living in the nation's capital, Olson earned his law degree from Columbian University, later George Washington University. He returned to Utah in 1901 to practice law and became active in local politics. He won a seat in the Utah legislature in 1916, the same year his cousin was first elected to the U.S. Senate, where King served until 1941.

In 1920, the progressive Democrat Olson moved his family to Los Angeles, California, where he began his law practice. The move was in large part Olson's reaction to the conservative political culture in Utah. By 1932, he had become the president of the Los Angeles Democratic Club, and he campaigned for Franklin Roosevelt that year. Two years later, he won a seat in the California senate and became the state Democratic chairman. Olson was a liberal who viewed the author UPTON SINCLAIR's campaign for the governorship favorably, in contrast to the more conservative WILLIAM MCADOO, who had been elected to the U.S. Senate on FDR's coattails during the 1932 landslide. While in the Republican-controlled California state senate, Olson remained a progressive.

In 1938, Olson became the first Democrat elected governor of California since 1894, easily defeating Republican Frank Merriam. Olson was then 62 years old, tall with a slender build, white hair, and Scandinavian fair skin and blue eyes. He looked the part of a governor, and he ran on a progressive reform platform. However, by the time he took office, the reform era in California politics had largely ended. In 1942, although he asked FDR to campaign for him, the president stayed out of the campaign. Olson had the misfortune of running against the pop-

ular state attorney general Earl Warren, who decisively defeated him by running a less partisan campaign that supported FDR's war policy. It was Olson's final political campaign. He died two decades later on April 13, 1962.

Olson, Floyd Bjornstjerne
(1891–1936) *Minnesota governor*

Floyd Olson was born on November 13, 1891, in Minneapolis, Minnesota, the son of an immigrant railroad worker, and brought up in the poor section of North Minneapolis. In high school he earned a name for himself as a debater and actor. He entered the University of Minnesota in 1910, majoring in pre-law, but had to drop out of college in 1911 due to financial difficulties. For a short time afterward, he was an itinerant worker in Alaska, Canada, and Washington, where he briefly joined the "Wobblies," as the Industrial Workers of the World were called. After he returned to Minneapolis in 1913, he worked as a legal clerk while completing his law degree at night during two years at Northwestern Law College. After he graduated, he joined a local law firm.

Olson entered the political world in 1919 when he was appointed as the assistant county attorney for the state's most populous county. The year before, he had unsuccessfully sought the Democratic nomination for Congress. In 1920, he again failed in his bid for Congress, but that same year he was appointed the county attorney following impeachment of the incumbent. He was reelected to that position in 1922 and 1926. During his tenure as county attorney, he developed a reputation for pragmatism, honesty, generosity, and hard work. His speaking ability, first exhibited in high school, attracted public attention.

In 1924, Olson narrowly lost the Minnesota gubernatorial election as the candidate of the new Farmer-Labor Association, but after the Wall Street crash in 1929, he easily won the 1930 election and served as governor until 1936. He was the first Minnesota governor to win on that ticket. Although the Farmer-Labor Party never controlled the legislature, he was able to pass bills for public-works projects, regulation of securities, conservation of natural resources, and worker cooperatives, implementing a "Little New Deal" for Minnesota.

Olson was a leftist critic of the New Deal who thought it should promote socialism, but he admired Franklin Roosevelt and supported him in 1932 and 1936. In 1933, Olson himself attracted national attention by threatening to declare martial law and seize private property unless his relief measures were passed. In 1934, he upset state employees by declaring martial law after the strikers agreed to mediation of a trucker's strike that had shut down Minneapolis. He initiated a campaign for the 1936 U.S. Senate election, but died of pancreatic cancer on August 22, 1936, at the Mayo Clinic in Rochester, Minnesota.

Owens, Jesse
(1913–1980) *U.S. Olympic track champion*

Even before the military clash between democracy and fascism in World War II, the theoret-

Jesse Owens winning the 220-yard low hurdles and setting a world record at the Big Ten meet in Ann Arbor, Michigan, on May 25, 1935 *(National Archives)*

ically apolitical world of Olympic sports became a politically charged symbol of these opposing forces, a foreshadowing of the ultimate outcome of the battle between the rivals. Ironically, African Americans from the Deep South who had personally endured racism—sports legends Joe Louis and Jesse Owens—struck the initial blows for democratic superiority.

Owens was born to sharecroppers on September 12, 1913, in Oakville, Alabama, literally and figuratively a world away from the global stage he would occupy in Germany during the 1936 Olympics. His family became part of the largest internal migration in history after World War I by leaving the South for the North with its opportunities for a better life in Cleveland, Ohio. There Owens attended local schools and was a track star in secondary school. In 1932, he narrowly missed winning a place on the U.S. Olympic team. Before beginning Ohio State University, he won several track events at the 1933 National Interscholastic Championships.

The stage was set for the Olympics in early August 1936. Owens stole the show by winning four gold medals at the Olympic Games in Berlin, intended by ADOLF HITLER to showcase the new Nazi Third Reich. Owens broke the world record in the 220-meter sprint, the long jump, and the final leg of the U.S. team's record-breaking 400-meter relay, and he tied the Olympic record for the 100-meter sprint. His triumph, witnessed by Hitler, provided a severe blow to the self-proclaimed racially superior Nazis and an inspiration to African Americans.

The world of art became enmeshed in the worlds of sports and politics through the Olympics. Leni Riefenstahl (1902–2003), condemned as "Hitler's filmmaker" due to the propaganda she produced for the dictator through her work, made Owens the hero of her 1936 documentary of the event, *Olympische Spiele*, despite Hitler's racial prejudice.

Always a Republican, Owens received a financial stipend from Republican presidential candidate ALF LANDON in 1936 to campaign for black votes in the fall election. Later that year, he was voted Athlete of the Year by the Associated Press.

During World War II, Owens became a supervisor of black workers at the Ford Motor Company in Detroit following several short assignments for the government. During the postwar period, he became a successful public speaker. In 1974, he was enshrined in the Track and Field Hall of Fame, and he was presented the Medal of Freedom by Republican president Gerald Ford in 1976, the nation's bicentennial year. Owens died on March 31, 1980, in Tucson, Arizona.

P

Patman, Wright
(1893–1976) *U.S. congressman*

The child of tenant farm parents, Wright Patman was born on August 6, 1893, in Patman's Switch in northeastern Texas. He attended local public schools and in 1913 began a correspondence law course while working as a tenant farmer. Subsequently he went to Cumberland University in Lebanon, Tennessee, and graduated with his law degree in 1916. He returned to Hughes Springs, Texas, where he had attended high school, and opened a law practice. Later that year, he became an assistant county attorney but left that position in July 1917 to enter the U.S. Army, serving as a machine-gun officer until 1919. After his tour with the army ended, he began another law practice in Linden, Texas, until he was elected as a Democrat to the Texas legislature in 1920. In 1923, he was appointed district attorney, leaving to serve in the U.S. House of Representatives after he won election in 1928. He served in Congress for 47 years.

Patman was a 20th-century populist, usually loyal to the New Deal and always loyal to veterans and poor farmers. Suspicious of banks, railroads, and corporations, he sponsored antitrust action. Despite FDR's veto, which the Congress overrode, Patman saw a compromise soldiers' bonus bill enacted in 1936. The next year, he became a member of the Banking and Currency Committee and helped to enact federal credit unions. During World War II, he helped to create a special committee on small business, which he then chaired. As a champion of small businesses, he helped to establish the Smaller Plants Corporation, which was designed to make loans to encourage small businesses to change to war production.

Patman finally attained the chairmanship of the Banking and Currency Committee in 1963. His tendency to hog committee time eventually led to the five-minute rule for questioners in the House. His autocratic style nearly led to a committee rebellion in 1965, but it was not until a decade later, in January 1975, that liberal reform Democrats defied the seniority system and unseated Patman as well as the other three oldest committee chairmen from their chairmanships. Patman died on March 7, 1976, in Bethesda, Maryland.

Patton, George Smith
(1885–1945) *army general*

George Patton was born the son of an attorney in San Gabriel, California, on November 11, 1885. His paternal grandfather had been a

Confederate colonel who had died during the Civil War; his maternal grandfather was a rancher, military hero, and politician. Raised on his grandfather's ranch, Patton did not begin formal school until he was 12 years old, yet he was a reader. He spent one year at the Virginia Military Institute before he entered the U.S. Military Academy at West Point in 1904. Math was hard for him, and it took him five years to graduate; he ranked 46th in a class of 103 graduates. In 1910, following his graduation from West Point, he married Beatrice Ayer. The couple had three children.

Patton entered the cavalry, and he spent his first years at Fort Sheridan, Illinois. The athletic Patton competed in the pentathlon at the 1912 Olympic Games in Stockholm and then spent six weeks at the French cavalry school in Saumur, France. After his next tour of duty at Fort Myer, Virginia, he returned to Saumur for another summer. An expert with the saber, he was appointed as an instructor in swordsmanship at the Mounted Service School in Fort Riley, Kansas.

Patton became an aide to General John J. Pershing during the army's unsuccessful 1916–17 expedition to Mexico to capture Pancho Villa. In 1917, Pershing promoted Patton to captain and again made him an aide and headquarters commandant with the American Expeditionary Forces in World War I. In November 1917, Patton became one of the first American officers to be assigned to tanks. Promoted to major, he organized the American Tank Center in Langres, France. Early in 1918, he became a lieutenant colonel and was named the commander of the 304th Tank Brigade. Wounded in late September of that year, he was promoted to colonel and received the Distinguished Service Cross.

During the interim between World War I and World War II, Patton was briefly at Camp Meade, Maryland, in 1918–19 before joining the 3rd Cavalry at Fort Myer, Virginia, from 1920 to 1922. The next year, he graduated from the Cavalry School at Fort Riley, and in 1924 he completed the Command and General Staff School there. In 1931, he attended the Army War College, and in 1932 he served under General DOUGLAS MACARTHUR in quashing the Bonus Army veterans in Washington, D.C. These were veterans from World War I who were camped in the capital seeking early payment of promised pensions. Patton also wrote many articles for military journals during this period.

In 1940, Patton was made a brigade commander of the newly formed 2nd Armored Division at Fort Benning, Georgia, and promoted to brigadier general. By the end of the year, he was a major general and the division commander. He became commander of the I Armored Corps in early 1942 and trained his troops at Desert Training Center in California. Later that year, he was selected as the commander of the Western Tank Force of Torch for the invasion of northwest Africa. General DWIGHT EISENHOWER reassigned Patton in 1943 and gave him the task of rebuilding II Corps after it had been badly mauled by the Nazis in Tunisia. After Patton restored the unit, Omar Bradley assumed command, and Patton was promoted to lieutenant general. He then commanded the U.S. Seventh Army, which, along with the British Eighth Army under General Bernard Montgomery, invaded Sicily in July 1943.

After the successful 38-day Allied campaign in Sicily, Patton was visiting hospitalized soldiers who had been wounded in the combat when he lost his temper and verbally abused two soldiers who were not physically wounded but had complained of battle fatigue. He struck one of them across the face with his glove, a blow that galvanized public attention. Suddenly the hero lionized for his ability to gain ground on the battlefield and deliver victories against foreign enemies was under public attack in the press. Eisenhower required Patton to apologize publicly and relieved him from active fighting for nearly a year. Nonetheless, Eisenhower recognized Patton's military strength and quietly gave him command of the Third Army in England, which did not become operational until August 1, 1944.

Though Patton was now subordinate to Omar Bradley, who had served under him in Sicily, he accepted the role reversal without complaint. GEORGE C. MARSHALL now had his winning team of EISENHOWER, Bradley, and Patton together again for the invasion of France. Patton's Third Army arrived a month after D-Day and quickly moved across France, but he was often in conflict with the more methodical British field marshal Montgomery. By April 1945, Patton had received his fourth star. He was appointed the military governor in Bavaria, but his outspoken nature led to his removal, and he became the commander of the Fifteenth Army, a largely ceremonial post.

Patton was fatally injured in an automobile accident near Mannheim in early December and died on December 21, 1945, in a Heidelberg hospital. He was buried near Hamm, Luxembourg.

Pecora, Ferdinand
(1882–1971) *chief counsel to the Senate Banking and Currency Committee, Securities and Exchange Commission member, New York Supreme Court justice*

Born in Nicosia, Cyprus, on January 6, 1882, Ferdinand Pecora came from a family of cobblers. He immigrated to the United States with his family when he was five years old and grew up in New York City. After studying at St. Stephen's College and the City College of New York, he went to New York Law School and received his degree in 1906. He practiced law for several years before becoming an assis-

tant district attorney in New York County, serving from 1918 to 1922 until he became chief assistant district attorney, a position he held from 1922 to 1930. He returned to private law practice in 1930. Pecora had supported Theodore Roosevelt's 1912 presidential comeback bid, but he became a Democrat afterward.

Pecora's entrance to the administration of Franklin Roosevelt came through congressional action that followed 1929 stock-market crash and the onset of the Great Depression. Even before FDR assumed the presidency, Senator Peter Norbeck, a Republican from New Jersey who was chairman of the Senate Banking and Currency Committee, had hired Pecora to serve as chief legal counsel for the committee's investigation into banking and securities fraud after the previous two counsels had failed. Pecora concluded that more hearings were needed before he could prepare the committee's final report. When the new Democratic administration took over the Senate in March 1933, Senator Duncan U. Fletcher of Florida, the new committee chairman, deferred to the remarkable chief counsel so much that the hearings, which lasted from February 1933 to June 1934, became known as the "Pecora Wall Street Investigation." It proved to be a virtuoso performance by Pecora.

The investigation led to the resignation of the president of National City Bank in New York; revealed that J. P. Morgan, Jr., had paid no income taxes in 1930–31; and caused Chase Manhattan Bank to separate its banking and securities activities. It also contributed to the Glass-Steagall Banking Act of 1933, which separated commercial and investment banking; the Securities Act of 1933, which required corporations to provide accurate information to stock purchasers; the Securities and Exchange Act of 1934, which regulated the stock exchange; and the Public Utility Holding Act of 1935.

Because he was so involved in the investigation, Pecora did not have time to campaign for the New York County district attorney position, and he lost it in 1933. After serving six months on the new Securities and Exchange Commission, he resigned in January 1935 to accept appointment by Governor HERBERT LEHMAN to the New York Supreme Court. He was elected later that year to serve a 14-year term and was reelected in 1949. He resigned the next year to make an unsuccessful bid to become mayor of New York City. Pecora then returned to private law practice. He died on December 7, 1971, in New York City.

Peek, George Nelson

(1873–1943) *head, Agricultural Adjustment Administration, special adviser to the president on foreign trade; president, Export-Import Bank*

George Peek, born November 19, 1873, in northern Illinois, was the son of a livestock merchant who was also a local sheriff. A dozen years later, the family moved to a farm near Oregon, Illinois. After attending Northwestern University in 1891 for a year, Peek began working for the John Deere Plow Company. In 1901, he moved to Omaha, Nebraska, to become general manager of the company, and in 1909 he helped convert the firm into Deere and Company. He moved to the company headquarters in Moline, Illinois, in 1914 as vice president in charge of sales.

Peek began his government service during World War I with an appointment as the industrial representative on the War Industries Board (WIB), which oversaw the conversion from peacetime manufacturing to war production. After BERNARD BARUCH became WIB chairman, he made Peek commissioner of finished products. In February 1919, W. C. Redfield, the secretary of commerce, appointed Peek as chairman of the Industrial Board of the

Department of Commerce, which was designed to cushion price declines during demobilization. However, Peek resigned the next month in a dispute over rail tariffs. It was the first of several disputes in which the strong-willed Peek would become embroiled while working with bureaucracies. From 1919 to 1923, he served as president and general manager of the Moline Plow Company, but in 1923 he fought with its vice president, his former WIB colleague General HUGH JOHNSON. Peek resigned but later won a large lawsuit against the company for violation of his management contract.

A lifelong Republican, Peek endorsed AL SMITH in his failed presidential bid, heading the Smith Independent Organization after the Republican national convention of 1928, but he did not support Smith's agriculture proposals. In 1932, Peek campaigned for Franklin Roosevelt, who named him the first head of the Agricultural Adjustment Administration in May 1933. Peek next clashed with Secretary of Agriculture HENRY WALLACE and his chief counsel, JEROME FRANK, who favored production controls, which he opposed. FDR finally had to replace him on December 6, 1933. To assuage Peek's ego, he was made a special presidential adviser on foreign trade and president of the government's Export-Import Bank. However, he soon came up against Secretary of State CORDELL HULL, who advocated a most-favored-nation trade policy instead of bilateral trade agreements. After Peek negotiated a cotton barter with Nazi Germany, FDR criticized it, and Peek resigned from his government posts.

For the rest of his life, Peek criticized the New Deal and FDR's farm program. In 1936 and 1940, he supported Republican presidential candidates, and in 1940, he joined the isolationist America First Committee. Peek died on December 17, 1943, in Rancho Santa Fe, California.

Pegler, Westbrook
(Francis Westbrook Pegler, James Westbrook Pegler)
(1894–1969) *syndicated newspaper columnist*

A journalist's son born on August 2, 1894, in Minneapolis, Minnesota, Francis Westbrook Pegler later changed his first name to James. He attended grade school in Excelsior near Minneapolis until his family moved to Chicago when he was 10 years old. Because he failed to do well in grade school, Pegler was placed in a technical school to learn a trade. In 1910, he worked for a year as an office boy in the United Press (UP) bureau in Chicago while attending Loyola Academy, a Jesuit preparatory school from which he earned his high-school diploma. His experience with UP motivated him to become a journalist like his father, and he rejoined UP in 1913. He subsequently worked in UP offices in Des Moines, St. Louis, New York, and Dallas. During World War I, he served as a UP foreign correspondent in England and France until he ran into trouble with military censors. He then enlisted in the U.S. Navy and served in England until the war ended.

After the war, Pegler resumed his career with the UP in New York, writing a sports column under the byline of Westbrook Pegler for the first time instead of using his initials. He often wrote stories for other sections of the paper as well. In 1922, he and newspaper reporter Julia Harpman married but the couple was childless. From 1925 to 1933, though he lived in New York, he was a sportswriter for the *Chicago Tribune*, owned by archconservative ROBERT MCCORMICK. Once again his stories branched into areas beyond sports, suggesting he still had not found his niche.

When the New Deal began, Pegler hit his stride as a journalist after he became a daily columnist in the *New York World-Telegram* and other newspapers in the Scripps-Howard and United Features syndicates. His column, "Fair Enough," established his national reputation as a conservative reactionary. He dubbed Franklin Roosevelt "Little Lord Fautleroy" and "Moosejaw" and harpooned ELEANOR ROOSEVELT as "La Boca Grande"—the big mouth—and later "the Widow." He was aggressively pro-lynching, anti-HEYWOOD BROUN, and antiunion. Still, the "True Crusader" of the press, as he modestly called himself, won a Pulitzer Prize in 1941 for the investigation of labor racketeers in Hollywood.

During World War II, Pegler created a column using fictional characters that permitted him to inject venom into his articles while protecting his publishers from lawsuits. After he attacked one of the syndicate's publishers in print, however, his contract was not renewed. He then joined the Hearst Corporation's King Features Syndicate, which distributed his column "As Pegler Sees It." A prolific journalist, he remained popular among readers as well as his colleagues.

Pegler's postwar years were not good ones. He supported Senator Joseph McCarthy's anticommunist witch hunt. His wife died in 1955, and he remarried four years later only to divorce the following year and remarry almost immediately to his longtime secretary Maude Towart. Those marriages, too, were childless.

In the early 1960s, Pegler's attack on the Hearst Corporation led to the dissolution of that contract, and he then moved to the journalistic fringes with *American Opinion*, the monthly magazine of the right-wing extremist John Birch Society. Even that periodical ended its contract with him as he became even more paranoid than the John Birchers. He died on June 24, 1969, in Tucson, Arizona.

Pendergast, Thomas Joseph
(1872–1945) *Kansas City Democratic Party boss*

Born to Irish immigrant parents on July 22, 1872, in St. Joseph, Missouri, Thomas Pendergast moved to Kansas City in the early 1890s. There he began working for his shopkeeper brother, who was an alderman representing the poor section of town. In 1896, Pendergast, who had developed a reputation as a good street fighter, was appointed deputy city marshal, a post he held until 1900. He was elected county marshal in 1902 and served until 1904. The short and ever-energetic politician was appointed as street commissioner twice, 1900–02 and 1908–10. He began his last elected office in 1910, serving as an alderman until 1915. After his brother died in 1911, he took over his brother's organization and expanded it into a citywide Democratic machine. By the late 1920s, he controlled not only Kansas City but also most of surrounding Jackson County. He ran the city and county as if they were his own personal business.

Pendergast's influence expanded under the New Deal, and he acquired federal patronage in the state. He replaced the Republican state director of federal reemployment with HARRY TRUMAN; the machine sent Truman to the U.S. Senate in 1934. Postmaster General JAMES FARLEY and presidential assistant HARRY HOPKINS allowed Pendergast to control Works Progress Administration (WPA) jobs and federal contracts for WPA projects. Because Pendergast controlled Missouri's electoral votes, FDR chose to ignore local corruption as long as the urban machine remained in control.

Pendergast's decline began during FDR's second term after a new governor, Lloyd C. Stark, decided to appease reformers by having the U.S. Treasury Department investigate crime in Kansas City. Despite Truman's objection, FDR allowed the investigation to proceed. In May 1939, Pendergast pled guilty to two counts of federal income-tax evasion. While he served a year in prison, his political machine collapsed. He died on January 26, 1945, in Kansas City.

Pepper, Claude Denson
(1900–1989) *U.S. senator, U.S. congressman*

The son of farmers, Claude Pepper was born in Dudleyville, Alabama, on September 8, 1900. When he was 10 years old, his family moved to Camp Hill, Alabama, and he graduated from high school there in 1917. He taught school for a year before entering the University of Alabama. Like many southern students, Pepper enrolled in the Student Army Training Corp to become eligible for veterans' benefits. After he graduated from the University of Alabama, he used a Veterans Administration program for financially disadvantaged students to gain entrance to Harvard Law School. His southern background combined with his lack of financial means or family pedigree made him an outsider at the elitist institution. In 1924, he earned his law degree, and he then taught for a year at the University of Arkansas Law School.

Pepper, a gifted orator, moved next to Perry, Florida, where in 1928 he was elected as a Democrat to the Florida House of Representatives. His liberal views led to his defeat when he ran for reelection, so he moved to Tallahassee in 1930 to practice law. He served on the state board of public welfare in 1931–32 and on the state board of law examiners in 1933. The next year, he ran for the U.S. Senate, nearly unseating the incumbent. In 1936, both of Florida's U.S. Senators died, and he was elected without opposition to one of the unexpired two-year terms. That same year, he and Mildred Webster were married. They had no children.

Pepper became an ardent New Dealer and one of the most liberal members of the Senate, except in racial matters. By 1939, he had become vocal about the threat of ADOLF HITLER at a time when the Congress was isolationist. He was the only member of the Senate Foreign Relations Committee to vote in May 1940 in favor of the lend-lease proposal to aid

Great Britain. Isolationists picketed him, and he was hung in effigy for his unpopular view.

With active support from Franklin Roosevelt, Pepper easily won reelection to a full six-year term in 1938 in a race against a single conservative opponent. However, in 1944, Pepper drew opponents in the Democratic primary. He won with 52 percent of the vote, although big business considered Pepper too liberal, as did arch-segregationists. At the 1944 National Democratic Convention, Pepper led an unsuccessful effort to keep HENRY WALLACE as the vice-presidential candidate. Both Wallace and Pepper advocated closer ties with the Soviet Union.

After World War II, Pepper continued to move further left, blaming HARRY TRUMAN for the cold war and even praising JOSEPH STALIN. In the 1950 Democratic primary, he lost to Representative George A. Smathers in one of the most vicious campaigns in politics to that time. Dismissed as the "Red Pepper," he never again won a statewide election, although he ran again in 1958. Four years later, after the creation of a new congressional district that included liberal Miami and other parts of Dade County, Pepper become one of only a few former senators to be elected to the U.S. House of Representatives.

Although he was a sharp critic of Truman, Pepper came to share at least one trait with him: they outlived their opponents so that their reputations were transformed from that of the most unpopular politicians of the early 1950s into folk heroes. Pepper's popularity was reflected by his appearance on the front cover of *Time* in 1938 and again 45 years later in 1983. He developed lung cancer and died on May 30, 1989, in Washington, D.C., while still serving in the House.

Perkins, Frances Coralie
(1880–1965) *secretary of labor*

Born to a Boston, Massachusetts, businessman and his wife on April 10, 1880, Frances Perkins

Frances Perkins *(Library of Congress)*

earned a degree in chemistry and physics at Mount Holyoke College. While at college, in keeping with her belief in the Social Gospel aspect of the progressive movement in which Protestants demonstrated their faith by helping the poor, she established a chapter of the National Consumers League, which worked to abolish sweatshops and child labor. After her graduation in 1902, she taught in Connecticut, Massachusetts, and Illinois; she also worked at Jane Addam's Hull House settlement in Chicago. In 1907, she became secretary of the Philadelphia Research and Protective Association, which assisted immigrant girls as well as African Americans from the South. During this same time, she studied economics and sociology at the University of Pennsylvania.

With a fellowship from the Russell Sage Foundation, Perkins moved to New York City in 1909 to study at the New York School of Philanthropy. She received her master's degree in sociology from Columbia University the next year and then became the executive secretary of the New York City Consumers' League and taught at Adelphi College.

The Triangle Shirtwaist Company's fire on March 25, 1911, killed 146 garment workers and propelled Perkins into state politics. She left her position with the Consumers League to become the executive secretary of the committee investigating the fire. Her work brought her into the political careers of AL SMITH, ROBERT WAGNER, and trade unionist Samuel Gompers. When Smith became governor, he named her to New York's Industrial Commission in 1919. She became the first woman to hold the post and received the highest salary for a state employee in the nation. That beginning served as her entrée to Franklin Roosevelt, who appointed her head of the New York State labor department following his election as governor. They often rode together on the train from New York City to the state capital.

After FDR's election to the White House, he appointed Perkins as secretary of labor, the first woman ever to hold a cabinet post. She served as labor secretary from 1933 to 1945, holding the post longer than anyone else in its history. Though organized labor was initially lukewarm about her nomination because she favored social justice legislation rather than unionization to help workers, she was confirmed easily. She organized the group that wrote the Social Security Act of 1935 and also assisted in development of the Fair Labor Standards Act of 1938, which established a federal minimum wage and a maximum work week of 40 hours.

Perkins' lifelong honesty, efficiency, and competence, as well as deliberately conservative dress worked in her favor during her pio-neering tenure as secretary of labor. She resigned on July 1, 1945, and HARRY TRUMAN appointed her later that year to the Civil Service Commission where she served until 1953. She then taught at the Cornell School of Industrial Relations from 1958 until her death on May 14, 1965, in New York City.

Pittman, Key
(1872–1940) *president pro tempore of the U.S. Senate*

A native of East Carroll Parish in extreme northeast Louisiana, an area of rural poverty, Key Pittman was born on September 12, 1872. His father, an attorney, was a Confederate Civil War veteran. His mother, whose maiden name was Key, died when he was eight, and his father died when he was 11. Pittman had been raised in Vicksburg, Mississippi, but he went to live with relatives in Afton, Louisiana, when he was orphaned. He attended Southwestern Presbyterian University in Clarksville, Tennessee, from 1887 to 1890 but did not graduate. After he left college, he moved to Seattle, Washington, where he clerked in a law office and was admitted to the state bar in 1892. He moved to Alaska in 1897 and eventually became the city attorney in Nome. Three years later, he married Mimosa Gates, who had been a prospector in the Klondike gold mines. Their marriage was childless.

After the Nevada gold fields were discovered in 1901, the Pittmans moved the next year to Tonopah, Nevada, where he practiced law and became active in Democratic politics. Pittman's first bid for the U.S. Senate in 1910 failed, but two years later he won a seat following the death of an incumbent. He easily won reelection in 1916, 1922, and 1928. His reelection campaigns in 1934 and 1940 were unsuccessfully challenged by the PATRICK MCCARRAN faction of the state Democratic

Party. As a loyal Democrat, Pittman supported Woodrow Wilson's domestic and foreign policies, but he ultimately voted against the League of Nations.

As a native southerner who spent his adult life out west, Pittman was generally well liked and often called on to mediate factional differences in the Democratic Party. He supported Franklin Roosevelt's presidential bid in 1932, and after the Democrats captured control of the Congress, he became president pro tempore of the Senate. Pittman supported the vast majority of the New Deal and became the the de facto leader of the Senate's silver bloc to protect the silver-mining industry. He was selected as a delegate to the London Monetary and Economic Conference in 1933, persuading FDR to ratify the Silver Agreement that emerged from it as well as to sign the Silver Purchase Act of 1934. In 1937, Pittman backed FDR's Court-packing plan.

Pittman also served as the chairman of the Senate Foreign Relations Committee from 1933 to 1940. Even though he authored the measure to permit export of goods and arms on a cash-and-carry basis in 1937, he was the first Senate leader to back FDR's request to repeal it in January 1939. He was also a leader in condemning Japanese aggression in China and called for economic sanctions in 1937. By fall 1940, the State Department supported this position.

Unfortunately, Pittman had a series of financial and marital problems during his Senate years and developed a serious alcohol-abuse problem. He was ill during his fall 1940 reelection campaign and required hospitalization on the eve of his election victory. Five days later, he died on November 10, 1940, in Reno, Nevada. His funeral was the largest in the state's history. Despite Pittman's enormous popularity in life, it was not enough after his death to offset McCarran's political strength. McCarran was able to block Pittman's youngest brother, Vail, from fill-

ing the vacant Senate seat, although the younger Pittman later became Nevada's governor.

Pressman, Lee
(1906–1969) *federal government legal counsel, national union legal counsel*

Lee Pressman, born on July 1, 1906, was the son of immigrant Russian parents who lived on New York City's Lower East Side. In 1926, he graduated from Cornell University, where he had developed an interest in labor issues during an economics course. He went on to attend Harvard Law School, where he became one of FELIX FRANKFURTER's best students and edited the *Harvard Law Review*. From 1929 to 1933, Pressman practiced law in New York City in the prestigious Wall Street firm of Chadbourne, Stanchfield, and Levy. During this period, he developed expertise in corporate reorganization, and he married Sophia Platnick in 1931. The couple had three children.

In 1932, Pressman became a member of the International Juridical Association, which included Marxists and liberal lawyers with an interest in labor law. The following year, a senior member of his law firm, JEROME FRANK, recruited Pressman to come with him to the nation's capital to become assistant general counsel to the Agricultural Adjustment Administration (AAA). Pressman joined the Communist Party in 1934 but left it the following year. He worked closely with Frank, who was the AAA's general counsel, and in 1935 both were fired by Secretary of Agriculture HENRY WALLACE because they sought to have the AAA support sharecroppers. Pressman went on to become general counsel to the Works Progress Administration and the Resettlement Administration, serving from 1935 to 1936.

In 1936, Pressman briefly returned to private practice, but he was soon recruited by JOHN L. LEWIS, the president of the United

Mine Workers of America, to work first for the new Committee of Industrial Organizations, then as general counsel to the new Steel Workers Organizing Committee (SWOC), and ultimately as general counsel to the national Congress of Industrial Organizations (CIO), the successor to the Committee of Industrial Organizations. Lewis wanted Pressman and other radicals to help him build a union from among the unorganized mass-production workers, who were ignored by the more conservative American Federation of Labor (AFL). Both Lewis and PHILIP MURRAY used Pressman's legal talent, but he lacked a personal power base within the union. His mission-oriented personality worked to his disadvantage, making him feared both inside and outside of the union. Although he had severed his relationship with the Communist Party after a short time, he retained a narrow ideological outlook. Instead of taking a convivial approach with others, he acted as a hired gun of the CIO. Pressman demanded financial compensation at a level appropriate to his background and skill.

In 1937, Pressman obtained the lifting of court injunctions on sit-down strikers in Flint, Michigan. Knowing how to use the law for the benefit of workers, he made the sit-down strikes a union tool. That same year, he was responsible for the first contract between SWOC and U.S. Steel, a contract that served as the model for other CIO recognition agreements. He also successfully litigated the case for reinstating strikers who participated in the 1937 strike and awarding them back pay. In 1940, he drafted the CIO resolution that supported the Lend-Lease Act and condemned totalitarian government. The next year, he drafted the contract with the Little Steel Formula, which for the first time linked wages and prices to inflation in a contract.

The postwar years were less positive for Pressman. After Murray moved to rid the CIO of communists, Pressman was forced to resign in 1948. That same year, he lost his bid for election to the House of Representatives on the Progressive Party ticket and was called before the House Un-American Activities Committee (HUAC) as a witness in the investigation of Alger Hiss. Pressman, who had worked with Hiss at the AAA, took the Fifth Amendment. In 1950, he was again called before the HUAC. To the consternation of both anticommunists and communists, he named only individuals in the Department of Agriculture who already had been identified as communists by several witnesses. His public life was ended, and he returned to the practice of law in New York City. He died in Mount Vernon, New York, on November 19, 1969.

R

Randolph, Asa Philip
(1889–1979) *labor and civil-rights leader,*
National Negro Congress president

Born in Crescent City, Florida, on April 15, 1889, Philip Randolph was the son of an itinerant preacher father. He was sent to the Cookman Institute in Jacksonville (later Bethune-Cookman College), graduating in 1907, but rejected parental pressure to become a minister. Instead, he moved to New York City in 1911, and two years later he married beauty-shop owner Lucille Campbell Green, a widow six years his senior who would support his labor and civil-rights work. In 1925, he was asked to organize the 10,000 Pullman train sleeping-car porters, considered an elite group of African-American workers with a near-monopoly on the occupation. Within a year, more than half of them had joined the Brotherhood of Sleeping Car Porters (BSCP).

As a result of Franklin Roosevelt's National Industrial Recovery Act (NIRA) of 1933, there was a resurgence of membership in the BSCP, which had decreased in the late 1920s. In 1935, the BSCP received a charter from the American Federation of Labor (AFL) and Randolph became the president of the National Negro Congress. Two years later, the Pullman Company signed a contract with the nation's first African-American union, earning Randolph the title of "Mr. Black Labor." Influenced by the sit-down strike of the labor movement and Mahatma Gandhi's nonviolence, Randolph proposed a march on Washington in 1941 to promote defense jobs for African Americans, who were blocked from them by racial discrimination. The threat of such a march on the segregated national capital prompted FDR to create a temporary wartime Fair Employment Practices Committee, chaired by FIORELLA LA GUARDIA. The La Gaurdia committee recommended an executive order on nondiscrimination, which FDR issued on June 25, 1941, creating the Fair Employment Practices Commission (FEPC). Randolph rejected an offer to serve on the FEPC, and he declined to run for Congress in 1944.

During the postwar era, Randolph helped encourage HARRY TRUMAN to integrate the military in July 1948. In 1955, after the merger of the AFL with the Congress of Industrial Organizations (CIO), Randolph became a vice president in the organization. He retired as president of the BSCP in 1968 due to failing health and died on May 16, 1979.

Rankin, John Elliott
(1882–1960) *U.S. congressman*

John Rankin was an economic liberal and social reactionary from the Deep South whose congressional career represented those contending populist tensions during the New Deal and into the postwar era. The son of a schoolteacher, he was born on March 29, 1882, in Itawamba County, Mississippi, and attended local schools in Itawamba and Lee counties before going to the University of Mississippi, where he received his law degree in 1910. Rankin first practiced law in West Point, Mississippi, but moved to Tupelo to practice with a partner in a new firm. By 1912, he was the prosecuting attorney for Lee County, a position he held for four years. He then made three unsuccessful runs for electoral office, once for district attorney and twice for the Democratic nomination for Congress.

During World War I, Rankin enlisted as a private in the U.S. Army and was assigned to field artillery, but he had served only a short time when the war ended. He returned to Tupelo, where he edited a weekly newspaper. In 1919, he married Annie Laurie Burrous, with whom he had one child. The next year he made his third attempt to win a seat in the U.S. Congress and was elected. He went on to win reelection to 15 consecutive terms, facing only minimal opposition in any contest. During his long tenure, he focused on public-power projects, veteran benefits, white supremacy, and anticommunism. The first two issues earned him a progressive reputation and improved the lives of his mostly white rural constituency in northeastern Mississippi; the latter two brought out the bigot and bully in him.

Rankin began as an ardent Democratic supporter of Franklin Roosevelt in 1932. As a southern populist, he was highly suspicious of concentrated economic power, especially that held by banks, railroads, and public utilities.

Therefore, like SAM RAYBURN, he championed workers and farmers. Rankin served as the leader of the public-power bloc in the House and, with Senator GEORGE NORRIS (R-Nebr.), cosponsored the Tennessee Valley Authority (TVA) Act of 1933. Although Tupelo was located outside the Tennessee River basin, Rankin persuaded DAVID LILIENTHAL, the first TVA director, to include his entire district within the agency's jurisdiction. Tupelo became the first municipality in the nation to receive TVA-generated electricity, and Rankin greeted FDR there in 1934 to commemorate the historic introduction by hydroelectric power. Rankin was also the key congressional sponsor in 1936 of the Rural Electrification Administration (REA), which enabled farms across the country to have inexpensive electrical power. In 1939, the REA was reorganized as a division of the U.S. Department of Agriculture.

As a southern populist and World War I veteran, Rankin championed bonuses for fellow veterans of that war. As chairman of the House Veterans Committee from 1931 onward, he led the fight to override FDR's veto of the bonus bill. During World War II, he sponsored legislation to more than double military base pay. He also supported FDR's decision to relocate Japanese Americans; in fact, he favored moving them all to concentration camps. A white supremacist to the core, Rankin believed segregation was necessary for different races to survive. He opposed all antilynching and antipoll-tax bills as well as any legislation that might enhance the status of African Americans. (It was perhaps the ultimate irony that John Rankin was the name of a prominent Ohio abolitionist reputed to have been the most active "conductor" on the Underground Railroad of the previous century.)

During the postwar period from 1945 to 1950, Rankin confirmed his reputation for bigotry by his membership on the House Un-American Activities Committee (HUAC). He used his seniority and parliamentary skills to make the HUAC a permanent committee with enlarged membership. Rankin bullied witnesses and ranted about a Jewish-communist conspiracy against American government to such a degree that even newspapers in his home state rebuked him. In 1948, he lost a senatorial bid, and in 1952 he lost his congressional seat after it was redistricted. When he left office in January 1953, he held the record for longevity in Congress up to that point. He returned to Tupelo to resume his law practice and died there on November 26, 1960.

Raskob, John Jakob
(1879–1950) *industrialist*

A native of Lockport, New York, John Raskob was born on March 19, 1879, to a cigar manufacturer. He attended Clark's Business College in Lockport and then moved to Lorain, Ohio, in 1899. The next year, he became the personal secretary to Pierre S. du Pont, a real-estate and street-railway executive. In 1902, du Pont persuaded Raskob to relocate with him to Wilmington, Delaware, to help operate the family firm, E. I. du Pont de Nemours Company. Raskob pioneered the use of statistical analysis in making management decisions. After a series of mergers and stock acquisitions, the business was transformed into a major gunpowder and dynamite maker. He married Helena Springer Green of Galina, Maryland in 1906, and the couple had 13 children.

Within a decade of working for the company, Raskob had taken over his former boss's position, and in 1914 he was formally named the company's treasurer. Intrigued by the emerging automobile industry, Raskob bought stock in the new General Motors Corporation and persuaded du Pont to invest in it as well. In 1915, he joined the board of the General Motors Corporation, and du Pont became board chairman. During World War I, Raskob directed the company's expansion and then resigned his position after the war to become chairman of its finance committee. While serving in that capacity, he began the General Motors Acceptance Corporation (GMAC) to provide credit to automobile dealers and purchasers. He also initiated the same modern accounting methods that du Pont was already using in its own operations.

In 1920, ALFRED P. SLOAN, JR., was brought in to manage General Motors. Raskob became a multimillionaire and began to write about finance in the popular press, which made him a business celebrity. He advocated installment purchases and the five-day work week. Despite the fact that he had voted for Calvin Coolidge in 1924, he developed a friendship with fellow Catholic AL SMITH, who named Raskob as chairman of the Democratic National Committee (DNC) during the Smith's presidential bid in 1928. Smith and Raskob helped to move the party to enlarge its base from its traditional rural ties by forming ties to the offspring of millions of immigrants who lived in the nation's largest cities. Raskob remained active in Democratic politics after Smith's electoral loss that fall by establishing the DNC's first permanent headquarters in the nation's capital.

Raskob tried to prevent Franklin Roosevelt, whom he considered too radical, from capturing the party's 1932 presidential nomination. He went on reluctantly to back FDR during the presidential campaign, urging him to say as little as possible about what he would do if elected. It was advice that FDR largely heeded. Raskob also recommended a national sales tax to help balance the budget. Though he appreciated how FDR saved the nation's banks in 1933, Raskob disliked the public-works programs and other New Deal proposals.

After Smith's 1928 electoral disaster, Raskob, Smith, and others had joined to build and manage the Empire State Building. In 1934, he again joined Smith and other conservatives in openly breaking with FDR to form the Liberty League, an organization of business executives disgruntled with the New Deal. Along with Smith, Sloan, and others, Raskob believed that the New Deal would lead the country to ruin. He never regained his prominence in the postwar political or business worlds and died on October 15, 1950, at his farm near Centerville, Maryland.

Rayburn, Sam
(1882–1961) *U.S. congressman, Speaker of the House*

The eighth of 11 children, Sam Rayburn was born on January 6, 1882, in Roane County, Tennessee, to poor farmer parents. Five years later, the family moved to northeast Texas and settled near Bonham. Rayburn attended country schools before enrolling in East Texas Normal College; he graduated in 1903 with a degree in education and then taught for three years.

Rayburn's interest in politics grew from watching Joseph W. Bailey, his local state senator. An observant student of politics, Rayburn was first elected in 1906 to the Texas House of Representatives, where he served three terms, and was Speaker during his final term. Short, stocky, balding, and always energetic, Rayburn took courses at the University of Texas Law School. He passed the bar exam in 1908 and then became a member of a law firm in Bonham.

Rayburn's entrance on the national political stage came in 1912 with his election to the U.S. House of Representatives during Woodrow Wilson's landslide. He soon became a friend of fellow Texas congressman JOHN NANCE GAR-

NER, who would mentor Rayburn for the next two decades. Rayburn became chairman of the Interstate and Foreign Commerce Committee in 1931, coinciding with Garner's rise to Speaker of the House. When Garner ran for the presidency in 1932, his faithful protégé Rayburn served as campaign manager and represented his mentor in the negotiations that resulted in Garner's becoming Franklin Roosevelt's vice-presidential candidate.

From 1933 to 1937, Rayburn worked closely with New Deal lawyers BENJAMIN COHEN and THOMAS CORCORAN to draft and enact some of FDR's most important initiatives: the Emergency Railroad Transportation Act of 1933, the Truth in Securities Act of 1933, the Stock Exchange Act of 1934, the Public Utility Holding Company Act of 1935, and the Rural Electrification Act of 1936. He was a workhorse in the House and brought the bacon home to his district. Whenever he

Speaker of the House Sam Rayburn sits as Madame Chiang Kai-shek addresses the House in 1943. *(Library of Congress)*

returned there, he dressed like a farmer and maintained an open-door policy toward his constituents.

After Speaker Henry T. Rainey died in 1934, Rayburn challenged heir-apparent JOSEPH BYRNS for the slot and was overwhelmingly defeated for the coveted position. But Rayburn learned from his political mistakes, and after Byrns died in 1936, he did not challenge WILLIAM BANKHEAD, who moved up to the top leadership rung. Instead, Rayburn won the post of majority leader, and after Bankhead died in 1940, he was elected Speaker. As Speaker, Rayburn used his personality and reputation for fairness, loyalty, honesty, and integrity—along with his knowledge of House rules—to bind colleagues to him. His friendships and astute parliamentary skills won the extension of the military draft by one vote in August 1941.

Rayburn had a fierce temper, but he was never an autocrat. He was a democrat who knew how to work with others without seeking credit or publicity. He grew more progressive as he aged. The longest-serving Speaker of the U.S. House of Representatives, he had served nearly 49 years as a congressman when he died on November 16, 1961, in Bonham.

Reed, Stanley Forman

(1884–1980) *U.S. solicitor general, U.S. Supreme Court justice*

Stanley Reed was born the son of a physician on December 31, 1884, in Minerva, Kentucky. He attended local private schools and received undergraduate degrees from Kentucky Wesleyan College in 1902 and from Yale University in 1906. He then studied law at the University of Virginia, Columbia University, and the Sorbonne but never obtained a law degree. Regardless, he was admitted to the bar and began practicing law in Kentucky. Always interested in Democratic Party politics, Reed

was soon elected to the state legislature, serving two consecutive terms from 1912 to 1916. He continued his legal practice until 1929, except for during his brief service in the army during World War I.

Reed's entry into national politics occurred during the HERBERT HOOVER administration. Because he had been the general counsel for the Farm Cooperative, Reed was appointed general counsel to the Federal Farm Board in 1929. In 1932, he was appointed general counsel to the Reconstruction Finance Corporation, where he eventually worked closely with THOMAS CORCORAN. Franklin Roosevelt first named Reed as a special assistant to Attorney General HOMER CUMMINGS when the "gold cases" came before the Supreme Court. The so-called gold cases involved four that challenged the constitutionality of the 1933 Emergency Banking Act, and the Joint Resolution of June 1933, which repudiated the gold clause in private and government obligations. CHARLES EVANS HUGHES upheld these congressional actions. Later in 1935, FDR named Reed as the U.S. solicitor general. In this role, Reed won 11 of the 13 cases in support of federal regulation of the economy that he argued before the U.S. Supreme Court. One of the two cases that he lost was the 1935 "sick chicken case" (*Schechter Poultry Corporation v. U.S.*), in which the Court unanimously held that the National Industrial Recovery Act was unconstitutional. During his three-year tenure with the Department of Justice, Reed also recruited a talented pool of young New Deal lawyers that included ROBERT JACKSON, Alger Hiss, Charles Wyzanski, and Paul Freund.

After GEORGE SUTHERLAND, one of the four most conservative justices on the Supreme Court, retired in 1935, FDR picked Reed as his replacement. Reed was the president's second appointment to the nation's highest tribunal, and he performed as FDR anticipated the rural, border-state appointee would. He was liberal on economic matters but more conservative on civil liberties and civil rights. During the postwar period, Reed was the last justice to join the Court's unanimous decision in *Brown v. Board of Education* (1954). He retired from the Court three years later but went on to live longer than any other justice in Supreme Court history, dying at age 95 on April 3, 1980, in Huntington, New York.

Reno, Milo

(1866–1936) *union leader*

The son of farmers, Milo Reno was born on January 5, 1866, in Agency, Iowa. He attended local public schools before briefly attending William Penn College, a Quaker school in Oskaloosa, Iowa, with the intent of becoming a minister. However, he left college to become a salesman in South Dakota and California. He returned to Iowa in the late 1890s and for two decades was a farmer near his birthplace as well as a popular rural Campbellite minister. He soon learned to combine politics and fiery sermons, preaching social justice for farmers and other underdogs in society. He joined the fraternal organization called the Grange, championed the Populist Party, and ran unsuccessfully for the Iowa legislature.

In 1918, Reno's new cause became the National Farmers' Union (NFU), which he joined that year; he was elected secretary-treasurer two years later. He was president of its Iowa branch by 1921 and held a leadership position in the NFU until his death. His guiding principle was to "secure for the farming industry the cost of production plus a reasonable profit." To achieve that, he endorsed AL SMITH's bid for the presidency in 1928. In May 1932, 3,000 Iowa farmers met in Des Moines and elected Reno as head of the National Farmers' Holiday Association (NFHA). He had selected inclusion of the word *holiday* to mock the use of *bank holidays*, the euphemistic term for closing banks to prevent runs on them.

Reno believed both major parties were corrupt and that direct action was necessary. In August 1932, he called for a peaceful strike among Iowa farmers that quickly escalated into a national strike by desperate farmers in several states. Reno soon called a truce and then used the NFHA councils to intervene in disputes over farm rents and mortgages. Marches on state legislatures led to the passage of mortgage moratorium legislation.

At the urging of Minnesota governor FLOYD OLSON, Reno called off a strike in May 1933. On May 13, Congress passed the Agricultural Adjustment Act (AAA), but it did not include a cost-of-production plan. By that fall, Reno was denouncing New Deal legislation that emphasized controlling overproduction rather than underconsumption. As a result, both he and Secretary of Agriculture HENRY WALLACE developed a mutual animosity. Reno had doubts about the incorporation of Extension Service (county) agents into the AAA since he viewed them as allies of the American Farm Bureau Federation, which was the main rival of the NFU. His call for a strike in the fall of 1933 soon fizzled, and the NFHA's demise quickly followed. As it was, most farmers were willing to give the New Deal a chance, especially after cash payments were made to them in return for their pledges to reduce their planted acreage in 1934. Reno subsequently turned to supporting other panaceas such as Dr. FRANCIS TOWNSEND's old-age pension plan. He died on May 5, 1936, in Excelsior Springs, Missouri.

Reuther, Walter Philip

(1907–1970) *United Auto Workers executive board member*

The son of immigrant German parents, Walter Reuther was born on September 1, 1907, in

Wheeling, West Virginia. Reuther's father had been a socialist, and at age 11, Walter had accompanied him to visit Socialist Party leader Eugene Debs in prison. One of five children, Reuther attended local public schools but dropped out at age 16 to begin working. He moved to Detroit in 1927 to take advantage of the high wages and five-day workweek at Ford Motor Company. He became one of Ford's highest-paid mechanics and completed his high-school education while working the night shift. He then enrolled in Detroit City College along with two of his younger brothers.

The Great Depression politicized the Reuther brothers. During the 1932 presidential campaign, Walter Reuther traveled extensively to campaign for Socialist candidate NORMAN THOMAS. In 1933, he quit his job to tour Europe, including Nazi Germany, with a brother. For two years, he worked in the Ford-equipped auto factory in Gorky, USSR. After he returned home in 1935, he channeled his abundant energy into organizing labor. The next year, the United Auto Workers (UAW) became independent from the American Federation of Labor (AFL), and Reuther was elected to the UAW's executive board. In December 1936, he helped to conduct a successful sit-down strike at the Kelsey-Hayes Wheel Company in Detroit. He helped plan the 1937 sit-down strike at the Ford plant in Flint, Michigan, and in the ensuing conflict he was beaten by company thugs but survived. This event transformed him into a national labor leader. Membership in the UAW, swelled and it became the nation's largest union.

After he broke his ties with communists and socialists in 1938, Reuther supported FDR during the 1940 and 1944 campaigns. In 1939, he became the UAW's vice president in charge of the General Motors Division. During World War II, the youthful, idealistic, and honest Reuther became a friend of ELEANOR ROOSEVELT, who shared his ideas with Franklin Roosevelt. Reuther called the First Lady "my secret weapon."

During the postwar period, Reuther won the presidency of the UAW in 1946. He survived an assassination attempt two years later, and in 1952 he became the head of the Congress of Industrial Organizations (CIO). He was instrumental in the CIO's 1955 merger with the AFL. Unlike other labor leaders, Reuther maintained a modest lifestyle. He also was a persistent supporter of black civil rights and desegregation. On May 9, 1970, he and his wife were among six persons killed in the crash of a plane en route to Detroit.

Richberg, Donald Randall
(1881–1960) *National Recovery Administration chief counsel and acting director*

Born on July 10, 1881, in Knoxville, Tennessee, Donald Richberg was the son of prosperous professional parents. He graduated in 1901 from the University of Chicago, and after completing Harvard Law School in 1904, he joined his father's Chicago law firm and became involved in local politics. Encounters with political corruption led him to advocate municipal reform and the progressive movement. Richberg campaigned for THEODORE ROOSEVELT in 1912 and for the next two years was the chairman of the National Legislative Reference Bureau of the Progressive Party. Like Roosevelt, who left the Republican Party in 1912, Richberg deserted the Progressive Party in 1916 when it endorsed CHARLES EVANS HUGHES—who was endorsed by Roosevelt, although he labeled Hughes "the bearded iceberg." Richberg instead campaigned for Woodrow Wilson's reelection.

During World War I and the 1920s, Richberg served as Chicago's special counsel, practiced law, and was chief counsel for the railway brotherhoods. Specializing in labor law, he was the principal draftsman of the Railway Labor

Act of 1926. In 1928, he supported AL SMITH's presidential bid, and in 1932 he worked with Senator GEORGE NORRIS (R-Nebr.) in supporting Franklin Roosevelt's presidential bid. He also helped RAYMOND MOLEY to draft speeches on labor relations during the 1932 campaign.

Richberg's entry into the FDR administration came through HUGH JOHNSON, who recruited Richberg to help draft the National Industrial Recovery Act of 1933, particularly its labor clauses. Johnson, who was director of the National Recovery Administration (NRA), named Richberg as its chief counsel. After Johnson's negative personality led to his retirement in 1934, Richberg served acting director of the NRA until the Supreme Court declared it unconstitutional on May 27, 1935. He then returned to private practice in Washington, D.C., and remained a supporter of FDR. Richberg basically wanted labor and management to resolve their differences without government intervention once labor gained the right to bargain collectively and to strike. During the postwar period, he wrote and spoke against "labor union monopoly," believing that the nation was on the road to the welfare state and socialism. He died on November 27, 1960, in Charlottesville, Virginia.

Rivera, Diego
(1886–1957) *Mexican muralist*

Born in Guanajuarto, Mexico, on December 8, 1886, Diego Rivera was 10 when he began studying art at Mexico City's National School of Fine Arts with Andrés Rios, Felix Parra, Santiago Rebull, and José Maria Velasco. Rivera exhibited an independent, if not rebellious, streak from an early age. When he was 13 he rebelled against his parents' demands that he attend a military academy and instead attended the Academy of San Carlos, where his first exhibition was held in 1906. The fol-

lowing year, he received a grant to study in Europe, where he spent the next 14 years and came under the influence of the impressionists.

Rivera's first mural, *Creation* (1922), was painted for the Bolivar Amphitheater at the University of Mexico. It is widely considered the first great mural in the Americas during the 20th century. His subsequent murals in the 1920s chronicled Mexican history and culture. His frescoes appeared in the Ministry of Education Building in Mexico City, in the auditorium of the National School of Agriculture in Chapingo, and in the Palace of Cortés in Cuernavaca.

In 1929, Rivera married fellow painter Frida Kahlo. The next year, he traveled to the United States, where his bold murals influenced a nation mired in the Great Depression. He first painted murals for the New York Stock Exchange Luncheon Club and the California School of Fine Arts. In 1932, the Museum of Modern Art in New York City staged an exhibit of his works. During the early New Deal years of 1932–33, he painted *Detroit Industry*, a cycle of 27 murals that depicted the history of the automobile industry at the indoor court of the Detroit Institute of Fine Arts. The murals reflected his belief in material progress and technology, themes he incorporated with Mexican mythology. While in Ford's automotive and aeronautical plants, he was at times accompanied by his wife.

In 1933, Nelson Rockefeller, art collector and heir to the family oil fortune, commissioned Rivera to paint a mural for the RCA Building in New York City. Rivera's portrayal of Soviet May Day celebrations proved too controversial for his patron, but he refused to paint out the portrait of Vladimir Lenin in the mural's center to make it acceptable. As a result, Rockefeller destroyed the mural. That event, coupled with the artistic expression in THOMAS HART BENTON's most famous mural at the Missouri state capitol, resulted in loss of commissions for their fellow New Deal muralists for the next decade.

While in New York, Rivera created frescoes for the Independent Labor Institute. Painted on movable panels, these frescoes captured the American spirit. Rivera also painted an anti-Nazi mural in 1933 for the newspaper office of *The Workers Age*. After he returned to Mexico City, Rivera replicated the destroyed RCA Building mural at the Palace of Fine Arts in 1934. His frescoes at the National Palace depicting Mexican history culminate in a symbolic image of Marx.

Rivera's artistic, political, and private life were turbulent. He married four times, and he was expelled from the Communist Party several times. After the Russian revolutionary and communist theorist Leon Trotsky was forced into exile by JOSEPH STALIN, Rivera hosted the political exile in his home briefly until they split over differences. Shortly thereafter, Stalin had Trotsky assassinated in Mexico City.

Some of Rivera's works were controversial in Mexico, as well. Four movable panels that he painted for the Hotel Reforma in 1936 caused such controversy that they were removed. In 1940, he returned to the United States to paint a mural for a junior college in San Francisco. His theme fused Latin American art with the industrial ingenuity of the United States. During the postwar period, the Palace of Fine Arts held a half-century retrospective of Rivera's work. During the McCarthy era, his murals in the United States had to be protected by armed guards. He continued painting and participating in left-wing politics until his death on November 25, 1957, in Mexico City.

Roberts, Owen Josephus

(1875–1955) *U.S. Supreme Court justice; chair, Presidential Commission on Pearl Harbor*

The son of a hardware merchant, Owen Roberts was born on May 2, 1875, in Germantown, Pennsylvania, and attended Germantown Academy. He graduated in 1895 from the University of Pennsylvania and then entered its law school. During law school, he became an associate editor of the *American Law Register*. After completing law school in 1898, Roberts simultaneously joined a Philadelphia law firm and began teaching at the University of Pennsylvania Law School. His career as a law-school professor continued for 22 years. From 1903 to 1905, he served as the first assistant district attorney for Philadelphia, an experience that led to his appointment by President Calvin Coolidge as special deputy U.S. attorney during World War I. He returned to federal service in 1924 to help prosecute the Teapot Dome and Elk Hills oil-reserve scandals, which had occurred during the Warren Harding administration. His work resulted in national attention.

The lifelong Republican was President HERBERT HOOVER's second-choice nominee in June 1930 to fill the U.S. Supreme Court vacancy created by the sudden death of associate justice Edward T. Stanford. Roberts joined the court at the same time that Hoover nominated CHARLES EVANS HUGHES as chief justice to fill the vacancy caused by the death of William Howard Taft.

Along with the new, moderate chief justice, Roberts became a "swing vote" on the court during the New Deal years. Both Hughes and Roberts sided with their liberal brethren to uphold emergency economic regulations (*Home Building and Loan Association v. Blaisdell*, 1934) placing a moratorium on the foreclosure of home mortgages in Minnesota. But in February 1935, Roberts wrote the 5-4 conservative majority opinion that invalidated the Railroad Retirement Act of 1933, which had provided pensions to railroad employees (*Railroad Retirement Board v. Alton*). He also sided with the conservatives in the "sick chicken" case (*Schechter v. United States*, 1935), which invalidated the National Industrial

Recovery Act, and he wrote the majority opinion for *Butler v. United States* (1936), which invalidated the first Agricultural Adjustment Act. Critics called the opinion an example of the "mechanical jurisprudence" that cloaked the Court's judicial activism. By late 1936, however, Roberts had become the "switch in time that saved nine." He voted with the liberal majority of five justices on the mid-1937 decisions that upheld the National Labor Relations Act (*NLRB v. Jones and Laughlin Steel Corp.*) and the state minimum-wage legislation (*West Coast Hotel v. Parrish*).

On December 18, 1941, FDR appointed Roberts to head the first of eight groups empaneled to investigate the nation's inadequate precautions before the Japanese attack on Pearl Harbor. The Presidential Commission on Pearl Harbor, better known as the Roberts Commission, reported on January 24, 1942.

Roberts's record was generally liberal in economic cases, but his record on civil rights and civil liberties was more divided. He wrote the majority opinion in *Betts v. Brady* (1942), which limited the right to counsel and was later reversed in *Gideon v. Wainwright* (1963), but dissented in the forced relocation of Japanese Americans during World War II (*Kormatsu v. United States*, 1944). When liberals sought to extend civil-liberties protections, Roberts was caught between the court's liberal and conservative factions. Frustrated, he retired in June 1945, the final pre-Roosevelt justice to depart from the bench. He died on May 17, 1955, in West Vincent Township, Chester, Pennsylvania.

Robeson, Paul
(1898–1976) *singer, actor*

Paul Robeson was born on April 9, 1898, in Princeton, New Jersey. His father, a Protestant minister, had been a runaway slave who had fought in the Civil War with Union troops.

Paul Robeson *(Library of Congress)*

His mother died when he was six years old. Robeson won a statewide scholarship to attend Rutgers College in 1915 and was the only black student enrolled. Academically and athletically exceptional, the 6'3", 215-pound Robeson excelled in debate and was named an All-America football player in both 1917 and 1918. After receiving his undergraduate degree in 1919, he moved to Harlem Preparatory before entering Columbia University Law School in 1920. He helped to pay for law school by playing for the Akron Pros and Milwaukee Badgers football teams from 1920 to 1922. After he earned his law degree in 1923, he joined a New York City law firm.

But Robeson lacked passion for either football or the law, and in 1920 he began acting in local theatrical productions. Four years later, before even taking the bar exam, he quit his law practice to pursue a full-time stage career. In

1925, he became the first soloist at Carnegie Hall to devote an entire concert to Negro spirituals. He achieved international success in London in 1930 as one of the first blacks to play Othello. During his career, he made more than 300 vocal recordings. He combined his singing and acting talents in several musicals from the late 1920s through World War II. He was best known for his rendition of "Ol' Man River" in *Show Boat*, released as a 1936 film. He appeared in 10 other motion pictures.

Robeson became involved in politics in 1928 after playwright George Bernard Shaw introduced him to the universal ideas behind socialism. Because of the racism that Robeson had endured during his academic, athletic, and acting experiences in the United States, he spent most of the 1930s in Europe. After a concert tour of the Soviet Union in 1934, he began to spend more time in Moscow, learned Russian, and came to oppose fascism, imperialism, and racism. During his years in Britain, he became interested in African culture and took courses at the University of London. He became active in the West African Students Union and met future African liberation leaders, including Jomo Kenyatta of Kenya and Kwame Nkrumah from the Gold Coast (Ghana). In 1938, he went to Spain to entertain the Republican troops fighting FRANCISCO FRANCO's fascists in the Spanish civil war. He returned to the United States the following year and became active in the national unionization movement.

Robeson achieved a career milestone in October 1943 when he became the first black actor to portray Othello in the United States. During the postwar anticommunist years, like many other actors and actresses Robeson was labeled a communist and communist sympathizer by the House Un-American Activities Committee. As a result, he was blacklisted as an entertainer. After enduring more than a dozen years of political harassment, his health suffered, and he attempted to commit suicide. He died on January 23, 1976, in Philadelphia.

Robinson, Joseph Taylor
(1872–1937) *U.S. senator, Senate majority leader*

Born near Lonoke, Arkansas, on August 26, 1872, Joseph Robinson was the son of a physician and Baptist minister. Although he had little formal schooling, he began to teach in rural schools near his hometown in 1889. He attended the Industrial University of Arkansas at Fayetteville for two years and then returned home to study law with a local judge before enrolling in the University of Virginia Law School. Even before he received his law degree in 1895, he had won a seat in the Arkansas state legislature (1894–96). After graduation from law school, Robinson returned to Lonoke to practice law and complete his statehouse term. In 1902, he won election to the U.S. House of Representatives and served in Congress for a decade before winning the Arkansas governorship. Shortly after becoming governor, he won a seat in the U.S. Senate on January 28, 1913. He was subsequently reelected to the Senate for four terms.

Conservative on fiscal and states' rights issues, Robinson was a progressive on economic issues. His support for religious rights earned him a national reputation. As a southerner, he defended Woodrow Wilson's foreign policy. He became Senate minority leader in the 1920s and chafed under Republican policies. Nonetheless, when he became the first elected Senate majority leader, he maintained cordial relations with Republican presidents Calvin Coolidge and HERBERT HOOVER. He served as chairman of the Democratic National Convention in 1920, 1928, and 1936 and was a presidential contender among the Democrats in 1924. He was the vice-presidential candidate selected by AL SMITH for the 1928 presidential race.

Robinson used his influence as Senate majority leader to serve Franklin Roosevelt's goals, even though his relationship with the president was more formal than personally friendly. Always the loyal Democrat, he muted his conservatism to implement the New Deal. FDR benefited greatly from Robinson's oratorical and legislative skills, his party loyalty, and his close ties to southern Democrats. Robinson's most significant personal legislative initiative was the Federal Anti-Price Discrimination Act of 1936, cosponsored with WRIGHT PATMAN in an effort to protect small merchants against chain stores.

Promised a spot on the U.S. Supreme Court by FDR, Robinson championed passage of the Judiciary Reorganization Act of 1937—the president's so-called Court-packing plan. But on July 14, 1937, during Senate debate on the bill, Robinson suffered a fatal heart attack. His death freed senators from their personal commitment to him that they would vote for the measure, effectively killing the bill.

Rockwell, Norman Perceval
(1894–1978) *illustrator*

Norman Rockwell was born in New York City on February 3, 1894. While he was growing up, his business manager father moved the family frequently to different Manhattan neighborhoods. Summers were spent in rural upstate New York. Neither Rockwell nor his older brother had a good relationship with either their aloof father or their self-indulgent mother. Instead, Rockwell identified with his maternal grandfather, a painter who loved to capture scenes from the natural world. Rockwell would come to paint idealized scenes of imagined family warmth. A skinny, pigeon-toed youth, he used his drawing skills as his venue to gain acceptance among his classmates. At age 14, he knew he wanted to be an illustrator, so he left Mamaroneck High School to study at the Chase School, also in New York City, for two years. After that, he was a student at the National Academy of Design in New York City and then studied at the Art Students League, where he developed his signature style, which combined details with an element of mirth.

Rockwell's first important job came in fall 1913 when he became an illustrator and art director for *Boy's Life*, the Boy Scout magazine. It was the start of his lifelong association with the Boy Scouts, as well as with Abraham Lincoln, the Boy Scout's adopted role model for good character. In 1915, he moved from New York City to New Rochelle to be among other illustrators there. For a time, he shared a studio with an artist and cartoonist whom Rockwell later credited for his characteristic humorous treatment of children with their families. He married Irene O'Connor in 1916, the same year that he began his long and important association with the *Saturday Evening Post*, illustrating its cover for the first time. Over the next half-century, his illustrations appeared on 321 covers, linking Rockwell's name with the magazine for two generations of Americans.

After World War I was declared, Rockwell enlisted and served one year in the U.S. Navy. He was stationed in Charleston, South Carolina, where he was art editor of the base publication.

Snobbish art critics loved to dismiss Rockwell as a mere illustrator, but he took pride in his work and kept pace with changes in the printing process. He also maintained a healthy appreciation for both the classic painters and contemporary ones, including Pablo Picasso. Many of his paintings depict small-town Americana, but Rockwell was personally cosmopolitan and made a number of trips to Europe in the 1920s and 1930s. Moreover, he was a serious worker who devoted seven days a week to his illustrations. By 1926, he was painting in color rather than using just black and white.

In contrast to the mounting success in his professional life with *Boy's Life*, the *Saturday Evening Post*, *Life*, *Literary Digest*, and *Country Gentleman*, Rockwell's personal life was disintegrating. His childless marriage ended in divorce in 1930, and he remarried that same year to Mary Barstow, with whom he had three sons. Rockwell hit his stride as an illustrator during the 1930s and 1940s. In addition to his magazine art, he began doing commercial art for many companies, including Hallmark and Ford Motor Company, and in 1935 he received a commission from Heritage Press to illustrate Mark Twain's classic novels. By 1939, he and

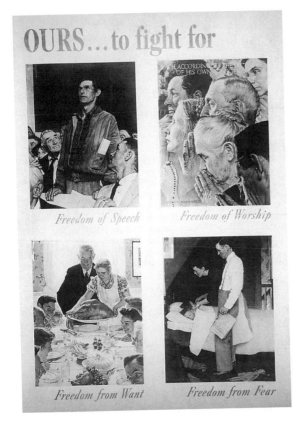

Freedom of Speech *Freedom of Worship*

Freedom from Want *Freedom from Fear*

Poster displaying the Norman Rockwell paintings depicting the four freedoms *(Library of Congress)*

his family had moved to Arlington, Vermont, which, like New Rochelle, contained a community of illustrators.

Though he was not a partisan figure, Rockwell painted at least six U.S. presidents. His first illustration was of "The Young Lawyer" Lincoln in 1927. His most famous work may have been his series of four posters in 1943 that illustrated the "four freedoms" referred to in the FDR's famous "Four Freedoms" speech before Congress on January 6, 1941, which outlined what eventually became the goals of American participation in World War II. The four illustrations were featured in the *Saturday Evening Post* and became symbolic of democracy and decency: freedom of speech, freedom of worship, freedom from want, and freedom from fear. These four paintings were reproduced as posters distributed by the Office of War Information and also were used in the campaign to raise war bonds.

The postwar period was anticlimactic for Rockwell. His wife underwent treatment for depression before her death in 1959. He underwent psychiatric therapy and two years later married a retired school teacher, Mary "Molly" Punderson. Rockwell, by now an American icon, in 1977 received the nation's highest peacetime honor, the Presidential Medal of Freedom, from Gerald Ford, who had been an Eagle Scout. For the nation's 1976 bicentennial, Rockwell had painted his 50th and final Boy Scouts of America calendar. He died on November 8, 1978, in Stockbridge, Massachusetts.

Rogers, Will
(William Penn Adair Rogers)
(1879–1935) *entertainer, humorist, social commentator*

Blessed with instinctive intelligence and biting wit, Will Rogers served as a transitional entertainment figure who mirrored American life as it evolved after the Civil War with the closing of the American frontier and the onset of the Great Depression. Rather than offering ideological panaceas, Rogers honed a persona of a simple cowboy who used humor to navigate successfully the emerging modern urban life and its associated traumas. Moderate bipartisan humor from a seemingly frontier naïf played well when juxtaposed with Franklin Roosevelt's more elegant and sophisticated upbeat confidence.

The son of ranchers of part-Cherokee heritage, Rogers was born on November 4, 1879, near Oologah, Oklahoma, in what was then Indian Territory. His father played a major role in Oklahoma politics before and after its statehood in 1907. Rogers grew up in a comfortable household. Always spirited, he was sent to the Kemper Military School in Missouri to have discipline instilled, but he ran away in 1898 to become an independent cowboy, with financial help from his prosperous father.

After four years of working as a cowboy and ranch hand, Rogers left the United States in 1902 to ride with the gauchos in Argentina. He then joined a circus as part of its Wild West Show and toured South Africa, Australia, and New Zealand. Representing the romantic image of the American cowboy abroad, he appealed to an earlier, simpler era of bygone days. He returned to the United States and continued to travel with Wild West shows while slowly transforming his trick-roping act into one that also spotlighted his distinctive Oklahoma twang. He married in 1908 and had three sons and one daughter with wife Betty Blake.

In 1916, Rogers joined the *Ziegfeld Follies*, and his folksy cowboy routine was transformed. During a program in Baltimore, Maryland, with President Woodrow Wilson in the audience, Rogers had the self-confidence and boldness to poke fun at General John J. Pershing's unsuccessful recent raid into Mexico to capture Pancho Villa. The forerunner of the

celebrity roast was born when Wilson joined in the laughter. Rogers had found his public voice as a humorous commentator on current event and political affairs. He performed with the *Follies* in 1916–18, 1922, and 1924–25. His cowboy humor was recorded in two small books published in 1919 by Harpers that contained his incisive comments on World War I and Prohibition.

In the early 1920s, Rogers expanded his entertainment routines into a good-natured newspaper column. He covered the national presidential nominating conventions for the McNaught Syndicate from 1920 to 1932. By 1926, he had launched a daily newspaper feature, "Will Rogers Says," that reached 40 million readers daily at its peak. He became a contributor to the *Saturday Evening Post*, which often featured cover illustrations by NORMAN ROCKWELL, whose visual commentary on American life also contained humor. Rogers was sent as a foreign correspondent to Europe in 1927 and to the Far East in 1934. He endorsed democratic values at home and advocated avoidance of foreign entanglements abroad, but he favored a strong military, especially an air corps. His flying friends included General William "Billy" Mitchell and fellow Oklahoman and pilot Wiley Post.

The energetic and talented Rogers managed to parlay his popularity into a Hollywood acting career while he toured and wrote. This career began in 1918, and he made nearly 50 silent comedies and travel films featuring his persona as a wise innocent who could pierce the pretensions of the self-designated sophisticates. His first sound film, *They Had to See Paris*, premiered in 1929 and elevated him to Hollywood star status. He starred in *A Connecticut Yankee* in 1931. In 1933's *State Fair*, he was a down-to-earth farmer, and he played the lead role in another 1933 release, *David Harum*, about a small-town banker; Rogers's own father had been the first local banker in their area. The next year he starred in *Judge Priest*, playing a rural politician, again like his father had been. Many of Rogers's films were directed by the legendary John Ford.

The resourceful Rogers also turned his talents to radio in the 1930s. He exploited his written work and spontaneous wit during his *Good Gulf Show*, which aired from 1933 to 1935, and a dozen radio programs for the E. R. Squibb drug company that focused on personalities such as CHARLES LINDBERGH, HERBERT HOOVER, AL SMITH, and HENRY FORD.

Rogers's popularity was so great that he was offered the Democratic nomination for governor of Oklahoma, but he declined. However, he did serve as the mayor of Beverly Hills, California. His most famous political line was that he was "not a member of any organized party; I'm a Democrat." He campaigned for Franklin Roosevelt in 1932. He found flaws in FDR's New Deal, especially his "brain trust," and chastised the Supreme Court for its role in blocking efforts to regulate the economy. He expressed hope that the experimental New Deal's deficit spending might work to restore the economy.

Rogers and his friend Wiley Post died in a plane crash in Alaska that occurred on August 15, 1935, while they were en route to the Far East.

Roosevelt, Eleanor
(Anna Eleanor Roosevelt)
(1884–1962) *First Lady of the United States*

Considered by scholars to be America's greatest First Lady, Eleanor Roosevelt expanded the nonconstitutional role of the president's wife from that of ceremonial hostess to a public figure whose political clout at times rivaled that of the president. Not content to be the traditional political wife who remained unobtrusively in the background and served solely as a helpmate and hostess for her husband,

Eleanor Roosevelt pioneered a new political dimension for the First Lady. At times, she acted as an equal partner in fulfilling the president's role and served—as FDR acknowledged—as his "spur."

Born into a life of material privilege on October 11, 1884, in New York City, Anna Eleanor Roosevelt was psychologically deprived from infancy. Her mother was a beautiful socialite who married the alcoholic younger brother of THEODORE ROOSEVELT. Eleanor's mother openly criticized her daughter's physical appearance and was emotionally unavailable for her. Her father, in contrast, was emotionally available but often physically absent. Compounding her childhood difficulties were the deaths of her parents, her mother when she was eight and her father two years later. The 10-year-old Eleanor was left in the care of her maternal grandmother, who met only her physical needs.

At age 15, Roosevelt was sent to the Allenswood School in England, run by Marie Souvestre, the liberal founding headmistress and daughter of a radical French philosopher. Under Souvestre's tutelage and attention, Roosevelt began her slow transformation from a self-conscious teenager into a young woman with a social conscience. After three years abroad, she returned to New York City to make her requisite social debut.

Roosevelt never attended college, but her Allenswood background equipped her with the skills needed to teach. She soon demonstrated her penchant for helping the underprivileged by teaching at the Rivington Settlement House and working for social reform. Unlike most of her debutante peers who were merely status conscious, Roosevelt was already exhibiting the strong sense of noblesse oblige that was her trademark throughout her activist life.

In late 1902, shortly after her return from England, Eleanor began seeing Franklin Delano Roosevelt, her childhood playmate and distant

Eleanor Roosevelt *(National Archives)*

When the socially prominent couple married in 1905, President Theodore Roosevelt gave away the bride. They had six children, five of whom survived infancy. In the tradition of the wealthy, the Roosevelt offspring were reared largely by servants, and until Sara Delano Roosevelt died, she ruled as the family's matriarch.

In contrast to many wives who found the political world of their husbands stifling, Eleanor Roosevelt found politics liberating. First, FDR was elected to the New York legislature, allowing them to move to Albany. The distance between Albany and Hyde Park loosened the grip that Eleanor's mother-in-law had on her. FDR next was appointed as assistant secretary of the navy in the Woodrow Wilson administration, requiring them to relocate to Washington, D.C., and giving Eleanor the opportunity to resume her volunteer work with Navy Relief and the Red Cross during World War I. It was during this period that she discovered her husband's infidelity, which ended their physical intimacy but not their marriage, which would evolve into a political partnership. That partnership was reinforced during FDR's seven-year struggle with polio, which necessitated Eleanor's assuming a more active role in the political arena to keep her husband politically viable.

Her incredible energy matched his. Roosevelt's organizational talent led to her involvement with the League of Women Voters, the Women's Trade Union League, the Women's City Club, and the Women's Division of the New York State Democratic Committee. She networked with activist women and helped buy the Todhunter School for Girls in New York City, where she taught government and literature. In 1926, FDR built Val-Kill, a house for her near their Hyde Park estate. For FDR, the residence provided only a pool in which to exercise, but for Eleanor it provided a sense of home away from her mother-in-law.

cousin. The somewhat diffident and still socially insecure Eleanor contrasted with the supremely outgoing and serene Franklin. On the surface, they appeared to be an unlikely pair, but Eleanor shared certain key traits with Franklin's adored mother, Sara Delano Roosevelt. Both women were bright, energetic, and empathetic to the less fortunate. For Franklin, Eleanor possessed still another attraction: she was the favorite niece of his political hero, Theodore Roosevelt, and FDR was painstakingly emulating TR's path to politics. Further, at the time that FDR and Eleanor were seeing each other, Eleanor was more attractive than TR's only daughter, who was jealous of her cousin.

After FDR's election as New York governor in 1928, Eleanor continued to support social reform and champion the appointment of women to governmental positions. She would continue this work in the White House after FDR won the presidency in 1932. She worked especially closely with MARY DAWSON, director of the Women's Division of the Democratic National Committee. In 1935, Roosevelt began writing her popular "My Day" newspaper column as well as magazine articles that advocated support for New Deal policies. She also instituted regular White House press conferences for women reporters only in an era when newsrooms were dominated by men. As the New Deal developed, her scope of interest broadened beyond the feminist agenda. She became an advocate for black civil rights and for the poor and others who had no political voice and were powerless. Her efforts helped to humanize both the New Deal and the subsequent war effort.

The president and First Lady were viewed favorably as a political partnership by most of the public. Eleanor Roosevelt became increasingly political, and in 1940 FDR sent her to the lectern at the Democratic National Convention, where she successfully quelled the protest against HENRY WALLACE as his vice-presidential running mate. Though her brief service as assistant director of the Office of Civil Defense was unsuccessful, her unflagging support for the New Deal reforms sometimes made her more popular than FDR. She set the benchmark against which other First Ladies are measured, acting sometimes as the conscience for her spouse and sometimes goading him.

During the postwar years, Roosevelt's continued work at the United Nations, especially the UN Declaration of Human Rights enacted in 1948, won for her the title "the First Lady of the World." She died in New York City on November 7, 1962.

Roosevelt, Elliott
(1910–1990) *third son of Eleanor and Franklin D. Roosevelt*

Born on September 23, 1910, in New York City, Elliott Roosevelt was the fourth of six children born to Franklin and ELEANOR ROOSEVELT; he was named for his mother's beloved father. From 1923 to 1929, he attended Groton School in Connecticut, as his father had done, and he then attended Hun School in Princeton, New Jersey, in 1929–30. Instead of following family tradition by going to Harvard, Roosevelt entered the world of business. From 1930 to 1932, he worked with advertising firms, and he was aviation editor for the *Los Angeles Examiner* from 1933 to 1935 during his father's first presidential term. He continued his career in journalism, working from 1936 to 1940 for Hearst newspapers and radio networks in the Southwest.

Roosevelt once again bucked family tradition during World War II by joining the Army Air Corps instead of the U.S. Navy. He served as a successful reconnaissance pilot over the North Atlantic. Both he and his brother, FRANKLIN DELANO ROOSEVELT, JR., who was four years younger, served as presidential aides to their father at three of his most important conferences: the Atlantic Charter Conference with WINSTON CHURCHILL in August 1941, the Casablanca Conference in January 1943, and the Cairo-Tehran Conference in November 1944.

During his military career, Roosevelt flew 300 combat missions, and he participated in the invasions of North Africa, Sicily, and Normandy. Wounded twice, he was a highly decorated brigadier general when he left the service.

His military performance was an outstanding success, but Roosevelt's personal life was just the opposite. He married five times. His first marriage, to Elizabeth Donner in 1932, produced one child. He married his second wife, Ruth Googins, in 1932, and they had three children. His third marriage, to actress Faye Emerson, took place in 1944 and was childless. He married his fourth wife, Minnewa Bell, in 1951, and they had no children. In 1960, he married his fifth wife, Patricia Peabody Whitehead, and he adopted her four children.

During the postwar years, Roosevelt returned to his writing and published several books. Although he never attempted to follow in his father's footsteps in national elective politics, he was mayor of Miami from 1965 to 1969 and was on the Democratic National Committee. He bred Arabian horses in Portugal during the early 1970s, and he also wrote a series of popular mysteries that featured Eleanor Roosevelt as a detective. He died on October 27, 1990, in Scottsdale, Arizona.

Roosevelt, Franklin Delano
(1882–1945) *president of the United States*

The 32nd president of the United States was born on January 30, 1882, at Hyde Park, New York. Franklin Delano Roosevelt was the second son of James Roosevelt, vice president of the Delaware and Hudson Railroad. The elder Roosevelt and his much-younger second wife, Sara Delano, the strong-willed daughter of a wealthy businessman, doted on their only child. Secure in the total love of his parents, young Franklin enjoyed a privileged, serene childhood despite his father's delicate health. Initially tutored privately, Roosevelt attended Groton Academy, a Massachusetts preparatory school that he did not enter until later than his peers. He attended the school from 1896 to 1900, and while there he learned to debate. In 1900, he entered Harvard University, where the young, athletic, and handsome student became editor of the *Crimson*, the school newspaper. Interested in politics and keenly aware that his distant cousin THEODORE ROOSEVELT had enjoyed academic and social success at Harvard, Franklin proved to be a rather average student unable to match his cousin's standard.

After FDR graduated from Harvard in 1904, he enrolled at Columbia University to study law but found it dull and failed two courses. After he passed the New York bar in 1907, he dropped out in his third year. By then, he was already married, having wed his fifth cousin, ELEANOR ROOSEVELT, of the Republican Oyster Bay Roosevelts and niece of Theodore Roosevelt, on St. Patrick's Day in 1905. He had married her despite his mother's initial objection. The marriage ultimately produced six children; their third child, Franklin Delano, Jr., died in infancy, and several years later another son was named FRANKLIN DELANO ROOSEVELT, JR. Their other children were Anna Eleanor, James, ELLIOTT ROOSEVELT, and John.

Roosevelt, the young husband and father who had found law school boring, joined one of New York City's elite law firms and worked in its admiralty division. He proceeded to follow in Theodore Roosevelt's footsteps with a resolve to exceed his hero's accomplishments and become the greatest American president of the 20th century. As an initial step, he passed the New York State bar exam, which Theodore had not done. FDR possessed the same legendary high-energy level of his distant cousin, and he channeled it into a successful bid for the New York State Senate in 1910, the same year that Woodrow Wilson was elected governor of New Jersey. FDR was reelected in 1912, and Wilson was elected president, having squeaked into the White House only because of the 1912 Republican Party split that had resulted from Teddy Roosevelt's Bull Moose third-party challenge. FDR parlayed his ambition and name into an appointment by Wilson as assistant secretary of the navy—the same job that Teddy Roosevelt had held in the McKinley administration—from 1913 to 1920. In 1920, he continued to follow TR's political development and became the 1920 vice presidential running mate to Ohio governor James M. Cox. Although the Cox/FDR team lost to Warren G. Harding and

Calvin Coolidge, FDR's political star was still in its ascendancy.

At the same time, however, Roosevelt's personal life was less stellar. By August 1921, when he contracted polio while vacationing at Campobello, Newfoundland, FDR and Eleanor's marriage had become hollow. In 1918, Eleanor had learned of his unfaithfulness with Lucy Mercer (later LUCY MERCER RUTHERFORD), but the resolution of the marital crisis was a decision not to divorce and to maintain a public facade of wedded harmony. Ironically, his polio served to strengthen their bond of political partnership, as Eleanor worked to keep his career viable while he struggled against the polio. Even under such tragic circumstances, Teddy Roosevelt—who had almost died of asthma in his youth—served as FDR's model.

When he was stricken with polio, FDR already had an established a network of loyal supporters, and Eleanor and LOUIS HOWE worked to keep their support while he recovered. Although the paralysis left him unable to walk, a condition that he masterfully concealed from the public, FDR never abandoned his presidential ambition. He twice nominated AL SMITH for president, first in 1924 with his "Happy Warrior" speech and then again in 1928. Meanwhile, Smith recruited FDR to run as his successor as New York governor in 1928. FDR won that election and was reelected in 1930. While governor, he initiated what would become his trademark "fireside chats" to listeners on the radio. His second term, especially, proved to be a training ground for his eventual presidency in terms of experience in providing emergency relief, public works, and unemployment compensation.

Armed with the magical Roosevelt name and well known as governor of the nation's most populous state, FDR was ready to seek the 1932 presidential nomination. Aided by many former Bull Moosers, FDR's team struck a deal with the Texas delegation to make JOHN NANCE GARNER, Speaker of the U.S. House of Representatives, his vice-presidential running mate. On the fourth ballot, FDR won the Democratic nomination. The "Square Deal" that Theodore Roosevelt had espoused was appropriated and modified into FDR's "New Deal for the American people." The 1929 stock-market crash and subsequent Great Depression had assured a Roosevelt landslide, despite FDR's contradictory and vague—but strenuous—campaign. The Roosevelt-Garner ticket carried 57 percent of the vote, won all but six states, and carried overwhelming congressional majorities with it. FDR's ebullience and winning smile convinced the nation that better days were just around the corner, just as his inner optimism kept him from letting his paralysis dominate his life.

The Democratic Congress acceded to FDR's initial 100 days of executive activism that introduced into the nation's vocabulary a host of new alphabet agencies created to regulate and reform the national economy. Some of the legislation passed during that period may be traced to Teddy Roosevelt's radical 1912 presidential campaign. Even more of it can be traced to the lasting influence on TR and FDR of Harvard professor William James, founder of the unique American brand of philosophy known as pragmatism. The Civilian Conservation Corps, one of the few pieces of legislation that FDR initiated, owed much to America's first conservation president, Theodore Roosevelt. The most radical piece of legislation, the Tennessee Valley Authority Act, helped to transform an entire impoverished region. During FDR's first term, two landmark acts, among the most significant pieces of legislation to be passed in the history of the Congress, were enacted. These were the Social Security Act of 1935, which established the basis of the modern welfare state, and the National Labor Relations Act of 1935, known as "Labor's Magna Carta."

The president was easily renominated in 1936 and achieved the greatest electoral victory among his four elections by winning 61 percent of the vote and carrying all but two states; the Republican ticket of ALF LANDON and FRANK KNOX carried only Maine and Vermont. The battle against the "economic royalists" that resulted in this landslide victory also spawned the hubris that caused FDR to make one of his two greatest blunders in office. On February 5, 1937, without engaging in his characteristic consultation of others before acting, he proposed his Supreme Court–packing plan as a means to quell the judicial activism of conservative justices who had struck down key pieces of New Deal legislation. Despite the Court suddenly beginning to reverse itself and supporting the New Deal legislation by a one-vote margin instead of rejecting it by one vote, FDR suffered his first major legislative defeat when the Court-packing plan failed to win congressional approval. It was the opening for which conservative Democrats and Republicans who opposed him had been waiting. His legislative defeat was compounded by his subsequent failed attempt in 1938 to purge those he considered anti–New Deal Democrats from the party. FDR's misjudgment resulted in a backlash that increased the number of Republicans in the House of Representatives from 88 to 170 and from 17 to 25 in the U.S. Senate in the midterm elections.

Nevertheless, Roosevelt had inspired the American people during their greatest internal crisis since the Civil War. At his best, FDR never lost sight of the ball within the international arena. He adjusted to his physical limitation and relaxed with his hobby of philately as he kept track of world politics. He faced the reality of the Fascist threat in Europe and the Japanese militarists in Asia at a time when most in post–World War I America had retreated into isolationism. On the domestic front, FDR confronted the issue of a third term in an era when opponents perceived him as a rising dictator because of his attempted Court–packing plan.

Ever the student of Theodore Roosevelt, FDR learned from his distant cousin's mistakes as well as his successes and avoided TR's costly

blunder of declaring after his initial election that he would not seek another term. At his political zenith, FDR simply rigged the Democratic convention in 1940. He used HARRY HOPKINS and Chicago Mayor ED KELLY to manipulate it so that FDR appeared to have received a popular draft. However, the results of the 1940 election showed that his public support had slipped. He and running mate HENRY WALLACE drew only 55 percent of the vote to beat WENDELL WILLKIE and CHARLES MCNARY, and the Democratic team carried only 38 states.

In his third term, FDR continued to prepare his isolationist nation for war. The Pearl Harbor attack on December 7, 1941, unified the nation behind him. His wartime leadership was exemplified on the world stage as he worked to maintain relations with Great Britain and the Soviet Union. The "invalid" president who flew to the historic Tehran conference in November 1943 with WINSTON CHURCHILL and JOSEPH STALIN displayed the same vigor that his outdoorsy "Uncle Ted" had exhibited as he charged

This 1941 photograph shows President Roosevelt asking Congress to declare war on Japan the day after Pearl Harbor. *(Library of Congress)*

up San Juan Hill. FDR signed the third most important piece of legislation of his administration, the GI Bill, in June 1944 during the Normandy invasion.

Consummately adaptable, FDR ran with HARRY S. TRUMAN against THOMAS E. DEWEY and JOHN W. BRICKER in 1944. His fourth term was secured with only 53 percent of the vote, FDR's smallest margin of victory; he carried 36 states. Although the grueling war effort had sapped his strength and health, FDR flew to Yalta in January 1945 to meet with Churchill and Stalin. Roosevelt, who was planning for a United Nations that would avoid the mistakes made by Woodrow Wilson after World War I, then left Washington for his vacation home in Warm Springs, Georgia, with its therapeutic waters. While there, the 63-year-old president suffered a cerebral hemorrhage and died on April 12, 1945.

As he set out to do, FDR had eclipsed the presidential record of his distant cousin. He left the greatest American democratic legacy since Abraham Lincoln. Not only had he been elected four times, but he had successfully confronted the Great Depression and the Axis powers of World War II. His active and flexible personality had allowed him to transform the nation's capital, the institution of the presidency, and the nation itself. Franklin Delano Roosevelt had made the United States the world's preeminent modern democratic nation.

Roosevelt, Franklin Delano, Jr.
(1914–1988) *fourth son of Eleanor and Franklin D. Roosevelt*

Born on Campobello Island, New Brunswick, Canada, on August 17, 1914, Franklin Delano Roosevelt, Jr., was the fifth of six children born to Franklin and ELEANOR ROOSEVELT. He was the second son to be named Franklin Delano Roosevelt, Jr.; the first had died in infancy in 1909. Following family tradition, FDR Jr. graduated from Groton School in Massachusetts in 1933 and Harvard University in 1937. He graduated three years later from the University of Virginia Law School, and his father gave the commencement address. He practiced law only briefly before he began his military service in March 1941 in the Naval Reserves. By the end of World War II, he had risen through the ranks from ensign to lieutenant commander and received many awards, including the Purple Heart. He and his older brother ELLIOTT ROOSEVELT served during the war as presidential aides to their father at three of his most important international conferences: the Atlantic Charter Conference with WINSTON CHURCHILL in August 1941, the Casablanca Conference in January 1943, and the Cairo-Tehran Conference in November 1944.

Like Elliott, Franklin D. Roosevelt, Jr., married five times. In 1937, he married his first wife, heiress Ethel du Pont, with whom he had two children. He married Suzanne Perrin in 1949, and there were two children born to that marriage. In 1970, he and third wife Felicia Schiff Warburg Sarnoff, were married; they had no children. Patricia Oakes became his fourth wife in 1977, and they had one son. His fifth and final marriage was to Linda Stevenson Weicker in 1984, and it was childless.

FDR Jr.'s good looks caused him to be dubbed early on as the "glamour boy" of the family, and he was considered most likely to follow in his father's political footsteps. He looked and sounded like FDR, and he tried to live up to his father's legacy in the postwar period but failed. He became actively involved in the liberal American Veterans' Committee and used it as his springboard for becoming a political contender. In 1947, HARRY TRUMAN made FDR Jr. vice chairman of his Committee on Civil Rights. Two years later, Roosevelt became the Liberal Party's candidate for the

20th Congressional District of New York. He was elected as the Democratic Party's candidate and served in Congress from 1949 to 1955.

In 1954, Roosevelt sought and lost his bid for the Democratic nomination for New York governor, a post that his father had held early in his career. Instead, he was nominated for the state's attorney general post, but lost in the general election. His support for John Kennedy's presidential bid in 1960 led to his appointment as undersecretary of commerce in 1963. Two years later, Lyndon Johnson appointed FDR Jr. the first chairman of the Equal Opportunity Commission. After his failed second attempt to gain the governorship of New York, he quit politics. He died on his 74th birthday, August 17, 1988, in Poughkeepsie, New York.

Roosevelt, Theodore
(1858–1919) *president of the United States*

Two dozen years and partisan loyalties divided the Oyster Bay and Hyde Park Roosevelts before the clans were bridged by the 1905 marriage of distant cousins ELEANOR ROOSEVELT and Franklin Delano Roosevelt. Even before that union, however, FDR had already begun applying his even greater personal flexibility and learning curve with the intention to emulate his older fifth cousin's political success and then to surpass it. Theodore Roosevelt was not only FDR's distant cousin, he also was his primary role model as well as a major source for FDR's serene political sense in facing the successive crises of the Great Depression and World War II.

Born on October 27, 1858, in New York City to a prosperous businessman and his southern-belle wife, Theodore Roosevelt was reared feeling the tensions from the American Civil War through his parents and their differing allegiances. To TR's later consternation, his father bought his way out of active military service during the Civil War in deference to TR's Georgia-born mother, whose brothers were Confederates. Young Theodore was the antithesis of the robust adult, a physical outsider among his childhood peers: frail, sickly, and nearsighted. Nonetheless, he was determined that strong will could triumph over a weak body, and as a teenager he embraced the physical regimen that his father set out. It became his first step along what would be a lifelong journey down the road of the "strenuous life" that he used to compensate for his earlier deficiencies, which at the same time transformed him into a model of physical fitness.

After being privately tutored for his primary and secondary education, Theodore Roosevelt entered Harvard University in 1876 as the United States celebrated its centennial. Not only a good student, he was also an energetic equestrian, boxer, and marksman. He graduated in 1880, ranked 20th in his class of 171. Despite learning that year that asthma and exercise had strained his heart, he defied medical advice to adopt a sedentary life by keeping his medical condition secret and pressing on with his active—even strenuous—activities. Exercise became a form of play for him for the remainder of his life.

Roosevelt entered Columbia University Law School in fall 1880 and married Alice Hathaway Lee that same year. Breaking with tradition among his social class, he simultaneously sought—and won election to—the New York Assembly, but he continued in law school. When Columbia lengthened its requirement to three years of study and the state changed its licensing procedure, Roosevelt quit law school. While later serving as vice president, he considered resuming his study of the law.

In 1882, Theodore Roosevelt completed his first of many books, *The Naval War of 1812*, inspired by his Confederate naval veteran relatives. Midway through his third legislative term, personal tragedy struck when his wife died in February 1884 after giving birth to their daughter, also named Alice. Compounding his grief was the death that same day of his mother, who had lived in the same house with the couple. He took refuge in ranching in western Dakota while he hunted, wrote, and maintained his high-energy lifestyle. On his return east, he ran unsuccessfully for the New York City mayor's seat in 1886. He soon married Edith Kermit Carow, a childhood friend, with whom he had four sons and another daughter.

In 1889, Roosevelt moved to the nation's capital for the first time after President Benjamin Harrison named him to the United States Civil Service Commission. He continued in that position under President Grover Cleveland until 1895, when he returned to New York City to become president of its Police Commission. Two years later, he returned to Washington after President William McKinley appointed him assistant secretary of the navy, the same slot that would first bring FDR to the nation's capital during the Woodrow Wilson administration. During the Spanish-American War, TR seized the opportunity to compensate for his father's lack of active military service during the American Civil War. He resigned from the Navy Department to lead the "Rough Riders" to victory in Cuba and was celebrated as a national hero. Just as he rode his horse up San Juan Hill in that fabled charge, Teddy Roosevelt rode public acclaim to victory as governor of New York in November 1898.

Roosevelt entered office as an energetic reform governor, making the state Republican machine eager to rid itself of the new, young governor. The opportunity came when McKinley's vice president died in office; TR was virtually pushed out of the state to accept the nomination as McKinley's running mate in 1900. Less than a year later, McKinley was assassinated, and on September 14, 1901, Theodore Roosevelt became the youngest

president in American history. He was elected to a term on his own in 1904, but on election night he committed a major political blunder that would later haunt him: he announced that he would not seek reelection in 1908.

During his $7\frac{1}{2}$-year administration, Roosevelt was a model of political and personal activity. He fought for a "Square Deal" for all Americans, wanting to create a modern administrative state in which nonpartisan experts would regulate corporations. He battled from his "bully pulpit" against "the malefactors of great wealth" at home and became the United States's first conservation president, despite his own party blocking his initiatives during the last two years of his administration. He advocated use of the American "big stick" of power to influence affairs abroad. For example, his "Roosevelt Corollary" to the Monroe Doctrine meant the United States would police Latin America. Yet despite his activist rhetoric, he mediated an end to the Russo-Japanese War in 1905, for which he won the Novel Peace Prize the following year.

On March 17, 1905, Roosevelt made time to give away his brother's daughter, Eleanor, in her New York City wedding to his fifth cousin, Franklin Delano Roosevelt. TR had treated his niece paternally after her parents died while she was still young, and he was generous in accepting FDR into the Oyster Bay branch of the Roosevelts. FDR lacked TR's multiple talents but was inspired by him to pursue politics in an even more focused way and learned from TR's political mistakes as well as his successes.

After leaving the presidency, Roosevelt was miserable out of power and sought a third term in the 1912 presidential election. He swept the newly created state primaries, but the conservative Republican Party bosses ignored his showing and renominated William Howard Taft as their candidate. Roosevelt then bolted the GOP and founded the Progressive Party, dubbed the Bull Moose Party in his honor. His platform for that campaign was later incorporated into FDR's New Deal. Although TR lost the 1912 election, he was instrumental in determining its outcome because his candidacy divided the Republican Party and enabled Democrat Woodrow Wilson to win the presidency.

On January 6, 1919, Theodore Roosevelt died in his home, Sagamore Hill, at Oyster Bay, Long Island, New York. As the Republican Party grew increasingly conservative and isolationist, it took fifth cousin FDR, who used TR's career as his political roadmap, to carry on TR's Bull Moose legacy by adapting it within the Democratic Party.

Rosenman, Samuel Irving
(1896–1973) *New York Supreme Court justice, speechwriter, special counsel to the president*

Samuel Rosenman was born on February 13, 1896, in San Antonio, Texas, the youngest of four children whose parents were Ukrainian-Jewish immigrants. His family resettled in New York, and he attended public schools in Manhattan. A talented student, he graduated from Columbia University in 1915 and then entered its law school. His legal training was interrupted in the third year by his enlistment in the U.S. Army during World War I. After his military service, he completed his law degree and was admitted to the New York bar in 1920. Rosenman then turned his attention to politics, becoming part of the Tammany Hall political machine and serving in the New York Assembly from 1921 to 1926. In 1924, he married Dorothy Reuben, with whom he had two children. His wife would become a housing expert, serving as chairman of the National Committee on Housing in 1941.

In 1926, Rosenman accepted appointment to the state Legislative Bill Drafting Commission, which led to his acquaintance with New York governor AL SMITH, who in 1928 gave him the task of assisting Smith's handpicked successor, Franklin D. Roosevelt. Rosenman became a close FDR aide and was one of the candidate's main speechwriters. After FDR's election as governor, Rosenman was designated general counsel to the governor, serving both as speechwriter and liaison with Tammany Hall. He played a major role in FDR's 1932 presidential campaign and was instrumental in establishing FDR's legendary "brain trust" of academic advisers. He also coined "the new deal" phrase that Roosevelt used at the 1932 National Democratic Convention in Chicago.

Before FDR left the governorship in 1932, he appointed Rosenman to the New York State Supreme Court. Tammany Hall denied his nomination to a full term, but New York governor HERBERT LEHMAN reappointed him the next year, and he then won election to a four-year term. Eventually FDR crowned him "Sammy the Rose" for his intelligence, personality, experience, and ability to work for Lehman and serve on the bench while continuing to work for FDR. In 1936, Rosenman became the president's chief speechwriter, and the next year FDR selected him as editor for what would become the 13-volume *Public Papers and Addresses of Franklin D. Roosevelt*, published between 1938 and 1950.

Rosenman's influence peaked during World War II, and he resigned from the bench in 1943 to become special counsel to the president. He helped to create the Office of Production Management, the National Housing Agency, the War Manpower Commission, and the Office of Economic Stabilization that was headed by JAMES BYRNES, with whom he had many conflicts. In 1946, Rosenman returned to private law practice in New York City but remained active in public life, serving as an adviser to the Truman administration and to Democratic governors. He died in New York City on June 24, 1973.

Ross, C. Ben
(Charles Benjamin Ross)
(1876–1946) *Idaho governor*

Charles Benjamin Ross was born in Parma, Idaho, on December 21, 1876, as the American centennial was drawing to a close. His parents were ranchers, and he left school after the sixth grade to work on the family ranch. As a teenager, he worked on several large ranches in Oregon, and from that experience he earned the lifelong nickname of "Cowboy" Ben Ross. From 1894 to 1897, he attended business colleges in Boise, Idaho, and Portland, Oregon. He then returned to the family ranch, which he managed with his brother for the next 16 years. In 1900, he married Edna Reavis, a schoolteacher and Democratic Party activist. They did not have children, but they raised four foster children.

During the 1896 presidential election, Ross was enamored of William Jennings Bryan's populist platform and abandoned his family's traditional Republican Party ties to become a Democrat. He was vice president of the Riverside Irrigation District from 1906 to 1915 and then became chairman of the Board of County Commissioners of Canyon County from 1915 to 1921. He helped to organize the State Farm Bureau after World War I and served as its president from 1921 to 1923. It was his springboard for later statewide office.

Always ambitious and energetic, Ross moved his family in 1921 to a farm in Bannock County near Pocatello, then Idaho's second-largest city. Two years later, he was elected mayor, serving until 1930. He made a failed bid for the governorship in 1928 but succeeded in 1930. His ideology was closer to the Populist Party of the 1890s than what would become the New Deal. Nonetheless, he became the first Democrat and native son to win three successive terms, serving from 1931 to 1937.

As Idaho's New Deal governor, Ross favored the Agricultural Adjustment Act of 1933, the Civilian Conservation Corps, and federal relief programs. On the other hand, he was openly critical of White House bureaucrat HARRY HOPKINS, Vice President HENRY WALLACE, Secretary of the Interior HAROLD ICKES, and even FDR on occasion. Often controversial because of maverick stances, the "Cowboy Governor" spoke the farmers' language and conducted colorful campaigns. In 1934, he received more votes than had ever been cast for an Idaho political candidate and carried every county.

Ross made the mistake in 1936 of challenging WILLIAM BORAH for his U.S. Senate seat, which the Republican had held since 1907. Ross was defeated in a landslide and retired from politics, only to make one last comeback effort in 1938, when he won the Democratic nomination for governor but was defeated in the fall election. Ross died on March 31, 1946, in Boise.

Rutherford, Lucy Mercer
(1891–1948) *social secretary to Eleanor Roosevelt, FDR companion*

Lucy Mercer was born on April 26, 1891, in Washington, D.C., and attended private schools. Her father, who had served with THEODORE ROOSEVELT's Rough Riders, and her independent-minded mother, who had been married previously, separated when she was 12 years old. Her association with the Franklin D. Roosevelt family began when she was hired as ELEANOR ROOSEVELT's social secretary in 1914. She had been recommended for the position by Theodore Roosevelt's sister, who lived in the same capital-city neighborhood near Dupont Circle and whose house Franklin and Eleanor rented when he was appointed as assistant secretary of the navy during Woodrow Wilson's administration. Mercer was 22 years old when she became Eleanor's social secretary, and she developed a reputation for efficiency and an ability to get along with everyone, including the Roosevelt children. Over time, she came to be regarded as almost a member of the family and occasionally filled in as hostess when Eleanor was too busy.

By 1917, Eleanor had discharged Mercer on the pretext of the need for economy during World War I. Mercer then enlisted in the Navy Department and served in the office building where FDR worked. In September 1918, Eleanor discovered the true nature of the intimate relationship between her husband and former social secretary. She offered FDR a divorce, but, responding to pressure from his mother and close adviser LOUIS HOWE, he remained with Eleanor. Franklin's infidelity had forever altered the nature of their relationship and spurred Eleanor to independence. Eight years later, Mercer married Winthrop Rutherford, a wealthy Catholic widower twice her age with six children. She gave birth to a daughter two years later.

Although their affair ostensibly had ended after Eleanor's discovery, Lucy Mercer Rutherford remained in contact with Franklin and attended all four of his presidential inaugurations. After more than two decades, on June 5, 1941, while Eleanor was away from the White House, Lucy began seeing FDR again. The visits increased over time, especially following the death of her 82-year-old husband on March 19, 1944. FDR always enjoyed the company of women, and Rutherford was more willing to listen to him than Eleanor, who had pursued her own agenda since her discovery of the affair. Rutherford was with FDR at the Little White House in Warm Springs, Georgia, when he suffered his fatal cerebral hemorrhage, leaving immediately after he was stricken. Eleanor learned the circumstances

only later. Lucy Rutherford died of leukemia on July 31, 1948, in New York City.

Rutledge, Wiley Blount
(1894–1949) *U.S. Supreme Court justice*

Born on July 20, 1894, in Cloverport, Kentucky, Wiley Rutledge was the oldest child of a fundamentalist Baptist minister and his wife. In his youth, he battled tuberculosis, the same disease that killed his mother when he was only nine years old. A member of the football team at Marysville College in Tennessee, he began an affair with his Greek instructor, Annabel Person. Rutledge transferred to the University of Wisconsin, where he received a B.A. in 1914. He then taught high school in Indiana, at the same time attending Indiana University Law School. The stress of doing both broke his health, and in 1915, he entered a tuberculosis sanitarium in Ashville, North Carolina. In 1917, he married Person, with whom he had three children. Later that same year, he and his wife moved to Albuquerque, New Mexico, in the hope of restoring his health. Named secretary to the Albuquerque school board, he taught high school until 1920, when he began law school at the University of Colorado while again teaching school. After he earned a law degree in 1922, he briefly practiced law in Boulder, Colorado, until joining the university's law faculty two years later. He moved to Missouri to teach law at Washington University in St. Louis and became dean (1931–35) of its law school. He became dean of the University of Iowa's law school in 1935.

Though born in the conservative South, Rutledge was a liberal who backed Franklin Roosevelt and the New Deal while he was a resident of segregated Missouri. He also became a vocal supporter of FDR's Court-packing plan in 1937, agreeing to testify on behalf of it when asked by the administration to do so. During the next few years he was seriously considered for openings on the bench that FELIX FRANKFURTER and WILLIAM O. DOUGLAS eventually received. Instead, in 1939, Rutledge was named to the U.S. Court of Appeals for the District of Columbia. In 1943, he became FDR's ninth and final appointee to the Supreme Court after the resignation of justice JAMES F. BYRNES. His confirmation was overwhelmingly approved by the Senate. While on the bench, Rutledge quickly joined the liberal bloc composed of HUGO BLACK, Douglas, and FRANK MURPHY. He supported the administration's efforts to regulate the economy and increasingly supported civil liberties during his tenure. After six years on the Court, Rutledge suffered a cerebral hemorrhage and died on September 10, 1949, while on vacation in York, Maine.

Sinclair, Upton Beall, Jr.
(Upton Bell, Sinclair, Jr.)
(1878–1968) *novelist, reformer, politician*

Upton Sinclair was born on September 20, 1878, in Baltimore, Maryland, the son of an alcoholic father. He attended elementary schools in New York City and graduated in 1898 from City College there. Sinclair, filled with restless energy and suffering from depression, would be married three times. He became a socialist in 1902 and embarked on a critically acclaimed career as a novelist highlighted by a Pulitzer Prize in 1943.

Sinclair's idealism was reflected in his 1904 historical novel *Manassas: A Novel of the War*, in which the hero meets Abraham Lincoln and other Civil War–era figures. A socialist magazine editor spurred him to write a similar novel of the 20th century dealing with the wage slavery of unregulated capitalism. As a result, *The Jungle*, an exposé of the meat-packing industry in Chicago, followed in 1905 and catapulted him into international prominence. Even though THEODORE ROOSEVELT considered Sinclair a "muckraker," he invited the novelist to the White House after reading *The Jungle*. The Pure Food and Drug Act and the Meat Inspection Act were passed because of the public reaction to Sinclair's book.

During the 1920s, Sinclair turned his energies to politics. He ran twice for governor of California as a Socialist but received few votes. By 1933, he had launched a campaign for governor as a Democrat, for which he penned *I, Governor of California, and How I Ended Poverty: A True Story of the Future*. To the surprise of many, his End Poverty in California (EPIC) platform led to his primary win. A tireless campaigner who made effective use of radio broadcasts, he garnered nearly 44 percent of the vote and gained the attention of Franklin D. Roosevelt. Following his defeat in the general election, he wrote *I, Candidate for Governor, And How I Got Licked* (1935). He quickly returned to writing fiction to justify his political behavior and won his Pulitzer for *Dragon's Teeth* (1942), the third in his 11-volume Lanny Budd series. Sinclair's last work of fiction was *What Didymus Did* (1954), and he published his autobiography in 1962. He died on November 25, 1968, in New Jersey.

Sloan, Alfred Pritchard, Jr.
(1875–1966) *industrialist*

The oldest of five siblings in a prosperous New Haven, Connecticut, business family, Alfred P. Sloan, Jr., was born on May 23, 1875. When he was 10 years old, his family moved to Brooklyn, New York. He became a serious student interested in mechanics and engineering and earned his undergraduate degree from the Massachusetts Institute of Technology in 1895, the youngest member of his class. He married Irene Jackson two years later; the couple was childless, and she died in 1956.

With help from his father, Sloan became a businessman first as a draftsman and then as the general manager of the Hyatt Roller Bearing Company. Lacking hobbies or children, he became a workaholic and was a millionaire by 1916. In 1918, he became a vice president of General Motors (GM), and he transformed that corporation in the 1920s using his managerial and marketing expertise. He subsequently became president of GM, which by the late 1920s had replaced Ford Motor Company as the leader in the automobile industry. Under Sloan's leadership, GM became the world's largest and most profitable bureaucracy.

Despite his business success, the 1930s proved to be a mixed blessing for Sloan. Franklin Roosevelt publicly chastised him for opposing unionization. He refused to talk to WALTER REUTHER, United Auto Workers head, after the UAW organized a sit-down strike at GM's Fisher Body Plant in Flint, Michigan. He unsuccessfully maneuvered to have Governor FRANK MURPHY use the National Guard to remove the strikers during the 44-day protest. As a result, Sloan stepped down from the presidency in favor of the GM vice president, who negotiated a settlement.

In late 1937, after the Department of the Treasury reported that Sloan had avoided paying nearly $2 million in taxes, he established the Alfred P. Sloan Foundation. He became known as a philanthropist as well as for instituting the concept of "planned obsolescence" into the modern American economy. He died in New York City on February 17, 1966.

Smith, Al
(Alfred Emanuel Smith)
(1873–1944) *New York governor*

Al Smith was born Alfred Emanuel Smith in a tenement in New York City's immigrant Lower East Side on December 30, 1873. His mother was an Irish Catholic, and his father, a veteran of the Union Army, was a truckman. He attended parochial school through the eighth grade, but his father died when he was 12, and he quit to go to work full-time. Married in 1900, he and his wife had five children.

The high-energy Smith possessed a gift for oratory, and he used it when he became involved in the local Tammany political organization, moving up quickly in the Democratic machine. He held several appointments before winning a state assembly seat in 1903, and in 1913 he was elected speaker of the state assembly. He left that office in 1915 to become sheriff of New York.

It was the tragic fire at the lower Manhattan Triangle Shirtwaist Company factory on March 26, 1911, killing nearly 150 workers, that turned Smith into a progressive, and he made a name for himself while serving on the investigating commission. He was nominated as the Democratic candidate for governor in 1918, over the opposition of WILLIAM RANDOLPH HEARST, and won the election. He lost the reelection in 1920, but regained the governorship in 1922 and held it until 1928.

Smith's years in office were consistent with the progressive policies that would be implemented by Franklin D. Roosevelt. Smith relied on the advice of public-policy experts as well as the advice of several knowledgeable women, including FRANCES PERKINS and Belle Moskowitz. In 1928, Smith ran for president as the Democratic nominee, the first Roman Catholic to be nominated by a major political party. He had made a previously unsuccessful bid for the Democratic nomination in 1924, when Roosevelt placed the name of the "Happy Warrior" before the Democratic convention. Smith had brought FDR back into active politics after his polio-imposed absence, recruiting him to run as his gubernatorial successor in the 1928 campaign. In the presidential campaign, although Smith almost doubled the popular Democratic vote from the 1924 election and won the nation's dozen largest cities, he was badly beaten by HERBERT HOOVER. The nation was not ready for an urban Irish Catholic.

FDR recognized the proverbial writing on the wall and maneuvered himself into the liberal wing of the Democrats against the conservatives such as Smith. The former governor became president of the company that operated the Empire State Building after he and a group of friends had erected it. Though he eventually supported FDR's campaign in 1932, Smith became estranged from the Roosevelt administration and was an outspoken critic. He helped to form the anti–New Deal Liberty League and even endorsed Republican presidential candidates in 1936 and 1940. He died in New York City in 1944.

Smith, Ellison DuRant
(Cotton Ed)
(1864–1944) *U.S. senator*

Born on August 1, 1864, near Lynchburg, South Carolina, to a Methodist Episcopal minister, Ellison DuRant Smith was brought up on his family's 2,000-acre cotton plantation. After he graduated in 1889 from Wofford College, a Methodist institution located in Spartanburg, he returned home to manage the cotton farm. He married Martha Cornelia Moorer in 1892, but she died the next year after having their only child. In 1906, Smith married Annie Brunson Farley, with whom he had four more children.

Smith became involved in local politics and was elected in 1896 to the South Carolina legislature, serving two terms. Influenced by the populists of the period, he ran for a congressional seat in 1901 but lost. He then became the principal organizer of the Southern Cotton Association, from which he received his nickname "Cotton Ed." The organization was short-lived, but Smith's defense of cotton interests remained throughout his life.

Smith shared the Populist Party desire to regulate big business and federal programs to help the rural South. His record on human rights issues, even in an era when they were only emerging, was abysmal. He opposed suffrage for women and favored restrictive immigration.

In 1908, Smith won election to the U.S. Senate; he was reelected five times, which was one of the longest tenure records up to that time in Senate history. He is best remembered for championing white supremacy and the poll tax while opposing antilynching laws, but he also was a founding member of the congressional agricultural bloc. In keeping with his racist views, he walked out of the National Democratic Convention held in Philadelphia in 1936 after an African-American minister was asked to deliver the invocation.

Smith was a progressive in opposing high tariffs, attacking Wall Street, favoring additional antitrust legislation, supporting Woodrow Wilson's New Freedoms, using federal aid to combat the boll weevil, supporting the federal government's Muscle Shoals development of hydroelectric facilities in Alabama, and backing public development of the Tennessee Valley. Following Franklin Roosevelt's landslide victory in 1932, Smith became chairman of the Senate Agriculture Committee. While he favored FDR's Tennessee Valley Authority, which was enacted on May 18, 1933, he opposed the appointment of REXFORD TUGWELL as undersecretary of agriculture in FDR's administration.

By 1935, Smith had publicly broken with the New Deal over the Public Utility Holding Company Act in its effort to dissolve holding companies that could not justify themselves. He went on to become one of FDR's most severe critics, opposing the 1937 Supreme Court–packing plan and fighting all minimum-wage and pro-union laws. In turn, he became one of FDR's prime targets in 1938 when the president sought to purge disloyal Democrats from the party. He encouraged South Carolina's young Democratic governor Olin Johnston to denounce the openly racist Smith, who was at that time the longest-serving member of the Senate. FDR endorsed Johnston and withdrew federal patronage from Smith. Nonetheless, Smith won the Democratic primary with 55 percent of the vote, presumably due to voter backlash against FDR's intervention in the state's politics.

Ultimately, "Cotton Ed," born during the Civil War, was mired in the past and unable or unwilling to move forward. Opposed to FDR's wartime-preparedness program, he increasingly lost touch with his constituents and lost his bid for a seventh term when he was defeated for renomination in August 1944. Even though he had spent more than three decades in the Senate, he left a legacy of minimal legislation and maximum reactionary behavior. In failing health, he returned to his lifelong plantation home and died there on November 17, 1944.

Smith, Gerald Lyman Kenneth
(1898–1976) *minister, orator*

Born in Pardeeville, Wisconsin, on February 27, 1898, Gerald L. K. Smith was the son of a farmer/traveling salesman and a schoolteacher. He grew up in rural towns and won prizes in high school for track as well as oratory. In 1918, he graduated from Valparaiso University with a degree in oratory. Smith's grandfather and father had been part-time ministers in the Christian (Disciples of Christ) Church, and Smith opted to become a full-time minister, serving churches of the same denomination in small Wisconsin towns. He married Elna M. Sorenson in 1922, and the couple eventually adopted a son who was named after his adoptive father. Smith's successful oratory and fund-raising led him to larger congregations in the Midwest and then in the South after his wife contracted tuberculosis.

In 1929, Smith became a minister of the Kings Highway Christian Church in Shreveport, Louisiana. Repeating his earlier successes in oratory and fund-raising, he nearly doubled the church's membership. He became associated with populist HUEY LONG, who had lived in Shreveport, after the senator helped to save mortgaged homes of Smith's congregants from foreclosure. However, because of his support of Long, and given the strong anti-Long sentiment in much of Shreveport, Smith was forced to resign as minister in 1933. This drove him into full-time association with Long, with whom he helped to organize the Share Our Wealth Society. Following Long's assassination in 1935, Smith delivered his eulogy at the largest funeral in Louisiana's history. Afterward, he became associated with a series of increasingly anti–New Deal and reactionary movements. First he joined Dr. FRANCIS TOWNSEND's national old-age pension plan and then Father CHARLES COUGHLIN's National Union for Social Justice. Smith and Townsend backed Coughlin's Union Party, which ran North Dakota congressman WILLIAM LEMKE's failed presidential bid in 1936.

After moving to Detroit, Smith became a friend of HENRY FORD and helped to found the America First Party. An isolationist in foreign policy and supporter of fascist causes, Smith made a failed bid for the U.S. Senate in 1942. He ran for president on his own racist and anti-Semitic Christian Nationalist Front three times, beginning in 1944. Donations to his right-wing causes eventually made him a millionaire and even more extreme in his political views. He died in 1976 in Los Angeles and was buried in Eureka Springs, Arkansas, at the foot of a seven-story statue of Jesus, the Christ of the Ozarks.

Smith, Hilda Jane Worthington
(1888–1984) *director, Workers Education Program, Works Progress Administration*

Born in New York City to affluent parents in 1888, Hilda Smith received her early education in private schools. She graduated from Bryn Mawr College in 1910 and the next year received her master's degree from the same college. She went on to complete further graduate work at Columbia University and what is now the New York School of Social Work, where she received her second master's degree in 1915. She became an active suffragette and part of the Philadelphia settlement house project working with factory women. It was a background of social responsibility that she shared with ELEANOR ROOSEVELT, FRANCES PERKINS, and HARRY HOPKINS, and they applied it to social reform during the progressive era in American politics.

Smith, who never married, became dean of Bryn Mawr College in 1919. From 1921 to 1933, she ran a summer program for female factory workers with support from the Women's Trade Union League and the Young Women's Christian Association (YWCA). In 1925, Eleanor Roosevelt visited the program, and it was this work that led to Smith's later involvement with the New Deal. In September 1933, Hopkins hired her as a specialist in workers' education in the Federal Emergency Relief Administration. The next year, she began teacher-training programs in the Workers Emergency Program of the Works Progress Administration (WPA), and in 1935 became its director. Eleanor Roosevelt described a visit to the White House by WEP supervisors in her

January 29, 1936, "My Day" column, noting the importance of workers' education, and did so again on June 27, 1939. It was in 1939 that critics began forcing cutbacks in the program, and FLORENCE KERR, who had become Smith's supervisor, began cutting Smith's staff. The Workers Service Program was terminated when it was merged with the WPA War Services Division. By September 1942, Smith's work with the WPA had ended.

Smith had drafted plans for a women's alternative to the Civilian Conservation Corps camps for young men. Eleanor Roosevelt supported the initiative by hosting a White House conference on Camps for Unemployed Women that was held on April 30, 1934. Rather than earning wages for physical work, women remained at the camps for short stays and received free housing, vocational counseling, and moral support. By 1936, 90 so-called she-she-she camps had provided services to 5,000 women. The camps were transferred in 1935 to the National Youth Administration and then terminated in 1937 due to budget cuts.

After 1942, Smith sought to create a permanent Workers Education Program with the Labor Extension Service in the Federal Public Housing Administration but the WPA phased out the program in 1943. After 1943, she also helped to found the National Committee for the Extension of Labor Education. From 1965 until her retirement from federal service in 1972, Smith worked as an analyst for the Office of Economic Opportunity. She died in Washington, D.C., on March 13, 1984.

Smith, Howard Worth
(1883–1976) *U.S. congressman*

Howard Smith was born in Broad Run, Virginia, on February 2, 1883, to farmer parents who lived on a Shenandoah Valley plantation. His cousin was Virginia congressman John F. Rixey (served

1897–1907). Smith completed law school at the University of Virginia in 1903 and began practicing law and investing in real estate. He became involved in Democratic Party politics and quickly rose to become a city councilman, state attorney, and judge. He married in 1913 and had two children by his first wife, who died in the 1919 flu epidemic. Four years later, he married the young woman who looked after his children.

In 1930, Smith began a 36-year career as a congressman representing northern Virginia in the U.S. House of Representatives. "Judge Smith" reached national power as a member of the House Rules Committee. By the late 1930s, he headed the conservative coalition of Republicans and southern Democrats following the 1937 defeat of Franklin Roosevelt's Court-packing plan. The coalition blocked social legislation in the House for 20 years. FDR's efforts to purge Smith in the 1938 Democratic primary failed. In 1940, Congress passed Smith's first major bill, the Alien Registration Act, better known as the Smith Act, which required registration by and fingerprinting of all aliens and outlawed the advocacy of violence against the federal government. Smith sought to prevent strikes in defense industries during World War II by cosponsoring with Senator THOMAS CONNALLY the 1943 Smith-Connally Anti-Strike Act, aimed at preventing wartime strikes. The legislation was enacted despite FDR's veto.

Smith eventually became chairman of the House Rules Committee (1955–67), but he narrowly lost his seat in the 1966 Democratic primary. He died on October 3, 1976, in Alexandria, Virginia.

Stalin, Joseph
(Iosif Vissarionovich Dzhugashvili)
(1879–1953) *Soviet leader*

Born Iosif Vissarionovich Dzhugashvili on December 21, 1879, Joseph Stalin (Russian for "steel") was the son of peasants in Gori, Georgia, an imperial colony of czarist Russia. He attended religious schools until he was 19, then joined the radical Bolshevik wing of the Community Party led by Vladimir Lenin, who made him a member of the Central Committee and editor of the party newspaper, *Pravda*, in 1912. The next year he changed his name to avoid czarist authorities and adopted his revolutionary name, "Stalin." Arrested several times and sent into internal exile in Siberia (1913–17), Stalin participated in the Bolshevik revolution in October 1917 and served as a military leader during the Russian civil war (1918–20). He served as commissioner of nationalities (1917–25) and became a member of the Politburo when he was made the general secretary of the party in April 1922, a post he retained until his death.

Stalin was physically short (5'2"), with a deformed arm, and poorly educated. Enormously energetic and insecure, he used his political positions to eliminate potential rivals. He first aligned himself with Nikolai Bukharin. However, after Lenin's death in January 1924, Stalin purged Leon Trotsky, Grigory Zinoviev, and then Bukharin. (Trotsky was forced into exile in 1929 and in 1940 while in Mexico, he was assassinated by an ice-pick stabbed into his brain. The assassination was ordered by Stalin.)

Like the French revolutionaries before Napoleon, Stalin had an abstract belief that he could create a different society. Unlike them, however, he accomplished his aims, albeit through a reign of terror, transforming a backward Russia into a modern industrial giant in a mere three decades. He collectivized agriculture and deported "kulaks"—wealthy peasant farmers—to Siberia. Ever ruthless, he assassinated his heir-apparent, Sergei Kirvov, in December 1934, a prelude to his Great Purge of 1936–38, which included the mock "Moscow Show Trials," leading to the executions of Zinoviev, Soviet marshal Mikhail N. Tukhachevsky, and thousands more.

Stalin had method to his madness. The Soviets tried to maintain alliances to prevent invasions, of which they were historically fearful. Stalin made Maxim Litvinov his commissar of foreign affairs (1930–39), and the Soviet Union established diplomatic relations with the United States under President Franklin Roosevelt, in 1933 and became a member of the League of Nations in 1934. Yet the West failed to include either the Soviet Union or Czechoslovakia when an appeasement policy toward ADOLF HITLER was implemented in 1938. With the Soviet Union left to fend for itself, Stalin dismissed Litvinov and replaced him with Vyacheslav Molotov, who worked to accommodate Hitler. In August 1939, the Nazi-Soviet Nonaggression Pact was concluded. It allowed a division of Poland between the two powers, the "Winter War," against Finland (November 1939–March 1940), and the annexation of the Baltic States and Bessarabia from Romania in 1940.

This arrangement changed after Hitler invaded the Soviet Union on June 22, 1941. Stalin created a "Grand Alliance with the British" and, after December 1941, with the United States and smaller nations and exiled governments. Stalin met with Franklin Roosevelt and WINSTON CHURCHILL in Tehran (November–December 1943) and again at Yalta in February 1945. The leaders generally accepted Stalin's territorial gains as a fait accompli in exchange for Soviet entry into the war against Japan, a division of postwar Germany, and agreement on the role of superpowers in a postwar United Nations. He continued to seek the extension of Soviet influence abroad leading to the cold war and the deterioration of Soviet relations with the West. Soviet military budgets increased as did his paranoia. Stalin died on March 5, 1953.

Steinbeck, John Ernst, Jr.
(1902–1968) *novelist*

One of America's best-known novelists, who graphically captured the plight of farmers and migrants during the Great Depression in universal themes, John Ernst Steinbeck, Jr., was born in Salinas, California, on February 27, 1902. The only son of a businessman father and former schoolteacher mother, he grew up in the "Salad Bowl of the Nation," the agriculturally fertile Salinas Valley. By age 15, he had decided that he wanted to become a writer, and he spent seven years off and on at Stanford University before finally leaving in 1925 without a degree. His factory work with migrants and itinerants became the source of his best writing during the 1930s. Three novels of this period constituted a labor trilogy: *In Dubious Battle* (1936), about a farm strike; *Of Mice and Men* (1937), which was made into the critically acclaimed Broadway play that made Steinbeck a household name; and *The Grapes of Wrath* (1939), which won both the Pulitzer Prize and the National Book Award. *The Grapes of Wrath*, turned into an equally acclaimed film by director John Ford in 1940, portrayed the plight of Oklahoma farmers driven from their land by the Dust Bowl and the Great Depression. The novel, considered the prototype of later "road novels," depicted a modern tale of America's westward destiny.

Always restless and energetic, as well as sensitive to criticism, Steinbeck married three times. He briefly met Franklin Roosevelt in 1940 and worked in several government information and intelligence agencies. He also served as a war correspondent during World War II. He won the Nobel Prize in literature in 1962. Steinbeck died on December 20, 1968, in New York City.

Stettinius, Edward Reilly, Jr.

(1900–1949) steel executive, wartime production manager, Lend-Lease administrator, undersecretary of state; secretary of state

Edward Stettinius was born on October 22, 1900, into a privileged Chicago, Illinois, family. His father, a business partner in J. P. Morgan and Company, had been assistant secretary of war during World War I. Stettinius grew up in Chicago and New York and was sent to the Pomfret School in Connecticut. He attended the University of Virginia, spending his undergraduate years in social work with the Appalachian poor. Although he lacked an undergraduate degree, Stettinius was offered a position with the Hyatt Roller Bearing Company, a division of General Motors, by a family acquaintance who was a General Motors vice president. He married Virginia Gordon Wallace in 1924, and the couple had three sons.

Stettinius's business acumen and concern for his employees led him to become the administrative assistant to General Motors president ALFRED P. SLOAN, JR. By 1931, the energetic and personable Stettinius was General Motors vice president in charge of industrial and public relations. The social conscience that during college prompted him to do social work with the poor later led him to do volunteer work with the unemployed, which brought him to the attention of Franklin Roosevelt. FDR made him a liaison between the National Industrial Recovery Administration in Washington, D.C., and the Industrial Advisory Board.

In 1934, Stettinius accepted a position with the United States Steel Corporation, where he engaged in reorganization, public relations, and plant production as well as employee welfare. Four years later, he was named the chairman of the board of U.S. Steel. In 1940, he left the company to become chairman of the War Resources Board, and the next year he was named director of priorities in the Office of Production. He thus brought business credibility to the New Deal.

Stettinius next turned his attention from government efficiency to diplomacy. In 1942, he became the administrator of the Lend-Lease Administration, winning friends abroad, especially among Allied diplomats. The following year, he replaced SUMNER WELLES as undersecretary of state. Stettinius was responsible for organizing the August 1944 Dumbarton Oaks conference in Washington, D.C., that led to the creation of the United Nations. After Secretary of State CORDELL HULL resigned in November 1944, Stettinius was easily confirmed as his successor. He accompanied FDR to the Yalta Conference in February 1945 and shortly afterward was named to head the U.S. delegation to the UN Conference on International Organization in San Francisco. Due to his energy and diplomatic skills, the UN Charter was finally approved on June 26, 1945. President HARRY S. TRUMAN appointed a new secretary of state to replace Stettinius but named him as the first U.S. representative to the UN General Assembly. Stettinius resigned in June 1946 and died on October 31, 1949, in Greenwich, Connecticut.

Stimson, Henry Lewis

(1867–1950) secretary of war

During his reelection campaign, emulating the actions of Abraham Lincoln, Franklin Roosevelt instituted an outreach effort aimed at undermining isolationism and preparing the nation for bipartisan support of World War II. One facet of his plan to gain bipartisan approval was the appointment of Henry Stimson, a leading Republican internationalist, as secretary of war in July 1940. Stimson thus became the highest-ranking Republican in FDR's administration.

President Franklin D. Roosevelt is seen looking on as a blindfolded Secretary of War Henry L. Stimson draws the first numbers in the Selective Service lottery. *(National Archives)*

Stimson, born in New York City on September 21, 1867, was the son of a prominent father who was a surgeon and stockbroker. His mother died when he was young, and his grandparents reared him. After attending Phillips Academy in Andover, Massachusetts, Stimson entered Yale, graduating in 1888. He then earned a master's degree from Harvard Law School in 1890. After being admitted to the New York bar, he became a member of Elihu Root's law firm. He had an enduring but childless marriage to Mabel White.

As a Wall Street lawyer associated with Root, THEODORE ROOSEVELT's future secretary of war, Stimson became a member of TR's conservation-prone Boone and Crockett hunt-ing club. He was appointed U.S. attorney for the Southern District of New York and, in 1910, ran unsuccessfully for New York's governorship as a progressive Republican. The following year, President William Howard Taft appointed Stimson as secretary of war, in part to bridge the emerging gap between Teddy Roosevelt and Taft. Stimson volunteered for military service in World War I and served on active duty in France despite his age. He subsequently served in diplomatic posts during the administrations of Calvin Coolidge and HERBERT HOOVER, who named him secretary of state in 1929. He functioned as a liaison between the Hoover and Roosevelt administrations.

To gain the desired bipartisan support for his foreign-policy initiatives, FDR named his Republican friend Stimson as secretary of war and former Republican vice-presidential candidate FRANK KNOX as secretary of the navy. Stimson favored instituting selective service for the military and came to work closely with General GEORGE C. MARSHALL. He played a central role in the relocation of Japanese Americans on the West Coast and defended segregation in the military. Stimson was given oversight of the project to develop an atomic bomb, and he argued effectively against Secretary of the Treasury HENRY MORGENTHAU, JR.'s proposal to reduce Germany to a postwar agricultural society as a means to prevent another German war. He retired as secretary of war in September 1945 and died on Long Island, New York, on October 20, 1950.

Stone, Harlan Fiske
(1872–1946) *U.S. Supreme Court chief justice*

Harlan Fiske Stone became the first U.S. Supreme Court justice to occupy in succession all nine seats on the highest bench, which are assigned by seniority, during his tenure, which began in the Calvin Coolidge administration and ended early in the HARRY TRUMAN presidency. Born October 11, 1872, in Chesterfield, New Hampshire, to a farmer father and former schoolteacher mother, Stone was one of four children. Brought up near Amherst, Massachusetts, he attended Massachusetts Agricultural College for two years before being expelled for a prank. Accepted at Amherst College, he graduated in 1894 and taught for a year. He entered Columbia Law School in 1895 and graduated in 1898. The next year he married Agnes Harvey, with whom he had two children.

Stone practiced law and developed a long association with Columbia, first as a popular professor and then as dean of the law school

(1910–23). His former students included WILLIAM O. DOUGLAS, who was later a colleague on the Court. During his deanship, Columbia served as a center for the new jurisprudence known as legal realism, which favored going beyond precedent to use the best knowledge available to justify a judicial decision.

Stone's life changed forever after his Republican former classmate President Calvin Coolidge nominated him as the attorney general to clean up the Teapot Dome scandal from the Warren Harding administration. Stone named J. EDGAR HOOVER as head of the agency that would become the Federal Bureau of Investigation (FBI). In January 1925, Coolidge nominated Stone as an associate justice of the Supreme Court to replace Joseph McKenna. Stone, the first Court nominee to appear personally before the Senate Judiciary Committee to defend his record, was confirmed on March 2, 1925, by a vote of 71 to 6.

As a justice, Stone practiced legal realism and typically deferred to the elected branches of government. He most often aligned himself with LOUIS BRANDEIS, Oliver Wendell Holmes, Jr., and BENJAMIN CARDOZO, who practiced similar values. His most famous decisions included a dissent in *United States v. Butler* (1936), when the conservative activist majority struck down the Agricultural Administration Act. He also pioneered a role in protecting racial, political, and religious minority rights in his famous footnote in *United States v. Carolene Products Co.* (1938), which established the doctrine of preferred inalienable freedoms over property rights. His lone dissent in *Minersville School District v. Gobitis* (1940), forcing children of Jehovah's Witness persuasion to salute the flag, became the basis for the majority *West Virginia State Board of Education v. Barnette* (1943), which reversed *Gobitis*.

Franklin Roosevelt named Stone as the replacement for Chief Justice CHARLES EVANS

HUGHES after Hughes retired in June 1941 as a bipartisan unity gesture with the approach of world war. Stone was confirmed unanimously.

While scholars typically rank Stone among the dozen greatest justices, his five-year tenure as chief justice proved a disappointment since he was unable to mediate the differences among his hot-tempered colleagues including WILLIAM O. DOUGLAS, HUGO BLACK, FRANK MURPHY, and FELIX FRANKFURTER. The brethren on the high tribunal became the most publicly combative during this time. Stone died on April 22, 1946, in Washington, D.C.

Stryker, Roy Emerson
(1893–1975) *director, Information Division, Historical Section, Resettlement Administration*

Roy Stryker was born on May 11, 1893, in Grand Bend, Kansas, to parents who were ranchers, farmers, and populists. In 1896, his family moved to Montrose, Colorado, where he grew up. After he graduated from high school in 1912, he attended the Colorado School of Mines and served in the infantry in France during World War I but did not see combat. He and his wife, Alice Frasier, married in 1921, and they had one daughter. The newlyweds moved to New York so Stryker could study economics at Columbia University. He received his undergraduate degree in 1924 and then became a graduate assistant at Columbia. While there, he met economics professor REXFORD TUGWELL, who was his mentor for years. Tugwell assigned Stryker the task of collecting photographs to illustrate his new textbook in American economics.

After Tugwell became head of the Resettlement Administration in 1935, he decided to use photography to document the need for social reform. That year he made Stryker the director of the Information Division of the Resettlement Administration's Historical Section. Stryker recruited a group of talented photographers to chronicle rural conditions, including DOROTHEA LANGE, WALKER EVANS, and Ben Shahn. Two years later, Tugwell resigned, and the Resettlement Administration became the Farm Security Administration (FSA). In 1943, the FSA was transferred to the Office of War, and the next year its funding was cut so that photography was used only to document the war effort.

The most important photographic series were the work of Evans, who traveled through Alabama with writer JAMES AGEE in July and August 1937. In 1941, Agee's *Let Us Now Praise Famous Men* contained 31 of Evans's photographs and is considered a literary and photographic classic. Ironically, Stryker considered Evans to be a "problem child" and fired him in late 1937.

Before Stryker left government service in 1943, he arranged with his friend ARCHIBALD MACLEISH, the Librarian of Congress, to donate the 250,000 photographs that had been gathered during his eight-year tenure to the Library of Congress. The collection included a series of photographs by Russell Lee that documented the 1942 forcible transfer of Japanese Americans from their homes to temporary assembly centers and finally to "relocation camps."

After his government service, Stryker worked on photographic projects for private industry, including Standard Oil of New Jersey and the Jones and Laughlin Steel Corporation. He returned to his childhood home in Colorado in 1959. Stryker died on September 26, 1975, in Grand Junction, Colorado.

Sullivan, Mark
(1874–1952) *journalist*

Mark Sullivan was born in Avondale, Pennsylvania, on September 10, 1874, and received his early education at West Chester State Normal

School. He entered Harvard University, where he earned his undergraduate degree in 1900 and his law degree in 1903. Four years later, he married Marie McMechen Buchanan, with whom he had four children.

Sullivan's journalism career had its roots in his high-school years, and it continued to develop while he was at Harvard, both as an undergraduate and as a law school student. A muckraker, Sullivan supported THEODORE ROOSEVELT, including his 1912 Bull Moose presidential bid. From 1914 to 1917, Sullivan was editor of *Collier's*. He covered the Paris Peace Conference for *Collier's* and later was the Washington, D.C., correspondent for the *New York Evening Post*.

After HERBERT HOOVER directed the Belgian food relief effort from the Abraham Lincoln room in the luxurious Savoy Hotel in London and became the U.S. food administrator, Sullivan became his enthusiastic admirer. He even joined the unsuccessful Hoover-for-President effort in 1920. Following the appointment of Hoover as secretary of commerce in the cabinet of Warren G. Harding in 1921, Sullivan and Hoover became close friends. When Hoover became the 31st president, Sullivan was the White House's favorite journalist.

During the 1920s, Sullivan emerged as one of the nation's first syndicated news columnists, so that by the 1930s his three-times-weekly column ran in more than 100 newspapers across the United States. He ranked with ARTHUR KROCK, WALTER LIPPMANN, David Lawrence, and Frank Kent as the nation's most important print commentators on political events. As a progressive Republican and Hoover's friend, he opposed Franklin Roosevelt's presidential bid in 1932. However, like most other journalists, during the new administration's first hundred days, Sullivan gave FDR and the New Deal the benefit of the doubt. Nonetheless, he remained highly suspicious of the radicals in FDR's administration, including HENRY WALLACE,

REXFORD TUGWELL, and MORDECAI EZEKIEL. By fall 1933, Sullivan's conservative values had kicked in, and he concluded that the New Deal reforms were slowing economic recovery. By 1937, he was constantly critical and feared that FDR was moving in a dictatorial direction. However, unlike many political commentators of his time, Sullivan remained a relative moderate toward the policies and personalities that he covered.

From the late 1920s to 1935, Sullivan wrote six volumes of contemporary American history that he had covered as a journalist. Scribner's published the series as *Our Time: The United States, 1900–1925*. He retired to his Avondale farm during the postwar period and continued to write his syndicated columns until his death on August 13, 1952.

Sutherland, George
(1862–1942) *U.S. Supreme Court justice*

Born on March 25, 1862, in England to Mormon parents who subsequently recanted their religion, Alexander George Sutherland's family moved to Utah when he was two. After graduating in 1881 from the Brigham Young Academy (later Brigham Young University), in Provo, Sutherland studied law for a single term at the University of Michigan, where he was influenced by the natural rights philosophy of Thomas McIntyre Cooley. Sutherland then returned to Utah where he married Rosamond Lee, with whom he had three children.

Initially, Sutherland practiced law with his father in Provo but then moved to larger law practices. He soon became active in politics. In 1896 was elected as a Republican to Utah's first state legislature, and in 1900 to the U.S. House of Representatives as the state's only representative. During his single congressional term he allied himself with the politics of Theodore Roosevelt. In January 1905, he became a United States senator for two terms. During his Senate career he introduced a woman suffrage amendment to the U.S. Constitution. After losing a third term senate bid in 1916, he practiced law in Washington, D.C., and was elected president of the American Bar Association. He became an adviser to Warren G. Harding, and was nominated by Harding to the United States Supreme Court on September 5, 1922, being confirmed without discussion. He found the Court suitable to his conservative judicial philosophy with William Howard Taft as the chief justice.

Though a conservative who favored individual liberty and minimal government power, Sutherland maintained cordial relations with his other brethren. In *United States v. Curtiss-Wright Export Corp.* (1936), he wrote for the majority that the president is "the sole organ" of the federal government in international relations. Yet on domestic legislation during the 1930s, as one of the so-called Four Horsemen, he became a conservative activist who ruled against the New Deal. He was the most intellectual of these justices. Despite poor health, Sutherland remained on the high bench until the defeat of FDR's Court-packing scheme, retiring on January 18, 1938. He died four years later in Stockbridge, Massachusetts.

T

Taft, Robert Alphonso
(1889–1953) *U.S. senator*

Robert Alphonso Taft was born September 8, 1889, into a well-known and conventional political family in Cincinnati, Ohio. He was the eldest son of Helen and William Howard Taft, the 27th president of the United States and subsequent chief justice of the U.S. Supreme Court. His grandfather, Alphonso Taft, had served under President Ulysses Grant as secretary of war and attorney general. Raised in Cincinnati, Taft attended Taft School in Connecticut, followed by Yale University and Harvard Law School. First in his class at both institutions, he graduated from Yale in 1910 and Harvard in 1913. In 1914, he married Martha Wheaton Bowers, with whom he had four children.

During World War I, Taft served with HERBERT HOOVER in the U.S. Food Administration. Both his father and Hoover were major influences on his traditional political ideas, opposing both governmental regulation of the economy and U.S. involvement in European political affairs. Taft quickly became involved in state politics in postwar Ohio, serving six years (1920–26) in the statehouse and gaining a reputation for partisanship against Democrats and insurgent Republicans as the Republican floor leader and speaker. He served a single term in the state senate from 1931 to 1932. He lost his bid for reelection in the 1932 Democratic landslide, but during the subsequent 1938 Republican sweep in Ohio, he was elected to the U.S. Senate.

Although he lacked charisma and was noted as a poor speaker on the campaign trail, Taft rose quickly in the U.S. Senate, where his name and intelligence made him a Republican presidential contender in 1940. However, he lost on the sixth ballot to relatively unknown WENDELL WILLKIE, the interventionist candidate, after Taft and THOMAS E. DEWEY had blocked each other. It was the first of Taft's three presidential bids—the others were 1948 and 1952—in which liberal interventionist Republicans thwarted his presidential ambitions. His hard work within the Senate, straightforward style, and partisan combativeness continued to inspire his conservative base so that he became the most powerful Republican in Congress, earning him the nickname of "Mr. Republican" among his colleagues. He died from cancer on July 31, 1953, in New York City.

Talmadge, Eugene
(1884–1946) *Georgia governor*

The son of a cotton planter, Eugene Talmadge was born on September 23, 1884, in Forsyth,

Georgia. He attended the Hilliard Institute for Boys and then entered the University of Georgia, where he received his undergraduate degree in 1904. After Talmadge completed law school at the University of Georgia in 1907, he briefly practiced in Atlanta. However, he was characteristically restless and moved two years later to southern Georgia, where he married the recently widowed Mattie "Mitt" Thurmand Peterson. She had one son from her first marriage and three more children with Talmadge. They moved to McCrae, Georgia, where Talmadge developed what would be a lifelong interest in both farmers and courthouse politics. He served briefly as the county attorney before launching his first bid for electoral office. He lost two consecutive elections for the state legislature in 1920 and 1922.

Talmadge's association with rural voters allowed him to appreciate their anxiety as the

Eugene Talmadge *(Library of Congress)*

South modernized, despite attempts to cling to the past. He also soon came to be a master of the state's unusual county unit system of electoral politics which favored underpopulated rural counties. In 1926, he relied on this system and his bonding with rural voters to capture the first of his three terms as state agricultural commissioner. He would dominate Georgia politics for the next 20 years, and his campaigns featured "Farmer Gene's" political road show.

In 1932, Talmadge used his rural base to capture the governor's mansion. He ran on populist panaceas and practiced conservative politics, preferring confrontation to compromise and executive decrees to legislative action. Reelected in 1934, he refused to institute a "Little New Deal" as other governors did in attempts to ameliorate the effects of the Great Depression on their states. Instead, Talmadge ran on a platform opposing Franklin Roosevelt's New Deal. He hated relief programs, the Civilian Conservation Corps, the Bankhead Cotton Control Act of 1934, and unions.

FDR's frequent trips to Warm Springs, Georgia, which had begun after he had contracted polio, did not make him more acceptable as president to Talmadge. Conservative Democrats backed Talmadge's December 1935 national speaking tour that was intended to position him to challenge FDR at the 1936 Democratic National Convention. His anti-Roosevelt campaign, dubbed the Southern Committee to Uphold the Constitution, culminated in a convention hall in Macon, Georgia, on January 29, 1936. This so-called Grass Roots Convention brought together former HUEY LONG supporters, national Share the Wealth Club director GERALD SMITH, Texas oilman John Henry Kirby, and Thomas Dixon, author of *The Clansman* (1905). Businessmen JOHN RASKOB, ALFRED SLOAN, Pierre du Pont, and others financed the convention. It marked the peak of Talmadge's political power.

The effort backfired, however. New Deal Democrats united to defeat Talmadge's 1936 bid to take Richard Russell's Senate seat, and Walter George defeated his second Senate bid in 1938. By 1940, Talmadge had toned down his anti–New Deal rhetoric, but he grew increasingly racist and reactionary. In 1942, he lost the governorship to Ellis Arnall. His supporters then formed a Klan-like group called the Vigilantes that intimidated Talmadge's opponents during the remainder of World War II.

In 1946, Talmadge ran his last political campaign. His son, Herman Talmadge, managed his father' racist and populist campaign to victory, but the governor-elect died on December 21, 1946, in Atlanta, a month before he would have become governor of Georgia for the fourth time.

Thomas, Norman Mattoon
(1884–1968) *Socialist presidential candidate*

Franklin Roosevelt faced demagogues on the extreme left and right. Norman Mattoon Thomas was a moral leader on the left who competed against both FDR's moderate reforms of the New Deal and a divided left. Born on November 20, 1884, he was the son of a Presbyterian minister in Marion, Ohio, where he grew up. He transferred from Bucknell University to Princeton University as a predivinity student and studied there with political scientist Woodrow Wilson and Social Gospel economist Walter Wyckoff. He was valedictorian in 1905 and for a while did social work in New York City, where he discovered the plight of working families. In 1910, he married Frances Violet Stewart, with whom he had six children. In 1911, he graduated from Union Theological Seminar, headquarters of Social Gospel learning, and became a Presbyterian minister at a church in Harlem. A dozen years after their marriage, his wife inherited a trust that provided a comfortable lifestyle for the family.

After his onetime professor-turned-president Wilson crushed dissent during World War I, Thomas helped to found the American Civil Liberties Union, in part because his brother was a conscientious objector. He resigned from the Presbyterian pulpit and formally joined the Socialist Party in 1918, becoming an editor of *The Nation*. His wife's inheritance permitted him to become a full-time politician, and he ran on the Socialist Party ticket in presidential elections from 1928 to 1948. His idealist appeal peaked in 1932, at the height of the Great Depression, when he won nearly 1 million votes.

An excellent speaker with a sense of humor, Thomas was inept as an organizer among the divided radical left. Compounding that deficit, he underestimated the political skills of Franklin Roosevelt, whose New Deal undermined the idealism of the Socialist Party program. In 1934, on a tour of Arkansas in support of the Southern Tenant Farmers Union, Thomas was chased out of town by thugs that the planters had hired. He initially spoke against U.S. entry into World War II but modified his pacifism. On the other hand, he helped to persuade Franklin Roosevelt to intervene on behalf of socialist leaders abroad to prevent their executions by ADOLF HITLER. Thomas's qualified support for America's war effort after the December 1941 Pearl Harbor attack ran counter to the patriot impulses of most Americans and undermined his utopian goals. He also spoke out against the Japanese-American relocation camp program and advocated racial equality, neither stance popular in mainstream America.

The moralistic appeal of Thomas, an empathetic spouse, father, and socialist, was restricted to a limited personal following and never developed into a mass organization. Despite his limited success in contemporary

America, his call for a welfare state was eventually achieved. He died on December 19, 1968, in Huntington, New York.

Tolley, Howard Ross
(1889–1958) *Agricultural Adjustment Administration program planner, Bureau of Agricultural Economics chief*

The son of schoolteachers, Howard Tolley was born on September 30, 1889, in Howard County, Indiana. He attended Marion Normal College and then studied mathematics at Indiana University, graduating in 1910. He taught high-school math only briefly before he pursued a more rewarding opportunity with the U.S. Interior Department's Coast and Geodetic Survey, where he worked for three years. He married Zora Hazlett in 1912, and the couple had three sons, all of whom became economists.

In 1915, Tolley moved his family to Washington, D.C., to work for the Department of Agriculture, and he joined the Bureau of Agricultural Economics (BAE). The BAE used social-science analysis to help create the new field of agricultural economics, which relied on quantitative data and eventually became the basis for econometrics. Tolley began to publish his findings in 1916, a practice that he continued for the rest of his career. Although by 1928 he was the assistant chief of the BAE, he moved to California in 1930 to become director of the Giannini Foundation at the University of California and to head the agricultural economics program there.

The advent of the New Deal brought Tolley back to the nation's capital. From 1933 to 1935, he was director of program planning in the Agricultural Adjustment Administration (AAA). In 1936, on the recommendation of Secretary of Agriculture HENRY WALLACE, Franklin Roosevelt named Tolley to replace Chester Davis as director of the AAA. He was a great architect of New Deal farm programs but a poor administrator for the AAA, refusing to allow political considerations in farm policy. Wallace replaced him with Rudolf M. Evans, and Tolley returned to the BAE as its chief from 1938 to 1946. During World War II, Tolley helped found the United Nations Food and Agricultural Organization (FAO). He left federal service in 1946 to become director of the FAO's economics and statistics division, a position he held until 1952. In that post, he worked to increase agricultural production worldwide. In 1952, he began to work as a consultant for the Ford Foundation, where he promoted one of its spinoff foundation's, the Resources for the Future. He died on September 18, 1958, in Alexandria, Virginia.

Townsend, Francis Everett
(1867–1960) *pension plan creator*

Born near Fairbury, Illinois, on January 13, 1867, Francis Townsend was the son of religious parents who were poor Midwest farmers. He graduated from high school in Nebraska and worked his way through Omaha Medical College (1899–1903), then moved to South Dakota and began a family practice. In 1906, he married Wilhelmina "Minnie" Mollie Brogue, a widowed nurse, with whom he had two children. During World War I, he served as an army physician. In 1919, for health reasons, the family moved to Long Beach, California. At the beginning of the Great Depression, Townsend served briefly as assistant director of the city's health office, identifying with the plight of older Americans like himself.

In September 1933, Townsend began writing a series of letters to the local newspaper calling for Americans aged 60 and older to receive a monthly pension of $200 that they would be required to spend each month. His pension panacea would be based on a 2 percent tax on business transactions. Professional economists ridiculed the proposal, but the Townsend Plan found a receptive public audience at a time when only 28 states provided any type of old-age pension. Within four months, 3,000 Townsend Clubs had sprung up. After the plan was marketed by Robert E. Clements, a young real-estate broker who was Townsend's friend, the number of clubs more than doubled during the next year.

In 1935, John Steven McGroarty, a Democratic California congressman from 1935 to 1939, introduced the Townsend Plan in the U.S. House of Representatives. Supporters collected 20 million signatures, but New Deal opposition led to its defeat. New Dealers countered with legislation for the Social Security Act, which may have resulted in its quick passage in 1935 despite Townsend's personal opposition to it. He considered it a mere palliative, while economists considered Townsend's scheme of providing the elderly a monthly pension of $200 unsound. A congressional investigation began into the Townsend Club's finances to determine if Townsend was profiting from the plight of the elderly. Congress found him guilty of contempt for refusing to testify before it, but FDR commuted the sentence in 1937.

In 1936, GERALD SMITH and Townsend worked together in support of Father CHARLES COUGHLIN's new Union Party. However, by the fall, Townsend had split with Coughlin and instead endorsed ALF LANDON for president. Townsend supported Republican presidential candidates for the rest of his life. The Social Security Act and World War II undermined the Townsend movement. He died in Los Angeles, California, on September 1, 1960.

Truman, Harry S.
(1884–1972) U.S. senator, vice president of the United States, 33rd president of the United States

A native of Lamar, Missouri, Harry S. Truman was born into a family of ardent Democrats on May 8, 1884. His father was a farmer, livestock trader, and grain speculator, and his mother, a major influence on his life, was a devout Baptist. Truman was seven when his family moved to Independence, Missouri, about 10 miles from Kansas City. He learned to play the piano and attended public schools, graduating from high school in 1901. He held a number of jobs before he turned for a decade to farming, which he did not enjoy.

World War I changed Truman's life. After having served in the National Guard as an artilleryman from 1905 to 1911, he resigned. When World War I was declared, he rejoined the National Guard, where he was elected an officer. By 1918, Truman was a captain and had served as a field artillery officer in France. Returning home the next year, he married Bess Wallace, and they had a daughter, Margaret. His haberdashery in Kansas City was unsuccessful, and he went deeply into debt, but he slowly repaid his creditors.

Truman was active in civic affairs, especially the Reserve Officers Association and the American Legion. His political career began in 1922 with his election as a Jackson County court judge, similar to a county commissioner, for the largest county in Missouri. He lost his reelection bid due to an intraparty conflict but was elected president of the county court in 1926 and held that post for eight years. An honest and serious politician who worked well with others, he built a modern road system and traveled to Shreveport, Louisiana, to inspect its new parish (county) courthouse, ultimately using it as a model for the new downtown Kansas City courthouse.

With the support of the THOMAS PEN-DERGAST political machine, Truman won a seat in the U.S. Senate in 1934. A consistent supporter of Franklin Roosevelt's domestic and foreign policies, he enjoyed popularity among his colleagues because of his work ethic, modesty, and conviviality. He won reelection to the Senate in 1940 while Boss Pendergast was in prison, and he earned his national reputation by chairing the Truman Committee, which investigated waste in defense production.

In 1944, National Democratic Committee chairman JAMES FARLEY and others offered Truman as a compromise candidate to replace HENRY WALLACE as vice president. Truman's border-state ties appealed to the South and conservatives, while his New Deal support won backing from labor and liberals. FDR thought Truman's popularity in Congress could be an asset in ratification of treaties, thereby avoiding the problems that Woodrow Wilson had faced during the post–World War I period. Truman's vice presidency lasted only 83 days before he assumed the presidency after FDR's death on April 12, 1945. Though FDR had kept him on the periphery during both his senatorial and his vice-presidential days, Truman believed in a strong executive and soon demonstrated that philosophy as president. He was reelected president in 1948, famously beating THOMAS DEWEY in a close race. He left office in 1953 and retired with his wife, Bess, to Independence. When he died on December 26, 1972, in Kansas City, he had outlived most of his sharpest critics.

Tugwell, Rexford Guy
(Rex the Red)
(1891–1979) *assistant secretary of agriculture, Resettlement Administration director, Puerto Rico governor*

Rex Tugwell, son of well-to-do upstate New York parents, was born on July 10, 1891. He received all three of his college economic degrees from the University of Pennsylvania's Wharton School. In 1914, he married Florence E. Arnold, with whom he had two children. From 1920 to 1936, he taught at Columbia University and became a prolific writer on American economic issues.

Tugwell's Columbia University colleague RAYMOND MOLEY recruited him for Franklin Roosevelt's Brain Trust, and he soon came to be regarded as one of the most radical New Dealers. He served as the assistant secretary of agriculture in 1933–34 and was director of the Resettlement Administration from 1935 to 1936. In these early positions, Tugwell was a major contributor to New Deal legislation that aimed to bring business, labor, and government together for a national recovery plan. He believed that big business was inevitable and that it needed big government to regulate it for the common good. His bureaucratic battles led to the resignation of GEORGE PEEK as Director of the Agricultural Adjustment Administration (AAA) at the end of 1933. Peek had favored marketing agreements rather than implementing the AAA's domestic allotment provisions. Two years later, Chester Davis, Peek's replacement, purged Tugwell's supporters JEROME FRANK, Alger Hiss, and others who had advocated the rights of southern sharecroppers over those of planters.

Tugwell's support of conservation measures, especially in relation to farmland, had favorably impressed FDR, who appointed him as the first head of the Resettlement Administration (RA), which relocated farmers from poor land and resettled and retrained them, in addition to creating "greenbelt towns" (also called "garden cities") for industrial workers. Tugwell's liberalism earned him the nickname Rex the Red and the enmity of opponents who viewed him as too arrogant. As a result, he was too great a political liability to be allowed to actively participate in FDR's 1936 reelection campaign. He resigned from the RA at the end of 1936. Afterward, he was blocked from returning to academia. His 1938 divorce from his first wife and marriage to Grace Falke, with whom he had two children, further alienated others from him.

After Tugwell had served several years on the New York City Planning Commission, Secretary of the Interior HAROLD ICKES brought him back in 1940 to federal service to do a study on land holding in Puerto Rico. FDR named Tugwell governor of Puerto Rico, and he served in that post from 1941 to 1946. From 1946 to 1957, he taught at the University of Chicago, and then at other academic institutions. He wrote *The Brains Trust* in 1968. Tugwell died on July 21, 1979, in Santa Barbara, California.

Tully, Grace George
(1900–1984) *FDR personal assistant and secretary*

Grace Tully, born on August 9, 1900, in Bayonne, New Jersey, was the daughter of Democratic Irish-Catholic parents. Her father, a businessman, and her mother, a former actress, sent her to Catholic boarding schools. Tully's father died while she was still young, so she took secretarial training at the Grace Institute in New York City, graduating in 1918. She worked for a decade in New York City for the Catholic Church and then began working with the Democratic National Committee in Manhattan.

Tully first worked as a secretary to ELEANOR ROOSEVELT, becoming part of Franklin Roosevelt's staff during his campaign for governor of New York. She was made an assistant to MISSY LEHAND from 1928 to 1941, a career that spanned FDR's governorship into the presidency. LeHand and Tully became close personal friends and worked together as equals until LeHand's illness. In 1941, Tully replaced LeHand as FDR's personal secretary. She never married and was admitted to Roosevelt's inner circle and treated as family. She handled FDR's correspondence, and he dictated his speeches to her. She was with him at Warm Springs, Georgia, when he died on April 12, 1945.

Following FDR's death, Tully became the executive secretary of the FDR Foundation. In 1949, she published her memoir, *FDR—My Boss*, which recounted her happy days with the Roosevelts. Tully died in Washington, D.C., on June 15, 1984.

Tydings, Millard Evelyn
(1890–1961) *U.S. senator*

Millard Tydings was born in Havre de Grace, Maryland, on April 6, 1890. He graduated from Maryland Agricultural College in 1910 with a degree in mechanical engineering and went on to earn his law degree from the University of Maryland in 1913. The energetic Democrat was elected to the Maryland state legislature in 1915, and he served there until 1922, except during his World War I military service. He won election in 1922 to the U.S. House of Representatives and served there until 1927, when he was elected to the U.S. Senate, where he served until 1951. In 1935, he married Eleanor Davies Cheesborough, daughter of Joseph E. Davies, FDR's second ambassador to the Soviet Union. Tydings adopted his wife's two children from her previous marriage.

An early supporter of FDR, the colorful, fiscally conservative, and acid-tongued Tydings was an antiprohibitionist who came to oppose the New Deal for its deficit spending. He joined fellow Democrat BURTON WHEELER of Montana in blocking FDR's 1937 Court-packing scheme. His opposition to New Deal labor and housing led FDR to campaign against Tydings's third term by openly supporting his

Democratic opponent in the 1938 primary. The president's attempt to purge him from the Senate failed, and Tydings became a leader of the southern conservative Democrats who tried to block FDR's 1940 bid for a third term and continued to oppose the president's domestic policies during World War II.

Ironically, for all his political prowess, FDR had been unable to defeat Tydings's reelection, but Republican senator Joseph McCarthy of Wisconsin helped successfully to prevent his reelection in 1950 after Tydings had condemned his activities. Tydings died in Maryland on February 9, 1961.

Vandenberg, Arthur Hendrick
(1884–1951) *U.S. senator*

Arthur Vandenberg was born on March 22, 1884, into a Grand Rapids, Michigan, business family. He graduated from public high school in Grand Rapids and attended the University of Michigan Law School from 1900 to 1901 before becoming the young editor of his hometown newspaper. He and Elizabeth Watson married in 1906 and had three children before her death in 1917. The next year, he married Hazel Whittaker.

Although Vandenberg admired THEODORE ROOSEVELT, he supported William Howard Taft after TR's 1912 third-party bid. During World War I, Vandenberg supported Woodrow Wilson's foreign policy. In the 1920s he authored three books on Alexander Hamilton, first secretary of the Treasury. He was appointed to the Senate in 1928 to fill an unexpired term when the incumbent died. He won election later that year and served in the Senate until his death.

Although he was a conservative Republican, Vandenberg did not become an anti–New Deal leader. With Representative Henry Steagall of Alabama, he cosponsored the guaranteed bank-deposit plan that became the Federal Deposit Insurance Corporation in the Banking Act of 1933. A Midwestern isolationist in the 1930s, he served with GERALD NYE, the North Dakota Republican, in an investigation of the munitions industry. However, after the December 1941 Pearl Harbor attack, Vandenberg changed his position and became a champion of bipartisan international cooperation. As a result, Franklin Roosevelt made him the ranking Republican delegate to the April 1945 San Francisco conference to draft the United Nations Charter. He died on April 18, 1951, in Grand Rapids.

Van Devanter, Willis
(1859–1941) *U.S. Supreme Court justice*

The son of a Republican lawyer, Willis Van Devanter never deviated from the traditional family values instilled during his youth. Born April 17, 1859, in Marion, Indiana, he attended Indiana Asbury (later DePaul) University. After graduating in 1879 from the University of Cincinnati Law School, he practiced law with his father for three years. In 1883, he married Dellice "Dollie" Paige Burhans, with whom he eventually had two sons, and the next year they moved to Wyoming after his brother-in-law was made chief justice of its territorial court. Van Devanter quickly became involved in Republican politics there. He was Cheyenne's city attorney in 1887 and the next year began serving in the territorial legislature. From 1889 to 1890, he was chief justice of Wyoming.

Van Devanter campaigned for William McKinley in his successful bid for the presidency in 1896 and the next year was appointed as an assistant attorney general in the Interior Department. In 1903, Theodore Roosevelt named him to the Eighth Circuit Court of Appeals, where he served until 1910, when President William Howard Taft named him as an associate justice on the U.S. Supreme Court.

Van Devanter would leave a legacy as one of the least productive justices, and his opinions are remembered less than his role in drafting the Judiciary Act of 1925. Nevertheless, both Edward Douglass White and Taft, as chief justice of the Supreme Court, valued Van Devanter's commentary in conference. He supported property rights, states' rights, and laissez-faire. During the 1930s, he joined his brethren PIERCE BUTLER, JAMES MCREYNOLDS, and GEORGE SUTHERLAND in the conservative bloc nicknamed the "Four Horsemen," which consistently opposed New Deal legislation.

Without the knowledge of the other six justices, Van Devanter and LOUIS BRANDEIS supported Chief Justice CHARLES EVANS HUGHES's unprecedented letter to the Senate Judiciary Committee opposing Franklin Roosevelt's 1937 scheme to pack the high bench with six additional justices. To further undermine congressional approval of FDR's scheme, Van Devanter announced his retirement from the bench on May 18, 1937. Though his retirement may have helped defeat FDR's Court-packing plan, in ratings of Supreme Court justices, scholars generally rank Van Devanter as a failure. He died on April 8, 1941, in Washington, D.C.

Vinson, Frederick Moore
(1890–1953) *U.S. congressman, federal judge, director of Office of Economic Stabilization and Office of War Mobilization and Reconversion*

Born on January 22, 1890, in a small town in eastern Kentucky, a Civil War border state, Vinson was the fourth and youngest child of a well-read mother and county jailer father. His grandfather was murdered when Vinson was five years old, and his father devoted the next six years to a crusade to bring the murderer to justice. Consequently, the young Vinson was largely raised by his mother from age five to 11. He attended local public schools in his hometown of Louisa, Kentucky, including the two-year training college from which he was graduated in 1908. Always a gifted athlete, Vinson also was a talented student with a

Frederick Moore Vinson *(United States Supreme Court)*

near-photographic memory. He attended the private liberal arts Centre College in Danville, Kentucky, earning his undergraduate degree in one year and his law degree two years later. He played on the college baseball team, taught history and math, and worked as the law librarian to help finance his legal education. Almost immediately after graduation, he signed a contract to play baseball for Lexington in the Blue Grass League, but his mother persuaded him to return home and practice law instead. His career continued for the next decade, interrupted by brief military service near the end of World War I.

Vinson's love for baseball competed with his legal career for the first five years of his practice, and he played shortstop for Louisa's semiprofessional team during that time. In 1913, he won the office of city attorney and held the position for only one year, but through it he found in politics a substitute for baseball. He reentered elective office in 1921 as district attorney. In 1923, he married Roberta Dixon, with whom he had two children. He won election to the U.S. House of Representatives in 1924, but he managed AL SMITH's presidential campaign in 1928 and subsequently went down in defeat with his candidate. It was Vinson's only electoral defeat. He regained his seat in 1930 after the Great Depression hit.

The congenial border-state politician with a gift for numbers quickly won over House leaders JOHN NANCE GARNER and SAM RAYBURN and led to his appointment to the influential Ways and Means Committee. This was followed quickly by chairmanship of its tax subcommittee, enabling him to help shape New Deal policy. A team player, he coauthored revenue bills and the Guffey Coal Act of 1935. He played a key role in passage of the Social Security Act (1935), the National Labor Relations Act (1935), and reciprocal trade agreements. Vinson introduced Franklin Roosevelt's Court-packing plan in 1937, and he supported the Fair Labor Standards Act (1938). In return for his loyal support, his district received roughly half of the Civilian Conservation Corps camps in his state.

As further reward for Vinson's loyalty, in May 1938 FDR appointed him to the second most important national tribunal, the U.S. Court of Appeals in Washington, D.C. Vinson stepped down in May 1943 to serve in a series of economic positions in the administrations of poker pals FDR and HARRY TRUMAN. That year, he became the director of the Office of Economic Stabilization, where he successfully worked to control inflation. In March 1945, FDR named him the federal loan administrator and then a month later used him as the replacement for JAMES BYRNES as director of the Office of War Modernization and Reconversion. By then Vinson had become a household name.

In July 1945, after Truman became president, he named Vinson as secretary of the Treasury and the next year appointed him as chief justice of the U.S. Supreme Court to fill the vacancy left by the unexpected death of HARLAN FISKE STONE. By this time the once-thin natural athlete was an overweight chain smoker who ridiculed the notion of exercise. He died unexpectedly of a heart attack on September 8, 1953, in Washington, D.C.

W

Wagner, Robert Ferdinand
(1877–1953) *U.S. senator*

Members of both houses of Congress played a significant role in the development of the New Deal, as illustrated by the U.S. Senate career of Robert F. Wagner. He was born in Nastatten, Germany, on June 8, 1877, to working-class parents who immigrated to New York in 1886. He graduated in 1898 from City College of New York and from New York Law School in 1900. In 1908, after he had converted to Catholicism, he married Margaret Marie McTague, and the couple had one child before she died in 1919.

Wagner mixed his Upper East Side law practice with Tammany Hall politics. He served in the New York legislature (1904–05, 1906–18), where he was a floor leader in 1913 and president pro tempore of the senate at the same time that his friend AL SMITH was majority leader of the assembly. Both were reformers and served on the Factory Investigating Commission that investigated the deadly Manhattan Triangle Shirtwaist Company factory fire, which had killed 150 workers in March 1911.

Wagner was elected in 1919 to the New York State Supreme Court, where he upheld progressive legislation. In 1926, he won election to the U.S. Senate and easily won reelection three times. Seniority gained him the chairmanship of the Committee on Banking and Currency, and he became the second-ranking member on the Foreign Affairs Committee. He drafted the National Industrial Recovery Act of 1933, which guaranteed labor's right to bargain collectively. After the U.S. Supreme Court struck down the legislation in 1935, Congress passed the historic National Labor Relations Act, popularly known as the Magna Carta of Labor. Also referred to as the Wagner Act, it established the National Labor Relations Board, which Wagner chaired.

Wagner also was one of the sponsors of the Social Security Act of 1935. In 1937, he helped to create the U.S. Housing Authority. Ill health forced his retirement in 1949, and he died of heart disease on May 4, 1953, in the New York City home of his namesake son, who served in the New York State Assembly (1937–41) and later in 1953 became mayor of New York City.

Wallace, Henry Agard
(1888–1965) *secretary of agriculture, vice president of the United States, secretary of commerce*

Born on October 7, 1888, near Orient, Iowa, Henry Wallace was brought up in a staunch Republican family. His father was a professor at the University of Iowa and also edited a family-run farm journal. His grandfather had served on THEODORE ROOSEVELT's Country Life Commission. In 1912, the two elder Wallaces supported Roosevelt's third-party bid for the presidency. During the Warren Harding and Calvin Coolidge administrations, Wallace's father was secretary of agriculture.

Henry Wallace graduated in 1910 from Iowa State College and worked with his father on the family farm journal. A successful plant geneticist, he made the first hybrid seed corn for commercial use in 1923 and three years later founded the Hi-Bred Seed Company, serving as its president until 1933. He broke with the Republican Party in 1928 and went on to support Franklin Roosevelt's successful presidential bid in 1932. The next year, FDR made him secretary of agriculture, and he became the first son to follow his father in that position.

Wallace's service in the Agriculture Department was loyal to the New Deal but turbulent. His assistant secretary was REXFORD TUGWELL, and together they helped to prepare the Agricultural Adjustment Act of 1933. Two years later, Wallace purged JEROME FRANK from the department after Frank and other radical liberal lawyers tried to aid tenant farmers who had been hurt when southern landowners reduced their crops in exchange for government benefits. The actions of the radical lawyers threatened to undo the New Deal congressional coalition. Nonetheless, Wallace assisted in the passage of the Bankhead-Jones Farm Tenancy Act of 1937.

Wallace also struggled with GEORGE PEEK, the first administrator of the Agricultural Adjustment Administration (AAA). FDR was forced to give Peek a new position in 1933, but Peek was a vocal critic of the New Deal when he left the administration two years later. The

This photograph shows retiring vice president John Nance Garner administer the oath of office to his successor, Henry A. Wallace, as President Roosevelt and others observe, at the U.S. Capitol, Washington, D.C., January 20, 1941. *(Library of Congress)*

Supreme Court declared the AAA unconstitutional in early 1936, but Wallace gained passage of the Soil Conservation and Domestic Allotment Act, which used crop reduction as a conservation measure. This was followed by passage of the second Agricultural Adjustment Act in early 1938, which established the successful idea of the "Ever-Normal Granary." The next year he began food-stamp and school-lunch programs.

Wallace's liberal positions appealed to FDR, who liked to consider himself a gentleman farmer, and the president forced through his choice of Wallace as his running mate in 1940, against the wishes of the leaders of the urban political machines and Southern wing of the Democratic Party. Though FDR won a third term with Wallace as his vice president, by 1944 the urban bosses and Southern Democrats were able to exert enough pressure on him to substitute HARRY S. TRUMAN for Wallace on the ticket. Wallace was made secretary of commerce in 1945 to appease him.

Wallace was bright and idealistic, and he called for "the century of the common man," but he was not a natural politician and failed to establish a political base for his ideas. Truman finally replaced him as his commerce secretary in September 1946. Wallace made a subsequent failed bid for the presidency in 1948 on the new Progressive Party ticket. Defeated, he returned to private life and died on November 18, 1965.

Welles, Orson
(George Orson Welles)
(1915–1985) *actor, writer, director*

Born in Kenosha, Wisconsin, on May 6, 1915, to talented parents—his father was an inventor and his mother a concert pianist—Orson Welles was considered a "boy genius." He made his first film while a student, at the Todd School for Boys in Woodstock, Illinois. It starred the woman who would become his first wife, Virginia Nicholson. After acting in bit parts in Ireland, Welles formed the Mercury Theater company with John Houseman in the United States, serving as actor, director, and writer and working with a talented company of actors that included Agnes Morehead, Joseph Cotton, and Houseman. In 1938, the Mercury Theater's broadcast of H. G. Wells's classic story "War of the Worlds" created panic across the country when thousands of radio listeners were frightened into believing that the United States was in imminent danger of invasion by Martians.

While this broadcast led to a Hollywood contract, Welles's greatest accomplishment, the film *Citizen Kane*, almost ended his movie career before it began. Made in 1941, the film was loosely based on the life of newspaper mogul WILLIAM RANDOLPH HEARST and his mistress Marion Davies, and it was boycotted by the vast Hearst media empire.

Welles seemed to have peaked at age 36 after these successes. He made other movies, but with his penchant of editing and reediting, going vastly over budget and disappearing during production, studio bosses lost interest in the former boy genius who never seemed to fulfill the promise of his early successes. Toward the end of his life, hugely obese, he could be seen on television hawking a variety of products including wine, hot dogs, and mail-order degrees. He died of a heart attack on October 10, 1985, at age 70.

Welles, Sumner
(Benjamin Sumner Welles)
(1892–1961) *assistant secretary of state, undersecretary of state*

The son of wealthy parents, Benjamin Sumner Welles was born in New York City on October 14, 1892. Related to former abolitionist senator

Charles Sumner from Massachusetts, he preferred to be known by his middle name. The Welleses and the Roosevelts were friends, and Sumner Welles roomed with ELEANOR ROOSEVELT's brother in boarding school; he carried her wedding-gown train at her marriage to Franklin Roosevelt in 1905. A bright student who avoided athletics as well as social endeavors, Welles graduated from Harvard University in 1914 and, heeding the advice of his friend FDR, began pursuing a foreign-service career.

Welles served two years in Japan and then began to specialize in Latin American affairs, becoming fluent in Spanish. He often seemed vindictive toward others, was considered by many to be vain, and frequently drank to excess. He would resign three times from the Department of State during his diplomatic career, and during periods of unemployment he wrote books on foreign affairs. The first, published in 1928, was on the history of the Dominican Republic. FDR liked it and made Welles his main adviser on Latin American affairs.

After FDR was elected as president, he made Welles assistant secretary of state. Welles became a major formulator of the Good Neighbor policy, and in 1934 he successfully negotiated the treaty terminating the Platt Amendment, which had allowed the United States to intervene in Cuba's foreign affairs. Two years later, he persuaded FDR to convene the inter-American peace conference in Buenos Aires to end the Chaco War between Paraguay and Bolivia, establishing a precedent for collective consultation in Latin America.

FDR promoted Welles to undersecretary of state in 1937, but Secretary of State CORDELL HULL resented Welles's close relationship with the president. In February 1940, FDR dispatched Welles to Europe to demonstrate the administration's desire for peace and to stall an expected Nazi attack on the Allies. In August 1941, Welles attended the first conference between FDR and WINSTON CHURCHILL near Newfoundland, and he helped to draft the Atlantic Charter.

Welles was eased out of the State Department at the end of September 1943, and he returned to his writing. His marriage to his first wife had produced two sons before they divorced, and he had married twice more. He died on September 24, 1961.

Wheeler, Burton Kendall
(1882–1975) *U.S. senator*

Born in Hudson, Massachusetts, on February 27, 1882, Burton Wheeler worked his way through college and received his law degree from the University of Michigan in 1905. He moved to Butte, Montana, to practice law, and in 1907 he married Lula M. White, with whom he had six children. Wheeler soon turned to Democratic politics, serving one term in the Montana legislature (1910–12). Woodrow Wilson appointed him as U.S. district attorney for Montana in 1913 and he held that position until 1918, while at the same time protecting civil liberties during the hysteria of World War I. In 1920, Wheeler won the Democratic bid for governor but lost the race badly after he was labeled as "Bolshevik Burt" by his more conservative opponents. He championed the interests of farmers and workers against big business. Two years later, he won election to the U.S. Senate and subsequently served four terms.

Wheeler first won national attention for bringing corruption charges against President Warren Harding's attorney general, Harry M. Daugherty. He served as prosecutor during the subsequent Senate investigation, which forced Daugherty's resignation. In 1924, he became the running mate of ROBERT M. LA FOLLETTE on the Progressive Party presidential ticket.

Wheeler was the first national figure to support Franklin Roosevelt's presidential bid in 1932. He initially favored most of the early

New Deal legislation but broke with FDR in 1937 over the Supreme Court–packing plan. Wheeler led the opposition to the Court-packing bill, which resulted in Roosevelt's first major legislative defeat. Some argue that Wheeler's life became the model for Jefferson Smith in FRANK CAPRA's classic 1939 film *Mr. Smith Goes to Washington.*

Wheeler also opposed FDR's foreign policy and led the opposition to the Lend-Lease Act of 1941. Both he and his wife actively supported the America First Committee, although he supported the war effort after the December 1941 attack on Pearl Harbor. Wheeler was defeated in the 1946 Democratic primary, despite his endorsement by President HARRY TRUMAN, with whom he had worked closely in the Senate. After leaving politics, he practiced law with his son, Robert, in Washington, D.C., until his death on January 6, 1975.

White, Walter Francis

(1893–1955) *executive secretary, National Association for the Advancement of Colored People*

Born in Atlanta, Georgia, on July 1, 1893, to a mail-carrier father and teacher mother, Walter White was one of seven children whose skin was light enough for them to pass as white; however, they regarded themselves as African American. He graduated from Atlanta University in 1916 and then worked briefly for Standard Life Insurance Company. White helped to establish the Atlanta branch of the National Association for the Advancement of Colored People (NAACP) and in 1918 was recruited by James Weldon Johnson, NAACP field secretary, to serve as his assistant in New York City. White kept that position until 1929, when he was made the association's acting secretary. In 1931, he was made the permanent executive secretary, and he held that position until 1955.

White promoted the work of African-American writers and artists and was himself the author of two novels published in the mid-1920s. He also wrote the classic investigative study of lynching, *Rope and Faggot: A Biography of Judge Lynch* (1929). He helped with passage of antilynching legislation in 1922, 1937, and 1939 in the U.S. House of Representatives, but the Senate blocked it each time. Nonetheless, White assisted with establishment of the NAACP Legal Defense and Education Fund, which challenged discrimination in the law. During the 1930s, he fought competition from the Communist Party to represent the needs of African Americans. That struggle led to his later anticommunist position during the cold war.

White became an important member of a group of prominent African Americans in Washington, D.C., including MARY MCLEOD BETHUNE and Robert Weaver, who associated with leading New Deal liberals such as HAROLD ICKES, AUBREY WILLIAMS, and ELEANOR ROOSEVELT. He built a variety of coalitions to fight racial discrimination and contributed to the establishment of the 1941 Fair Employment Practices Committee, which was set up to promote equal hiring practices in defense industries during World War II.

White died on March 21, 1955, in New York City.

Wickard, Claude Raymond

(1893–1967) *federal agricultural administrator, secretary of agriculture*

Born near Flora, Indiana, on February 28, 1893, Claude Wickard attended a local high school and then entered Purdue University in 1910. He graduated in 1915 with a degree in agriculture and a strong belief in scientific farming. He took over the family farm and was granted an occupational deferment during

World War I. In 1918, he married Louise Eckert, with whom he had two daughters.

Wickard mixed Democratic Party politics with his farmwork when he was elected to the presidency of the local county Farm Bureau. In 1932, he was elected to a senate seat in the Indiana legislature, and by the next year he had been tapped as the assistant to the chief of the Corn Hog Section of the federal Agricultural Adjustment Administration; he became the section's chief in 1935. In 1937, HENRY WALLACE, the secretary of agriculture, made him head of the North Central Division of the Department of Agriculture. Wicker admired Wallace's views, including those on parity, the "Ever-Normal Granary," and acreage reduction. Wicker's loyalty to those concepts led Wallace to appoint him as undersecretary of agriculture on March 1, 1940. Six months later, Wickard was named secretary of agriculture to replace Wallace after he became Franklin Roosevelt's 1940 vice-presidential running mate.

Wickard loyally supported FDR's shift to wartime preparedness and the corresponding changes in agricultural policy necessary to effect the shift. He essentially became the president's food administrator during the early years of World War II. Despite his loyalty, he was heavily criticized, and FDR responded by appointing a separate war food administrator in early 1943. Nonetheless, Wickard cooperated with the new "food czars" and remained as agriculture secretary until after FDR's death. HARRY S. TRUMAN then appointed him as the head of the Rural Electrification Administration (REA) following refusal by the U.S. Senate to confirm the more controversial AUBREY WILLIAMS. Wickard remained with the REA until after the 1952 election. He then returned to his Indiana farm but remained politically active until his death in an automobile accident on April 19, 1967, while traveling to Indiana.

Williams, Aubrey Willis
(1890–1965) *federal programs administrator*

The son of working-class parents, Aubrey Williams was born in Springville, Alabama, on August 23, 1890, six months before his family moved to Birmingham. He and his six siblings quit after elementary school to go to work and help support their family. Williams was 21 years old before he entered Maryville College in Tennessee. After five years, he transferred to the University of Cincinnati in 1916, and in 1918 he joined the army while in Europe during World War I. He returned to the University of Cincinnati in 1919 and graduated in 1920. That same year, he married Anita Schreck, and the couple had four children.

Williams served as executive director of the Wisconsin Conference of Social Work from 1922 until 1932, when he became a field consultant for the Reconstruction Finance Corporation. He established relief administrations in several states, including Mississippi and Texas. In 1933, HARRY HOPKINS recruited Williams first as a field representative for the Federal Emergency Relief Administration and then as his deputy administrator in Washington, D.C. The two, who soon became close friends, helped with the Civil Works Administration, and in 1935 they administered the Works Progress Administration (WPA). Williams also administered the National Youth Administration (NYA). Through his work he became friends with ELEANOR ROOSEVELT and Lyndon B. Johnson, the Texas NYA administrator. Williams also appointed MARY MCLEOD BETHUNE to the NYA staff.

Nevertheless, Williams's passion for the underdog had made him so controversial that Franklin Roosevelt was unable to make him head of the WPA after Hopkins was named commerce secretary in 1938. The NYA was separated from the WPA, and Congress finally terminated it in 1943. Southern Democrats then blocked Williams's nomination as director of the Rural Electrification Administration in 1945.

Williams returned to Alabama for more than a decade, where he was active in the civil rights movement. In ill health he moved back to Washington, D.C., in 1963 and died there on March 3, 1965.

Willkie, Wendell Lewis

(1892–1944) *business executive, Republican presidential candidate*

Wendell Willkie, the son of lawyers, was born on February 18, 1892, in Elwood, Indiana, and attended local schools. A lifelong avid reader, he graduated from Indiana University in 1913 and its law school in 1916. He married Edith Wilk, a librarian, before serving with the army in France during World War I. The couple had one child.

A Wilsonian Democrat, Willkie moved from Indiana to Akron, Ohio, in 1920 to work on the legal staff of the Firestone Tire and Rubber Company. In 1929, he moved to New York City to become a corporate lawyer for the newly formed Commonwealth and Southern Corporation, a utilities holding company, becoming vice president in 1933. After the passage of the Public Utilities Holding Act of 1935, he became a critic of Franklin Roosevelt and the New Deal. Willkie's utility company battled the Tennessee Valley Authority, which finally had to buy out the utility in 1939 in a $78 million settlement. That same year, he became a registered Republican. His attacks on FDR's New Deal, coupled with his personality and speaking skills, made him popular with businessmen as well as ordinary Republican voters. On the sixth ballot, he became the Republican Party's dark-horse nominee for president in 1940. Despite the loss of Willkie and his vice-presidential running mate, CHARLES MCNARY, who took 45 percent of the popular vote to the FDR-Wallace team's 55 percent, it was the best showing for a Republican in two decades.

Willkie was soon cooperating with Franklin Roosevelt through his active support of the Lend-Lease Act of 1941. By 1943, he had written a best seller, *One World*, which argued against colonialism and imperialism. He promoted civil rights and counted WALTER WHITE among his friends. Willkie sought the Republican nomination in 1944 but had to drop out of the race after his poor showing in the Wisconsin primary, dominated by isolationist voters. Six months later, on October 8, 1944, he died in New York City.

Wood, Grant DeVolson

(1891–1942) *painter*

Born near Anamosa, Iowa, on February 13, 1891, Grant Wood was the son of farmers. After his father died in 1901, the family moved to Cedar Rapids, Iowa, where a decade later Wood studied metalwork and jewelry at the Minneapolis School of Design and Handicraft and Normal Arts. In addition, he took art classes at the University of Iowa, Iowa City, and in 1913 he enrolled at the Art Institute of Chicago. During World War I, he entered military service but remained stateside. He returned to Cedar Rapids after his military service and taught in elementary and high schools there.

Upon Wood's return to Cedar Rapids, he became the town's de facto artist, living with his mother in a studio apartment above a funeral parlor that was owned by his major patron. It also served as a quasi Latin Quarter in Cedar Rapids where artists and writers could spend time together. During the 1920s, Wood made several trips to Europe to study art. By 1927, his regionalist art style had emerged as an original American approach to painting. His works ignored contemporary social and political reality by focusing on the imagined simplicities of earlier times.

Wood's most famous painting was created in 1930. Entitled *American Gothic*, it appears at first glance to depict a dour midwestern married couple standing in front of their farmhouse. In actuality, the two subjects are an Iowa farmer and his spinster daughter, modeled after Wood's dentist and his own sister, Nan Wood Graham. Noted for Wood's incorporation of subtle humor and satire into his paintings, *American Gothic* captures old-fashioned midwesterners with Victorian-era attitudes. However, some critics perceive it as a satire of close-minded, small-town morality—a canvas version of Sherwood Anderson's *Winesburg, Ohio*. *American Gothic* won an award at the 1930 Art Institute of Chicago's annual exhibit of American paintings, and the Institute purchased it for $300.

In 1931, Wood painted a similar satirical work, *Birthplace of Herbert Hoover*, which poked fun at Iowa's first president and his campaign that stressed his "humble beginnings." During the summers of 1932 and 1933, as Franklin Roosevelt's national momentum accelerated, Wood helped to run an art school in Stone City to celebrate the state's and the region's Midwest identity. He became the Iowa director of the Public Works of Art Project (PWAP), which provided work relief and art production, holding the position for six months until the program was terminated in June that year. The PWAP was the first national art project sponsored by the federal government among the New Deal programs that emerged.

Wood then became an associate professor of fine arts at the University of Iowa. The December 24, 1934, issue of *Time* showcased the regionalist art movement in its lead story, elevating it to nearly a household term. THOMAS HART BENTON, Wood, and others were portrayed as rejecting modern abstraction in favor of regionalist art.

In 1935, Wood married Sara Sherman Maxon, who not only was older than he but already a grandmother when they wed. The couple struck some as a real-life parody of *American Gothic*. Wood and his new wife bought a house in Iowa City, where they lavishly entertained visitors to the university campus, including poets Robert Frost and Carl Sandburg. They had no children during their marriage, which ended in divorce in 1939.

In 1940, Wood's portrait of FDR's secretary of agriculture, HENRY WALLACE, was reproduced on the front cover of *Time*. He was appointed the following year as the first faculty member to hold a special chair as University Professor of Fine Arts at the University of Iowa. He died from liver cancer on February 12, 1942.

Wright, Richard Nathaniel
(1908–1960) *novelist*

Richard Wright was born in rural Mississippi between Roxie and Natchez on September 4, 1908, to an illiterate sharecropper and his schoolteacher wife. When Wright was five years old, his father abandoned the family, forcing his mother to take domestic jobs. For a time, he and his brother were sent to an orphanage, and after his mother suffered a stroke when he was about 12 years old, he went to live with his maternal grandparents. They were very religious but illiterate and kept books out of their house. Although Wright managed to graduate from junior high school in 1925, he dropped out of high school almost immediately. The same year he completed junior high school, he moved to Memphis, where he worked as a dishwasher and delivery boy and began reading contemporary American literature as well as commentary by H. L. MENCKEN. In December 1927, he boarded a train to Chicago and left the South for good, cutting his ties to his early identity.

Wright spent a decade in Chicago working at the post office and a variety of other jobs. During the Great Depression, he joined the John Reed Club in 1932 and the Communist Party the next year. By 1935, he had found temporary professional work with the Federal Negro Theater in Chicago, part of the Federal Writers' Project in the Works Progress Administration. Although he wrote short stories and a novel during this period, they were not published until after his death.

In 1937, the restless and active Wright migrated to New York City, where he was the Harlem editor of the *Daily Worker* and also worked on other leftist publications. His big break occurred in 1938 when his short-story collection, *Uncle Tom's Children*, garnered first prize in the *Story* magazine contest for best book-length manuscript, a competition open to authors in the Federal Writers' Project. The New Deal, in essence, had launched his literary career. Also in 1938, *Harper's* published a Wright manuscript, *Uncle Tom's Children*, that related the effects of racism on American society. The volume, supplemented by more of his stories, was reissued in 1940. That same year, Wright published *Native Son*, which holds the distinction of dual "firsts." It was the first best-selling novel by an African-American as well as the first Book-of-the-Month selection by an African-American author. Most critics consider *Native Son* to be Wright's masterpiece. It also made him the wealthiest African-American writer in the nation up to that time. The book's protagonist, Bigger Thomas, was presented as a product of a racist nation.

In *Native Son*, Wright faulted the Communist Party for failing to help the very people it relied on for support. Disillusioned with the party, he quit it in 1942, relating his experience in an article, "I Tried to be a Communist," for the *Atlantic Monthly* in 1944. The article was part of *The God That Failed*, published in 1949 by disenchanted former communists. Wright

had for the second time in his life cut his ties to the group with which he had identified.

Wright collaborated in writing a stage adaptation of *Native Son* the same year it was published. Produced by John Houseman and staged by ORSON WELLES, the play opened for its Broadway run in spring 1941. Wright's autobiography, *Black Boy*, was published in 1945, giving him another best seller and Book-of-the Month Club selection.

Wright's first brief marriage had taken place in 1939 when he wed Dhimah Rose Meadman, a Russian-Jewish ballerina. He divorced her the next year, and in 1941 he married Ellen Poplar, who was white and a Communist Party member. The couple had two daughters. In 1947, the family moved permanently to Paris, France, and they never returned to the United States. Wright had again cut ties to his former life.

In 1953, Wright published an existential novel, *The Outsider*, which captured the author's personal views of life. Though he continued to publish and travel to developing nations, he found himself in the same situation as many leaders of newly independent African nations who had left colonial Africa to be educated abroad and then returned home to lead their nations to independence, only to become marginal outsiders in the process. In Wright's case, the move to Europe had served to alienate him from African Americans, while at the same time he was never fully accepted by native Africans. He died in Paris on November 28, 1960, from a heart attack.

Wyzanski, Charles Edward, Jr.
(1906–1986) *federal lawyer, National Defense Mediation Board member, U.S. district judge*

Born on May 27, 1906, in Boston, Massachusetts, Charles Wyzanski was the son of a real-estate developer. He was raised in the upper-middle-class suburb of Brookline and attended Phillips Exeter Academy. He entered Harvard University, graduating in 1927, and then enrolled in Harvard Law School, where he served on the law review. His professors included JAMES LANDIS and FELIX FRANK-FURTER, who recommended him following his 1930 graduation for clerkships on the United States Court of Appeals for the Second Circuit. Wyzanski served clerkships with Augustus Hand in 1931 and Learned Hand in 1932. The next year, he became a "Happy Hotdog" after Frankfurter endorsed him as the solicitor of the Department of Labor with FRANCES PERKINS, even though Wyzanski had voted for HERBERT HOOVER in 1932.

Wyzanski was a social liberal and a constitutional conservative. As Perkins's top lawyer, he helped to draft the public works and labor portions of the National Industrial Recovery Act of June 16, 1933. He opposed New York senator ROBERT WAGNER's Labor Disputes Act of 1934, and he helped to draft the charter of the International Labor Organization. He also worked to modernize immigration law. Perkins transferred him to the Justice Department in 1935, and he successfully defended several New Deal court cases, especially *National Labor Relations Board v. Jones & Laughlin Steel Corpo-ration* (1937), and he helped to prepare a defense of the Social Security Act of 1935.

Wyzanski was infuriated by Franklin Roosevelt's Court-packing plan of 1937 but remained silent and returned to private practice in Boston at the end of that year. In 1941, he returned to the federal government as a member of the National Defense Mediation Board, resigning that position later in the year to accept FDR's nomination as U.S. district judge for Massachusetts. He held that position for 45 years, declining the opportunity in 1943 to move to the federal court of appeals. He married Gisela Warburg in 1943, and they had two children.

In 1965, Wyzanski became the chief judge of the U.S. District Court for Massachusetts. He served in that capacity until 1971, when he assumed senior status on the court. An extremely able and well-read judge, in the eyes of scholars he became the judicial equal of not only Augustus and Learned Hand, for whom he had clerked years earlier, but also of Oliver Wendell Holmes, Jr., who had recommended to him that he become a lawyer, and of justices LOUIS BRAN-DEIS and Frankfurter, his former teacher and mentor. Wyzanski helped to shape the law on the bench, like fellow judge JEROME FRANK, until his death on September 3, 1986, in Boston.

CHRONOLOGY

1882

January 30—Roosevelt is born at Hyde Park, New York, the only child of Sara Delano Roosevelt, second wife of James Roosevelt, becoming his second son.

1884

October 11—Anna Eleanor Roosevelt is born in New York City.

1896

September—FDR enters Groton School in Groton, Massachusetts

1899

June—FDR graduates from Groton.

1900

September—FDR enters Harvard University, Cambridge, Massachusetts.

December 8—James Roosevelt, his father, dies at age 72.

1903

June 24—FDR graduates from Harvard University.

1904

September—FDR enters Columbia Law School, New York City.

1905

March 17—Marries Anna Eleanor Roosevelt, the niece of Theodore Roosevelt and FDR's own fifth cousin once removed, in New York City.

1906

May 6—Anna Eleanor, the first child of Eleanor and Franklin, is born.

1907

Spring—FDR is admitted to the bar, New York City.

December 23—James, the second child of Eleanor and Franklin, is born.

1909

March 18—Franklin Delano, Jr. (lst), the third child of Eleanor and Franklin, is born.

November 8—Franklin Delano, Jr. (lst) dies.

1910

September 23—Elliott, the fourth child of Eleanor and Franklin, is born.

November 8—FDR is elected to New York State Senate.

1912

September—FDR becomes ill and asks Louis McHenry Howe to take over his political campaign for reelection to the state senate.

November 5—FDR is reelected state senator with 62 percent of the vote.

1913

March 17—FDR is appointed assistant secretary of the navy by President Woodrow Wilson.

April—Franklin and Eleanor move to Washington, D.C.

1914

August 17—Franklin Delano, Jr. (2nd), the fifth child of Eleanor and Franklin, is born.

September 28—FDR is defeated in the Democratic primary for a U.S. Senate seat from New York by Tammany Hall's candidate, James Gerard.

1916

March 13—John Aspinwall, the sixth child of Eleanor and Franklin, is born.

March—FDR begins a love affair with Lucy Mercer (Rutherford), his wife's social secretary.

1917

March—FDR attempts to enlist in the navy.

April 6—The United States enters World War I.

1918

July–September—FDR tours Europe, including the western front of the war and contracts influenza.

Eleanor Roosevelt discovers evidence of her husband's affair with Lucy Mercer.

July 6—FDR is nominated for vice president at the Democratic National Convention held in San Francisco, California.

August 6—FDR resigns as assistant secretary of the navy.

November 2—In a landslide Republicans Warren Harding and Calvin Coolidge defeat the James Cox-FDR, the Democratic ticket.

1921

August 10—FDR contracts an anterior poliomyelitis, Campobello, New Brunswick, Canada.

1924

June 26—FDR makes nominating speech for Alfred E. Smith, dubbing him "the Happy Warrior," at the Democratic National Convention held in New York City.

1927

FDR establishes the Georgia Warm Springs Foundation to treat individuals with polio.

1928

June 28—FDR nominates Alfred E. Smith at the Democratic National Convention, held in Houston, Texas.

November 6—FDR is elected governor of New York with 50.3 percent of the vote.

1929

October—The stock market crash marks the beginning of the Great Depression.

1930

November 4—FDR is reelected governor of New York with 63 percent of the vote.

1932

July 1—FDR is nominated for president at the Democratic National Convention, held in Chicago, Illinois.

July 2—FDR flies from Albany to Chicago to accept the nomination. He calls for a "new deal," and sets precedent by appearing at the convention rather than waiting for the formal ceremony.

November 8—FDR defeats President Herbert Hoover by winning 57.4 percent of the vote.

1933

February 15—Assassination attempt on FDR in Miami by Giuseppe Zangara.

March 4—FDR is inaugurated 32nd president of the United States.

He announces his "Good Neighbor policy" toward Latin America and also says "that the only thing we have to fear is fear itself." Frances Perkins becomes the first female cabinet secretary in U.S. history.

March 5—Congress convenes in emergency session.

March 6—"Bank holiday" declared until March 13. Eleanor Roosevelt starts weekly press conferences.

March 8—FDR holds his first press conference, agreeing to meet with the press twice weekly. He ends the written question rule that had begun in 1921.

March 9—First "Hundred Days" congressional session continues until June 16; FDR signs the Emergency Banking Act.

March 12—FDR delivers his first of 27 "Fireside Chat" radio addresses. In the first, dealing with the banking crisis, he reassures the country that the banks are safe.

March 20—Economy Act requires balanced budget (cuts government salaries and veterans' benefits).

March 22—FDR signs the Beer Tax Act. This act amended the Volstead Act of 1919, legalizing beer and wine that contained no more than 3.2 percent of alcohol.

March 27—Executive order creates Farm Credit Administration.

March 31—FDR signs the Civilian Conservation Corps (CCC) Reforestation Act. It creates road construction, soil erosion, flood control, park, and reforestation jobs for men between ages of 18 and 25.

April 5—Executive order creates the CCC, the first of the New Deal programs.

May 12—FDR signs Federal Emergency Relief Act (FERA), creating a national relief system overseen by Harry L. Hopkins, and the Emergency Farm Mortgage Act.

May 13—FDR signs the Agricultural Adjustment Act (AAA) raising farm prices through cash subsidies and rental payments in exchange for production limits and parity prices for basic commodities.

May 15—Tennessee Valley Authority (TVA) Act created with three-person board of directors.

May 18—FDR signs the Tennessee Valley Act to build dams and power plants that will sell electric power and nitrogen fertilizers in seven states.

May 27—FDR signs the Federal Securities Act requiring new securities issues to be registered with the Federal Trade Commission (FTC).

June 5—Abandonment of the Gold Act takes the United States off the gold standard.

June 6—National Employment Act.

June 12—London Economic Conference convenes and continues until July 28.

June 13—Home Owners Refinancing Act.

June 16—FDR signs the National Industrial Recovery Act (NIRA), creating the National Recovery Administration (NRA), and the Banking Act of 1933. The Glass-Steagall Act creates the Federal Deposit Insurance Corporation (FDIC), which guarantees deposits under $5,000, separated investment from commercial banking, and broadened the powers of the Federal Reserve Board. FDR also signs the Farm Credit Act, consolidating the Farm Credit Administration, the Federal Farm Board, and Federal Farm Loan Board; and the Railroad

Transportation Act. The Public Works Administration (PWA) is established.

July 8—Harold Ickes is named Federal Emergency Administrator of Public Works.

July 9—Cotton Textile National Industrial Relations Board created.

July 11—Emergency Council (National Emergency Council) created.

July 27—Central Statistical Board created.

July 30—National Planning Board established.

August 4—Coal Arbitration Board established.

August 5—National Labor Board established.

August 28—Petroleum Administration Board established.

October 16—Commodity Credit Corporation established.

November 7—FDR receives Maxim M. Litvinov, Soviet commissar of foreign affairs, at the White House.

November 8—FDR appoints Harry L. Hopkins as head of the Civil Works Administration (CWA), an emergency unemployment relief program providing jobs on federal, state and local projects.

November 16—The United States recognizes the USSR.

November 17—National Emergency Council established.

December 5—Federal Alcohol Control Administration established; Twenty-first Amendment ratified, repealing Prohibition; Eighteenth Amendment repealed.

December 10—Public Works Art Project established.

December 19—Electric Home and Farm Authority, Petroleum Labor Board established.

December 21—London Agreement on Silver of 1933 ratified.

1934

January 1—Francis Townsend founds Old Age Revolving Pensions organization.

January 3—FDR delivers his first State of the Union message to Congress.

January 8—FDR receives credentials of the first Soviet ambassador, Alexander Troyanovsky.

January 27—FDR signs the Railway Labor Act creating a national adjustment board, upholding workers rights to organize and bargain collectively.

January 28—FDR signs the National Housing Act creating the Federal Housing Administration (FHA), which insured loans for new construction, repairs, and improvements on farms and in small businesses.

January 30—Gold Reserve Act devalues the dollar.

January 31—Farm Mortgage Refinancing Act enacted.

February 2—Export-Import Bank established.

February 9—U.S. Army begins carrying air mail.

February 23—Crop Loan Act enacted; Huey Long delivers "Every Man a King" speech on national radio.

March 7—National Recovery Review Board established.

March 10—Conservation of Fish Act enacted to protect native fish from federal water development projects.

March 12—Second Export-Import Bank established.

March 24—Philippine Independence Act provides for independence in 1946.

March 27—Vinson Naval Parity Act permits naval buildup.

March 28—Independent Offices Appropriations Act enacted over FDR's veto. Election year politics forced Congress to increase salaries of government employees and allowances of World War I veterans.

April 4—Soviet Nonaggression Pact with Poland and the Baltic States.

April 7—FDR signs the Jones-Connally Relief Act.

April 13—Johnson Debt Default Act forbids U.S. loans to nations in default of obligations to the United States.

April 21—Bankhead Cotton Control Act passed.

April 27—Home Owner's Loan Act passed.

May 2—Title I of Emergency Railroad Act extended.

May 9—FDR signs the Jones-Costigan Sugar Act.

May 18—Crime Control Laws enacted; Emergency Cattle Purchase Program established.

May 24—FDR signs the Municipal Bankruptcy Act.

May 31—U.S. Cuban Treaty repeals Platt Amendment.

June 6—Securities Exchange Act creates five-member Securities and Exchange Commission (SEC). Joseph Kennedy is named the first chairman.

June 07—FDR signs the Corporate Bankruptcy Act.

June 12—Reciprocal Tariff Act for three-year period passed.

June 18—FDR signs the Indian Reorganization Act.

June 19—First National Labor Relations Board established; Silver Purchase Act passed; Federal Communications Commission (FCC) created.

June 21—FDR signs the Railway Labor Act.

June 26—National Longshoremen's Board established.

June 27—National Pension Act for Railroad Employees passed.

June 30—Industrial Emergency Committee, National Resources Board, Federal Prison Industries established.

July 5—National Power Policy Committee established.

July 10—FDR becomes the first president to visit South America while in office when he flies to Colombia.

July 25—FDR becomes the first president to visit Hawaii.

August 19—Plebiscite gives Adolf Hitler total power and title of führer.

August 22—Liberty League announced.

September 11—Agricultural Adjustment Act extended.

September 26—Textile Labor Relations Board established.

October 16—Federal Tender Board established.

November 6—Democrats strengthen their control of Congress with an increase of nine House seats; they control 69 seats in the U.S. Senate and all but seven governorships. This marks the first time in U.S. history that the party in the White House has gained House seats in Congress since a midterm election during the Civil War; it will not happen again until 1978.

December 5—FDR establishes the Federal Alcohol Administration to regulate the alcohol industry. It ended after the Supreme Court invalidated the National Recovery Act (NRA) in May 1935.

December 19—Japan renounces Naval Agreements of 1922 and 1930.

1935

January 4—FDR delivers the Second State of the Union message to Congress, calling for national public works projects, unemployment and old-age insurance, slum clearance and new housing, and improved use of natural resources.

January 7—In the first major Supreme Court case dealing with the New Deal, *Panama Refin-*

ing Company v. Ryan, invalidates a section of the NIRA that gave presidential power to regulate petroleum shipments.

January 16—FDR sends special message to Congress asking United States adherence to the World Court.

March 16—Germany renounces clauses of Versailles Treaty concerning disarmament.

March 24—FDR signs Philippine Independence Act.

April 8—Emergency Relief Appropriation Act creates Works Progress Administration (WPA) with the largest single appropriation in U.S. history.

April 27—Soil Conservation Act passed, placing the Soil Conservation Service on a permanent basis in the Department of Agriculture, and establishing soil conservation districts.

April 30—Resettlement Administration is established to grant loans for the purchase of farms by sharecroppers and tenants; assist in preventing soil erosion, floods; and reforestation.

May 6—FDR creates Works Progress Administration (WPA) by executive order—the most enduring New Deal symbol. *Railroad Retirement Board v. Alton* overturns the Railroad Retirement Act of 1934.

May 11—Rural Electrification Administration (REA) established to finance electricity production and building light and power lines in rural areas not served by private utility companies.

May 27—*Schechter Poultry Corporation v. U.S.* invalidates the NIRA.

June 7—National Resources Committee established; "Second Hundred Days" begins now and ends in August.

June 15—National Labor Relations Board established.

June 19—FDR sends "wealth tax" proposal to Congress.

June 26—National Youth Administration (NYA) established as part of the Works Progress Administration (WPA), to provide work relief and employment for those between the ages of 16 and 25.

July 5—FDR signs National Labor Relations Act (Wagner Act) which gives labor the right to organize and bargain collectively. It establishes a new National Labor Relations Board to supervise elections at employee request, certify trade unions, and issue cease and desist orders to employers adjudged unfair.

July 31—National Labor Relations Board extended.

August 2—Federal Art Project, Federal Music Project, Federal Theater Project, Federal Writers Project established.

August 9—FDR signs the Motor Carrier Act, dramatically increasing the scope of the Interstate Commerce Commission (ICC).

August 12—A new Electric Home and Farm Authority created.

August 14—FDR signs Social Security Act establishing a federal-state system of unemployment compensation, and an old-age pension plan on the national level.

August 23—FDR signs Banking Act, one of the most important pieces of banking legislation in United States history.

August 24—FDR signs the Potato Control Act.

August 26—Federal Power Commission established under Public Utility Holding Act.

August 27—Indian Arts and Crafts Board established.

August 28—FDR signs the Mortgage Moratorium Act; Public Utility Holding Company Act gives SEC power to regulate public utilities.

August 29—Congress passes the Federal Alcohol Administration Act that abolishes the Federal Alcohol Administration, replacing it with the Federal Alcohol Administration until 1940, when it is transferred to the Internal Revenue Service. FDR signs the Railroad Retirement Act of 1935 in response to the Supreme Court invalidating the Railroad Retirement Act of 1934.

August 30—FDR signs the Bituminous Coal Stabilization Act; Wealth Tax Act passed.

August 31—FDR signs the Neutrality Act of 1935 prohibiting loans to belligerents and embargoing shipments of munitions to them.

September 8—Senator Huey Long is shot in Louisiana, dies two days later.

October 3—Italian invasion of Ethiopia.

October 7—U.S. Supreme Court opened its first term in its new and current location across from the Capitol.

November 16—Historical Records Survey established in the Works Progress Administration; Federal Surplus Relief Corporation established.

December 21—National Recovery Administration terminated.

December 30—Eleanor Roosevelt begins her "My Day" newspaper column.

1936

January 3—FDR delivers his third State of the Union message to Congress, challenging New Deal critics to repeal the administration's programs if they could.

January 6—*U.S. v. Butler* invalidates the Agricultural Adjustment Act of 1933 as an invasion of states' rights.

February 17—*Ashwander v. TVA* upholds the Tennessee Valley Authority.

February 29—Neutrality Act, Soil Conservation and Domestic Allotment Act passed (SCDA). The SCDA replaced the Agricultural Adjustment Act (AAA) by substituting payments to farmers practicing soil conservation.

March 4—FDR pushes button putting Norris Dam (TVA) at Norris, Tennessee, into operation.

March 6—The Works Progress Administration (WPA) establishes an independent Federal Dance Program with Don Oscar Becque as its director.

April 3—FDR increases the spending limits imposed on the Emergency Relief Appropriation Act of 1935.

April 4—Labor Non-Partisan League announced.

April 20—Rural Electrification Act passed.

May 1—FDR signs the Alaska Reorganization Act.

May 16—*Carter v. Carter Coal Company* invalidates the Bituminous Coal Stabilization Act of 1935.

June 1—*Morehead v. Tipaldo* invalidates New York's minimum-wage law for women.

June 2—Republican National Convention in Cleveland nominates Alf Landon for president and Frank Knox for vice president.

June 15—FDR signs the Flood Control Act.

June 19—Father Charles Coughlin calls for Union Party.

June 20—FDR signs the Federal Anti-Price Discrimination Act.

June 27—Democratic National Convention in Philadelphia renominates the FDR–John Nance Garner ticket. In his acceptance speech, FDR says, "This generation of Americans has a rendezvous with destiny."

June 29—Merchant Marine Act provides for Maritime Commission and ship subsidies.

June 30—FDR signs the Public Contracts Act.

August 7—The United States announces strict neutrality in the Spanish civil war.

October 29—Alf Landon charges FDR has plan to "pack" U.S. Supreme Court.

November 1—Rome-Berlin Axis formed.

November 3—FDR reelected in landslide (60.8 percent) over Alf Landon, the worst showing for the Republican Party since 1856. Democrats win 331 seats in the U.S. House of Representatives (89 Republicans), 76 seats in the U.S. Senate (16 Republicans).

November 25—Anti-Comintern Pact signed by Germany, Italy, and Japan.

December 1—FDR and Secretary of State Cordell Hull attend Pan-American Conference in Buenos Aires, Argentina. FDR is the first sitting president to tour Southern Hemisphere.

December 30—The United Auto Workers (UAW) begin sit-down strike at the General Motors plant in Flint, Michigan.

1937

January 6—FDR delivers fourth State of the Union message to Congress, saying a constitutional amendment was unnecessary to achieve the goal of his administration.

January 8—FDR signs joint congressional resolution placing an embargo on shipment of arms and munitions to Spain.

January 12—FDR sends special message to Congress requesting legislation to reorganize the executive branch as a result of the Louis Brownlow report that stated "the president needs help."

January 20—FDR inaugurated and in his address says, "I see one-third of a nation ill-housed, ill-clad, and ill-nourished."

February 7—Supreme Court–packing plan (Judicial Reform Act) sent to Congress; controversy continues until July.

March 9—During a Fireside Chat FDR tries to justify the Supreme Court "packing plan."

March 12—UAW sit-down strike at General Motors, Flint, Michigan, plant resolved.

March 29—*West Coast Hotel v. Parrish* decision reflects new voting realignment on the Supreme Court upholding New Deal legislation; this is the so-called switch in time saves the nine case.

April 12—*NLRB v. Jones & Laughlin Steel Corp.* upholds the Wagner Act.

April 26—FDR signs the Bituminous Coal Act.

May 1—FDR signs the Neutrality Act of 1937, the third Neutrality Act passed by joint resolution.

May 18—Farm Forestry Act.

May 24—Conservative justice Willis Van Devanter announces his retirement; Supreme Court upholds Social Security Act of 1935.

May 27—Columbia River Basin Anti-Speculation Act passed.

May 28—Neville Chamberlain becomes British prime minister.

June 29—Emergency Relief Appropriation Act, Railroad Retirement Act passed.

July 7—Outbreak of hostilities between Japan and China.

July 14—Senate majority leader Joe Robinson of Arkansas dies.

July 22—Farm Tenancy Act passed; Senate rejects Court-packing plan in 20-70 vote.

August 5—National Cancer Institute Act passed creating a new branch of the National Institute of Health in Bethesda, Maryland.

August 8—Japanese take Beijing.

August 12—FDR nominates Hugo Black to the Supreme Court.

August 20—Bonneville Power Administration Act passed to deal with the electric power produced by the new Bonneville Dam in Oregon.

August 26—FDR signs the Revenue Act, and the Judicial Procedures Reform Act. The Judicial Procedures Reform Act was a face-saving measure after Congress rejected the proposal to increase the number of justices on the Supreme Court.

August 28—FDR signs the Water Facilities Act.

September 1—Farm Security Administration established by secretary of agriculture Henry A. Wallace to supervise the programs of the Resettlement Administration and the farm ownership program.

September 2—FDR signs the Wagner-Steagall Housing Act, creating the U.S. Housing Authority.

September 16—National Emergency Council, which FDR had created on November 17, 1933, abolished.

September 25—Benito Mussolini begins three-day visit to Berlin.

October 5—FDR delivers "Quarantine" speech in Chicago challenging isolationism.

October 12—Special session of Congress on business recession.

November 9—Japanese capture Shanghai.

December 13—Nanjing (Nanking) falls to Japanese.

December 24—Japanese take Hangchow.

December 27—National Emergency Council extended.

1938

January 6—FDR opposes the Louis Ludlow proposed amendment to require a national vote prior to the declaration of war except in the event of an attack on or invasion of the United States.

January 10—U.S. House of Representatives narrowly defeats the Ludlow Amendment by a 209-188 vote.

January 15—After Justice George Sutherland, one of the four most conservative members of the Supreme Court, retires, FDR nominates Stanley F. Reed, the solicitor general, to replace him.

January 28—FDR sends special defense armaments message to Congress.

February 3—FDR signs Housing Act.

February 10—Federal National Mortgage Association established.

February 16—A new Agricultural Adjustment Act (AAA) is passed after the first was invalidated by Supreme Court; Federal Crop Insurance Act passed.

March 13—Hitler declares Austria a province of the German Reich.

April 16—Anglo-Italian Pact, in which British recognize Italian sovereignty over Ethiopia, is agreed.

May 17—FDR signs Naval Expansion Act authorizing a 10-year construction program.

May 26—Military officers assume preeminence in Japanese cabinet.

May 27—Revenue Act enacted without FDR's support.

June 21—National Gas Act passed; FDR signs the Emergency Relief Appropriation Act allocating $3 billion for new jobs.

June 22—FDR signs the Chandler Act to protect small investors.

June 23—FDR signs the Civil Aeronautics Act moving the Bureau of Air Commerce from the Commerce Department and renames it the Civil Aeronautics Authority.

June 24—FDR announces his plan to actively participate in the Democratic primaries and to defeat conservative incumbents. The so-called purge fails.

June 25—FDR signs the Fair Labor Standards Act setting a mandatory minimum wage and maximum work hours per week; Food, Drug, and Cosmetics Act passed.

August 13—U.S. Film Service established.

September 26—FDR appeals to European leaders to negotiate the Czechoslovakian crisis.

September 27—FDR appeals to Adolf Hitler for a peaceful resolution.

September 30—Mussolini, Neville Chamberlain, and Édouard Daladier give Sudetenland to Germany; Chamberlain proclaims Munich meeting has achieved "peace in our time."

November 8—In midterm elections, Democrats suffer first electoral setback during FDR administration, losing 71 seats in the U.S. House, seven in the U.S. Senate, and 13 governorships.

November 17—Conclusion of trade agreements among Britain, Canada, and the United States.

December 10—FDR announces plans for his eventual presidential library at Hyde Park, New York.

December 24—Declaration of Lima at the Pan-American conference adopted by 21 nations in the Americas, affirming solidarity and opposition to foreign intervention.

1939

January 14—Federal Real Estate Board established.

January 30—Supreme Court upholds the TVA.

February 26—Eleanor Roosevelt resigns from the Daughters of the American Revolution after it denies Marian Anderson a booking in Constitutional Hall.

March 20—After Justice Louis D. Brandeis retires, FDR nominates William O. Douglas to the Supreme Court.

April 1—FDR recognizes Franco Spain.

April 3—FDR signs the Administrative Reorganization Act, which had been stalled due to the Supreme Court–packing plan. It establishes the Office of the White House, institutionalizing the modern presidency.

April 7—Italian invasion of Albania.

April 9—Opera singer Marian Anderson gives performance at Lincoln Memorial.

April 14—FDR asks Adolf Hitler and Benito Mussolini not to attack or invade European and Middle Eastern nations.

April 26—FDR sends special message to Congress requesting immediate construction of additional naval bases in the United States, Alaska, Puerto Rico, and the Pacific.

May 16—Food Stamp Plan implemented.

June 7–11—The first-ever visit by the king and queen of Great Britain to the United States for five days.

June 30—FDR signs the Emergency Relief Appropriation Act.

July 1—Executive Branch Reorganization implemented; Federal Loan Agency, Federal Security Agency, Federal Works Agency, National Resources Planning Board established.

July 6—Monetary Act passed.

July 18—FDR requests revisions to the Neutrality Act.

August 2—FDR signs the Hatch Act regarding the political activity of classified federal employees.

August 4—FDR signs the Reclamation Project Act.

August 23—Germany and USSR sign nonaggression pact in Moscow.

August 24—FDR appeals to Adolf Hitler and President Ignaz Moszicki of Poland to resolve differences through peaceful means.

September 1—Nazi Germany invades Poland; France and Great Britain declare war two days later, and World War II in Europe begins.

September 5—The United States proclaims its neutrality in European war.

September 8—Bureau of the Budget established in the new executive office of the president. FDR issues proclamation of limited national emergency.

September 11—Title II of the Sugar Act of 1937 suspended.

September 21—FDR urges repeal of embargo provisions of Neutrality Act during address to Congress.

September 29—Germany and the USSR divide Poland between them.

October 21—First meeting of the President's Advisory Committee on Uranium.

November 4—Neutrality Act is modified to allow belligerent nations to buy U.S. arms on cash-and-carry basis.

November 30—Soviet army invades Poland.

December 1—FDR condemns Soviet invasion of Finland.

1940

January 3—FDR delivers the seventh State of the Union message to Congress warning against foreign entanglements.

January 4—After the death of Justice Pierce Butler, one of the four most conservative justices on the Supreme Court, FDR names attorney general Frank Murphy to replace him.

February 13—FDR sends special message to Congress calling for an immediate appropriation for strategic war materials.

March 30—Japanese set up puppet Chinese government headed by Wang Ching-wei (Wang Jingwei) in Nanking (Nanjing).

April 4—Winston Churchill is given general direction over British defense program.

April 9—Nazi forces occupy Denmark and invade Norway.

April 22—*Thornhill v. Alabama* restricts power of states to interfere with right of labor to picket peacefully.

May 10—Nazi forces cross into Belgium, Holland, and Luxembourg; Winston Churchill becomes prime minister of Great Britain.

May 26—During a Fireside Chat FDR emphasizes the need for a national defense program.

May 31—FDR sends special message to Congress requesting an additional appropriation for national defense and the authority to call up the National Guard and Reserves.

June 10—FDR issues proclamation of neutrality in war between Italy and France and Britain.

June 13—Congress passes the Military Supply Act.

June 22—France signs armistice with Nazi Germany; Vichy government created.

June 24—FDR signs the Emergency Relief Appropriation Act.

June 27—FDR declares national emergency.

June 28—Congress passes the Alien Registration Act; Republican National Convention in Philadelphia nominates Wendell Willkie of New York for president and Charles McNary of Oregon for vice president.

July 5—Vichy government severs relations with Britain. FDR suggests Four Freedoms during a press conference.

July 6—FDR meets with National Democratic Committee chairman James Farley and informs him of plan to seek third term.

July 9—U.S. Senate confirms Republican Henry Stimson as secretary of war.

July 10—U.S. Senate confirms Republican Frank Knox, Alf Landon's running mate in 1936, as secretary of the navy.

July 18—FDR is nominated for unprecedented third term, with Henry Wallace for vice president; Eleanor Roosevelt addresses the convention, helping to unite the Democratic Party after FDR's advocacy of Henry Wallace on the ticket.

July 19—Second Hatch Act passed; FDR signs the Two-Ocean Navy Expansion Act.

July 25—The United States announces it will no longer export oil and scrap metal to nations outside Western hemisphere, except Great Britain.

August 18—FDR and Prime Minister William Lyon MacKenzie King of Canada set up joint board of defense.

August 22—Investment Advisers Act passed.

September 3—FDR announces "destroyers-for-bases" deal with Great Britain.

September 16—FDR signs the Selective Service Act of 1940, which creates local draft boards.

September 18—FDR signs the Transportation Act.

September 22—Japanese begin occupation of Indochina.

September 26—FDR places embargo on export of scrap iron and steel, especially aimed at Japan.

September 27—Nazi Germany, Italy, and Japan sign the Tripartite Pact.

October 16—Registration for selective service begins.

October 28—Italy invades Greece.

November 5—FDR defeats Republican Wendell Willkie with 54.8 percent of the vote, winning a third term in office.

November 20—Britain and the United States agree to partial standardization of military weapons and equipment.

December 10—FDR announces further limits on iron and steel exports, which deprive Japan of needed material.

December 20—FDR names four-member Defense Board.

December 23—Anthony Eden becomes British foreign secretary; Lord Halifax named British ambassador to the United States.

1941

January 6—FDR delivers his "Four Freedoms" State of the Union address, which defines his concept of America's role in the world.

January 8—FDR appoints four-member Office of Production Management.

January 20—FDR is inaugurated for his third presidential term.

February 3—*U.S. v. Darby* upholds the Fair Labor Standards Act.

March 11—FDR signs the Lend-Lease Act.

June 12—After Justice George Sutherland, the last of the four most conservative justices retires, FDR names James F. Byrnes to the Supreme Court. Harlan F. Stone replaces Charles Evans Hughes as chief justice, and attorney general Robert H. Jackson is nominated to replace Stone's former position as a justice. Though FDR lost the so-called Supreme Court–packing plan, he wins the larger battle to reconstitute the membership of the Court.

May 27—FDR proclaims unlimited state of national emergency because of crisis in Europe.

June 14—FDR freezes all German and Italian assets in the United States.

June 16—FDR closes all German and Italian consulates in the United States.

June 22—Nazi Germany attacks USSR (Operation Barbarossa); U.S. extends lend-lease program.

June 24—FDR promises aid to the Soviet Union.

June 25—FDR creates the Committee on Fair Employment Practice, mandates the end of racial discrimination on defense contracts and government employment.

June 30—FDR dedicates the Franklin D. Roosevelt Library, Hyde Park, New York.

July 7—FDR announces occupation of Iceland on invitation of government.

July 13—FDR sends Harry L. Hopkins to confer with Winston Churchill in London.

July 26—FDR freezes Japanese assets in the United States in response to the Japanese occupation of Indochina.

August 1—FDR stops exportation of oil and aviation in Western Hemisphere except for Great Britain.

August 9–12—FDR and Churchill meet at Placentia Bay, Newfoundland, and agree to Atlantic Charter.

August 18—FDR signs bill permitting U.S. Army to keep men in service one month longer.

September 7—Sara Delano Roosevelt, FDR's mother, dies at age 85.

September 22—Eleanor Roosevelt appointed assistant director of the Office of Civilian Defense (OCD).

October 16—Hideki Tojo becomes Japan's new prime minister.

October 28—FDR establishes the Lend-Lease Administration.

November 6—The United States extends $1 million lend-lease credit to USSR.

November 7—FDR declares the defense of the Soviet Union vital to the United States.

November 24—*Edwards v. California* invalidates California's so-called Okie Law statute.

December 6—FDR sends personal appeal to Emperor Hirohito of Japan for peace.

December 7—Japan attacks Pearl Harbor.

December 8—Congress declares war against Japan.

December 11—Nazi Germany and Italy declare war on the United States. FDR sends special message to Congress asking that a state of war be recognized between Germany and Italy and the United States.

December 12—Japanese capture Guam.

December 15—Congress passes appropriation of over $800 million for defense and lend-lease.

December 18—FDR appoints commission with Owen Roberts at its head to investigate Pearl Harbor attack.

December 22—Churchill arrives in Washington, D.C., for the Arcadia Conference to discuss war strategy with FDR until January 14; combined Chiefs of Staff to coordinate Anglo-American war policy.

December 23—Free French take possession of St. Pierre and Miquelon off coast of Newfoundland.

December 25—Hong Kong captured by Japanese.

1942

January 1—FDR signs joint declaration of United Nations at the White House pledging cooperation for victory in the war.

January 2—Manila, Philippines, falls to the Japanese.

January 9—FDR delivers his ninth State of the Union message to Congress stating the war was started by militarists in Berlin and Tokyo.

January 12—FDR establishes National War Labor Board with power to adjudicate labor disputes requiring mediation.

January 16—FDR establishes War Production Board.

January 24—The Roberts Commission submits its report on the Pearl Harbor attack.

January 26—First American troops arrive in Great Britain.

January 30—FDR signs Price Control Act to limit inflation.

February 1—Vidkun Quisling named head of Nazi puppet government in Norway.

February 7—FDR approves Lend-Lease aid to China, and establishes War Shipping Administration.

February 15—Japanese take Singapore.

February 19—FDR issues Executive Order 9066 authorizing the removal of Japanese Americans from the West Coast.

February 24—FDR establishes National Housing Agency.

March 8—The United States and Great Britain name General Joseph Stillwell to command an Allied force in Burma.

March 11—FDR orders General Douglas MacArthur to leave the Philippines and go to Australia to assume command of the Allied forces in the Southwest Pacific.

March 18—FDR issues executive order establishing War Relocation Authority.

April 4—U.S. War Production Board halts all nonessential building.

April 9—Filipino and American troops surrender to Japanese on Bataan.

April 18—Lieutenant Colonel James Doolittle leads air attack on Tokyo.

May 8—The Battle of the Coral Sea takes place; the Japanese lose many aircraft.

May 14—Women's Auxiliary Air Corps authorized.

June 4—The Battle of Midway Island in the Pacific is turning point for the United States in the Pacific.

June 9—The United States and Great Britain pool resources and production.

June 13—FDR establishes Office of Strategic Services (OSS).

June 18—Churchill confers with FDR at White House; disagreement between them on first Allied offensive.

June 30—Congress appropriates $42 million for defense.

July 6—Argentina declares neutrality.

July 16—War Labor Board decrees wage stabilization plan.

July 25—FDR and Churchill agree on Americans to join British Eighth Army in North Africa by an American landing behind German lines in the west; Dwight Eisenhower named commander in charge.

July 30—Women Appointed for Voluntary Emergency Services (WAVES), the women's branch of the navy, is established.

August 7—U.S. Marines land in Guadalcanal in the Solomon Islands in the Pacific.

November 3—The United States severs relations with Vichy government.

November 3—In midterm elections, the Democrats lose 55 seats in the U.S. House.

November 7—Operation Torch begins with the landing of American forces in French North Africa led by Dwight Eisenhower; they occupy Casablanca and Oran by November 11.

November 12—Naval battle in Solomon Islands ends in U.S. victory.

December 1—With U.S. and British approval, Admiral Jean-Louis-Xavier-François Darlan is appointed head of state in French North Africa.

December 2—Enrico Fermi and other scientists at the University of Chicago achieve the first human-made atomic reactor, marking the first step in developing the atomic bomb. FDR establishes Petroleum Administration for War.

December 4—FDR terminates the WPA with war production at full steam.

December 24—Admiral Darlan assassinated.

1943

January 7—FDR delivers his tenth State of the Union message to Congress, detailing progress on military and naval production.

January 11—After Justice James F. Byrnes resigns from the Supreme Court, FDR names Wiley B. Rutledge to replace him. It is FDR's ninth and final appointee to the Court.

January 14–23—FDR and Churchill meet for 10 days at Casablanca, Morocco, Conference and demand unconditional surrender terms for Axis powers.

January 20—Japanese begin to withdraw from Guadalcanal.

January 28—FDR and President Vargas of Brazil meet at Natal, Brazil.

February 2—Nazi troops surrender at Stalingrad.

March 12—Congress extends lend-lease another year.

April 8—FDR freezes wages and prices to combat inflation.

May 1—FDR issues executive order to secretary of the interior to seize coal mines after a general strike begins.

May 2—FDR gives fireside chat on mine seizure.

May 12—FDR and Churchill meet at White House for the Trident Conference and secretly agree on May 1944 as date for invasion of France.

May 27—FDR establishes the Office of War Mobilization to coordinate war effort in the United States.

May 28—President Edwin Barclay of Liberia becomes the first chief executive of a sub-Sahara African nation to address the U.S. Congress.

June 9—FDR signs a pay-as-you-go income tax act with a 20 percent withholding of taxable income for wage and salary earners.

June 23—FDR calls the action of the United Mine Workers (UMW) "intolerable" after the third interruption of coal production.

June 25—War Labor Disputes Act passed over FDR's veto. The Smith-Connally Anti-Strike Act made illegal strikes in plants seized by the government.

July 10—British and American invasion of Sicily begins.

July 16—FDR establishes Office of Economic Warfare.

July 24—Italian Grand Council removes Mussolini from power.

August 11—First Quebec conference with FDR and Churchill begins.

August 25—FDR becomes the first president to visit Ottawa, Ontario, the capital of Canada. He arrives from Quebec, where he confers with Churchill.

September 3—Italy surrenders to the Allies.

October 9—Yugoslav guerrilla forces under Marshall Tito open offensive against Axis troops in Trieste region.

October 12—Nazis withdraw to north of Naples, Italy.

October 13—Italy's new leader, Marshall Pietro Badoglio, declares war on Nazi Germany.

November 9—UN Relief and Rehabilitation Administration established by 44 nations at Washington, D.C.

November 22–24—Cairo, Egypt, conference with FDR, Churchill, and Chiang Kai-shek begins; Allied commitment to invade Burma made.

November 28–December 1—FDR, Churchill, and Josef Stalin meet together for the first time at the Tehran conference and agree on the invasion of southern France; Stalin commits Soviet troops against Japan after Nazis are defeated.

December 4—The second Cairo conference is held with FDR, Churchill, and President Ismet Inonu of Turkey reaffirming friendship among the United States, Great Britain, Turkey, and the Soviet Union.

December 27—FDR orders Secretary of War Henry Stimson to assume control of railroads until dispute between owners and unions is resolved.

1944

January 11—FDR sends the eleventh State of the Union message to Congress, his only one not delivered in person. He outlines an "Economic Bill of Rights," and asks for a national service law.

January 18—FDR opens the fourth war loan drive.

January 19—Railroads returned to private control after the owners and unions resolve issues.

January 22—Allied forces land at Anzio, Italy.

January 27—Argentina severs relations with Nazi Germany and Japan after discovery of espionage plot.

March 6—U.S. bombing raids of Berlin begin.

June 4—Rome becomes first occupied European capital to be liberated.

June 6—Allied invasion of Normandy begins ("D-Day"). Operation Overlord, the invasion of France, is the largest amphibious military operation in history.

June 12—FDR opens the fourth war loan drive.

June 20—Soviet offensive against Finland begins.

June 22—FDR signs the G.I. Bill of Rights (Servicemen's Readjustment Act).

June 28—Republican National Convention held in Chicago selects New York governor Thomas Dewey for president and U.S. senator John Bricker of Ohio for vice president.

July 11—The United States recognizes French Committee of National Liberation, headed by Charles de Gaulle; FDR announces at news conference he is willing to seek a fourth presidential term.

July 18—General Tojo and his cabinet resign.

July 20—FDR is renominated for president at the Democratic National Convention in Chicago.

August 7—Dumbarton Oaks conference begins in Washington, D.C., with representatives of the United States, Britain, USSR, and China planning the groundwork for the United Nations. The conference will run to October.

August 11—Recapture of Guam by U.S. forces.

August 12—Florence, Italy, taken by Allies.

August 25—Allied troops liberate Paris.

September 2—Allies liberate Belgium.

September 4—Morganthau Plan for Germany completed.

September 11–16—Second Quebec Conference is held; Churchill and FDR discuss postwar policy toward Germany.

September 23—FDR delivers the "Fala" speech at Teamsters Union dinner in Washington, D.C.

October 5—FDR calls for the end of poll taxes.

October 13—Athens occupied by Allied forces.

November 7—FDR reelected in the closest of his four presidential bids. He defeats Thomas E. Dewey.

November 27—Edward Stettinius succeeds Cordell Hull as secretary of state.

December 16—Battle of the Bulge in southern Belgium.

1945

January 6—The largest single beach assault in the Pacific takes place at Lingayen Gulf, Philippines.

January 20—FDR delivers his fourth inaugural address, a six-minute speech, the first held at the White House under the South Portico.

February 3—Battle for Manila begins; it takes Allied troops 20 days to capture the city.

February 4–11—Yalta Conference in the Crimea with FDR, Churchill, and Stalin. They agree to occupation zones in postwar Germany, a freely elected Polish government, and a UN conference in San Francisco.

February 19—Iwo Jima Marine assault begins; American flag raised atop Mt. Suribachi on February 23.

February 21–March 8—Inter-American Conference on Problems of War and Peace in Chapultepec, Mexico.

February 28—FDR appoints delegates to the UN conference.

March 1—FDR addresses Congress on Yalta Conference.

March 23—American forces cross Rhine at Remagen.

March 27—Argentina declares war on Nazi Germany and Japan.

April 1—U.S. Marines and Army invade Okinawa.

April 5—Soviets renounce five-year nonaggression pact with Japan. FDR holds his final press conference at the Little White House in Warm Springs, Georgia.

April 11—U.S. Ninth Army reaches the Elbe.

April 12—FDR dies in Warm Spring, Georgia. Harry S. Truman succeeds to the presidency.

Principal U.S. Government Officials of the FDR Years

Supreme Court

Charles Evans Hughes, Chief Justice,
   1930–1941
Harlan Fiske Stone, Associate Justice,
   1925–1941; Chief Justice, 1941–1946
Hugo L. Black, 1937–1971
Louis D. Brandeis, 1916–1939
Pierce Butler, 1923–1939
James F. Byrnes, 1941–1942
Benjamin N. Cardozo, 1932–1938

Felix Frankfurter, 1939–1962
Robert H. Jackson, 1941–1954
James C. McReynolds, 1914–1941
Frank Murphy, 1940–1949
Stanley F. Reed, 1938–1957
Owen J. Roberts, 1930–1945
Wiley B. Rutledge, 1943–1949
George Sutherland, 1922–1938
Willis Van Devanter, 1911–1937

Executive Departments

Department of Agriculture
Secretary of Agriculture
   Henry A. Wallace, 1933–1940
   Claude R. Wickard, 1940–1941
   Clinton Anderson, 1945–1948

Department of Commerce
Secretary of Commerce
   Daniel C. Roper, 1933–1938
   Harry L. Hopkins, 1938–1940
   Jesse H. Jones, 1941–1945
   Henry A. Wallace, 1945–1946

Department of the Interior
Secretary of the Interior
   Harold L. Ickes, 1933–1946

Department of Justice
Attorney General
   Homer S. Cummings, 1933–1938
   Frank Murphy, 1939
   Robert H. Jackson, 1940
   Francis Biddle, 1941–1945

Department of Labor
Secretary of Labor
   Frances Perkins, 1933–1945

Department of State
Secretary of State
   Cordell Hull, 1933–1944
   Edward R. Stettinius, 1944–1945

Department of the Treasury

Secretary of the Treasury
William A. Woodin, 1933
Henry Morgenthau, Jr., 1934–1945

Department of War

Secretary of War
George H. Dun, 1933–1936
Harry Woodring, 1936–1940
Henry L. Stimson, 1940–1945

Secretary of the Navy
Claude Swanson, 1933–1939
Charles Edison, 1939–1940
Frank Knox, 1940–1944
James Forrestal, 1944–1947

Bureau of the Budget

Daniel W. Bell, Acting Director,
1933–1938
Harold D. Smith, Director, 1939–1946

Regulatory Commissions and Independent Agencies

Federal Reserve Board

Marriner S. Eccles, Chair, 1934–1948
Eugene R. Black, Governor, 1933
Charles S. Hamlin, 1933–1935
George R. James, 1933–1935
Adolph Miller, 1933–1934
M. S. Szymczak, 1933–1941
J. J. Thomas, 1933–1945
Joseph A. Broderick, 1936
Chester C. Davis, 1936–1940

Securities and Exchange Commission

Joseph P. Kennedy, Chair, 1934
James M. Landis, Chair, 1935–1936
William O. Douglas, Chair, 1937–1938
Jerome N. Frank, Chair, 1939–1940
Edward C. Eicher Chair, 1941–1942
Ganson Purcell, 1941–1946

Other Agencies

Agricultural Adjustment Administration

George N. Peek, Administrator, 1933
Chester C. Davis, Administrator,
1934–1935
Howard R. Tolley, Administrator,
1936–1938
Rudolph M. Evans, Administrator,
1938–1941

Automobile Labor Board

Richard Byrd, 1934

Nicholas Kelley, 1934
Leo Wolman, 1934

Board of Economic Warfare

Henry A. Wallace, Chair, 1942–1944

Bureau of Indian Affairs

John Collier, Commissioner, 1933–1944

Civil Aeronautics Authority

Edward J. Noble, Chair, 1938–1939

Robert H. Hinckley, Chair, 1939–1940

J. Welch Pogue, Chair, 1944

Donald H. Connolly, Administrator of Civil Aeronautics, 1940–1942

Harllee Branch, Chair, Civil Aeronautics Board

Civilian Conservation Corps

Robert Fechner, Director, 1933–1939

J. J. McEntee, Director, 1940–1941

Civil Works Administration

Harry L. Hopkins, Administrator, 1933–1934

Commodity Credit Corporation

Lynn P. Talley, President, 1933–1938

Carl B. Robbins, President, 1939–1940

J. B. Hutson, President, 1941

Comptroller of the Currency

J. F. T. O'Connor, 1933–1937

Preston Delano, 1938–1941

Cotton Textile Board

John G. Winant, Chair, 1934

Marion Smith, 1934

Raymond V. Ingersoll, 1934

Cotton Textile National Industrial Relations Board

Robert W. Bruere, Chair, 1933–1934

George L. Berry, 1933–1934

B. E. Green, 1933–1934

C. M. Fox, 1934

Arthur Dixon, 1934

Electric Home and Farm Authority

Emil Schram, President, 1936–1940

A. T. Hobson, President, 1941

Export-Import Bank of Washington

George N. Peek, President, 1935

Warren Lee Pierson, President, 1936–1941

Leo Crowley, Chair, 1944–1945

Farm Credit Administration

Henry Morgenthau, Jr., Governor, 1933

William I. Myers, Governor, 1934–1937

F. F. Hill, Governor, 1938–1939

Albert G. Black, Governor, 1940–1941

Farm Security Administration

Will W. Alexander, Administrator, 1937–1939

C. B. Baldwin, Administrator, 1940–1941

Federal Alcohol Administration

Franklin Chase Hoyt, Administrator, 1935

Wilford S. Alexander, Administrator, 1936–1940

Federal Art Project

Holger Cahill, Director, 1935–1941

Federal Bureau of Investigation

J. Edgar Hoover, Director, 1933–1972

Federal Communications Commission

Eugene O. Sykes, Chair, 1934; Member, 1935–1938

Anning S. Prall, Chair, 1935–1936

Frank R. McNinck, Chair, 1937–1938

James Lawrence Fly, Chair, 1939–1944

Thad H. Brown, 1934–1939

Norman S. Case, 1934–1941

Hampson Gary, 1934

George Henry Payne, 1934–1941

Irvin Stewart, 1934–1936

Paul A. Walker, 1934–1941

T. A. M. Craven, 1936–1941

Frederick I. Thompson, 1939–1940

R. C. Wakefield, 1941

Paul Potter, 1945

Federal Crop Insurance Corporation

Leroy K. Smith, Manager, 1938–1941

Federal Dance Project

Don Becque, Supervisor, 1935–1936

Lincoln Kirstein, Supervisor, 1937,
  resigned after one day
Stephen Karnot, Administrative Assistant,
  1937–1938
Evelyn David, Coordinator of Dance
  Activities, 1938–1939

Federal Deposit Insurance Corporation
Walter J. Cummings, Chair, 1933
Leo T. Crowley, Chair, 1934–1941

Federal Emergency Relief Administration
Harry L. Hopkins, Administrator,
  1933–1938

Federal Farm Mortgage Corporation
William I. Myers, President, 1934–1937
F. F. Hill, President, 1938
A. T. Esgate, Executive Vice President,
  1939
J. H. Guill, Vice President, 1940–1941

Federal Housing Administration
James Moffett, Administrator, 1934
Stewart McDonald, Administrator,
  1935–1940
Abner H. Ferguson, Administrator,
  1941–1944
Raymond Foley, Commissioner, 1945

Federal Loan Agency
Jesse H. Jones, 1939–1942

Federal Music Project
Nikolai Sokoloff, Director, 1935–1939

Federal National Mortgage Association
Sam H. Husbands, President, 1938–1944

Federal Power Commission
Frank R. McNinch, Chair, 1933–1936
Herbert H. Drane, 1933–1936
Claude L. Draper, 1933–1941
Basil Manly, 1933–1941; Acting Chair, 1944

George O. Smith, 1933
Clyde L. Seavey, 1934–1939; Chair,
  1937–1939
John W. Scott, 1937–1941
Leland Olds, 1939–1941, Chair,
  1940–1942, 1945
Leon M. Fuquay, 1939–1941

Federal Prison Industries, Inc.
Sanford Bates, President, 1935–1941

Federal Real Estate Board
D. H. Sawyer, Chair, 1939–1941
John K. McKee, 1936–1941
Ronald Ransom, 1936–1941
Ernest G. Draper, 1938–1941

Federal Savings and Loan Insurance Corporation
Nugent Fallon, General Manager,
  1934–1940
Oscar R. Kreutz, General Manager, 1941

Federal Security Agency
Paul V. McNutt, Administrator, 1939–1942
Watson R. Miller, Administrator, 1945

Federal Surplus Commodities Corporation
Chester C. Davis, President, 1935
Francis R. Wilcox, President, 1936
Jesse W. Tapp, President, 1937–1938
Milo Perkins, President, 1939;
  Administrator, 1940–1941

Federal Surplus Relief Corporation
Harry L. Hopkins, 1934

Federal Theatre Project
Hallie V. Flanagan, Director, 1935–1939

Federal Trade Commission
Charles H. March, 1934–1940; Chair,
  1933, 1936, 1941
Garland S. Ferguson, 1933–1941; Chair,
  1934, 1938

Ewin L. Davis, 1933–1941; Chair, 1935, 1940
William A. Ayres, 1934–1941; Chair, 1937
Robert E. Freer, 1935–1941; Chair, 1939, 1944, 1945
William E. Humphrey, 1933
Otis Johnson, 1933–1940
Raymond Stevens, 1933

Federal Works Agency

John M. Carmody, Administrator, 1939–1941
Philip B. Fleming, Chair, 1942–1945

Federal Writers Project

Henry G. Alsberg, Director, 1935–1939

First Export-Import Bank

George N. Peek, President, 1934–1935

First National Labor Relations Board

Lloyd Garrison, Chair, 1934
Francis Biddle, Chair, 1935
Harry A. Mills, 1934
Edwin S. Smith, 1934

Historical Records Survey

Luther H. Evans, National Director, 1935–1939
Sargent P. Childs, National Director, 1940–1941

Home Owners Loan Corporation

William F. Stevenson, Chair, 1933
John H. Fahey, Chair, 1934–1938
Charles A. Jones, General Manager, 1939–1941
Charles F. Cotter, General Manager, 1942

Indian Arts and Crafts Board

Louis C. West, General Manager, 1936–1937
Rene d'Harnoncourt, General Manager, 1937–1941

Interstate Commerce Commission

Patrick J. Farrell, 1933–1934; Chair, 1933
William E. Lee, 1933–1941; Chair, 1934
Hugh M. Tate, 1933–1936; Chair, 1935
Charles D. Mahaffie, 1933–1936; Chair, 1936
Carroll Miller, 1933–1941; Chair, 1937
Walter M. Splawn, 1934–1941; Chair, 1938
Joseph B. Eastman, 1933–1941; Chair, 1939–1941
William J. Patterson, 1939–1944; Chair, 1944
Ezra Brainerd, Jr., 1933
Balthassal Meyer, 1933–1938
Clyde B. Atchison, 1933–1941
Frank McManamy, 1933–1938
Claude Porter, 1933–1941
Marion Caskie, 1935–1938
John Rogers, 1937–1941
J. Haden Alldridge, 1939–1941
J. Monroe Johnson, 1940–1941

Maritime Labor Board

Robert W. Bruere, Chair, 1938–1942
Louis Block, 1938–1941
Claude E. Seehorn, 1938–1941

National Bituminous Coal Commission

John M. Paris, Chair, 1935
C. F. Hosford, Jr., Chair, 1935–1936

National Bituminous Coal Labor Board

Judge J. D. Acuff, 1933–1935
John M. Carmody, 1933–1935
T. S. Hogan, 1933–1935
M. S. Johnson, 1933–1935
John A. Lapp, 1933–1935

National Defense Advisory Commission

Edward R. Stettinius, 1940

National Emergency Council

Donald Richberg, Executive Director, 1934

Frank C. Walker, Executive Director, 1935
Eugene S. Leggett, Acting Executive
Director, 1936–1937
Lowell Mellett, Executive Director,
1938–1939

National Institute of Health
George W. McCoy, 1933–1937
Lewis R. Thompson, 1938–1941

National Labor Board
Senator Robert Wagner, Chair, 1933–1934
Henry S. Dennison, 1933–1934
Ernst Draper, 1933–1934
Pierre S. du Pont, 1933–1934
William Green, 1933–1934
Dr. Francis J. Hass, 1933–1934
Louis E. Kirstein, 1933–1934
John L. Lewis, 1933–1934
Leon C. Marshall, 1933–1934
Walter C. Teagle, 1933–1934
S. Clay Williams, 1933–1934
Leo Wolman, 1933–1934

National Longshoremen's Labor Board
Archbishop Edward J. Hanna, 1934–1935
Edward F. McGrady, 1934–1935
D. K. Cushing, 1934–1935

National Planning Board
Frederic A. Delano, Chair, 1933–1943

National Recovery Administration
Hugh S. Johnson, Administrator, 1933
Clay Williams, Administrator, 1934
Laurence J. Martin, Acting Administrator,
1935

National Resources Board
Harold L. Ickes, Chair, 1934
Frederic A. Delano, Chair, 1935–1938

National Resources Planning Board
Frederic A. Delano, Chair, 1939–1941

National Steel Labor Relations Board
Judge Walter Stacy, Chair, 1934–1935
Dr. James Mullenback, 1934–1935
Rear Admiral Henry Wiley, 1934–1935

National Youth Administration
Aubrey Williams, Executive Director,
1935–1941

Office of Civilian Defense
Fiorello H. LaGuardia, Director,
1942–1944
Eleanor Roosevelt, Assistant Director,
1942–1944
William N. Haskell, Director, 1944–1945

Office of Economic Stabilization
James F. Byrnes, Director, 1943
Fred M. Vinson, Director, 1944
William H. Davis, Director, 1945

Office of Price Administration
Leon Henderson, Administrator, 1941–1942
Prentiss H. Brown, Administrator, 1943
Chester Bowles, Administrator,
1944–1945

Office of Production Management
William Knudsen, 1941
Sidney Hillman, 1941

Office of War Mobilization and Reconversion
James F. Byrnes, Director, 1944–1945

Petroleum Labor Policy Board
Nathan R. Margold, Chair, 1933–1934
Seth W. Candee, 1933–1934
H. C. Fleming, 1933–1934
Charles C. Jones, 1933–1934
R. H. Ivory, 1933–1934
Dr. George W. Stocking, 1933–1934
R. R. Zimmerman, 1933–1934
Dr. John A. Lapp, 1935–1936
James P. Pope, 1939–1940

Public Works Administration
Harold L. Ickes, Administrator, 1933–1939
Colonel E. W. Clark, Commissioner of
Public Works, 1939–1940
Maurice Gilmore, Commissioner of Public
Works, 1941–1942

Reconstruction Finance Corporation
Jesse H. Jones, Chair, 1933–1938
Emil Schram, Chair, 1939–1940
Charles B. Henderson, Chair, 1941–1944

Resettlement Administration
Rexford G. Tugwell, Administrator,
1935–1936

Rural Electrification Administration
Morris L. Cooke, Administrator,
1935–1936
John M. Carmody, Administrator,
1937–1938
Harry Slattery, Administrator, 1939–1941

Second Export-Import Bank
George N. Peek, President, 1934–1935

Second National Bituminous Coal Commission
C. F. Hosgood, Chair, 1937
Percy Tetlow, Chair, 1938
Howard A. Gray, Director, 1939–1941

Second National Labor Relations Board
Joseph Warren Madden, Chair,
1935–1939
Harry A. Mills, Chair, 1941
John M. Carmody, 1935
Edwin S. Smith, 1935–1941
Donald W. Smith, 1936–1939
William Leiserson, 1939–1941

Social Security Board
John G. Winant, Chair, 1935–1936
Arthur J. Altmeyer, 1935–1941, Chair,
1937–1944

Vincent M. Miles, 1935–1936
George E. Bigge, 1937–1941
Mary Dewson, 1937–1938
Ellen S. Woodward, 1939–1941

Tennessee Valley Authority
Arthur E. Morgan, Chair, 1934–1937
Harcourt A. Morgan, 1934–1941; Chair,
1938–1941
David Lilienthal, Chair, 1934–1941, 1945
James P. Pope, 1939–1941

Textile Labor Relations Board
Judge Walker P. Stacy, Chair, 1934–1935
James Mullenback, 1934
Admiral Henry Wiley, 1934–1935
Frank P. Douglas, 1935

United States Employment Service
W. Frank Persons, Director, 1933–1939

United States Film Service
Pare Lorentz, 1938–1940

United States Housing Authority
Nathan Straus, Administrator, 1937–1942

United States Maritime Commission
Rear Admiral Henry A. Wiley, Chair, 1936
Joseph P. Kennedy, Chair, 1937
Rear Admiral Emory S. Land, Chair,
1938–1945

War Production Board
Donald M. Nelson, Chair, 1942–1944
Julius A. Krug, Chair, 1944–1945
J. A. Keco, Chair, 1945

War Resources Board
Edward R. Stettinius, Chair, 1939
Walter S. Gifford, 1939
John Pratt, 1939
Robert E. Wood, 1939
Karl Compton, 1939

Works Progress Administration
Harry L. Hopkins, Administrator, 1935–1938
Colonel F. C. Harrington, Commissioner of Work Projects, 1939

Howard Hunter, Commissioner of Work Projects, 1940–1941
Emory Land, Chair, 1945

UNITED STATES HOUSE OF REPRESENTATIVES

73rd Congress (1933–1935)

Speaker of the House
Henry T. Rainey (D-Illinois)

Majority Leader
Joseph H. Brynes (D-Tennessee)

Minority Leader
Bertrand H. Snell (R-New York)

Majority Whip
Arthur H. Greenwood (D-Indiana)

Minority Whip
Harry L. Englebright (R-California)

74th Congress (1935–1937)

Speaker of the House
Joseph W. Byrns (D-Tennessee)
William B. Bankhead (D-Alabama)

Majority Leader
William B. Bankhead (D-Alabama)

Minority Leader
Bertrand H. Snell (R-New York)

Majority Whip
Patrick J. Boland (D-Pennsylvania)

Minority Whip
Harry L. Englebright (R-California)

75th Congress (1937–1939)

Speaker of the House
William B. Bankhead (D-Alabama)

Majority Leader
Sam Rayburn (D-Texas)

Minority Leader
Bertrand H. Snell (R-New York)

Majority Whip
Patrick J. Boland (D-Pennsylvania)

Minority Whip
Harry L. Englebright (R-California)

76th Congress (1939–1941)

Speaker of the House
William B. Bankhead (D-Alabama)
Sam Rayburn (D-Texas)

Majority Leader
Sam Rayburn (D-Texas)
John W. McCormack (D-Massachusetts)

Minority Leader
Joseph W. Martin (R-Massachusetts)

Majority Whip
Patrick J. Boland (D-Pennsylvania)

Minority Whip
Harry L. Englebright (R-California)

77th Congress (1941–1943)

Speaker of the House
Sam Rayburn (D-Texas)

Majority Leader
John W. McCormack (D-Massachusetts)

Minority Leader
Joseph W. Martin (R-Massachusetts)

Majority Whip
Robert Ramspeck (D-Georgia)

Minority Whip
   Leslie C. Arends (R-Illinois)

78th Congress (1943–1945)
Speaker of the House
   Sam Rayburn (D-Texas)

Majority Leader
   John W. McCormack (D-Massachusetts)

Minority Leader
   Joseph W. Martin, Jr. (R-Massachusetts)

Majority Whip
   Robert Ramspeck (D-Georgia)

UNITED STATES SENATE

73rd Senate (1933–1935)
President
   John Nance Garner (D-Texas)

President Pro Tempore
   Key Pittman (D-Nevada)

Majority Leader
   Joseph T. Robinson (D-Arkansas)

Minority Leader
   Charles L. McNary (R-Oregon)

Majority Whip
   J. Hamilton Lewis (D-Illinois)

Minority Whip
   Felix Hebert (R-Rhode Island)

74th Senate (1935–1937)
President
   John Nance Garner (D-Texas)

President Pro Tempore
   Key Pittman (D-Nevada)

Majority Leader
   Joseph T. Robinson (D-Arkansas)

Minority Leader
   Charles L. McNary (R-Oregon)

Majority Whip
   J. Hamilton Lewis (D-Illinois)

Minority Whip
   None

75th Senate (1937–1939)
President
   Henry A. Wallace (D-Iowa)

President Pro Tempore
   Key Pittman (D-Nevada)

Majority Leader
   Joseph T. Robinson (D-Arkansas)

   Alben W. Barkley (D-Kentucky)

Minority Leader
   Charles L. McNary (R-Oregon)

Majority Whip
   J. Hamilton Lewis (D-Illinois)

Minority Whip
   None

76th Senate (1939–1941)
President
   Henry A. Wallace (D-Iowa)

President Pro Tempore
   Key Pittman (D-Nevada)
   William King (D-Utah)

Majority Leader
   Alben W. Barkley (D-Kentucky)

Minority Leader
   Charles L. McNary (R-Oregon)

Majority Whip
   Sherman Minton (D-Indiana)

77th Senate (1941–1943)

President
Harry S. Truman (D-Missouri)

President Pro Tempore
Pat Harrison (D-Mississippi)

Majority Leader
Alben W. Barkley (D-Kentucky)

Minority Leader
Charles L. McNary (R-Oregon)

Majority Whip
Lister Hill (D-Alabama)

Minority Whip
Kenneth Wherry (R-Nebraska)

78th Senate (1943–1944)

President
Harry S. Truman (D-Missouri)

President Pro Tempore
Carter Glass (D-Virginia)

Majority Leader
Alben W. Barkley (D-Kentucky)

Minority Leader
*Wallace H. White, Jr. (R-Maine)

Majority Whip
(Joseph) Lister Hill (D-Alabama)

Minority Whip
Kenneth S. Wherry (R-Nebraska)

*During Charles L. McNary's illness, White served as acting leader and was elected Republican leader in January 4, 1945.

SELECTED PRIMARY DOCUMENTS

1. "The Forgotten Man"—Radio Address, New York, April 7, 1932

2. "Bold, Persistent Experimentation"—Address at Oglethorpe University, May 22, 1932

3. Roosevelt's Address to the Democratic National Convention Accepting the Nomination, Chicago, Illinois, July 2, 1932

4. "Progressive Government Speech"—Address at the San Francisco Commonwealth Club, September 23, 1932

5. Speech on the Federal Budget, Pittsburgh, Pennsylvania, October 19, 1932

6. First Inaugural Address, March 4, 1933

7. First Fireside Chat—On the Bank Crisis, March 12, 1933

8. Fifth Fireside Chat—"On Economic Progress," June 28, 1934

9. Sixth Fireside Chat—On Moving Forward to Greater Freedom and Security, September 30, 1934

10. Speech to the Democratic National Convention, June 27, 1936

11. "I Hate War" Speech, Chautauqua, New York, August 14, 1936

12. "We Have Only Just Begun to Fight"—Campaign Address at Madison Square Garden, New York City, October 31, 1936

13. Second Inaugural Address, January 20, 1937

14. Democratic Victory Dinner Address, Washington, D.C., March 4, 1937

15. Ninth Fireside Chat—On Reorganization of the Judiciary, March 9, 1937

16. "Quarantine" Speech, Chicago, Illinois, October 5, 1937

17. Thirteenth Fireside Chat—On Party Primaries ("Purge" Chat), June 24, 1938

18. Fourteenth Fireside Chat—On the European War, September 3, 1939

19. The "Dagger Speech"—Address at the University of Virginia, Charlottesville, June 10, 1940

20. Campaign Address at Madison Square Garden, New York City, October 28, 1940

21. Campaign Speech, Boston, Massachusetts, October 30, 1940

22. FDR on Lend-Lease—Press Conference, December 17, 1940

23. Sixteenth Fireside Chat—On National Security ("Great Arsenal" Chat), December 29, 1940

24. The "Four Freedoms"—FDR's Annual Address to Congress, January 6, 1941

25. Third Inaugural Address, January 20, 1941

26. Eighteenth Fireside Chat—On Maintaining Freedom of the Seas, September 11, 1941

27. Message to Congress on the Japanese Attack at Pearl Harbor, December 8, 1941

28. The "Fala Speech"—Campaign Address at the Teamsters' Union Dinner, September 23, 1944

29. Address to the Foreign Policy Association Dinner, New York City, October 21, 1944

30. Fourth Inaugural Address, January 20, 1945

1. "The Forgotten Man"—Radio Address, Albany, New York, April 7, 1932

FDR delivered his "Forgotten Man" address on the radio from Albany, New York, during his campaign to receive the 1932 presidential nomination by the Democrats. He identifies with the victims of the Great Depression. The speech was largely written by Raymond Moley.

Although I understand that I am talking under the auspices of the Democratic National Committee, I do not want to limit myself to politics. I do not want to feel that I am addressing an audience of Democrats or that I speak merely as a Democrat myself. The present condition of our national affairs is too serious to be viewed through partisan eyes for partisan purposes.

. . . The generalship of that moment [World War I] conceived of a whole Nation mobilized for war, economic, industrial, social and military resources gathered into a vast unit capable of and actually in the process of throwing into the scales ten million men equipped with physical needs and sustained by the realization that behind them were the united efforts of 110,000,000 human beings. It was a great plan because it was built from bottom to top and not from top to bottom.

In my calm judgment, the Nation faces today a more grave emergency than in 1917.

It is said that Napoleon lost the battle of Waterloo because he forgot his infantry—he staked too much on the more spectacular but less substantial cavalry. The present administration in Washington provides a close parallel. It has either forgotten or it does not want to remember the infantry of our economic army.

These unhappy times call for the building of plans that rest upon the forgotten, the unorganized but the indispensable units of economic power, for plans like those of 1917 that build from the bottom up and not from the top down, that put their faith once more in the forgotten man at the bottom of the economic pyramid. . . .

. . . A real economic cure must go to the killing of the bacteria in the system rather than to the treatment of external symptoms. . . .

Such objectives as these three, restoring farmers' buying power, relief to the small banks and homeowners and a reconstructed tariff policy, are only a part of ten or a dozen vital factors. But they seem to be beyond the concern of a national administration which can think in terms only of the top of the social and economic structure. It has sought temporary relief from the top down rather than permanent relief from the bottom up. It has totally failed to plan ahead in a comprehensive way. It has waited until something has cracked and then at the last moment has sought to prevent total collapse.

It is high time to get back to fundamentals. It is high time to admit with courage that we are in the midst of an emergency at least equal to that of war. Let us mobilize to meet it.

Source: Samuel I. Rosenman, ed., *The Public Papers and Addresses of Franklin D. Roosevelt* (1939; reprint, New York: Russell and Russell, 1969, 1: 624–627.

2. "Bold, Persistent Experimentation"— Address at Oglethorpe University, May 22, 1932

This speech, written by Ernest Lindley, was delivered at Oglethorpe University in Atlanta, Georgia. FDR attacked Herbert Hoover and promised to redistribute income without saying how he would do it.

President Jacobs, members and friends of Oglethorpe University and especially you, my fellow members of the Class of 1932:

For me, as for you, this is a day of honorable attainment. For the honor conferred upon me I am deeply grateful, and I felicitate you on yours, even though I cannot share with you that greater satisfaction which comes from a laurel worked for and won. For many of you, doubtless, this mark of distinction which you have received today has meant greater sacrifice by your parents or by yourselves, than you anticipated when you matriculated almost four years ago. The year 1928 does not seem far in the past, but since that time, as all of us are aware, the world about us has experienced significant changes. Four years ago, if you heard and believed the tidings of the time, you could expect to take your place in a society well supplied with material things and could look forward to the not too distant time when you would be living in your own homes, each (if you believed the politicians) with a two-car garage; and, without great effort, would be providing yourselves and your families with all the necessities and amenities of life, and perhaps in addition, assure by your savings their security and your own in the future. Indeed, if you were observant, you would have seen that many of your elders had discovered a still easier road to material success. They had found that once they had accumulated a few dollars they needed only to put them in the proper place and then sit back and read in comfort the hieroglyphics called stock quotations which proclaimed that their wealth was mounting miraculously without any work or effort on their part. Many who were called and who are still pleased to call themselves the leaders of finance celebrated and assured us of an eternal future for this easy-chair mode of living. And to the stimulation of belief in this dazzling chimera were lent not only the voices of some of our public men in high office, but their influence and the material aid of the very instruments of Government which they controlled.

How sadly different is the picture which we see around us today! If only the mirage had vanished, we should not complain, for we should all be better off. But with it have vanished, not only the easy gains of speculation, but much of the savings of thrifty and prudent men and women, put by for their old age and for the education of their children. With these savings has gone, among millions of our fellow citizens, that sense of security to which they have rightly felt they are entitled in a land abundantly endowed with natural resources and with productive facilities to convert them into the necessities of life for all of our population. More calamitous still, there has vanished, with the expectation of future security the certainty of today's bread and clothing and shelter.

Some of you—I hope not many—are wondering today how and where you will be able to earn your living a few weeks or a few months hence. Much has been written about the hope of youth. I prefer to emphasize another quality. I hope that you who have spent four years in an institution whose fundamental purpose, I take it, is to train us to pursue truths relentlessly and to look at them courageously, will face the unfortunate state of the world about you with greater clarity of vision than many of your elders.

As you view this world of which you are about to become a more active part, I have no doubt that you have been impressed by its chaos, its lack of plan. Perhaps some of you have used stronger language. And stronger language is justified. Even had you been graduating, instead of matriculating, in these rose-colored days of 1928, you would, I believe, have perceived this condition. For beneath all the happy optimism of those days there existed lack of plan and great waste.

This failure to measure true values and to look ahead extended to almost every industry, every profession, every walk of life. Take, for example, the vocation of higher education itself.

If you had been intending to enter the profession of teaching, you would have found that the universities, the colleges, the normal schools of our country were turning out annually far more trained teachers than the schools of the country could possibly use or absorb. You and I know that the number of teachers needed in the Nation is a relatively stable figure, little affected by the depression and capable of fairly accurate estimate in advance with due consideration for our increase in population. And yet, we have continued to add teaching courses, to accept every young man or young woman in those courses without any thought or regard for the law of supply and demand. In the State of New York alone, for example, there are at least seven thousand qualified teachers who are out of work, unable to earn a livelihood in their chosen profession just because nobody had the wit or the forethought to tell them in their younger days that the profession of teaching was gravely oversupplied.

Take, again, the profession of the law. Our common sense tells us that we have too many lawyers and that thousands of them, thoroughly trained are either eking out a bare existence or being compelled to work with their hands, or are turning to some other business in order to keep themselves from becoming objects of charity. The universities, the bar, the courts themselves have done little to bring this situation to the knowledge of young men who are considering entering any one of our multitude of law schools. Here again foresight and planning have been notable for their complete absence.

In the same way we cannot review carefully the history of our industrial advance without being struck with its haphazardness, the gigantic waste with which it has been accomplished, the superfluous duplication of productive facilities, the continual scrapping of still useful equipment, the tremendous mortality in industrial and commercial undertakings, the thousands of dead-end trails into which enterprise has been lured, the profligate waste of natural resources. Much of this waste is the inevitable by-product of progress in a society which values individual endeavor and which is susceptible to the changing tastes and customs of the people of which it is composed. But much of it, I believe, could have been prevented by greater foresight and by a larger measure of social planning. Such controlling and directive forces as have been developed in recent years reside to a dangerous degree in groups having special interests in our economic order, interests which do not coincide with the interests of the Nation as a whole. I believe that the recent course of our history has demonstrated that, while we may utilize their expert knowledge of certain problems and the special facilities with which they are familiar, we cannot allow our economic life to be controlled by that small group of men whose chief outlook upon the social welfare is tinctured by the fact that they can make huge profits from the lending of money and the marketing of securities—an outlook which deserves the adjectives "selfish" and "opportunist."

You have been struck, I know, by the tragic irony of our economic situation today. We have not been brought to our present state by any natural calamity—by drought or floods or earthquakes or by the destruction of our productive machine or our man power. Indeed, we have a superabundance of raw materials, a more than ample supply of equipment for manufacturing these materials into the goods which we need, and transportation and commercial facilities for making them available to all who need them. But raw materials stand unused, factories stand idle, railroad traffic continues to dwindle, merchants sell less and less, while millions of able-bodied men and women, in dire need, are clamoring for the opportunity to work. This the awful paradox with which we are confronted, a stinging rebuke that challenges our power to operate the economic machine which we have created.

We are presented with a multitude of views as to how we may again set into motion that economic machine. Some hold to the theory that the periodic slowing down of our economic machine is one of its inherent peculiarities—a peculiarity which we must grin, if we can, and bear because if we attempt to tamper with it we shall cause even worse ailments. According to this theory, as I see it, if we grin and bear long enough, the economic machine will eventually begin to pick up speed and in the course of an indefinite number of years will again attain that maximum number of revolutions which signifies what we have been wont to miscall prosperity, but which, alas, is but a last ostentatious twirl of the economic machine before it again succumbs to that mysterious impulse to slow down again. This attitude toward our economic machine requires not only greater stoicism, but greater faith in immutable economic law and less faith in the ability of man to control what he has created than I, for one, have. Whatever elements of truth lie in it, it is an invitation to sit back and do nothing; and all of us are suffering today, I believe, because this comfortable theory was too thoroughly implanted in the minds of some of our leaders, both in finance and in public affairs.

Other students of economics trace our present difficulties to the ravages of the World War and its bequest of unsolved political and economic and financial problems. Still others trace our difficulties to defects in the world's monetary systems. Whether it be an original cause, an accentuating cause, or an effect, the drastic change in the value of our monetary unit in terms of the commodities is a problem which we must meet straightforwardly. It is self-evident that we must either restore commodities to a level approximating their dollar value of several years ago or else that we must continue the destructive process of reducing, through defaults or through deliberate writing down, obligations assumed at a higher price level.

Possibly because of the urgency and complexity of this phase of our problem some of our economic thinkers have been occupied with it to the exclusion of other phases of as great importance.

Of these other phases, that which seems most important to me in the long run is the problem of controlling by adequate planning the creation and distribution of those products which our vast economic machine is capable of yielding. It is true that capital, whether public or private, is needed in the creation of new enterprise and that such capital gives employment.

But think carefully of the vast sums of capital or credit which in the past decade have been devoted to unjustified enterprises—to the development of unessentials and to the multiplying of many products far beyond the capacity of the Nation to absorb. It is the same story as the thoughtless turning out too many school teachers and too many lawyers.

Here again, the field of industry and business many of those whose primary solicitude is confined to the welfare of what they call capital have failed to read the lessons of the past few years and have been moved less by calm analysis of the needs of the Nation as a whole than by a blind determination to preserve their own special stakes in the economic order. I do not mean to intimate that we have come to the end of this period of expansion. We shall continue to need capital for the production of newly invented devices, for the replacement of equipment worn out or rendered obsolete by our technical progress; we need better housing in many of our cities and we still need in many parts of the country more good roads, canals, parks and other improvements.

But it seems to me probable that our physical economic plant will not expand in the future at the same rate at which it has expanded in the past. We may build more factories, but the fact remains that we have enough now to supply all of our domestic needs, and more, if they are used. With these factories we can now make more shoes, more textiles, more steel, more radios, more automobiles, more of almost everything than we can use.

No, our basic trouble was not an insufficiency of capital. It was an insufficient distribution of buying power coupled with an oversufficient speculation in production. While wages rose in many of our industries, they did not as a whole rise proportionately to the reward to capital, and at the same time the purchasing power of other great groups of our population was permitted to shrink. We accumulated such a superabundance of capital that our great bankers were vying with each other, some of them employing questionable methods, in their efforts to lend this capital at home and abroad.

I believe that we are at the threshold of a fundamental change in our popular economic thought, that in the future we are going to think less about the producer and more about the consumer. Do what we may have to do to inject life into our ailing economic order, we cannot make it endure for long unless we can bring about a wiser, more equitable distribution of the national income.

It is well within the incentive capacity of man, who has built up this great social and economic machine capable of satisfying the wants of all, to insure that all who are willing and able to work receive from it at least the necessities of life. In such a system, the reward for a day's work will have to be greater, on the average, than it has been, and the reward to capital, especially capital which is speculative, will have to be less. But I believe that after the experience of the last three years, the average citizen would rather receive a smaller return upon his savings in return for a greater security for the principal, than experience for a moment the

thrill or the prospect of being a millionaire only to find the next moment that his fortune, actual or expected, has withered in his hand because the economic machine has again broken down.

It is toward that objective that we must move if we are to profit by our recent experiences. Probably few will disagree that the goal is desirable. Yet many, of faint heart, fearful of change, sitting tightly on the roof-tops in the flood, will sternly resist striking out for it, lest they fail to attain it. Even among those who are ready to attempt the journey there will be violent differences of opinion as to how it should be made. So complex, so widely distributed over our society are the problems which confront us that men and women of common aim do not agree upon the method of attacking them. Such disagreement leads to doing nothing, to drifting. Agreement may come too late.

Let us not confuse objectives with methods. Too many so-called leaders of the Nation fail to see the forest because of the trees. Too many of them fail to recognize the vital necessity of planning for definite objectives. True leadership calls for the setting forth of the objectives and the rallying of public opinion in support of these objectives.

Do not confuse objects with methods. When the Nation becomes substantially united in favor of planning the broad objectives of civilization, then true leadership must unite thought behind definite methods.

The country needs and, unless I mistake its temper, the country demands bold, persistent experimentation. It is common sense to take a method and try it: If it fails, admit it frankly and try another. But above all, try something. The millions who are in want will not stand by silently forever while the things to satisfy their needs are within easy reach.

We need enthusiasm, imagination and the ability to face facts, even unpleasant ones, bravely. We need to correct, by drastic means if necessary, the faults in our economic system from which we now suffer. We need the courage of the young. Yours is not the task of making your way in the world, but the task of remaking the world which you will find before you. May every one of us be granted the courage, the faith and the vision to give the best that is in us to that remaking!

Source: *The Public Papers and Addresses of Franklin D. Roosevelt*, Vol. 1 (New York: Macmillan Company, 1938), 639–647.

3. Roosevelt's Address to the Democratic National Convention Accepting the Nomination, Chicago, Illinois, July 2, 1932

FDR's acceptance speech for the Democratic nomination in Chicago was dramatic for he became the first presidential nominee to deliver it in person at a national convention. Moreover, by flying from Albany to Chicago, he demonstrated his physical vigor. The most famous line in the speech, "I pledge you, I pledge myself, to a new deal for the American people," was written by Samuel Rosenman.

Chairman Walsh, my friends of the Democratic National Convention of 1932:

I appreciate your willingness after these six arduous days to remain here, for I know well the sleepless hours which you and I have had. I regret that I am late, but I have no control over the winds of Heaven and could only be thankful for my Navy training.

The appearance before a National Convention of its nominee for President, to be formally notified of his selection, is unprecedented and unusual, but these are unprecedented and unusual times. I have started out on the tasks that lie ahead by breaking the absurd traditions that the candidate should remain in professed ignorance of what has happened for weeks until he is formally notified of that event many weeks later.

My friends, may this be the symbol of my intention to be honest and to avoid all hypocrisy or sham, to avoid all silly shutting of the eyes to the truth in this campaign. You have nominated me and I know it, and I am here to thank you for the honor.

Let it also be symbolic that in so doing I broke traditions. Let it be from now on the task of our Party to break foolish traditions. We will break foolish traditions and leave it to the Republican leadership, far more skilled in that art, to break promises.

Let us know and here highly resolve to resume the country's interrupted march along the path of real progress, of real justice, or real equality for all of our citizens, great and small. Our indomitable leader in that interrupted march is no longer with us, but there still survives today his spirit. Many of his captains, thank God, are still with us, to give us wise counsel. Let us feel that in everything we do there still lives with us, if not the body, the great indomitable, unquenchable, progressive soul of our Commander-in-Chief, Woodrow Wilson.

I have many things on which I want to make my position clear at the earliest possible moment in this campaign. That admirable document, the platform which you have adopted, is clear. I accept it 100 percent.

And you can accept my pledge that I will leave no doubt or ambiguity on where I stand on any question of moment in this campaign.

As we enter this new battle, let us keep always present with us some of the ideals of the Party: The fact that the Democratic Party by tradition and by the continuing logic of history, past and present, is the bearer of liberalism and of progress and at the same time of safety to our institutions. And if this appeal fails, remember well, my friends that a resentment against the failure of Republican leadership— and note well that in this campaign I shall not use the word "Republican Party," but I shall use, day in and day out, the words, "Republican leadership"—the failure of Republican leaders to solve our troubles may degenerate into unreasoning radicalism.

The great social phenomenon of this depression, unlike others before it, is that it has produced but a few of the disorderly manifestations that too often attend upon such times.

Wild radicalism has made few converts, and the greatest tribute that I can pay to my countrymen is that in these days of crushing want there persists an orderly and hopeful spirit on the part of the millions of our people who have suffered so much. To fail to offer them a new chance is not only to betray their hopes but to misunderstand their patience.

To meet by reaction that danger of radicalism is to invite disaster. Reaction is no barrier to the radical. It is a challenge, a provocation. The way to meet that danger is to offer a workable program of reconstruction, and the party to offer it is the party with clean hands.

This, and this only, is a proper protection against blind reaction on the one hand and an improvised, hit-or-miss, irresponsible opportunism on the other.

There are two ways of viewing the Government's duty in matters affecting economic and social life. The first sees to it that a favored few are helped and hopes that some of their prosperity will leak through, sift through, to labor, to the farmer, to the small business man. That theory belongs to the party of Toryism, and I had hoped that most of the Tories left this country in 1776.

But it is not and never will be the theory of the Democratic Party. This is no time for fear, for reaction or for timidity. Here and now I invite those nominal Republicans who find that their conscience cannot be squared with the groping and the failure of their party leaders to join hands with us; here and now, in equal measure, I warn those nominal Democrats who squint at the future with their faces turned toward the past, and who feel no responsibility to the demands of the new time, that they are out of step with their Party.

Yes, the people of this country want a genuine choice this year, not a choice between two names for the same reactionary doctrine. Ours must be a party of liberal thought, of planned action, of enlightened international outlook, and of the greatest good to the greatest number of our citizens.

Now it is inevitable—and the choice is that of the times—it is inevitable that the main issue of this campaign should revolve about the clear fact of our economic condition, a depression so deep that it is without precedent in modern history. It will not do merely to state, as do Republican leaders to explain their broken promises of continued inaction, that the depression is worldwide. That was not their explanation of the apparent prosperity of 1928. The people will not forget the claim made by them then that prosperity was only a domestic product manufactured by a Republican President and a Republican Congress. If they claim paternity for the one they cannot deny paternity for the other.

I cannot take up all the problems today. I want to touch on a few that are vital. Let us look a little at the recent history and the simple economics, the kind of economics that you and I and the average man and woman talk.

In the years before 1929 we know that this country had completed a vast cycle of building and inflation; for ten years we expanded on the theory of repairing the wastes of the War, but actually expanding far beyond that, and also beyond our natural and normal growth. Now it is worth remembering, and the cold figures of finance prove it, that during that time there was little or no drop in the prices that the consumer had to pay, although those same figures proved that the cost of production fell very greatly; corporate profit resulting from this period was enormous; at the same time little of that profit was devoted to the reduction of prices. The consumer was forgotten. Very little of it went into increased wages; the worker was forgotten, and by no means an adequate proportion was even paid out in dividends—the stockholder was forgotten.

And, incidentally, very little of it was taken by taxation to the beneficent Government of those years.

What was the result? Enormous corporate surpluses piled up—the most stupendous in history. Where, under the spell of delirious speculation, did those surpluses go? Let us talk economics that the figures prove and that we can understand. Why, they went chiefly in two directions: first, into new and unnecessary plants which now stand stark and idle; and second, into the call-money market of Wall Street, either directly by the corporations, or indirectly through the banks. Those are the facts. Why blink at them?

Then came the crash. You know the story. Surpluses invested in unnecessary plants became idle. Men lost their jobs; purchasing power dried up; banks became frightened and started calling loans. Those who had money were afraid to part with it. Credit contracted. Industry stopped. Commerce declined, and unemployment mounted.

And there we are today.

Translate that into human terms. See how the events of the past three years have come home to specific groups of people: first, the group dependent on industry; second, the group dependent on agriculture; third, and made up in large part of members of the first two groups, the people who are called "small investors and depositors." In fact, the strongest possible tie between the first two groups, agriculture and industry, is the fact that the savings and to a degree the security of both are tied together in that third group—the credit structure of the Nation.

Never in history have the interests of all the people been so united in a single economic problem. Picture to yourself, for instance, the great groups of property owned by millions of our citizens, represented by credits issued in the form of bonds and mortgages—Government bonds of all kinds, Federal, State, county, municipal; bonds of industrial companies, of utility companies; mortgages on real estate in farms and cities, and finally the vast investments of the Nation in the railroads. What is the measure of the security of each of those groups? We know that well that in our complicated, interrelated credit structure if any one of these credit groups collapses they may all collapse. Danger to one is danger to all.

How, I ask, has the present Administration in Washington treated the interrelationship of these credit groups? The answer is clear: It has not recognized that interrelationship existed at all. Why, the Nation asks, has Washington failed to understand that all of these groups, each and every one, the top of the pyramid and the bottom of the pyramid, must be considered together, that each and every one of them is dependent on every other; each and every one of them affecting the whole financial fabric?

Statesmanship and vision, my friends, require relief to all at the same time. Just one word or two on taxes, the taxes that all of us pay toward the cost of Government of all kinds.

I know something of taxes. For three long years I have been going up and down this country preaching that Government—Federal and State and local—costs too much. I shall not stop that preaching. As an immediate program of action we must abolish useless offices. We must eliminate unnecessary functions of Government—functions, in fact, that are not definitely essential to the continuance of Government. We must merge, we must consolidate subdivisions of Government, and, like the private citizen, give up luxuries which we can no longer afford.

By our example at Washington itself, we shall have the opportunity of pointing the way of economy to local government, for let us remember well that out of every tax dollar in the average State in this nation, 40 cents enter the treasury in Washington, D.C., 10 or 12 cents only go the State capitals, and 48 cents are consumed by the costs of local government in counties and cities and towns.

I propose to you, my friends, and through you, that Government of all kinds, big and little, be made solvent and that the example be set by the President of the United States and his Cabinet.

And talking about setting a definite example, I congratulate this convention for having had the courage fearlessly to write into its declaration of principles what an overwhelming majority here assembled really thinks about the 18th Amendment. This convention wants repeal. Your candidate wants repeal. And I am confident that the United States of America wants repeal.

Two years ago the platform on which I ran for Governor the second time contained substantially the same provision. The overwhelming sentiment of the people of my State, as shown by the vote of that year, extends, I know, to the people of many of the other States. I say to you now that from this date on the 18th Amendment is doomed. When that happens, we as Democrats must and will, rightly and morally, enable the States to protect themselves against the importation of intoxicating liquor where such importation may violate their State laws. We must rightly and morally prevent the return of the saloon.

To go back to this dry subject of finance, because it all ties in together—the 18th Amendment has something to do with finance, too—in a comprehensive planning for the reconstruction of the great credit groups, including Government credit. I list an important place for that prize statement of principle in the platform here adopted calling for the letting in of the light of day on issues of securities, foreign and domestic, which are offered for sale to the investing public.

My friends, you and I as common-sense citizens know that it would help to protect the savings of the country from the dishonesty of crooks and from the lack of honor of some men in high financial places. Publicity is the enemy of crookedness.

And now one word about unemployment, and incidentally about agriculture. I have favored the use of certain types of public works as a further emergency means of stimulating employment and the issuance of bonds to pay for such public works, but I have pointed out that no economic end is served if we merely build without building for a necessary purpose. Such works, of course, should insofar as possible be self-sustaining if they are to be financed by the issuing of bonds. So as to spread the points of all kinds as widely as possible, we must take definite steps to shorten the working day and the working week.

Let us use common sense and business sense. Just as one example, we know that a very hopeful and immediate means of relief, both for the unemployed and for agriculture, will come from a wide plan of the converting of many millions of acres of marginal and unused land into timberland through reforestation. There are tens of millions of acres east of the Mississippi River alone in abandoned farms, in cut-over land, now growing up in worthless brush. Why, every European Nation has a definite land policy, and has had one for generations. We have none. Having none, we face a future of soil erosion and timber famine. It is clear that economic foresight and immediate employment march hand in hand in the call for the reforestation of these vast areas.

In so doing, employment can be given to a million men. That is the kind of public work that is self-sustaining, and therefore capable of being financed by the issuance of bonds which are made secure by the fact that the growth of tremendous crops will provide adequate security for the investment.

Yes, I have a very definite program for providing employment by that means. I have done it, and I am doing it today in the State of New York. I know that the Democratic Party can do it successfully in the Nation. That will put men to work, and that is an example of the action that we are going to have.

Now as a further aid to agriculture, we know perfectly well—but have we come out and said so clearly and distinctly?—we should repeal immediately those provisions of law that compel the Federal Government to go into the market to purchase, to sell, to speculate in farm products in a futile attempt to reduce farm surpluses. And they are the people who are talking of keeping Government out of business. The practical way to help the farmer is by an arrangement that will, in addition to lightening some of the impoverishing burdens from his back, do something toward the reduction of the surpluses of staple commodities that hang on the market. It should be our aim to add to the world prices of staple products the amount of reasonable tariff protection, to give agriculture the same protection that industry has today.

And in exchange for this immediately increased return I am sure that the farmers of this Nation would agree ultimately to such planning of their production as would reduce the surpluses and make it unnecessary in later years to depend on dumping those surpluses abroad in order to support domestic prices. That result has been accomplished in other Nations; why not in America, too?

Farm leaders and farm economists, generally, agree that a plan based on that principle is a desirable first step in the reconstruction of agriculture. It does not in itself furnish a complete program, but it will serve in great measure in the long run to remove the pall of a surplus without the continued perpetual threat of world dumping. Final voluntary reduction of surplus is a part of our objective, but the long continuance and the present burden of existing surpluses make it necessary to repair great damage of the present by immediate emergency measures.

Such a plan as that, my friends, does not cost the Government any money, nor does it keep the Government in business or in speculation.

As to the actual wording of a bill, I believe that the Democratic Party stands ready to be guided by whatever the responsible farm groups themselves agree on. That is a principle that is sound; and again I ask for action.

One more word about the farmer, and I know that every delegate in this hall who lives in the city knows why I lay emphasis on the farmer. It is because one-half of our population, over 50,000,000 people, are dependent on agriculture; and, my friends, if those 50,000,000 people have no money, no cash, what is produced in the city, the city suffers to an equal or greater extent.

That is why we are going to make the voters understand this year that this Nation is not merely a Nation of independence, but it is, if we are to survive, bound to be a Nation of interdependence—town and city, and North and South, East and West. That is our goal, and that goal will be understood by the people of this country no matter where they live.

Yes, the purchasing power of that half of our population dependent on agriculture is gone. Farm mortgages reach nearly ten billions of dollars today and interest charges on that alone are $560,000,000 a year. But that is not all. The tax burden caused by extravagant and inefficient local government is an additional factor. Our most immediate concern should be to reduce the interest burden on these mortgages.

Rediscounting of farm mortgages under salutary restrictions must be expanded and should, in the future, be conditioned on the reduction of interest rates. Amortization payments, maturities should likewise in the crisis be extended before rediscount is permitted where the mortgagor is sorely pressed. That, my friends, is another example of practical, immediate relief: Action.

I aim to do the same thing, and it can be done, for the small home-owner in our cities and villages. We can lighten his burden and develop his purchasing power. Take away, my friends, that spectre of too high an interest rate. Take away that spectre of the due date just a short time away. Save homes; save homes for thousands of self-respecting families, and drive out that spectre of insecurity from our midst.

Out of all the tons of printed paper, out of all the hours of oratory, the recriminations, the defenses, the happy-thought plans in Washington and in every State, there emerges one great, simple, crystal-pure fact that during the past ten years a Nation of 120,000,000 people has been led by the Republican leaders to erect an impregnable barbed wire entanglement around its borders through the instrumentality of tariffs which have isolated us from all the other human beings in all the rest of the round world. I accept that admirable tariff statement in the platform of this convention. It would protect American business and American labor. By our acts of the past we have invited and received the retaliation of other Nations. I propose an invitation to them to forget the past, to sit at the table with us, as friends, and to plan with us for the restoration of the trade of the world. Go into the home of the business man. He knows what the tariff has done for him. Go into the home of the factory worker. He knows why goods do not move. Go into the home of the farmer. He knows how the tariff has helped to ruin him.

At last our eyes are open. At last the American people are ready to acknowledge that Republican leadership was wrong and that the Democracy is right.

My program, of which I can only touch on these points, is based upon this simple moral principle: the welfare and the soundness of a Nation depend first upon what the great mass of the people wish and need; and second, whether or not they are getting it.

What do the people of America want more than anything else? To my mind, they want two things: work, with all the moral and spiritual values that go with it; and with work, a reasonable measure of security—security for themselves and for their wives and children. Work and security—these are more than words. They are more than facts. They are the spiritual values, the true goal toward which our efforts of reconstruction should lead. These are the values that this program is intended to gain; these are the values we have failed to achieve by the leadership we now have.

Our Republican leaders tell us economic laws—sacred, inviolable, unchangeable—cause panics which no one can prevent. But while they prate of economic laws, men and woman are starving. We must lay hold of the fact that economic laws are not made by nature. They are made by human beings.

Yes, when—not if—when we get the chance, the Federal Government will assume bold leadership in distress relief. For years Washington has alternated between putting its head in the sand and saying there is no large number of destitute people in our midst who need food and clothing, and then saying the States should take care of them, if there are. Instead of planning two and half years ago to do what they are now trying to do, they kept putting it off from day to day, week to week, and month to month, until the conscience of America demanded action.

I say that while primary responsibility for relief rests with localities now, as ever, yet the Federal Government has always had and still has a continuing responsibility for the broader public welfare. It will soon fulfill that responsibility.

And now, just a few words about our plans for the next four months. By coming here instead of waiting for a formal notification, I have made it clear that I believe we should eliminate expensive ceremonies and that we should set in motion at once, tonight, my friends, the necessary machinery for an adequate presentation of the issues to the electorate of the Nation.

I myself have important duties as Governor of a great State, duties which in these times are more arduous and more grave than at any previous period. Yet I feel confident that I shall be able to make a number of short visits to several parts of the Nation. My trips will have as their first objective the study at first hand, from the lips of men and women of all parties and all occupations, of the actual conditions and needs of every part of an interdependent country.

One word more: Out of every crisis, every tribulation, every disaster, mankind rises with some share of greater knowledge, of higher decency, of purer purpose. Today we shall have come through a period of loose thinking, descending morals, an era of selfishness, among individual men and women and among Nations. Blame not Governments alone for this. Blame ourselves in equal share. Let us be frank in acknowledgment of the truth that many amongst us have made obeisance to Mammon, that the profits of speculation, the easy road without toil, have lured us from the old barricades. To return to higher standards we must abandon the false prophets and seek new leaders of own choosing.

Never before in modern history have the essential differences between the two major American parties stood out in such striking contrast as they do today. Republican leaders not only failed in material things, they have failed in national vision, because in disaster they held out no hope, they have pointed out no path for the people below to climb back to places of security and of safety in our American life.

Thoughout the Nation, men and women, forgotten in the political philosophy of the Government of the last years look to us here for guidance and for more equitable opportunity to share in the distribution of national wealth.

On the farms, in the large metropolitan areas, in the smaller cities, and in the villages, millions of our citizens cherish the hope that their old standards of living and of thought have not gone forever. Those millions cannot and shall not hope in vain.

I pledge you, I pledge myself, to a new deal for the American people. Let us all here assembled constitute ourselves prophets of a new order of competence and of courage. This is more than a political campaign; it is a call to arms. Give me your help, not to win votes alone, but to win in this crusade to restore America to its own people.

Source: "Roosevelt's Nomination Address, Chicago, Ill., July 2, 1932." New Deal Network—Works of Franklin D. Roosevelt. Available online. URL: http://newdeal.feri.org/speeches/1932b.htm.

4. "Progressive Government"— Commonwealth Club Address, San Francisco, California, September 23, 1932

FDR's most definitive statement on the role of government and presidential leadership was delivered in his so-called Progressive Government speech. Written by Adolph Berle and revised by the Brain Trust, it outlined the approach that the New Deal and FDR's leadership would eventually take: "Government includes the art of formulating policy and using the political technique to attain so much of the policy as will receive general support; persuading, leading, sacrificing, teaching always, because the greatest duty of a statesman is to educate."

I count it a privilege to be invited to address the Commonwealth Club. It has stood in the life of this city and state, and it is perhaps accurate to add, the nation, as a group of citizen leaders interested in fundamental problems of government, and chiefly concerned with achievement of progress in government through non-partisan means. The privilege of addressing you, therefore, in the heat of a political campaign, is great. I want to respond to your courtesy in terms consistent with your policy.

I want to speak not of politics but of government. I want to speak not of parties, but of universal principles. They are not political, except in that larger sense in which a great American once expressed a definition of politics, that nothing in all of human life is foreign to the science of politics . . .

The issue of government has always been whether individual men and women will have to serve some system of government or economics, or whether a system of government and economics exists to serve individual men and women. This question has persistently dominated the discussion of government for many generations. On questions relating to these things men have differed, and for time immemorial it is probable that honest men will continue to differ.

The final word belongs to no man; yet we can still believe in change and in progress. Democracy, as a dear old friend of mine in India, Meredith Nicholson, has called it, is a quest, a never-ending seeking for better things, and in the seeking for these things and the striving for them, there are many roads to follow. But, if we map the course of these roads, we find that there are only two general directions.

When we look about us, we are likely to forget how hard people have worked to win the privilege of government. The growth of the national governments of Europe was a struggle for the development of a centralized force in the nation, strong enough to impose peace upon ruling barons. In many instances the victory of the central government, the creation of a strong central government, was a haven of refuge to the individual. The people preferred the master far away to the exploitation and cruelty of the smaller master near at hand.

But the creators of national government were perforce ruthless men. They were often cruel in their methods, but they did strive steadily toward something that society needed and very much wanted, a strong central state, able to keep the peace, to stamp out civil war, to put the unruly nobleman in his place, and to permit the bulk of individuals to live safely. The man of ruthless force had his place in developing a pioneer country, just as he did in fixing the power of the central government in the development of nations. Society paid him well for his services and its development. When the development among the nations of Europe, however, has been completed, ambition, and ruthlessness, having served its term tended to overstep its mark.

There came a growing feeling that government was conducted for the benefit of a few who thrived unduly at the expense of all. The people sought a balancing—a limiting force. There came gradually, through town councils, trade guilds, national parliaments, by constitution and by popular participation and control, limitations on arbitrary power.

Another factor that tended to limit the power of those who ruled, was the rise of the ethical conception that a ruler bore a responsibility for the welfare of his subjects.

The American colonies were born in this struggle. The American Revolution was a turning point in it. After the revolution the struggle continued and shaped itself in the public life of the country. There were those who because they had seen the confusion which attended the years of war for American independence surrendered to the belief that popular government was essentially dangerous and essentially unworkable. They are honest people, my friends, and we cannot deny that their experience had warranted some measure of fear. The most brilliant, honest and able exponent of this point of view was Hamilton. He was too impatient of slow moving methods. Fundamentally he believed that the safety of the republic lay in the autocratic strength of its government, and that fundamentally a great and strong group of central institutions, guided by a small group of able and public spirited citizens could best direct all government.

But Mr. Jefferson, in the summer of 1776, after drafting the Declaration of Independence turned his mind to the same problem and took a different view. He did not deceive himself with outward forms. Government to him was a means to an end, not an end in itself; it might be either a refuge and a help or a threat and a danger, depending on the circumstances. We find him carefully analyzing the society for which he was to organize a government. "We have no paupers. The great mass of our population is of laborers, our rich who cannot live without labor, either manual or professional, being few and of moderate wealth. Most of the laboring class possess property, cultivate their own lands, have families and from the demand for their labor, are enabled to exact from the rich and the competent such prices as enable them to feed abundantly, clothe above mere decency, to labor moderately and raise their families."

These people, he considered, had two sets of rights, those of "personal competency," and those involved in acquiring and possessing property. By "personal competency" he meant the right of free thinking, freedom of forming and expressing opinions, and freedom of personal living each man according to his own rights. To insure the first set of rights, a government must so order its functions as not to interfere with the individual. But even Jefferson realized that the exercise of the property rights might so interfere with the rights of the individual that the government, without whose assistance the property rights could not exist, must intervene, not to destroy individualism but to protect it.

You are familiar with the great political duel which followed, and how Hamilton, and his friends, building towards a dominant centralized power were at length defeated in the great election of 1800, by Mr. Jefferson's party. Out of that duel came the two parties, Republican and Democratic, as we know them today.

So began, in American political life, the new day, of the individual against the system, the day in which individualism was made the great watchword of American life. The happiest of economic conditions made that day long and splendid. On the Western frontier, land was substantially free. No one, who did not shirk the task of earning a living, was entirely without opportunity to do so. Depressions could, and did, come and go; but they could not alter the fundamental fact that most of the people lived partly by selling their labor and partly by extracting their livelihood from the soil, so that starvation and dislocation were practically impossible. At the very worst there was always the possibility of climbing into a covered wagon and moving west where the untilled prairies afforded a haven for men to whom the East did not provide a place. So great were our natural resources that we could offer this relief not only to our own people, but to the distressed of all the world; we could invite immigration from Europe, and welcome it with open arms. Traditionally, when a depression came, a new section of land was opened in the West; and even our temporary misfortune served our manifest destiny.

It was the middle of the 19th century that a new force was released and a new dream created. The force was what is called the industrial revolution, the advance of steam and machinery and the rise of the forerunners of the modern industrial plant. The dream was the dream of an economic machine, able to raise the standard of living for everyone; to bring luxury within the reach of the humblest; to annihilate distance by steam power and later by electricity, and to release everyone from the drudgery of the heaviest manual toll. It was to be expected that this would necessarily affect government. Heretofore, government had merely been called upon to produce conditions within which people could live happily, labor peacefully, and rest secure. Now it was called upon to aid in the consummation of this new dream. There was, however, a shadow over the dream. To be made real, it required use of the talents of men of tremendous will, and tremendous ambition, since by no other force could the problems of financing and engineering and new developments be brought to a consummation.

So manifest were the advantages of the machine age, however, that the United States fearlessly, cheerfully, and, I think, rightly, accepted the bitter with the sweet. It was thought that no price was too high to pay for the advantages which we could draw from a finished industrial system.

The history of the last half century is accordingly in large measure a history of a group of financial Titans, whose methods were not scrutinized with too much care, and who were honored in proportion as they produced the results, irrespective of the means they used. The financiers who pushed the railroads to the Pacific were always ruthless, we have them today. It has been estimated that the American investor paid for the American railway system more than three times over in the process; but despite the fact the net advantage was to the United States. As long as we had free land; as long as population was growing by leaps and bounds; as long as our industrial plants were insufficient to supply our needs, society chose to give the ambitious man free play and unlimited reward provided only that he produced the economic plant so much desired.

During this period of expansion, there was equal opportunity for all and the business of government was not to interfere but to assist in the development of industry. This was done at the request of businessmen themselves. The tariff was originally imposed for the purpose of "fostering our infant industry", a phrase I think the older among you will remember as a political issue not so long ago. The railroads were subsidized, sometimes by grants of money, oftener by grants of land; some of the most valuable oil lands in the United States were granted to assist the financing of the railroad which pushed through the Southwest. A nascent merchant marine was assisted by grants of money, or by mail subsidies, so that our steam shipping might ply the seven seas. Some of my friends tell me that they do not want the Government in business. With this I agree; but I wonder whether they realize the implications of the past. For while it has been American doctrine that the government must not go into business in competition with private enterprises, still it has been traditional particularly in Republican administrations for business urgently to ask the government to put at private disposal all kinds of government assistance.

The same man who tells you that he does not want to see the government interfere in business—and he means it, and has plenty of good reasons for saying so—is the first to go to Washington and ask the government for a prohibitory tariff on his produce. When things get just bad enough—as they did two years ago—he will go with equal speed to the United States government and ask for a loan; and the Reconstruction Finance Corporation is the outcome of it. Each group has sought protection from the government for its own special interest, without realizing that the function of government must be to favor no small group at the expense of its duty to protect the rights of personal freedom and of private property of all its citizens.

In retrospect we can now see that the turn of the tide came with the turn of the century. We were reaching our last frontier; there was no more free land and our industrial combinations had become great uncontrolled and irresponsible units of power within the state. Clear-sighted men saw with fear the danger that opportunity would no longer be equal; that the growing corporation, like the feudal baron of old, might threaten the economic freedom of individuals to earn a living. In that hour, our antitrust laws were born. The cry was raised against the great corporations. Theodore Roosevelt, the first great Republican progressive, fought a Presidential campaign on the issue of "trust busting" and talked freely about male-factors of great wealth. If the government had a policy it was rather to turn the clock back, to destroy the large combinations and to return to the time when every man owned his individual small business.

This was impossible; Theodore Roosevelt, abandoning the idea "good" trusts and "bad" trusts. The Supreme Court set forth the famous "rule of reason" by which it seems to have meant that a concentration of industrial power was permissible if the method by which it got its power, and the use it made of that power, was reasonable.

Woodrow Wilson, elected in 1912, saw the situation more clearly. Where Jefferson had feared the encroachment of political power on the lives of individuals, Wilson knew that the new power was financial. He saw, in the highly centralized economic system, the depot of the twentieth century, on whom great masses of individuals relied for their safety and their livelihood, and whose irresponsibility and greed (if it were not controlled) would reduce them to starvation and penury. The concentration of financial power had not proceeded so far in 1912 as it has today; but it had grown far enough for Mr. Wilson to realize fully its implications. It is interesting, now, to read his speeches.

What is called "radical" today (and I reason to know whereof I speak) is mild compared to the campaign of Mr. Wilson. "No man can deny," he said, "that the lines of endeavor have more and more narrowed and stiffened; no man who knows anything about the development of industry in this country can have failed to observe that the larger kinds of credit are more and more difficult to obtain unless you obtain them upon terms of uniting your efforts with those who already control the industry of the country, and nobody can fail to observe that every man who tries to set himself up in competition with any process of manufacture which has taken place under the control of large combinations of capital will presently find himself either squeezed out or obliged to sell and allow himself to be absorbed."

Had there been no World War—had Mr. Wilson been able to devote eight years to domestic instead of to international affairs—we might have had a wholly different situation at the present time. However, the then distant roar of European cannon, growing ever louder, forced him to abandon the study of this issue. The problem he saw so clearly is left with us as a legacy; and no one of us on either side of the political controversy can deny that it is a matter of grave concern to the government.

A glance at the situation today only too clearly indicates the equality of opportunity as we have known it no longer exists. Our industrial plant is built; the problem just now is whether under existing conditions it is not overbuilt. Our last frontier has long since been reached, and there is practically no more free land. More than half of our people do not live on the farms or on lands and cannot derive a living by cultivating their own property. There is no safety valve in the form of a Western prairie to which those thrown out of work by the Eastern economic machines can go for a new start. We are not able to invite the immigration from Europe to share our endless plenty. We are now providing a drab living for our own people.

Our system of constantly rising tariffs has at least reached against us to the point of closing our Canadian frontier on the north, our European markets on the east, many of our Latin American markets to the south, and a goodly proportion of our Pacific markets on the west, through the retaliatory tariffs of those countries. It has forced many of our great industrial institutions who exported their surplus production to such countries, to establish plants in such countries within the tariff walls. This has resulted in the reduction of the operation of their American plants, and opportunity for employment.

Just as freedom to farm has ceased, so also the opportunity in business has narrowed. It still is true that men can start small enterprises, trusting to native shrewdness and ability to keep abreast of competitors; but area after area has been preempted altogether by the great corporations, and even in the fields which still have no great concerns, the small man starts with a handicap. The unfeeling statistics of the past three decades show that the independent business man is running a losing race. Perhaps he is forced to the wall; perhaps he cannot command credit; perhaps he is "squeezed out," in Mr. Wilson's words, by highly organized corporate competitors, as your corner grocery man can tell you.

Recently a careful study was made of the concentration of business in the United States. It showed that our economic life was dominated by some six hundred odd corporations who controlled two-thirds of American industry. Ten million small business men divided the other third. More striking still, it appeared that if the process of concentration goes on at the same rate, at the end of another century we shall have all American industry controlled by a dozen corporations, and run by perhaps a hundred men. Put plainly, we are steering a steady course toward economic oligarchy, if we are not there already.

Clearly, all this calls for a re-appraisal of values. A mere builder of more industrial plants, a creator of more railroad systems, and organizer of more corporations, is as likely to be a danger as a help. The day of the great promoter or the financial Titan, to whom we granted anything if only he would build, or develop, is over. Our task now is not discovery or exploitation of natural resources, or necessarily producing more goods. It is the soberer, less dramatic business of administering resources and plants already in hand, of seeking to reestablish foreign markets for our surplus production, of meeting the problem of under consumption, of adjusting production to consumption, of distributing wealth and products more equitably, of adapting existing economic organizations to the service of the people. The day of enlightened administration has come.

Just as in older times the central government was first a haven of refuge, and then a threat, so now in a closer economic system the central and ambitious financial unit is no longer a servant of national desire, but a danger. I would draw the parallel one step further. We did not think because national government had become a threat in the 18th century that therefore we should abandon the principle of national government. Nor today should we abandon the principle of strong economic units called corporations, merely because their power is susceptible of easy abuse. In other times we dealt with the problem of an unduly ambitious central government by modifying it gradually into a constitutional democratic government. So today we are modifying and controlling our economic units.

As I see it, the task of government in its relation to business is to assist the development of an economic declaration of rights, an economic constitutional order. This is the common task of statesman and business man. It is the minimum requirement of a more permanently safe order of things.

Every many has a right to life; and this means that he has also a right to make a comfortable living. He may by sloth or crime decline to exercise that right; but it may not be denied him. We have no actual famine or death; our industrial and agricultural mechanism can produce enough and to spare. Our government formal and informal, political and economic, owes to every one an avenue to possess himself of a portion of that plenty sufficient for his needs, through his own work.

Every man has a right to his own property; which means a right to be assured, to the fullest extent attainable, in the safety of his savings. By no other means can men carry the burdens of those parts of life which, in the nature of things afford no chance of labor; childhood, sickness, old age. In all thought of property, this right is paramount; all other property rights must yield to it. If, in accord with this principle, we must restrict the operations of the speculator, the manipulator, even the financier, I believe we must accept the restriction as needful, not to hamper individualism but to protect it.

These two requirements must be satisfied, in the main, by the individuals who claim and hold control of the great industrial and financial combinations which dominate so large a part of our industrial life. They have undertaken to be, not business men, but princes—princes of property. I am not prepared to say that the system which produces them is wrong. I am very clear that they must fearlessly and competently assume the responsibility which goes with the power. So many enlightened business men know this that the statement would be little more than a platitude, were it not for an added implication.

This implication is, briefly, that the responsible heads of finance and industry instead of acting each for himself, must work together to achieve the common end. They must, where necessary, sacrifice this or that private advantage; and in reciprocal self-denial must seek a general advantage. It is here that formal government—political government, if you choose, comes in. Whenever in the pursuit of this objective the lone wolf, the unethical competitor, the reckless promoter, the Ishmael or Insull whose hand is against every man's, declines to join in achieving an end recognized as being for the public welfare, and threatens to drag the industry back to a state of anarchy, the government may properly be asked to apply restraint. Likewise, should the group ever use its collective power contrary to public welfare, the government must be swift to enter and protect the public interest.

The government should assume the function of economic regulation only as a last resort, to be tried only when private initiative, inspired by high responsibility, with such assistance and balance as government can give, has finally failed. As yet there has been no final failure, because there has been no attempt, and I decline to assume that this nation is unable to meet the situation.

The final term of the high contract was for liberty and the pursuit of happiness. We have learned a great deal of both in the past century. We know that individual liberty and individual happiness mean nothing unless both are ordered in the sense that one man's meat is not another man's poison. We know that the old "rights of personal competency"—the right to read, to think, to speak, to choose, and live a mode of life, must be respected at all hazards. We know that liberty to do anything which deprives others of those elemental rights is outside the protection of any compact; and that government in this regard is the maintenance of a balance, within which every individual may have a place if he will take it; in which every individual may find safety if he wishes it; in which every individual may attain such power as his ability permits, consistent with his assuming the accompanying responsibility . . .

Faith in America, faith in our tradition of personal responsibility, faith in our institutions, faith in ourselves demands that we recognize the new terms of the old social contract. We shall fulfill them, as we fulfilled the obligation of the apparent Utopia which Jefferson imagined for us in 1776, and which Jefferson, Roosevelt and Wilson sought to bring to realization. We must do so, lest a rising tide of misery engendered by our common failure, engulf us all. But failure is not an American habit; and in the strength of great hope we must all shoulder our common load.

Source: Howard F. Bremer, ed. *Franklin Delano Roosevelt 1882–1945*. Dobbs Ferry, N.Y.: Oceana Publications, Inc. 1971.

5. Speech on the Federal Budget, Pittsburgh, Pennsylvania, October 19, 1932

During the fall campaign, FDR delivered a speech to appeal to conservatives that would come back to haunt him in 1936. He attacked President Herbert Hoover for deficit spending, while promising to balance the federal budget without saying how, if he were elected.

To my friends of Pennsylvania:

It is fitting that I should chose Pittsburgh to sound a solemn note of warning, addressed not only to the Republican leaders, but also to the rank and file of American voters of all parties. There are some prices too high for the country to pay for the propaganda spread abroad in a Presidential election.

That, my friends, is proved when, as now, the Republican campaign management and people like Henry Ford and General Atterbury of the Pennsylvania Railroad are guilty of spreading the gospel of fear.

That is true when in a desperate, futile, last-minute effort to dam the tide of popular disapproval that is steadily growing against the Administration, they become alarmists and panic breeders.

This policy of seeking to win by fear of ruin is selfish in its motive, brutal in its method and false in its promise. It is a policy that will be resented as such by men and women of all parties in every section of the country on November eighth.

It is an insult to the intelligence of the American voters to think that they can be fooled by shifting the boast of the full dinner pail made in 1928, to the threat of the continued empty dinner pail in 1932.

I assure the badly advised and fear-stricken leaders of the Republican Party that not only Democrats but also the rank and file of their own party, who are properly dissatisfied with that leadership, are still American patriots and that they still cherish in their hearts, as I do, the safety of the country, the welfare of its people and the continuance of its institutions.

What is the normal and sensible thing to do when your neighbor gets all excited and starts calling you and your family bad names over the back fence? I take it that nothing is gained by your calling your neighbor worse names or by losing your own temper. As a matter of fact, the peace of the community is best served by sitting down and quietly discussing the problems without raising one's voice. That is why I decline to answer vituperation merely by more vituperation.

Sometime, somewhere in this campaign, I have to talk about dollars and cents. It is a terrible thing to ask you people to listen for forty-five minutes to the story of the Federal budget, but I am going to ask you to do it; and I am going to talk to you about "dollars and cents" in terms that I think not only public accountants, but everybody else can understand.

One of these great problems—and a very vital one to my family and your family and to the whole community—is the financial problem of making both ends meet. I want to discuss this problem with you tonight. To do so sincerely I must tell you the facts as they are and conceal nothing from you. It is not a pretty picture, but if we know that picture and face it we have nothing to fear. This country is the richest and most resourceful Nation in the world. It can and will meet successfully every problem which it faces; but it can do so only through intelligent leadership working unselfishly for the good of all people. That it has not had such leadership in its financial affairs will become obvious from the facts I am going to relate to you tonight.

We all know that our own family credit depends in large part on the stability of the credit of the United States. And here, at least, is one field in which all business—big business and little business and family business and the individual's business—is at the mercy of our big Government down at Washington, D.C.

What I should like to do is to reduce, in so far as possible, the problem of our national finances to the terms of a family budget.

The credit of the family depends chiefly on whether that family is living within its income. And that is equally true of the Nation. If the Nation is living within its income, its credit is good. If, in some crises, it lives beyond its income for year or two, it can usually borrow temporarily at reasonable rates. But if, like a spendthrift, it throws discretion to the winds, and is willing to make no sacrifice at all in spending; if it extends its taxing to the limit of the people's power to pay and continues to pile up deficits, then it is on the road to bankruptcy.

For over two years our Federal Government has experienced unprecedented deficits, in spite of increased taxes. We must not forget that there are three separate governmental spending and taxing agencies in the United States—the national Government in Washington, the State Government and the local government. Perhaps because the apparent national income seemed to have spiraled upward from about 35 billions a year in 1913, the year before the outbreak of the World War, to about 90 billions in 1928, four years ago, all three of our governmental units became reckless; and, consequently, the total spending in all three classes, national, state and local, rose in the same period from about three billions to nearly thirteen billions, or from 8 1/2 percent of income to 14 1/2 percent of income.

"Come-easy-go-easy" was the rule. It was all very merry while it lasted. We did not greatly worry. We thought we were getting rich. But when the crash came, we were shocked to find that while income melted away like snow in the spring, governmental expense did not drop at all. It is estimated that in 1932 our total national income will not much exceed 45 billions, or half of what it used to be, while our total cost of Government will likely be considerably in excess of 15 billions. This simply means that the 14 percent that Government cost has risen to has now become 331/3 percent of our national income. Take it in terms of human beings: It means that we are paying for the cost of our three kinds of Government $125 a year for every man, woman and child in the United States, or $625 a year for the average family of five people. Can we stand that? I do not believe it.

That is a perfectly impossible economic condition. Quite apart from every man's own tax assessment, that burden is a brake on any return to normal business activity. Taxes are paid in the sweat of every man who labors because they are a burden on production and are paid through production. If those taxes are excessive, they are reflected in idle factories, in tax-sold farms, in hordes of hungry people, tramping the streets and seeking jobs in vain. Our workers may never see a tax bill, but they pay. They pay in deductions from wages, in increased cost of what they buy, or—as now—in broad unemployment throughout the land. There is not an unemployed man, there is not a struggling farmer, whose interest in this subject is not direct and vital. It comes home to every one of us!

Let me make it perfectly clear, however, that if men or women or children are starving in the United States—anywhere—I regard it as a positive duty of the Government—of the national Government if local and State Governments have not the cash—to raise by taxes whatever sums may be necessary to keep them from starvation.

What I am talking about are the taxes which go to the ordinary costs of conducting Government year in and year out. That is where the question of extravagance comes in. There can be no extravagance when starvation is in question; but extravagance does apply to the mounting budget of the Federal Government in Washington during these past four years.

The most obvious effect of extravagant Government spending is its burden on farm and industrial activity, and, for that nearly every Government unit in the United States is to blame. But when we come to consider prodigality and extravagance in the Federal Government, as distinguished from State or local government, we are talking about something even more dangerous. For upon the financial stability of the United States Government depends the stability of trade and employment, and of the entire banking, savings and insurance system of the Nation.

To make things clear, to explain the exact nature of the present condition of the Federal pocketbook, I must go back to 1929.

Many people throughout the land—rich and poor—have believed the fairy story which has been painstakingly circulated by this Administration, that the routine spending of our Federal Government has been kept on a fairly even keel during these past five years. It was perhaps easy to give this impression because the total outlay each year up to the emergency appropriations of this year did not increase alarmingly. But the joker in this is that the total outlay includes interest and sinking fund on the public debt; and those charges were going down steadily, right up to this year.

On the plain question of frugality of management, if we want to compare routine Government outlay for 1927 with that for 1931 for example—for years later—we must subtract this so-called "debt service charge" from the total budget in each year. If we do this, we find that the expenditure for the business of Government in 1927 was $2,187,000,000, and in 1931, $3,168,000,000.

That represents an increase of actual administrative spending in those four years of approximately one billion dollars, or roughly, 50 percent; and that, I may add, is the most reckless and extravagant past that I have been able to discover in the statistical record of any peacetime Government anywhere, any time.

It is an ultimate fact proved by the record which is the exact reverse of the thing announced as fact by Republican leaders.

Let me repeat those figures so that the whole country can get them clearly in mind. Leaving out "debt service charges" in both instances, the cost of carrying on the usual business of the United States was $2,187,000,000 in 1927 and $3,168,000,000 in 1931—an increase in four years of one billion dollars!

That, my friends, is the story on the spending side of the ledger. But you and I know that there are always two sides—or ought to be—to a ledger that is supposed to balance. It is bad enough—that story on the spending side, and a billion dollar increase, that 50 percent increase in four years! But it is less than half of the whole appalling story. And I am telling the Nation that on the income side of our ledger, the record is worse.

Unlike other taxing agencies, the Federal Government does not levy a direct tax on property. Therefore, you do not have to be an expert to know that when anything happens that violently contracts sales and incomes and the prices of securities and commodities, there is sure to be a similar violent contraction of Federal income and that a Government charged with maintaining the financial stability not only of the United States itself, but of the whole American Nation under all conditions, is under a very solemn duty, in such an event, to take immediate steps to avoid a deficit.

Although six weeks had elapsed since the worst economic crash in history, the panic of 1929, the Federal budget that was submitted by the President in December, 1929, did not even refer to it. It estimated receipts for the year ending June 30, 1931, at 4.2 billions, actually more than they had been in the preceding year of economic fantasy, a figure which obviously could not possibly be attained without an immediate return to the exaggerated speculations of 1929. The Administration advised no economy. On the contrary, it proposed a reduction of taxes and it blandly and cheerfully remarked—here are its own words: "Our finances are in sound condition. . . . Our estimated expenditures . . . are well within our expected receipts." That was six weeks after the panic had broken!

Against those estimated receipts, placed at 4.2 billions by the Secretary of the Treasury, the sad fact is that the actual revenue turned out to be 3.3 billions, or nearly a billion short of the estimate.

I recite that 1929 Federal incident to clarify what happened at Washington in the next two years, in 1930 and 1931. In December of 1930 a new budget appeared. Vast declines in every form of business activity were at that time deadly certain. In fact, the national income was in a nosedive, or perhaps it was in a tailspin. It was therefore certain that Federal income was

on the verge of catastrophe. Yet, that new budget of December, 1930, recommended neither increased taxes nor decreased expenditures, although upon its recommendations depended the credit standing of the United States.

The Budget Message of the President asserted that the deficit for 1931 would be only $180,000,000; and it contained the statements: "Nor do I look with great concern upon this moderate deficit," and, again, "Our Government finances are in a sound condition." He actually estimated a surplus for the year 1932.

At this time the President and his Secretary of the Treasury had had plenty of experience with falling tax receipts—just as you and I had had with falling income.

The astonishing and inescapable fact is that no such results as those estimated could have been achieved without an immediate and complete business recovery from the practical paralysis then existing. That 1930 budget cannot fairly be called an estimate at all. It was an extreme hazard on the hope of an economic miracle, a gamble, if you please, a gamble with your money and mine—and a hidden one at that.

There is something much more than mere error in that kind of thing. Our people and the world are entitled to reasonable accuracy and reasonable prudence; and above all they are entitled to complete frankness. They have a right and a duty to place in retirement those who conceal realities, those who abuse confidence.

I am going to talk more about figures—but figures talk.

We remember these simple facts: On December 3, 1930, the President estimated that the following summer there would be a deficit of $180,000,0000, but that in the summer of 1932 there would be a profit of $30,000,000, or a total estimated deficit for the two years of $150,000,000.

Now, I am going to give you good people a real shock. Instead of the Government running into the red for those two years to the tune of $150,000,000, the deficit on June 30, 1932, was, for the two fiscal years, three and three-quarters billion dollars.

No, I fear we cannot call this budget an estimate—or even a fair gamble. I do not know what to call that kind of representation or that kind of fact, but the name for it certainly is not candor.

Nineteen hundred and thirty-one proved to be the worst year experienced in the depression up to that time. For my distinguished opponent, 1931 was the year in which all his distinctive 1928 economic heresies seemed to come home to roost, all at the same time.

Let us call the roll of those economic heresies:

1. Those famous loans to "backward and crippled countries," which he said would provide uninterrupted employment and uninterrupted industrial activity by expanding our export trade, no longer could be made.

2. Retaliation against his monstrous Grundy tariff—and you people in Pennsylvania ought to know something about that—against which the best economic and industrial thought in the country had stood in almost unanimous protest, and against which it once more protested within the past week, and which was to cure our agriculture and maintain our industry, had already begun to strangle the world trade of all Nations, including our own.

3. Debtor Nations, no longer sustained by our improvident loans and no longer able to export goods, were drained of gold for debts and, one by one, were forced to abandon specie payments.

4. Finally, as a direct result of all these influences, our export markets dried up, our commodity prices slumped and our own domestic business itself declined at a more rapid rate than business in some of the backward and crippled countries.

Unemployment began to rise here in even greater proportions than in Europe. To top this ruin of all these seductive 1928 theories—which were to bring the millennium of abolished poverty and the chicken, or maybe it was two of them, in every pot—came the complete collapse of the 1929 and 1930 Administration fiscal policy.

The truth about the shattering effect of all these homing heresies began to leak out as the summer of 1931 advanced; and it is my opinion that in the conduct of national finances, as in the conduct of corporation finances or family budgets, if things are not going as well as one had hoped, it is far better to face the truth than to try to hide it. That is why, when history comes to be written, it will be shown that it was far more harmful to the Nation last autumn—in 1931—and all through this year of 1932, to have the facts leak out, than it would have been to have had them boldly and frankly disclosed to us when they were actually taking place.

The result of such a combination of disquieting revelations was inevitable. The very basis of confidence in our economic and financial structure both here and abroad was impaired. A fresh wave of liquidation ensued. Foreigners took $1,000,000,000 of their gold back in that black year of 1931.

I emphasize this history because our opponents have now become almost frantic in their insistence that this entire sequence of events originated abroad. I do not know where; they have never located "abroad," but I think it is somewhere near Abyssinia. They insist that no American policy was in the least to blame, and that to say otherwise is what they call "hideous misrepresentation." The "foreign cause" alibi is just like ascribing measles on our little boy to the spots on his chest, instead of to the contagious germ that he has picked up somewhere.

No, we need not look abroad for scapegoats. We had ventured into the economic stratosphere—which is a long way up—on the wings of President Hoover's novel, radical and unorthodox economic theories of 1928, the complete collapse of which brought the real crash in 1931. The Grundy tariff accelerated the drop. As hard reality rushed up to meet our fall, this Administration did not see fit to adapt its fiscal policies to this inevitable consequence. It is a responsibility which no campaign alibi can avert, and less than three weeks off, the day of reckoning will come.

The Administration's recent strategy in this campaign is a direct appeal to public sympathy for its agony of spirit in the dark hours of last year and this year, when retribution for our chasing after strange economic gods overtook us. It protests against any assessment of just blame. But it protests in vain.

I want to say, with all sincerity, that I recite this record with reluctance. No man with a spark of decency or humanity can fail to sympathize with our responsible leaders in hours of crisis. Politics or no politics, I pay my tribute to the devotion of the President of the United States. It is not true to say that he has not been unremitting in his efforts, and I for one have never heard it said.

But I do indict his Administration for wrong action, for delayed action, for lack of frankness and for lack of courage. Before the Administration partisans complain of this arraignment, they must remember that the American people are now about to exercise their democratic right of self-determination of their own fate and their own future. They must make a choice. That appeal for sympathy is not based on any frank acknowledgement of the failure of the policies so clearly portrayed by these tragic events. On the contrary, it is a denial that these principles have failed. It persists in the same course and even presumes to ask admiration for the stubborn ruggedness of that persistence.

Under those circumstances I should fail utterly in my duty to the American people, if I did not fearlessly portray these errors and link them directly to the havoc which they have brought and which they threaten to continue.

The autumn of 1931 witnessed the complete wreckage of the Administration program to that date, the collapse of its entire economic philosophy. The convening of the 72nd Congress last December started the last phase. The President appeared with his December, 1931 Budget Message. It was a fateful moment. That was the time—last December—for an honest demonstration to the world that might have set the whole world trend of economic events in an upward direction or at least checked the decline. All that it was necessary to do was finally to end once and for all the two years of vacillation and secretiveness, to tell the truth to the Congress of the United States, and to rely on that Congress to balance the budget and establish American credit in the eyes of the world.

In a way the Administration did acknowledge the necessity for that. It started off by saying that it was going to balance the budget. Fine! Then it said it was balancing the budget. Fine! And finally, it said it had balanced the budget. Better yet! And now, months later, it insists that because it has balanced the budget, it has saved the Gibraltar of world stability and prevented the overthrow of our form of Government.

If all that is true, the Administration has done well. If it not true, then the Administration stands convicted of a new and fatal trifling with the welfare of our people and the credit of our country.

Let me not waste words. I now quote from the daily Treasury statement, made three weeks ago, on the result of the first three months of operation under the new budget this year, the statement covering the months of July, August and September, the first quarter of the fiscal year. Here is what it says:

"Excess of expenditures over receipts, $402,043,002." There you are!

For the corresponding quarter of last year the deficit was only $380,495,584, but at the end of the year it was $2,885,000,000. There is, therefore, strong indication that we are in for another staggering deficit. If the present rate on that budget continues, the true deficit as of June 30th next year will be over $1,600,000,000—a deficit so great that it makes us catch our breath.

I regret to say that the appeal of this Administration for applause for its soundness and courage last winter is simply not based on facts. The budget is not balanced and the whole job must be done over again in the next session of Congress.

I have shown how unreliable these constant reassurances are. It is not seemly to conjecture motives, but I think it is fair to say the whole record of Administration policy in the last four years reveals that it has been afraid to trust the people of the United States with the true facts about their affairs. That is a fundamental error which shows unfamiliarity with the true basis of American character.

While the President claims that he did finally recommend new taxes, I fear this courage came two years too late and in far too scanty measure. Perhaps it explains the underlying thought of the phrase "prosperity is just around the corner." Perhaps it explains two complete concealments of deficits and the insufficiency of the action taken last winter. It is an error of weakness and an error which I assure you I will not make.

Our Federal extravagance and improvidence bear a double evil; first, our people and our business cannot carry these excessive burdens of taxation; second, our credit structure is impaired by the unorthodox Federal financing made necessary by the unprecedented magnitude of these deficits.

Instead of financing the billion-dollar deficit of 1931 in the regular way, the Government simply absorbed that much of the lending capacity of the banks and by so much impaired the credit available for business. In that year the amount of Government obligations held by our banks increased by a little more than one billion dollars.

You and I know that this Administration's claims that it has provided credit for industry and agriculture by pouring credit into banks are not wholly frank. Commercial credit has continuously contracted and is contracting now. The truth is that our banks are financing these great deficits and that the burden is absorbing their resources. All this is highly undesirable and wholly unnecessary. It arises from one cause only, and that is the unbalanced budget and the continued failure of this Administration to take effective steps to balance it. If that budget had been fully and honestly balanced in 1930, some of the 1931 troubles would have been avoided. Even if it had been balanced in 1931, much of the extreme dip in 1932 would have been obviated. Every financial man in the country knows why this is true. He knows the unnecessary muddle that has accumulated and is still accumulating in Washington.

Now, how can we continue to countenance such a condition? That is a practical question. In all conscience, can an Administration which has so frequently failed in a matter so directly touching its own responsibilities ask for your support and trifle with your common sense by these campaign alibis about mysterious foreign forces and by this specious talk about sound fiscal policies? Would it not be infinitely better to clear this whole subject of obscurity, to present the facts squarely to the Congress and the people of the United States, and to secure the one sound foundation of permanent economic recovery—a complete and honest balancing of the Federal budget? In all earnestness I leave the answer to your common sense and judgment.

The other bad effect of this fiscal mismanagement is not the least bit technical. It is the burden of high cost on the backs of all our people. I can state the condition best by quoting one paragraph from a document published a week ago and signed by both Calvin Coolidge and Alfred E. Smith. They say:

"All the costs of local, State and national Government must be reduced without fear and without favor. Unless the people, through unified action, arise and take charge of their Government, they will find that their Government has taken charge of them."

Every word of that warning is true; and the first and most important and necessitous step in balancing our Federal budget is to reduce expense.

The air is now surcharged with Republican death-bed repentance on the subject of economy, but it is too late. We must look deeper than these eleventh-hour pronouncements. You cannot go very far with any real Federal economy, without a complete change of concept of what are the proper functions and limits of the Federal Government itself.

Perhaps we can get some glimpse of the President's underlying philosophy about the Federal Government by going back and opening the volume of his 1928 speeches. He proposed, you remember, as he said, "a new thing in Government." He says that he "reorganized the Department of Commerce on a greater scale than has ever been attempted or achieved by any Government in the world." In his book, called *The New Day*, he says this: "A Nation which is spending ninety billions a year can well afford a few hundred million for a workable program."

I could go on quoting for a good many minutes, but perhaps the point could be made clearer by recalling that the Department of Commerce went through even the heavy war strain, back in the days of the World War, on about 13 millions a year. When Secretary Hoover left it, it was spending 39 millions a year; and this year it is estimated that it will be spending 43 millions a year. And the Department of Commerce is now housed in that great marble building which is facetiously called in Washington the "Temple of Fact Finding," which cost the people considerably more than the Capitol of the United States.

That little example, my friends, may explain the 50 percent increase in Government overhead in four years, 1927–1931, and I am sure that the whole group of quotations reveal why you can never expect any important economy from this Administration. It is committed to the idea that we ought to center control of everything in Washington as rapidly as possible—Federal control. That was the idea that increased the cost of Government by a billion dollars in four years. Ever since the days of Thomas Jefferson, that has been the exact reverse of the democratic concept, which is to permit Washington to take from the States nothing more than is necessary to keep abreast of the march of our changing economic situation.

In the latter philosophy, and not in the philosophy of Mr. Hoover—which I think is responsible for so much of our trouble—I shall approach the problem of carrying out the plain precept of our Party, which is to reduce the cost of current Federal Government operations by 25 percent.

Of course that means a complete realignment of the unprecedented bureaucracy that has assembled in Washington in the past four years. I am no stranger to Washington. I knew it firsthand during the administrations of President Roosevelt and President Taft. I served in Washington for seven and a half years under President Wilson. I have some familiarity with the national Government. In addition to that, for more than four years I have been conducting the Administration and the policies of a State that has thirteen million inhabitants.

Now, I am going to disclose to you a definite personal conclusion which I reached the day after I was nominated in Chicago. Here it is: Before any man enters my Cabinet he must give me a two-fold pledge:

1. Absolute loyalty to the Democratic platform and especially to its economy plank.
2. Complete cooperation with me, looking to economy and reorganization in his Department.

I regard reduction in Federal spending as one of the most important issues in this campaign. In my opinion it is the most direct and effective contribution that Government can make to business.

In accordance with this fundamental policy it is equally necessary to eliminate from Federal budget-making during this emergency all new items except such as relate to direct relief of unemployment.

As part of that phase of the budget problem, I take note that former President Coolidge is reported as having said in a speech in New York City:

"An early and timely word from the Democratic candidate for President that he would reject the proposal to increase the national debt by $2,300,000,000 to pay a bonus would have been a great encouragement to business, reduced unemployment, and guaranteed the integrity of the national credit. While he remained silent economic recovery was measurably impeded."

That charge is baseless and absurd for the very good reason that last April my views on the subject were widely published and have been subsequently frequently quoted. I said this:

"I do not see how, as a matter of practical sense, a Government running behind two billion dollars annually can consider the anticipation of bonus payment until it has a balanced budget, not only on paper, but with a surplus of cash in the treasury."

No one, for political purposes or otherwise, has the right in the absence of explicit statement from me to assume that my views have changed. They have not. So much for another effort by Republican leaders to preach an unwarranted gospel of fear and panic to the American electorate.

I have sought to make two things clear: First, that we can make savings by reorganization of existing departments, by eliminating functions, by abolishing many of those innumerable boards and those commissions which, over a long period of years, have grown up as a fungus growth on American Government. These savings can properly be made to total many hundreds and thousands of dollars a year.

Second, I hope that it will not be necessary to increase the present scale of taxes, and I call definite attention to the fact that just as soon as the Democratic platform pledge is enacted into legislation modifying the Volstead Act, a source of new revenue amounting to several hundred millions of dollars a year will be made available toward the balancing of the budget. I refer specifically to a Federal tax on beer, which would be raised through the sale of beer in those States and those States only which by State law allow the sale of beer. At the same time I reiterate the simple language of the Democratic platform which in good faith opposes the return of the old-time saloon:

"We urge the enactment of such measures by the several States as will actually promote temperance, effectively prevent the return of the saloon and bring the liquor traffic into the open under complete supervision and control by the State."

The above two categorical statements are aimed at a definite balancing of the budget. At the same time, let me repeat from now to election day so that every man, woman and child in the United States will know what I mean: If starvation and dire need on the part of any of our citizens make necessary the appropriation of additional funds which would keep the budget out of balance, I shall not hesitate to tell the American people the full truth and ask them to authorize the expenditure of that additional amount.

These have been unhealthy years for prophets, and I hasten to disclaim such a role. But one thing I know: A powerful cause contributing to economic disaster has been this inexcusable fiscal policy and the obscurity and uncertainty that have attended and grown out of it. There it remains for all to see—a veritable cancer in the body politic and economic. Is it prophecy to assure you that if we remove that destructive growth we shall move on to better health and better life?

To my mind, that is so plain and persuasive as scarcely to be open to argument. As I said in the beginning, this is the one field in which business is wholly in the grip of Government. It is a field where Government can make a great contribution to recovery.

To that contribution I here pledge the utmost of my faith and my ability. I am as certain as mortal man can be certain of anything in the future, that from the moment that you and I set our hands openly and frankly and courageously to that problem, we shall have reached the end of our long, hard, downward road. We shall have started on the upward trail. We shall have built for economic recovery a firm footing, on a path that is broad, true and straight. Join me, and "let's go!"

Source: *The Public Papers and Addresses of Franklin D. Roosevelt,* Vol. 1 (New York: Macmillan Company, 1938), 795–811.

6. First Inaugural Address, March 4, 1933

FDR's First Inaugural Address is one of the most famous speeches in American history. Its most famous line, "the only thing we have to fear is fear itself," helped to inspire the public. He stressed the necessity of interdependence and the role of government in promoting the general welfare of society.

I am certain that my fellow Americans expect that on my induction into the Presidency I will address them with a candor and a decision which the present situation of our Nation impels. This is preeminently the time to speak the truth, the whole truth, frankly and boldly. Nor need we shrink from honestly facing conditions in our country today. This great Nation will endure as it has endured, will revive and will prosper. So, first of all, let me assert my firm belief that the only thing we have to fear is fear itself—nameless, unreasoning, unjustified terror which paralyzes needed efforts to convert retreat into advance. In every dark hour of our national life a leadership of frankness and vigor has met with that understanding and support of the people themselves which is essential to victory. I am convinced that you will again give that support to leadership in these critical days.

In such a spirit on my part and on yours we face our common difficulties. They concern, thank God, only material things. Values have shrunken to fantastic levels; taxes have risen; our ability to pay has fallen; government of all kinds is faced by serious curtailment of income; the means of exchange are frozen in the currents of trade; the withered leaves of industrial enterprise lie on every side; farmers find no markets for their produce; the savings of many years in thousands of families are gone.

More important, a host of unemployed citizens face the grim problem of existence, and an equally great number toil with little return. Only a foolish optimist can deny the dark realities of the moment.

Yet our distress comes from no failure of substance. We are stricken by no plague of locusts. Compared with the perils which our forefathers conquered because they believed and were not afraid, we have still much to be thankful for. Nature still offers her bounty and human efforts have multiplied it. Plenty is at our doorstep, but a generous use of it languishes in the very sight of the supply. Primarily this is because the rulers of the exchange of mankind's goods have failed, through their own stubbornness and their own incompetence, have admitted their failure, and abdicated. Practices of the unscrupulous money changers stand indicted in the court of public opinion, rejected by the hearts and minds of men.

True they have tried, but their efforts have been cast in the pattern of an outworn tradition. Faced by failure of credit they have proposed only the lending of more money. Stripped of the lure of profit by which to induce our people to follow their false leadership, they have resorted to exhortations, pleading tearfully for restored confidence. They know only the rules of a generation of self-seekers. They have no vision, and when there is no vision the people perish.

The money changers have fled from their high seats in the temple of our civilization. We may now restore that temple to the ancient truths. The measure of the restoration lies in the extent to which we apply social values more noble than mere monetary profit.

Happiness lies not in the mere possession of money; it lies in the joy of achievement, in the thrill of creative effort. The joy and moral stimulation of work no longer must be forgotten in the mad chase of evanescent profits. These dark days will be worth all they cost us if they teach us that our true destiny is not to be ministered unto but to minister to ourselves and to our fellow men.

Recognition of the falsity of material wealth as the standard of success goes hand in hand with the abandonment of the false belief that public office and high political position are to be valued only by the standards of pride of place and personal profit; and there must be an end to a conduct in banking and in business which too often has given to a sacred trust the

likeness of callous and selfish wrongdoing. Small wonder that confidence languishes, for it thrives only on honesty, on honor, on the sacredness of obligations, on faithful protection, on unselfish performance; without them it cannot live.

Restoration calls, however, not for changes in ethics alone. This Nation asks for action, and action now.

Our greatest primary task is to put people to work. This is no unsolvable problem if we face it wisely and courageously. It can be accomplished in part by direct recruiting by the Government itself, treating the task as we would treat the emergency of a war, but at the same time, through this employment, accomplishing greatly needed projects to stimulate and reorganize the use of our natural resources.

Hand in hand with this we must frankly recognize the overbalance of population in our industrial centers and, by engaging on a national scale in a redistribution, endeavor to provide a better use of the land for those best fitted for the land. The task can be helped by definite efforts to raise the values of agricultural products and with this the power to purchase the output of our cities. It can be helped by preventing realistically the tragedy of the growing loss through foreclosure of our small homes and our farms. It can be helped by insistence that the Federal, State, and local governments act forthwith on the demand that their cost be drastically reduced. It can be helped by the unifying of relief activities which today are often scattered, uneconomical, and unequal. It can be helped by national planning for and supervision of all forms of transportation and of communications and other utilities which have a definitely public character. There are many ways in which it can be helped, but it can never be helped merely by talking about it. We must act and act quickly.

Finally, in our progress toward a resumption of work we require two safeguards against a return of the evils of the old order; there must be a strict supervision of all banking and credits and investments; there must be an end to speculation with other people's money, and there must be provision for an adequate but sound currency.

These are the lines of attack. I shall presently urge upon a new Congress in special session detailed measures for their fulfillment, and I shall seek the immediate assistance of the several States.

Through this program of action we address ourselves to putting our own national house in order and making income balance outgo. Our international trade relations, though vastly important, are in point of time and necessity secondary to the establishment of a sound national economy. I favor as a practical policy the putting of first things first. I shall spare no effort to restore world trade by international economic readjustment, but the emergency at home cannot wait on that accomplishment.

The basic thought that guides these specific means of national recovery is not narrowly nationalistic. It is the insistence, as a first consideration, upon the interdependence of the various elements in all parts of the United States—a recognition of the old and permanently important manifestation of the American spirit of the pioneer. It is the way to recovery. It is the immediate way. It is the strongest assurance that the recovery will endure.

In the field of world policy I would dedicate this Nation to the policy of the good neighbor—the neighbor who resolutely respects himself and, because he does so, respects the rights of others—the neighbor who respects his obligations and respects the sanctity of his agreements in and with a world of neighbors.

If I read the temper of our people correctly, we now realize as we have never realized before our interdependence on each other; that we can not merely take but we must give as well; that

if we are to go forward, we must move as a trained and loyal army willing to sacrifice for the good of a common discipline, because without such discipline no progress is made, no leadership becomes effective. We are, I know, ready and willing to submit our lives and property to such discipline, because it makes possible a leadership which aims at a larger good. This I propose to offer, pledging that the larger purposes will bind upon us all as a sacred obligation with a unity of duty hitherto evoked only in time of armed strife.

With this pledge taken, I assume unhesitatingly the leadership of this great army of our people dedicated to a disciplined attack upon our common problems.

Action in this image and to this end is feasible under the form of government which we have inherited from our ancestors. Our Constitution is so simple and practical that it is possible always to meet extraordinary needs by changes in emphasis and arrangement without loss of essential form. That is why our constitutional system has proved itself the most superbly enduring political mechanism the modern world has produced. It has met every stress of vast expansion of territory, of foreign wars, of bitter internal strife, of world relations.

It is to be hoped that the normal balance of executive and legislative authority may be wholly adequate to meet the unprecedented task before us. But it may be that an unprecedented demand and need for undelayed action may call for temporary departure from that normal balance of public procedure.

I am prepared under my constitutional duty to recommend the measures that a stricken nation in the midst of a stricken world may require. These measures, or such other measures as the Congress may build out of its experience and wisdom, I shall seek, within my constitutional authority, to bring to speedy adoption.

But in the event that the Congress shall fail to take one of these two courses, and in the event that the national emergency is still critical, I shall not evade the clear course of duty that will then confront me. I shall ask the Congress for the one remaining instrument to meet the crisis—broad Executive power to wage a war against the emergency, as great as the power that would be given to me if we were in fact invaded by a foreign foe.

For the trust reposed in me I will return the courage and the devotion that befit the time. I can do no less.

We face the arduous days that lie before us in the warm courage of the national unity; with the clear consciousness of seeking old and precious moral values; with the clean satisfaction that comes from the stern performance of duty by old and young alike. We aim at the assurance of a rounded and permanent national life.

We do not distrust the future of essential democracy. The people of the United States have not failed. In their need they have registered a mandate that they want direct, vigorous action. They have asked for discipline and direction under leadership. They have made me the present instrument of their wishes. In the spirit of the gift I take it.

In this dedication of a Nation we humbly ask the blessing of God. May He protect each and every one of us. May He guide me in the days to come.

Source: "First Inaugural Address of Franklin D. Roosevelt, Saturday, March 4, 1933." The Avalon Project at Yale Law School. Available online. URL: http://www.yale.edu/lawweb/avalon/presiden/inaug/froos1.htm.

7. First Fireside Chat— On the Bank Crisis, March 12, 1933

FDR's first radio address to the American people may have been his most important of the approximately 30 that he delivered during his four terms. He used it to restore confidence in the banking system by explaining the crisis in understandable terms, relying on his warm, melodious voice. Many listeners felt he was talking to them personally.

I want to talk for a few minutes with the people of the United States about banking—with the comparatively few who understand the mechanics of banking but more particularly with the overwhelming majority who use banks for the making of deposits and the drawing of checks. I want to tell you what has been done in the last few days, why it was done, and what the next steps are going to be. I recognize that the many proclamations from State capitals and from Washington, the legislation, the Treasury regulations, etc., couched for the most part in banking and legal terms, should be explained for the benefit of the average citizen. I owe this in particular because of the fortitude and good temper with which everybody has accepted the inconvenience and hardships of the banking holiday. I know that when you understand what we in Washington have been about I shall continue to have your cooperation as fully as I have had your sympathy and help during the past week.

First of all, let me state the simple fact that when you deposit money in a bank the bank does not put the money into a safe deposit vault. It invests your money in many different forms of credit—bonds, commercial paper, mortgages and many other kinds of loans. In other words, the bank puts your money to work to keep the wheels of industry and of agriculture turning around. A comparatively small part of the money you put into the bank is kept in currency—an amount which in normal times is wholly sufficient to cover the cash needs of the average citizen. In other words, the total amount of all the currency in the country is only a small fraction of the total deposits in all of the banks.

What, then, happened during the last few days of February and the first few days of March? Because of undermined confidence on the part of the public, there was a general rush by a large portion of our population to turn bank deposits into currency or gold—a rush so great that the soundest banks could not get enough currency to meet the demand. The reason for this was that on the spur of the moment, it was, of course, impossible to sell perfectly sound assets of a bank and convert them into cash except at panic prices far below their real value.

By the afternoon of March third scarcely a bank in the country was open to do business. Proclamations temporarily closing them in whole or in part had been issued by the Governors of almost all the States.

It was then that I issued the proclamation providing for the nationwide bank holiday, and this was the first step in the Government's reconstruction of our financial and economic fabric.

The second step was the legislation promptly and patriotically passed by the Congress confirming my proclamation and broadening my powers so that it became possible in view of the requirement of time to extend the holiday and lift the ban of that holiday gradually. This law also gave authority to develop a program of rehabilitation of our banking facilities. I want to tell our citizens in every part of the Nation that the national Congress—Republicans and Democrats alike—showed by this action a devotion to public welfare and a realization of the emergency and the necessity for speed that is difficult to match in our history.

The third stage has been the series of regulations permitting the banks to continue their functions to take care of the distribution of food and household necessities and the payment of payrolls.

This bank holiday, while resulting in many cases in great inconvenience, is affording us the opportunity to supply the currency necessary to meet the situation. No sound bank is a dollar worse off than it was when it closed its doors last Monday. Neither is any bank which may turn out not to be in a position for immediate opening. The new law allows the twelve Federal Reserve Banks to issue additional currency on good assets and thus the banks which reopen will be able to meet every legitimate call. The new currency is being sent out by the Bureau of Engraving and Printing in large volume to every part of the country. It is sound currency because it is backed by actual, good assets.

A question you will ask is this: why are all the banks not to be reopened at the same time? The answer is simple. Your Government does not intend that the history of the past few years shall be repeated. We do not want and will not have another epidemic of bank failures.

As a result, we start tomorrow, Monday, with the opening of banks in the twelve Federal Reserve Bank cities—those banks which on first examination by the Treasury have already been found to be all right. This will be followed on Tuesday by the resumption of all their functions by banks already found to be sound in cities where there are recognized clearing houses. That means about two hundred and fifty cities of the United States.

On Wednesday and succeeding days banks in smaller places all through the country will resume business, subject, of course, to the Government's physical ability to complete its survey. It is necessary that the reopening of banks be extended over a period in order to permit the banks to make applications for necessary loans, to obtain currency needed to meet their requirements and to enable the Government to make common sense checkups.

Let me make it clear to you that if your bank does not open the first day you are by no means justified in believing that it will not open. A bank that opens on one of the subsequent days is in exactly the same status as the bank that opens tomorrow.

I know that many people are worrying about State banks not members of the Federal Reserve System. These banks can and will receive assistance from member banks and from the Reconstruction Finance Corporation. These State banks are following the same course as the National banks except that they get their licenses to resume business from the State authorities, and these authorities have been asked by the Secretary of the Treasury to permit their good banks to open up on the same schedule as the national banks. I am confident that the State Banking Departments will be as careful as the national Government in the policy relating to the opening of banks and will follow the same broad policy.

It is possible that when the banks resume a very few people who have not recovered from their fear may again begin withdrawals. Let me make it clear that the banks will take care of all needs—and it is my belief that hoarding during the past week has become an exceedingly unfashionable pastime. It needs no prophet to tell you that when the people find that they can get their money—that they can get it when they want it for all legitimate purposes—the phantom of fear will soon be laid. People will again be glad to have their money where it will be safely taken care of and where they can use it conveniently at any time. I can assure you that it is safer to keep your money in a reopened bank than under the mattress.

The success of our whole great national program depends, of course, upon the cooperation of the public—on its intelligent support and use of a reliable system.

Remember that the essential accomplishment of the new legislation is that it makes it possible for banks more readily to convert their assets into cash than was the case before. More liberal provision has been made for banks to borrow on these assets at the Reserve Banks and more liberal provision has also been made for issuing currency on the security of these good assets. This currency is not fiat currency. It is issued only on adequate security, and every good bank has an abundance of such security.

One more point before I close. There will be, of course, some banks unable to reopen without being reorganized. The new law allows the Government to assist in making these reorganizations quickly and effectively and even allows the Government to subscribe to at least a part of new capital which may be required.

I hope you can see from this elemental recital of what your Government is doing that there is nothing complex, or radical, in the process.

We had a bad banking situation. Some of our bankers had shown themselves either incompetent or dishonest in their handling of the people's funds. They had used the money entrusted to them in speculations and unwise loans. This was, of course, not true in the vast majority of our banks, but it was true in enough of them to shock the people for a time into a sense of insecurity and to put them into a frame of mind where they did not differentiate, but seemed to assume that the acts of a comparative few had tainted them all. It was the Government's job to straighten out this situation and do it as quickly as possible. And the job is being performed.

I do not promise you that every bank will be reopened or that individual losses will not be suffered, but there will be no losses that possibly could have been avoided; and there would have been more and greater losses had we continue to drift. I can even promise you salvation for at least some of the sorely pressed banks. We shall be engaged not merely in reopening sound banks but in the creation of sound banks through reorganization.

It has been wonderful to me to catch the note of confidence from all over the country. I can never be sufficiently grateful to all the people for the loyal support they have given me in their acceptance of the judgment that has dictated our course, even though all our processes may not have seemed clear to them.

After all, there is an element in the readjustment of our financial system more important than currency, more important than gold, and that is the confidence of the people. Confidence and courage are the essentials of success in carrying out our plan. You people must have faith; you must not be stampeded by rumors or guesses. Let us unite in banishing fear. We have provided the machinery to restore our financial system; it is up to you to support and make it work.

It is your problem no less than it is mine. Together we cannot fail.

Source: B. D. Zevin, ed. *Nothing to Fear: The Selected Addresses of Franklin Delano Roosevelt, 1932–1945.* Boston: Houghton Mifflin, 1946.

8. Fifth Fireside Chat—"On Economic Progress" June 28, 1934

FDR's fifth Fireside Chat dealt with the New Deal as most of them did. He focused on whether the New Deal was working. His response was put in a rhetorical question, "Are you better off now than you were last year?" He fully understood that his audience would answer in the affirmative.

It has been several months since I have talked with you concerning the problems of government. Since January, those of us in whom you have vested responsibility have been engaged in the fulfillment of plans and policies which had been widely discussed in previous months. It seemed to us our duty not only to make the right path clear but also to tread that path.

As we review the achievements of this session of the Seventy-third Congress, it is made increasingly clear that its task was essentially that of completing and fortifying the work it had begun in March, 1933. That was no easy task, but the Congress was equal to it. It has been well said that while there were a few exceptions, this Congress displayed a greater freedom from mere partisanship than any other peace-time Congress since the Administration

of President Washington himself. The session was distinguished by the extent and variety of legislation enacted and by the intelligence and good will of debate upon these measures.

I mention only a few of the major enactments. It provided for the readjustment of the debt burden through the corporate and municipal bankruptcy acts and the farm relief act. It lent a hand to industry by encouraging loans to solvent industries unable to secure adequate help from banking institutions. It strengthened the integrity of finance through the regulation of securities exchanges. It provided a rational method of increasing our volume of foreign trade through reciprocal trading agreements. It strengthened our naval forces to conform with the intentions and permission of existing treaty rights. It made further advances towards peace in industry through the labor adjustment act. It supplemented our agricultural policy through measures widely demanded by farmers themselves and intended to avert price destroying surpluses. It strengthened the hand of the Federal Government in its attempts to suppress gangster crime. It took definite steps towards a national housing program through an act which I signed today designed to encourage private capital in the rebuilding of the homes of the Nation. It created a permanent Federal body for the just regulation of all forms of communication, including the telephone, the telegraph and the radio. Finally, and I believe most important, it reorganized, simplified and made more fair and just our monetary system, setting up standards and policies adequate to meet the necessities of modern economic life, doing justice to both gold and silver as the metal bases behind the currency of the United States.

In the consistent development of our previous efforts toward the saving and safeguarding of our national life, I have continued to recognize three related steps. The first was relief, because the primary concern of any Government dominated by the humane ideals of democracy is the simple principle that in a land of vast resources no one should be permitted to starve. Relief was and continues to be our first consideration. It calls for large expenditures and will continue in modified form to do so for a long time to come. We may as well recognize that fact. It comes from the paralysis that arose as the after-effect of that unfortunate decade characterized by a mad chase for unearned riches and an unwillingness of leaders in almost every walk of life to look beyond their own schemes and speculations. In our administration of relief we follow two principles: First, that direct giving shall, wherever possible, be supplemented by provision for useful and remunerative work and, second, that where families in their existing surroundings will in all human probability never find an opportunity for full self-maintenance, happiness and enjoyment, we will try to give them a new chance in new surroundings.

The second step was recovery, and it is sufficient for me to ask each and every one of you to compare the situation in agriculture and in industry today with what it was fifteen months ago.

At the same time we have recognized the necessity of reform and reconstruction—reform because much of our trouble today and in the past few years has been due to a lack of understanding of the elementary principles of justice and fairness by those in whom leadership in business and finance was placed—reconstruction because new conditions in our economic life as well as old but neglected conditions had to be corrected.

Substantial gains well known to all of you have justified our course. I could cite statistics to you as unanswerable measures of our national progress—statistics to show the gain in the average weekly pay envelope of workers in the great majority of industries—statistics to show hundreds of thousands reemployed in private industries and other hundreds of thou-sands given new employment through the expansion of direct and indirect government assistance of many kinds, although, of course, there are those exceptions in professional pursuits whose economic improvement, of necessity, will be delayed. I also could cite statistics to show the great rise in the value of farm products—statistics to prove the demand for consumers' goods, ranging all the way from food and clothing to automobiles and of late to prove the rise in the demand for durable goods—statistics to cover the great increase in bank deposits and to show the scores of thousands of homes and of farms which have been saved from foreclosure.

But the simplest way for each of you to judge recovery lies in the plain facts of your own individual situation. Are you better off than you were last year? Are your debts less burdensome? Is your bank account more secure? Are your working conditions better? Is your faith in your own individual future more firmly grounded?

Also, let me put to you another simple question: Have you as an individual paid too high a price for these gains? Plausible self-seekers and theoretical die-hards will tell you of the loss of individual liberty. Answer this question also out of the facts of your own life. Have you lost any of your rights or liberty or constitutional freedom of action and choice? Turn to the Bill of Rights of the Constitution, which I have solemnly sworn to maintain and under which your freedom rests secure. Read each provision of that Bill of Rights and ask yourself whether you personally have suffered the impairment of a single jot of these great assurances. I have no question in my mind as to what your answer will be. The record is written in the experiences of your own personal lives.

In other words, it is not the overwhelming majority of the farmers or manufacturers or workers who deny the substantial gains of the past year. The most vociferous of the doubting

Thomases may be divided roughly into two groups: First, those who seek special political privilege and, second, those who seek special financial privilege. About a year ago I used as an illustration the 90% of the cotton manufacturers of the United States who wanted to do the right thing by their employees and by the public but were prevented from doing so by the 10% who undercut them by unfair practices and un-American standards. It is well for us to remember that humanity is a long way from being perfect and that a selfish minority in every walk of life—farming, business, finance and even Government service itself—will always continue to think of themselves first and their fellow-being second.

In the working out of a great national program which seeks the primary good of the greater number, it is true that the toes of some people are being stepped on and are going to be stepped on. But these toes belong to the comparative few who seek to retain or to gain position or riches or both by some short cut which is harmful to the greater good.

In the execution of the powers conferred on it by Congress, the Administration needs and will tirelessly seek the best ability that the country affords. Public service offers better rewards in the opportunity for service than ever before in our history—not great salaries, but enough to live on. In the building of this service there are coming to us men and women with ability and courage from every part of the Union. The days of the seeking of mere party advantage through the misuse of public power are drawing to a close. We are increasingly demanding and getting devotion to the public service on the part of every member of the Administration, high and low.

The program of the past year is definitely in operation and that operation month by month is being made to fit into the web of old and new conditions. This process of evolution is well illustrated by the constant changes in detailed organization and method going on in the National Recovery Administration. With every passing month we are making strides in the orderly handling of the relationship between employees and employers. Conditions differ, of course, in almost every part of the country and in almost every industry. Temporary methods of adjustment are being replaced by more permanent machinery and, I am glad to say, by a growing recognition on the part of employers and employees of the desirability of maintaining fair relationships all around.

So also, while almost everybody has recognized the tremendous strides in the elimination of child labor, in the payment of not less than fair minimum wages and in the shortening of hours, we are still feeling our way in solving problems which relate to self-government in industry, especially where such self government tends to eliminate the fair operation of competition.

In this same process of evolution we are keeping before us the objectives of protecting on the one hand industry against chiselers within its own ranks, and on the other hand the consumer through the maintenance of reasonable competition for the prevention of the unfair sky-rocketing of retail prices.

But, in addition to this our immediate task, we must still look to the larger future. I have pointed out to the Congress that we are seeking to find the way once more to well-known, long-established but to some degree forgotten ideals and values. We seek the security of the men, women and children of the Nation.

That security involves added means of providing better homes for the people of the Nation. That is the first principle of our future program.

The second is to plan the use of land and water resources of this country to the end that the means of livelihood of our citizens may be more adequate to meet their daily needs.

And, finally, the third principle is to use the agencies of government to assist in the establishment of means to provide sound and adequate protection against the vicissitudes of modern life—in other words, social insurance.

Later in the year I hope to talk with you more fully about these plans. A few timid people, who fear progress, will try to give you new and strange names for what we are doing. Sometimes they will call it "Fascism," sometimes "Communism," sometimes "Regimentation," sometimes "Socialism." But, in so doing, they are trying to make very complex and theoretical something that is really very simple and very practical.

I believe in practical explanations and in practical policies. I believe that what we are doing today is a necessary fulfillment of what Americans have always been doing—a fulfillment of old and tested American ideals.

Let me give you a simple illustration: While I am away from Washington this summer, a long needed renovation of and addition to our White House office building is to be started. The architects have planned a few new rooms built into the present all too small one-story structure. We are going to include in this addition and in this renovation modern electric wiring and modern plumbing and modern means of keeping the offices cool in the hot Washington summers. But the structural lines of the old Executive Office Building will remain. The artistic lines of the White House buildings were the creation of master builders when our Republic was young. The simplicity and the strength of the structure remain in the face of every modern test. But within this magnificent pattern, the necessities of modern government business require constant reorganization and rebuilding.

If I were to listen to the arguments of some prophets of calamity who are talking these days, I should hesitate to make these alterations. I should fear that while I am away for a few weeks the architects might build some strange new Gothic tower or a factory building or perhaps a replica of the Kremlin or of the Potsdam Palace. But I have no such fears. The architects and builders are men of common sense and of artistic American tastes. They know that the principles of harmony and of necessity itself require that the building of the new structure shall blend with the essential lines of the old. It is this combination of the old and the new that marks orderly peaceful progress—not only in building buildings but in building government itself.

Our new structure is a part of and a fulfillment of the old.

All that we do seeks to fulfill the historic traditions of the American people. Other nations may sacrifice democracy for the transitory stimulation of old and discredited autocracies. We are restoring confidence and well-being under the rule of the people themselves. We remain, as John Marshall said a century ago, "emphatically and truly, a government of the people." Our government "in form and in substance . . . emanates from them. Its powers are granted by them, and are to be exercised directly on them, and for their benefits."

Before I close, I want to tell you of the interest and pleasure with which I look forward to the trip on which I hope to start in a few days. It is a good thing for everyone who can possibly do so to get away at least once a year for a change of scene. I do not want to get into the position of not being able to see the forest because of the thickness of the trees.

I hope to visit our fellow Americans in Puerto Rico, in the Virgin Islands, in the Canal Zone and in Hawaii. And, incidentally, it will give me an opportunity to exchange a friendly word of greeting to the Presidents of our sister Republics: Haiti, Colombia and Panama.

After four weeks on board ship, I plan to land at a port in our Pacific northwest, and then will come the best part of the whole trip, for I am hoping to inspect a number of our new great national projects on the Columbia, Missouri and Mississippi Rivers, to see some of our national parks and, incidentally, to learn much of actual conditions during the trip across the continent back to Washington.

While I was in France during the War our boys used to call the United States "God's country." Let us make it and keep it "God's country."

Source: Franklin D. Roosevelt, "Review of the Achievements of the Seventy-third Congress." New Deal Network—Reagan's Fireside Chats. Available online. URL: http://newdeal.feri.org/chat/chat05.htm.

9. Sixth Fireside Chat—On Moving Forward to Greater Freedom and Security, September 30, 1934

FDR's sixth Fireside Chat was a spirited defense of the National Recovery Act, which had been offered as the backbone of the New Deal in response to the critical economic conditions of 1933.

Three months have passed since I talked with you shortly after the adjournment of the Congress. Tonight I continue that report, though, because of the shortness of time, I must defer a number of subjects to a later date.

Recently the most notable public questions that have concerned us all have had to do with industry and labor and with respect to these, certain developments have taken place which I consider of importance. I am happy to report that after years of uncertainty, culminating in the collapse of the spring of 1933, we are bringing order out of the old chaos with a greater certainty of the employment of labor at a reasonable wage and of more business at a fair profit. These governmental and industrial developments hold promise of new achievements for the Nation.

Men may differ as to the particular form of governmental activity with respect to industry and business, but nearly all are agreed that private enterprise in times such as these cannot be left without assistance and without reasonable safeguards lest it destroy not only itself but also our processes of civilization. The underlying necessity for such activity is indeed as strong now as it was years ago when Elihu Root said the following very significant words:

"Instead of the give and take of free individual contract, the tremendous power of organization has combined great aggregations of capital in enormous industrial establishments working through vast agencies of commerce and employing great masses of men in movements of production and transportation and trade, so great in the mass that each individual concerned in them is quite helpless by himself. The relations between the employer and the employed, between the owners of aggregated capital and the units of organized labor, between the small producer, the small trader, the consumer, and the great transporting and manufacturing and distributing agencies, all present new questions for the solution of which the old reliance upon the free action of individual wills appears quite inadequate. And in many directions, the intervention of that organized control which we call government seems necessary to produce the same result of justice and right conduct which obtained through the attrition of individuals before the new conditions arose."

It was in this spirit thus described by Secretary Root that we approached our task of reviving private enterprise in March, 1933. Our first problem was, of course, the banking situation because, as you know, the banks had collapsed. Some banks could not be saved but the great majority of them, either through their own resources or with Government aid, have been restored to complete public confidence. This has given safety to millions of depositors in these banks. Closely following this great constructive effort we have, through various Federal agencies, saved debtors and creditors alike in many other fields of enterprise, such as loans on farm mortgages and home mortgages; loans to the railroads and insurance companies and, finally, help for home owners and industry itself.

In all of these efforts the Government has come to the assistance of business and with the full expectation that the money used to assist these enterprises will eventually be repaid. I believe it will be.

The second step we have taken in the restoration of normal business enterprise has been to clean up thoroughly unwholesome conditions in the field of investment. In this we have had assistance from many bankers and business men, most of whom recognize the past evils in the banking system, in the sale of securities, in the deliberate encouragement of stock gambling, in the sale of unsound mortgages and in many other ways in which the public lost billions of dollars. They saw that without changes in the policies and methods of investment there could be no recovery of public confidence in the security of savings. The country now enjoys the safety of bank savings under the new banking laws, the careful checking of new securities under the Securities Act and the curtailment of rank stock speculation through the Securities Exchange Act. I sincerely hope that as a result people will be discouraged in unhappy efforts to get rich quick by speculating in securities. The average person almost always loses. Only a very small minority of the people of this country believe in gambling as a substitute for the old philosophy of Benjamin Franklin that the way to wealth is through work.

In meeting the problems of industrial recovery the chief agency of the Government has been the National Recovery Administration. Under its guidance, trades and industries covering over 90 percent of all industrial employees have adopted codes of fair competition, which have been approved by the President. Under these codes, in the industries covered, child labor has been eliminated. The work day and the work week have been shortened. Minimum wages have been established and other wages adjusted toward a rising standard of living. The emergency purpose of the N.R.A. was to put men to work and since its creation more than four million persons have been reemployed, in great part through the cooperation of American business brought about under the codes.

Benefits of the Industrial Recovery Program have come, not only to labor in the form of new jobs, in relief from overwork and in relief from underpay, but also to the owners and managers of industry because, together with a great increase in the payrolls, there has come a substantial rise in the total of industrial profits—a rise from a deficit figure in the first quarter of 1933 to a level of sustained profits within one year from the inauguration of N.R.A.

Now it should not be expected that even employed labor and capital would be completely satisfied with present conditions. Employed workers have not by any means all enjoyed a return to the earnings of prosperous times, although millions of hitherto underprivileged workers are today far better paid than ever before. Also, billions of dollars of invested capital have today a greater security of present and future earning power than before. This is because of the establishment of fair, competitive standards and because of relief from unfair competition in wage cutting which depresses markets and destroys purchasing power. But it is an undeniable fact that the restoration of other billions of sound investments to a reasonable earning power could not be brought about in one year. There is no magic formula, no economic panacea, which could simply revive overnight the heavy industries and the trades dependent upon them.

Nevertheless the gains of trade and industry, as a whole, have been substantial. In these gains and in the policies of the Administration there are assurances that hearten all forward-looking men and women with the confidence that we are definitely rebuilding our political and economic system on the lines laid down by the New Deal—lines which as I have so often made clear, are in complete accord with the underlying principles of orderly popular government which Americans have demanded since the white man first came to these shores. We count, in the future as in the past, on the driving power of individual initiative and the incentive of fair private profit, strengthened with the acceptance of those obligations to the public interest which rest upon us all. We have the right to expect that this driving power will be given patriotically and whole-heartedly to our Nation.

We have passed through the formative period of code making in the National Recovery Administration and have effected a reorganization of the N.R.A. suited to the needs of the next phase, which is, in turn, a period of preparation for legislation which will determine its permanent form.

In this recent reorganization we have recognized three distinct functions: first, the legislative or policy-making function; second, the administrative function of code making and revision; and, third, the judicial function, which includes enforcement, consumer complaints and the settlement of disputes between employers and employees and between one employer and another.

We are now prepared to move into this second phase, on the basis of our experience in the first phase under the able and energetic leadership of General Johnson.

We shall watch carefully the working of this new machinery from the second phase of the N.R.A., modifying it where it needs modification and finally making recommendations to the Congress, in order that the functions of N.R.A. which have provided their worth may be made a part of the permanent machinery of government.

Let me call your attention to the fact that the National Industrial Recovery Act gave business men the opportunity they had sought for years to improve business conditions through what has been called self-government in industry. If the codes which have been written have been too complicated, if they have gone too far in such matters as price fixing and limitation of production, let it be remembered that so far as possible, consistent with the immediate public interest of this past year and the vital necessity of improving labor conditions, the representatives of trade and industry were permitted to write their ideas into the codes. It is now time to review these actions as a whole to determine through deliberative means in the light of experience, from the standpoint of the good of the industries themselves, as well as the general public interest, whether the methods and policies adopted in the emergency have been best calculated to promote industrial recovery and a permanent improvement of business and labor conditions. There may be a serious question as to the wisdom of many of those devices to control production, or to prevent destructive price cutting which many business organizations have insisted were necessary, or whether their effect may have been to prevent that volume of production which would make possible lower prices and increased employment. Another question arises as to whether in fixing minimum wages on the basis of an hourly or weekly wage we have reached into the heart of the problem which is to provide annual earnings for the lowest paid worker as will meet his minimum needs. We also question the wisdom of extending code requirements suited to the great industrial centers and to large employers, to the great number of small employers in the smaller communities.

During the last twelve months our industrial recovery has been to some extent retarded by strikes, including a few of major importance. I would not minimize the inevitable losses to employers and employees and to the general public through such conflicts. But I would point out that the extent and severity of labor disputes during this period have been far less than in any previous comparable period.

When the business men of the country were demanding the right to organize themselves adequately to promote their legitimate interests; when the farmers were demanding legislation which would give them opportunities and incentives to organize themselves for a common advance, it was natural that the workers should seek and obtain a statutory declaration of their constitutional right to organize themselves for collective bargaining as embodied in Section 7-A of the National Industrial Recovery Act.

Machinery set up by the Federal Government has provided some new methods of adjustment. Both employers and employees must share the blame of not using them as fully as they should. The employer who turns away from impartial agencies of peace, who denies freedom of organization to his employees, or fails to make every reasonable effort at a peaceful solution of their differences, is not fully supporting the recovery effort of his Government. The workers who turn away from these same impartial agencies and decline to use their good offices to gain their ends are likewise not fully cooperating with their Government.

It is time that we made a clean-cut effort to bring about that united action of management and labor, which is one of the high purposes of the Recovery Act. We have passed through more than a year of education. Step by step we have created all the Government agencies necessary to insure, as a general rule, industrial peace, with justice for all those willing to use these agencies whenever their voluntary bargaining fails to produce a necessary agreement.

There should be at least a full and fair trial given to these means of ending industrial warfare; and in such an effort we should be able to secure for employers and employees and con-sumers the benefits that all derive from the continuous, peaceful operation of our essential enterprises.

Accordingly, I propose to confer within the coming month with small groups of those truly representative of large employers of labor and of large groups of organized labor, in order to seek their cooperation in establishing what I may describe as a specific trial period of industrial peace.

From those willing to join in establishing this hoped-for period of peace, I shall seek assurances of the making and maintenance of agreements, which can be mutually relied upon, under which wages, hours and working conditions may be determined and any later adjustments shall be made either by agreement or, in case of disagreement, through the mediation or arbitration of State or Federal agencies. I shall not ask either employers or employees permanently to lay aside the weapons common to industrial war. But I shall ask both groups to give a fair trial to peaceful methods of adjusting their conflicts of opinion and interest, and to experiment for a reasonable time with measures suitable to civilize our industrial civilization.

Closely allied to the N.R.A. is the program of public works provided for in the same Act and designed to put more men back to work, both directly on the public works themselves, and indirectly in the industries supplying the materials for these public works. To those who say that our expenditures for public works and other means for recovery are a waste that we cannot afford, I answer that no country, however rich, can afford the waste of its human resources. Demoralization caused by vast unemployment is our greatest extravagance. Morally, it is the greatest menace to our social order. Some people try to tell me that we must make up our minds that for the future we shall permanently have millions of unemployed just as other countries have had them for over a decade. What may be necessary for those countries is not my responsibility to determine. But as for this country, I stand or fall by my refusal to accept as a necessary condition of our future a permanent army of unemployed. On the contrary, we must make it a national principle that we will not tolerate a large army of unemployed and that we will arrange our national economy to end our present unemployment as soon as we can and then to take wise measures against its return. I do not want to think that it is the destiny of any American to remain permanently on relief rolls.

Those, fortunately few in number, who are frightened by boldness and cowed by the necessity for making decisions, complain that all we have done is unnecessary and subject to great risks. Now that these people are coming out of their storm cellars, they forget that there ever was a storm. They point to England. They would have you believe that England has made progress out of her depression by a do-nothing policy, by letting nature take her course. England has her peculiarities and we have ours, but I do not believe any intelligent observer can accuse England of undue orthodoxy in the present emergency.

Did England let nature take her course? No. Did England hold to the gold standard when her reserves were threatened? No. Has England gone back to the gold standard today? No. Did England hesitate to call in ten billion dollars of her war bonds bearing 5 percent interest, to issue new bonds therefore bearing only 3 1/2 percent interest, thereby saving the British Treasury one hundred and fifty million dollars a year in interest alone? No. And let it be recorded that the British bankers helped. Is it not a fact that ever since the year 1909, Great Britain in many ways has advanced further along the lines of social security than the United States? Is it not a fact that relations between capital and labor on the basis of collective bargaining are much further advanced in Great Britain than in the United States? Is it perhaps not strange that the conservative British press has told us with pardonable irony that much of our New Deal program is only an attempt to catch up with English reforms that go back ten years or more.

Nearly all Americans are sensible and calm people. We do not get greatly excited nor is our peace of mind disturbed, whether we be business men or workers or farmers, by awesome pronouncements concerning the unconstitutionality of some of our measures of recovery and relief and reform. We are not frightened by reactionary lawyers or political editors. All of these cries have been heard before. More than twenty-one years ago, when Theodore Roosevelt and Woodrow Wilson were attempting to correct abuses in our national life, the great Chief Justice White said;

"There is a great danger it seems to me to arise from the constant habit which prevails where anything is opposed or objected to, of referring without rhyme or reason to the Constitution as a means of preventing its accomplishment, thus creating the general impression that the Constitution is but a barrier to progress instead of being the broad highway through which alone true progress may be enjoyed."

In our efforts for recovery we have avoided, on the one hand, the theory that business should and must be taken over into an all-embracing Government. We have avoided, on the other hand, the equally untenable theory that it is an interference with liberty to offer reasonable help when private enterprise is in need of help. The course we have followed fits the American practice of Government, a practice of taking action step by step, of regulating only to meet concrete needs, a practice of courageous recognition of change. I believe with Abraham Lincoln, that "The legitimate object of Government is to do for a community of people whatever they need to have done but cannot do at all or cannot do so well for themselves in their separate and individual capacities."

I am not for a return to that definition of liberty under which for many years a free people were being gradually regimented into the service of the privileged few. I prefer and I am sure you prefer that broader definition of liberty under which we are moving forward to greater freedom, to greater security for the average man than he has ever known before in the history of America."

Source: *The Public Papers and Addresses of Franklin D. Roosevelt*, Vol. 3 (New York: Macmillan Company), 413–422.

10. Speech to the Democratic National Convention, June 27, 1936

In 1936, in Philadelphia, Pennsylvania, FDR was in the position that Herbert Hoover held in 1932. Campaigning for reelection, he delivered his opening salvo. He used Stanley High's phrase condemning the rich "economic royalists" and promised Americans they had a "rendezvous with destiny," a phrase coined by Tommy Corcoran.

. . . America will not forget these recent years, will not forget that the rescue was not a mere party task. It was the concern of all of us. In our strength we rose together, rallied our energies together, applied the old rules of common sense, and together survived.

In those days we feared fear. That was why we fought fear. And today, my friends, we have won against the most dangerous of our foes. We have conquered fear.

But I cannot, with candor, tell you that all is well with the world. Clouds of suspicion, tides of ill-will and intolerance gather darkly in many places. In our own land we enjoy indeed a fullness of life greater than that of most Nations. But the rush of modern civilization itself has raised for us new difficulties, new problems which must be solved if we are to preserve to the United States the political and

economic freedom for which Washington and Jefferson planned and fought. . . .

Throughout the Nation, opportunity was limited by monopoly. Individual initiative was crushed in the cogs of a great machine. The field open for free business was more and more restricted. Private enterprise, indeed, became too private. It became privileged enterprise, not free enterprise.

An old English judge once said: "Necessitous men are not free men." Liberty requires opportunity to make a living—a living decent according to the standard of the time, a living which gives man not only enough to live by, but something to live for.

For too many of us the political equality we once had won was meaningless in the face of economic inequality. A small group had concentrated into their own hands an almost complete control over other people's property, other people's money, other people's labor—other people's lives. For too many of us life was no longer free; liberty no longer real; men could no longer follow the pursuit of happiness.

Against economic tyranny such as this, the American citizen could appeal only to the organized power of Government. The collapse of 1929 showed up the despotism for what it was. The election of 1932 was the people's mandate to end it. Under that mandate it is being ended.

The royalists of the economic order have conceded that political freedom was the business of the Government, but they have maintained that economic slavery was nobody's business. They granted that the Constitution could protect the citizen in his right to vote, but they denied that the Government could do anything to protect the citizen in his right to work and his right to live.

Today we stand committed to the proposition that freedom is no half-and-half affair. If the average citizen is guaranteed equal opportunity in the polling place, he must have equal opportunity in the market place.

These economic royalists complain that we seek to overthrow the institutions of America. What they really complain of is that we seek to take away their power. Our allegiance to American institutions requires the overthrow of this kind of power. In vain they seek to hide behind the Flag and the Constitution. In their blindness they forget what the Flag and the Constitution stand for. Now, as always, they stand for democracy, not tyranny; for freedom, not subjection; and against a dictatorship by mob rule and the overprivileged alike. . . .

We seek not merely to make Government a mechanical implement, but to give it the vibrant personal character that is the very embodiment of human charity. . . .

Governments can err, Presidents do make mistakes, but the immortal Dante tells us that divine justice weighs the sins of the cold-blooded and the sins of the warm-hearted in different scales.

Better the occasional faults of Government that lives in the spirit of charity than the consistent omissions of a Government frozen in the ice of its own indifference.

There is a mysterious cycle in human events. To some generations much is given. Of other generations much is expected. This generation of Americans has a rendezvous with destiny. . . .

Source: Samuel I. Rosenman, comp. *The Public Papers and Addresses of Franklin D. Roosevelt*, Vol. 5 (1938; reprint, New York: Russell and Russell, 1969), 230–236.

11. "I Hate War" Speech, Chautauqua, New York, August 14, 1936

Facing the Spanish civil war and the Neutrality Act of 1935, FDR was caught between his international outlook and an isolationist Congress. He turned the tables on the isolationists asserting that he rather than the Republicans, many of whom were isolationists, could prevent war. He claimed that war profiteers or Republican economic royalists favored war but that he would fight for peace.

As many of you who are here tonight know, I formed the excellent habit of coming to Chautauqua more than twenty years ago. After my Inauguration in 1933, I promised Mr. Bestor that during the next four years I would come to Chautauqua again. It is in fulfillment of this that I am with you tonight.

A few days ago I was asked what the subject of this talk would be; and I replied that for two good reasons I wanted to discuss the subject of peace: First, because it is eminently appropriate in Chautauqua and second, because in the hurly-burly of domestic politics it is important that our people should not overlook problems and issues which, though they lie beyond our borders, may, and probably will, have a vital influence on the United States of the future.

Many who have visited me in Washington in the past few months may have been surprised when I have told them that personally and because of my own daily contacts with all manner of difficult situations I am more concerned and less cheerful about international world conditions than about our immediate domestic prospects.

I say this to you not as a confirmed pessimist but as one who still hopes that envy, hatred and malice among Nations have reached their peak and will be succeeded by a new tide of peace and good-will. I say this as one who has participated in many of the decisions of peace and war before, during and after the World War; one who has traveled much; and one who has spent a good portion of every twenty-four hours in the study of foreign relations.

Long before I returned to Washington as President of the United States, I had made up my mind that pending what might be called a more opportune moment on other continents, the United States could best serve the cause of a peaceful humanity by setting an example.

That was why on the 4th of March 1933, I made the following declaration:

"In the field of world policy I would dedicate this Nation to the policy of the good neighbor—the neighbor who resolutely respects himself and, because he does so, respects the rights of others—the neighbor who respects his obligations and respects the sanctity of his agreements in and with a world of neighbors."

This declaration represents my purpose; but it represents more than a purpose, for it stands for a practice. To a measurable degree it has succeeded; the whole world now knows that the United States cherishes no predatory ambitions. We are strong; but less powerful Nations know that they need not fear our strength. We seek no conquest; we stand for peace.

In the whole of the Western Hemisphere our good-neighbor policy has produced results that are especially heartening.

The noblest monument to peace and to neighborly economic and social friendship in all the world is not a monument in bronze or stone, but the boundary which unites the United States and Canada—3,000 miles of friendship with no barbed wire, no gun or soldier, and no passport on the whole frontier.

Mutual trust made that frontier. To extend the same sort of mutual trust throughout the Americas was our aim.

The American Republics to the south of us have been ready always to cooperate with the United States on the basis of equality and mutual respect, but before we inaugurated the good-neighbor policy there were among them resentment and fear, because certain Administrations in Washington had slighted their national pride and their sovereign rights.

In pursuance of the good-neighbor policy, and because in my younger days I had learned many lessons in the hard school of experience, I stated that the United States was opposed definitely to armed intervention.

We have negotiated a Pan-American convention embodying the principle of non-intervention. We have abandoned the Platt Amendment which gave us the right to intervene in the international affairs of the Republic of Cuba. We have withdrawn American marines from Haiti. We have signed a new treaty which places our relations with Panama on a mutually satisfactory basis. We have undertaken a series of trade agreements with other American countries to our mutual commercial profit. At the request of two neighboring Republics, I hope to give assistance in the final settlement of the last serious boundary dispute between any of the American nations.

Throughout the Americas the spirit of the good neighbor is a practical and living fact. The twenty-one American Republics are not only living together in friendship and in peace; they are united in the determination so to remain.

To give substance to this determination a conference will meet on December 1, 1936, at the capital of our great Southern neighbor, Argentina, and it is, I know, the hope of all Chiefs of State of the Americas that this will result in measures which will banish wars forever from this vast portion of the earth.

Peace, like charity, begins at home; that is why we have begun at home. But peace in the Western world is not all that we seek.

It is our hope that knowledge of the practical application of the good-neighbor policy in this hemisphere will be borne home to our neighbors across the seas.

For ourselves we are on good terms with them—terms in most cases of straightforward friendship, of peaceful understanding.

But, of necessity, we are deeply concerned about tendencies of recent years among many of the Nations of other continents. It is a bitter experience to us when the spirit of agreements to which we are a party is not lived up to. It is an even more bitter experience for the whole company of Nations to witness not only the spirit but the letter of international agreements violated with impunity and without regard to the simple principles of honor. Permanent friendships between Nations as between men can be sustained only by scrupulous respect for the pledged word.

In spite of all this we have sought steadfastly to assist international movements to prevent war. We cooperated to the bitter end—and it was a bitter end—in the work of the General Disarmament Conference. When it failed we sought a separate treaty to deal with the manufacture of arms and the international traffic in arms. That proposal also came to nothing. We participated—again to the bitter end—in a conference to continue naval limitations, and when it became evident that no general treaty could be signed because of the objections of other Nations, we concluded with Great Britain and France a conditional treaty of qualitative limitation which, much to my regret, already shows signs of ineffectiveness.

We shun political commitments which might entangle us in foreign wars; we avoid connection with the political activities of the League of Nations; but I am glad to say that we have cooperated whole-heartedly in the social and humanitarian work at Geneva. Thus we are part of the world effort to control traffic in narcotics, to improve international health, to help child welfare, to eliminate double taxation and to better working conditions and laboring hours throughout the world.

We are not isolationists except in so far as we seek to isolate ourselves completely from war. Yet we must remember that so long as war exists on earth there will be some danger that even the Nation which most ardently desires peace may be drawn into war.

I have seen war. I have seen war on land and sea. I have seen blood running from the wounded. I have seen men coughing out their gassed lungs. I have seen the dead in the mud. I have seen cities destroyed. I have seen two hundred limping, exhausted men come out of line—the survivors of a regiment of one thousand that went forward forty-eight hours before. I have seen children starving. I have seen the agony of mothers and wives. I hate war.

I have passed unnumbered hours, I shall pass unnumbered hours, thinking and planning how war may be kept from this Nation.

I wish I could keep war from all Nations; but that is beyond my power. I can at least make certain that no act of the United States helped to produce or to promote war. I can at least make clear that the conscience of America revolts against war and that any Nation which provokes war forfeits the sympathy of the people of the United States.

Many causes produce war. There are ancient hatred, turbulent frontiers, the "legacy of old forgotten, far-off things, and battles long ago." There are new-born fanaticisms, convictions on the part of certain peoples that they have become the unique depositories of ultimate truth and right.

A dark old world was devastated by wars between conflicting religions. A dark modern world faces war between conflicting economic and political fanaticisms in which are intertwined race hatreds. To bring it home, it is as if within the territorial limits of the United States, forty-eight Nations with forty-eight forms of government, forty-eight custom barriers, forty-eight languages, and forty-eight eternal and different verities, were spending their time and their substance in a frenzy of effort to make ourselves strong enough to conquer their neighbors or strong enough to defend themselves against their neighbors.

In one field, that of economic barriers, the American policy may be, I hope, of some assistance in discouraging the economic source of war and therefore a contribution toward the peace of the world. The trade agreements which we are making are not only finding outlets for the products of the American fields and American factories, but are also pointing the way to the elimination of embargoes, quotas and other devices which place such pressure on Nations not possessing great natural resources that to them the price of peace seems less terrible than the price of war.

We do not maintain that a more liberal international trade will stop war; but we fear that without a more liberal international trade, war is a natural sequence.

The Congress of the United States has given me certain authority to provide safeguards of American neutrality in case of war.

The President of the United States, who, under our Constitution, is vested with primary authority to conduct our international relations, thus has been given new weapons with which to maintain our neutrality.

Nevertheless—and I speak from long experience—the effective maintenance of American neutrality depends today, as in the past, on the wisdom and determination of whoever at the moment occupy the offices of President and Secretary of State.

It is clear that our present policy and measures passed by the Congress would, in the event of a war on some other continent, reduce war profits which would otherwise accrue to American citizens. Industrial and agricultural production for a war market may give immense fortunes to a few men; for the nation as a whole it produces disaster. It was the prospect of war profits that made our farmers in the West plow up prairie land that should never have been plowed, but should have been left for grazing cattle. Today we are reaping the harvest of those war profits in dust storms which have devastated those war-plowed areas.

It was the prospect of war profits that caused the extension of monopoly and unjustified expansion of industry and a price level so high that the normal relationship between debtor and creditor was destroyed.

Nevertheless, if war should break out again in another continent, let us not blink the fact that we would find in this country thousands of Americans who, seeking immediate riches— fools' gold—would attempt to break down or evade our neutrality.

They would tell you—and, unfortunately, their views would get wide publicity—that if they could produce and ship this and that and the other article to belligerent Nations, the unemployed of America would all find work. They would tell you that if they could extend credit to warring Nations that credit would be used in the United States to build homes and factories and pay our debts. They would tell you that America once more would capture the trade of the world.

It would be hard to resist that clamor; it would be hard for many Americans, I fear, to look beyond—to realize the inevitable penalties, the inevitable day of reckoning, that come from a false prosperity. To resist the clamor of that greed, if war should come, would require the unswerving support of all Americans who love peace.

If we face the choice of profits or peace, the Nation will answer—must answer—"We choose peace." It is the duty of all of us to encourage such a body of public opinion in this country that the answer will be clear and for all practical purposes unanimous.

With that wise and experienced man who is our Secretary of State, whose statesmanship has met with such wide approval, I have thought and worked long and hard on the problem of keeping the United States at peace. But all the wisdom of America is not to be found in the White House or in the Department of State; we need the meditation, the prayer, and the positive support of the people of America who go along with us in seeking peace.

No matter how well we are supported by neutrality legislation, we must remember that no laws can be provided to cover every contingency, for it is impossible to imagine how every future event may shape itself. In spite of every possible forethought, international relations involve of necessity a vast uncharted area. In that safe area sailing will depend on the knowledge and the experience and the wisdom of those who direct our foreign policy. Peace will depend on their day-to-day decisions.

At this late date, with the wisdom which is so easy after the event and so difficult before the event, we find it possible to trace the tragic series of small decisions which led Europe into the Great War in 1914 and eventually engulfed us and many other Nations.

We can keep out of war if those who watch and decide have a sufficiently detailed understanding of international affairs to make certain that the small decisions of each day do not lead toward war and if, at the same time, they possess the courage to say "no" to those who selfishly or unwisely would let us go to war.

Of all the Nations of the world today we are in many ways most singularly blessed. Our closest neighbors are good neighbors. If there are remoter Nations that wish us not good but ill, they know that we are strong; they know that we can and will defend ourselves and defend our neighborhood.

We seek to dominate no other Nation. We ask no territorial expansion. We oppose imperialism. We desire reduction in world armaments.

We believe in democracy; we believe in freedom; we believe in peace. We offer to every Nation of the world the handclasp of the good neighbor. Let those who wish our friendship look us in the eye and take our hand.

Source: "Franklin D. Roosevelt at Chautauqua, New York (I Hate War Speech), August 14, 1936." The Authentic History Center. Available online. URL: http://www.authentichistory.com/audio/1930s/history/19360814_FDR_At_Chautauqua_NY.html.

12. "We Have Only Just Begun to Fight"—Campaign Address at Madison Square Garden, New York City, October 31, 1936

FDR delivered his so-called John Paul Jones speech—his last major address during the fall 1936 campaign. It was written by Samuel Rosenman, Tommy Corcoran, Stanley High, and Donald Richberg. Naval enthusiast Roosevelt incorporated John Paul Jones's famous retort from the Revolutionary War to the captain of a British warship, "we have only just begun to fight." FDR sided with the people against "the Interests," claiming he welcomed the hatred of the business community, and scored Hooverism with the famous monkey metaphor, "hear-nothing, see-nothing, do-nothing Government."

Senator Wagner, Governor Lehman, ladies and gentlemen:

On the eve of a national election, it is well for us to stop for a moment and analyze calmly and without prejudice the effect on our Nation of a victory by either of the major political parties.

The problem of the electorate is far deeper, far more vital than the continuance in the Presidency of any individual. For the greater issue goes beyond units of humanity—it goes to humanity itself.

In 1932 the issue was the restoration of American democracy; and the American people were in a mood to win. They did win. In 1936 the issue is the preservation of their victory. Again they are in a mood to win. Again they will win.

More than four years ago in accepting the Democratic nomination in Chicago, I said: "Give me your help not to win votes alone, but to win in this crusade to restore America to its own people."

The banners of that crusade still fly in the van of a Nation that is on the march.

It is needless to repeat the details of the program which this Administration has been hammering out on the anvils of experience. No amount of misrepresentation or statistical contortion can conceal or blur that record. Neither the attacks of unscrupulous enemies nor the exaggerations of over-zealous friends will serve to mislead the American people.

What was our hope in 1932? Above all other things the American people wanted peace. They wanted peace of mind instead of gnawing fear.

First, they sought escape from the personal terror which had stalked them for three years. They wanted the peace that comes from security in their homes: safety for their savings, permanence in their jobs, a fair profit from their enterprise.

Next, they wanted peace in the community, the peace that springs from the ability to meet the needs of community life: schools, playgrounds, parks, sanitation, highways—those things which are expected of solvent local government. They sought escape from disintegration and bankruptcy in local and state affairs.

They also sought peace within the Nation: protection of their currency, fairer wages, the ending of long hours of toil, the abolition of child labor, the elimination of wild-cat speculation, the safety of their children from kidnappers.

And, finally, they sought peace with other Nations—peace in a world of unrest. The Nation knows that I hate war, and I know that the Nation hates war.

I submit to you a record of peace; and on that record a well-founded expectation for future peace—peace for the individual, peace for the community, peace for the Nation, and peace with the world.

Tonight I call the roll—the roll of honor of those who stood with us in 1932 and still stand with us today.

Written on it are the names of millions who never had a chance—men at starvation wages, women in sweatshops, children at looms.

Written on it are the names of those who despaired, young men and women for whom opportunity had become a will-o'-the-wisp.

Written on it are the names of farmers whose acres yielded only bitterness, business men whose books were portents of disaster, home owners who were faced with eviction, frugal citizens whose savings were insecure.

Written there in large letters are the names of countless other Americans of all parties and all faiths. Americans who had eyes to see and hearts to understand, whose consciences were burdened because too many of their fellows were burdened, who looked on these things four years ago and said, "This can be changed. We will change it."

We still lead that army in 1936. They stood with us then because in 1932 they believed. They stand with us today because in 1936 they know. And with them stand millions of new recruits who have come to know.

Their hopes have become our record.

We have not come this far without a struggle and I assure you we cannot go further without a struggle.

For twelve years this Nation was affiliated with hear-nothing, see-nothing, do-nothing Government. The Nation looked to Government but the Government looked away. Nine mocking years with the golden calf and three long years in the breadlines! Nine mad years of mirage and three long years of despair! Powerful influences strive today to restore that kind of government with its doctrine that that Government is best which is most indifferent.

For nearly four years you have had an Administration which instead of twirling its thumbs has rolled up its sleeves. We will keep our sleeves rolled up.

We had to struggle with the old enemies of peace—business and financial monopoly, speculation, reckless banking, class antagonism, sectionalism, war profiteering.

They had begun to consider the Government of the United States as a mere appendage to their own affairs. We know now that Government by organized money is just as dangerous as Government by organized mob.

Never before in all our history have these forces been so united against one candidate as they stand today. They are unanimous in their hate for me—and I welcome their hatred.

I should like to have it said of my first Administration that in it the forces of selfishness and of lust for power met their match. I should like to have it said of my second Administration that in it these forces met their master.

The American people know from a four-year record that today there is only one entrance to the White House—by the front door. Since March 4, 1933, there has been only one pass-key to the White House. I have carried that key in my pocket. It is there tonight. So long as I am President, it will remain in my pocket.

Those who used to have pass-keys are not happy. Some of them are desperate. Only desperate men with their backs to the wall would descend so far below the level of decent citizenship as to foster the current pay-envelope campaign against America's working people. Only reckless men, heedless of the consequences, would risk the disruption of the hope for a new peace between worker and employer by returning to the tactics of the labor spy.

Here is an amazing paradox! The very employers and politicians and publishers who talk most loudly of class antagonism and the destruction of the American system now undermine that system by this attempt to coerce the votes of the wage earners of this country. It is the 1936 version of the old threat to close down the factory or the office if a particular candidate does not win. It is an old strategy of tyrants to delude their victims into fighting their battles for them.

Every message in a pay envelope, even if it is the truth, is a command to vote according to the will of the employer. But this propaganda is worse—it is deceit.

They tell the worker his wage will be reduced by a contribution to some vague form of old-age insurance. They carefully conceal from him the fact that for every dollar of premium he pays for that insurance the employer pays another dollar. That omission is deceit.

They carefully conceal from him the fact that under the federal law, he receives another insurance policy to help him if he loses his job, and that the premium of the policy is paid 100 percent by the employer and not one cent by the worker. They do not tell him that the insurance policy that is bought for him is far more favorable to him than any policy that any private insurance company could afford to issue. That omission is deceit.

They imply to him that he pays all the cost of both forms of insurance. They carefully conceal from him the fact that for every dollar put up by him his employer puts up three dollars—three for one. And that omission is deceit.

But they are guilty of more than deceit. When they imply that the reserves thus created against both these policies will be stolen by some future Congress, diverted to some wholly foreign purpose, they attack the integrity and honor of American Government itself. Those who suggest that, are already aliens to the spirit of American democracy. Let them emigrate and try their lot under some foreign flag in which they have more confidence.

The fraudulent nature of this attempt is well shown by the record of votes on the passage of the Social Security Act. In addition to an overwhelming majority of Democrats in both Houses, seventy-seven Republican Representatives voted for it and only eighteen against it and fifteen Republican Senators voted for it and only five against it. Where does this last-minute drive of the Republican leadership leave these Republican Representatives and Senators who helped enact this law?

I am sure the vast majority of law-abiding businessmen who are not parties to this propaganda fully appreciate the extent of the threat to honest business contained in this coercion.

I have expressed indignation at this form of campaigning and I am confident that the overwhelming majority of employers, workers and the general public share that indignation and will show it at the polls on Tuesday next.

Aside from this phase of it, I prefer to remember this campaign not as bitter but only as hard-fought. There should be no bitterness or hate where the sole thought is the welfare of the United States of America. No man can occupy the office of President without realizing that he is President of all the people.

It is because I have sought to think in terms of the whole Nation that I am confident that today, just as four years ago, the people want more than promises.

Our vision for the future contains more than promises.

This is our answer to those who, silent about their own plans, ask us to state our objectives.

Of course we will continue to seek to improve working conditions for the workers of America—to reduce hours over-long, to increase wages that spell starvation, to end the labor of children, to wipe out sweatshops. Of course we will continue every effort to end monopoly in business, to support collective bargaining, to stop unfair competition, to abolish dishonorable trade practices. For all these we have only just begun to fight.

Of course we will continue to work for cheaper electricity in the homes and on the farms of America, for better and cheaper transportation, for low interest rates, for sounder home financing, for better banking, for the regulation of security issues, for reciprocal trade among nations, for the wiping out of slums. For all these we have only just begun to fight.

Of course we will continue our efforts in behalf of the farmers of America. With their continued cooperation we will do all in our power to end the piling up of huge surpluses which spelled ruinous prices for their crops. We will persist in successful action for better land use, for reforestation, for the conservation of water all the way from its source to the sea, for drought and flood control, for better marketing facilities for farm commodities, for a definite reduction of farm tenancy, for encouragement of farmer cooperatives, for crop insurance and a stable food supply. For all these we have only just begun to fight.

Of course we will provide useful work for the needy unemployed; we prefer useful work to the pauperism of a dole.

Here and now I want to make myself clear about those who disparage their fellow citizens on the relief rolls. They say that those on relief are not merely jobless—that they are worthless. Their solution for the relief problem is to end relief—to purge the rolls by starvation. To use the language of the stock broker, our needy unemployed would be cared for when, as, and if some fairy godmother should happen on the scene.

You and I will continue to refuse to accept that estimate of our unemployed fellow Americans. Your Government is still on the same side of the street with the Good Samaritan and not with those who pass by on the other side.

Again—what of our objectives?

Of course we will continue our efforts for young men and women so that they may obtain an education and an opportunity to put it to use. Of course we will continue our help for the crippled, for the blind, for the mothers, our insurance for the unemployed, our security for the aged. Of course we will continue to protect the consumer against unnecessary price spreads, against the costs that are added by monopoly and speculation. We will continue our successful efforts to increase his purchasing power and to keep it constant.

For these things, too, and for a multitude of others like them, we have only just begun to fight.

All this—all these objectives—spell peace at home. All our actions, all our ideals, spell also peace with other nations.

Today there is war and rumor of war. We want none of it. But while we guard our shores against threats of war, we will continue to remove the causes of unrest and antagonism at home which might make our people easier victims to those for whom foreign war is profitable. You know well that those who stand to profit by war are not on our side in this campaign.

"Peace on earth, good will toward men"—democracy must cling to that message. For it is my deep conviction that democracy cannot live without that true religion which gives a nation a sense of justice and of moral purpose. Above our political forums, above our market places stand the altars of our faith—altars on which burn the fires of devotion that maintain all that is best in us and all that is best in our Nation.

We have need of that devotion today. It is that which makes it possible for government to persuade those who are mentally prepared to fight each other to go on instead, to work for and to sacrifice for each other. That is why we need to say with the Prophet: "What doth the Lord require of thee—but to do justly, to love mercy and to walk humbly with thy God." That is why the recovery we seek, the recovery we are winning, is more than economic. In it are included justice and love and humanity, not for ourselves as individuals alone, but for our Nation.

That is the road to peace.

Source: "Franklin D. Roosevelt Speeches—Madison Square Garden (October 31, 1936)." Miller Center of Public Affairs, Scripps Library and Multimedia Archive. Available online. URL: http://www.millercenter.virginia.edu/scripps/diglibrary/prezspeeches/roosevelt/fdr_1936_1031.html.

13. Second Inaugural Address, January 20, 1937

Compared to his First Inaugural address, FDR's second was more philosophical than action oriented. It was drafted by Donald Richberg, Samuel Rosenman, and Roosevelt himself, who wrote its best line: "I see one-third of a nation ill-housed, ill-clad, ill-nourished."

When four years ago we met to inaugurate a President, the Republic, single-minded in anxiety, stood in spirit here. We dedicated ourselves to the fulfillment of a vision—to speed the time when there would be for all the people that security and peace essential to the pursuit of happiness. We of the Republic pledged ourselves to drive from the temple of our ancient faith those who had profaned it; to end by action, tireless and unafraid, the stagnation and despair of that day. We did those first things first.

Our covenant with ourselves did not stop there. Instinctively we recognized a deeper need—the need to find through government the instrument of our united purpose to solve for the individual the ever-rising problems of a complex civilization. Repeated attempts at their solution without the aid of government had left us baffled and bewildered. For, without that aid, we had been unable to create those moral controls over the services of science which are necessary to make science a useful servant instead of a ruthless master of mankind. To do this we knew that we must find practical controls over blind economic forces and blindly selfish men.

We of the Republic sensed the truth that democratic government has innate capacity to protect its people against disasters once considered inevitable, to solve problems once considered unsolvable. We would not admit that we could not find a way to master economic epidemics just as, after centuries of fatalistic suffering, we had found a way to master epidemics of disease. We refused to leave the problems of our common welfare to be solved by the winds of chance and the hurricanes of disaster.

In this we Americans were discovering no wholly new truth; we were writing a new chapter in our book of self-government.

This year marks the one hundred and fiftieth anniversary of the Constitutional Convention which made us a nation. At that Convention our forefathers found the way out of the chaos which followed the Revolutionary War; they created a strong government with powers of united action sufficient then and now to solve problems utterly beyond individual or local solution. A century and a half ago they established the Federal Government in order to promote the general welfare and secure the blessings of liberty to the American people.

Today we invoke those same powers of government to achieve the same objectives.

Four years of new experience have not belied our historic instinct. They hold out the clear hope that government within communities, government within the separate States, and government of the United States can do the things the times require, without yielding its democracy. Our tasks in the last four years did not force democracy to take a holiday.

Nearly all of us recognize that as intricacies of human relationships increase, so power to govern them also must increase—power to stop evil; power to do good. The essential democracy of our Nation and the safety of our people depend not upon the absence of power, but upon lodging it with those whom the people can change or continue at stated intervals through an honest and free system of elections. The Constitution of 1787 did not make our democracy impotent.

In fact, in these last four years, we have made the exercise of all power more democratic; for we have begun to bring private autocratic powers into their proper subordination to the public's government. The legend that they were invincible—above and beyond the processes of a democracy—has been shattered. They have been challenged and beaten.

Our progress out of the depression is obvious. But that is not all that you and I mean by the new order of things. Our pledge was not merely to do a patchwork job with secondhand materials. By using the new materials of social justice we have undertaken to erect on the old foundations a more enduring structure for the better use of future generations.

In that purpose we have been helped by achievements of mind and spirit. Old truths have been relearned; untruths have been unlearned. We have always known that heedless self-interest was bad morals; we know now that it is bad economics. Out of the collapse of a prosperity whose builders boasted their practicality has come the conviction that in the long run economic morality pays. We are beginning to wipe out the line that divides the practical from the ideal; and in so doing we are fashioning an instrument of unimagined power for the establishment of a morally better world.

This new understanding undermines the old admiration of worldly success as such. We are beginning to abandon our tolerance of the abuse of power by those who betray for profit the elementary decencies of life.

In this process evil things formerly accepted will not be so easily condoned. Hard-headedness will not so easily excuse hardheartedness. We are moving toward an era of good feeling. But we realize that there can be no era of good feeling save among men of good will.

For these reasons I am justified in believing that the greatest change we have witnessed has been the change in the moral climate of America.

Among men of good will, science and democracy together offer an ever-richer life and ever-larger satisfaction to the individual. With this change in our moral climate and our rediscovered ability to improve our economic order, we have set our feet upon the road of enduring progress.

Shall we pause now and turn our back upon the road that lies ahead? Shall we call this the promised land? Or, shall we continue on our way? For "each age is a dream that is dying, or one that is coming to birth."

Many voices are heard as we face a great decision. Comfort says, "Tarry a while." Opportunism says, "This is a good spot." Timidity asks, "How difficult is the road ahead?"

True, we have come far from the days of stagnation and despair. Vitality has been preserved. Courage and confidence have been restored. Mental and moral horizons have been extended.

But our present gains were won under the pressure of more than ordinary circumstances. Advance became imperative under the goad of fear and suffering. The times were on the side of progress.

To hold to progress today, however, is more difficult. Dulled conscience, irresponsibility, and ruthless self-interest already reappear. Such symptoms of prosperity may become portents of disaster! Prosperity already tests the persistence of our progressive purpose.

Let us ask again: Have we reached the goal of our vision of that fourth day of March 1933? Have we found our happy valley?

I see a great nation, upon a great continent, blessed with a great wealth of natural resources. Its hundred and thirty million people are at peace among themselves; they are making their country a good neighbor among the nations. I see a United States which can demonstrate that, under democratic methods of government, national wealth can be translated into a spreading volume of human comforts hitherto unknown, and the lowest standard of living can be raised far above the level of mere subsistence.

But here is the challenge to our democracy: In this nation I see tens of millions of its citizens—a substantial part of its whole population—who at this very moment are denied the greater part of what the very lowest standards of today call the necessities of life.

I see millions of families trying to live on incomes so meager that the pall of family disaster hangs over them day by day.

I see millions whose daily lives in city and on farm continue under conditions labeled indecent by a so-called polite society half a century ago.

I see millions denied education, recreation, and the opportunity to better their lot and the lot of their children.

I see millions lacking the means to buy the products of farm and factory and by their poverty denying work and productiveness to many other millions.

I see one-third of a nation ill-housed, ill-clad, ill-nourished.

It is not in despair that I paint you that picture. I paint it for you in hope—because the Nation, seeing and understanding the injustice in it, proposes to paint it out. We are determined to make every American citizen the subject of his country's interest and concern; and we will never regard any faithful law-abiding group within our borders as superfluous. The test of our progress is not whether we add more to the abundance of those who have much; it is whether we provide enough for those who have too little.

If I know aught of the spirit and purpose of our Nation, we will not listen to Comfort, Opportunism, and Timidity. We will carry on.

Overwhelmingly, we of the Republic are men and women of good will; men and women who have more than warm hearts of dedication; men and women who have cool heads and willing hands of practical purpose as well. They will insist that every agency of popular government use effective instruments to carry out their will.

Government is competent when all who compose it work as trustees for the whole people. It can make constant progress when it keeps abreast of all the facts. It can obtain justified support and legitimate criticism when the people receive true information of all that government does.

If I know aught of the will of our people, they will demand that these conditions of effective government shall be created and maintained. They will demand a nation uncorrupted by cancers of injustice and, therefore, strong among the nations in its example of the will to peace.

Today we reconsecrate our country to long-cherished ideals in a suddenly changed civilization. In every land there are always at work forces that drive men apart and forces that draw men together. In our personal ambitions we are individualists. But in our seeking for economic and political progress as a nation, we all go up, or else we all go down, as one people.

To maintain a democracy of effort requires a vast amount of patience in dealing with differing methods, a vast amount of humility. But out of the confusion of many voices rises an understanding of dominant public need. Then political leadership can voice common ideals, and aid in their realization.

In taking again the oath of office as President of the United States, I assume the solemn obligation of leading the American people forward along the road over which they have chosen to advance.

While this duty rests upon me I shall do my utmost to speak their purpose and to do their will, seeking Divine guidance to help us each and every one to give light to them that sit in darkness and to guide our feet into the way of peace.

Source: "Second Inaugural Address of Franklin D. Roosevelt, Wednesday, January 20, 1937." The Avalon Project of Yale Law School. Avail-able online. URL: http://www.yale.edu/lawweb/avalon/presiden/inaug/froos2.htm.

14. Democratic Victory Dinner Address, Washington, D.C., March 4, 1937

At the Mayflower Hotel in Washington, D.C., FDR gave one of his best fighting speeches. Appealing directly to the public over the heads of Congress, he tried to pressure representatives to support his Supreme Court–packing plan. He acknowledged that the conservative bench had overturned essential New Deal legislation.

On this fourth of March, 1937, in millions of homes, the thoughts of American families are reverting to the March 4th of another year. That day in 1933 represented the death of one era and the birth of another.

At that time we faced and met a grave national crisis. Now we face another crisis—of a different kind but fundamentally even more grave than that of four years ago. Tonight I want to begin with you a discussion of that crisis. I shall continue that discussion on Tuesday night in a nation-wide broadcast and thereafter, from time to time, as may be necessary. For I propose to follow my custom of speaking frankly to the Nation concerning our common problems.

I speak at this Victory Dinner not only as the head of the Democratic Party but as the representative of all Americans who have faith in political and economic democracy.

Our victory was not sectional. It did not come from compromises and bargains. It was the voice of twenty-seven million voters—from every part of the land.

The Democratic Party, once a minority party, is today the majority party by the greatest majority any party ever had.

It will remain the majority party so long as it continues to justify the faith of millions who had almost lost faith—so long as it continues to make modern democracy work—so long and no longer. We are celebrating the 1936 victory. That was not a final victory. It was a victory whereby our party won further opportunity to lead in the solution of the pressing problems that perplex our generation. Whether we shall celebrate in 1938, 1940, and in 1944, as we celebrate tonight, will deservedly depend upon whether the party continues on its course and solves those problems.

And if I have aught to say it will continue on its course and it will solve those problems.

After election day in 1936, some of our supporters were uneasy lest we grasp the excuse of a false era of good feeling to evade our obligations. They were worried by the evil symptom that the propaganda and the epithets of last Summer and Fall had died down.

Today, however, those who placed their confidence in us are reassured. For the tumult and the shouting have broken forth anew—and from substantially the same elements of opposition. This new roar is the best evidence in the world that we have begun to keep our promises, that we have begun to move against conditions under which one-third of this Nation is still ill-nourished, ill-clad, ill-housed.

We gave warning last November that we had only just begun to fight. Did some people really believe we did not mean it? Well—I meant it, and you meant it.

A few days ago, a distinguished member of the Congress came to see me to talk about national problems in general and about the problem of the Judiciary in particular.

I said to him:

"John, I want to tell you something that is very personal to me—something that you have a right to hear from my own lips. I have a great ambition in life."

My friend pricked up his ears.

I went on: "I am by no means satisfied with having twice been elected President of the United States by very large majorities. I have an even greater ambition."

By this time, my friend was sitting on the edge of his chair.

I continued: "John, my ambition relates to January 20, 1941." I could feel just what horrid thoughts my friend was thinking. So in order to relieve his anxiety, I went on to say: "My great ambition on January 20, 1941, is to turn over this desk and my chair in the White House to my successor, whoever he may be, with the assurance that I am at the same time turning over to him as President, a Nation intact, a Nation at peace, a Nation prosperous, a Nation clear in its knowledge of what powers it has to serve its own citizens, a Nation that is in a position to use those powers to the full in order to move forward steadily to meet the modern needs of humanity—a Nation which has thus proved that the democratic form and methods of national government can and will succeed.

"In these coming years I want to provide such assurance. I want to get the nation as far along the road of progress as I can. I do not want to leave it to my successor in the condition in which Buchanan left it to Lincoln."

My friends, that ambition of mine for my successor can well be the serious ambition of every citizen who wants his United States to be handed down intact to his children and grandchildren.

I spoke in the dead earnestness of anxiety. I speak to you tonight in the same earnestness. For no one who sees as a whole today's picture of this Nation and the world can help but feel concern for the future.

To the President of the United States there come every day thousands of messages of appeal, of protest, of support, of information and advice, messages from rich and poor, from business man and farmer, from factory employee and relief worker, messages from every corner of our wide domain.

Those messages reflect the most striking feature of the life of this generation—the feature which men who live mentally in another generation can at least understand—the ever-accelerating speed with which social forces now gather headway.

The issue of slavery, for example, took at least forty years—two generations—of argument, discussion and futile compromise, before it came to a head in the tragic war between the States.

But economic freedom for the wage earner and the farmer and the small business man will not wait, like emancipation, for forty years. It will not wait for four years. It will not wait at all.

After the World War, there arose everywhere insistent demands upon government that human needs be met. The unthinking, or those who dwell in the past, have tried to block them. The wise who live in the present have recognized their innate justice and irresistible pressure—and have sought to guide them.

In some countries, a royalist form of government failed to meet these demands—and fell. In other countries, a parliamentary form of government failed to meet these demands—and fell. In still other countries, governments have managed to hold on, but civil strife has flared or threats of upheaval persist.

Democracy in many lands has failed for the time being to meet human needs. People have become so fed up with futile debate and party bickerings over methods that they have been willing to surrender democratic processes and principles in order to get things done. They have forgotten the lessons of history that the ultimate failures of dictatorships cost humanity far more than any temporary failures of democracy.

In the United States democracy has not yet failed and does not need to fail. And we propose not to let it fail!

Nevertheless, I cannot tell you with complete candor that in these past few years democracy in the United States has fully succeeded. Nor can I tell you, under present circumstances, just where American democracy is headed nor just what it is permitted to do in order to insure its continued success and survival. I can only hope.

For as yet there is no definite assurance that the three horse team of the American system of government will pull together. If three well-matched horses are put to the task of ploughing up a field where the going is heavy, and the team of three pull as one, the field will be ploughed. If one horse lies down in the traces or plunges off in another direction, the field will not be ploughed.

What you and I call the principles of the New Deal did not originate on the fourth of March, 1933. We think of that date as their beginning, because it was not until then that the social demands they represented broke through the inertia of many years of failure to improve our political and economic processes.

What were those demands and needs? How far did we succeed in meeting them? What about them today?

Ever since the World War the farmers of America had been beating off ever-mounting disasters. This Administration tried to help them effectively where no other Administration had dared to take that risk.

The Agricultural Adjustment Act testified to our full faith and confidence that the very nature of our major crops makes them articles of commerce between the States.

The AAA testified also to our full faith and confidence that the preservation of sound agriculture is essential to the general welfare—that the Congress of the United States had full constitutional authority to solve the national economic problems of the Nation's agriculture. By overwhelming votes, the Congress thought so too!

You know who assumed the power to veto, and did veto that program.

In the campaign of 1936, I said: "Of course we will continue our efforts in behalf of the farmers of America. With their continued cooperation we will do all in our power to end the piling up of huge surpluses which spell ruinous prices for their crops. We will persist in successful action for better land use, for reforestation . . . for better marketing facilities for farm commodities, for a definite reduction of farm tenancy, for encouragement of farmer cooperatives, for crop insurance and a stable food supply. For all these things we have only just begun to fight."

Neither individually nor as a party can we postpone and run from that fight on advice of defeatist lawyers. But I defy anyone to read the majority opinion invalidating of the AAA and tell us what we can do for agriculture in this session of the Congress with any reasonable certainty that what we do will not be nullified as unconstitutional.

The farmers were not the only people in distress in 1932. There were millions of workers in industry and in commerce who had lost their jobs, young people who had never been able to find their first job, and more millions whose jobs did not return them and their families enough to live on decently.

The Democratic Administration and the Congress made a gallant, sincere effort to raise wages, to reduce hours, to abolish child labor, to eliminate unfair trade practices.

We tried to establish machinery to adjust the relations between the employer and employee.

And what happened?

You know who assumed the power to veto, and did veto that program.

The Railroad Retirement Act, the National Recovery Act and the Guffey Coal Act were successively outlawed as the Child Labor Statute had been outlawed twenty years before.

Soon thereafter the Nation was told by a judicial pronunciamento that although the Federal Government had thus been rendered powerless to touch the problem of hour and wages, the States were equally helpless; and that it pleased the "personal economic predilections"

of a majority of the Court that we live in a Nation where there is no legal power anywhere to deal with its most difficult practical problems—a No Man's Land of final futility.

Furthermore, court injunctions have paralyzed the machinery which we created by the National Labor Relations Act to settle great disputes raging in the industrial field, and, indeed, to prevent them for ever arising. We hope that this Act may yet escape final condemnation in the highest court. But so far the attitude and language of the courts in relation to many other laws have made the legality of this Act also uncertain, and have encouraged corporations to defy rather than obey it.

In the campaign of 1936, you and I promised this to working men and women:

"Of course we will continue to seek to improve working conditions for the workers of America—to reduce hours over-long, to increase wages that spell starvation, to end the labor of children, to wipe out sweatshops. . . . We will provide useful work for the needy unemployed. For all these things we have only just begun to fight."

And here again we cannot afford, either individually or as a party, to postpone or run from the fight on the advice of defeatist lawyers.

But I defy anyone to read the opinions concerning AAA, the Railroad Retirement Act, the National Recovery Act, the Guffey Coal Act and the New York Minimum Wage Law, and tell us exactly what, if anything, we can do for the industrial worker in this session of the Congress with any reasonable certainty that what we do will not be nullified as unconstitutional.

During the course of the past four years the Nation has been overwhelmed by disasters of flood and drought.

Modern science knows how to protect our land and our people from the recurrence of such catastrophes, and knows how to produce as a by-product the blessing of cheaper electric power. With the Tennessee Valley Authority we made a beginning of that kind of protection on an intelligent regional basis. With only two of its nine projected dams completed there was no flood damage in the valley of the Tennessee this winter.

But how can we confidently complete that Tennessee Valley project or extend the idea to the Ohio and other valleys while the lowest courts have not hesitated to paralyze its operations by sweeping injunctions?

The Ohio River and the Dust Bowl are not conversant with the habits of the Interstate Commerce Clause. But we shall never be safe in our lives, in our property, or in the heritage of our soil, until we have somehow made the Interstate Commerce Clause conversant with the habits of the Ohio River and the Dust Bowl.

In the campaign of 1936, you and I and all who supported us did take cognizance of the Ohio River and the Dust Bowl. We said: "Of course we will continue our efforts . . . for drought and flood control. . . . For these things we have only just begun to fight."

Here, too, we cannot afford, either individually or as a party, to postpone or run away from that fight on the advice of defeatist lawyers. Let them try that advice on sweating men piling sandbags on the levees at Cairo.

But I defy anyone to read the opinions in the T.V.A. case, the Duke Power case and the AAA case and tell us exactly what we can do as a National Government in this session of the Congress to control flood and drought and generate cheap power with any reasonable certainty that what we do will not be nullified as unconstitutional.

The language of the decisions already rendered and the widespread refusal to obey law incited by the attitude of the courts, create doubts and difficulties for almost everything else for which we have promised to fight—help for the crippled, for the blind, for the moth-

ers—insurance for the unemployed—security for the aged—protection of the consumer against monopoly and speculation—protection of the investor—the wiping out of slums—cheaper electricity for the homes and on the farms of America. You and I owe it to ourselves individually, as a party, and as a Nation to remove those doubts and difficulties.

In this fight, as the lawyers themselves say, time is of the essence. In three elections during the past five years great majorities have approved what we are trying to do. To me, and I am sure to you, those majorities mean that the people themselves realize the increasing urgency that we meet their needs now. Every delay creates risks of intervening events which make more and more difficult an intelligent, speedy, and democratic solution of our difficulties.

As Chief Executive and as the head of the Democratic Party, I am unwilling to take those risks—to the country and to the party—of postponing one moment beyond absolutely necessity the time when we can free from legal doubt those policies which offer a progressive solution of our problems.

Floods and droughts and agricultural surpluses, strikes and industrial confusion and disorder, cannot be handled forever on a catch-as-catch-can basis.

I have another ambition—not so great an ambition as that which I have for the country, but an ambition which as a lifelong Democrat, I do not believe unworthy. It is an ambition for the Democratic Party.

The Party, and its associates, have had the imagination to perceive essential unity below the surface of apparent diversity. We can, therefore, long remain a natural rallying point for the cooperative effort of all of those who truly believe in political and economic democracy.

It will take courage to let our minds be bold and find the ways to meet the needs of the Nation. But for our Party, now as always, the counsel of courage is the counsel of wisdom.

If we do not have the courage to lead the American people where they want to go, someone else will.

Here is one-third of a Nation ill-nourished, ill-clad, ill-housed—NOW!

Here are thousands upon thousands of farmers wonder whether next year's prices will meet their mortgage interest—NOW!

Here are thousands upon thousands of men and women laboring for long hours in factories for inadequate pay—NOW!

Here are thousands upon thousands of children who should be at school, working in mines and mills—NOW!

Here are strikes more far-reaching than we have ever known, costing millions of dollars—NOW!

Here are Spring floods threatening to roll again down our river valleys—NOW!

Here is the Dust Bowl beginning to blow again—NOW!

If we would keep faith with those who had faith in us, if we would make democracy succeed, I say we must act—NOW!

Source: *The Public Papers and Addresses of Franklin D. Roosevelt*, Vol. 6. (New York: Macmillan Company), 113–121.

15. Ninth Fireside Chat— On Reorganization of the Judiciary, March 9, 1937

FDR made a second fighting speech on the radio in another effort to appeal directly to the American people to pressure their representatives to support his Court-packing plan. The speech is defensive in tone, trying to reassure the public that they could trust him "to make democracy succeed."

Last Thursday I described in detail certain economic problems which everyone admits now face the Nation. For the many messages which have come to me after that speech, and which it is physically impossible to answer individually, I take this means of saying "thank you."

Tonight, sitting at my desk in the White House, I make my first radio report to the people in my second term of office.

I am reminded of that evening in March, four years ago, when I made my first radio report to you. We were then in the midst of the great banking crisis.

Soon after, with the authority of the Congress, we asked the Nation to turn over all of its privately held gold, dollar for dollar, to the Government of the United States.

Today's recovery proves how right that policy was.

But when, almost two years later, it came before the Supreme Court its constitutionality was upheld only by a five-to-four vote. The change of one vote would have thrown all the affairs of this great Nation back into hopeless chaos. In effect, four Justices ruled that the right under a private contract to exact a pound of flesh was more sacred than the main objectives of the Constitution to establish an enduring Nation.

In 1933 you and I knew that we must never let our economic system get completely out of joint again—that we could not afford to take the risk of another great depression.

We also became convinced that the only way to avoid a repetition of those dark days was to have a government with power to prevent and to cure the abuses and the inequalities which had thrown that system out of joint.

We then began a program of remedying those abuses and inequalities—to give balance and stability to our economic system—to make it bomb-proof against the causes of 1929.

Today we are only part-way through that program—and recovery is speeding up to a point where the dangers of 1929 are again becoming possible—not this week or month perhaps, but within a year or two.

National laws are needed to complete that program. Individual or local or state effort alone cannot protect us in 1937 any better than ten years ago.

It will take time—and plenty of time—to work out our remedies administratively even after legislation is passed. To complete our program of protection in time, therefore, we cannot delay one moment in making certain that our National Government has power to carry through.

Four years ago action did not come until the eleventh hour. It was almost too late.

If we learned anything from the depression we will not allow ourselves to run around in new circles of futile discussion and debate, always postponing the day of decision.

The American people have learned from the depression. For in the last three national elections an overwhelming majority of them voted a mandate that the Congress and the President begin the task of providing that protection not after long years of debate, but now.

The Courts, however, have cast doubts on the ability of the elected Congress to protect us against catastrophe by meeting squarely our modern social and economic conditions.

We are at a crisis in our ability to proceed with that protection. It is a quiet crisis. There are no lines of depositors outside closed banks. But to the far sighted it is far reaching in its possibilities of injury to America.

I want to talk with you very simply about the need for present action in this crisis, the need to meet the unanswered challenge of one-third of a nation ill-nourished, ill-clad, ill-housed.

Last Thursday, I described the American form of Government as a three horse team provided by the Constitution to the American people so that their field might be plowed. The three horses are, of course, the three branches of government—the Congress, the Executive and the Courts. Two of the horses are pulling in unison today; the third is not. Those who have intimated that the President of the United States is trying to drive that team, overlook the simple fact that the President, as Chief Executive, is himself one of the three horses.

It is the American people themselves who are in the driver's seat.

It is the American people themselves who want the furrow plowed.

It is the American people themselves who expect the third horse to pull in unison with the other two.

I hope that you have re-read the Constitution of the United States in these past few weeks. Like the Bible, it ought to be read again and again.

It is an easy document to understand when you remember that it was called into being because the Articles of Confederation under which the original thirteen States tried to operate after the Revolution showed the need of a national government with power enough to handle national problems. In its Preamble, the Constitution states that it was intended to form a more perfect Union and promote the general welfare; and the powers given to the Congress to carry out those purposes can be best described by saying that they were all the powers needed to meet each and every problem which then had a national character and which could not be met by merely local action.

But the framers went further. Having in mind that in succeeding generations many other problems then undreamed of would become national problems, they gave to the Congress the ample broad powers "to levy taxes . . . and provide for the common defense and general welfare of the United States."

That, my friends, is what I honestly believe to have been the clear and underlying purpose of the patriots who wrote a Federal Constitution to create a National Government with national power, intended as they said, "to form a more perfect union . . . for ourselves and our posterity."

For nearly twenty years there was no conflict between the Congress and the Court.

Then Congress passed a statute, which, in 1803, the Court said violated an express provision of the Constitution. The Court claimed the power to declare it unconstitutional and did so declare it. But a little later the Court itself admitted that it was an extraordinary power to exercise and through Mr. Justice Washington laid down this limitation upon it: "It is but a decent respect due to the wisdom, the integrity and the patriotism of the legislative body, by which any law is passed, to presume in favor of its validity until its violation of the Constitution is proved beyond all reasonable doubt."

But since the rise of the modern movement for social and economic progress through legislation, the Court has more and more often and more and more boldly asserted a power to veto laws passed by the Congress and State Legislatures in complete disregard of this original limitation.

In the last four years the sound rule of giving statutes the benefit of all reasonable doubt has been cast aside. The Court has been acting not as a judicial body, but as a policy-making body.

When the Congress has sought to stabilize national agriculture, to improve the conditions of labor, to safeguard business against unfair competition, to protect our national resources, and in many other ways, to serve our clearly national needs, the majority of the Court has been assuming the power to pass on the wisdom of these acts of the Congress—and to approve or disapprove the public policy written into these laws.

That is not only my accusation. It is the accusation of most distinguished justices of the present Supreme Court. I have not the time to quote to you all the language used by dissenting justices in many of these cases. But in the case holding the Railroad Retirement Act unconstitutional, for instance, Chief Justice Hughes said in a dissenting opinion that the majority opinion was "a departure from sound principles," and placed "an unwarranted limitation upon the commerce clause." And three other justices agreed with him.

In the case of holding the AAA unconstitutional, Justice Stone said of the majority opinion that it was a "tortured construction of the Constitution." And two other justices agreed with him.

In the case holding the New York minimum wage law unconstitutional, Justice Stone said that the majority were actually reading into the Constitution their own "personal economic predilections," and that if the legislative power is not left free to choose the methods of solving the problems of poverty, subsistence, and health of large numbers in the community, then "government is to be rendered impotent." And two other justices agreed with him.

In the face of these dissenting opinions, there is no basis for the claim made by some members of the Court that something in the Constitution has compelled them regretfully to thwart the will of the people.

In the face of such dissenting opinions, it is perfectly clear that, as Chief Justice Hughes has said, "We are under a Constitution, but the Constitution is what the judges say it is."

The Court, in addition to the proper use of its judicial functions, has improperly set itself up as a third house of the Congress—a superlegislature, as one of the justices has called it, reading into the Constitution words and implications which are not there, and which were never intended to be there.

We have, therefore, reached the point as a nation where we must take action to save the Constitution from the Court and the Court from itself. We must find a way to take an appeal from the Supreme Court to the Constitution itself. We want a Supreme Court which will do justice under the Constitution and not over it. In our courts we want a government of laws and not of men.

I want, as all Americans want, an independent judiciary as proposed by the framers of the Constitution. That means a Supreme Court that will enforce the Constitution as written, that will refuse to amend the Constitution by the arbitrary exercise of judicial power—in other words by judicial say-so. It does not mean a judiciary so independent that it can deny the existence of facts which are universally recognized.

How then could we proceed to perform the mandate given us? It was said in last year's Democratic platform, "If these problems cannot be effectively solved within the Constitution, we shall seek such clarifying amendment as will assure the power to enact those laws, adequately to regulate commerce, protect public health and safety, and safeguard economic security." In other words, we said we would seek an amendment only if every other possible means by legislation were to fail.

When I commenced to review the situation with the problem squarely before me, I came by a process of elimination to the conclusion that, short of amendments, the only method which was clearly constitutional, and would at the same time carry out other much needed reforms, was to infuse new blood into all our Courts. We must have men worthy and equipped to carry out impartial justice. But, at the same time, we must have Judges who will bring to the Courts a present-day sense of the Constitution—Judges who will retain in the Courts the judicial functions of a court, and reject the legislative powers which the courts have today assumed.

In forty-five out of the forty-eight States of the Union, Judges are chosen not for life but for a period of years. In many States Judges must retire at the age of seventy. Congress has provided financial security by offering life pensions at full pay for Federal Judges on all Courts who are willing to retire at seventy. In the case of Supreme Court Justices, that pension is $20,000 a year. But all Federal Judges, once appointed, can, if they choose, hold office for life, no matter how old they may get to be.

What is my proposal? It is simply this: whenever a Judge or Justice of any Federal Court has reached the age of seventy and does not avail himself of the opportunity to retire on a pension, a new member shall be appointed by the President then in office, with the approval, as required by the Constitution, of the Senate of the United States.

That plan has two chief purposes. By bringing into the judicial system a steady and continuing stream of new and younger blood, I hope, first, to make the administration of all Federal justice speedier and, therefore, less costly; secondly, to bring to the decision of social and economic problems younger men who have had personal experience and contact with modern facts and circumstances under which average men have to live and work. This plan will save our national Constitution from hardening of the judicial arteries.

The number of Judges to be appointed would depend wholly on the decision of present Judges now over seventy, or those who would subsequently reach the age of seventy.

If, for instance, any one of the six Justices of the Supreme Court now over the age of seventy should retire as provided under the plan, no additional place would be created. Consequently, although there never can be more than fifteen, there may be only fourteen, or thirteen, or twelve. And there may be only nine.

There is nothing novel or radical about this idea. It seeks to maintain the Federal bench in full vigor. It has been discussed and approved by many persons of high authority ever since a similar proposal passed the House of Representatives in 1869.

Why was the age fixed at seventy? Because the laws of many States, the practice of the Civil Service, the regulations of the Army and Navy, and the rules of many of our Universities and of almost every great private business enterprise, commonly fix the retirement age at seventy years or less.

The statute would apply to all the courts in the Federal system. There is general approval so far as the lower Federal courts are concerned. The plan has met opposition only so far as the Supreme Court of the United States itself is concerned. If such a plan is good for the lower courts it certainly ought to be equally good for the highest Court from which there is no appeal.

Those opposing this plan have sought to arouse prejudice and fear by crying that I am seeking to "pack" the Supreme Court and that a baneful precedent will be established.

What do they mean by the words "packing the Court"?

Let me answer this question with a bluntness that will end all honest misunderstanding of my purposes.

If by that phrase "packing the Court" it is charged that I wish to place on the bench spineless puppets who would disregard the law and would decide specific cases as I wished them to be decided, I make this answer: that no President fit for his office would appoint, and no Senate of honorable men fit for their office would confirm, that kind of appointees to the Supreme Court.

But if by that phrase the charge is made that I would appoint and the Senate would confirm Justices worthy to sit beside present members of the Court who understand those modern conditions, that I will appoint Justices who will not undertake to override the judgment of the Congress on legislative policy, that I will appoint Justices who will act as Justices and not as legislators—if the appointment of such Justices can be called "packing the Courts," then I say that I and with me the vast majority of the American people favor doing just that thing—now.

Is it a dangerous precedent for the Congress to change the number of the Justices? The Congress has always had, and will have, that power. The number of justices has been changed several times before, in the Administration of John Adams and Thomas Jefferson—both signers of the Declaration of Independence—Andrew Jackson, Abraham Lincoln and Ulysses S. Grant.

I suggest only the addition of Justices to the bench in accordance with a clearly defined principle relating to a clearly defined age limit. Fundamentally, if in the future, America cannot trust the Congress it elects to refrain from abuse of our Constitutional usages, democracy will have failed far beyond the importance to it of any kind of precedent concerning the Judiciary.

We think it so much in the public interest to maintain a vigorous judiciary that we encourage the retirement of elderly Judges by offering them a life pension at full salary. Why then should we leave the fulfillment of this public policy to chance or make independent on upon the desire or prejudice of any individual Justice?

It is the clear intention of our public policy to provide for a constant flow of new and younger blood into the Judiciary. Normally every President appoints a large number of District and Circuit Court Judges and a few members of the Supreme Court. Until my first term practically every President of the United States has appointed at least one member of the Supreme Court. President Taft appointed five members and named a Chief Justice; President Wilson, three; President Harding, four, including a Chief Justice; President Coolidge, one; President Hoover, three, including a Chief Justice.

Such a succession of appointments should have provided a Court well-balanced as to age. But chance and the disinclination of individuals to leave the Supreme bench have now given us a Court in which five Justices will be over seventy-five years of age before next June and one over seventy. Thus, a sound public policy has been defeated.

I now propose that we establish by law an assurance against any such ill-balanced Court in the future. I propose that hereafter, when a Judge reaches the age of seventy, a new and younger Judge shall be added to the Court automatically. In this way I propose to enforce a sound public policy by law instead of leaving the composition of our Federal Courts, including the highest, to be determined by chance or the personal indecision of individuals.

If such a law as I propose is regarded as establishing a new precedent, is it not a most desirable precedent?

Like all lawyers, like all Americans, I regret the necessity of this controversy. But the welfare of the United States, and indeed of the Constitution itself, is what we all must think about first. Our difficulty with the Court today rises not from the Court as an institution but from human beings within it. But we cannot yield our constitutional destiny to the personal judgment of a few men who, being fearful of the future, would deny us the necessary means of dealing with the present.

This plan of mine is no attack on the Court; it seeks to restore the Court to its rightful and historic place in our Constitutional Government and to have it resume its high task of building anew on the Constitution "a system of living law." The Court itself can best undo what the Court has done.

I have thus explained to you the reasons that lie behind our efforts to secure results by legislation within the Constitution. I hope that thereby the difficult process of constitutional amendment may be rendered unnecessary. But let us examine the process.

There are many types of amendment proposed. Each one is radically different from the other. There is no substantial group within the Congress or outside it who are agreed on any single amendment.

It would take months or years to get substantial agreement upon the type and language of the amendment. It would take months and years thereafter to get a two-thirds majority in favor of that amendment in both Houses of the Congress.

Then would come the long course of ratification by three-fourths of all the States. No amendment which any powerful economic interests or the leaders of any powerful political party have had reason to oppose has ever been ratified within anything like a reasonable time. And thirteen states which contain only five percent of the voting population can block ratification even though the thirty-five States with ninety-five percent of the population are in favor of it.

A very large percentage of newspaper publishers, Chambers of Commerce, Bar Association, Manufacturers' Associations, who are trying to give the impression that they really do want a constitutional amendment would be the first to exclaim as soon as an amendment was proposed, "Oh! I was for an amendment all right, but this amendment you proposed is not the kind of amendment that I was thinking about. I am therefore, going to spend my time, my efforts and my money to block the amendment, although I would be awfully glad to help get some other kind of amendment ratified."

Two groups oppose my plan on the ground that they favor a constitutional amendment. The first includes those who fundamentally object to social and economic legislation along modern lines. This is the same group who during the campaign last Fall tried to block the mandate of the people.

Now they are making a last stand. And the strategy of that last stand is to suggest the time-consuming process of amendment in order to kill off by delay the legislation demanded by the mandate.

To them I say: I do not think you will be able long to fool the American people as to your purposes.

The other group is composed of those who honestly believe the amendment process is the best and who would be willing to support a reasonable amendment if they could agree on one.

To them I say, we cannot rely on an amendment as the immediate or only answer to our present difficulties. When the time comes for action, you will find that many of those who pretend to support you will sabotage any constructive amendment which is proposed. Look at these strange bed-fellows of yours. When before have you found them really at your side in your fights for progress?

And remember one thing more. Even if an amendment were passed, and even if in the years to come it were to be ratified, its meaning would depend upon the kind of Justices who would be sitting on the Supreme Court Bench. An amendment, like the rest of the Constitution, is what the Justices say it is rather than what its framers or you might hope it is.

This proposal of mine will not infringe in the slightest upon the civil or religious liberties so dear to every American.

My record as Governor and President proves my devotion to those liberties. You who know me can have no fear that I would tolerate the destruction by any branch of government of any part of our heritage of freedom.

The present attempt by those opposed to progress to play upon the fears of danger to personal liberty brings again to mind that crude and cruel strategy tried by the same opposition to frighten the workers of America in a pay-envelope propaganda against the Social Security Law. The workers were not fooled by that propaganda then. The people of America will not be fooled by such propaganda now.

I am in favor of action through legislation, First, because I believe that it can be passed at this session of the Congress. Second, because it will provide a reinvigorated, liberal-minded Judiciary necessary to furnish quicker and cheaper justice from bottom to top. Third,

because it will provide a series of Federal Courts willing to enforce the Constitution as written, and unwilling to assert legislative powers by writing into it their own political and economic policies.

During the past half century the balance of power between the three great branches of the Federal Government, has been tipped out of balance by the Courts in direct contradiction of the high purposes of the framers of the Constitution. It is my purpose to restore that balance.

You who know me will accept my solemn assurance that in a world in which democracy is under attack, I seek to make American democracy succeed. You and I will do our part.

Source: "Fireside Chat on Reorganization of the Judiciary." Franklin D. Roosevelt Presidential Library and Museum. Available online. URL: http://www.fdrlibrary.marist.edu/030937.html.

16. "Quarantine" Speech, Chicago, Illinois, October 5, 1937

In Chicago FDR tried to find a way to resolve the fact that he was ahead of public opinion in terms of preparation for war. After war broke out between Japan and China in 1937, he suggested in this rather vague speech that aggressor nations should be treated as if they were carriers of infectious disease. It was his first major effort to mold public opinion to endorse international action.

I am glad to come once again to Chicago and especially to have the opportunity of taking part in the dedication of this important project of civic betterment.

On my trip across the continent and back I have been shown many evidences of the result of common-sense cooperation between municipalities and the federal government, and I have been greeted by tens of thousands of Americans who have told me in every look and word that their material and spiritual well-being has made great strides forward in the past few years.

And yet, as I have seen with my own eyes the prosperous farms, the thriving factories, and the busy railroads, as I have seen the happiness and security and peace which covers our wide land, almost inevitably I have been compelled to contrast, our peace with very different scenes being enacted in other parts of the world.

It is because the people of the United States under modern conditions must, for the sake of their own future, give thought to the rest of the world, that I, as the responsible executive head of the nation, have chosen this great inland city and this gala occasion to speak to you on a subject of definite national importance.

The political situation in the world, which of late has been growing progressively worse, is such as to cause grave concern and anxiety to all the peoples and nations who wish to live in peace and amity with their neighbors.

Some fifteen years ago the hopes of mankind for a continuing era of international peace were raised to great heights when more than sixty nations solemnly pledged themselves not to resort to arms in furtherance of their national aims and policies. The high aspirations expressed in the Briand-Kellogg peace pact and the hopes for peace thus raised have of late given way to a haunting fear of calamity. The present reign of terror and international lawlessness began a few years ago.

It began through unjustified interference in the internal affairs of other nations or the invasion of alien territory in violation of treaties, and has now reached a stage where the very foundations of civilization are seriously threatened. The landmarks and traditions which have marked the progress of civilization toward a condition of law, order, and justice are being wiped away.

Without a declaration of war and without warning or justification of any kind, civilians, including vast numbers of women and children, are being ruthlessly murdered with bombs from the air. In times of so-called peace, ships are being attacked and sunk by submarines without cause or notice. Nations are fomenting and taking sides in civil warfare in nations that have never done them any harm. Nations claiming freedom for themselves deny it to others.

Innocent peoples, innocent nations, are being cruelly sacrificed to a greed for power and supremacy which is devoid of all sense of justice and humane consideration. . . .

The peace-loving nations must make a concerted effort in opposition to those violations of treaties and those ignorings of humane instincts which today are creating a state of international anarchy and instability from which there is no escape through mere isolation or neutrality.

Those who cherish their freedom, and recognize and respect the equal right of their neighbors to be free and live in peace, must work together for the triumph of law and moral principles in order that peace, justice, and confidence may prevail in the world. There must be a return to a belief in the pledged word, in the value of a signed treaty. There must be recognition of the fact that national morality is as vital as private morality. . . .

There is a solidarity and interdependence about the modern world, both technically and morally, which makes it impossible for any nation completely to isolate itself from economic and political upheavals in the rest of the world, especially when such upheavals appear to be spreading and not declining. There can be no stability or peace either within nations or between nations except under laws and moral standards adhered to by all. International anarchy destroys every foundation for peace. It jeopardizes either the immediate or the future security of every nation, large or small. It is, therefore, a matter of vital interest and concern to the people of the United States that the sanctity of international treaties and the maintenance of international morality be restored. . . .

In those nations of the world which seem to be piling armament on armament for purposes of aggression, and those other nations which fear acts of aggression against them and their security, a very high proportion of their national income is being spent directly for armaments. It runs from 30 to as high as 50 percent. We are fortunate. The proportion that we in the United States spend is far less—11 or 12 percent.

How happy we are that circumstances of the moment permit us to put our money into bridges and boulevards, dams and reforestation, the conservation of our soil, and many other kinds of useful works rather than into huge standing armies and vast supplies of implements of war.

I am compelled and you are compelled, nevertheless, to look ahead. The peace, the freedom, and the security of 90 percent of the population of the world is being jeopardized by the remaining 10 percent who are threatening a breakdown of all international order and law. Surely the 90 percent who want to live in peace under law in accordance with moral standards that have received almost universal acceptance through the centuries can and must find some way to make their will prevail. . . .

It seems to be unfortunately true that the epidemic of world lawlessness is spreading.

When an epidemic of physical disease starts to spread, the community approves and joins in a quarantine of the patients in order to protect the health of the community against the spread of the disease.

It is my determination to pursue a policy of peace. It is my determination to adopt every practicable measure to avoid involvement in war. It ought to be inconceivable that in this modern era, and in the face of experience, any

nation could be so foolish and ruthless as to run the risk of plunging the whole world into war by invading and violating, in contravention of solemn treaties, the territories of other nations that have done them no real harm and are too weak to protect themselves adequately. Yet the peace of the world and the welfare and security of every nation, including our own, is today being threatened by that very thing.

War is a contagion, whether it be declared or undeclared. It can engulf states and peoples remote from the original scene of hostilities. We are determined to keep out of war, yet we cannot insure ourselves against the disastrous effects of war and the dangers of involvement. We are adopting such measures as will minimize our risk of involvement, but we cannot have complete protection in a world of disorder in which confidence and security have broken down.

If civilization is to survive, the principles of the Prince of Peace must be restored. Trust between nations must be revived.

Most important of all, the will for peace on the part of peace-loving nations must express itself to the end that nations that may be tempted to violate their agreements and the rights of others will desist from such a course. There must be positive endeavors to preserve peace.

America hates war. America hopes for peace. Therefore, America actively engages in the search for peace.

Source: Samuel I. Rosenman, comp. *The Public Papers and Addresses of Franklin D. Roosevelt*, Vol. 6 (1941; reprint, New York: Russell and Russell, 1969), 406–411.

17. Thirteenth Fireside Chat—On Party Primaries ("Purge" Chat), June 24, 1938

Frustrated over congressional reaction to his Supreme Court–packing plan, in his Thirteenth Fire-

side Chat, FDR announced his decision to purge conservatives from the Democratic Party. Yet his charge remained vague in the address and voters saw him as interfering in state and local matters. The purge failed.

. . . Our Government, happily, is a democracy. As part of the democratic process, your President is again taking an opportunity to report on the progress of national affairs to the real rulers of this country—the voting public.

The Seventy-fifth Congress, elected in November, 1936, on a platform uncompromisingly liberal, has adjourned. Barring unforeseen events, there will be no session until the new Congress, to be elected in November, assembles next January.

On the one hand, the Seventy-fifth Congress has left many things undone.

For example, it refused to provide more businesslike machinery for running the Executive Branch of the Government. The Congress also failed to meet my suggestion that it take the far-reaching steps necessary to put the railroads of the country back on their feet.

But, on the other hand, the Congress, striving to carry out the Platform on which most of its members were elected achieved more for the future good of the country than any Congress between the end of the World War and the spring of 1933.

I mention tonight only the more important of these achievements.

1. It improved still further our agricultural laws to give the farmer a fairer share of the national income, to preserve our soil, to provide an all-weather granary, to help the farm tenant toward independence, to find new uses for farm products, and to begin crop insurance.
2. After many requests on my part the Congress passed a Fair Labor Standards Act, commonly called the Wages and Hours Bill. That Act—applying to

products in interstate commerce—ends child labor, sets a floor below wages and a ceiling over hours of labor.

Except perhaps for the Social Security Act, it is the most far-reaching, far-sighted program for the benefit of workers ever adopted here or in any other country. Without question it starts us toward a better standard of living and increases purchasing power to buy the products of farm and factory.

Do not let any calamity-howling executive with an income of $1,000 a day, who has been turning his employees over to the Government relief rolls in order to preserve his company's undisturbed reserves, tell you—using his stockholders' money to pay the postage for his personal opinions—that a wage of $11 a week is going to have a disastrous effect on all American industry. Fortunately for business as a whole, and therefore for the Nation, that type of executive is a rarity with whom most business executives heartily disagree.

3. The Congress has provided a fact-finding Commission to find a path through the jungle of contradictory theories about wise business practices—to find the necessary facts for any intelligent legislation on monopoly, on price-fixing and on the relationship between big business and medium-sized business and little business. Different from a great part of the world, we in America persist in our belief in individual enterprise and in the profit motive; but we realize we must continually seek improved practices to insure the continuance of reasonable profits, together with scientific progress, individual initiative, opportunities for the little fellow, fair prices, decent wages and continuing employment.

4. The Congress has coordinated the supervision of commercial aviation and air mail by establishing a new Civil Aeronautics Authority; and it has placed all postmasters under the civil service for the first time in our history.

5. The Congress set up the United States Housing Authority to help finance large-scale slum clearance and provide low rent housing for the low income groups in our cities. And by improving the Federal Housing Act, the Congress made it easier for private capital to build modest homes and low rental dwellings.

6. The Congress has properly reduced taxes on small corporate enterprises, and has made it easier for the Reconstruction Finance Corporation to make credit available to all business. I think the bankers of the country can fairly be expected to participate in loans where the Government, through the Reconstruction Finance Corporation, offers to take a fair portion of the risk.

7. The Congress has provided additional funds for the Works Progress Administration, the Public Works Administration, the Rural Electrification Administration, the Civilian Conservation Corps and other agencies in order to take care of what we hope is a temporary additional number of unemployed and to encourage production of every kind by private enterprise.

   All these things together I call our program for the national defense of our economic system. It is a program of balanced action—of moving on all fronts at once in intelligent recognition that all our economic problems, of every group, of every section, are essentially one problem.

8. Finally, because of increasing armaments in other nations and an international situation which is definitely disturbing to all of us, the Congress has authorized important additions to the national armed defense of our shores and our people.

On another important subject, the net result of a struggle in the Congress, has been an important victory for the people of the United States—a battle lost which won a war.

You will remember that on February 5, 1937, I sent a message to the Congress dealing with the real need of Federal Court reforms of several kinds. In one way or another, during the sessions of this Congress, the ends—the real objectives—sought in that message, have been substantially attained.

The attitude of the Supreme Court toward constitutional questions is entirely changed. Its recent decisions are eloquent testimony of a willingness to collaborate with the two others branches of Government to make democracy work. The Government has been granted the right to protect its interests in litigation between private parties involving the constitutionality of Federal statutes, and to appeal directly to the Supreme Court in all cases involving the constitutionality of Federal statutes; and no single judge is any longer empowered to suspend a Federal statute on his sole judgment as to its constitutionality. Justices of the Supreme Court may now retire at the age of seventy after ten years service; a substantial number of additional judgeships have been created in order to expedite the trial of cases; and greater flexibility has been added to the Federal judicial system by allowing judges to be assigned to congested districts.

Another indirect accomplishment of this Congress has been its response to the devotion of the American people to a course of sane consistent liberalism. The Congress has understood that under modern conditions government has a continuing responsibility to meet continuing problems, and that Government cannot take a holiday of a year, a month, or even a day just because a few people are tired or frightened by the inescapable pace of this modern world in which we live.

Some of my opponents and some of my associates have considered that I have a mistakenly sentimental judgment as to the tenacity of purpose and the general level of intelligence of the American people.

I am still convinced that the American people, since 1932, continue to insist on two requisites of private enterprise, and the relationship of Government to it. The first is complete honesty at the top in looking after the use of other people's money, and in apportioning and paying individual and corporate taxes according to ability to pay. The second is sincere respect for the need of all at the bottom to get work—and through work to get a really fair share of the good things of life, and a chance to save and rise.

After the election of 1936 I was told, and the Congress was told, by an increasing number of politically—and worldly—wise people that I should coast along, enjoy an easy Presidency for four years, and not take the Democratic platform too seriously. They told me that people were getting weary of reform through political effort and would no longer oppose that small minority which, in spite of its own disastrous leadership in 1929, is always eager to resume its control over the Government of the United States.

Never in our lifetime has such a concerted campaign of defeatism been thrown at the heads of the President and Senators and Congressmen as in the case of this Seventy-fifth Congress. Never before have we had so many Copperheads—and you will remember that it was the Copperheads who, in the days of the War Between the States, tried their best to make Lincoln and his Congress give up the fight, let the Nation remain split in two and return to peace—peace at any price.

This Congress has ended on the side of the people. My faith in the American people—and their faith in themselves—have been justified. I congratulate the Congress and the leadership thereof and I congratulate the American people on their own staying power.

One word about our economic situation. It makes no difference to me whether you call it a recession or a depression. In 1932, the total national income of all the people in the country had reached the low point of thirty-eight billion dollars in that year. With each succeeding year it rose. Last year, 1937, it had risen to seventy billion dollars—despite definitely worse business and agricultural prices in the last four months of last year. This year, 1938, while it is too early to do more than give an estimate, we hope that the national income will not fall below sixty billion dollars. We remember also that banking and business and farming are not failing apart like the one-hoss shay, as they did in the terrible winter of 1932–1933.

Last year mistakes were made by the leaders of private enterprise, by the leaders of labor and by the leaders of Government—all three.

Last year the leaders of private enterprise pleaded for a sudden curtailment of public spending, and said they would take up the slack. But they made the mistake of increasing their inventories too fast and setting many of their prices too high for their goods to sell.

Some labor leaders, goaded by decades of oppression of labor, made the mistake of going too far. They were not wise in using methods which frightened many well-wishing people. They asked employers not only to bargain with them but to put up with jurisdictional disputes at the same time.

Government, too, made mistakes—mistakes of optimism in assuming that industry and labor would themselves make no mistakes—and Government made a mistake of timing, in not passing a farm bill or a wage and hour bill last year.

As a result of the lessons of all these mistakes we hope that in the future private enterprise—capital and labor alike—will operate more intelligently together, and in greater cooperation with their own Government than they have in the past. Such cooperation on the part of both of them will be very welcome to me. Certainly at this stage there should be a united stand on the part of both of them to resist wage cuts which would further reduce purchasing power.

Today a great steel company announced a reduction in prices with a view to stimulating business recovery, and I was gratified to know that this reduction involved no wage cut. Every encouragement should be given to industry which accepts a large volume of high wage policy.

If this is done, it ought to result in conditions which will replace a great part of the Government spending which the failure of cooperation made necessary this year.

From March 4, 1933, down, not a single week has passed without a cry from the opposition "to do something, to say something, to restore confidence." There is a very articulate group of people in this country, with plenty of ability to procure publicity for their views, who have consistently refused to cooperate with the mass of the people, whether things were going well or going badly, on the ground that they required more concessions to their point of view before they would admit having what they called "confidence."

These people demanded "restoration of confidence" when the banks were closed—and again when the banks were reopened.

They demanded "restoration of confidence" when hungry people were thronging the streets—and again when the hungry people were fed and put to work.

They demanded "restoration of confidence" when droughts hit the country—again now when our fields are laden with bounteous yields and excessive crops.

They demanded "restoration of confidence" last year when the automobile industry was running three shifts and turning out more cars than the country could buy—and again this year when the industry is trying to get rid of an automobile surplus and has shut down its factories as a result.

It is my belief that many of these people who have been crying aloud for "confidence" are beginning today to realize that that hand has been overplayed, and that they are now willing to talk cooperation instead. It is my belief that the mass of the American people do have confidence in themselves—have confidence in their ability, with the aid of Government, to solve their own problems.

It is because you are not satisfied, and I am not satisfied, with the progress we have made in finally solving our business and agricultural and social problems that I believe the great majority of you want your own Government to keep on trying to solve them. In simple frankness and in simple honesty, I need all the help I can get—and I see signs of getting more help in the future from many who have fought against progress with tooth and nail.

And now, following out this line of thought, I want to say a few words about the coming political primaries.

Fifty years ago party nominations were generally made in conventions—a system typified in the public imagination by a little group in a smoke-filled room who made out the party slates.

The direct primary was invented to make the nominating process a more democratic one—to give the party voters themselves a chance to pick their party candidates.

What I am going to say to you tonight does not relate to the primaries of any particular political party, but to matters of principle in all parties—Democratic, Republican, Farmer-Labor, Progressive, Socialist, or any other. Let that be clearly understood.

It is my hope that everybody affiliated with any party will vote in the primaries, and that every such voter will consider the fundamental principles for which his party is on record. That makes for a healthy choice between the candidates of the opposing parties on Election Day in November.

An election cannot give a country a firm sense of direction if it has two or more national parties which merely have different names but are as alike in their principles and aims as peas in the same pod.

In the coming primaries in all parties, there will be many clashes between two schools of thought, generally classified as liberal and conservative. Roughly speaking, the liberal school of thought recognizes that the new conditions throughout the world call for new remedies.

Those of us in America who hold to this school of thought, insist that these new remedies can be adopted and successfully maintained in this country under our present form of government if we use government as an instrument of cooperation to provide these remedies. We believe that we can solve our problems through continuing effort, through democratic processes instead of Fascism or Communism. We are opposed to the kind of moratorium on reform which, in effect, is reaction itself.

Be it clearly understood, however, that when I use the word "liberal," I mean the believer in progressive principles of democratic, representative government and not the wild man who, in effect, leans in the direction of Communism, for that is just as dangerous as Fascism.

The opposing or conservative school of thought, as a general proposition, does not recognize the need for Government itself to step in and take action to meet these new problems. It believes that individual initiative and private philanthropy will solve them—that we ought to repeal many of the things we have done and go back, for instance, to the old gold standard, or stop all this business of old age pensions and unemployment insurance, or repeal the Securities and Exchange Act, or let monopolies thrive unchecked—return, in effect, to the kind of Government we had in the twenties.

Assuming the mental capacity of all the candidates, the important question which seems to me the primary voter must ask is this: "To which of these general schools of thought does the candidate belong?"

As President of the United States, I am not asking the voters of the country to vote for Democrats next November as opposed to Republicans or members of any other party. Nor am I, as President, taking part in Democratic primaries.

As the head of the Democratic Party, however, charged with the responsibility of carrying out the definitely liberal declarations of principles set forth in the 1936 Democratic platform, I feel that I have every right to speak in those few instances where there may be a clear issue between candidates for a Democratic nomination involving these principles, or involving a clear misuse of my own name.

Do not misunderstand me. I certainly would not indicate a preference in a State primary merely because a candidate, otherwise liberal in outlook, had conscientiously differed with me on any single issue. I should be far more concerned about the general attitude of a candidate toward present day problems and his own inward desire to get practical needs attended to in a practical way. We all know that progress may be blocked by outspoken reactionaries and also by those who say "yes" to a progressive objective, but who always find some reason to oppose any specific proposal to gain that objective. I call that type of candidate a "yes, but" fellow.

And I am concerned about the attitude of a candidate or his sponsors with respect to the rights of American citizens to assemble peaceably and to express publicly their views and opinions on important social and economic issues. There can be no constitutional democracy in any community which denies to the individual his freedom to speak and worship as he wishes. The American people will not be deceived by anyone who attempts to suppress individual liberty under the pretense of patriotism.

This being a free country with freedom of expression—especially with freedom of the press—there will be a lot of mean blows struck between now and Election Day. By "blows" I mean misrepresentation, personal attack and appeals to prejudice. It would be a lot better, of course, if campaigns everywhere could be waged with arguments instead of blows.

I hope the liberal candidates will confine themselves to argument and not resort to blows. In nine cases out of ten the speaker or writer who, seeking to influence public opinion, descends from calm argument to unfair blows hurts himself more than his opponent.

The Chinese have a story on this—a story based on three or four thousand years of civilization: Two Chinese coolies were arguing heatedly in the midst of a crowd. A stranger expressed surprise that no blows were being struck. His Chinese friend replied: "The man who strikes first admits that his ideas have given out."

I know that neither in the summer primaries nor in the November elections will the American voters fail to spot the candidate whose ideas have given out.

Source: *The Public Papers and Addresses of Franklin D. Roosevelt*, Vol. 7 (New York: Macmillan Company, 1941), 391–400.

18. Fourteenth Fireside Chat—On the European War, September 3, 1939

In addition to using his Fireside Chats to develop support for the New Deal, FDR used them to prepare the nation for war. In his fourteenth he pledged

that the United States would remain neutral and there would be "no black-out of peace."

My fellow Americans and my friends:

Tonight my single duty is to speak to the whole of America.

Until four-thirty this morning I had hoped against hope that some miracle would prevent a devastating war in Europe and bring to an end the invasion of Poland by Germany.

For four long years a succession of actual wars and constant crises have shaken the entire world and have threatened in each case to bring on the gigantic conflict which is today unhappily a fact.

It is right that I should recall to your minds the consistent and at times successful efforts of your Government in these crises to throw the full weight of the United States into the cause of peace. In spite of spreading wars I think that we have every right and every reason to maintain as a national policy the fundamental moralities, the teachings of religion and the continuation of efforts to restore peace—for some day, though the time may be distant, we can be of even greater help to a crippled humanity.

It is right, too, to point out that the unfortunate events of these recent years have, without question, been based on the use of force and the threat of force. And it seems to me clear, even at the outbreak of this great war, that the influence of America should be consistent in seeking for humanity a final peace which will eliminate, as far as it is possible to do so, the continued use of force between nations.

It is, of course, impossible to predict the future. I have my constant stream of information from American representatives and other sources throughout the world. You, the people of this country, are receiving news through your radios and your newspapers at every hour of the day.

You are, I believe, the most enlightened and the best informed people in all the world at this moment. You are subjected to no censorship of news, and I want to add that your Government has no information which it withholds or which it has any thought of withholding from you.

At the same time, as I told my press conference on Friday, it is of the highest importance that the press and the radio use the utmost caution to discriminate between actual verified fact on the one hand, and mere rumor on the other.

I can add to that by saying that I hope the people of this country will also discriminate most carefully between news and rumor. Do not believe of necessity everything that you hear or read. Check up on it first.

You must master at the outset a simple but unalterable fact in modern foreign relations between nations. When peace has been broken anywhere, the peace of all countries everywhere is in danger.

It is easy for you and for me to shrug our shoulders and to say that conflicts taking place thousands of miles from the continental United States, and, indeed, thousands of miles from the whole American hemisphere, do not seriously affect the Americas—and that all the United States has to do is to ignore them and go about its own business. Passionately though we may desire detachment, we are forced to realize that every word that comes through the air, every ship that sails the sea, every battle that is fought, does affect the American future.

Let no man or woman thoughtlessly or falsely talk of America sending its armies to European fields. At this moment there is being prepared a proclamation of American neutrality. This would have been done even if there had been no neutrality statute on the books, for this proclamation is in accordance with international law and in accordance with American policy.

This will be followed by a Proclamation required by the existing Neutrality Act. And I trust that in the days to come our neutrality can be made a true neutrality.

It is of the utmost importance that the people of this country, with the best information in the world, think things through. The most dangerous enemies of American peace are those who, without well-rounded information on the whole broad subject of the past, the present and the future, undertake to speak with assumed authority, to talk in terms of glittering generalities, to give the nation assurances or prophesies which are of little present or future value.

I myself cannot and do not prophesy the course of events abroad—and the reason is that, because I have of necessity such a complete picture of what is going on in every part of the world, I do not dare to do so. And the other reason is that I think it is honest for me to be honest with the people of the United States.

I cannot prophesy the immediate economic effect of this new war on our nation, but I do say that no American has the moral right to profiteer at the expense of his fellow citizens or of the men, the women and the children who are living and dying in the midst of war in Europe.

Some things we do know. Most of us in the United States believe in spiritual values. Most of us, regardless of what church we belong to, believe in the spirit of the New Testament—a great teaching which opposes itself the use of force, of armed force, of marching armies and falling bombs. The overwhelming masses of our people seek peace—peace at home, and the kind of peace in other lands which will not jeopardize our peace at home.

We have certain ideas and certain ideals of national safety, and we must act to preserve that safety today, and to preserve the safety of our children in future years.

That safety is and will be bound up with the safety of the Western Hemisphere and of the seas adjacent thereto. We seek to keep war from our own firesides by keeping war from coming to the Americas. For that we have historic precedent that goes back to the days of the Administration of President George Washington. It is serious enough and tragic enough to every American family in every State in the Union to live in a world that is torn by wars on other continents. Those wars today affect every American home. It is our national duty to use every effort to keep them out of the Americas.

And at this time let me make the simple plea that partisanship and selfishness be adjourned; and that national unity be the thought that underlies all others.

This nation will remain a neutral nation, but I cannot ask that every American remain neutral in thought as well. Even a neutral has a right to take account of facts. Even a neutral cannot be asked to close his mind or his conscience.

I have said not once, but many times, that I have seen war and that I hate war. I say that again and again.

I hope the United States will keep out of this war. I believe that it will. And I give you assurance and reassurance that every effort of your Government will be directed toward that end.

As long as it remains within my power to prevent, there will be no black-out of peace in the United States.

Source: *The Public Papers and Addresses of Franklin D. Roosevelt*, Vol. 8 (New York: Macmillan Company, 1941), 460–464.

19. The "Dagger Speech"—Address at the University of Virginia, Charlottesville, June 10, 1940

In his commencement address at the University of Virginia, FDR reacted to Benito Mussolini's invasion of France with Nazi Germany. In an impromptu rhetorical stab at Il Duce, FDR commented "the hand that held the dagger has plunged it into the back of its neighbor."

President Newcomb, my friends at the University of Virginia . . .

Every generation of young men and women in America has questions to ask the world. Most of the time they are the simple but nevertheless difficult questions of work to do, opportunities to find, ambitions to satisfy.

But every now and again in the history of the republic a different kind of question presents itself—a question that asks, not about the future of an individual or even of a generation, but about the future of the country, the future of the American people. . . .

There is such a time again today. Again today the young men and the young women of America ask themselves with earnestness and with deep concern this same question: "What is to become of the country we know?"

Now they ask it with even greater anxiety than before. They ask, not only what the future holds for this republic, but what the future holds for all peoples and all nations that have been living under democratic forms of government—under the free institutions of a free people.

It is understandable to all of us, I think, that they should ask this question. They read the words of those who are telling them that the ideal of individual liberty, the ideal of free franchise, the ideal of peace through justice is a decadent idea!

They read the word and hear the boast of those who say that a belief in force—force directed by self-chosen leaders—is the new and vigorous system which will overrun the earth. They have seen the ascendancy of the philosophy of force in nation after nation where free institutions and individual liberties were once maintained.

It is natural and understandable that the younger generation should first ask itself what the extension of the philosophy of force to all the world would lead to ultimately. We see today, for example, in stark reality some of the consequences of what we call the machine age.

Where control of machines has been retained in the hands of mankind as a whole, unrelated benefits have accrued to mankind. For mankind was then the master: The machine was the servant.

But in this new system of force the master of the machine is not in the hands of mankind. It is in the control of infinitely small groups of individuals who rule without a single one of the democratic sanctions that we have known.

The machine in the hands of the irresponsible conquerers becomes the master; mankind is not only the servant, it is the victim too. Such mastery abandons with deliberate contempt all of the moral values to which even this young country for more than 300 years has been accustomed and dedicated.

Surely the new philosophy proves from month to month that it could have no possible conception of the way of life or the way of thought of a nation whose origins go back to Jamestown and Plymouth Rock.

And conversely, neither those who sprang from that ancient stock nor those who have come hither in later years can be indifferent to the destruction of freedom in their ancestral lands across the sea.

Perception to danger to our institution may come slowly or it may come with a rush and shock as it has to the people of the United States in the past few months. This perception of danger—danger in a worldwide arena—has come to us clearly and overwhelmingly. We perceive the peril in this world-wide arena—an arena that may become so narrow that only the Americans will retain the ancient faiths.

Some indeed still hold to the now somewhat obvious delusion that we of the United States can safely permit the United States to become a lone island in a world dominated by the philosophy of force.

Such an island may be the dream of those who still talk and vote as isolationists. Such an island represents to me and to the overwhelming majority of Americans today a helpless nightmare, the helpless nightmare of a people without freedom. Yes, the nightmare of a people lodged in prison, handcuffed, hungry, and fed through the bars from day to day by the contemptuous, unpitying masters of other continents.

It is natural also that we should ask ourselves how now we can prevent the building of that prison and the placing of ourselves in the midst of it.

Let us not hesitate—all of us—to proclaim certain truths. Overwhelmingly we, as a nation, and this applies to all the other American nations, we are convinced that military and naval victory for the gods of force and hate would endanger the institutions of democracy in the Western World—and that equally, therefore, the whole of our sympathies lie with those nations that are giving their life blood in combat against those forces.

The people and Government of the United States have seen with the utmost respect and with grave disquiet the decision of the Italian Government to engage in the hostilities now raging in Europe.

More than three months ago the chief of the Italian Government sent me word that because of the determination of Italy to limit, so far as might be possible, the spread of the European conflict, more than two hundred millions of people in the region of the Mediterranean had been enabled to escape the suffering and the devastation of war.

I informed the chief of the Italian Government that this desire on the part of Italy to prevent the war from spreading met with full sympathy and response on the part of the government and the people of the United States, and I expressed the earnest hope of this government and of this people that this policy on the part of Italy might be continued. I made it clear that in the opinion of the Government of the United States any extension of hostilities in the region of the Mediterranean might result in the still greater enlargement of the scene of the conflict, the conflict in the Near East and in Africa, and that if this came to pass no one could foretell how much greater the theatre of the war eventually might become.

Again, upon a subsequent occasion, not so far ago, recognizing that certain aspirations of Italy might form the basis of discussions between the powers most specifically concerned, I offered, in a message addressed to the chief of the Italian government, to send to the Governments of France and Great Britain such specific indications of the desires of Italy to obtain readjustments with regard to her position as the chief of the Italian Government might desire to transmit through me.

While making it clear that the government of the United States in such an event could not and would not assume responsibility for the nature of the proposals submitted nor for agreements which might thereafter be reached, I proposed that if Italy would refrain from entering the war I would be willing to ask assurances from the other powers concerned that they would faithfully execute any agreement so reached, and that Italy's voice in any future peace conference would have the same authority as if Italy had actually taken part in the war as a belligerent.

Unfortunately, unfortunately to the regret of all of us, and to the regret of humanity, the chief of the Italian Government was unwilling to accept the procedure suggested, and he has made no counter proposal. This government directed its efforts to doing what it could to work for the preservation of peace in the Mediterranean area, and it likewise expressed its willingness to endeavor to cooperate with the government of Italy when the appropriate occasion arose for the creation of a more stable world order, through the reduction of armaments and through the construction of a more liberal international economic system which would assure to all powers equality of opportunity in the world markets and in the securing of raw materials on equal terms.

I have likewise, of course, felt it necessary in my communications to Signor Mussolini to express the concern of the government of the United States because of the fact that any extension of the war in the region of the Mediterranean would inevitably result in great prejudice to the ways of life and government and to the trade and commerce of all the American republics.

The government of Italy has now chosen to preserve what it terms its "freedom of action" and to fulfill what it states are its promises to Germany. In so doing it has manifested disregard for the rights and serenity of other nations, disregard for the lives of the peoples of those nations which are directly threatened by the spread of this war; and has evidenced its unwillingness to find the means through pacific negotiations for the satisfaction of what it believes are its legitimate aspirations.

On this 10th day of June, 1940, the hand that held the dagger has struck it into the back of its neighbor.

On this 10th day of June, 1940, in this university founded by the first great American teacher of democracy we send forth our prayers and our hopes to those beyond the seas who are maintaining with magnificent valor their battle for freedom.

In our unity, in our American unity, we will pursue two obvious and simultaneous courses; we will extend to the opponents of force the material resources of the nation and, at the same time, we will harness and speed up the use of those resources in order that we ourselves in the Americas may have equipment and training equal to the task of any emergency and every defense.

All roads leading to the accomplishment of those objectives must be kept clear of obstructions. We will not slow down or detour. Signs and signals call for speed—full speed ahead.

Yes, it is right that each new generation should ask questions. But in recent months the principal question has been somewhat simplified. Once more the future of the nation and the future of the American people is at stake.

We need not and we will not, in any way, abandon our continuing efforts to make democracy work within our borders. Yes, we still insist on the need for vast improvements in our own social and economic life.

But that, that is a component part of national defense itself.

The program unfolds swiftly and into that program will fit the responsibility and the opportunity of every man and woman in the land to preserve our heritage in days of peril.

I call for effort, courage, sacrifice, devotion. Granting the love of freedom, all of these are possible.

And the love of freedom is still fierce, still steady in the nation today.

Source: "Franklin D. Roosevelt Address at Charlottesville, Virginia, June 10, 1940—The 'Hand that held the dagger' Speech." Available online. URL: http://www.sagehistory.net/worldwar2/docs/FDRUVaSpeech.htm.

20. Campaign Address at Madison Square Garden, New York City, October 28, 1940

In his fall 1940 reelection campaign for an unprecedented third term, FDR reveled in poking fun at "Martin, Barton, and Fish," the Republican members of Congress who had voted against the repeal of the embargo of arms for the Allies.

Mr. Chairman, Governor Lehman, ladies and gentlemen:

No campaign can possibly be complete without this great Garden meeting.

I have had a very wonderful day in New York, in all five boroughs But, as you know, I have had an anxious day too, because three or four times during the day I have had to be in touch with the Department of State and with the Secretary of State, Cordell Hull, because, unfortunately, it seems that another war has broken out on the other side of the ocean. I am quite sure that all of you will feel the same sorrow in your hearts that I feel—sorrow for the Italian people and the Grecian people, that they should have been involved together in conflict.

Tonight, for the second time, I take up the public duty—the far from disagreeable duty—of answering major campaign falsifications with facts.

Last week in Philadelphia, which is supposed to be the City of Brotherly Love, but isn't always, I nailed the falsehood about some fanciful secret treaties to dry on the barn door. I nailed that falsehood and other falsehoods the way when I was a boy up in Dutchess County we used to nail up the skins of foxes and weasels. And, incidentally, I think it was a kinsman of mine, about thirty years ago, who invented the term, "weasel words."

Tonight I am going to nail up the falsifications that have to do with our relations with the rest of the world and with the building up of our Army, our Navy and our air defense. It is a very dangerous thing to distort facts about things like that, because if repeated over and over again, it is apt to create a sense of fear and doubt in the minds of some of the American people.

I now brand as false the statement being made by Republican campaign orators, day after day and night after night, that the rearming of America is slow, that it is hamstrung and impeded, that it will never be able to meet threats from abroad. Those are the whisperings of appeasers.

That particular misstatement has a history. It came into the world last June, just about the time of the Republican National Convention.

Before that, the responsible Republican leaders had been singing an entirely different song. For almost seven years the Republican leaders in Congress kept on saying that I was placing too *much* emphasis on national defense.

And now today these men of great vision have suddenly discovered that there is a war going on in Europe and another one in Asia. And so, now, always with their eyes on the good old ballot box, they are charging that we have placed to *little* emphasis on national defense.

But, unlike them, the printed pages of the Congressional Record cannot be changed or suppressed at election time. And based on that permanent record of their speeches and their votes, I make this assertion—that if the Republican leaders had been in control of the Congress of the United States during the past seven years, the important measures for our defense would not now be law; and the Army and Navy of the United States would still be in almost the same condition in which I found them in 1933.

Remember, I am making those charges against the responsible political leadership of the Republican Party. But there are millions—millions and millions—of patriotic Republicans who have at all times been in sympathy with the efforts of this Administration to arm the nation adequately for purposes of defense.

To Washington in the past few months have come not two or three or a dozen but several hundred of the best business executives in the United States—Republicans and Democrats alike. Not holding company executives or lawyers, but men experienced in actual production—production of all the types of machines and tools and steel and everything else that has made this Nation the industrial leader of the world.

I have asked Mr. Knudsen and Mr. Stettinius and Mr. Harriman and Mr. Budd and the many others to serve their Government because I certainly believe that they are among the ablest men in the nation in their own fields. I do not know their politics. I do not care about their politics. All I know is that they are cooperating one hundred per cent with this Administration in our efforts for national defense. And, the other way around, this Government is cooperating with them—one hundred per cent.

All these men—all American industry and American labor—are doing magnificent and unselfish work. The progress of today proves it.

I shall have occasion on Wednesday or Friday or Saturday of this week to tell more about the work they are doing and about the progress that has been made in our whole picture of defense.

When the first World War broke out, we were pretty weak, but by the end of it we were one of the strongest naval and military powers in the world. When this Administration first came into office fifteen years later, we were one of the weakest.

As early as 1933 the storm was gathering in Europe and in Asia. Year by year I reported the warnings of danger from our listening posts in foreign lands. But I was only called "an alarmist" by the Republican leadership, and by the great majority of the Republican newspapers of the country.

Year by year I asked for more and more defense appropriations. In addition, I allocated hundreds of millions of dollars for defense work from relief funds. The C.C.C. helped, the Public Works helped—as was understood by the Congress when the money was voted by them.

Today our Navy is at a peak of efficiency and fighting strength. Ship for ship, man for man, it is as powerful and efficient as any single navy that ever sailed the seas in history. But it is not as powerful as combinations of other navies that might be put together in an attack upon us. Our Army and our air forces are now at the highest level that they have ever been in peacetime. But in the light of existing dangers they are not great enough for the absolute safety of America at home.

While this great, constructive work was going forward, the Republican leaders were definitely and beyond peradventure of doubt trying to block our efforts toward national defense. They not only voted against these efforts; but they stated time and again through the years that they were unnecessary and extravagant, that our armed strength was sufficient for any emergency.

I propose now to indict these Republican leaders out of their own mouths—these leaders who now disparage our defenses—with what they themselves said in the days before this election year, about how adequate our defenses already were.

Listen to this for instance:

"The facts are that we have the largest and most powerful Navy we ever had, except for two years after the World War, and the greatest air forces we ever had and a match for any nation."

Now, who do you suppose made that statement a little over two years ago? It was not I. It was not even a member of this Administration. It was the ranking Republican member of the House Committee on Foreign Affairs, Republican Leader, Hamilton Fish.

And now listen to the only living ex-President of the United States. He said in that same year, two years ago:

"We shall be expending nine hundred million dollars more than any nation on earth. We are leading in the arms race."

And now listen to Republican leader Senator Vandenberg, also speaking at that time. He said that our defense expenditures had already brought us "an incomparably efficient Navy" and he said further, "I rise in opposition to this super-super Navy bill. I do not believe it is justified by any conclusive demonstration of national necessity."

And now listen to what Republican leader Senator Taft—the runner-up for the Republican Presidential nomination this year—said this past February, 1940:

"The increase of the Army and Navy over the tremendous appropriations of the current year seems to be unnecessary if we are concerned solely with defense."

There is the record on that; the permanent crystal clear record. Until the present political campaign opened, Republican leaders, in and out of the Congress shouted from the housetops that our defenses were fully adequate.

Today they proclaim that this Administration has starved our armed forces, that our Navy is anemic, our Army puny, our air forces piteously weak.

Yes, it is a remarkable somersault.

I wonder if the election could have something to do with it. And this seems to be what they would have called "logic" when I was at school: If the Republican leaders were telling the truth in 1938 and 1939, then—out of their own mouths—they stand convicted of inconsistency today. And, as we used to say, per contra, if they are telling the truth today, they stand convicted of inconsistency in 1938 and 1939.

The simple truth is that the Republican Party, through its leadership, played politics with defense, the defense of the United States, in 1938 and 1939. And they are playing politics with the national security of America today.

That same group would still control their party in Congress at the next session. It is the Congress which passes the laws of the United States. The record of those Republican leaders shows what a slim chance the cause of strong defense would have, if they were in control.

Not only in their statements but in their votes is written their record of sabotage of this Administration's continual efforts to increase our defenses to meet the dangers that loomed ever larger and larger upon the horizon.

For example, deeply concerned over what was happening in Europe, I asked the Congress in January, 1938, for a naval expansion of twenty per cent—forty-six additional ships and nine hundred and fifty new planes.

What did the Republican leaders do when they had this chance to increase our national defense almost three years ago? You would think from their present barrage of verbal pyrotechnics [*laughter*], that they rushed in to pass that bill, or that they even demanded a larger expansion of the Navy.

But, ah! my friends, they were not in a national campaign for votes then.

In those days they were trying to build up a different kind of political fence.

In those days they thought that the way to win votes was by representing this Administration as extravagant in national defense, indeed as hysterical, and as manufacturing panics and inventing foreign dangers.

But now, in the serious days of 1940, all is changed! Not only because they are serious days, but because they are election days as well.

On the radio these Republican orators swing through the air with the greatest of ease; but the American people are not voting this year for the best trapeze performer.

The plain fact is that when that naval bill I was speaking about was submitted to the Congress, the Republican leaders jumped in to fight it.

Who were they? There was the present Republican candidate for Vice President, Senator McNary. There were Senator Vandenberg and Senator Nye. And there was the man who would be the Chairman of the House Committee on Foreign Affairs, Congressman Fish.

The first thing they did was to try to eliminate the battleships from the bill. The Republicans in the House voted sixty-seven to twenty against building them; and in the Senate, where they had a much smaller number, the Republicans voted seven to four against building them.

The record is perfectly clear that back in 1938 they were positive in their own minds that we needed no more battleships. The naval

expansion bill, of course, was passed; but it was passed by Democratic votes in the Congress—in spite of the Republicans.

You see, I am talking by the book. Again, in March, 1939, the Republican Senators voted twelve to four against the bill for one hundred and two million dollars to buy certain strategic war materials which we did not have in this country.

In March, 1939, the Republicans in the Senate voted eleven to eight against increasing the authorized number of planes in the Navy.

In June, 1939, Republicans in the House voted one hundred and forty-four to eight in favor of reducing the appropriations for the Army Air Corps.

Now that proves this one simple fact: It proves that if the Republican leaders had been in control of the Congress in 1938 and 1939, these measures to increase our Navy and our Army and our air forces would have been defeated overwhelmingly.

I say that the Republican leaders played politics with defense in 1938 and 1939. I say that they are playing politics with our national security today.

Turn another page:

The Republican campaign orators and leaders are all now yelling "me too" on help to Britain. But this fall they had their chance to vote to give aid to Britain and other democracies—and they turned it down.

This chance came when I recommended that the Congress repeal the embargo on the shipment of armaments and munitions to nations at war, and permit such shipments on a "cash-and-carry basis." It is only because of the repeal of the embargo law that we have been able to sell planes and ships and guns and munitions to victims of aggression.

But how did the Republicans vote on the repeal of that embargo?

In the Senate the Republicans voted fourteen to six against it. In the House Republicans voted one hundred and forty to nineteen against it.

The Act was passed by Democratic votes, but it was over the opposition of the Republican leaders. And just to name a few, the following Republican leaders, among many others, voted against the Act: Senators McNary, Vandenberg, Nye and Johnson; now wait, a perfectly beautiful rhythm—Congressmen Martin, Barton and Fish.

Now, at the eleventh hour, they have discovered what we knew all along—that overseas success in warding off invasion by dictatorship forces means safety to the United States. It means also continued independence to those smaller nations which still retain their independence. And it means the restoration of sovereignty to those smaller nations which have temporarily lost it. As we know, one of the keystones of American policy is the recognition of the right of small nations to survive and prosper.

Great Britain and a lot of other nations would never have received one ounce of help from us—if the decision had been left to Martin, Barton and Fish.

And, finally, let me come down to something that happened two months ago.

In the Senate there was an amendment to permit the United States Government to prevent profiteering or unpatriotic obstruction by any corporation in defense work. It permitted the Government to take over, with reasonable compensation, any manufacturing plant which refused to cooperate in national defense. And the Republican Senators voted against this Russell-Overton Amendment on August 28, 1940, eight to six.

The bill was adopted all right—by Democratic votes. But the opposing vote of those eight Republican leaders showed what would happen if the National Government were turned over to their control. For their vote said, in effect, that they put money rights ahead of human lives—to say nothing of national security.

You and I, and the overwhelming majority of Americans, will never stand for that.

Outside the halls of Congress eminent Republican candidates began to turn new somersaults. At first they denounced the bill; then, when public opinion rose up to demand it, they seized their trapeze with the greatest of ease, and reversed themselves in mid-air.

This record of Republican leadership—a record of timidity, of weakness, of short-sightedness—is as bad in international as in military affairs.

It is the same record of timidity, of weakness, of short-sightedness which they showed in domestic affairs when they were in control before 1933.

But the Republican leaders' memories seem to have been short, in this, as in some other matters. And by the way—who was it said that an elephant never forgets?

It is the same record of timidity, of weakness and of short-sightedness that governed the policy of the confused, reactionary governments in France and England before the war.

That fact was discovered too late in France.

It was discovered just in time in England.

Pray God that, having discovered it, we won't forget it either.

For eight years our main concern, as you know and as the nation knows, has been to look for peace and the preservation of peace.

Back in 1935, in the face of growing dangers throughout the world, your Government undertook to eliminate certain hazards which in the past had led us into war.

By the Neutrality Act of 1935, and by other steps:

We made it possible to prohibit American citizens from traveling on vessels belonging to countries at war. Was that right?

We made it clear that American investors, who put their money into enterprises in foreign nations, could not call on American warships or American soldiers to bail out their investments. Was that right?

We made it clear that we would not use American armed forces to intervene in affairs of the sovereign republics to the south of us. Was that right?

We made it clear that ships flying the American flag could not carry munitions to a belligerent; and that they must stay out of war zones. Was that right?

In all these ways we made it clear to every American, and to every foreign nation that we would avoid becoming entangled through some episode beyond our borders.

Those were measures to keep us at peace. And through all the years since 1935, there has been no entanglement and there will be no entanglement.

And we have had plenty of chances to get into trouble. I know that well.

In July, 1937, Japan invaded China.

On January 3, 1938, I called the attention of the nation to the danger of the whole world situation.

It was clear that rearmament was now, unfortunately, a necessary implement of peace. I asked for large additions to American defenses. Yes, I was called an alarmist—and worse names than that. I have learned by now to take it on the chin.

In March, 1938, German troops marched into Vienna.

In September, 1938, came the Munich crisis. German, French and Czech armies were mobilized. The result was only an abortive armistice.

I said then: "It is becoming increasingly clear that peace by fear has no higher or more enduring quality than peace by the sword."

Three months later, in Lima, Peru, the twenty-one American Republics, including our own, solemnly agreed to stand together to defend the independence of each one of us.

That declaration at Lima was a great step toward peace. For unless the Hemisphere is safe, we are not safe.

Matters in Europe grew steadily worse. Czecho-Slovakia was overrun by the Nazis. General war seemed inevitable.

Yet even then, in the summer of 1939, the Republican leaders kept chanting, "There will be no war."

A few months later—on the first of September, 1939—war came.

The steps which we had carefully planned were put into effect.

American ships were kept from danger zones.

American citizens were helped to come home.

Unlike 1914, there was no financial upheaval.

Very soon, in a few weeks, the American Republics set up at Panama a system of patrolling the waters of the whole Western Hemisphere, with success.

I am asking the American people to support a continuance of this type of affirmative, realistic fight for peace. The alternative is to risk the future of the country in the hands of those with this record of timidity, weakness and short-sightedness or to risk it in the inexperienced hands of those who in these perilous days are willing recklessly to imply that our boys are already on their way to the transports.

This affirmative search for peace calls for clear vision. It is necessary to mobilize resources, minds and skills, and every active force for peace in all the world.

We have steadily sought to keep mobilized the greatest force of all—religious faith, devotion to God.

Your Government is working at all times with representatives of the Catholic, Protestant, and Jewish faiths. Without these three, all three of them, without them working with us toward that great end, things would not be as clear or as easy.

Shadows, however, are still heavy over the faith and the hope of mankind.

We—who walk in the ways of peace and freedom and light—have seen the tragedies enacted in one free land after another.

We have not been blind to the causes or the consequences of these tragedies.

We guard ourselves against all evils—spiritual as well as material—which may beset us. We guard against the forces of anti-Christian aggression, which may attack us from without, and the forces of ignorance and fear which may corrupt us from within.

Source: *The Public Papers and Addresses of Franklin D. Roosevelt*, Vol. 7 (New York: Macmillan Company, 1941), 391–400.

21. Campaign Speech, Boston, Massachusetts, October 30, 1940

Two days after his speech at Madison Square Garden in New York in which he ridiculed "Martin, Barton, and Fish," the Republican members of the Congress who had voted against the repeal of the embargo of arms for the Allies, FDR had only to mention "Martin" and the audience in unison responded with "Barton and Fish." He then went on to assert in this fall campaign address that "Your boys are not going to be sent into any foreign wars."

Mr. Mayor, my friends of New England:

I've had a glorious day here in New England. And I do not need to tell you that I have been glad to come back to my old stamping ground in Boston. There's one thing about this trip that I regret. I have to return to Washington tonight, without getting a chance to go into my two favorite states of Maine and Vermont.

In New York City two nights ago, I showed by the cold print of the Congressional Record how Republican leaders, with their votes and in their speeches, have been playing, and are still playing politics with national defense.

Even during the past three years, when the dangers to all forms of democracy throughout the world have been obvious, the Republican team in the Congress has been acting only as a Party team.

Time after time, Republican leadership refused to see that what this country needs is an all-American team.

Those side-line critics are now saying that we are not doing enough for our national defense. I say to you that we are going full speed ahead! . . .

And within the past two months your Government has acquired new naval and air bases in British territory in the Atlantic Ocean; extending all the way from Newfoundland in the north to that part of South America where the Atlantic Ocean begins to get narrow, with Africa not far away.

I repeat: Our objective is to keep any potential attacker as far from our continental shores as we possibly can. . . .

Campaign orators seek to tear down the morale of the American people when they make false statements about the Army's equipment. I say to you that we are supplying our Army with the best fighting equipment in the all the world.

Yes, the Army and the Defense Commission are getting things done with speed and efficiency. More than eight billion dollars of contracts for defense have been let in the past few months.

I am afraid that those campaign orators will pretty soon be under the painful necessity of coming down to Washington later on and eating their words. . . .

And while I am talking to you mothers and fathers, I give you one more assurance.

I have said this before, but I shall say it again and again and again:

Your boys are not going to be sent into any foreign wars.

They are going into training to form a force so strong that, by its very existence, it will keep the threat of war far away from our shores.

The purpose of defense is defense. . . .

In ten months this Nation has increased our engine output for planes 240 percent; and I am proud of it.

Remember, too, that we are scattering them all over the country. We are building brand new plants for airplanes and airplane engines in places besides the Pacific Coast and this coast.

We are also building them in centers in the Middle West.

Last spring and last winter this great production capacity program was stepped up by orders from overseas. In taking these orders for planes from overseas, we are following and were following hard-headed self-interest.

Building on the foundation provided by these orders, the British on the other side of the ocean are receiving a steady stream of airplanes. After three months of blitzkrieg in the air over there, the strength of the Royal Air Force is actually greater now than when the attack began. And they know and we know that that increase in strength despite battle losses is due in part to the purchases made from the American airplane industries. . . .

The productive capacity of the United States which has made it the greatest industrial country in the world, is not failing now. It will make us the strongest air power in the world. And that is not just a campaign promise!

I have been glad in the past two or three days to welcome back to the shores of America that Boston boy, beloved by all of Boston and a lot of other places, my Ambassador to the Court of St. James, Joe Kennedy.

Actually on the scene where planes were fighting and bombs were dropping day and night for many months, he has been telling me just what you and I have visualized from afar—that all the smaller independent nations of Europe—Sweden, Switzerland, Greece, Ire-

land and the others—have lived in terror of the destruction of their independence by Nazi military might.

And so, my friends, we are building up our armed defenses to their highest peak of efficiency for a very good reason, the reason of the possibility of real national danger to us; but these defenses will be inadequate unless we support them with a strong national morale, a sound economy, a sense of solidarity and economic and social justice.

When this Administration first came to office, the foundation of that national morale was crumbling. In the panic and misery of those days no democracy could have built up an adequate armed defense.

What we have done since 1933 has been written in terms of improvement in the daily life and work of the common man. . . .

I would not single him out except that he is national interest now, because at the time of his appointment as Republican National Chairman this handsome verbal bouquet, this expensive orchid, was pinned upon him: "In public life for many years Joe Martin has represented all that is finest in American public life."

Considering the source of that orchid, Martin must be slated for some Cabinet post. So let's look for a minute at the voting record of this representative of what they call, "all that is finest in American public life." Martin voted against the Public Utility Holding Company Act, the Tennessee Valley Authority Act, the National Securities Exchange Act, and the extension of the Civilian Conservation Corps Act. He voted against practically all relief and work relief measures, and against the appropriation for rural electrification.

Martin voted against the Civil Service Extension Act and against the United States Housing Act.

What I particularly want to say on the radio to the farmers of the Nation, and to you here in this hall, is that Republican National Chairman

Martin voted against every single one of the farm measures that were recommended by this Administration. Perhaps Brother Martin will be rewarded for this loyal service to the principles of his party by being appointed Secretary of Agriculture.

He is one of that great historic trio which has voted consistently against every measure for the relief of agriculture—Martin, Barton and Fish. [Bruce Barton and Hamilton Fish were conservative Republican congressmen.]

I have to let you in on a secret. It will come as a great surprise to you. And it's this:

I'm enjoying this campaign. I'm really having a fine time.

I think you know that the office of President has not been an easy one during the past years.

The tragedies of this distracted world have weighed heavily on all of us.

But—there is revival for every one of us in the sight of our own national community.

In our own American community we have sought to submerge all the old hatreds, all the old fears, of the old world.

We are Anglo-Saxon and Latin, we are Irish and Teuton and Jewish and Scandinavian and Slav—we are American. We belong to many races and colors and creeds—we are American.

And it seems to me that we are most completely, most loudly, most proudly American around Election Day.

Because it is then that we can assert ourselves—voters and candidates alike. We can assert the most glorious, the most encouraging fact in all the world today—the fact that democracy is alive—and going strong.

We are telling the world we are free—and we intend to remain free and at peace.

We are free to live and love and laugh.

We face the future with confidence and courage. We are American.

Source: Samuel I. Rosenman, comp., *The Public Papers and Addresses of Franklin D. Roosevelt*, Vol.

9. (1941; reprint, New York: Russell and Russell, 1969), 514–524.

22. FDR on Lend-Lease—Press Conference, December 17, 1940

FDR's impromptu eloquence is suggested in this press conference when he argued for the Lend-Lease program that he formally proposed the next month. He used familiar homey images to argue that sending aid to the British was just like lending a garden hose to a neighbor whose house was on fire. Moreover, it was not appropriate to ask how items would be repaid if they could not be returned. His ability to obfuscate technical and legal problems trumped the isolationists.

The President: When I came back yesterday I began to note intimations that this inaugural party was getting out of hand—all these chairmen, et cetera, trying to make a real party out of it, and I was trying not to. In other words, simplicity, I still think, should be the keynote; and I am trying to catch up and find out what people have been doing while I was away.

Outside of that I have been trying to catch up on quite a number of other things.

I don't think there is any particular news, except possibly one thing that I think is worth my talking about. In the present world situation of course there is absolutely no doubt in the mind of a very overwhelming number of Americans that the best immediate defense of the United States is the success of Great Britain in defending itself; and that, therefore, quite aside from our historic and current interest in the survival of democracy in the world as a whole, it is equally important from a selfish point of view of American defense, that we should do everything to help the British Empire to defend itself.

I have read a great deal of nonsense in the last few days by people who can only think in what we may call traditional terms about finances. Steve [Early] was asking me about it this morning, and I thought it was better that I should talk to you than for Steve to talk to you; but I gave him one line which he would have used this morning if anybody had asked him, and that was this: In my memory, and your memory, and in all history, no major war has ever been won or lost through lack of money.

I remember 1914 very well, and I will give you an illustration: In 1914 I was up at Eastport, Maine, with the family the end of July, and I got a telegram from the Navy Department that it looked as if war would break out in Europe the next day. Actually it did break out in a few hours, when Germany invaded Belgium. So I went across from the island and took a train down to Ellsworth, where I got on the Bar Harbor Express. I went into the smoking room. The smoking room of the Express was filled with gentlemen from banking and brokerage offices in New York, most of whom were old friends of mine; and they began giving me their opinion about the impending world war in Europe. These eminent bankers and brokers assured me, and made it good with bets, that there wasn't enough money in all the world to carry on a European war for more than three months—bets at even money; that the bankers would stop the war within six months—odds of 2 to 1; that it was humanly impossible—physically impossible—for a European war to last for six months—odds of 4 to 1; and so forth and so on. Well, actually, I suppose I must have won those—they were small, five-dollar bets—I must have made a hundred dollars. I wish I had bet a lot more.

There was the best economic opinion in the world that the continuance of the war was absolutely dependent on money in the bank. Well, you know what happened.

Now we have been getting stories, speeches, et cetera, in regard to this particular war that is going on, which go back a little bit to that attitude. It isn't merely a question of doing things the traditional way; there are lots of other ways of doing them. I am just talking background, informally; I haven't prepared any of this—I go back to the idea that the one thing necessary for American national defense is additional productive facilities; and the more we increase those facilities—factories, shipbuilding ways, munition plants, et cetera, and so on—the stronger American national defense is.

Orders from Great Britain are therefore a tremendous asset to American national defense; because they automatically create additional facilities. I am talking selfishly, from the American point of view—nothing else. Therefore, from the selfish point of view, that production must be encouraged by us. There are several ways of encouraging it—not just one, as the narrow-minded fellow I have been talking about might assume, and has assumed. He has assumed that the only way was to repeal certain existing statutes, the Neutrality Act and the old Johnson Act and a few other things like that; and then to lend the money to Great Britain to be spent over here—either lend it through private banking circles, as was done in the earlier days of the previous war, or make it a loan from this Government to the British Government.

Well, that is one type of mind that can think only of that method as somewhat banal.

There is another one which is also somewhat banal—we may come to it, I don't know—and that is a gift; in other words, for us to pay for all these munitions, ships, plants, guns, et cetera, and make a gift of them to Great Britain. I am not at all sure that that is a necessity, and I am not at all sure that Great Britain would care to have a gift from the taxpayers of the United States. I doubt it very much.

Well, there are other possible ways, and those ways are being explored. All I can do is to speak in very general terms, because we are in the middle of it. I have been at it now three or four weeks, exploring other methods of continuing the building up of our productive facilities and continuing automatically the flow of munitions to Great Britain. I will just put it this way, not as an exclusive alternative method, but as one of several other possible methods that might be devised toward that end.

It is possible—I will put it that way—for the United States to take over British orders, and, because they are essentially the same kind of munitions that we use ourselves, turn them into American orders. We have enough money to do it. And thereupon, as to such portion of them as the military events of the future determine to be right and proper for us to allow to go to the other side, either lease or sell the materials, subject to mortgage, to the people on the other side. That would be on the general theory that it may still prove true that the best defense of Great Britain is the best defense of the United States, and therefore that these materials would be more useful to the defense of the United States if they were used in Great Britain, than if they were kept in storage here.

Now, what I am trying to do is to eliminate the dollar sign. That is something brand new in the thoughts of practically everybody in this room, I think—get rid of the silly, foolish old dollar sign.

Well, let me give you an illustration: Suppose my neighbor's home catches fire, and I have a length of garden hose four or five hundred feet away. If he can take my garden hose and connect it up with his hydrant, I may help him to put out his fire. Now, what do I do? I don't say to him before that operation, "Neighbor, my garden hose cost me $15; you have to pay me $15 for it." What is the transaction that goes on? I don't want $15—I want my garden hose back after the fire is over. All right. If it goes through the fire all right, intact, without any damage to it, he gives it back to me and thanks me very much for the use of it. But suppose it gets smashed up—holes in it—during the fire; we don't have to have too much formality about it, but I say to him, "I was glad to lend you that hose; I see I can't use it any more, it's all smashed up." He says, "How many feet of it were there?" I tell him, "There were 150 feet of it." He says, "All right, I will replace it." Now, if I get a nice garden hose back, I am in pretty good shape.

In other words, if you lend certain munitions and get the munitions back at the end of the war, if they are intact—haven't been hurt—you are all right; if they have been damaged or have deteriorated or have been lost completely, it seems to me you come out pretty well if you have them replaced by the fellow to whom you have lent them.

I can't go into details; and there is no use asking legal questions about how you would do it, because that is the thing that is now under study; but the thought is that we would take over not all, but a very large number of, future British orders; and when they come off the line, whether they were planes or guns or something else, we would enter into some kind of arrangement for their use by the British on the ground that it was the best thing for American defense, with the understanding that when the show was over, we would get repaid sometime in kind, thereby leaving out the dollar mark in the form of a dollar debt and substituting for it a gentleman's obligation to repay in kind. I think you all get it.

Q. Mr. President, that suggests a question, all right; Would the title still be in our name?

The President: You have gone and asked a question I told you not to ask, because it would take lawyers much better than your or I to answer it. Where the legal title is would depend largely on what the lawyers say. Now, for example, if you get mixed up in the legal end of this, you get in all kinds of tangles. Let me ask you this simple question: You own, let us say, a house, a piece of property, a farm, and it is not encumbered in any way—there is no mortgage on it—but you have had some troubles, and you want to borrow four or five thousand dollars on it. You go to the bank and you say, "I want to borrow four or five thousand dollars on my house or my farm." They say, "Sure; give me a mortgage."

You give them a mortgage, if you think you will be able to pay it off in three or four years. In your mind you still think you own your own house; you still think it is your house or your farm; but from the strictly legalistic point of view, the bank is the owner. You deed your house over to the bank; you pledge it, like going to the pawnbroker. Let's take the other side of it: The title to your gold watch is vested in the pawnbroker. You can redeem it; you can pay off your mortgage and get title to your house.

On this particular thing—let's say it's a ship—I haven't the faintest idea at this moment in whom the legal title of that particular ship would be. I don't think that makes any difference in the transaction; the point of the transaction is that if that ship were returned to us in first-class condition, after payment of what might be called a reasonable amount for the ship during that time—the other people might have had legal title or the title might have remained in us; I don't know, and I don't care.

Q: Let us leave out the legal phase of it entirely; the question I have is whether you think this takes us any more into the war than we are?

The President: No, not a bit.

Q: Even though goods we own are being used?

The President: I don't think you go into a war for legalistic reasons; in other words, we are doing all we can at the present time.

Q: Mr. President, did you mean naval craft?

The President: No, no! I am talking about merchant ships.

Q: It is my understanding that this is all for purposes of background, but at one point here I was wondering whether you would attribute this to the necessity for facilities and for encouragement of production?

The President: I think you can attribute this—what we have been talking about—to me.

Q: Mr. President, would we take our own goods abroad?

The President: What do you mean—take our own goods?

Q: As long as this is being made to our account and we are lending it to Great Britain, would we deliver the goods in Great Britain that are going to be used in that way?

The President: Oh, I suppose it would depend on what flag was flying at the stern of the ship. You can work it out any way you want. It might even be a Bolivian flag. That question is a detail.

Q: Would it be an American flag?

The President: Not necessarily. That would bring up another subject; that would bring up a subject which might be a dangerous one, quite frankly, of American sailors and American passengers, et cetera, taking the

American flag into a war zone. You need not worry about that one bit, because you don't have to send an American flag and an American crew on an American vessel.

Q: I was backing into the question that this whole theory of yours doesn't involve amendment of the Neutrality Act.

The President: Right!

Q: You referred to future orders in this connection; as I understand it, the orders the British have given would go ahead on the basis of existing contracts and would be paid for?

The President: Yes, I think so. They have plenty of exchange, you know. There doesn't seem to be very much of a problem about payment for existing orders, but there might be a problem about paying for additions to those orders or for replacement of those orders now.

Q: Is this a safe conclusion on what you have said, that what the British are interested in is to have us lend them the supplies?

The President: That's the point. I am trying to eliminate the dollar mark.

Q: Does this require Congressional approval?

The President: Oh, yes, this would require various types of legislation, in addition to appropriation. Let me give you an example: Let's take anything—a shell factory; and the present shell factories are all filled up with orders a year—two years—ahead; but the British need more shells now, and the shell manufacturers say, "That is all very well, but we have got to get a new factory." And the United States Government has ordered several new factories and put up the money through the R.F.C. or some other way for the capital. Well, if the British wanted a new factory for additional shells, or went above present orders, if we take that order over we

would do the financing of the factory just the way we have done it for ourselves, thereby increasing the productive capacity for turning out shells.

Q: Mr. President, before you loan your hose to your neighbor you have to have the hose. I was wondering, have you any plans to build up supplies? There has been a good deal of discussion about the lack of authority to tell a manufacturer he should run two or three shifts a day. There is no one now that has that authority.

The President: Isn't there?

Q: I don't believe so.

The President: I think so, yes. After all, you have to follow certain laws of the land. Of course the law is, and always was that contracts by the Navy, for instance (I used to place a great many of them in the World War)—should be signed by the Secretary of the Navy or the Assistant Secretary of the Navy. Never, in the history of the United States, has that power been taken away from the two main contracting departments.

That is a pretty important thing to remember. A lot of people in the last week or two have forgotten that fact. There never has been one individual in this country, outside of the Army or Navy, who could do anything more than recommend very strongly that they do thus and so, and supervise it—supervise keeping the program up to date. If the program is not kept up to date, there are lots of things that have been done in the past, and would be done in the future. That is what was done in the World War.

The number of perfectly crazy assertions that have been made in the last couple of weeks by some people who didn't grow up until after the World War is perfectly extraordinary. They have assigned all kinds of authorities and powers to people in the

World War that never existed, except in the figment of their imagination. I went through it; I happen to know.

Q: Mr. President, on your statement that we never would get into war for legalistic reasons—would you amplify that a little?

The President: Only this, that I would not try, from what I have said, to make it appear—who was it who asked that question a while ago?

Mr. Early: Jim Wright

The President: Jim Wright asked whether any of these steps would be a greater danger to the United States of getting into war than the existing situation, and the answer it: "No, of course not." In other words, we are furnishing everything we possibly can at the present moment. This will make easier a continuation of that program. That's all there is to it.

Q: Mr. President, it is interesting about taking over the future orders for the British, but Mr. Knudsen says that the first half of that is crucial. Can you do anything more than you are doing?

The President: Except efficient people; that's what he is trying to do—push them.

Q: Mr. President, has the division of orders been changed? It was 50-50 the last time.

The President: That was rule of thumb. In some places it is 40-60, and in others 60-40.

Q: Mr. President, do any production delays at the present time indicate any need for authority to take over plants?

The President: That is a thing I asked Steve [Mr. Early] to look up this morning.

Mr. Early: No one is reporting today, sir.

The President: That is a thing I asked Steve to report on. No one is reporting today. But I think it is fair to say there are two or three companies under investigation.

Q: Mr. President, do you expect to place this general idea before this session of Congress?

The President: Either that or something similar.

Q: Within a few days?

The President: No, probably not until the 3rd, because the thing has not only to be worked out here, but in London too.

Q: Mr. President, is there any plan under consideration for building up our Defense Program because of this?

The President: Well, that's a pretty general question; on what, for example?

Q: I wondered if you had any specific program for building up any phase of defense.

The President: You can't answer a general question like that. If you ask about an article that is coming along in good shape, the answer is No. It depends on what you are talking about. Before I left, I think we talked about the Navy destroyer program which, in my judgment, was completely insufficient because a lot of the planned destroyers could not be laid down except in turn. In other words, after No. 1 Destroyer had been built and launched from the ways, then they would start No. 31 of the destroyers on the same ways, build that and launch it, and after that was launched they would put No. 61 on the same ways, so that No. 61 would not be launched for perhaps four years from now.

Well, now, the answer to that program, which was laid down by the Navy Department, was that in my judgment it was too darned slow. And how can you speed it up? By building more ways. So that was an illustration of how the program as laid down proved insufficient, and we are now studying how we can build more destroyer ways.

Q: Mr. President, Mr. Knudsen said that the whole Defense Program was lagging pretty severely; do you see anything in this picture that would require you to extend the present limited emergency?

The President: No; that again is largely a legalistic problem. It is a great question whether it would speed it up or not—a great technical question.

Q: Mr. President, when the Government refuses to take in a union man on a defense project, don't you think it is because the unions ask exorbitant fees?

The President: You would have to give me the name of the man and information about the case.

Q: How about eliminating the Friday to Monday blackout?

The President: It depends entirely on the particular type of industrial plant and the conditions in the locality, and the type of workmen that are used. There is no generalization that is possible; and the one thing we have to avoid, all of us, is generalization. Now for example—you take down here in the Washington Navy Yard, there are certain very, very skilled trades; and there is a shortage of labor in those trades. Because there is a shortage, because there is no relief, no additional labor in that trade, we probably have to employ the people in that particular trade, more than 40 hours; and for the extra hours they will get time and a half for overtime.

You take the other extreme—common labor; there's plenty of it. For common labor it is not necessary in that particular yard to work men overtime; and yet you can run the yard six days a week, or even seven days a week. It takes a lot more planning on the part of the management team

to work it out, but you can employ one group of common laborers the first five days in the week, 40 hours—that is 8 hours a day; and then another group you can employ on Tuesday, Wednesday, Thursday, Friday and Saturday and give them Sunday and Monday off; and another group you can employ Wednesday, Thursday, Friday, Saturday and Sunday and give them Monday and Tuesday off; and in that way you can keep a plant going seven days a week if you want to. It takes a little more—what shall I say?—figuring out on a sheet of paper, a little more trouble.

In that way some people will get their holiday in the middle of the week for a while, and others will get it at the end of the week; but it can be done, and it is being done—that is the point of it—in a great many plants in the United States. It is being done; and that can be extended to a great many other plants. It is a nuisance from the point of plant management; we all know that.

There is still another point to consider—there are plants which obviously could not run seven days a week; the plant that has to be laid up for repairs one day out of seven; or a part of the particular plant that has to be laid up for repairs and closed down one day out of seven. You see you can't apply a general rule. It's just plain immature to try to do it. The people that understand manufacturing will be the first to say you can't apply a general rule to this question.

Q: Mr. President, one argument that is advanced is where it is necessary for a man to work 55 hours a week, a trained man, and he can't be replaced; and since the public is begging for this armament, that is putting undue stress on the public's shoulders—time and a half.

The President: In the case of that particular man that is irreplaceable working 55 hours a week, we are trying, as you know, to train other people to fit into those positions. It takes time to do it, but gradually we are getting a large number of people trained to do these specialized jobs.

Q: Mr. President, on this defense setup, do we understand you to mean that you are not interested in appointing a chairman of the national defense?

The President: I would not draw any inferences on a detail. That is a pure detail.

Q: One more question: I believe Mr. Knudsen referred to the blackout of machine time rather than human time. I believe he was referring quite specifically to the fact that the machines were shut down between Friday and Monday.

The President: You have to tell me the machine, and the trade that runs the machine.

Q: He didn't say.

The President: In some cases, yes; in some cases, no. The objective is to keep all the machines that will run seven days a week in operation seven days a week.

Source: *The Public Papers and Addresses of Franklin D. Roosevelt*, Vol. 9 (New York: Macmillan Company, 1941), 604–615.

23. Sixteenth Fireside Chat— On National Security ("Great Arsenal" Chat, December 29, 1940)

FDR used his 16th Fireside Chat to promote his Lend-Lease progress in Congress and prepare the nation for war. To counter isolationists' fear that the United States would be dragged into war by giving aid to the Allies, he assured the public that they could "nail any talk about sending armies to Europe as deliberate untruths."

My Friends:

This is not a fireside chat on war. It is a talk on national security, because the nub of the whole purpose of your President is to keep you now, and your children later, and your grandchildren much later, out of a last-ditch war for the preservation of American independence and all of the things that American independence means to you and to me and to ours.

Tonight, in the presence of a world crisis, my mind goes back eight years to a night in the midst of a domestic crisis. It was a time when the wheels of American industry were grinding to a full stop, when the whole banking system of our country had ceased to function.

I well remember that while I sat in my study in the White House, preparing to talk with the people of the United States, I had before my eyes the picture of all those Americans with whom I was talking. I saw the workmen in the mills, the mines, the factories; the girl behind the counter; the small shopkeeper; the farmer doing his spring plowing; the widows and the old men wondering about their life's savings.

I tried to convey to the great mass of American people what the banking crisis meant to them in their daily lives. Tonight, I want to do the same thing, with the same people, in this new crisis which faces America.

We met the issue of 1933 with courage and realism.

We face this new crisis—this new threat to the security of our nation—with the same courage and realism.

Never before since Jamestown and Plymouth Rock has our American civilization been in such danger as now.

For, on September 27th, 1940, this year, by an agreement signed in Berlin, three powerful nations, two in Europe and one in Asia, joined themselves together in the threat that if the United States of America interfered with or blocked the expansion program of these three nations—a program aimed at world control—

they would unite in ultimate action against the United States.

The Nazi masters of Germany have made it clear that they intend not only to dominate all life and thought in their own country, but also to enslave the whole of Europe, and then to use the resources of Europe to dominate the rest of the world.

It was only three weeks ago their leader stated this: "There are two worlds that stand opposed to each other." And then in defiant reply to his opponents, he said this: "Others are correct when they say: With this world we cannot ever reconcile ourselves . . . I can beat any other power in the world." So said the leader of the Nazis.

In other words, the Axis not merely admits but the Axis proclaims that there can be no ultimate peace between their philosophy of government and our philosophy of government.

In view of the nature of this undeniable threat, it can be asserted, properly and categorically, that the United States has no right or reason to encourage talk of peace, until the day shall come when there is a clear intention on the part of the aggressor nations to abandon all thought of dominating or conquering the world.

At this moment, the forces of the states that are leagued against all peoples who live in freedom are being held away from our shores. The Germans and the Italians are being blocked on the other side of the Atlantic by the British, and by the Greeks, and by thousands of soldiers and sailors who were able to escape from subjugated countries. In Asia the Japanese are being engaged by the Chinese nation in another great defense. In the Pacific Ocean is our fleet.

Some of our people like to believe that wars in Europe and in Asia are of no concern to us. But it is a matter of most vital concern to us that European and Asiatic war-makers should not gain control of the oceans which lead to this hemisphere.

One hundred and seventeen years ago the Monroe Doctrine was conceived by our Government as a measure of defense in the face of a threat against this hemisphere by an alliance in Continental Europe. Thereafter, we stood guard in the Atlantic, with the British as neighbors. There was no treaty. There was no "unwritten agreement."

And yet, there was the feeling, proven correct by history, that we as neighbors could settle any disputes in peaceful fashion. And the fact is that during the whole of this time the Western Hemisphere has remained free from aggression from Europe or from Asia.

Does anyone seriously believe that we need to fear attack anywhere in the Americas while a free Britain remains our most powerful naval neighbor in the Atlantic? And does anyone seriously believe, on the other hand, that we could rest easy if the Axis powers were our neighbors there?

If Great Britain goes down, the Axis powers will control the continents of Europe, Asia, Africa, Australia, and the high seas—and they will be in a position to bring enormous military and naval resources against this hemisphere. It is no exaggeration to say that all of us, in all the Americas, would be living at the point of a gun—a gun loaded with explosive bullets, economic as well as military.

We should enter upon a new and terrible era in which the whole world, our hemisphere included, would be run by threats of brute force. And to survive in such a world, we would have to convert ourselves permanently into a militaristic power on the basis of war economy.

Some of us like to believe that even if Britain falls, we are still safe, because of the broad expanse of the Atlantic and of the Pacific. But the width of those oceans is not what it was in the days of clipper ships. At one point between Africa and Brazil the distance is less from Washington than it is from Washington to

Denver, Colorado—five hours for the latest type of bomber. And at the North end of the Pacific Ocean America and Asia almost touch each other.

Why, even today we have planes that could fly from the British Isles to New England and back again without refueling. And remember that the range of a modern bomber is ever being increased.

During the past week many people in all parts of the nation have told me what they wanted me to say tonight. Almost all of them expressed a courageous desire to hear the plain truth about the gravity of the situation. One telegram, however, expressed the attitude of the small minority who want to see no evil and hear no evil, even though they know in their hearts that evil exists. That telegram begged me not to tell again of the ease with which our American cities could be bombed by any hostile power which had gained bases in this Western Hemisphere. The gist of that telegram was: "Please, Mr. President, don't frighten us by telling us the facts."

Frankly and definitely there is danger ahead—danger against which we must prepare. But we well know that we cannot escape danger, or the fear of danger, by crawling into bed and pulling the covers over our heads.

Some nations of Europe were bound by solemn non-intervention pacts with Germany. Other nations were assured by Germany that they need never fear invasion.

Non-intervention pact or not, the fact remains that they were attacked, overrun, thrown into modern slavery at an hour's notice, or even without any notice at all. As an exiled leader of one of these nations said to me the other day, "The notice was a minus quantity. It was given to my Government two hours after German troops had poured into my country in a hundred places."

The fate of these nations tells us what it means to live at the point of a Nazi gun.

The Nazis have justified such actions by various pious frauds. One of these frauds is the claim that they are occupying a nation for the purpose of "restoring order." Another is that they are occupying or controlling a nation on the excuse that they are "protecting it" against the aggression of somebody else.

For example, Germany has said that she was occupying Belgium to save the Belgians from the British. Would she then hesitate to say to any South American country, "We are occupying you to protect you from aggression by the United States?"

Belgium today is being used as an invasion base against Britain, now fighting for its life. And any South American country, in Nazi hands, would always constitute a jumping-off place for German attack on any one of the other republics of this hemisphere.

Analyze for yourselves the future of two other places even nearer to Germany if the Nazis won. Could Ireland hold out? Would Irish freedom be permitted as an amazing pet exception in an unfree world? Or the Islands of the Azores which still fly the flag of Portugal after five centuries? You and I think of Hawaii as an outpost of defense in the Pacific. And yet, the Azores are closer to our shores in the Atlantic than Hawaii is on the other side.

There are those who say that the Axis powers would never have any desire to attack the Western Hemisphere. That is the same dangerous form of wishful thinking which has destroyed the powers of resistance of so many conquered peoples. The plain facts are that the Nazis have proclaimed, time and again, that all other races are their inferiors and therefore subject to their orders.

And most important of all, the vast resources and wealth of this American Hemisphere constitute the most tempting loot in all of the round world. Let us no longer blind ourselves to the undeniable fact that the evil forces which have crushed and undermined and corrupted so many others are already within our own gates. Your Government knows much about them and every day is ferreting them out.

Their secret emissaries are active in our own and in neighboring countries. They seek to stir up suspicion and dissension to cause internal strife. They try to turn capital against labor, and vice versa. They try to reawaken long slumbering racist and religious enmities which should have no place in this country. They are active in every group that promotes intolerance. They exploit for their own ends our own natural abhorrence of war. These trouble-breeders have but one purpose. It is to divide our people, to divide them into hostile groups and to destroy our unity and shatter our will to defend ourselves.

There are also American citizens, many of them in high places, who, unwittingly in most cases, are aiding and abetting the work of these agents. I do not charge these American citizens with being foreign agents. But I do charge them with doing exactly the kind of work that the dictators want done in the United States.

These people not only believe that we can save our own skins by shutting our eyes to the fate of other nations. Some of them go much further than that. They say that we can and should become the friends and even the partners of the Axis powers. Some of them even suggest that we should imitate the methods of the dictatorships. But Americans never can and never will do that. The experience of the past two years has proven beyond doubt that no nation can appease the Nazis. No man can tame a tiger into a kitten by stroking it.

There can be no appeasement with ruthlessness. There can be no reasoning with an incendiary bomb. We know now that a nation can have peace with the Nazis only at the price of total surrender.

Even the people of Italy have been forced to become accomplices of the Nazis, but at this moment they do not know how soon they will be embraced to death by their allies. The American appeasers ignore the warning to be found in the fate of Austria, Czechoslovakia, Poland, Norway, Belgium, the Netherlands, Denmark and France.

They tell you that the Axis powers are going to win anyway; that all of this bloodshed in the world could be saved, that the United States might just as well throw its influence into the scale of a dictated peace, and get the best out of it that we can.

They call it a "negotiated peace." Nonsense! Is it a negotiated peace if a gang of outlaws surrounds your community and on threat of extermination makes you pay tribute to save your own skins?

Such a dictated peace would be no peace at all. It would be only another armistice, leading to the most gigantic armament race and the most devastating trade wars in all history. And in these contests the Americas would offer the only real resistance to the Axis powers.

With all their vaunted efficiency, with all their parade of pious purpose in this war, there are still in their background the concentration camp and the servants of God in chains.

The history of recent years proves that the shootings and the chains and the concentration camps are not simply the transient tools but the very altars of modern dictatorships. They may talk of a "new order" in the world, but what they have in mind is only a revival of the oldest and the worst tyranny. In that there is no liberty, no religion, no hope.

The proposed "new order" is the very opposite of a United States of Europe or a United States of Asia. It is not a government based upon the consent of the governed. It is not a union of ordinary, self-respecting men and women to protect themselves and their freedom and their dignity from oppression. It is an unholy alliance of power and pelf to dominate and to enslave the human race. The British people and their allies today are conducting an active war against this unholy alliance. Our own future security is greatly dependent on the outcome of that fight. Our ability to "keep out of war" is going to be affected by that outcome.

Thinking in terms of today and tomorrow, I make the direct statement to the American people that there is far less chance of the United States getting into war if we do all we can now to support the nations defending themselves against attack by the Axis than if we acquiesce in their defeat, submit tamely to an Axis victory, and wait our turn to be the object of attack in another war later on.

If we are to be completely honest with ourselves, we must admit that there is risk in any course we may take. But I deeply believe that the great majority of our people agree that the course that I advocate involves the least risk now and the greatest hope for world peace in the future.

The people of Europe who are defending themselves do not ask us to do their fighting. They ask us for the implements of war, the planes, the tanks, the guns, the freighters which will enable them to fight for their liberty and for our security. Emphatically we must get these weapons to them, get them to them in sufficient volume and quickly enough, so that we and our children will be saved the agony and suffering of war which others have had to endure. Let not the defeatists tell us that it is too late. It will never be earlier. Tomorrow will be later than today.

Certain facts are self-evident. In a military sense Great Britain and the British Empire are today the spearhead of resistance to world conquest. And they are putting up a fight which will live forever in the story of human gallantry. There is no demand for sending an American Expeditionary Force outside our own borders. There is no intention by any member of your Government to send such a force. You can, therefore, nail—nail any talk about sending armies to Europe as deliberate untruth.

Our national policy is not directed toward war. Its sole purpose is to keep war away from our country and away from our people.

Democracy's fight against world conquest is being greatly aided, and must be more greatly aided, by the rearmament of the United States and by sending every ounce and every ton of munitions and supplies that we can possibly spare to help the defenders who are in the front lines. And it is no more unneutral for us to do that than it is for Sweden, Russia and other nations near Germany to send steel and ore and oil and other war materials into Germany every day in the week.

We are planning our own defense with the utmost urgency, and in its vast scale we must integrate the war needs of Britain and the other free nations which are resisting aggression.

This is not a matter of sentiment or of controversial personal opinion. It is a matter of realistic, practical military policy, based on the advice of our military experts who are in close touch with existing warfare. These military and naval experts and the members of Congress and the Administration have a single-minded purpose—the defense of the United States.

This nation is making a great effort to produce everything that is necessary in this emergency—and with all possible speed. And this great effort requires great sacrifice.

I would ask no one to defend a democracy which in turn would not defend everyone in the nation against want and privation. The strength of this nation shall not be diluted by the failure of the Government to protect the economic well-being of its citizens.

If our capacity to produce is limited by machines, it must ever be remembered that these machines are operated by the skill and the stamina of the workers. As the Government is determined to protect the rights of the workers, so the nation has a right to expect that the men who man the machines will discharge their full responsibilities to the urgent needs of defense.

The worker possesses the same human dignity and is entitled to the same security of position as the engineer or the manager or the owner. For the workers provide the human power that turns out the destroyers, and the planes and the tanks.

The nation expects our defense industries to continue operation without interruption by strikes or lockouts. It expects and insists that management and workers will reconcile their differences by voluntary or legal means, to continue to produce the supplies that are so sorely needed.

And on the economic side of our great defense program, we are, as you know, bending every effort to maintain stability of prices and with that the stability of the cost of living.

Nine days ago I announced the setting up of a more effective organization to direct our gigantic efforts to increase the production of munitions. The appropriation of vast sums of money and a well coordinated executive direction of our defense efforts are not in themselves enough. Guns, planes, ships and many other things have to be built in the factories and the arsenals of America. They have to be produced by workers and managers and engineers with the aid of machines which in turn have to be built by hundreds of thousands of workers throughout the land. In this great work there has been splendid cooperation between the Government and industry and labor, and I am very thankful.

American industrial genius, unmatched throughout all the world in the solution of production problems, has been called upon to bring its resources and its talents into action. Manufacturers of watches, of farm implements, of linotypes, and cash registers, and automobiles, and sewing machines, and lawn mowers and locomotives are now making fuses, bomb packing crates, telescope mounts, shells, and pistols and tanks.

But all of our present efforts are not enough. We must have more ships, more guns, more planes—more of everything. And this can only be accomplished if we discard the notion of "business as usual." This job cannot be done merely by superimposing on the existing productive facilities the added requirements of the nation for defense.

Our defense efforts must not be blocked by those who fear the future consequences of surplus plant capacity. The possible consequences of failure of our defense efforts now are much more to be feared.

And after the present needs of our defense are past, a proper handling of the country's peacetime needs will require all of the new productive capacity—if not still more.

No pessimistic policy about the future of America shall delay the immediate expansion of those industries essential to defense. We need them. I want to make it clear that it is the purpose of the nation to build now with all possible speed every machine, every arsenal, every factory that we need to manufacture our defense material. We have the men—the skill—the wealth—and above all, the will.

I am confident that if and when production of consumer or luxury goods in certain industries requires the use of machines and raw materials that are essential for defense purposes, then such production must yield, and will gladly yield, to our primary and compelling purpose.

So I appeal to the owners of plants—to the managers—to the workers—to our own Government employees—to put every ounce of effort into producing these munitions swiftly and without stint. With this appeal I give you the pledge that all of us who are officers of your Government will devote ourselves to the same whole-hearted extent to the great task that lies ahead.

As planes and ships and guns and shells are produced, your Government, with its defense experts, can then determine how best to use them to defend this hemisphere. The decision as to how much shall be sent abroad and how much shall remain at home must be made on the basis of our overall military necessities.

We must be the great arsenal of democracy. For us this is an emergency as serious as war itself. We must apply ourselves to our task with the same resolution, the same sense of urgency, the same spirit of patriotism and sacrifice as we would show were we at war.

We have furnished the British great material support and we will furnish far more in the future.

There will be no "bottlenecks" in our determination to aid Great Britain. No dictator, no combination of dictators, will weaken that determination by threats of how they will construe that determination.

The British have received invaluable military support from the heroic Greek army and from the forces of all the governments in exile. Their strength is growing. It is the strength of men and women who value their freedom more highly than they value their lives.

I believe that the Axis powers are not going to win this war. I base that belief on the latest and best of information.

We have no excuse for defeatism. We have every good reason for hope—hope for peace, yes, and hope for the defense of our civilization and for the building of a better civilization in the future.

I have the profound conviction that the American people are now determined to put forth a mightier effort than they have ever yet made to increase our production of all the implements of defense, to meet the threat to our democratic faith.

As President of the United States I call for that national effort. I call for it in the name of this nation which we love and honor and which we are privileged and proud to serve. I call

upon our people with absolute confidence that our common cause will greatly succeed.

Source: "On National Security," December 29, 1940. Franklin D. Roosevelt Presidential Library and Museum. Available online. URL: http://www.fdrlibrary.marist.edu/122940.html.

24. The "Four Freedoms"—FDR's Annual Address to Congress, January 6, 1941

In urging aid for Britain short of war, FDR delivered an eloquent pledge to the nation and the remainder of the free world in support of freedom of speech, freedom to worship God, freedom from want, and freedom from fear. In response, Congress passed the Lend-Lease program.

Mr. President, Mr. Speaker, Members of the Seventy-seventh Congress:

I address you, the Members of the Seventy-seventh Congress, at a moment unprecedented in the history of the Union. I use the word "unprecedented," because at no previous time has American security been as seriously threatened from without as it is today.

Since the permanent formation of our Government under the Constitution, in 1789, most of the periods of crisis in our history have related to our domestic affairs. Fortunately, only one of these—the four-year War Between the States—ever threatened our national unity. Today, thank God, one hundred and thirty million Americans, in forty-eight States, have forgotten points of the compass in our national unity.

It is true that prior to 1914 the United States often had been disturbed by events in other Continents. We had even engaged in two wars with European nations and in a number of undeclared wars in the West Indies, in the Mediterranean and in the Pacific for the maintenance of American rights and for the principles of peaceful commerce. But in no case had a serious threat been raised against our national safety or our continued independence.

What I seek to convey is the historic truth that the United States as a nation has at all times maintained clear, definite opposition, to any attempt to lock us in behind an ancient Chinese wall while the procession of civilization went past. Today, thinking of our children and of their children, we oppose enforced isolation for ourselves or for any other part of the Americas.

That determination of ours, extending over all these years, was proved, for example, during the quarter century of wars following the French Revolution. While the Napoleonic struggles did threaten interests of the United States because of the French foothold in the West Indies and in Louisiana, and while we engaged in the War of 1812 to vindicate our right to peaceful trade, it is nevertheless clear that neither France nor Great Britain, nor any other nation, was aiming at domination of the whole world.

In like fashion from 1815 to 1914—ninety-nine years—no single war in Europe or in Asia constituted a real threat against our future or against the future of any other American nation.

Except in the Maximilian interlude in Mexico, no foreign power sought to establish itself in this Hemisphere; and the strength of the British fleet in the Atlantic has been a friendly strength. It is still a friendly strength.

Even when the World War broke out in 1914, it seemed to contain only small threat of danger to our own American future. But, as time went on, the American people began to visualize what the downfall of democratic nations might mean to our own democracy.

We need not overemphasize imperfections in the Peace of Versailles. We need not harp on failure of the democracies to deal with problems of world reconstruction. We should remember that the Peace of 1919 was far less unjust than the kind of "pacification" which began even before Munich, and which is being carried on under the new order of tyranny that seeks to spread over every continent today. The American people have unalterably set their faces against that tyranny.

Every realist knows that the democratic way of life is at this moment being directly assailed in every part of the world—assailed either by arms, or by secret spreading of poisonous propaganda by those who seek to destroy unity and promote discord in nations that are still at peace.

During sixteen long months this assault has blotted out the whole pattern of democratic life in an appalling number of independent nations, great and small. The assailants are still on the march, threatening other nations, great and small.

Therefore, as your President, performing my constitutional duty to "give to the Congress information of the state of the Union," I find it, unhappily, necessary to report that the future and the safety of our country and of our democracy are overwhelmingly involved in events far beyond our borders.

Armed defense of democratic existence is now being gallantly waged in four continents. If that defense fails, all the population and all the resources of Europe, Asia, Africa and Australasia will be dominated by the conquerors. Let us remember that the total of those populations and their resources in those four continents greatly exceeds the sum total of the population and the resources of the whole of the Western Hemisphere-many times over.

In times like these it is immature—and incidentally, untrue—for anybody to brag that an unprepared America, single-handed, and with one hand tied behind its back, can hold off the whole world.

No realistic American can expect from a dictator's peace international generosity, or return of true independence, or world disarmament, or freedom of expression, or freedom of religion -or even good business.

Such a peace would bring no security for us or for our neighbors. "Those, who would give up essential liberty to purchase a little temporary safety, deserve neither liberty nor safety."

As a nation, we may take pride in the fact that we are softhearted; but we cannot afford to be soft-headed.

We must always be wary of those who with sounding brass and a tinkling cymbal preach the "ism" of appeasement.

We must especially beware of that small group of selfish men who would clip the wings of the American eagle in order to feather their own nests.

I have recently pointed out how quickly the tempo of modern warfare could bring into our very midst the physical attack which we must eventually expect if the dictator nations win this war.

There is much loose talk of our immunity from immediate and direct invasion from across the seas. Obviously, as long as the British Navy retains its power, no such danger exists. Even if there were no British Navy, it is not probable that any enemy would be stupid enough to attack us by landing troops in the United States from across thousands of miles of ocean, until it had acquired strategic bases from which to operate.

But we learn much from the lessons of the past years in Europe-particularly the lesson of Norway, whose essential seaports were captured by treachery and surprise built up over a series of years.

The first phase of the invasion of this Hemisphere would not be the landing of regular troops. The necessary strategic points would be occupied by secret agents and their dupes-and great numbers of them are already here, and in Latin America.

As long as the aggressor nations maintain the offensive, they-not we—will choose the time and the place and the method of their attack.

That is why the future of all the American Republics is today in serious danger.

That is why this Annual Message to the Congress is unique in our history.

That is why every member of the Executive Branch of the Government and every member of the Congress faces great responsibility and great accountability.

The need of the moment is that our actions and our policy should be devoted primarily-almost exclusively—to meeting this foreign peril. For all our domestic problems are now a part of the great emergency.

Just as our national policy in internal affairs has been based upon a decent respect for the rights and the dignity of all our fellow men within our gates, so our national policy in foreign affairs has been based on a decent respect for the rights and dignity of all nations, large and small.

And the justice of morality must and will win in the end.

Our national policy is this: First, by an impressive expression of the public will and without regard to partisanship, we are committed to all-inclusive national defense.

Second, by an impressive expression of the public will and without regard to partisanship, we are committed to full support of all those resolute peoples, everywhere, who are resisting aggression and are thereby keeping war away from our Hemisphere. By this support, we express our determination that the democratic cause shall prevail; and we strengthen the defense and the security of our own nation.

Third, by an impressive expression of the public will and without regard to partisanship, we are committed to the proposition that principles of morality and considerations for our own security will never permit us to acquiesce in a peace dictated by aggressors and sponsored by appeasers. We know that enduring peace cannot be bought at the cost of other people's freedom.

In the recent national election there was no substantial difference between the two great parties in respect to that national policy. No issue was fought out on this line before the American electorate. Today it is abundantly evident that American citizens everywhere are demanding and supporting speedy and complete action in recognition of obvious danger.

Therefore, the immediate need is a swift and driving increase in our armament production.

Leaders of industry and labor have responded to our summons. Goals of speed have been set. In some cases these goals are being reached ahead of time; in some cases we are on schedule; in other cases there are slight but not serious delays; and in some cases—and I am sorry to say very important cases—we are all concerned by the slowness of the accomplishment of our plans.

The Army and Navy, however, have made substantial progress during the past year. Actual experience is improving and speeding up our methods of production with every passing day. And today's best is not good enough for tomorrow.

I am not satisfied with the progress thus far made. The men in charge of the program represent the best in training, in ability, and in patriotism.

They are not satisfied with the progress thus far made. None of us will be satisfied until the job is done.

No matter whether the original goal was set too high or too low, our objective is quicker and better results. To give you two illustrations:

We are behind schedule in turning out finished airplanes; we are working day and night to solve the innumerable problems and to catch up.

We are ahead of schedule in building warships but we are working to get even further ahead of that schedule.

To change a whole nation from a basis of peacetime production of implements of peace to a basis of wartime production of implements of war is no small task. And the greatest difficulty comes at the beginning of the program, when new tools, new plant facilities, new assembly lines, and new ship ways must first be constructed before the actual materiel begins to flow steadily and speedily from them.

The Congress, of course, must rightly keep itself informed at all times of the progress of the program. However, there is certain information, as the Congress itself will readily recognize, which, in the interests of our own security and those of the nations that we are supporting, must of needs be kept in confidence.

New circumstances are constantly begetting new needs for our safety. I shall ask this Congress for greatly increased new appropriations and authorizations to carry on what we have begun.

I also ask this Congress for authority and for funds sufficient to manufacture additional munitions and war supplies of many kinds, to be turned over to those nations which are now in actual war with aggressor nations.

Our most useful and immediate role is to act as an arsenal for them as well as for ourselves. They do not need man power, but they do need billions of dollars worth of the weapons of defense.

The time is near when they will not be able to pay for them all in ready cash. We cannot, and we will not, tell them that they must surrender, merely because of present inability to pay for the weapons which we know they must have. I do not recommend that we make them a loan of dollars with which to pay for these weapons—a loan to be repaid in dollars.

I recommend that we make it possible for those nations to continue to obtain war materials in the United States, fitting their orders into our own program. Nearly all their materiel would, if the time ever came, be useful for our own defense.

Taking counsel of expert military and naval authorities, considering what is best for our own security, we are free to decide how much should be kept here and how much should be sent abroad to our friends who by their determined and heroic resistance are giving us time in which to make ready our own defense.

For what we send abroad, we shall be repaid within a reasonable time following the close of hostilities, in similar materials, or, at our option, in other goods of many kinds, which they can produce and which we need.

Let us say to the democracies: "We Americans are vitally concerned in your defense of freedom. We are putting forth our energies, our resources and our organizing powers to give you the strength to regain and maintain a free world. We shall send you, in ever-increasing numbers, ships, planes, tanks, guns. This is our purpose and our pledge."

In fulfillment of this purpose we will not be intimidated by the threats of dictators that they will regard as a breach of international law or as an act of war our aid to the democracies which dare to resist their aggression. Such aid is not an act of war, even if a dictator should unilaterally proclaim it so to be.

When the dictators, if the dictators, are ready to make war upon us, they will not wait for an act of war on our part. They did not wait for Norway or Belgium or the Netherlands to commit an act of war.

Their only interest is in a new one-way international law, which lacks mutuality in its observance, and, therefore, becomes an instrument of oppression.

The happiness of future generations of Americans may well depend upon how effective and how immediate we can make our aid felt. No one can tell the exact character of the emergency situations that we may be called upon to meet. The Nation's hands must not be tied when the Nation's life is in danger.

We must all prepare to make the sacrifices that the emergency—almost as serious as war itself—demands. Whatever stands in the way of speed and efficiency in defense preparations must give way to the national need.

A free nation has the right to expect full cooperation from all groups. A free nation has the right to look to the leaders of business, of labor, and of agriculture to take the lead in stimulating effort, not among other groups but within their own groups.

The best way of dealing with the few slackers or trouble makers in our midst is, first, to shame them by patriotic example, and, if that fails, to use the sovereignty of Government to save Government.

As men do not live by bread alone, they do not fight by armaments alone.

Those who man our defenses, and those behind them who build our defenses, must have the stamina and the courage which come from unshakable belief in the manner of life which they are defending. The mighty action that we are calling for cannot be based on a disregard of all things worth fighting for.

The Nation takes great satisfaction and much strength from the things which have been done to make its people conscious of their individual stake in the preservation of democratic life in America. Those things have toughened the fibre of our people, have renewed their faith and strengthened their devotion to the institutions we make ready to protect.

Certainly this is no time for any of us to stop thinking about the social and economic problems which are the root cause of the social revolution which is today a supreme factor in the world.

For there is nothing mysterious about the foundations of a healthy and strong democracy. The basic things expected by our people of their political and economic systems are simple. They are :

Equality of opportunity for youth and for others.

Jobs for those who can work. Security for those who need it.

The ending of special privilege for the few.

The preservation of civil liberties for all.

The enjoyment of the fruits of scientific progress in a wider and constantly rising standard of living.

These are the simple, basic things that must never be lost sight of in the turmoil and unbelievable complexity of our modern world. The inner and abiding strength of our economic and political systems is dependent upon the degree to which they fulfill these expectations.

Many subjects connected with our social economy call for immediate improvement.

As examples:

We should bring more citizens under the coverage of old-age pensions and unemployment insurance.

We should widen the opportunities for adequate medical care.

We should plan a better system by which persons deserving or needing gainful employment may obtain it.

I have called for personal sacrifice. I am assured of the willingness of almost all Americans to respond to that call.

A part of the sacrifice means the payment of more money in taxes. In my Budget Message I shall recommend that a greater portion of this great defense program be paid for from taxation than we are paying today. No person should try, or be allowed, to get rich out of this program; and the principle of tax payments in accordance with ability to pay should be constantly before our eyes to guide our legislation.

If the Congress maintains these principles, the voters, putting patriotism ahead of pocketbooks, will give you their applause.

In the future days, which we seek to make secure, we look forward to a world founded upon four essential human freedoms.

The first is freedom of speech and expression—everywhere in the world.

The second is freedom of every person to worship God in his own way—everywhere in the world.

The third is freedom from want—which, translated into world terms, means economic understandings which will secure to every nation a healthy peacetime life for its inhabitants—everywhere in the world.

The fourth is freedom from fear—which, translated into world terms, means a worldwide reduction of armaments to such a point and in such a thorough fashion that no nation will be in a position to commit an act of physical aggression against any neighbor—anywhere in the world.

That is no vision of a distant millennium. It is a definite basis for a kind of world attainable in our own time and generation. That kind of world is the very antithesis of the so-called new order of tyranny which the dictators seek to create with the crash of a bomb.

To that new order we oppose the greater conception—the moral order. A good society is able to face schemes of world domination and foreign revolutions alike without fear.

Since the beginning of our American history, we have been engaged in change—in a perpetual peaceful revolution—a revolution which goes on steadily, quietly adjusting itself to changing conditions—without the concentration camp or the quick-lime in the ditch. The world order which we seek is the cooperation of free countries, working together in a friendly, civilized society.

This nation has placed its destiny in the hands and heads and hearts of its millions of free men and women; and its faith in freedom under the guidance of God.

Freedom means the supremacy of human rights everywhere.

Our support goes to those who struggle to gain those rights or keep them.

Our strength is our unity of purpose. To that high concept there can be no end save victory.

Source: "Our Documents: Franklin Roosevelt's Annual Address to Congress—The 'Four Freedoms.'" Franklin D. Roosevelt Presidential Library and Museum. Available online. URL: http://www.fdrlibrary.marist.edu/online14.html, http://website_online_version/od4frees.html.

25. Third Inaugural Address, January 20, 1941

FDR's Third Inaugural address was less successful than his first two. He wrote out a draft in longhand in which he compared the nation's needs to the mind, body, and spirit of humanity. Samuel Rosenman contributed to the philosophical speech that echoes the tension between the president's preference for belligerency and the nonbelligerency favored by the isolationists. The address failed to clarify what the president planned to do.

On each national day of inauguration since 1789, the people have renewed their sense of dedication to the United States.

In Washington's day the task of the people was to create and weld together a nation.

In Lincoln's day the task of the people was to preserve that Nation from disruption from within.

In this day the task of the people is to save that Nation and its institutions from disruption from without.

To us there has come a time, in the midst of swift happenings, to pause for a moment and take stock—to recall what our place in history has been, and to rediscover what we are and what we may be. If we do not, we risk the real peril of inaction.

Lives of nations are determined not by the count of years, but by the lifetime of the human spirit. The life of a man is three-score years and ten: a little more, a little less. The life of a nation is the fullness of the measure of its will to live.

There are men who doubt this. There are men who believe that democracy, as a form of Government and a frame of life, is limited or measured by a kind of mystical and artificial fate that, for some unexplained reason, tyranny and slavery have become the surging wave of the future—and that freedom is an ebbing tide.

But we Americans know that this is not true.

Eight years ago, when the life of this Republic seemed frozen by a fatalistic terror, we proved that this is not true. We were in the midst of shock—but we acted. We acted quickly, boldly, decisively.

These later years have been living years—fruitful years for the people of this democracy. For they have brought to us greater security and, I hope, a better understanding that life's ideals are to be measured in other than material things.

Most vital to our present and our future is this experience of a democracy which successfully survived crisis at home; put away many evil things; built new structures on enduring lines; and, through it all, maintained the fact of its democracy.

For action has been taken within the three-way framework of the Constitution of the United States. The coordinate branches of the Government continue freely to function. The Bill of Rights remains inviolate. The freedom of elections is wholly maintained. Prophets of the downfall of American democracy have seen their dire predictions come to naught.

Democracy is not dying.

We know it because we have seen it revive—and grow.

We know it cannot die—because it is built on the unhampered initiative of individual men and women joined together in a common enterprise—an enterprise undertaken and carried through by the free expression of a free majority.

We know it because democracy alone, of all forms of government, enlists the full force of men's enlightened will.

We know it because democracy alone has constructed an unlimited civilization capable of infinite progress in the improvement of human life.

We know it because, if we look below the surface, we sense it still spreading on every continent—for it is the most humane, the most advanced, and in the end the most unconquerable of all forms of human society.

A nation, like a person, has a body—a body that must be fed and clothed and housed, invigorated and rested, in a manner that measures up to the objectives of our time.

A nation, like a person, has a mind—a mind that must be kept informed and alert, that must know itself, that understands the hopes and the needs of its neighbors—all the other nations that live within the narrowing circle of the world.

And a nation, like a person, has something deeper, something more permanent, something larger than the sum of all its parts. It is that something which matters most to its future—which calls forth the most sacred guarding of its present.

It is a thing for which we find it difficult—even impossible—to hit upon a single, simple word.

And yet we all understand what it is—the spirit—the faith of America. It is the product of centuries. It was born in the multitudes of those who came from many lands—some of high degree, but mostly plain people, who sought here, early and late, to find freedom more freely.

The democratic aspiration is no mere recent phase in human history. It is human history. It permeated the ancient life of early peoples. It blazed anew in the middle ages. It was written in Magna Carta.

In the Americas its impact has been irresistible. America has been the New World in all tongues, to all peoples, not because this continent was a new-found land, but because all those who came here believed they could create upon this continent a new life—a life that should be new in freedom.

Its vitality was written into our own Mayflower Compact, into the Declaration of Independence, into the Constitution of the United States, into the Gettysburg Address.

Those who first came here to carry out the longings of their spirit, and the millions who followed, and the stock that sprang from them—all have moved forward constantly and consistently toward an ideal which in itself has gained stature and clarity with each generation.

The hopes of the Republic cannot forever tolerate either undeserved poverty or self-serving wealth.

We know that we still have far to go; that we must more greatly build the security and the opportunity and the knowledge of every citizen, in the measure justified by the resources and the capacity of the land.

But it is not enough to achieve these purposes alone. It is not enough to clothe and feed the body of this Nation, and instruct and inform its mind. For there is also the spirit. And of the three, the greatest is the spirit.

Without the body and the mind, as all men know, the Nation could not live.

But if the spirit of America were killed, even though the Nation's body and mind, constricted in an alien world, lived on, the America we know would have perished.

That spirit—that faith—speaks to us in our daily lives in ways often unnoticed, because they seem so obvious. It speaks to us here in the Capital of the Nation. It speaks to us through the processes of governing in the sovereignties of 48 States. It speaks to us in our counties, in our cities, in our towns, and in our villages. It speaks to us from the other nations of the hemisphere, and from those across the seas—the enslaved, as well as the free. Sometimes we fail to hear or heed these voices of freedom because to us the privilege of our freedom is such an old, old story.

The destiny of America was proclaimed in words of prophecy spoken by our first President in his first inaugural in 1789—words almost directed, it would seem, to this year of 1941: "The preservation of the sacred fire of liberty and the destiny of the republican model of government are justly considered . . . deeply, . . . finally, staked on the experiment intrusted to the hands of the American people."

If we lose that sacred fire—if we let it be smothered with doubt and fear—then we shall reject the destiny which Washington strove so valiantly and so triumphantly to establish. The preservation of the spirit and faith of the Nation does, and will, furnish the highest justification for every sacrifice that we may make in the cause of national defense.

In the face of great perils never before encountered, our strong purpose is to protect and to perpetuate the integrity of democracy.

For this we muster the spirit of America, and the faith of America.

We do not retreat. We are not content to stand still. As Americans, we go forward, in the service of our country, by the will of God.

Source: "Third Inaugural Address of Franklin D. Roosevelt, Monday, January 20, 1941." The Avalon Project at Yale Law School. Available online. URL: http://www.yale.edu/lawweb/avalon/presid/inaug/froos3.htm.

26. Eighteenth Fireside Chat— On Maintaining Freedom of the Seas, September 11, 1941

In his last Fireside Chat before the Pearl Harbor attack, FDR brought the nation into a de facto naval war with Nazi Germany as a result of the fact that a Nazi submarine had torpedoed the American destroyer Greer. He did not mention that the Nazi submarine had first been attacked by a British plane while working with the Greer.

My fellow Americans:

The Navy Department of the United States has reported to me that on the morning of September fourth, the United States destroyer *Greer*, proceeding in full daylight towards Iceland, had reached a point southeast of Greenland. She was carrying American mail to Iceland. She was flying the American flag. Her identity as an American ship was unmistakable.

She was then and there attacked by a submarine.

Germany admits that it was a German submarine. The submarine deliberately fired a torpedo at the *Greer*, followed later by another torpedo attack.

In spite of what Hitler's propaganda bureau has invented, and in spite of what any American obstructionist organization may prefer to believe, I tell you the blunt fact that the German submarine fired first upon this American destroyer without warning, and with deliberate design to sink her.

Our destroyer, at the time, was in waters which the Government of the United States had declared to be waters of self-defense—surrounding outposts of American protection in the Atlantic.

In the North of the Atlantic, outposts have been established by us in Iceland, in Greenland, in Labrador and in Newfoundland. Through these waters there pass many ships of many flags. They bear food and other supplies to civilians; and they bear material of war, for which the people of the United States are spending billions of dollars, and which, by Congressional action, they have declared to be essential for the defense of (their) our own land.

The United States destroyer, when attacked, was proceeding on a legitimate mission.

If the destroyer was visible to the submarine when the torpedo was fired, then the attack was a deliberate attempt by the Nazis to sink a clearly identified American warship. On the other hand, if the submarine was beneath the surface of the sea and, with the aid of its listening devices, fired in the direction of the sound of the American destroyer without even taking the trouble to learn its identity—as the official German communique would indicate then the attack was even more outrageous. For it indicates a policy of indiscriminate violence against any vessel sailing the seas—belligerent or non-belligerent.

This was piracy—piracy legally and morally. It was not the first nor the last act of piracy which the Nazi Government has committed against the American flag in this war. For attack has followed attack.

A few months ago an American flag merchant ship, the *Robin Moor*, was sunk by a Nazi submarine in the middle of the South Atlantic, under circumstances violating long-established international law and violating every principle of humanity. The passengers and the crew were forced into open boats hundreds of miles from land, in direct violation of international agreements signed by nearly all nations including the Government of Germany.

No apology, no allegation of mistake, no offer of reparations has come from the Nazi Government.

In July, 1941, nearly two months ago an American battleship in North American waters was followed by a submarine which for a long time sought to maneuver itself into a position of attack upon the battleship. The periscope of the submarine was clearly seen. No British or American submarines were within hundreds of miles of this spot at the time, so the nationality of the submarine is clear.

Five days ago a United States Navy ship on patrol picked up three survivors of an American-owned ship operating under the flag of our sister Republic of Panama—the S. S. *Sessa*. On August seventeenth, she had been first torpedoed without warning, and then shelled, near Greenland, while carrying civilian supplies to Iceland. It is feared that the other members of her crew have been drowned.

In view of the established presence of German submarines in this vicinity, there can be no reasonable doubt as to the identity of the flag of the attacker.

Five days ago, another United States merchant ship, the *Steel Seafarer*, was sunk by a German aircraft in the Red Sea two hundred and twenty miles south of Suez. She was bound for an Egyptian port.

So four of the vessels sunk or attacked flew the American flag and were clearly identifiable. Two of these ships were warships of the American Navy.

In the fifth case, the vessel sunk clearly carried the flag of our sister Republic of Panama.

In the face of all this, we Americans are keeping our feet on the ground. Our type of democratic civilization has outgrown the thought of feeling compelled to fight some other nation by reason of any single piratical attack on one of our ships. We are not becoming hysterical or losing our sense of proportion. Therefore, what I am thinking and saying tonight does not relate to any isolated episode.

Instead, we Americans are taking a long-range point of view in regard to certain fundamentals—a point of view in regard to a series of events on land and on sea which must be considered as a whole—as a part of a world pattern.

It would be unworthy of a great nation to exaggerate an isolated incident, or to become inflamed by some one act of violence. But it would be inexcusable folly to minimize such incidents in the face of evidence which makes it clear that the incident is not isolated, but is part of a general plan.

The important truth is that these acts of international lawlessness are a manifestation of a design—a design that has been made clear to the American people for a long time. It is the Nazi design to abolish the freedom of the seas, and to acquire absolute control and domination of (the) these seas for themselves.

For with control of the seas in their own hands, the way can obviously become clear for their next step—domination of the United States (and the) domination of the Western Hemisphere by force of arms. Under Nazi control of the seas, no merchant ship of the United States or of any other American Republic would be free to carry on any peaceful commerce, except by the condescending grace of this foreign and tyrannical power. The Atlantic Ocean which has been, and which should always be, a free and friendly highway for us would then become a deadly menace to the commerce of the United States, to the coasts of the United States, and even to the inland cities of the United States.

The Hitler Government, in defiance of the laws of the sea, (and) in defiance of the recognized rights of all other nations, has presumed to declare, on paper, that great areas of the seas—even including a vast expanse lying in the Western Hemisphere—are to be closed, and that no ships may enter them for any purpose, except at peril of being sunk. Actually they are sinking ships at will and without warning in widely separated areas both within and far outside of these far-flung pretended zones.

This Nazi attempt to seize control of the oceans is but a counterpart of the Nazi plots now being carried on throughout the Western Hemisphere—all designed toward the same end. For Hitler's advance guards—not only his avowed agents but also his dupes among us—have sought to make ready for him footholds, bridgeheads in the New World, to be used as soon as he has gained control of the oceans.

His intrigues, his plots, his machinations, his sabotage in this New World are all known to the Government of the United States. Conspiracy has followed conspiracy.

For example, last year a plot to seize the Government of Uruguay was smashed by the prompt action of that country, which was supported in full by her American neighbors. A like plot was then hatching in Argentina, and that government has carefully and wisely blocked it at every point. More recently, an endeavor was made to subvert the government of Bolivia. And within the past few weeks the discovery was made of secret air-landing fields in Colombia, within easy range of the Panama Canal. I could multiply instance(s) upon instance.

To be ultimately successful in world mastery, Hitler knows that he must get control of the seas. He must first destroy the bridge of ships which we are building across the Atlantic and over which we shall continue to roll the implements of war to help destroy him, (and) to destroy all his works in the end.

He must wipe out our patrol on sea and in the air if he is to do it. He must silence the British Navy.

I think it must be explained over and over again to people who like to think of the United States Navy as an invincible protection, that this can be true only if the British Navy survives. And that, my friends, is simple arithmetic. For if the world outside of the Americas falls under Axis domination, the shipbuilding facilities which the Axis powers would then possess in all of Europe, in the British Isles and in the Far East would be much greater than all the shipbuilding facilities and potentialities of all of the Americas—not only greater, but two or three times greater, enough to win.

Even if the United States threw all its resources into such a situation, seeking to double and even redouble the size of our Navy, the Axis powers, in control of the rest of the world, would have the manpower and the physical resources to outbuild us several times over.

It is time for all Americans, Americans of all the Americas to stop being deluded by the romantic notion that the Americas can go on living happily and peacefully in a Nazi-dominated world.

Generation after generation, America has battled for the general policy of the freedom of the seas. And that policy is a very simple one, but a basic, a fundamental one. It means that no nation has the right to make the broad oceans of the world at great distances from the actual theatre of land war, unsafe for the commerce of others.

That has been our policy, proved time and again, in all of our history.

Our policy has applied from the earliest days of the Republic—and still applies—not merely to the Atlantic but to the Pacific and to all other oceans as well.

Unrestricted submarine warfare in 1941 constitutes defiance—an act of aggression—against that historic American policy.

It is now clear that Hitler has begun his campaign to control the seas by ruthless force and by wiping out every vestige of international law, every vestige of humanity. His intention has been made clear. The American people can have no further illusions about it.

No tender whisperings of appeasers that Hitler is not interested in the Western hemisphere, no soporific lullabies that a wide ocean protects us from him—can long have any effect on the hard-headed, far-sighted and realistic American people.

Because of these episodes, because of the movements and operations of German warships, and because of the clear, repeated proof that the present government of Germany has no respect for treaties or for international law, that it has no decent attitude toward neutral nations or human life—we Americans are now face to face not with abstract theories but with cruel, relentless facts.

This attack on the *Greer* was no localized military operation in the North Atlantic. This was no mere episode in a struggle between two nations. This was one determined step towards creating a permanent world system based on force, on terror and on murder.

And I am sure that even now the Nazis are waiting, waiting to see whether the United States will by silence give them the green light to go ahead on this path of destruction.

The Nazi danger to our Western world has long ceased to be a mere possibility. The danger is here now—not only from a military enemy but from an enemy of all law, all liberty, all morality, all religion.

There has now come a time when you and I must see the cold inexorable necessity of saying to these inhuman, unrestrained seekers of world conquest and permanent world domination by the sword: "You seek to throw our children and our children's children into your form of terrorism and slavery. You have now attacked our own safety. You shall go no further."

Normal practices of diplomacy—note writing—are of no possible use in dealing with international outlaws who sink our ships and kill our citizens. One peaceful nation after another has met disaster because each refused to look the Nazi danger squarely in the eye until it had actually had them by the throat.

The United States will not make that fatal mistake.

No act of violence, no act of intimidation will keep us from maintaining intact two bulwarks of American defense: First, our line of supply of material to the enemies of Hitler; and second, the freedom of our shipping on the high seas.

No matter what it takes, no matter what it costs, we will keep open the line of legitimate commerce in these defensive water of ours.

We have sought no shooting war with Hitler. We do not seek it now. But neither do we want peace so much, that we are willing to pay for it by permitting him to attack our naval and merchant ships while they are on legitimate business.

I assume that the German leaders are not deeply concerned, tonight or any other time, by what we Americans or the American government say or publish about them. We cannot bring about the downfall of Nazi-ism by the use of long-range invective.

But when you see a rattlesnake poised to strike, you do not wait until he has struck before you crush him.

These Nazi submarines and raiders are the rattlesnakes of the Atlantic. They are a menace to the free pathways of the high seas. They are a challenge to our own sovereignty. They hammer at our most precious rights when they attack ships of the American flag—symbols of our independence, our freedom, our very life.

It is clear to all Americans that the time has come when the Americas themselves must now be defended. A continuation of attacks in our own waters or in waters that could be used for further and greater attacks on us, will inevitably weaken our American ability to repel Hitlerism.

Do not let us be hair-splitters. Let us not ask ourselves whether the Americas should begin to defend themselves after the first attack, or the fifth attack, or the tenth attack, or the twentieth attack.

The time for active defense is now.

Do not let us split hairs. Let us not say : "We will only defend ourselves if the torpedo succeeds in getting home, or if the crew and the passengers are drowned."

This is the time for prevention of attack.

If submarines or raiders attack in distant waters, they can attack equally well within sight of our own shores. Their very presence in any waters which America deems vital to its defense constitutes an attack.

In the waters which we deem necessary for our defense, American naval vessels and American planes will no longer wait until Axis submarines lurking under the water, or Axis raiders on the surface of the sea, strike their deadly blow—first.

Upon our naval and air patrol—now operating in large number over a vast expanse of the Atlantic Ocean—falls the duty of maintaining the American policy of freedom of the seas—now. That means, very simply, very clearly, that our patrolling vessels and planes will protect all merchant ships—not only American ships but ships of any flag—engaged in commerce in our defensive waters. They will protect them from submarines; they will protect them from surface raiders.

This situation is not new. The second President of the United States, John Adams, ordered the United States Navy to clean out European privateers and European ships of war which were infesting the Caribbean and South American waters, destroying American commerce.

The third President of the United States, Thomas Jefferson, ordered the United States Navy to end the attacks being made upon American and other ships by the corsairs of the nations of North Africa.

My obligation as President is historic; it is clear. Yes, it is inescapable.

It is no act of war on our part when we decide to protect the seas that are vital to American defense. The aggression is not ours. Ours is solely defense.

But let this warning be clear:

From now on, if German or Italian vessels of war enter the waters, the protection of which is necessary for American defense, they do so at their own peril.

The orders which I have given as Commander-in-Chief of the United States Army and Navy are to carry out that policy—at once.

The sole responsibility rests upon Germany. There will be no shooting unless Germany continues to seek it.

That is my obvious duty in this crisis. That is the clear right of this sovereign nation. This is the only step possible, if we would keep tight the wall of defense which we are pledged to maintain around this Western Hemisphere.

I have no illusions about the gravity of this step. I have not taken it hurriedly or lightly. It is the result of months and months of constant thought and anxiety and prayer. In the protection of your nation and mine it cannot be avoided.

The American people have faced other grave crises in their history—with American courage, with American resolution. They will do no less today. They know the actualities of the attacks upon us. They know the necessities of a bold defense against these attacks. They know that the times call for clear heads and fearless hearts.

And with that inner strength that comes to a free people conscious of their duty, (and) conscious of the righteousness of what they do, they will—with Divine help and guidance—stand their ground against this latest assault upon their democracy, their sovereignty, and their freedom.

Source: "On Maintaining Freedom of the Seas," September 11, 1941. Franklin D. Roosevelt Presidential Library and Museum. Available online. URL: http://www.fdrlibrary.marist.edu/091141.html.

27. Message to Congress on the Japanese Attack at Pearl Harbor, December 8, 1941

FDR delivered the best speech he ever wrote in this message, which was virtually all his own work, except for the ending line by Harry Hopkins. FDR dictated the first draft to Grace Tully, his secretary, and then made changes in the second draft. The sneak attack on Pearl Harbor on December 7, 1941, became "a date which will live in infamy."

Mr. Vice President, and Mr. Speaker, and Members of the Senate and House of Representatives:

Yesterday, December 7, 1941—a date which will live in infamy—the United States of America was suddenly and deliberately attacked by naval and air forces of the Empire of Japan.

The United States was at peace with that Nation and, at the solicitation of Japan, was still in conversation with its Government and its Emperor looking toward the maintenance of peace in the Pacific. Indeed, one hour after Japanese air squadrons had commenced bombing in the American Island of Oahu, the Japanese Ambassador to the United States and his colleague delivered to our Secretary of State a formal reply to a recent American message. And while this reply stated that it seemed useless to continue the existing diplomatic negotiations, it contained no threat or hint of war or of armed attack.

It will be recorded that the distance of Hawaii from Japan makes it obvious that the attack was deliberately planned many days or even weeks ago. During the intervening time the Japanese Government has deliberately sought to deceive the United States by false statements and expressions of hope for continued peace.

The attack yesterday on the Hawaiian Islands has caused severe damage to American naval and military forces. I regret to tell you that very many American lives have been lost. In addition American ships have been reported torpedoed on the high seas between San Francisco and Honolulu.

Yesterday the Japanese Government also launched an attack against Malaya.

Last night Japanese forces attacked Hong Kong.

Last night Japanese forces attacked Guam.

Last night Japanese forces attacked the Philippine Islands.

Last night the Japanese attacked Wake Island. And this morning the Japanese attacked Midway Island.

Japan has, therefore, undertaken a surprise offensive extending throughout the Pacific area. The facts of yesterday and today speak for themselves. The people of the United States have already formed their opinions and well understand the implications to the very life and safety of our Nation.

As Commander in Chief of the Army and Navy I have directed that all measures be taken for our defense.

But always will our whole Nation remember the character of the onslaught against us. No matter how long it may take us to overcome this premeditated invasion, the American people in their righteous might will win through to absolute victory. I believe that I interpret the will of the Congress and of the people when I assert that we will not only defend ourselves to the uttermost but will make it very certain that this form of treachery shall never again endanger us.

Hostilities exist. There is no blinking at the fact that our people, our territory, and our interests are in grave danger.

With confidence in our armed forces—with the unbounding determination of our people—we will gain the inevitable triumph—so help us God.

Source: "Address to Congress Requesting a Declaration of War (December 8, 1941)." Miller Center of Public Affairs. Scripps Library and Multimedia Archive. Available online: URL: http://millercenter.virginia.edu/scripps/diglibrary/prezspeches/roosevelt/fdr_1941_1208.html.

28. The "Fala Speech"—Teamsters' Union Dinner, September 23, 1944

FDR's so-called Fala Speech was delivered during the fourth term of his presidency. He responded to concerns over his health by using humor to disarm his critics and inspire the nation. Rebutting Republican distortions of his record, he used sarcasm and humor in defense of his dog, Fala, against alleged partisan attacks.

Well, here we are together again—after four years—and what years they have been! You know, I am actually four years older, which is a fact that seems to annoy some people. In fact, in the mathematical field there are millions of Americans who are more than eleven years older than we started in to clear up the mess that was dumped in our laps in 1933.

We all know that certain people who make it a practice to depreciate the accomplishments of labor—who even attack labor as unpatriotic—they keep this up usually for three years and six months in a row. But then, for some strange reason they change their tune—every four years—just before election day. When votes are at stake, they suddenly discover that they really love labor and that they are anxious to protect labor from its old friends.

I got quite a laugh, for example—and I am sure that you did—when I read this plank in the Republican platform adopted at their National Convention in Chicago last July:

"The Republican Party accepts the purposes of the National Labor Relations Act, the Wage and Hour Act, the Social Security Act and all other Federal statutes designed to promote and protect the welfare of American working men and women, and we promise a fair and just administration of these laws."

You know, many of the Republican leaders and Congressmen and candidates, who shouted enthusiastic approval of that plank in that Convention Hall would not even recognize these progressive laws if they met them in broad daylight. Indeed, they have personally spent years of effort and energy—and much money—in fighting every one of those laws in the Congress, and in the press, and in the courts, ever since this Administration began to advocate them and enact them into legislation. That is a fair example of their insincerity and of their inconsistency.

The whole purpose of Republican oratory these days seems to be to switch labels. The object is to persuade the American people that the Democratic Party was responsible for the 1929 crash and the depression, and that the Republican Party was responsible for all social progress under the New Deal.

Now, imitation may be the sincerest form of flattery—but I am afraid that in this case it is the most obvious common or garden variety of fraud.

Of course, it is perfectly true that there are enlightened, liberal elements in the Republican Party, and they have fought hard and honorably to bring the Party up to date and to get it in step with the forward march of American progress. But these liberal elements were not able to drive the Old Guard Republicans from their Republican positions.

Can the Old Guard pass itself off as the New Deal?

I think not.

We have all seen many marvelous stunts in the circus but no performing elephant could turn a hand-spring without falling flat on his back.

I need not recount to you the centuries of history which have been crowded into these four years since I saw you last.

There were some—in the Congress and out—who raised their voices against our preparations for defense—before and after 1939—objected to them, raised their voices against them as hysterical war mongering, who cried out against our help to the Allies as provocative and dangerous. We remember the voices. They would like to have us forget them now. But in 1940 and 1941—my, it seems a long time ago—they were loud voices. Happily they were a minority and—fortunately for ourselves, and for the world—they could not stop America.

There are some politicians who kept their heads buried deep in the sand while the storms of Europe and Asia were headed our way, who said that the lend-lease bill "would bring an end to free government in the United States," and who said, "only hysteria entertains the idea that Germany, Italy, or Japan contemplates war on us." "These very men are now asking the American people to entrust to them the conduct of our foreign policy and our military policy."

What the Republican leaders are now saying in effect is this:

"Oh, just forget what we used to say, we have changed our minds now—we have been reading the public opinion polls about these things and now we know what the American people want." And they say: "Don't leave the task of making the peace to those old men who first urged it and who have already laid the foundation for it, and who have had to fight all of us inch by inch during the last five years to do it. Why, just turn it over to us. We'll do it so skillfully that we won't lose a single isolationist vote or a single isolationist campaign contribution."

I think there is one thing that you should know: I am too old for that.

I cannot talk out of both sides of my mouth at the same time. . . .

And while I am on the subject of voting, let me urge every American citizen—man and woman—to use your sacred privilege of voting, no matter which candidate you expect to support. Our millions of soldiers and sailors and merchant seamen have been handicapped or prevented from voting by those politicians and candidates who think that they stand to lose by such votes. You here at home have the freedom of the ballot. Irrespective of the party, you should register and vote this November. I think that is a matter of plain good citizenship.

Words come easily, but they do not change the record. You are, most of you, old enough to remember what things were like for labor in 1932.

You remember the closed banks and the breadlines and the starvation wages; the foreclosures of homes and farms, and the bankruptcies of businesses; the "Hoovervilles," and the young men and women of the nation facing a hopeless, jobless future; the closed factories and mines and mills; the ruined and abandoned farms; the stalled railroads and the empty docks; the blank despair of a whole Nation—and the utter impotence of the Federal Government.

You remember the long, hard road, with its gains and its setbacks, which we have traveled together ever since those days.

Now there are some politicians who do not remember that far back, and there are some who remember but find it convenient to forget. No, the record is not to be washed away that easily.

The opposition this year has already imported into this campaign a very interesting thing, because it is foreign. They have imported the propaganda technique invented by the dictators abroad. Remember, a number of years ago, there was a book, *Mein Kampf*, written by Hitler himself. The technique was all set out in Hitler's book—and it was copied by the aggressors of Italy and Japan. According to that technique, you should never use a small falsehood; always a big one, for its very fantastic nature would make it more credible—if only you keep repeating it over and over and over again.

Well, let us take some simple illustrations that come to mind. For example, although I rubbed my eyes when I read it, we have been told that it was not a Republican depression, but a Democratic depression from which this nation was saved in 1933. That this administration—this one—today—is responsible for all the suffering and misery that the history books and the American people have always thought had been brought about during the twelve ill-fated years when the Republican party was in power.

Now, there is an old and somewhat lugubrious adage which says: "Never speak of rope in the house of a man who has been hanged." In the same way, if I were a Republican leader speaking to a mixed audience, the last word in the whole dictionary that I think I would use is that word "depression.". . .

But perhaps the most ridiculous of these campaign falsifications is the one that this Administration failed to prepare for the war that was coming. I doubt whether even Goebbels [Joseph Goebbels was the Nazi's propaganda and culture minister] would have tried that one. For even he would never have dared hope that the voters of American had already forgotten that many of the Republican leaders in the Congress and outside the Congress tried to thwart and block nearly every attempt that this Administration made to warn our people and to arm our Nation. Some of them called our 50,000 airplane program fantastic. Many of those very same leaders who fought every defense measure we proposed are still in control of the Republican party—look at their names—were in control of its National Convention in Chicago, and would be in control of the machinery of the Congress and of the Republican party, in the event of a Republican victory this fall.

These Republican leaders have not been content with attacks on me, or my wife, or my sons. No, not content with that, they now include my little dog, Fala. Well, of course, I don't resent attacks, and my family doesn't resent attacks, but Fala *does* resent them. You know, Fala is Scotch, and being a Scottie, as soon as he learned that the Republican fiction writers in Congress and out had concocted a story that I had left him behind on the Aleutian Islands and had sent a destroyer back to find him—at a cost to the taxpayers of two or three, or eight or twenty million dollars—his Scotch soul was furious. He has not been the same dog since. I am accustomed to hearing malicious falsehoods about myself—

such as that old, worm-eaten chestnut that I have represented myself as indispensable. But I think I have a right to resent, to object to libelous statements, about my dog.

Well, I think we all recognize the old technique. The people of this country know well the past too well to be deceived into forgetting. Too much is at stake to forget. There are tasks ahead of us which we must now complete with the same will and the same skill and intelligence and devotion that have already led us so far along the road to victory.

There is the task of finishing victoriously this most terrible of all wars as speedily as possible and with the least cost in lives.

There is a task of setting up international machinery to assure that the peace, once established, will not again be broken.

And there is the task that we face here at home—the task of reconverting our economy from the purposes of war to the purposes of peace.

These peace-building tasks were faced once before, nearly a generation ago. They were botched by a Republican administration. That must not happen this time. We will not let it happen this time.

Fortunately, we do not begin from scratch. Much has been done. Much more is under way. The fruits of victory this time will not be apples sold on street corners. . . .

This is not the time in which men can be forgotten as they were in the Republican catastrophe that we inherited. The returning soldiers, the workers by their machines, the farmers in the field, the miners, the men and women in offices and shops, do not intend to be forgotten.

No, they know that they are not surplus. Because they know that they are America.

We must set targets and objectives for the future which will seem impossible—like the airplanes—to those who live in and are weighted down by the dead past.

We are even now organizing the logistics of the peace, just as Marshall and King and Arnold, MacArthur, Eisenhower and Nimitz are organizing the logistics of this war.

I think that the victory of the American people and their allies in this war will be far more than a victory against Fascism and reaction and the dead hand of despotism of the past. The victory of the American people and their allies in this war will be a victory for democracy. It will constitute such an affirmation of the strength and power and vitality of government by the people as history has never before witnessed.

And so, my friends, we have had affirmation of the vitality of democratic government behind us, that demonstration of its resilience and its capacity for decision and for action—we have that knowledge of our own strength and power—we move forward with God's help to the greatest epoch of free achievement by free men that the world has ever known.

Source: Samuel I. Rosenman, comp., *The Public Papers and Addresses of Franklin D. Roosevelt*, Vol. 13 (1950; reprint, New York: Russell and Russell, 1969), 284–292.

29. Address to the Foreign Policy Association Dinner, New York City, October 21, 1944

In his 1944 campaign FDR preempted New York Governor Thomas Dewey's support for the United Nations by coming out in favor of it first.

General McCoy, My Old Friends, Ladies and Gentlemen:

Tonight I am speaking as the guest of the Foreign Policy Association, a nation-wide organization, a distinguished organization composed of Americans of every shade of political opinion.

I am going to talk about American foreign policy.

I am going to talk without rancor, without snap judgment.

And I am going to talk without losing my head or losing my temper.

When the first World War was ended, and it seems like a long time ago, I believed—I believe now—that enduring peace in the world has not a chance unless this nation, our America, is willing to cooperate in winning it and maintaining it. I thought back in those days of 1918 and 1919—and I know now—that we have to back our American words with American deeds.

A quarter of a century ago we helped to save our freedom but we failed to organize the kind of world in which future generations could live with freedom. Opportunity knocks again. There is no guarantee that opportunity will knock a third time.

Today, Hitler and the Nazis continue to fight desperately, inch by inch, and may continue to do so all the way to Berlin.

And, by the way, we have another important engagement in Tokyo. No matter how hard, how long the road we must travel, our forces will fight their way under the leadership of MacArthur and Nimitz.

All of our thinking about foreign policy in this war must be conditioned by the fact that millions of our American boys are today fighting many thousands of miles from home, for the first objective, the defense of our country, and the second objective, the perpetuation of our American ideals. And there are still many hard and bitter battles to be fought.

The leaders of this nation have always held—time out of mind—that concern for our national security does not end at our borders. President Monroe and every American President following him were prepared to use force, if necessary, to assure the independence of other American nations threatened by aggressors from across the seas.

That principle we've learned in childhood has not changed. The world has. Wars are no longer fought from horseback or from the decks of sailing ships.

It was with recognition of that fact, that way back in 1933 we took as the basis of our foreign relations the Good Neighbor Policy—the policy, the principle of the neighbor who, resolutely respecting himself, equally respects the rights of others.

We and the other American Republics have made the Good Neighbor Policy real, real in this hemisphere. And I want to say tonight that it is my conviction that this policy can be and should be made universal throughout the world.

At American, inter-American conferences beginning in Montevideo in 1933, and continuing down to date, we have made it clear, clear to this hemisphere at least, and I think to most of the world, that the United States of American practices what it preaches.

Our action in 1934, for example, with respect to Philippine independence was another step in making good the same philosophy that animated the Good Neighbor Policy of the year before.

And as I said two years ago: "I like to think that the history of the Philippine Islands in the last forty-four years provides in a very real sense a pattern for the future of other small nations in the world. It is a pattern of what men of good-will look forward to in the future to come."

And I cite as an illustration in the field of foreign policy something that I'm proud of—that was the recognition in 1933 of Soviet Russia.

And may I add a personal word.

In 1938, a certain lady who sits at a table in front of me came back from a trip on which she had attended the opening of a schoolhouse. And she had gone to the history class, history and geography, children of 8, 9 and 10, and she told me she had seen there a map of the world with a big white space upon it; no name, no information, and the teacher told her that it was blank with no name because the school board wouldn't let her say anything about that big blank space. Oh, there were only 180,000,000 to 200,000,000 people in it, it was called Soviet Russia, and there were a lot of children and they were told that the teacher was forbidden by the school board even to put the name of that blank space on the map.

For sixteen years before then the American people and the Russian people had no practical means of communicating with each other. We re-established those means, and today we are fighting with the Russians against common foes, and we know that the Russian contribution to victory has been, and will continue to be, gigantic.

However, we have to take a lot of things. Certain politicians, now very prominent in the Republican party, have condemned our recognition.

I am impelled to wonder how Russia would have survived, survived against the German attack, if these same people had had their way.

After the last war—in the political campaign of 1920—the isolationist Old Guard professed to be enthusiastic about international cooperation.

And—I remember very well, for I was running at the time—while campaigning for votes in that year of 1920 Senator Harding said that he favored with all his heart an Association of Nations, "so organized, so participated in"—I am quoting the language—"as to make the actual attainment of peace a reasonable possibility."

However, and this is history, too, after President Harding's election the Association of Nations was never heard of again.

However, we've got to look at people. One of the leading isolationists who killed international cooperation in 1920 was an old friend of mine—I think he supported me two or three times—Senator Hiram Johnson. Now, in the

event of Republican victory in the Senate this year, 1944, that same Senator Johnson, who is still a friend of mine—he would be chairman of the Senate Foreign Relations Committee. And I hope that the American voters will bear that in mind.

And it's fact, a plain fact; all you have to do is to go back through the files of the newspapers. During the years that followed 1920, the foreign policy of the Republican Administrations was dominated by the heavy hand of isolationism.

Much of the strength of our Navy, and I ought to know it, was scuttled, and some of the Navy's resources were handed over to friends in private industry—as in the unforgettable case of Teapot Dome.

Tariff walls went higher and higher—blocking international trade.

There was snarling at our former Allies and at the same time encouragement was given to American finance to invest two and one-half billion dollars in Germany—our former enemy.

All petitions that this nation joined the World Court were rejected or ignored.

We know that after this Administration took office, Secretary Hull and I replaced high tariffs with a series of reciprocal trade agreements under a statute of the Congress. The Republicans in the Congress opposed these agreements and tried to stop the extension of the law every three years.

In 1935 I asked the Congress to join the World Court. It so happens, and I put it that way, the Democrats in the Senate at the time voted for it, for joining, 43 to 20, the two-thirds. The Republicans voted against it 14 to 9. And the result was that we were prevented from obtaining the necessary two-thirds majority. I did my best.

In 1937, I asked that aggressor nations be quarantined. For this I was branded by isolationists in and out of public office as an "alarmist" and a "warmonger."

From that time on, as you well know, I made clear by repeated messages to the Congress of the United States, by repeated statements to the American people, the danger threatening from abroad—and the need of rearming to meet it.

Why, in, for example, in July, 1939, I tried to obtain the repeal of the Arms Embargo provisions of the Neutrality Law that tied our hands, tied us against selling arms to the European democracies in defense against Hitler and Mussolini.

I remember very well—I've got a note on it somewhere in my memoirs—the late Senator Borah told a group, which I called, all parties, which I called together in the White House, that his own private information from abroad was better than that of the State Department of the United States and that there would be no war in Europe.

And as it was made plain to Mr. Hull and me—and it was made plain to us at that time— that because of the isolationist vote in the Congress of the United States we could not possibly hope to obtain the desired revision of the Neutrality Act.

Now, this fact was also made plain to Adolf Hitler. A few weeks after Borah said that to me, he brutally attacked Poland, and the second World War began.

Let's get on. In 1941, this Administration proposed and the Congress passed, in spite of isolationist opposition, a thing called Lend-Lease Law—the practical and dramatic notice to the world that we intended to help those nations resisting aggression.

Bring it down to date, in these days—and now I am speaking of October 1944—I hear voices in the air attacking me for my "failure" to prepare this nation for this war, to warn the American people of the approaching tragedy.

It's rather interesting as a side thought that these same voices were not so very audible five years ago—or even four years ago—giving warning of the grave peril which we then faced.

There have been, and there still are, in the Republican party distinguished men and women of vision and courage, both in and out of public office, men and women who have vigorously supported our aid to our Allies and all the measures that we took to build up our national defense. And many of these Republicans have rendered magnificent services, services to our country in this war as members of my Administration. I am happy that one of these distinguished Americans is sitting here at this table tonight, our great Secretary of War— Henry Stimson.

And let us always remember that this very war might have been averted if Harry Stimson's views had prevailed when in 1931 the Japanese ruthlessly attacked and raped Manchuria.

Let's analyze a little more. The majority of the Republican members of the Congress voted—I'm just giving you a few, not many— voted against the Selective Service Law in 1940; they voted against Repeal of the Arms Embargo in 1939; they voted against the Lend-Lease Law in 1941, and they voted in August, 1941, against extension of the Selective Service, which meant voting against keeping our Army together—four months before Pearl Harbor.

You see, I'm quoting history to you. I'm going by the record, and I am giving you the whole story, and not a phrase here, and half a phrase there. In my reading copy is another half-sentence. You got the point and I'm not going to use it.

You know I happen to believe—I am sort of old-fashioned, I guess I am getting old—that even in a political campaign we ought to obey that ancient injunction—Thou shalt not bear false witness against they neighbor.

Now, the question of the men who will formulate and carry out the foreign policy of this country is in issue in this country, very much in issue. It is in issue not in terms of partisan application but in terms of sober solemn facts—the facts that are on the record.

If the Republicans were to win control of the Congress in this election—and it's only two weeks from next Tuesday and I occupy the curious position of being President of the United States and at the same time a candidate for the Presidency—if the Republicans were to win control of the Congress, inveterate isolationists would occupy positions of commanding influence and power. That's record, too.

I have already spoken of the ranking Republican member of the Senate Foreign Relations Committee, Senator Hiram Johnson.

One of the most influential members of the Senate Foreign Relations Committee—a man who'd also be chairman of the powerful Senate Committee on Appropriations—is Senator Gerald P. Nye. Well, I'm not going back to the old story of the last Presidential campaign, Martin and Barton and Fish. One of 'em's gone.

But in the House of Representatives the man who is the present leader of the Republicans there, and another friend of mine, and who'd undoubtedly be speaker is Joseph W. Martin. He voted, I'm not just giving you examples, he voted against repeal of the Arms Embargo; he voted against the Lend-Lease Bill, against the extension of the Selective Service Law, against the arming of merchant ships, against the Reciprocal Trade Agreements Act, and their extension.

The chairman of the powerful Committee on Rules is the other one, would be none other than Hamilton Fish.

These are like a lot of others in the Congress of the United States. Every one of them is now actively campaigning for the National Republican ticket this year.

Can any one really suppose that these isolationists have changed their minds about world affairs? That's a real question. Politicians who embraced the policy of isolationism—and who never raised their voices against it in our days

of peril—I don't think they're reliable custodians of the future of America.

Let's be fair. There have been Democrats in the isolationist camp, but they have been relatively few and far between, and so far they have not attained great positions of leadership.

And I am proud of the fact that this Administration does not have the support of the isolationist press. Well, for about a half a century, I've been accustomed to naming names—I mean specifically, to take the glaring examples, the McCormick, Patterson, Gannett and Hearst press.

You know the American people have gone through great national debates in the recent critical years. They were soul-searching debates. They reached from every city to every village and every home.

We have debated our principles, our determination to aid those fighting for freedom.

Obviously we could have come to terms with Hitler. We could have accepted a minor role in his totalitarian world. We rejected that!

We could have compromised with Japan and bargained for a place in the Japanese-dominated Asia, the Japanese-dominated Pacific, by selling out the heart's blood of the Chinese people. And we rejected that!

As I look back I am more and more certain that the decision not to bargain with the tyrants rose from the hearts and souls and sinews of the American people. They faced reality; they appraised reality; they knew what freedom meant.

The power which this nation has attained—the political, the economic, the military and above all the moral power—has brought to us the responsibility, and with it the opportunity, for leadership in the community of nations. In our own best interest, in the name of peace and humanity, this nation cannot, must not and will not shirk that responsibility.

Now there are some who hope to see a structure of peace, a structure of peace completely set up, set up immediately, with all of the apartments assigned to everybody's satisfaction, with the telephones in, and the plumbing complete, the heating system, the electric iceboxes all functioning perfectly, all furnished with linen and silver—and with the rent prepaid.

The United Nations have not yet produced such a comfortable dwelling place. But we have achieved a very practical expression of a common purpose on the part of four great nations, who are now united to wage this war, that they will embark together after the war on a greater and more difficult enterprise—on the enterprise of waging peace. We will embark on it with all the peace-loving nations of the world—large and small.

And our objective, as I stated ten days ago, is to complete the organization of the United Nations without delay, before hostilities actually cease.

You know peace, like war, can succeed only when there is a will to enforce it, and where there is available power to enforce it.

The Council of the League of Nations of the United Nations, must have the power to act quickly and decisively to keep the peace by force, if necessary.

I live in a small town, and I always think in small town terms, but this goes for small towns as well as for big towns. A policeman would not be a very effective policeman if, when he saw a felon break into a house, he had to go to the town hall and call a town meeting to issue a warrant before the felon could be arrested.

So to my simple mind, it is clear that, if the world organization is to have any reality at all, our American representative must be endowed in advance by the people themselves, by constitutional means through their representatives in Congress, with authority to act.

If we do not catch the international felon when we have our hands on him, if we let him get away with his loot, because the town council has not passed an ordinance authorizing his arrest, then we are not doing our share to prevent another world war. I think, and I have had some experience, that the people of this nation want their Government to work, they want their Government to act, and not merely talk, whenever and wherever there is a threat to world peace.

Now it is obvious that we cannot attain our great objectives by ourselves. Never again after cooperating with other nations in a world war to save our way of life can we wash our hands of maintaining the peace for which we fought.

The Dumbarton Oaks conference didn't spring up overnight. It was called by Secretary Hull and me after years of thought, discussion, preparation, consultation with our allies. Our State Department did a grand job in preparing for the conference and leading it to a successful termination. It was just another chapter in the long process of cooperations—beginning with the Atlantic Charter, that's a long time ago, and continuing through conferences at Casablanca, and Moscow, and Cairo and Teheran and Quebec and Washington.

It is my profound conviction that the American people know that Cordell Hull and I are thoroughly conversant with the Constitution of the United States and know that we cannot commit this nation to any secret treaties or any secret guarantees that in violation of that Constitution.

After my return from Teheran, I stated officially that no secret commitments had been made. The issue then is between my veracity and the continuing assertions of those who have no responsibility in the foreign field—or, perhaps I should say, a field foreign to them.

No President of the United States—there have been quite a lot of them, too—can or could have made the American contribution to preserve the peace without the constant, alert and conscious collaboration of the American people.

Only the determination of the people to use the machinery gives worth to the machinery. Remember that.

We believe that the American people have already made up their minds on this great issue; and this Administration has been able to press forward constantly with its plans.

We are thinking to avert and avoid war.

The very fact that we are now at work on the organization of the peace proves that the great nations are committed to trust each other. Put this proposition any way you want, it is bound to come out the same way; we either work with the other great nations, or we might some day have to fight them. And I am against that.

The kind of world order which we, the peace-loving nations must achieve, must depend essentially on friendly human relations, on acquaintance, on tolerance, on unassailable sincerity and goodwill and good faith. We have achieved that relationship to a very remarkable degree in our dealings with our Allies in this war—as I think the events of the war have proved.

It is a new thing in human history for allies to work together as we have done—so closely, so harmoniously, so effectively in fighting of a war, and at the same time in the building of a peace.

If we fail to maintain that relationship in the peace—if we fail to expand it and strengthen it—then there will be no lasting peace.

I digress for a moment. As for Germany, that tragic nation which has sown the wind and is now reaping the whirlwind, we and our Allies are entirely agreed that we shall not bargain with the Nazi conspirators, or leave them a shred of control—open or secret—of the instruments of government.

We shall not leave them a single element of military power—or a potential military power.

But I should be false to the very foundations of my religious and political convictions, if I should ever relinquish the hope—or even the faith—that in all peoples, without exception, there live some instinct for truth, some attrac-

tion toward justice, some passion for peace—buried as it may be in the German case under a brutal regime.

We bring no charge against the German race, as such, for we cannot believe that God has eternally condemned any race or humanity. We know in our own land, in the United States of America, how many good men and women of German ancestry have proved loyal, freedom-loving, and peace-loving citizens.

But there is going to be a stern punishment for all those in Germany directly responsible for this agony of mankind.

The German people are not going to be enslaved. Why? Because the United Nations do not traffic in human slavery. But it will be necessary for them to earn their way back—earn their way back into the fellowship of peace-loving and law-abiding nations. And, in their climb up that steep road, we shall certainly see to it that they are not encumbered by having to carry guns. We hope they will be relieved of that burden forever.

Now, the task ahead of us will not be easy. Indeed, it will be as difficult, complex, as any task which has ever faced any American Administration.

I will not say to you now, or ever, that we of the Democratic party know all the answers. I am certain, for myself, that I do not know how all the unforeseeable difficulties can be met. What I can say to you is this—that I have unlimited faith that the task can be done. And that faith, that faith, is based on knowledge, knowledge gained in the arduous practical and continuing experience of these past eventful years.

And so I speak to the present generation of Americans with a reverent participation in its sorrows and in its hopes. No generation has undergone a greater test, or has met that test with greater heroism, and, I think, greater wisdom, and no generation has had a more exalted mission.

For this generation must act not only for itself, but as a trustee for all those who fell in the last war—a part of their mission unfilled.

It must also act for all those who have paid the supreme price in this war—lest their mission, too, be betrayed.

And, finally, it must act for the generations to come—that must be granted a heritage of peace.

I do not exaggerate that mission. We are not fighting for, and we shall not attain a Utopia. Indeed, in our own land, the work to be done is never finished. We have yet to realize the full and equal enjoyment of our freedom. So, in embarking on the building of a world fellowship, we have set ourselves a long and arduous task, a task which will challenge our patience, our intelligence, our imagination, as well as our faith.

That task, my friends, calls for the judgment of a seasoned and mature people. This, I think, the American people have become. We shall not again be thwarted in our will to live as a mature nation, confronting limitless horizons. We shall bear our full responsibility, exercise our full influence, and bring our full help and encouragement to all who aspire to peace and freedom.

We now are, and we shall continue to be, strong brothers, strong brothers in the family of mankind, the family of the children of God.

Source: "Text of the Address by President Roosevelt at Dinner of the Foreign Policy Association Here," *New York Times*, October 22, 1944, 34.

30. Fourth Inaugural Address, January 20, 1945

Unlike his first three inaugurals which were delivered at the Capitol, FDR delivered the Fourth Inaugural at the White House. It is the second shortest in American history after George Washington's Second Inaugural Address. He used a draft written by Robert Sherwood but after several subsequent drafts had pared the original down to only 560 words. The President's philosophical address praised American communal values.

Mr. Chief Justice, Mr. Vice President, my friends, you will understand and, I believe, agree with my wish that the form of this inauguration be simple and its words brief.

We Americans of today, together with our allies, are passing through a period of supreme test. It is a test of our courage—of our resolve—of our wisdom—our essential democracy.

If we meet that test—successfully and honorably—we shall perform a service of historic importance which men and women and children will honor throughout all time.

As I stand here today, having taken the solemn oath of office in the presence of my fellow countrymen—in the presence of our God—I know that it is America's purpose that we shall not fail.

In the days and in the years that are to come we shall work for a just and honorable peace, a durable peace, as today we work and fight for total victory in war.

We can and we will achieve such a peace.

We shall strive for perfection. We shall not achieve it immediately—but we still shall strive. We may make mistakes—but they must never be mistakes which result from faintness of heart or abandonment of moral principle.

I remember that my old schoolmaster, Dr. Peabody, said, in days that seemed to us then to be secure and untroubled: "Things in life will not always run smoothly. Sometimes we will be rising toward the heights—then all will seem to reverse itself and start downward. The great fact to remember is that the trend of civilization itself is forever upward; that a line drawn through the middle of the peaks and the valleys of the centuries always has an upward trend."

Our Constitution of 1787 was not a perfect instrument; it is not perfect yet. But it provided a firm base upon which all manner of men, of all races and colors and creeds, could build our solid structure of democracy.

And so today, in this year of war, 1945, we have learned lessons—at a fearful cost—and we shall profit by them.

We have learned that we cannot live alone, at peace; that our own well-being is dependent on the well-being of other nations far away. We have learned that we must live as men, not as ostriches, nor as dogs in the manger.

We have learned to be citizens of the world, members of the human community.

We have learned the simple truth, as Emerson said, that "The only way to have a friend is to be one."

We can gain no lasting peace if we approach it with suspicion and mistrust or with fear.

We can gain it only if we proceed with the understanding, the confidence, and the courage which flow from conviction.

The Almighty God has blessed our land in many ways. He has given our people stout hearts and strong arms with which to strike mighty blows for freedom and truth. He has given to our country a faith which has become the hope of all peoples in an anguished world.

So we pray to Him now for the vision to see our way clearly—to see the way that leads to a better life for ourselves and for all our fellow men—to the achievement of His will to peace on earth.

Source: "Fourth Inaugural Address of Franklin D. Roosevelt, Saturday, January 20, 1945." The Avalon Project at Yale Law School. Available online. URL: www.yale.edu/lawweb/avalon/presid/inaug/froos4.htm.

SELECTED BIBLIOGRAPHY

Adams, Grace. *Workers on Relief.* New Haven, Conn.: Yale University Press, 1939.

Adams, Henry H. *Harry Hopkins: A Biography.* New York: Putnam, 1977.

———. *Thomas Hart Benton: An American Original.* New York: Knopf, 1989.

Adams, Stephen B. *Mr. Kaiser Goes to Washington: The Rise of a Government Entrepreneur.* Chapel Hill: University of North Carolina Press, 1997.

Agee, James. *Let Us Now Praise Famous Men: Three Tenant Families.* Boston: Houghton Mifflin, 1941.

Alldritt, Keith. *The Greatest of Friends: Franklin D. Roosevelt and Winston Churchill, 1941–1945.* London: Robert Hall, 1995.

Allswang, John. *The New Deal and American Politics: A Study in Political Change.* New York: Wiley, 1978.

Alsop, Joseph. *The 168 Days.* New York: Da Capo, 1973.

Alter, Jonathan. *The Defining Moment: FDR's Hundred Days and the Triumph of Hope.* New York: Simon and Schuster, 2006.

Ambrose, Stephen E. *Eisenhower: Soldier and President.* New York: Distican, 1990.

Amenta, Edwin. *Bold Relief: Institutional Politics and the Origins of Modern American Social Policy.* Princeton, N.J.: Princeton University Press, 1998.

Anderson, Marian. *My Lord, What a Morning: An Autobiography.* Madison: University of Wisconsin Press, 1992.

Argersinger, Jo Ann E. *Toward a New Deal in Baltimore: People and Government in the Great Depression.* Chapel Hill: University of North Carolina Press, 1988.

Arkes, Hadley. *The Return of George Sutherland: Restoring a Jurisprudence of Natural Rights.* Princeton, N.J.: Princeton University Press, 1994.

Badger, Anthony J. *The New Deal: The Depression Years, 1933–1940.* Lanham, Md.: Rowman and Littlefield, 2003.

Baker, Leonard. *Back to Back: The Duel Between FDR and the Supreme Court.* New York: Macmillan, 1967.

———. *Brandeis and Frankfurter: A Dual Biography.* New York: New York University Press, 1986.

Baker, William J. *Jesse Owens: An American Life.* London: Collier Macmillan, 1986.

Baldwin, Sidney. *Poverty and Politics: The Rise and Fall of the Farm Security Administration.* Raleigh: University of North Carolina Press, 1968.

Ball, Howard. *Hugo L. Black: Cold Steel Warrior.* New York: Oxford University Press, 1996.

Barber, James G. *Portraits from the New Deal.* Washington, D.C.: Smithsonian Institution Press, 1988.

Barber, William J. *Designs Within Disorder: Franklin D. Roosevelt, the Economists, and the Shaping of American Economic Policy, 1933–1945.* New York: Cambridge University Press, 1996.

Barfield, Ray E. *Listening to Radio, 1920–1950.* Westport: Conn.: Praeger, 1996.

Barnard, Rita. *The Great Depression and the Culture of Abundance: Kenneth Fearing, Nathanael West and Mass Culture in the 1930s.* New York: Cambridge University Press, 1995.

Barrow, Joe Louis, and Barbara Munder. *Joe Louis: 50 Years an American Hero.* New York: McGraw-Hill, 1988.

Bartlett, John H. *The Bonus March and the New Deal.* New York: M. A. Donohue, 1937.

Bassett, John. *Sherwood Anderson: An American Career.* Selinsgrove, Pa.: Susquehanna University Press, 2005.

Baughman, James L. *Henry R. Luce and the Rise of the American News Media.* Boston: Twayne, 1987.

Bauman, John F., and Thomas H. Coode. *In the Eye of the Great Depression: New Deal Reporters and the Agony of the American People.* DeKalb: Northern Illinois University Press, 1988.

Bayly, Christopher, and Tim Harper. *Forgotten Armies: The Fall of British Asia, 1941–1945.* Cambridge, Mass.: Harvard University Press, 2005.

Beasley, Maurine, Holly C. Shulman, and Henry R. Beasley, eds. *The Eleanor Roosevelt Encyclopedia.* Westport, Conn.: Greenwood, Press, 2001.

Beasley, Norman. *Frank Knox, American: A Short Biography.* Garden City, N.Y.: Doubleday, Doran, 1936.

Becker, Heather. *Art for the People: The Rediscovery and Preservation of Progressive and WPA-Era Murals in the Chicago Public Schools, 1904–1943.* San Francisco: Chronicle Books, 2003.

Becker, Marjorie. *Setting the Virgin on Fire: Lazaro Cárdenas, Michoacán Peasants, and the Redemption of the Mexican Revolution.* Berkeley: University of California Press, 1995.

Beckham, Sue B. *Depression Post Office Murals and Southern Culture: A Gentle Reconstruction.* Baton Rouge: Louisiana State University Press, 1989.

Bellows, Sidney. *Poverty and Politics: The Rise and Decline of the Farm Security Administration.* Chapel Hill: University of North Carolina Press, 1968.

Bellush, Bernard. *The Failure of the NRA.* New York: Norton, 1975.

Bennett, Davis H. *Demagogues in the Depression: American Radicals and the Union Party, 1932–1936.* New Brunswick, N.J.: Rutgers University Press, 1969.

Bennett, Edward M. *Franklin D. Roosevelt and the Search for Security: American-Soviet Relations, 1933–1939.* Wilmington, Del.: Scholarly Resources, 1985.

Bennett, Harry. *Ford: We Never Called Him Henry.* New York: Tom Doherty Associates, 1951.

Bentley, Joanne Davis. *Hallie Flanagan: A Life in the American Theatre.* New York: Knopf, 1988.

Benton, Thomas Hart. *An Artist in America.* Columbia: University of Missouri Press, 1983.

Berg, A. Scott. *Goldwyn: A Biography.* New York: Knopf, 1989.

———. *Lindbergh.* New York: Berkley, 1998.

Bergreen, Laurence. *As Thousands Cheer: The Life of Irving Berlin.* New York: Viking Penguin, 1990.

Berle, Adolf A. *The Modern Corporation and Private Property.* New York: Macmillan, 1933.

Bernstein, Irving. *The Lean Years: A History of the American Worker, 1920–1933.* Boston: Houghton Mifflin, 1960.

Bernstein, Michael A. *The Great Depression: Delayed Recovery and Economic Change in America, 1929–1939.* New York: Cambridge University Press, 1987.

Berthon, Simon. *Allies at War: The Bitter Rivalry Among Churchill, Roosevelt and DeGaulle.* New York: Carroll and Graf, 2001.

———— and Joanna Potts. *Warlords: An Extraordinary Recreation of World War II through the Eyes and Minds of Hitler, Roosevelt, Churchill, and Stalin*. New York: Da Capo, 2006.

Bertin, Amy. *Competition and Productivity in the Depression-Era Steel Industry*. Master's thesis, Harvard University, 1994.

Beschloss, Michael R. *Kennedy and Roosevelt: The Uneasy Alliance*. New York: W. W. Norton, 1980.

————. *The Conquerors: Roosevelt, Truman and the Destruction of Hitler's Germany, 1941–1945*. New York: Simon and Schuster, 2002.

Best, Gary D. *FDR and the Bonus Marchers, 1933–1935*. Westport, Conn.: Greenwood Press, 1992.

Best, Geoffrey. *Churchill: A Study in Greatness*. New York: Hambleton and London, 2001.

Bezner, Lili Corbus. *Photography and Politics in America: From the New Deal into the Cold War*. Baltimore: Johns Hopkins University Press, 1999.

Biddle, Francis. *In Brief Authority*. Garden City, N.J.: Greenwood Publishing, 1962.

Biles, Roger. *A New Deal for the American People*. Dekalb: Northern Illinois Press, 1991.

————. *Big City Boss in Depression and War: Mayor Edward J. Kelly of Chicago*. Dekalb: Northern Illinois University Press, 1984.

Bindas, Kenneth J. *All of This Music Belongs to the Nation: The WPA's Federal Music Project and American Society*. Knoxville: University of Tennessee Press, 1995.

Black, Allida. *Casting Her Own Shadow: Eleanor Roosevelt and the Shaping of Postwar Liberalism*. New York: Columbia University Press, 1996.

————. *Courage in a Dangerous World: The Political Writings of Eleanor Roosevelt*. New York: Columbia University Press, 1999.

————, ed. *What I Hope to Leave Behind: The Essential Essays of Eleanor Roosevelt*. Brooklyn, N.Y.: Carlson Publishing, 1995.

Black, Conrad. *Franklin D. Roosevelt: Champion of Freedom*. New York: Perseus, 2003.

Blackorby, Edward C. *Prairie Rebel: The Public Life of William Lemke*. Lincoln: University of Nebraska Press, 1963.

Blotner, Joseph Leo. *Robert Penn Warren: A Biography*. New York: Random House, 1997.

Blum, John Morton, ed. *Roosevelt and Morgenthau*. Boston: Houghton Mifflin, 1970.

Blum, Leon. *For All Mankind*. New York: Viking, 1946.

Bold, Christine. *The WPA Guides: Mapping America*. Jackson: University Press of Mississippi, 1999.

Borg, Dorothy. *The United States and the Far Eastern Crisis of 1933–1938*. Cambridge, Mass.: Harvard University Press, 1964.

Bosworth, R. J. B. *The Italian Dictatorship: Problems and Perspectives in the Interpretation of Mussolini and Fascism*. London: Arnold, 1998.

————. *Mussolini's Italy. Life Under the Fascist Dictatorship, 1915–1945*. New York: Penquin Press, 2006.

Brady, Frank. *Citizen Welles: A Biography of Orson Welles*. New York: Scribner, 1989.

Braeman, John, Robert Bremmer, and David Brody. *The New Deal*, Vol. 1. Columbus: Ohio State University Press, 1975.

————. *The New Deal: The National Level*. Columbus: Ohio State University Press, 1975.

Brecher, Jeremy. *Strike*. 2d ed. Boston: South End, 1997.

Breitman, Richard. *Official Secrets: What the Nazis Planned, What the British and Americans Knew*. New York: Hill & Wang, 1998.

Brian, Denis. *Einstein: A Life*. New York: Wiley, 1996.

Brinkley, Alan. *The End of Reform: New Deal Liberalism in Recession and War*. New York: Knopf, 1995.

————. *Voices of Protest: Huey Long, Father Coughlin, and the Great Depression*. New York: Knopf, 1982.

————. *The Transformation of New Deal Liberalism*. New York: Knopf, 1995.

Brinkley, David. *Washington Goes to War.* New York: Knopf, 1988.

Brinkley, Douglas, and David R. Facey-Crowther, eds. *The Atlantic Charter.* New York: St. Martin's, 1994.

Britton, Andrew. *Katharine Hepburn: Star as Feminist.* New York: Continuum, 1995.

Broadus, Mitchell. *Depression Decade: From New Era Through New Deal, 1929–1941.* New York: Harper & Row, 1947.

Brodsky, Alyn. *The Great Mayor: Fiorello LaGuardia and the Making of the City of New York.* New York: St. Martin's Press, 2003.

Browder, Laura. *Radical Culture in the 1930s.* Amherst: University of Massachusetts Press, 1998.

Brown, Francis Joseph. *The Social and Economic Philosophy of Pierce Butler.* Washington, D.C.: Catholic University of America Press, 1938.

Brown, Lorraine, and John O'Connor, eds. *Free, Adult, Uncensored: The Living History of the Federal Theatre Project.* Washington, D.C.: New Republic Books, 1978.

Brown, Peter Harry, and Pat H. Broeskie. *Howard Hughes: The Untold Story.* New York: Dutton, 1996.

Brown, Robert J. *Manipulating the Ether: The Power of Broadcast Radio in Thirties America.* Jefferson, N.C.: McFarland, 1998.

Brownlee, W. Elliot. *Federal Taxation in America: A Short History.* New York: Cambridge University Press, 1996.

Brownlow, Louis. *A Passion for Politics.* Chicago: University of Chicago Press, 1955.

Bryan, Ford R. *Henry's Lieutenants.* Detroit: Wayne State University Press, 1992.

Buechner, Thomas S. *Norman Rockwell, Artist and Illustrator.* New York: Abradale/Abrams, 1996.

Buhite, Russell D., and David W. Levy, eds. *FDR's Fireside Chats.* Norman: University of Oklahoma Press, 1992.

Bullock, Alan. *Hitler and Stalin.* London: Fontana Press, 1998.

Burner, David. *Herbert Hoover: A Public Life.* New York: Knopf, 1979.

———. *The Politics of Provincialism: The Democratic Party in Transition, 1918–1932.* New York: Norton, 1967.

Burns, Helen. *The American Banking Community and New Deal Banking Reforms: 1933–1935.* Westport, Conn.: Greenwood, 1974.

Burns, James MacGregor. *Roosevelt: The Lion and the Fox, 1882–1940.* New York: Harcourt Brace Jovanovich, 1956.

———. *Roosevelt: Soldier of Freedom.* New York: Harcourt Brace Jovanovich, 1972.

Burns, James MacGregor, and Susan Dunn. *The Three Roosevelts: Patrician Leaders who Transformed America.* New York: Atlantic Monthly Press, 2001.

Bustard, Bruce I. *A New Deal for the Arts.* Seattle: University of Washington Press, 1997.

Butler, Michael A. *Cautious Visionary: Cordell Hull and Trade Reform, 1933–1937.* Kent, Ohio: Kent State University Press, 1998.

Butler, Susan, ed. *My Dear Mr. Stalin: The Complete Correspondence Between Franklin D. Roosevelt and Joseph V. Stalin.* New Haven: Yale University Press, 2006.

Byrnes, James F. *All in One Lifetime.* New York: Harper, 1958.

Callow, Simon. *Orson Welles: The Road to Xanadu.* New York: Viking, 1996.

Canedy, Susan. *America's Nazis: A Democratic Dilemma: A History of the German American Bund.* Menlo Park, Calif.: Markgraf, 1990.

Cannadine, David. *In Churchill's Shadow: Confronting the Past in Modern Britain.* New York: Oxford University Press, 2002.

———, ed. *Blood, Toil, Tears, and Sweat: The Speeches of Winston Churchill.* Boston: Houghton Mifflin, 1989.

Cannistraro, Philip V. *Historical Dictionary of Fascist Italy.* Westport, Conn.: Greenwood, 1982.

Cannon, Brian Q. *Remaking the Agrarian Dream: New Deal Rural Resettlement in the*

Mountain West. Albuquerque: University of New Mexico Press, 1996.

Carew, Michael G. *The Power to Persuade. FDR, the Newsmagazine, and Going to War, 1939–1941.* Lanham, Md.: University Press of America, 2005.

Carlton, David L., and Peter A. Coclanis, eds. *Confronting Southern Poverty in the Great Depression: The Report on Economic Conditions of the South with Related Documents.* New York: Bedford Books of St. Martin's, 1996.

Carney, Raymond. *American Vision: The Films of Frank Capra.* New York: Cambridge University Press, 1987.

Caroli, Betty. *The Roosevelt Women.* New York: Basic Books, 1998.

Carringer, Robert L. *The Making of Citizen Kane.* Berkeley: University of California Press, 1996.

Carter, Dan. *Scottsboro: A Tragedy of the American South.* Baton Rouge: Louisiana State University Press, 1979.

Casey, Steven. *Cautious Crusade. Franklin D. Roosevelt, American Public Opinion, and the War Against Nazi Germany.* New York: Oxford University Press, 2001.

Cash, William M., and R. Daryl Lewis. *The Delta Council: Fifty Years of Service to the Mississippi Delta.* Stoneville, Miss.: Delta Council, 1986.

Cashman, Sean. *America in the Twenties and Thirties: The Olympian Age of Franklin Delano Roosevelt.* New York: New York University Press, 1989.

Cassella-Blackburn, Michael. *The Donkey, the Carrot, and the Club: William C. Bullitt and Soviet-American Relations, 1917–1948.* Westport: Praeger, 2004.

Cassels, Alan. *Fascism.* New York: Crowell, 1975.

Cayleff, Susan E. *Babe: The Life and Legend of Babe Didrikson Zaharias.* Urbana: University of Illinois Press, 1995.

Chadwin, Dean. *Those Damn Yankees: The Secret Life of America's Greatest Franchise.* New York: Verso, 1999.

Chafe, William H., ed. *The Achievements of American Liberalism: The New Deal and Its Legacies.* New York: Columbia University Press, 2003.

Chamberlain, Charles D. *Victory at Home: Manpower and Race in the American South during World War II.* Athens: University of Georgia Press, 2003.

Churchill, Winston. *While England Slept: A Survey of World Affairs, 1932–1938.* New York: Putnam, 1938.

Ciment, James, ed. *Encyclopedia of the Great Depression and the New Deal.* Armonk, N.Y.: M. E. Sharpe, 2001.

Clarke, Jeanne N. *Roosevelt's Warrior: Harold L. Ickes and the New Deal.* Baltimore: Johns Hopkins University Press, 1996.

Clausen, John A. *American Lives: Looking Back at the Children of the Great Depression.* New York: Free Press, 1993.

Clements, Cynthia. *George Burns and Gracie Allen: A Bio-Bibliography.* Westport, Conn.: Greenwood, 1996.

Clurman, Harold. *The Fervent Years: The Story of the Group Theatre and the Thirties.* New York: Harcourt Brace Jovanovich, 1975.

Coffey, Thomas M. *Lion by the Tail: The Story of the Italian-Ethiopian War.* New York: Viking, 1974.

Cohen, Elizabeth. *Making a New Deal: Industrial Workers in Chicago.* New York: Cambridge University Press, 1990.

Cohen, Robert, ed. *Dear Mrs. Roosevelt. Letters from the Children of the Great Depression.* Chapel Hill: University of North Carolina, 2002.

Cohen, Wilbur J., ed. *The New Deal Fifty Years After: A Historical Assessment.* Austin: University of Texas Press, 1984.

Cole, Olen, Jr. *The African-American Experience in the Civilian Conservation Corps.* Gainesville: University Press of Florida, 1999.

Cole, Wayne S. *America First: The Battle Against Intervention, 1940–1941.* New York: Octagon Books, 1971.

———. *Charles A. Lindbergh and the Battle Against American Intervention in World War II*. New York: Harcourt, Brace & Jovanovich, 1974.

———. *Determinism and American Foreign Relations during the Franklin D. Roosevelt Era*. Lanham, Md.: University Press of America, 1995.

———. *Roosevelt and the Isolationists, 1932–45*. Lincoln: University of Nebraska Press, 1983.

———. *Senator Gerald P. Nye and American Foreign Relations*. Minneapolis: University of Minnesota Press, 1962.

Collier, Peter, and David Horowitz. *The Roosevelts: An American Saga*. New York: Simon and Schuster, 1994.

Colton, Joel. *Leon Blum: Humanist in Politics*. New York: Knopf, 1966.

Congdon, Don, ed. *The 30's: A Time to Remember*. New York: Simon & Schuster, 1962.

Conkin, Paul. *The New Deal*. Arlington Heights, Ill.: Harlan Davidson, 1975.

Conn, Peter J. *Pearl S. Buck: A Cultural Biography*. New York: Cambridge University Press, 1996.

Conquest, Robert. *The Great Terror: A Reassessment*. New York: Oxford University Press, 1990.

Cook, Blanche W. *Eleanor Roosevelt: A Life*. New York: Viking Penguin, 1992.

———. *Eleanor Roosevelt: 1933–1938*. New York: Viking Penguin, 1999.

Cook, Sylvia J. *Erskine Caldwell and the Fiction of Poverty. The Flesh and Spirit*. Baton Rouge: Louisiana State University Press, 1991.

Copland, Aaron. *Copland on Music*. Garden City, N.Y.: Doubleday, 1960.

Cormier, Frank. *Reuther*. Englewood Cliffs, N.J.: Prentice-Hall, 1970.

Cowley, Malcolm. *The Dream of the Golden Mountains: Remembering the 1930s*. New York: Penguin, 1981.

Cramer, Clarence H. *Newton D. Baker: A Biography*. Cleveland: World Publishing Co., 1961.

Cramer, Richard Ben. *Joe Dimaggio: The Hero's Life*. New York: Simon & Schuster, 2000.

Creese, Walter L. *TVA's Public Planning: The Vision and the Reality*. Knoxville: University of Tennessee Press, 1990.

Crouse, Joan M. *The Homeless Transient in the Great Depression: New York State, 1929–1941*. Albany: State University of New York Press, 1986.

Crozier, Brian. *The Man Who Lost China: The First Full Biography of Chiang Kai-shek. His Life and Times*. New York: Scribner, 1981.

Culver, John C., and John Hyde. *American Dreamer: The Life and Times of Henry A. Wallace*. New York: Norton, 2000.

Curtis, Sandra R. *Alice and Eleanor: A Contrast in Style and Purpose*. Bowling Green, Ohio: Bowling Green University Popular Press, 1994.

Cushman, Barry. *Rethinking the New Deal Court: The Structure of a Constitutional Revolution*. New York: Oxford University Press, 1998.

Daily, David W. *Battle for the BIA: G.E.E. Lindquist and the Missionary Crusade Against John Collier*. Tempe: University of Arizona Press, 2004.

Dallek, Robert. *Franklin D. Roosevelt as a World Leader*. New York: Oxford University Press, 1995.

———. *Franklin D. Roosevelt and American Foreign Policy 1932–1945*. New York: Oxford University Press, 1979.

Danbom, David B. *Going It Alone: Fargo Grapples with the Great Depression*. Minneapolis: Minnesota Historical Society Press, 2005.

Danchev, Alex. *On Specialness: Essays in Anglo-American Relations*. New York: St. Martin's Press, 1998.

Danelski, David, and Joseph S. Tulchin, eds. *The Autobiographical Notes of Charles Evans Hughes*. Cambridge, Mass.: Harvard University Press, 1973.

Danese, Tracy E. *Claude Pepper and Ed Ball: Politics, Purpose, and Power.* Gainesville: University Press of Florida, 2000.

Daniel, Cletus E. *The ACLU and the Wagner Act: An Inquiry into the Depression-Era Crisis of American Liberalism.* Ithaca, N.Y.: Cornell University Press, 1980.

Daniel, Pete, et. al. *Official Images: New Deal Photography.* Washington, D.C.: Smithsonian Institution Press, 1987.

Daniels, Roger. *The Bonus March: An Episode of the Great Depression.* Westport, Conn.: Greenwood, 1971.

Danish, Max. *The World of David Dubinsky.* Cleveland: World, 1957.

Davidson, Eugene. *The Making of Adolf Hitler: The Birth and Rise of Nazism.* Columbia: University of Missouri Press, 1997.

Davis, Kenneth S. *The Hero.* London: Longmans, 1959.

———. *FDR: The New Deal Years, 1933–1937.* New York: Random House, 1986.

———. *FDR: The New York Years, 1928–1933.* New York: Random House, 1985.

———. *Into the Storm, 1937–1940.* New York: Random House, 1993.

———. *The War President, 1940–1945.* New York: Random House, 2000.

Davis, Kingsley. *Youth in the Depression.* Chicago: University of Chicago Press, 1935.

Davis, Polly Ann. *Alben W. Barkley: Senate Majority Leader and Vice President.* New York: Garland, 1979.

Davis, Ronald. *John Ford: Hollywood's Old Master.* Norman: University of Oklahoma Press, 1995.

Dawes, Charles G. *How Long Prosperity?* Chicago: A. N. Marquis, 1937.

Dawson, Robert M. *William Lyon Mackenzie King: A Political Biography.* Toronto: University of Toronto Press, 1958.

Daynes, Byron, William Pederson and Michael Riccards, eds. *The New Deal and Public Policy.* New York: St. Martin's Press, 1998.

Deakin, F. W. *The Brutal Friendship: Mussolini, Hitler and the Fall of Italian Fascism.* London: Weidenfeld & Nicolson, 1962.

Dear, I. C. B., ed. *The Oxford Companion to World War II.* New York: Oxford University Press, 1995.

DeDedts, Ralph. *The New Deal's SEC: The Formative Years.* New York: Columbia University Press, 1964.

DeGrand, Alexander J. *Italian Fascism: Its Origins and Development.* Lincoln: University of Nebraska Press, 1982.

Denning, Michael. *The Cultural Front: The Laboring of American Culture.* London: Verso, 1996.

Dennis, James M. *Grant Wood: A Study in American Art and Culture.* Columbia: University of Missouri Press, 1986.

DeNoon, Christopher. *Posters of the WPA.* Los Angeles: Wheatley, 1987.

Dewey, Thomas. *The Case Against the New Deal.* New York: Harper, 1940.

Diamond, Sander A. *The Nazi Movement in the United States, 1924–1941.* Ithaca, N.Y.: Cornell University Press, 1974.

Dickinson, Matthew J. *Bitter Harvest: FDR, Presidential Power and Growth of the Presidential Branch.* New York: Cambridge University Press, 1996.

Dierenfield, Bruce J. *Keeper of the Rules: Congressman Howard W. Smith of Virginia.* Charlottesville: University Press of Virginia, 1987.

Doan, Edward N. *The La Follettes and the Wisconsin Idea.* New York: Rinehart, 1947.

Doenecke, Justus D. *Storm on the Horizon: The Challenge to American Intervention, 1939–1941.* Lanham, Md.: Rowman and Littlefield, 2000.

Donaldson, Scott. *Archibald MacLeish. An American Life.* Boston: Houghton Mifflin, 1992.

Donn, Linda. *The Roosevelt Cousins.* New York: Random House, 2001.

Dorsett, Lyle W. *Franklin D. Roosevelt and the City Bosses.* Port Washington, N.Y.: Kennikat Press, 1977.

Douglas, William O. *Go East, Young Man: The Early Years: The Autobiography of William O. Douglas.* New York: Random House, 1974.

Doyle, Judith K. "Out of Step: Maury Maverick and the Politics of the Depression and the New Deal." Unpublished Ph.D. dissertation, University of Texas at Austin, 1989.

Doyle, Paul A. *Pearl S. Buck.* Boston: Twayne, 1980.

Draper, Theodore. *The Roots of American Communism.* New York: Viking, 1957.

Droze, Wilmon H. *High Dams and Slack Waters: TVA Rebuilds a River.* Baton Rouge: Louisiana State University Press, 1965.

Duberman, Martin B. *Paul Robeson.* New York: Knopf, 1989.

Dubinsky, David, and A. H. Raskin. *David Dubinsky: A Life with Labor.* New York: Simon & Schuster, 1977.

Dubofsky, Melvyn. *The New Deal: Conflicting Interpretations and Shifting Perspectives.* New York: Garland, 1992.

Dubofsky, Melvyn, and Foster Rhea Dulles. *Labor in America: A History.* Wheeling, Ill.: Harlan Davidson, 1999.

Dubofsky, Melvyn, and Stephen Burwood, eds. *The New Deal: Selected Articles on the Political Response to the Great Depression.* New York: Garland, Inc. 1990.

Dubofsky, Melvyn, and Warren Van Time. *John L. Lewis: A Biography.* Urbana: University of Illinois Press, 1986.

Dunn, Dennis J. *Caught Between Roosevelt & Stalin: America's Ambassadors to Moscow.* Lexington: University Press of Kentucky, 1998.

Dunning, John. *On the Air: The Encyclopedia of Old-Time Radio.* New York: Oxford University Press, 1998.

Eastman, Lloyd E. *The Abortive Revolution: China Under Nationalist Rule, 1927–1937.* Cambridge, Mass.: Harvard University Press, 1974.

———. *Seeds of Destruction: Nationalist China in War and Revolution, 1937–1940.* Stanford, Calif.: Stanford University Press, 1984.

Eccles, Marriner. *Beckoning Frontiers: Public and Personal Recollections.* New York: Knopf, 1951.

Edel, Leon, ed. *The Thirties: From Notebooks and Diaries of the Period: Edmund Wilson.* New York: Farrar, Straus and Giroux, 1980.

Eden, Robert T., ed. *The New Deal and Its Legacy: Critique and Reappraisal.* Westport, Conn.: Greenwood Press, 1989.

Edens, John A. *Eleanor Roosevelt: A Comprehensive Bibliography.* Westport, Conn.: Greenwood Press, 1994.

Edwards, Jerome E. *Pat McCarran: Political Boss of Nevada.* Reno: University of Nevada Press, 1982.

Egan, Timothy. *The Worst Hard Time. The Untold Story of Those Who Survived the Great Dust Bowl.* Boston: Houghton Mifflin, 2005.

Eichengreen, Barry. *Golden Fetters: The Gold Standard and the Great Depression, 1919–1939.* New York: Oxford University Press, 1992.

Eisner, Marc Allen. *From Warfare State to Welfare State.* University Park: Pennsylvania State University Press, 2000.

Ekirch, Arthur A., Jr. *Ideologies and Utopias: The Impact of the New Deal on American Thought.* Chicago: Quadrangle, 1969.

Elder, Glen H., Jr. *Children of the Great Depression: Social Change in Life Experience.* Chicago: University of Chicago Press, 1974.

Ellis, William E. *Robert Worth Bingham and the Southern Mystique: From the Old South to the New South and Beyond.* Kent, Ohio: Kent State University Press, 1997.

Elson, Robert T. *Time, Inc.: The Intimate History of a Publishing Enterprise, 1923–1941.* New York: Atheneum, 1968.

Emblidge, David, ed. *My Day: The Best of Eleanor Roosevelt's Acclaimed Newspaper Columns, 1936–1962.* New York: Da Capo Press, 2001.

Evans, Hugh E. *The Hidden Campaign. FDR's Health and the 1944 Election.* Armonk, N.Y.: M. E. Sharpe, 2002.

Faber, Doris. *The Life of Lorena Hickok: E.R.'s Friend.* New York: Morrow, 1980.

Farber, David R. *Sloan Rules: Alfred P. Sloan and the Triumph of General Motors.* Chicago: University of Chicago Press, 2002.

Farley, James A. *Jim Farley's Story: The Roosevelt Years.* New York: Whittlesey House, 1948.

Farnham, Barbara R. *Roosevelt and the Munich Crisis: A Study of Political Decision-making.* Princeton, N.J.: Princeton University Press, 1997.

Farrell, Nicholas. *Mussolini: A New Life.* London: Phoenix Press, 2005.

Fassett, John D. *New Deal Justice: The Life of Stanley Reed of Kentucky.* New York: Vantage, 1994.

Fausold, Martin L. *The Presidency of Herbert C. Hoover.* Lawrence: University Press of Kansas, 1985.

Fearon, Peter. *War, Prosperity and Depression: The US Economy 1917–1945.* Oxford, England: Philip Alan, 1987.

Feingold, Henry L. *The Politics of Rescue: The Roosevelt Administration and the Holocaust, 1938–1945.* New York: Holocaust Library, 1970.

Fenby, Jonathan. *China's Generalissmo and the Nation He Lost.* New York: Carroll & Graf, 2004.

Fensch, Thomas, ed. *Conversations with John Steinbeck.* Jackson: University Press of Mississippi, 1988.

Ferrell, Robert H. *American Diplomacy in the Great Depression: Hoover-Stimson Diplomacy, 1929–1933.* New Haven, Conn.: Yale University Press, 1957.

———. *The Dying President: Franklin D. Roosevelt, 1944–45.* Columbia: University of Missouri Press, 1998.

Finan, Christopher. *Alfred E. Smith. The Happy Warrior.* New York: Hill and Wang, 2002.

Fine, Sidney. *The Automobile Under the Blue Eagle.* Ann Arbor: University of Michigan Press, 1963.

———. *Frank Murphy.* Ann Arbor: University of Michigan Press, 1975.

———. *Sit-Down: The General Motors Strike of 1936–1937.* Ann Arbor: The University of Michigan Press, 1969.

Finegold, Kenneth, and Theda Skocpol. *State, Party and Policy: Industry and Agriculture in America's New Deal.* Madison: University of Wisconsin Press, 1995.

Fite, Gilbert C. *George N. Peek and the Fight for Farm Parity.* Norman: University of Oklahoma Press, 1954.

Flanagan, Hallie. *Arena.* New York: Duell, Sloan, and Pearce, 1940.

Flannery, Gerald V., ed. *Commissioners of the FCC, 1927–1994.* Lanham, Md.: University Press of America, 1995.

Fleischhauer, Carl, and Beverly W. Brannan, eds. *Documenting America, 1935–1943.* Berkeley: University of California Press, 1988.

Fleming, Thomas. *The New Dealers' War: FDR and the War Within World War II.* New York: Basic Books, 2001.

Flynn, Errol. *My Wicked, Wicked Ways.* London: Heinemann, 1960.

Foner, Philip, ed. *Paul Robeson Speaks: Writings, Speeches, Interviews, 1918–1974.* New York: Brunner/Mazel, 1978.

Forrest, Suzanne. *The Preservation of the Village: New Mexico Hispanics and the New Deal.* Albuquerque: University of New Mexico Press, 1989.

Fox, Richard Wrightman. *Reinhold Niebuhr: A Biography.* New York: Pantheon, 1985.

Fraser, Steve. "The 'Labor Question.'" In *The Rise and Fall of the New Deal Order, 1930–1980,* edited by Steve Fraser and Gary Gerstle. Princeton, N.J.: Princeton University Press, 1989, 44–84.

Freedman, Max, ed. *Roosevelt and Frankfurter: Their Correspondence, 1928–1945.* Boston: Little, Brown, 1967.

Freidel, Frank. *Franklin D. Roosevelt: Launching the New Deal.* Boston: Little, Brown, 1973.

———. *Franklin D. Roosevelt: A Rendezvous with Destiny.* Boston: Little, Brown, 1990.

Fried, Albert. *FDR and His Enemies.* New York: St. Martin's Press, 1999.

Fried, Richard M. *The Man Everybody Knew: Bruce Barton and the Making of Modern America.* New York: Ivan R. Dee, 2006.

Fromkin, David. *In the Time of the Americans: The Generation that Changed America's Role in the World.* New York: Knopf, 1995.

Fuchser, Larry William. *Neville Chamberlain and Appeasement: A Study in the Politics of History.* New York: Norton, 1982.

Furia, Philip. *Ira Gershwin: The Art of the Lyricist.* New York: Oxford University Press, 1996.

Furuya, Keiji. *Chiang Kai-shek: His Life and Times.* New York: St. John's University Press, 1981.

Galbraith, John Kenneth. *The Great Crash.* Boston: Houghton Mifflin, 1954.

Galbraith, John Kenneth, prep., assisted by G. G. Johnson, Jr. *The Economic Effects of the Federal Public Works Expenditures, 1933–1938.* Washington, D.C.: Government Printing Office, 1940.

Gall, Gilbert J. *Pursuing Justice: Lee Pressman, the New Deal and the CIO.* New York: State University of New York, 1999.

Gallagher, Hugh G. *FDR's Splendid Deception.* New York: St. Martin's Press, 1999.

Galloway, J. M. *The Public Life of Joseph W. Byrns.* Knoxville: University of Tennessee Press, 1962.

Gardner, Lloyd C. *Spheres of Influence: The Great Powers Partition Europe, From Munich to Yalta.* Chicago: Ivan R. Dee, 1993.

Garfinkel, Herbert. *When Negroes March: The March on Washington Movement in the Organizational Politics for FEPC.* New York: Atheneum, 1959.

Garraty, John A., and Mark C. Carnes, eds. *American National Biography.* New York: Oxford University Press, 1999.

Garwood, Darrell. *Artist in Iowa: A Life of Grant Wood.* New York: Atheneum, 1959.

Gellerman, Carol. *All the President's Words.* New York: Walker and Company, 1997.

Gellerman, William. *Martin Dies.* New York: John Day, 1944.

Gellman, Irwin F. *Good Neighbor Diplomacy: United States Policies in Latin America, 1933–1945.* Baltimore: Johns Hopkins University Press, 1995.

———. *Secret Affairs: Franklin Roosevelt, Cordell Hull, and Sumner Welles.* Baltimore: Johns Hopkins University Press, 1995.

Gérard, André. *The Gravediggers of France: Gamelin, Daladier, Reynaud, Pétain, and Laval.* Indianapolis: Bobbs-Merrill, 1940.

Gieske, Millard. *Minnesota Farmer-Laborism: The Third Party Alternative.* Minneapolis: University of Minnesota Press, 1979.

Gilbert, Martin. *Churchill: A Life.* London: Minerva, 1991.

Gilbert, Robert E. *The Mortal Presidency: Illness and Anguish in the White House.* New York: HarperCollins, 1992.

Glad, Betty. *Charles Evans Hughes and the Illusions of Innocence: A Study in American Diplomacy.* Urbana: University of Illinois Press, 1966.

Glantz, Mary E. *FDR and the Soviet Union: The President's Battles over Foreign Policy.* Lawrence: University Press of Kansas, 2005.

Glasco, Laurence A., ed. *The WPA History of the Negro in Pittsburgh.* Pittsburgh: University of Pittsburgh Press, 2004.

Glassford, Larry A. *Reaction and Reform: The Politics of the Conservative Party under R.B. Bennett, 1927–1938.* Toronto: University of Toronto Press, 1992.

Glendon, Mary Ann. *A World Made New: Eleanor Roosevelt and the Universal Declaration of Human Rights.* New York: Random House, 2001.

Glennon, Robert J. *The Iconoclast as Reformer. Jerome Frank's Impact on American Law.* Ithaca, N.Y.: Cornell University Press, 1985.

Glickman, Marty. *The Fastest Kid on the Block.* Syracuse, N.Y.: Syracuse University Press, 1996.

Godfrey, Donald G., and Frederic A. Leigh, eds. *Historical Dictionary of American Radio.* Westport, Conn.: Greenwood Press, 1998.

Godfrey, Hodgson. *The Colonel: The Life and Wars of Henry Stimson, 1867–1950.* New York: Knopf, 1990.

Goldberg, Vicki. *Margaret Bourke-White: A Biography.* New York: Harper & Row, 1986.

Goodwin, Doris K. *No Ordinary Time: Franklin and Eleanor Roosevelt: The Home Front in World War II.* New York: Simon and Schuster, 1994.

Gordon, Colin. *New Deals: Business, Labor and Politics in America, 1920–1935.* New York: Cambridge University Press, 1994.

Gottfried, Martin. *George Burns and the Hundred-Year Dash.* New York: Simon and Schuster, 1996.

Gould, Jean. *Walter Reuther: Labor's Rugged Individualist.* New York: Dodd, Mead, 1972.

Graham, Katharine. *Katharine Graham's Washington.* New York: Knopf, 2002.

Graham, Otis L. *An Encore for Reform: The Old Progressives and the New Deal.* New York: Oxford University Press, 1967.

Graham, Otis L., and Megan R. Wancker, eds. *Franklin D. Roosevelt, His Life and Times: An Encyclopedic View.* New York: Macmillan, 1985.

Green, Elne C., ed. *The New Deal and Beyond. Social Welfare in the South since 1930.* Columbus: University of Georgia Press, 2003.

Gregor, A. James. *Young Mussolini and the Intellectual Origins of Fascism.* Berkeley: University of California Press, 1979.

Gross, James. *The Making of the National Labor Relations Board.* Albany: State University of New York Press, 1974.

Grubbs, Donald H. *Cry from the Cotton: The Southern Tenant Farmers' Union and the New Deal.* Chapel Hill: University of North Carolina Press, 1971.

Guerrant, Edward O. *Roosevelt's Good Neighbor Policy.* Albuquerque: University of New Mexico Press, 1950.

Gugin, Linda C., and James E. St. Clair. *Shermon Minton. New Deal Senator, Cold War Justice.* Bloomington: Indiana University Press, 1997.

Gurewitsch, Edna P. *Kindred Souls: The Friendship of Eleanor Roosevelt and David Gurewitsch.* New York: St. Martin's Press, 2002.

Hair, William Ivy. *The Kingfish and His Realm.* Baton Rouge: Louisiana State University Press, 1991.

Hamby, Alonzo L. *For the Survival of Democracy: Franklin D. Roosevelt and the World Crisis of the 1930s.* New York: Free Press, 2004.

Hamilton, Alastair. *The Appeal of Fascism: A Study of Intellectuals and Fascism.* New York: Macmillan, 1971.

Hamilton, David E. *From New Day to New Deal: American Farm Policy from Hoover to Roosevelt, 1928–1933.* Chapel Hill: University of North Carolina Press, 1991.

Hargrove, Erwin, and Paul Conkin, eds. *TVA: Fifty Years of Grassroots Bureaucracy.* Urbana: University of Illinois Press, 1983.

Harper, Donna A. *Not So Simple: The Simple Stories of Langston Hughes.* Columbia: University of Missouri Press, 1995.

Harper, John L. *American Visions of Europe: Franklin D. Roosevelt, George F. Kennan, and Dean G. Acheson.* New York: Cambridge University Press, 1994.

Harris, Brice. *The United States and the Italo-Ethiopian Crisis.* Stanford, Calif.: Stanford University Press, 1964.

Harris, William Hamilton. *Keeping the Faith: A. Philip Randolph, Milton P. Webster, and the Brotherhood of Sleeping Car Porters, 1925–37.* Urbana: University of Illinois Press, 1991.

Hawley, Ellis W. *The New Deal and the Problem of Monopoly: A Study in Economic Ambivalence.* Bronx, N.Y.: Fordham University Press, 1995.

Hayes, Jack I., Jr. *South Carolina and the New Deal.* Columbia: University of South Carolina Press, 2001.

Hayes, Richard K. *Kate Smith: A Biography.* Jefferson, N.C.: McFarland, 1995.

Heinemann, Ronald L. *Harry Byrd of Virginia.* Charlottesville: University of Virginia Press, 1996.

Henderson, A. Scott. *Housing and the Democratic Ideal: The Life and Thought of Charles Abrams.* New York: Columbia University Press, 2000.

Henderson, Henry L., and David B. Woolner. *FDR and the Environment.* New York: Palgrave Macmillan, 2005.

Henderson, Richard B. *Maury Maverick, A Political Biography.* Austin: University of Texas Press, 1970.

Hendrickson, Kenneth D., ed. *Hard Times in Oklahoma: The Depression Years.* Oklahoma City: Oklahoma State Historical Society, 1983.

———. *The Life and Presidency of Franklin Delano Roosevelt. An Annotated Bibliography.* Lanham, Md.: Scarecrow Press, 2005.

Herspring, Dale R. *The Pentagon and the Presidency: Civil-Military Relations From FDR to George W. Bush.* Lawrence: University Press of Kansas, 2005.

Herzstein, Robert E. *Henry R. Luce: A Political Portrait of the Men Who Created the American Century.* New York: Scribners, 1994.

Hickok, Lorena A. *One-Third of a Nation: Lorena Hickok Reports on the Great Depression.* Urbana: University of Illinois Press, 1981.

Higham, Charles. *The Rise and Fall of an American Genius.* New York: St. Martin's Press, 1985.

Hilmes, Michele. *Radio Voices: American Broadcasting, 1922–1952.* Minneapolis: University of Minnesota Press, 1997.

Himmelberg, Robert. *The Origins of the National Recovery Administration: Business, Government, and the Trade Association Issue, 1921–1933.* New York: Fordham University Press, 1976.

Hirsch, Jerrold. *Portrait of America: A Cultural History of the Federal Writers' Project.* Chapel Hill: University of North Carolina Press, 2004.

Hobson, Archie, ed. *Remembering America: A Sampler of the WPA American Guide Series.* New York: Columbia University Press, 1985.

Hockett, Jeffrey D. *New Deal Justice: The Constitutional Jurisprudence of Hugo L. Black, Felix Frankfurter, and Robert H. Jackson.* Lanham, Md.: Rowman and Littlefield, 1996.

Hodges, Gabrielle A. *Franco: A Concise Biography.* New York: St. Martin's Press, 2003.

Hodgson, Godfrey. *The Colonel: The Life and Wars of Henry Stimson, 1867–1950.* New York: Knopf, 1990.

Hoffman, Abraham. *Unwanted Mexican Americans in the Great Depression.* Tucson: University of Arizona Press, 1974.

Hoff-Wilson, Joan. *Herbert Hoover: Forgotten Progressive.* Boston: Little, Brown, 1975.

Hofstadter, Richard. *The Age of Reform: From Byron to F.D.R.* New York: Vintage, 1955.

———. *The American Political Tradition.* New York: Vintage, 1948.

Holli, Melvin G. *The Wizard of Washington. Emil Hurja, Franklin Roosevelt, and the Birth of Public Opinion Polling.* New York: Palgrave McMillan, 2002.

Holmes, Richard. *In the Footsteps of Churchill: A Study in Character.* New York: Basic Books, 2005.

Holt, Rackham. *Mary McLeod Bethune: A Biography.* Garden City, N.Y.: Doubleday, 1964.

Holtzman, Abraham. *The Townsend Movement: A Political Study.* New York: Bookman Associates, 1963.

Hoopes, Townsend, and Douglas Brinkley. *FDR and the Creation of the United Nations.* New Haven, Conn.: Yale University Press, 1997.

Hoover, Herbert. *The Memoirs of Herbert Hoover: The Cabinet and the Presidency, 1920–1933.* New York: Macmillan, 1952.

———. *The Memoirs of the Great Depression, 1929–1941.* New York: Macmillan, 1952.

Hopkins, Harry Lloyd. *Spending to Save: The Complete Story of Relief.* New York: Norton, 1936.

Hopkins, June. *Harry Hopkins: Sudden Hero, Brash Reformer.* New York, N.Y.: St. Martin's, 1999.

Hopkins, Robert. *Witness to History: Recollections of a World War II Photographer.* Seattle: Castle Pacific Publishing, 2002.

Hosen, Frederick. E. *The Great Depression and the New Deal: Legislative Acts in Their Entirety (1932–1933) and Statistical Economic Data (1926–1946).* Jefferson, N.C.: McFarland and Co., 1992.

Houck, Davis W. *FDR and Fear Itself: The First Inaugural Address.* College Station Texas A and M University Press, 2002.

Howard, Donald S. *The WPA and Federal Relief Policy.* New York: Russell Sage Foundation, 1943.

Howard, Thomas C., and William D. Pederson, eds. *Franklin D. Roosevelt and the Formation of the Modern World.* Armonk, N.Y.: M. E. Sharpe, 2003.

Hughes, Charles Evans. *The Autobiographical Notes of Charles Evans Hughes.* Cambridge, Mass.: Harvard University Press, 1973.

Hull, Cordell. *The Memoirs of Cordell Hull.* 1948. Reprint, New York: Hill & Wang, 1993.

Hurley, Forrest Jack. *Portrait of a Decade: Roy Stryker and the Development of Documentary Photography in the Thirties.* Baton Rouge: Louisiana State University Press, 1972.

Hurston, Zora Neale. *Dust Tracks on a Road.* New York: Harper Perennial, 1996 (reprint).

———. *Folklore, Memoirs, and Other Writings.* New York: Library of America, 1995.

Huthmacher, J. Joseph. *Senator Robert F. Wagner and the Rise of Urban Liberalism.* New York: Atheneum, 1968.

Hyman, Sidney. *Marriner S. Eccles: Private Entrepreneur and Public Servant.* Stanford, Calif.: Stanford University Press, 1976.

Ickes, Harold L. *The Autobiography of a Curmudgeon.* New York: Reynal and Hitchcock, 1943.

———. *Back to Work: The Story of the PWA.* New York: Reynal and Hitchcock, 1943.

Ingalls, Robert P. *Herbert H. Lehman and New York's Little New Deal.* New York: New York University Press, 1975.

Irons, Peter. *The New Deal Lawyers.* Princeton, N.J.: Princeton University Press, 1982.

Irye, Akira. *Pearl Harbor and the Coming of the Pacific War: A Brief History with Documents and Essays.* Boston: Bedford/St. Martin's, 1999.

Isaacson, Walter, and Evan Thomas. *The Wise Men.* New York: Simon and Schuster, 1986.

Isakoff, Jack F. *The Public Works Administration.* Urbana: University of Illinois Press, 1938.

Jackson, Donald C. *Great American Bridges and Dams.* New York: Wiley, 1996.

Jackson, Julian. *The Politics of Depression in France, 1932–1936.* New York: Cambridge University Press, 1985.

———. *The Popular Front in France: Defending Democracy 1934–1938.* New York: Cambridge University Press, 1988.

Jackson, Robert H. *That Man: An Insider's Portrait of Franklin D. Roosevelt.* New York: Oxford University Press, 2003.

Janeway, Michael. *The Fall of the House of Roosevelt. Brokers of Ideas and Power from FDR to LBJ.* New York: Columbia University Press, 2004.

Jeansonne, Glen. *Gerald L. K. Smith, Minister of Hate.* New Haven, Conn.: Yale University Press, 1988.

———. *Messiah of the Masses: Huey P. Long and the Great Depression.* New York: HarperCollins, 1993.

Jenkins, Roy. *Churchill. A Biography.* New York: Farrar, Straus & Giroux, 2001.

———. *Franklin D. Roosevelt.* New York: Henry Holt, 2003.

Johnson, David Alan. *The Battle of Britain and the American Factor, July–October, 1940.* Conshohocken, Pa.: Combined Press, 1998.

Johnson, Donald Bruce. *The Republican Party and Wendell Willkie.* Urbana: University of Illinois Press, 1960.

Johnson, Hugh Samuel. *The Blue Eagle from Egg to Earth.* Garden City, N.Y.: Doubleday, Doran, 1935.

Johnston, Carol Ingalls. *Of Time and the Artist: Thomas Wolfe, His Novels, and the Critics.* Columbia, S.C.: Camden House, 1995.

Jones, Manfred. *Isolationism in America.* Ithaca, N.Y.: Cornell University Press, 1966.

Josephson, Matthew. *Sidney Hillman: Statesman of American Labor.* Garden City, N.Y.: Doubleday, 1952.

Kalfatovic, Martin R. *The New Deal Fine Arts Projects: A Bibliography, 1933–1992.* Lanham, Md.: Scarecrow, 1994.

Katznelson, Ira. *When Affirmative Action Was White. An Untold History of Racial Inequality in Twentieth-Century America.* New York: Norton, 2005.

Kaufman, Andrew L. *Cardozo.* Cambridge, Mass.: Harvard University Press, 1998.

Kazakoff, George. *Dangerous Theatre: The Federal Theatre Project as a Forum for New Plays.* New York: Peter Land, 1989.

Kearny, Edward N. *Thurmon Arnold, Social Critic.* Albuquerque: University of New Mexico Press, 1976.

Keene, Jennifer. *Doughboys, the Great War, and the Remaking of America.* Baltimore: Johns Hopkins University Press, 2000.

Keiji, Furuya. *Chiang Kai-shek: His Life and Times.* New York: St. John's University Press, 1981.

Keiler, Allan. *Marian Anderson: A Singer's Journey.* New York: Scribner, 2000.

Kelly, Lawrence C. *The Assault on Assimilation: John Collier and the Origins of Indian Policy Reform.* Albuquerque: University of New Mexico Press, 1983.

Kelly, Robin. *Hammer and Hoe: Alabama Communists During the Great Depression.* Chapel Hill: University of North Carolina Press, 1990.

Kendall, Kathleen. *Communication in the Presidential Primaries: The Candidate and the Media, 1912–2000.* Westport, Conn.: Praeger, 2000.

Kennedy, David M. *Freedom from Fear: The American People in Depression and War, 1929–1945.* New York: Oxford University Press, 1999.

Kershaw, Ian. *Hitler, 1889–1936: Hubris.* New York: W. W. Norton, 1999.

Kessner, Thomas. *Fiorello La Guardia and the Making of Modern New York.* New York: McGraw-Hill, 1989.

Kettenman, Andrea. *Diego Rivera (1886–1957): A Revolutionary Spirit in Modern Art.* New York: Taschen, 1997.

Keynes, John Maynard. *The Collected Writings of John Maynard Keynes.* New York: St. Martin's, 1971.

Khademian, Anne M. *SEC and Capital Market Regulation: The Politics of Expertise.* Pittsburgh: University of Pittsburgh Press, 1992.

Kimball, Warren F. *Forged in War: Roosevelt, Churchill, and the Second World War.* New York: William Morrow, 1997.

Kindleberger, C. *The World in Depression, 1929–1939.* Berkeley: University of California Press, 1986.

Kirby, John B. *Black Americans in the Roosevelt Era: Liberalism and Race.* Knoxville: University of Tennessee Press, 1980.

Kirkendall, Richard S. "The New Deal and Agriculture." In *The New Deal: The National Level,* edited by John Braeman, Robert H. Bremner, and David Brody. Columbus: Ohio State University Press, 1975, 83–109.

Kirkpatrick, Ivone, Sir. *Mussolini: A Study in Power.* New York: Avon, 1964.

Klehr, Harvey. *The Heyday of American Communism: The Depression Decade*. New York: Basic Books, 1984.

Klein, Jonas. *Beloved Island: Franklin and Eleanor and the Legacy of Campobello*. Forest Dale, Vt.: Ericksson, 2002.

Knepper, Cathy D. *Greenbelt, Maryland. A Living Legacy of the New Deal*. Baltimore: Johns Hopkins University Press, 2001.

Knox, John. *The Forgotten Memoir of John Knox: A Year in the Life of a Supreme Court Clerk in FDR's Washington*. Chicago: University of Chicago Press, 2002.

Koch, Stephen. *The Breaking Point. Hemingway, Dos Passos, and the Murder of José Robles*. New York: Counterpoint, 2005.

Koistinen, Paul A. *Arsenal of World War II: The Political Economy of American Warfare, 1940–1945*. Lawrence: University of Kansas Press, 2004.

Konefsky, Samuel Joseph. *Chief Justice Stone and the Supreme Court*. New York: Macmillan, 1946.

Koskoff, David E. *Joseph P. Kennedy: A Life and Times*. Englewood Cliffs, N.J.: Prentice-Hall, 1974.

Kraus, Henry. *Heroes of Unwritten Story: The UAW, 1934–1939*. Urbana: University of Illinois Press, 1993.

Kuehl, Warren F. *Keeping the Covenant: American Internationalists and the League of Nations, 1920–1939*. Kent, Ohio: Kent State University Press, 1997.

Lacouture, Jean. *DeGaulle: The Rebel, 1890–1944*. New York: W. W. Norton, 1990.

Lacy, Leslie Alexander. *The Soil Soldiers: The Civilian Conservation Corps in the Great Depression*. Radnor, Pa.: Chilton, 1976.

La Guardia, Fiorello. *The Making of an Insurgent*. Philadelphia: Lippincott & Crowell, 1948.

Landis, Arthur H. *Death in the Olive Groves: American Volunteers in the Spanish Civil War, 1936–1939*. New York: Paragon House, 1989.

Lange, Dorothea. *An American Exodus: A Record of Human Erosion in the Thirties*. Rev. ed. New Haven, Conn.: Yale University Press, 1969.

Langer, William L., and S. Everett Gleason. *The Undeclared War: 1940–1941*. New York: Harper, 1953.

Lash, Joseph P. *Dealers and Dreamers: A New Look at the New Deal*. New York: Doubleday, 1988.

———. *Eleanor and Franklin: The Story of Their Friendship*. New York: Norton, 1971.

Lasser, William. *Benjamin V. Cohen. Architect of the New Deal*. New Haven, Conn.: Yale University Press, 2002.

Lawson, Don. *The Abraham Lincoln Brigade: Americans Fighting Fascism in the Spanish Civil War*. New York: Crowell, 1989.

Lear, Linda. *Harold Ickes*. London: Taylor and Francis, 1981.

Lee, Mordecai. *The First Presidential Communications Agency: FDR's Office of Government Reports*. New York: State University of New York Press, 2005.

Lee, Stephen J. *Stalin and the Soviet Union*. New York: Routledge, 1999.

Leff, Mark H. *The Limits of Symbolic Reform: The New Deal and Taxation*. Cambridge: Cambridge University Press, 1984.

Leibovitz, Clement. *In Our Time: The Chamberlain-Hitler Collusion*. New York, N.Y.: Monthly Review, 1998.

Lekachman, Robert. *The Age of Keynes*. New York: Vintage, 1968.

Leonard, Charles A. *A Search for a Judicial Philosophy: Mr. Justice Roberts and the Constitutional Revolution of 1937*. Port Washington, N.Y.: Kennikat Press, 1971.

Leuchtenburg, William E. *Franklin D. Roosevelt and the New Deal*. New York: Harper and Row, 1963.

———. *The FDR Years: On Roosevelt and His Legacy*. New York: Columbia University Press, 1995.

———. *In the Shadow of FDR: From Harry Truman to Bill Clinton.* Ithaca, N.Y.: Cornell University Press, 1993.

———. *The Supreme Court Reborn: Constitutional Revolution in the Age of Roosevelt.* New York: Oxford University Press, 1995.

Levine, Rhonda F. *Class Struggle and the New Deal: Industrial Labor, Industrial Capital, and the State.* Lawrence: University of Kansas Press, 1988.

Levy, Beryl Harold. *Cardozo and Frontiers of Legal Thinking, with Selected Opinions.* Cleveland: Press of Case Western Reserve University, 1969.

Lichtenstein, Nelson. *The Most Dangerous Man in Detroit: Walter Reuther and the Fate of American Labor.* New York: Basic Books, 1995.

Lindbloom, Charles. *Politics and Markets.* New York: Basic Books, 1977.

Lisio, Donald J. *The President and Protest: Hoover, Conspiracy, and the Bonus Riot.* Columbia: University of Missouri Press, 1974.

Littlewood, Thomas B. *Horner of Illinois.* Evanston: Northwestern University Press, 1969.

Lobdell, George H., Jr. "A Biography of Frank Knox." Unpublished Ph.D. dissertation, University of Illinois, 1954.

Lofaro, Michael A., and Hugh Davis. *James Agee Rediscovered: The Journals of "Let Us Now Praise Famous Men" and Other Manuscripts.* Knoxville: University of Tennessee Press, 2005.

Long, Frank W. *Confessions of a Depression Muralist.* Columbia: University of Missouri Press, 1997.

Louchheim, Katie. *The Making of the New Deal: The Insiders Speak.* Cambridge, Mass.: Harvard University Press, 1983.

Louvish, Simon. *Man on the Flying Trapeze: The Life and Times of W. C. Fields.* New York: Norton, 1997.

———. *Monkey Business: The Lives and Legends of the Marx Brothers: Groucho, Chico, Harpo,* *Zeppo, with added Gummo.* London: Faber & Faber, 1999.

Lower, Richard. *A Bloc of One: The Political Career of Hiram W. Johnson.* Stanford, Calif.: Stanford University Press, 1993.

Lowitt, Richard. *George Norris: The Making of a Progressive, 1861–1912.* Urbana: University of Illinois Press, 1963.

Luconi, Stefano. *Little Italies e New Deal ia coalizione rooseveltiana e il voto italo-americano a Filadelfia e Pittsburgh.* Milan: Franco Angeli, 2002.

Ludlow, Louis. *Hell or Heaven.* Boston: Stratford Press, 1937.

Lukacs, John. *The Hitler of History.* New York: Knopf, 1997.

———. *The Rise of Hitler.* New York: Knopf, 1997.

Lunt, Richard D. *The High Ministry of Government: The Political Career of Frank Murphy.* Detroit: Wayne State University Press, 1965.

Maddox, Robert J. *William E. Borah and American Foreign Policy.* Baton Rouge: Louisiana State University Press, 1969.

Maland, Charles J. *Frank Capra.* New York: Twayne, 1995.

Manchester, William R. *American Caesar: Douglas MacArthur, 1880–1964.* Boston: Little, Brown, 1978.

Mandell, Richard D. *The Nazi Olympics.* New York: Macmillan, 1971.

Maney, Patrick J. *The Roosevelt Presence. A Biography.* New York: Twayne Publishers, 1992.

———. *"Young Bob" La Follette: A Biography of Robert La Follette, Jr., 1895–1953.* Columbia: University of Missouri Press, 1978.

Mangione, Jerre G. *The Dream and the Deal: The Federal Writer's Project, 1935–1943.* Philadelphia: University of Pennsylvania Press, 1983.

Mann, Arthur. *La Guardia: A Fighter Against His Times.* Philadelphia: Lippincott, 1959.

Margolick, David. *Beyond Glory: Joe Louis vs. Max Schmeling and a World on the Brink.* New York: Knopf, 2005.

Marling, Karal Ann. *Wall-to-Wall America: A Cultural History of Post-Office Murals in the Great Depression.* Minneapolis: University of Minnesota Press, 1982.

Marolda, Edward J. *FDR and the U.S. Navy.* New York: St. Martin's, 1998.

Marquis, Alice G. *Hope and Ashes: The Birth of Modern Times 1929–1939.* New York: Free Press, 1986.

Martin, George W. *Madam Secretary: Frances Perkins.* Boston: Houghton Mifflin, 1976.

Martin-Perdue, Nancy J., and Charles L. Perdue, Jr. *Talk About Trouble: A New Deal Portrait of Virginians in the Great Depression.* Chapel Hill: University of North Carolina Press, 1996.

Mason, Alpheus Thomas. *Harlan Fiske Stone: Pillar of the Law.* New York: Viking, 1956.

Mayer, George H. *The Political Career of Floyd B. Olson.* Minneapolis: University of Minnesota Press, 1951.

McBrien, William. *Cole Porter: A Biography.* New York: Knopf, 1998.

McCabe, John. *Cagney.* New York: Knopf, 1997.

McCann, Graham. *Cary Grant: A Class Apart.* New York: Columbia University Press, 1996.

McCarthy, Todd. *Howard Hawks: The Grey Fox of Hollywood.* New York: Grove, 1997.

McCarty, Clifford. *The Complete Films of Humphrey Bogart.* Secaucus, N.J.: Carol Publishing Group, 1995.

McCluskey, Audrey Thomas, and Elaine M. Smith, eds. *Mary McLeod Bethune: Building a Better World: Essays and Selected Documents.* Bloomington: Indiana University Press, 1999.

McCoy, Donald R. *Angry Voices: Left-of-Center Politics in the New Deal Era.* Lawrence: University of Kansas Press, 1958.

———. *Landon of Kansas.* Lincoln: University of Nebraska Press, 1966.

McCraw, Thomas. *Prophets of Regulation: Charles Francis Adams, Louis D. Brandeis, James M. Landis, and Alfred Kahn.* Cambridge, Mass.: Harvard University Press, 1984.

McDannell, Colleen. *Picturing Faith: Photography and the Great Depression.* New Haven, Conn.: Yale University Press, 2005.

McDonald, William F. *Federal Relief Administration and the Arts: The Origins and Administrative History of the Arts Projects of the Works Progress Administration.* Columbus: Ohio State University Press, 1969.

McDonough, Frank. *Neville Chamberlain: Appeasement and the British Road to War.* New York: St. Martin's, 1998.

McElvaine, Robert S. *The Depression and the New Deal: A History in Documents.* New York: Oxford University Press, 2000.

———. *Franklin D. Roosevelt.* Washington, D.C.: CQ Press, 2002.

———. *The Great Depression: America, 1929–1941.* New York: Oxford University Press, 1984.

———, ed. *Encyclopedia of the Great Depression.* New York: Hale, 2004.

McFarland, Kevin D. and David L. Roll. *Louis Johnson and the Arming of America: The Roosevelt and Truman Years.* Bloomington: Indiana University Press, 2005.

McGovern, James R. *And a Time for Hope: Americans in the Great Depression.* Westport, Conn.: Praeger, 2000.

McJimsey, George. *Harry Hopkins: Ally of the Poor and Defender of Democracy.* Cambridge, Mass.: Harvard University Press, 1987.

———. *The Presidency of Franklin Delano Roosevelt.* Lawrence: University Press of Kansas, 2000.

McKean, David. *Tommy the Cork: Washington's Ultimate Insider from Roosevelt to Reagan.* Hanover, N.H.: WestGroup, 2004.

McKinzie, Richard D. *The New Deal for Artists.* Princeton, N.J.: Princeton University Press, 1973.

McMahon, Kevin J. *Reconsidering Roosevelt on Race: How the Presidency Paved the Road to Brown.* Chicago: University of Chicago Press, 2004.

Meacham, Jon. *Frank and Winston: An Intimate Portrait of the Epic Friendship.* New York: Random House, 2003.

Mead, Chris. *Champion—Joe Louis: Black Hero in White America.* New York: Scribner, 1985.

Mee, Charles L. *Meeting at Potsdam.* New York: Harper's, 1995.

Meisner, Maurice. *Marxism, Maoism and Utopianism: Eight Essays.* Madison: University of Wisconsin Press, 1982.

Meltzer, Milton. *Dorothea Lange: A Photographer's Life.* Syracuse, N.Y.: Syracuse University Press, 2000.

Menand, Louis. *The Metaphysical Club.* New York: Farrar, Straus & Giroux, 2001.

Merkley, Paul. *Reinhold Niebuhr: A Political Account.* Montreal: McGill-Queen's University Press, 1975.

Merrill, Hugh. *Esky: The Early Years at Esquire.* New Brunswick: N.J.: Rutgers University Press, 1995.

Merrill, Perry H. *Roosevelt's Forest Army: A History of the Civilian Conservation Corps.* Barre, Vt.: Northlight Studio, 1981.

Mettler, Susanne. *Dividing Citizens: Gender and Federalism in New Deal Public Policy.* Ithaca, N.Y.: Cornell University Press, 1998.

Meyers, Jeffrey. *Edmund Wilson: A Biography.* Boston: Houghton Mifflin, 1995.

Michaelis, Meir. *Mussolini and the Jews: German-Italian Relations and the Jewish Question in Italy, 1922–1945.* New York: Oxford University Press, 1978.

Milkis, Sidney. *The President and the Parties: The Transformation of the American Party System Since the New Deal.* New York: Oxford University Press, 1993.

Miller, Dan B. *Erskine Caldwell: The Journey from Tobacco Road: A Biography.* New York: Knopf, 1995.

Miller, Dwight, and Timothy M. Walch, eds. *Herbert Hoover and Franklin D. Roosevelt: A Documentary History.* Westport, Conn.: Greenwood Press, 1998.

Miller, John E. *Governor Philip F. La Follette: The Wisconsin Progressives, and the New Deal.* Columbia: University of Missouri Press, 1982.

Milner, E. R. *The Lives and Times of Bonnie and Clyde.* Carbondale: Southern Illinois University Press, 1996.

Minter, David. *William Faulkner: His Life and Work.* Baltimore: Johns Hopkins University Press, 1980.

Mintz, Frank P. *The Liberty Lobby and the American Right: Race, Conspiracy, and Culture.* Westport, Conn.: Greenwood, 1985.

Mitchell, Broadus. *Depression Decade: From New Era through New Deal, 1929–1941.* New York: Harper & Row, 1947.

Mitchell, Greg. *The Campaign of the Century: Upton Sinclair's Race for Governor of California and the Birth of Media Politics.* New York: Random House, 1992.

Moley, Raymond. *After Seven Years.* New York: Harper, 1939.

Moley, Raymond, and Eliot A. Rosen. *The First New Deal.* New York: Harcourt, Brace & World, 1966.

Monroy, Douglas. *Rebirth: Mexican Los Angeles from the Great Migration to the Great Depression.* Berkeley: University of California Press, 1999.

Mooney, Booth. *Roosevelt and Rayburn: A Political Partnership.* Philadelphia: Lippincott, 1971.

Moore, Clayton, and Frank Thompson. *I Was That Masked Man.* Dallas, Tex.: Taylor, 1996.

Moore, Jesse Thomas. *A Search for Equality: The National Urban League, 1910–1961.* University Park: Pennsylvania State University Press, 1981.

Moore, John Robert. *Senator Josiah William Bailey of North Carolina.* Durham, N.C.: Duke University Press, 1968.

Moorehead, Caroline. *Gellhorn: A Twentieth-Century Life.* New York: Holt, 2003.

Mora, Gilles. *Walker Evans: The Hungry Eye.* New York: Abrams, 1993.

Moreo, Dominic W. *Schools in the Great Depression.* New York: Garland, 1996.

Morgan, Ted. *FDR: A Biography.* New York, N.Y.: Simon and Schuster, 1985.

———. *Reds: McCarthyism in Twentieth-Century America.* New York: Random House, 2004.

Morison, Elting Elmore. *Turmoil and Tradition: A Study of the Life and Times of Henry L. Stimson.* New York: Atheneum, 1964.

Morse, Arthur D. *While Six Million Died: A Chronicle of American Apathy.* New York: Random House, 1968.

Morwood, William. *Duel for the Middle Kingdom: The Struggle Between Chiang Kai-shek and Mao Tse-tung for Control of China.* New York: Everest House, 1980.

Moser, John E. *Right Turn: John T. Flynn and the Transformation of American Liberalism.* New York: New York University Press, 2005.

Mosley, Leonard. *Marshall: Hero for Our Times.* New York: Hearst, 1982.

Murphy, Bruce A. *Wild Bill: The Legend and Life of William O. Douglas.* New York: Random House, 2003.

Murray, Williamson, and Allan R. Millet. *A War to be Won: Fighting the Second World War.* Cambridge, Mass.: Harvard University Press, 2000.

Muscio, Giuliana. *Hollywood's New Deal.* Philadelphia: Temple University Press, 1997.

Naison, Mark. *Communists in Harlem during the Depression.* New York: Grove, 1983.

Namorato, Michael V. *Rexford G. Tugwell: A Biography.* New York: Praeger, 1988.

Nasaw, David. *The Chief: The Life of William Randolph Hearst.* Boston: Houghton Mifflin, 2000.

Nash, Gerald. *The Great Depression and World War II: Organizing America, 1933–1945.* New York: St. Martin's, 1979.

Neal, Steve. *Happy Days are Here Again: The 1932 Democratic Convention, the Emergence of FDR and How America Was Changed Forever.* New York: Morrow, 2004.

Neatby, H. Blair. *The Politics of Chaos: Canada in the Thirties.* Toronto: Copp, Clark, Pitman, 1986.

Nelson, Brace. *Workers on the Waterfront: Seamen, Longshoremen and Unionism in the 1930s.* Urbana: University of Illinois Press, 1988.

Newman, Roger K. *Hugo Black: A Biography.* New York: Oxford University Press, 1994.

Newton, Verne W., ed. *FDR and the Holocaust.* New York: St. Martin's Press, 1995.

Nordin, Dennis S. *The New Deal's Black Congressman: A Life of Arthur Wergs Mitchell.* Columbia: University of Missouri Press, 1997.

Norris, George. *Fighting Liberal: The Autobiography of George W. Norris.* New York: Macmillan, 1945.

Novkov, Julie. *Constitution Workers, Protecting Women: Gender, Law, and Labor in the Progressive and New Deal Years.* Ann Arbor: University of Michigan Press, 2001.

O'Connor, F. V. *The New Deal Art Projects: An Anthology of Memoirs.* Washington, D.C.: Smithsonian Institution Press, 1972.

O'Connor, Richard. *Heywood Broun: A Biography.* New York: Putnam, 1975.

———. *The First Hurrah: A Biography of Alfred E. Smith.* New York: Putnam, 1970.

Offner, Arnold A. *American Appeasement: United States Foreign Policy and Germany, 1933–1938.* New York: Norton, 1969.

Ogden, August R. *The Dies Committee: A Study of the Special House Committee for the Investigation of Un-American Activities, 1938–1944.* Washington, D.C.: Murray and Heister, 1945.

Ohl, John K. *Hugh Johnson and the New Deal.* DeKalb: Northern Illinois University Press, 1985.

Olson, James S. *Herbert Hoover and the Reconstruction Finance Corporation, 1931–1933*. Ames: Iowa State University Press, 1977.

———. *Saving Capitalism: The Reconstruction Finance Corporation and the New Deal*. Ames: Iowa State University Press, 1988.

———, ed. *Historical Dictionary of the New Deal. From Inauguration to Preparations for War*. Westport, Conn.: Greenwood Press, 1985.

Ottanelli, Fraser. *The Communist Party of the United States: From the Depression to World War II*. New Brunswick, N.J.: Rutgers University Press, 1991.

Owens, Jesse, and Paul G. Neimark. *Blackthink: My Life as Black Man and White Man*. New York: Morrow, 1970.

Owens, Louis. *John Steinbeck's Re-vision of America*. Athens: University of Georgia Press, 1985.

Paige, Leroy, and David Lipman. *Maybe I'll Pitch Forever: A Great Baseball Player Tells the Hilarious Story Behind the Legend*. Lincoln: University of Nebraska Press, 1993.

Palmer, Frederick. *This Man Landon: The Record and Career of Governor Alfred M. Landon of Kansas*. New York: Dodd, Mead, 1936.

Parini, Jay. *John Steinbeck: A Biography*. New York: Holt, 1995.

Paris, Barry. *Garbo: A Biography*. New York: Random House, 1995.

Parish, Michael E. *Felix Frankfurter and His Times: The Reform Years*. New York: Free Press, 1982.

Parker, R. A. C., ed. *Winston Churchill: Studies in Statesmanship*. Washington, D.C.: Brassey's, 1995.

Parrish, Michael E. *Anxious Decades: America in Prosperity and Depression, 1920–1941*. New York: Norton, 1992.

Patterson, James T. *Congressional Conservatism and the New Deal: The Growth of the Conservative Coalition in Congress, 1933–1939*. Lexington: University Press of Kentucky, 1967.

Paulson, George. A *Living Wage for the Forgotten Man: The Quest for Fair Labor Standards, 1933–1941*. Selinsgrove, Pa.: Susquehanna University Press, 1996.

Paxton, Robert O. *The Anatomy of Fascism*. New York: Knopf, 2004.

Payne, Stanley G. *A History of Fascism, 1914–1945*. Madison: University of Wisconsin Press, 1995.

Pederson, William, and Ann M. McLaurin, eds. *The Rating Game in American Politics*. New York: Irvington Publishers, 1987.

Pederson, William D., ed. *The "Barberian" Presidency: Theoretical and Empirical Readings*. New York: Peter Lang, 1989.

Pederson, William D., and Norman W. Provizer, eds. *Great Justices of the U.S. Supreme Court: Ratings and Case Studies*. New York: Peter Lang, 1993.

———. *Leaders of the Pack: Polls and Case Studies of Great Supreme Court Justices*. New York: Peter Lang, 2003.

Pederson, William D. and Frank J. Williams, eds. *Franklin D. Roosevelt and Abraham Lincoln: Competing Perspectives on Two Great Presidencies*. Armonk, N.Y.: M. E. Sharpe, 2003.

Peek, George N. *Why Quit Our Own*. New York: Van Nostrand, 1936.

Pepper, Claude. *Pepper: Eyewitness to a Century*. San Diego: Harcourt Brace Jovanovich, 1987.

Perisco, Joseph E. *Roosevelt's Secret War: FDR and World War II Espionage*. New York: Random House, 2001.

Perkins, Frances. *The Roosevelt I Knew*. New York: Viking, 1946.

Perras, Galen R. *Franklin D. Roosevelt and the Origins of the Canadian-American Security Alliance, 1933–1945: Necessary, But Not Necessary Enough*. Westport, Conn.: Praeger, 1998.

Peters, Charles. *Five Days in Philadelphia. Wendell Willkie, FDR, and the 1940 Convention that Saved the Western World*. New York: Public Affairs, 2005.

Peterson, N. H. *From Hitler's Doorstep.* University Park: Pennsylvania State University Press, 1996.

Pfeffer, Paula F. *A Philip Randolph: Pioneer of the Civil Rights Movement.* Baton Rouge: Louisiana State University Press, 1990.

Phelen, Craig. *William Green: Biography of a Labor Leader.* Albany: State University of New York Press, 1989.

Philip, Kenneth R. *John Collier's Crusade for Indian Reform, 1920–54.* Tucson: University of Arizona Press, 1981.

Phillips, Susan M., and J. Richard Zecher. *The SEC and the Public Interest.* Cambridge, Mass.: MIT Press, 1981.

Pike, Frederick. *FDR's Good Neighbor Policy: Sixty Years of Generally Gentle Chaos.* Austin: University of Texas Press, 1995.

Plotke, David. *Building a Democratic Order: Reshaping American Liberalism in the 1930s and 1940s.* Princeton, N.J.: Princeton University Press, 1996.

Polenberg, Richard. *The Era of Franklin D. Roosevelt, 1933–1945: A Brief History with Documents.* New York: St. Martin's Press, 2000.

———. *War and Society: The United States, 1941–1945.* Philadelphia: Lippincott, 1972.

———. *The World of Benjamin Cardozo: Personal Values and the Judicial Process.* Cambridge, Mass.: Harvard University Press, 1987.

Pollack, Howard. *Aaron Copland: The Life and Work of an Uncommon Man.* New York: Holt, 1999.

Potter, Claire Bond. *War on Crime: Bandits, G-Men, and the Politics of Mass Culture.* New Brunswick, N.J.: Rutgers University Press, 1998.

Pratt, Julius William. *Cordell Hull, 1933–1944.* New York: Cooper Square, 1964.

Preston, Paul. *Franco: A Biography.* London: HarperCollins, 1994.

Pringle, Henry Fowles. *Alfred E. Smith: A Critical Study.* New York: AMS, 1970.

Provizer, Norman, and William Pederson, eds. *Grassroots Constitutionalism,* Lanham, Md.: University Press of America, 1988.

Pusey, Merlo John. *Charles Evans Hughes.* New York: Macmillan, 1951.

Radford, Gail. *Modern Housing for America: Policy Struggles in the New Deal Era.* Chicago: University of Chicago Press, 1996.

Rappoport, Helen. *Joseph Stalin: A Biographical Companion.* Santa Barbara, Calif.: ABC-CLIO, 1999.

Rathbone, Belinda. *Walker Evans.* Boston: Houghton Mifflin, 1995.

Rauch, Basil. *The History of the New Deal, 1933–1938.* New York: Creative Age Press, 1944.

Reiman, Richard A. *The New Deal and American Youth: Ideas and Ideals in a Depression Decade.* Athens: University of Georgia Press, 1992.

Renwick, R., *Fighting With Allies,* London: Times Books, 1996.

Ribuffo, Leo. *The Old Christian Right: The Protestant Far Right from the Great Depression to the Cold War.* Philadelphia: Temple University Press, 1983.

Richardson, R. Dan. *Comintern Army: The International Brigades and the Spanish Civil War.* Lexington: University Press of Kentucky, 1982.

Ridley, Jasper Godwin. *Mussolini.* New York: St. Martin's Press, 1998.

Rivas-Rodriguez, Maggie, ed. *Mexican Americans and World War II.* Austin: University of Texas Press, 2005.

Ritchie, Donald A. *James M. Landis: Dean of the Regulators.* Cambridge, Mass.: Harvard University Press, 1980.

Roberts, Owen J. *The Court and the Constitution.* Cambridge, Mass.: Harvard University Press, 1951.

Roberts, Ron E. *John L. Lewis: Hard Labor and Wild Justice.* Dubuque, Iowa: Kendall/Hunt, 1994.

Robertson, David. *Sly and Able: A Political Biography of James F. Byrnes.* New York: W. W. Norton, 1994.

Robinson, Greg. *By Order of the President: FDR and the Internment of Japanese Americans.* Cambridge, Mass.: Harvard University Press, 2001.

Rock, William R. *Chamberlain and Roosevelt: British Foreign Policy and the United States, 1937–1940.* Columbus: Ohio State University Pres, 1988.

Roddick, Nick. *A New Deal in Entertainment: Warner Brothers in the 1930s.* London: British Film Institute, 1983.

Rodger, Streitmatter, ed. *Empty Without You: The Intimate Letters of Eleanor Roosevelt and Lorena Hickok.* New York: Free Press, 1998.

Rodgers, Marion E. *Mencken: The American Iconoclast.* New York: Oxford University Pres, 2005.

Rollins, Alfred B. *Roosevelt and Howe.* New York: Knopf, 1962.

Rollyson, Carl. *Nothing Ever Happens to the Brave: The Story of Martha Gellhorn.* New York: St. Martin's Press, 1990.

Romasco, Albert U. *The Politics of Recovery: Roosevelt's New Deal.* New York: Oxford University Press, 1983.

Roosevelt, Eleanor. *Autobiography.* New York: Harper & Row, 1961.

Roosevelt, Franklin. *The Public Papers and Addresses of Franklin D. Roosevelt.* 13 vols. Compiled by Samuel I. Rosenman. New York: Random House, 1938–50.

Rose, Nancy E. *Put to Work: Relief Programs in the Great Depression.* New York: Monthly Review Press, 1994.

Rosen, Elliot A. *Hoover, Roosevelt, and the Brains Trust: From Depression to New Deal.* New York: Columbia University Press, 1977.

———. *Roosevelt, the Great Depression, and the Economics of Recovery.* Charlottesville: University of Virginia Press, 2006.

Rosen, Robert N. *Saving the Jews. Franklin D. Roosevelt and the Holocaust.* Thunder's Mouth: Avalon, 2006.

Rosenbaum, Herbert D., and Elizabeth Bartelme, eds. *Franklin D. Roosevelt: The Man, the Myth and the Era, 1882–1945.* Westport, Conn.: Greenwood Press, 1987.

Rosenhof, Theodore. *Economics in the Long Run: New Deal Theorists and Their Legacies, 1933–1993.* Chapel Hill: University of Carolina Press, 1997.

——— *Working with Roosevelt.* New York: Harper, 1952.

Rosenstone, Robert A. *Crusade of the Left: The Lincoln Battalion in the Spanish Civil War.* New York: Pegasus, 1969.

Rossi, Mario. *Roosevelt and the French.* Westport, Conn.: Praeger, 1993.

Rozell, Mark J., and William D. Pederson, eds. *FDR and the Modern Presidency: Leadership and Legacy.* Westport, Conn.: Praeger, 1997.

Rubinstein, William D. *The Myth of Rescue: Why the Democrats Could Not Have Saved More Jews from the Nazis.* New York: Routledge, 1997.

Ruddy, T. Michael. *The Cautious Diplomat: Charles E. Bolen and the Soviet Union, 1929–69.* Kent, Ohio: Kent State University Press, 1986.

Ryan, James G. *Earl Browder: The Failure of American Communism.* Tuscaloosa: University of Alabama Press, 1997.

Ryan, Halford R. *Franklin Roosevelt's Rhetorical Presidency.* Westport, Conn.: Greenwood Press, 1988.

Sachs, Bernard. "Recreation After Fifty," *Recreation* 308 (August 1937): 332–333.

Sainsbury, Keith. *Churchill and Roosevelt at War: The War They Fought and the Peace They Hoped to Make.* New York: New York University Press, 1994.

St. Clair, James E., and Linda C. Gugin. *Chief Justice Fred M. Vinson of Kentucky: A Political*

12and the Transformation of the Supreme Court. Armonk, N.Y.: M. E. Sharpe, 2004.

Salmond, John A. *The Civilian Conservation Corps, 1932–1942: A New Deal Case Study.* Durham, N.C.: Duke University Press, 1967.

———. *A Southern Rebel: The Life and Times of Aubrey Willis Williams, 1890–1965.* Chapel Hill: University of North Carolina Press, 1983.

Saloutos, Theodore. *The American Farmer and the New Deal.* Ames: Iowa State University Press, 1982.

Samuel, Lawrence R. *Pledging Allegiance: American Identity and the Bond Drive of World War II.* Washington, D.C.: Smithsonian Institution Press, 1997.

Santelli, Robert, and Emily Davidson, eds. *Hard Travelin': The Life and Legacy of Woody Guthrie.* Hanover, N.H.: University Press of New England, 1999.

Sarti, Roland. *Fascism and the Industrial Leadership in Italy, 1919–1940: A Study in the Expansion of Private Power under Fascism.* Berkeley: University of California Press, 1971.

Savage, Sean J. *Roosevelt: the Party Leader, 1932–1945.* Lexington: University Press of Kentucky, 1991.

Schaller, Michael. *Douglas MacArthur: The Far Eastern General.* New York: Oxford University Press, 1989.

———. *The U.S. Crusade in China, 1938–1945.* Lexington: University Press of Kentucky, 1991.

Schapsmeier, Edward L., and Frederick H. Schapsmeier. *Henry A. Wallace of Iowa: The Agrarian Years, 1910–1940.* Ames: Iowa State University Press, 1968.

Scharf, Lois. *To Work and to Wed: Female Employment, Feminism, and the Great Depression.* Westport, Conn.: Greenwood, 1980.

Schivelbusch, Wolfgang. *Three New Deals: Roosevelt's America, Mussolini's Italy, Hitler's Germany, and the Rise of State Power in the 1930s.* New York: Holt, 2006.

Schlesinger, Arthur A., Jr. *The Age of Roosevelt: The Crisis of the Old Order, 1919–1933.* Boston: Houghton Mifflin, 1957.

———. *The Coming of the New Deal.* Vol. 2. Boston: Houghton Mifflin, 1958.

———. *The Politics of Upheaval.* Boston: Houghton Mifflin, 1959.

Schlup, Leonard C., and Donald W. Whisenhunt, eds. *It Seems to Me: Selected Letters of Eleanor Roosevelt.* Lexington: University Press of Kentucky, 2001.

Schonbach, Morris. *Native American Fascism During the 1930s and 1940s.* New York: Garland, 1985.

Schorer, Mark. *Sinclair Lewis: An American Life.* New York: McGraw-Hill, 1961.

Schrecker, Ellen. *Many Were the Crimes: McCarthyism in America.* Princeton, N.J.: Princeton University Press, 1998.

Schwarz, Jordan A. *The Interregnum of Despair: Hoover, Congress and the Depression.* Urbana: University of Illinois Press, 1970.

———. *Liberal: Adolf A. Berle and the Vision of An American Era.* New York: Free Press, 1987.

———. *The Speculator: Bernard M. Baruch in Washington, 1917–1965.* Chapel Hill: University of North Carolina Press, 1981.

Sealander, Judith. *Private Wealth and Public Life: Foundation Philanthropy and the Reshaping of American Social Policy from the Progressive Era to the New Deal.* Baltimore: Johns Hopkins University Press, 1997.

Seidler, Murray B. *Norman Thomas: Respectable Rebel.* 2d ed. Syracuse, N.Y.: Syracuse University Press, 1967.

Seligman, Joel. *The SEC and the Future of Finance.* New York: Praeger, 1985.

Service, Robert. *Stalin: A Biography.* Cambridge, Mass.: Belknap/Harvard, 2005.

Shamir, Ronen. *Managing Legal Uncertainty. Elite Lawyers in the New Deal.* Durham, N.C.: Duke University Press, 1995.

Shaw, Stephen K., William D. Pederson, and Frank J. Williams, eds. *Franklin D. Roosevelt and the Transformation of the Supreme Court.* Armonk, N.Y.: M. E. Sharpe, 2004.

Sheldon, Marcus. *Father Coughlin: The Tumultuous Life of the Priest of the Little Flower.* Boston: Little, Brown, 1973.

Sheridan, James E. *China in Disintegration: The Republican Era in Chinese History, 1912–1949.* New York: Free Press, 1975.

Sherrow, Victoria. *Hardship and Hope: America and the Great Depression.* New York: Twenty-First Century Books, 1997.

Sherwood, Robert Emmet. *Roosevelt and Hopkins: An Intimate History.* New York: Harper, 1950.

Shirer, William. *The Rise and Fall of the Third Reich: A History of Nazi Germany.* New York: Simon & Schuster, 1990.

Shogan, Robert. *Hard Bargain: How FDR Twisted Churchill's Arm, Evaded the Law, and Changed the Role of the American Presidency.* New York: Scribner, 1995.

Short, Philip. *Mao: A Life.* New York: Holt, 2000.

Simmonds, Roy. *John Steinbeck: The War Years, 1939–1995.* Lewisburg, Pa.: Bucknell University Press, 1996.

Simon, James F. *Independent Journey: The Life of William O. Douglas.* New York: Harper & Row, 1980.

Sinclair, Upton. *The Autobiography of Upton Sinclair.* New York: Harcourt, Brace & World, 1962.

Sirgiovanni, George. *An Undercurrent of Suspicion: Anti-Communism in America During World War II.* New Brunswick, N.J., and London: Transaction Publishers, 1990.

Sitkoff, Harvard. *A New Deal for Blacks: The Emergence of Civil Rights as a National Issue. Vol. 1.: The Depression Years.* New York: Oxford University Press, 1978.

Skidelsky, Robert J. *John Maynard Keynes: A Biography.* 2 vols. London: Macmillan, 1983.
———. *Keynes.* New York: Oxford University Press, 1996.

Slayton, Robert A. *Empire Statesman. The Rise and Redemption of Al Smith.* New York: Free Press, 2001.

Smith, Amanda, ed. *Hostage to Fortune: The Letters of Joseph P. Kennedy,* New York: Viking Press, 2001.

Smith, Gene. *The Shattered Dream: Herbert Hoover and the Great Depression.* New York: Greenwood, 1986.

Smith, Grover Cleveland. *Archibald MacLeish.* Minneapolis: University of Minnesota Press, 1971.

Smith, Richard Norton. *The Colonel: The Life and Legend of Robert R. McCormick, 1880–1955.* Boston: Houghton Mifflin, 1997.
———. *Thomas E. Dewey and His Times.* New York: Simon and Schuster, 1982.

Smith, Rixey. *Carter Glass: A Biography.* New York: Longmans, 1939.

Smith, Sally Bedell. *Reflected Glory: The Life of Pamela Churchill Harriman.* New York: Simon & Schuster, 1996.

Smith, Wendy. *Real Life: The Group Theatre and America, 1931–1940.* New York: Knopf, 1990.

Smook, Diane, and Kelli Peduzzi. *Shaping a President: Sculpting for the Roosevelt Memorial.* Riverside, N.J.: Millbrook Press, 1998.

Sneed, Betty M. *Hattie Wright Caraway. United States Senator, 1931–1945.* Fayetteville: University of Arkansas Press, 1975.

Snellgrove, Laurene E. *Franco and the Spanish Civil War.* New York: McGraw-Hill, 1968.

Snow, Edgar. *Red Star Over China.* New York: Random House, 1938.

Snyder, Robert L. *Pare Lorentz and the Documentary Film.* Norman: University of Oklahoma Press, 1968.

Somerville, Mollie. *Eleanor Roosevelt as I Knew Her.* McLean, Va.: EPM Publications, 1996.

Speer, Albert. *Inside the Third Reich: Memoirs.* Translated by Richard Winston and Clara Winston. New York: Simon & Schuster, 1997.

Sperber, Ann M. *Bogart.* New York: Morrow, 1997.

Steel, Ronald. *Walter Lippman and the American Century.* Boston: Little, Brown, 1980.

Stefancic, Jean, and Richard Delgado. *How Lawyers Lose Their Way: A Profession Fails its Creative Minds.* Durham, N.C.: Duke University Press, 2005.

Steinberg, Alfred. *Sam Rayburn: A Biography.* New York: Hawthorn, 1975.

Sternsher, Bernard, ed. *Hitting Home: The Great Depression in Town and Country.* Chicago: Quadrangle, 1970.

———. *Hope Restored: How the New Deal Worked in Town and Country.* Chicago: Ivan R. Dee Publisher, 1999.

Stiles, Lela Mae. *The Man Behind Roosevelt: The Story of Louis McHenry Howe.* Cleveland: World, 1954.

Stillman, Richard J., II. *Creating the American State: The Moral Reformers and the Modern Administrative World They Made.* Tuscaloosa: University of Alabama Press, 2002.

Stimson, Henry L. *On Active Service in Peace and War.* New York: Harper, 1948.

Stinnett, Robert B. *Day of Deceit: The Truth About FDR and Pearl Harbor.* New York: Free Press, 1999.

Stock, Catherine McNicol. *Main Street in Crisis: The Great Depression and the Old Middle Class on the Northern Plains.* Chapel Hill: University of North Carolina Press, 1992.

Stolberg, Mary M. *Fighting Organized Crime: Politics, Justice, and The Legacy of Thomas E. Dewey.* Boston: Northeastern University Press, 1995.

Stoler, Mark A. *George C. Marshall: Soldier-Statesman of the American Century.* Boston: Twayne, 1989.

Storb, Ilse. *Louis Armstrong: The Definitive Biography.* New York: Peter Lang, 1999.

Storrs, Landon R. Y. *Civilizing Capitalism.* Chapel Hill: University of North Carolina Press, 2000.

Stott, William. *Documentary Expression and Thirties America.* Chicago: University of Chicago Press, 1973.

Stowe, David W. *Swing Changes: Big Band Jazz in New Deal America.* Cambridge, Mass.: Harvard University Press, 1994.

Strum, Philippa. *Brandeis: Beyond Progressivism.* Lawrence: University of Kansas Press, 1993.

Stryker, Roy Emerson. *In This Proud Land: America 1935–1943 as Seen in the FSA Photographs.* Boston: New York Graphic Society, 1973.

Sullivan, Patricia. *Days of Hope: Race and Democracy in the New Deal Era.* Chapel Hill: University of North Carolina Press, 1996.

Sunstein, Cass R. *The Second Bill of Rights: FDR's Unfinished Revolution and Why We Need It More than Ever.* New York: Basic Books, 2004.

Swain, Martha H. *Ellen S. Woodward. New Deal Advocate for Women.* Jackson: University Press of Mississippi, 1995.

Swanberg, W. A. *Citizen Hearst: A Biography of William Randolph Hearst.* New York: Scribner, 1961.

———. *Norman Thomas: The Last Idealist.* New York: Scribner, 1976.

Swenson, Karen. *Greta Garbo: A Life Apart.* New York: Scribner, 1997.

Swiss, Cheryl Diane. *Hallie Flanagan and the Federal Theatre Project: An Experiment in Form.* Madison: University of Wisconsin Press, 1982.

Szalay, Michael. *New Deal Modernism: American Literature and the Invention of the Welfare State.* Durham, N.C.: Duke University Press, 2000.

Tauranac, John. *The Empire State Building: The Making of a Landmark.* New York: Scribner, 1995.

Teatro, William. *Mackenzie King: Man of Mission.* Don Mills, Ontario: T. Nelson and Sons, 1979.

Terkel, Studs. *Hard Times: An Oral History of the Great Depression.* New York: Pantheon, 1970.

Terrill, Ros. *Mao: A Biography*. New York: Harper & Row, 1980.

Thelan, David P. *Robert M. La Follette and the Insurgent Spirit*. Boston: Little, Brown, 1976.

Theoharis, Athan, et al. *The FBI: A Comprehensive Reference Guide*. New York: Checkmark, 2000.

Thomas, Hugh. *The Spanish Civil War*. 3d ed. London: Hamish Hamilton, 1977.

Thomas, Jerry B. *An Appalachian New Deal. West Virginia in the New Deal:* Lexington: University Press of Kentucky, 1998.

Thomson, David. *Rosebud: The Story of Orson Welles*. New York: Knopf, 1996.

Tierney, Kevin. *Darrow: A Biography*. New York: Crowell, 1978.

Timmons, Bascom Nolly. *Garner of Texas: A Personal History*. New York: Harper, 1948.

Tindall, George Brown. *The Emergence of the New South 1913–1945*. Baton Rouge: Louisiana University Press, 1967.

Tobey, Ronald C. *Technology as Freedom: The New Deal and the Electrical Modernization of the American Home*. Berkeley: University of California Press, 1996.

Townsend, Francis. *New Horizons*. Chicago: J. L. Stewart, 1943.

Townsend, William C. *Lazaro Cardenas, Mexican Democrat*. Ann Arbor, Mich.: George Wahr, 1952.

Tucker, Robert C. *Stalin in Power: The Revolution from Above, 1928–1941*. New York: Norton, 1990.

Tugwell, Rexford G. *The Brains Trust*. New York: Viking, 1968.

———. *The Diary of Rexford G. Tugwell: The New Deal: 1932–1935*. New York: Greenwood, 1992.

Tull, Charles J. *Father Coughlin and the New Deal*. Syracuse, N.Y.: Syracuse University Press, 1984.

Tyack, David B. *Great Depression and Recent Years*. Cambridge, Mass.: Harvard University Press, 1984.

Underhill, Robert. *FDR and Harry: Unparalleled Lives*. Westport, Conn.: Praeger, 1996.

Underwood, Thomas A., ed. *The Southern Agrarians and the New Deal*. Charlottesville: University of Virginia Press, 2001.

Unger, Nancy C. *Fighting Bob La Follette: The Righteous Reformer*. Chapel Hill: University of North Carolina Press, 2000.

Urofksy, Melvin I. *Felix Frankfurter: Judicial Restraint and Individual Liberties*. Boston: Twayne, 1991.

———. *Louis D. Brandeis and the Progressive Tradition*. Boston: Little, Brown, 1981.

Uys, Errol Lincoln. *Riding the Rails: Teenagers on the Move during the Great Depression*. New York: TV Books, 1999.

Van Minnen, Cornelis A., and John F. Sears, eds. *FDR and His Contemporaries: Foreign Perceptions of an American President*. New York: St. Martin's Press, 1992.

Van Rijn, Guido. *Roosevelt Blues: Black Blues and Gospel Songs on FDR*. Oxford: University Press of Mississippi, 1997.

Venn, Fiona. *The New Deal*. Edinburgh: Edinburgh University Press, 2001.

Volanto, Keith J. *Texas, Cotton, and the New Deal*. College Station: Texas A & M University Press, 2005.

Waddell, Brian. *The War Against the New Deal*. DeKalb: Northern University Press, 2001.

Walch, Timothy, and Dwight M. Miller, eds. *Herbert Hoover and Franklin Roosevelt. A Documentary History*. Westport, Conn.: Greenwood Press, 1998.

Wallace, Henry Agard. *The Century of the Common Man*. Edited by Russell Lord. New York: Reynal & Hitchcock, 1943.

Ward, Geoffrey C. *Before the Trumpet: Young Franklin Roosevelt, 1882–1905*. New York: Perennial Library, 1986.

———. *A First-Class Temperament: The Emergence of Franklin Roosevelt*. New York: Harper and Row, 1989.

———, ed. *Closest Companion. The Unknown Story of the Intimate Friendship Between Franklin Roosevelt and Margaret Suckley*. New York: Houghton Mifflin, 1995.

Ware, Gilbert. *William Hastie: Grace Under Pressure.* New York: Oxford University Press, 1984.

Ware, Susan. *Beyond Suffrage: Women in the New Deal.* Cambridge, Mass.: Harvard University Press, 1981.

———. *Partner and I: Molly Dawson, Feminism, and New Deal Politics.* Cambridge, Mass.: Harvard University Press, 1987.

Warren, Donald I. *Radio Priest: Charles Coughlin, the Father of Hate Radio.* New York: Free Press, 1996.

Warren, Harris G. *Herbert Hoover and the Great Depression.* New York: Oxford University Press, 1959.

Watkins, Floyd C. *The Hungry Years: A Narrative History of the Great Depression* in America. New York: Holt, 1999.

Watkins, Floyd C., John T. Hiers, and Mary Louise Weaks. *Talking with Robert Penn Warren.* Athens: University of Georgia Press, 1990.

Watkins, T. H. *The Great Depression: America in the 1930s.* New York: Back Bay, 1993.

———. *Righteous Pilgrim: The Life and Times of Harold L. Ickes, 1874–1952.* New York: Holt, 1990.

Watts, Steven. *The People's Tycoon: Henry Ford and the American Century.* New York: Knopf, 2005.

Weatherson, Michael A., and Hal Bochin. *Hiram Johnson: A Bio-Bibliography.* Westport, Conn.: Greenwood Press, 1988.

Weber, Debra. *Dark Sweat, White Gold: California Farm Workers, Cotton and the New Deal.* Berkeley and Los Angeles: University of California Press, 1994.

Weed, Clyde P. *The Nemesis of Reform: The Republican Party During the New Deal.* New York: Columbia University Press, 1994.

Weinberg, Arthur, and Lola Weinberg. *Clarence Darrow. A Sentimental Rebel.* New York: Atheneum, 1980.

Weinberg, Gerhard L. *A World at Arms: A Global History of World War II.* Cambridge: Cambridge University Press, 1994.

———. *Visions of Victory. The Hope of Eight World War II Leaders.* New York: Cambridge University Press, 2005.

Weisenberger, Bernard. A., ed. *The WPA Guides to America: the Best of 1930s America as Seen by the Federal Writer's Project.* New York: Pantheon, 1985.

Weiss, Nancy J. *Farewell to the Party of Lincoln: Black Politics in the Age of FDR.* Princeton, N.J.: Princeton University Press, 1983.

Weiss, Stuart L. *The President's Man: Leo Crowley and Franklin Roosevelt in Peace and War.* Carbondale: Southern Illinois University Press, 1996.

Weller, Cecil Edward. *Joe T. Robinson: Always a Loyal Democratic.* Fayetteville: University of Arkansas Press, 1998.

Welles, Benjamin. *Sumner Welles: FDR's Global Strategist: Biography.* New York: St. Martin's Press, 1997.

Welles, Sumner. *The Time for Decision.* New York: Harper, 1944.

Whalen, Richard J. *The Founding Father: The Story of Joseph P. Kennedy.* New York: New American Library, 1964.

Whealey, Robert H. *Hitler and Spain: The Nazi Role in the Spanish Civil War 1936–1939.* Lexington: University Press of Kentucky, 1989.

Wheeler, Burton K., and Paul F. Healy. *Yankee from the West: The Candid, Turbulent Life Story of the Yankee-born U.S. Senator from Montana.* Garden City, N.Y.: Doubleday, 1962.

White, G. Edward. *The Constitution and the New Deal.* Cambridge, Mass.: Harvard University Press, 2001.

White, Graham. *FDR and the Press.* Chicago: University of Chicago Press, 1979.

White, Graham and John Maze. *Harold L. Ickes.* Cambridge, Mass.: Harvard University Press, 1985.

White, Michael, and John Gribbin. *Einstein: A Life in Science.* New York: Dutton, Plume, 1994.

White, Walter Francis. *A Man Called White: The Autobiography of Walter White.* New York: Viking Press, 1948.

Willis, Rese. *FDR and Lucy: Lovers and Friends.* New York: Routledge, 2004.

Wicker, Elmus. *The Banking Panics of the Great Depression.* New York: Cambridge University Press, 1996.

Williams, Thomas Harry. *Huey Long.* New York: Random House, 1981.

Williamson, Philip. *Stanley Baldwin: Conservative Leadership and National Values.* New York: Cambridge University Press, 1999.

Wilson, Joan Hoff. *Herbert Hoover: Forgotten Progressive.* New York: HarperCollins, 1975.

Windeler, Robert. *The Films of Shirley Temple.* New York: Citadel, 1995.

Winfield, Betty H. *FDR and the News Media.* Champaign: University of Illinois Press, 1991.

Witham, Barry B. *The Federal Theatre Project: A Case Study.* Cambridge, Mass.: Cambridge University Press, 2003.

Witte, Edwin E. *The Development of the Social Security Act.* Madison: University of Wisconsin Press, 1962.

Wolf, Thomas P., William D. Pederson, and Byron W. Daynes, eds. *Franklin D. Roosevelt and Congress. The New Deal and Its Aftermath.* Armonk, N.Y.: M. E. Sharpe, 2001.

Wong, K. Scott. *Americans First: Chinese Americans and the Second World War.* Cambridge, Mass.: Harvard University Press, 2005.

Wolters, Raymond. *Negroes and the Great Depression: The Problem of Economic Recovery.* Westport, Conn.: Greenwood, 1970.

Wood, Bryce. *The Making of the Good Neighbor Policy.* New York: Columbia University Press, 1961.

Worster, Donald. *Dust Bowl: The Southern Plains in the 1930s.* New York: Oxford University Press, 1979.

Ybarra, Michael J. *Washington Gone Crazy: Senator Pat McCarran and the Great American Communist Hunt.* New York: Steerforth, 2004.

Yoshihake, Takehiko. *Conspiracy in Manchuria: The Rise of the Japanese Military.* New Haven, Conn.: Yale University, 1963.

Young, Louise. *Japan's Total Empire: Manchuria and the Culture of Wartime Imperialism.* Berkeley: University of California Press, 1998.

Young, Nancy B., William D. Pederson, and Byron W. Daynes, eds. *Franklin D. Roosevelt and the Shaping of American Political Culture.* Armonk, N.Y.: M. E. Sharpe, 2001.

Zevin, B. D. *Nothing to Fear: The Selected Addresses of Franklin Delano Roosevelt, 1932–1945.* Boston: Houghton Mifflin, 1946.

Ziegler, Robert H. *John L. Lewis: Labor Leader.* New York: Macmillan, 1988.

———. *The CIO: 1935–1955.* Chapel Hill: University of North Carolina Press, 1995.

INDEX

Boldface page numbers indicate primary discussions. *Italic* page numbers indicate illustrations.